Archaeology of Oceania: Australia and the Pacific Islands

Edited by

Ian Lilley

D1601986

Blackwell
Publishing

BLACKWELL PUBLISHING
350 Main Street, Malden, MA 02148-5020, USA
9600 Garsington Road, Oxford OX4 2DQ, UK
550 Swanston Street, Carlton, Victoria 3053, Australia

The right of Ian Lilley to be identified as the Author of the Editorial Material in this Work has been asserted in accordance with the UK Copyright, Designs, and Patents Act 1988.

First published 2006 by Blackwell Publishing Ltd

1   2006

Library of Congress Cataloging-in-Publication Data

Archaeology of Oceania : Australia and the Pacific Islands / edited by Ian Lilley.
    p. cm. — (Blackwell studies in global archaeology)
    Includes bibliographical references and index.
    ISBN-13: 978-0-631-23082-3 (hard cover : alk. paper)
    ISBN-10: 0-631-23082-3 (hard cover : alk. paper)
    ISBN-13: 978-0-631-23083-0 (pbk. : alk. paper)
    ISBN-10: 0-631-23083-1 (pbk. : alk. paper)   1. Oceania—Antiquities.   2. Australia—Antiquities.
3. Islands of the Pacific—Antiquities.   I. Lilley, Ian.   II. Series.

    DU28.A73 2006
    995—dc22

                                                                                    2005011633

A catalogue record for this title is available from the British Library.

Set in 10 on 12.5 pt Plantin
by SNP Best-set Typesetter Ltd, Hong Kong
Printed and bound in India
by Replika Press

The publisher's policy is to use permanent paper from mills that operate a sustainable forestry policy, and which has been manufactured from pulp processed using acid-free and elementary chlorine-free practices. Furthermore, the publisher ensures that the text paper and cover board used have met acceptable environmental accreditation standards.

For further information on
Blackwell Publishing, visit our website:
www.blackwellpublishing.com

Contents

Series Editors' Preface   viii

List of Figures   ix

List of Tables   xii

Notes on Contributors   xiii

Acknowledgments   xix

  1 Archaeology in Oceania: Themes and Issues   1
     Ian Lilley

Part 1 Australia

  2 Revisiting the Past: Changing Interpretations of Pleistocene Settlement
     Subsistence and Demography in Northern Australia   31
     Sue O'Connor and Peter Veth

  3 Archaeology and the Dreaming: Toward an Archaeology of Ontology   48
     Bruno David

  4 Blunt and to the Point: Changing Technological Strategies in
     Holocene Australia   69
     Peter Hiscock

  5 Rock Art and Social Identity: A Comparison of Holocene Graphic
     Systems in Arid and Fertile Environments   96
     Jo McDonald and Peter Veth

  6 Closing the Distance: Interpreting Cross-Cultural Engagements through
     Indigenous Rock Art   116
     Anne Clarke and Ursula Frederick

Part II   The Pacific

  7 Archaeology in Melanesia: A Case Study from the Western Province of
     the Solomon Islands   137
     Richard Walter and Peter Sheppard

  8 Envisaging Early Agriculture in the Highlands of New Guinea   160
     Tim Denham

  9 Late Pleistocene Complexities in the Bismarck Archipelago   189
     Matthew Leavesley

 10 Life before Lapita: New Developments in Melanesia's Long-Term History 205
     Christina Pavlides

 11 The First Millennium B.C. in Remote Oceania: An Alternative
     Perspective on Lapita   228
     Jean-Christophe Galipaud

 12 Ethnoarchaeology in Polynesia   240
     Eric Conte

 13 The Formation of Hawaiian Territories   259
     Thegn Ladefoged and Michael Graves

 14 Ritual and Domestic Architecture, Sacred Places, and Images:
     Archaeology in the Marquesas Archipelago, French Polynesia   284
     Sidsel Millerstrom

 15 The Archaeology of the Conical Clan in Micronesia   302
     Paul Rainbird

Part III   Politics

 16 What is Archaeology for in the Pacific? History and Politics in
     New Caledonia   321
     Christophe Sand, Jacques Bole, and André Ouetcho

 17 Levuka, Fiji: A Case Study in Pacific Islands Heritage Management   346
     Anita Smith

 18 Last Words   363
     A Few Words about Archaeology in French Polynesia   363
     Mickaelle-Hinanui Cauchois

Shaking the Pillars   367
Mark Dugay-Grist

What is the Future of our Past? Papua New Guineans and
Cultural Heritage   379
Herman Mandui

Index   383

 # Series Editors' Preface

This series was conceived as a collection of books designed to cover central areas of undergraduate archaeological teaching. Each volume in the series, edited by experts in the area, includes newly commissioned articles written by archaeologists actively engaged in research. By commissioning new articles, the series combines one of the best features of readers, the presentation of multiple approaches to archaeology, with the virtues of a text conceived from the beginning as intended for a specific audience. While the model reader for the series is conceived of as an upper-division undergraduate, the inclusion in the volumes of researchers actively engaged in work today will also make these volumes valuable for more advanced researchers who want a rapid introduction to contemporary issues in specific subfields of global archaeology.

Each volume in the series will include an extensive introduction by the volume editor that will set the scene in terms of thematic or geographic focus. Individual volumes, and the series as a whole, exemplify a wide range of approaches in contemporary archaeology. The volumes uniformly engage with issues of contemporary interest, interweaving social, political, and ethical themes. We contend that it is no longer tenable to teach the archaeology of vast swaths of the globe without acknowledging the political implications of working in foreign countries and the responsibilities archaeologists incur by writing and presenting other people's pasts. The volumes in this series will not sacrifice theoretical sophistication for accessibility. We are committed to the idea that usable teaching texts need not lack ambition.

Blackwell Studies in Global Archaeology aims to immerse readers in fundamental archaeological ideas and concepts, but also to illuminate more advanced concepts, exposing readers to some of the most exciting contemporary developments in the field.

Lynn Meskell and Rosemary A. Joyce

Figures

1.1	Oceania	3
2.1	Map showing location of sites and major deserts mentioned in the text	33
2.2	Veth's (1989) biogeographic model showing hypothesized "refuges" from aridity, "corridors" between refuges, and "barriers" to movement (after Veth 1989)	34
2.3	Graph of all calibrated radiocarbon dates CG1 and CG3	36
2.4	Graph of all calibrated radiocarbon dates from nine coastal Kimberley sites	38
2.5	Graph of all calibrated radiocarbon dates from the Pilbara uplands	40
3.1	Ngarrabullgan, showing Initiation Cave in foreground	52
3.2	Map showing locations of Djungan, Arrernte, and Wardaman country	53
3.3	The Lightning Brothers, Yagjagbula and Jabirringi, at Yiwarlarlay	59
3.4	Garnawala, Shelter 1, showing the paintings that relate to the Rainbow Serpent/Two Sisters story	60
4.1	Changes in scraper morphology during reduction (after Hiscock and Attenbrow 2002)	75
4.2	Changes in point morphology during reduction (illustration of one possible sequence as an example)	77
4.3	Examples of backed artifact morphology	79
4.4	Models of the extension–abundance continuum. A) Illustration showing the continuum of possible artifact forms that play off reduction potential against production rate. B) Plot of some Australian artifact types using proxies for reduction potential (specimen weight) and production rate (number of specimens per kilogram)	82

5.1   Map of Australia showing locations of Sydney–Hawkesbury
         Basin and Calvert Ranges in the Western Desert (after Layton
         1992)   97
5.2   Map showing Sydney Basin languages following Capell (1970)   101
6.1   Groote Eylandt, showing places mentioned in the text   118
6.2   The Marngkala Cave site showing superimposition of praus   125
6.3   Prau with 68 people   127
7.1   Roviana Lagoon, New Georgia Island, Western Province of the
         Solomon Islands   144
7.2   A model of the flow of power in the late period Roviana Chiefdom 146
8.1   Map showing location of archaeological sites in the Highlands of
         New Guinea. Inset depicts wetland sites   172
8.2   Composite plan of 1975–1977 and 1998 excavations at Kuk
         Swamp showing Phase 1 paleosurface adjacent to paleochannel
         (101; modified version of Denham 2004, Fig. 7)   175
8.3   Composite plan of 1975–1977 and 1998 excavations at Kuk
         Swamp showing Phase 2 paleosurface cut by later paleochannel
         (107)   177
8.4   Summary plan of Phase 3 ditch networks and contemporary
         paleochannels (102, 103, 106, and 107) at Kuk Swamp. Inset
         A depicts early and late sub-phase ditch complexes and Inset B
         depicts an early Phase 3 ditched enclosure (reproduced with
         permission from Denham, Golson, and Hughes 2004, Fig. 16)   178
9.1   New Guinea, the Bismarck Archipelago, and the Solomon Islands,
         showing places mentioned in the text (derived from Allen and
         Gosden 1996)   190
10.1   The rain forest study area and other sites mentioned in the text 209
10.2   The bifacial stemmed and waisted and unifacial stemmed tools
         (dorsal view)   217
12.1   French Polynesia   252
13.1   The four Hawaiian chiefdoms at European contact (after Cordy
         1981)   261
13.2   The districts of Molokaʻi, Oʻahu, Kauaʻi, Maui, and Hawaiʻi Island 264
13.3   The ahupuaʻa of North Kohala with labels on the 35 ahupuaʻa
         that are analyzed   270
13.4   Level 1 grouping, ahupuaʻa classified into 29 groups   271
13.5   Level 2 grouping, ahupuaʻa classified into 25 groups   272
13.6   Level 3 grouping, ahupuaʻa classified into 19 groups   273
13.7   Level 4 grouping, ahupuaʻa classified into 15 groups   274
13.8   Level 5 grouping, ahupuaʻa classified into 11 groups   275
13.9   Level 6 grouping, ahupuaʻa classified into 9 groups   276
13.10   GPS data depicting suspected early, intermediate, and late phase
         walls and trails in the Kehena 1, Kaupalaoa, and Makeanehu area 277
14.1   Marquesas Islands, French Polynesia   285
14.2   Anthropomorphic stick figure, Anaho, Nuku Hiva   287

14.3   Anthropomorphic face (*mata komoe*), Taipivai Valley, Nuku Hiva   288
14.4   Map of Hatiheu Valley showing zones I–III and Tohua Hikoku'a (1),
        Tohua Kamuihei II (2), Tohua Kamuihei I (3), Tohua Tahakia (4),
        Tohua Maikuku (5), Tohua Pa'aha'ua (6), Tohua Ninauhi (7),
        and Tohua Pahumano (8)   295
14.5   High-status residential unit with megalithic breadfruit pits (*ua ma*) 297
15.1   Entrance to Nan Douwas Islet, Nan Madol, Pohnpei   305
15.2   Plan of Nan Madol indicating "mortuary area"   307
15.3   Plan of Leluh, Kosrae   310
16.1   New Caledonia   323
16.2   Examples of reconstructed Lapita pottery   324
16.3   Abandoned taro terraces, La Grande Terre   330
16.4   Abandoned raised yam fields, La Grande Terre   330
17.1   Location of Levuka and Ovalau in relation to the principal
        Fiji Islands   347
17.2   Beach Street, Levuka   348
18.1   The author and Gunia/Kurni community members surveying
        Lake Glenmaggie. L–R Mick Harding, Mark Dugay-Grist, Tim
        Farnham, and Chris Johnson. (Photograph courtesy of the
        Aboriginal Affairs Victoria Library)   378

Tables

2.1   Estimated artifact discard rates from Western Desert sites in pre-
       LGM–LGM Pleistocene levels versus late Holocene levels of
       deposits. (Artifact numbers summarized from *a*. O'Connor et al.
       1998:17, *b*. Smith 1988:108, Table 4.4, *c*. Thorley 1998b:41)   41
2.2   Mean weight of amorphous retouched artifacts in grams, Puritjarra
       (data derived from Smith 1988:108, 119, Tables 4.4, 4.9). Numbers
       in brackets give the numbers of artifacts in the sample that the
       mean weights are based on   41
2.3   Mean weight of total artifacts in grams, Puritjarra, Pit N10 (from
       Smith 1988:119, Table 4.10)   42
10.1   Archaeological units and known tephras at the Yombon rain forest
       sites (Pavlides 1999)   210

Notes on Contributors

Mickaelle-Hinanui Cauchois received her M.A. in Anthropology from the University of Hawai'i at Manoa in 2004 and is now a Ph.D. candidate in the same university. She previously worked as Assistant Archaeologist at the former Department of Archaeology in Tahiti (now Service de la Culture et du Patrimoine). Her Ph.D. research focuses on inland valley systems as areas of refuge in the Society Islands, especially the island of Mo'orea, in comparison with other Polynesian areas such as the Cook Islands and Samoa. Mickaelle-Hinanui's other research interests are settlement patterns, household archaeology, ancient horticultural systems, and archaeological heritage management in the Pacific.

Anne Clarke lectures in Heritage Studies at the University of Sydney in Australia. She previously taught at the Australian National University, where she also obtained her Ph.D. and held two Postdoctoral Fellowships, one working through the Northern Australian Research Unit in Darwin. Her dissertation concerned the archaeology of cross-cultural contact on Groote Eylandt and her other research interests include community archaeology and popular collecting. She has co-edited five volumes, covering archaeobotany, heritage management, and contact archaeology. Her latest book is *Negotiating Difference* (with Robin Torrence, 2000).

Eric Conte gained his doctorate and Habilitation à diriger des recherches from the Sorbonne in Paris. He is Maître de Conférences at the University of French Polynesia in Tahiti and directs the Oceanic Prehistory program at the Sorbonne. Since 1980, he has undertaken ethnoarchaeological and archaeological research in all the archipelagoes of French Polynesia. His Ph.D. concerned pre-European fishing techniques and he has published several works on Polynesian archaeology.

Bruno David is Queen Elizabeth II Fellow in the Programme for Australian Indigenous Archaeology at Monash University, Australia. He has led archaeological and multidisciplinary research teams in Australia, Vanuatu and the USA. He is currently working with Torres Strait Islanders, researching the archaeology of rituals. His other research interests include the social entanglement of objects, the archaeology of place, and the archaeology of spiritscapes. His latest books are *Landscapes, Rock-art and the Dreaming* (2002), and the co-edited volume *The Social Archaeology of Indigenous Societies* (2005).

Tim Denham is an Honorary Research Associate in the School of Geography and Environmental Science, Monash University, Australia. He recently completed his Ph.D. dissertation on early and mid-Holocene plant exploitation at Kuk Swamp in the Papua New Guinea highlands. He first undertook fieldwork in the highlands in 1990, and has since undertaken archaeological projects across the Pacific. He is currently continuing his research of early agricultural and arboricultural practices in New Guinea and has initiated an environmental history of the Adelaide Hills, South Australia.

Ursula Frederick is an archaeologist and art historian based at the Centre for Cross-Cultural Research, Australian National University. Her research interests are interdisciplinary and include art, mobility, culture contact, cultural heritage, and the social life of things. She is also engaged in the research and production of visual media.

Jean-Christophe Galipaud is based in New Caledonia as a Director of Research at the Institute of Research for Development (IRD, previously ORSTOM). He works within the multidisciplinary framework of the research group ADENTRHO (Adaptation to tropical environments during the Holocene), studying the initial settlement of the islands of Oceania. Since 1980 he has conducted fieldwork in New Caledonia, Vanuatu, Solomons, Tahiti and central Micronesia. His Ph.D. dissertation, completed at the Sorbonne, proposed a chronological sequence for New Caledonia in a regional context. It helped lay the foundations for cultural heritage management services in New Caledonia and Vanuatu. Jean-Christophe's other research interests include historical settlement of the islands and he has recently been working on Vanikoro studying the survivor's camp of the shipwrecked men of the La Pérouse expedition.

Michael Graves is Chair of the Department of Anthropology at the University of Hawai'i-Manoa where he has taught for nearly two decades. He gained his Ph.D. from the University of Arizona and previously taught at the University of Guam. His archaeological research interests focus on the explanation of the evolution of social complexity in Hawai'i and elsewhere in Oceania, the development of models linking geographical information systems to agricultural practices, and the application of stylistic analyses to explain the evolution of social units and patterns of diversification. In 2002 he published *Pacific Landscapes* (with Thegn Ladefoged).

Mark Dugay-Grist is an Aboriginal man from the Werigia, Nyeri Nyeri, and Wamba Wamba peoples of northwest Victoria, Australia. He has a B.A. Honours in archaeology from the Australian National University and is Manager of the

Statewide Heritage Program for Aboriginal Affairs Victoria. He has worked as a government Cultural Heritage Officer, a consulting archaeologist, and Curator of Southeastern Australia at the Museum of Victoria in Melbourne. Mark's research interests include lithic procurement and technology, Aboriginal skeletal anatomy, Aboriginal educational needs in cultural heritage management, cultural heritage legislation, curatorial practices concerning Indigenous cultural property, and the social history of southeastern Australia.

Peter Hiscock is a Reader in the School of Archaeology and Anthropology at the Australian National University. He is a leading researcher into prehistoric stone technology, with a record of developing models about ancient technology, both in Australia and elsewhere. He has worked extensively on Australian artifacts, and is the most published author on the subject of the ancient lithic technologies in Australia. His current focus is the analysis of Middle Paleolithic technologies in Europe. He has published more than a hundred journal articles and three books, including Blackwell's *Desert Peoples* (with Mike Smith and Peter Veth, 2004).

Thegn Ladefoged is a Senior Lecturer in Archaeology at the University of Auckland in New Zealand. He received his Ph.D. from the University of Hawai'i in 1993, studying the evolutionary ecology of agricultural and socio-political development on Rotuma. He has worked in the Kohala fieldsystem in Hawai'i for the past eight years, most recently as a member of a multidisciplinary team researching the ecodynamics of the area. He is currently also studying agricultural development and socio-political transformations on Rapa Nui, and in the past has also worked in New Zealand. He recently published *Pacific Landscapes* (with Michael Graves, 2002).

Matthew Leavesley read Melanesian archaeology at La Trobe University in Australia, before undertaking graduate studies in the School of Archaeology and Anthropology at The Australian National University. His recent Ph.D. dissertation investigated late Pleistocene hunting strategies in New Ireland, Papua New Guinea. He is currently a Postdoctoral Research Fellow at the Leverhulme Centre for Human Evolutionary Studies, Cambridge University. He is working within the Pioneers of Island Melanesia Project investigating the spatial distribution of material culture in Bougainville.

Ian Lilley is Reader in Aboriginal and Torres Strait Islander Studies at the University of Queensland, Australia, and Secretary of the World Archaeological Congress. He has worked in archaeology and cultural heritage throughout Australia and in Papua New Guinea, and is currently developing a research program with French and New Caledonian colleagues in the Loyalty Islands. His other interests include archaeology and social identity, and archaeology's place in contemporary society. His recent books include *Histories of Old Ages. Essays in honour of Rhys Jones* (with A. Anderson and S. O'Connor, 2001), *Native Title and the Transformation of Archaeology in the Postcolonial World* (2000), and *Le Pacifique de 5000 à 2000 avant le présent* (with J-C Galipaud, 1999).

Jo McDonald is a cultural heritage management consultant based in Sydney, Australia. Her consulting work focuses on archaeology and rock art in southeastern Australia but has also involved a Native Title claim in Central Australia. Her Ph.D. dissertation examined the extensive rock art assemblages around Sydney. She has published many papers and several books on this art and her doctoral thesis will soon appear as a *Terra Australis* monograph. Her current research focus is on Australia's Western Desert, where she is involved in a project to date the region's engraved and pigment art. She is also currently working on the scientific values assessment report for the World Heritage nomination of the Dampier Archipelago in northwestern Australia.

Herman Mandui graduated from the University of Papua New Guinea, Waigani Main Campus with a B.A. Degree in Archaeology, Physical Geography and Environmental Sciences in 1993. He was employed by the Papua New Guinea National Museum in 1994 as the country's first Salvage Archaeologist and worked in the mining, petroleum, agroforestry, and infrastructural sectors until 1999 when he was appointed as the Deputy Head of Archaeology with the Papua New Guinea National Museum, the position he currently maintains. Herman's other interests include research in early agriculture, prehistoric pottery manufacture, and settlement of Melanesian peoples in New Guinea and the Pacific.

Sidsel Millerstrom was born in Norway. She earned her Ph.D. in anthropology from the University of California at Berkeley. The majority of her archaeological research has been conducted in Oceania, in Hawai'i, Easter Island, and especially in French Polynesia. One of her numerous passions is rock art and architecture, a subject that has led her to many remote locations. Currently she is focusing her research on ritual places in the Marquesas Islands. A book on the Marquesan research is soon to be published in French in Tahiti. When not exploring the world she teaches and lives in California with her family.

Sue O'Connor is a Senior Research Fellow in the Department of Archaeology and Natural History, Research School of Pacific and Asian Studies at the Australian National University. Her Ph.D. focused on Aboriginal colonization of northern Australia and Pleistocene change and adaptation. While teaching at the University of Western Australia she investigated the prehistory of offshore islands and contemporary Aboriginal use of islands and marine resources on the Kimberley coast. Sue has since undertaken a series of field projects in eastern Indonesia and East Timor. In 2003 she began a collaborative project on the north coast of New Guinea. Her books include *30,000 years of Aboriginal Occupation, Kimberley, Northwest Australia* (1999) and *East Of Wallace's Line* with Peter Veth (2000).

Christina Pavlides is a Postdoctoral Research Fellow with the Institute of Archaeology, Oxford University. She has worked in New Britain since 1987, completing her Ph.D. on the prehistory of the Yombon area in the central lowland rainforests in 2000. Her interests include prehistoric flaked stone technology and its relationship with other economic activities, the origins of agriculture in Melanesia, early adaptations to living in lowland tropical rainforests, and prehistoric and modern-day exchange activities in New Guinea. Currently she is part of a multidisciplinary European research team investigating the origins and development of non-Austronesian culture in Melanesia.

Paul Rainbird is Senior Lecturer and Head of the Department of Archaeology and Anthropology at the University of Wales, Lampeter. He holds degrees from the University of Sheffield and the University of Sydney and has conducted archaeological fieldwork in the Pacific, Australia, and Europe. His book *The Archaeology of Micronesia* was published by Cambridge University Press in 2004.

Christophe Sand, Jacques Bole, and André Ouetcho created the Department of Archaeology in the New Caledonia Museum in 1991. They have conducted numerous projects on the prehistory and colonial history of the archipelago, while also carrying out archaeological programs in Fiji. Promoting awareness of New Caledonia's history amongst the population of New Caledonia, the team's research themes have over the years led to work on topics linked to first settlement (Lapita) sites, prehistoric cultural dynamics, intensification processes during the last millennium before European contact, and the consequences of European settlement in the Pacific.

Peter Sheppard is Head of the Department of Anthropology at the University of Auckland in New Zealand. He started in Auckland as a Postdoctoral Fellow researching geoarchaeological sourcing of chert and obsidian in Lapita assemblages from the Solomon Islands. He expanded this interest to include Oceanic basalts from Samoa and the Cook Islands after he was appointed to teach in Archaeological Science, including geoarchaeology. He now leads major multidisciplinary projects among both Oceanic Austronesian and non-Austronesian societies in the Central Solomons. These projects focus on processes of social transformation in this region and more generally through the Solomons.

Anita Smith is a Post-Doctoral Fellow and Lecturer in graduate programs in cultural heritage and museum studies in the Cultural Heritage Centre for Asia and the Pacific at Deakin University, Australia. Her Ph.D. focused on West Polynesia. Anita's principal research interest now is in Pacific Island cultural landscapes and heritage management. She is currently working in association with UNESCO in training Pacific Island heritage managers and with the Fijian government on their World Heritage nomination for the colonial capital of Levuka.

Peter Veth has carried out research within the arid zone of Australia for over 20 years. His work has focused on the dynamism and flexibility inherent in hunter-gatherer adaptations to "marginal" environments. He has published collaboratively on issues concerning the emergence of desert societies, their symbolic, graphic and language systems, and also their totemic geography. Recently he co-edited the first review of the emergence of desert hunter-gatherer groups in the 2004 Blackwell volume *Desert Peoples* (with Peter Hiscock and Mike Smith). Peter is Director of Research at the Australian Institute of Aboriginal and Torres Strait Islander Studies and holds an Adjunct Senior Research Fellowship at the Australian National University.

Richard Walter received his Ph.D. from the University of Auckland in New Zealand in 1991. His dissertation looked at the prehistoric colonization of East Polynesia using the archaeological record of the Cook Islands as a case study. Richard is an historical anthropologist with archaeological interests in exchange systems, landscape archaeology, material culture studies, prehistoric fishing, and the use of tradition in archaeology. Richard has current research projects in New Zealand, the Cook Islands and the Solomon Islands.

Acknowledgments

This volume had an extended gestation. It allowed us to take advantage of a great deal of new information which appeared in 2003–2004 but made the process a long one for many of those involved. I would like to thank the contributors who patiently saw it through from the beginning as well as those who came on board, often at short notice, as things progressed. Thanks, too, to Jane Huber, Emily Martin and the other staff at Blackwell, as well as the series editors Lynn Meskell and Rosemary Joyce, for their help and cheerful forbearance. Michael Williams, Director of the Aboriginal and Torres Strait Islander Studies Unit in the University of Queensland, offered a conducive atmosphere in which to work. Sean Ulm, the Unit's Senior Researcher, graciously provided skilled assistance with the illustrations and Simon Haberle of Monash University supplied our up-to-the-minute environmental data.

I
Archaeology in Oceania: Themes and Issues

Ian Lilley

Introduction

The archaeology of Oceania is shaped by five overlapping themes: colonization, interaction, cultural diversification, environmental change, and, on a different but no less fundamental plane, contemporary politics. The participants in this volume examine aspects of these themes as they played and continue to play out across the region. Our goal is to introduce you to the diversity of current approaches to the intellectual and technical challenges of archaeology in Australia and the Pacific Islands. In this chapter I define central terms, sketch the thematic background against which the other contributions are set and fill in some of the key details that a wide-ranging but selective survey of this sort inevitably misses.

Scope

We canvas cross-cultural entanglement and colonial heritage but deal primarily with pre-European (i.e., pre-contact, prehistoric) archaeology. While the division between prehistoric and text-aided (i.e., historical) archaeology is a false one that is being undermined in Oceania as much as anywhere (e.g., Clarke and Patterson 2003; Kirch and Sahlins 1992; Torrence and Clarke 2000), their integration is still too far off for us to present them here seamlessly joined. Our focus is also specifically *archaeological*. Thus while the findings of research into human biology, historical linguistics, and paleoenvironmental change are critical to understanding many of the issues in focus, they will only be outlined rather than detailed. Finally, the book shows where early to mid-career researchers from a range of backgrounds are taking archaeology in Oceania. You will be directed to major syntheses by established scholars for detailed references to past research. Here you will read about new discoveries, conceptual innovations, and the dynamics of postcolonial *realpolitik*. As you read, bear in mind that most of Oceania remains under-researched, with many regions lacking reliable basic chronologies let alone more sophisticated study. This introduces some unevenness to the volume. Some chapters provide detailed treatments of specific issues arising from intensive, long-term research, but others concern the simple questions that are asked at the earliest stages of investigation. Some of the perspectives challenge orthodox models. This means a few contributions are much longer than the others, owing to the need to clear their conceptual and technical paths. All describe works very much in progress – something underlined by the number of references to unpublished Masters, Ph.D. and even Honors dissertations – and emphasize that as yet there is little settled knowledge in the archaeology of Oceania.

The work is divided broadly by geography and time. Chapters 2–6 cover Australia, beginning with the Pleistocene after initial colonization and ending with European contact. Chapters 7–15 address issues in Pacific archaeology, first in Melanesia, then Polynesia and finally Micronesia. The last section, chapters 16–18, addresses the contemporary politics of archaeology and cultural heritage.

Definition of terms

We include Australia as well as the other islands of the Pacific in "Oceania" (Figure 1.1). Some writers exclude Australia (e.g., Kirch 2000:5), but our definition has long been used by the region's premier professional journal *Archaeology in Oceania*. As the journal's editor has noted, Pleistocene low sea-levels joined Australia and New Guinea (and Tasmania) as dry land for at least eighty percent of the region's human history (White with O'Connell 1982). One thus cannot consider this very large part of Oceanic archaeology without Australia, or vice versa.

This basic fact is acknowledged in most general texts on one or the other topic. Yet no one has ever dealt with the postglacial histories of Australia and the rest of Oceania in the same volume except in the most generalized global works. The Holocene histories of Australia and the Pacific differed significantly but they were not unconnected. As discussed below, new evidence from Torres Strait is beginning to tie Australia to late Holocene developments in Island Melanesia and the wider Pacific as well as mainland New Guinea in ways unimagined by most Australian and Pacific archaeologists until now. Like the shared Pleistocene history, the fascinating possibilities surrounding more recent links such as these strengthen the case for treating Australia and the Pacific in the same volume rather than continuing to promote their separation.

Other terms which need to be defined are "Melanesia" (the "black islands"), "Micronesia" (the "small islands"), and "Polynesia" (the "many islands") (Figure 1.1). Melanesia includes mainland New Guinea and, excluding Micronesian Nauru, all of the islands south of the equator out to and including Fiji in the east and New Caledonia in the south. "Island Melanesia" refers to Melanesia without mainland New Guinea. The Indonesian province of Papua covers the western half

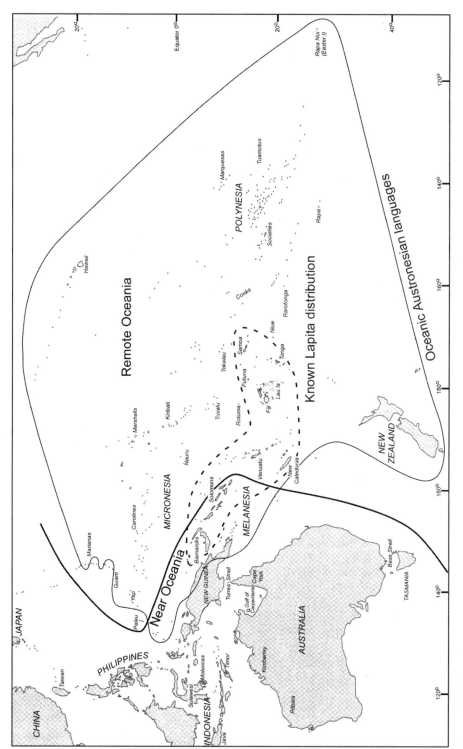

Figure 1.1 Oceania

of New Guinea. The eastern half comprises the mainland provinces of Papua New Guinea, which also includes the islands of the Bismarck Archipelago and northern Solomons (Figure 9.1). Micronesia includes all the islands north of or straddling the equator between Palau and the Marianas in the west and the Marshalls and Kiribati in the east. "Triangle Polynesia" encompasses the area between Hawai'i, Aotearoa/New Zealand, and Rapa Nui/Easter Island, including Tuvalu (Figures 12.1, 13.1, 14.1). It subsumes "West Polynesia," formed by Tuvalu, Tonga, and Samoa, and "East Polynesia," which covers all of the remainder. New Zealand and nearby islands are increasingly separated as "South Polynesia," as is the case in this chapter. The "Polynesian Outliers" are Polynesian communities in Melanesia and Micronesia resulting from recent westerly back-migration, while the "Mystery Islands," not discussed further, are those with signs of prehistoric use which were unpopulated when first found by Europeans (e.g., Di Piazza and Pearthree 2001).

For reasons detailed in Walter and Sheppard's chapter, archaeologists often replace the Melanesia–Micronesia–Polynesia schema with the terms "Near Oceania" and "Remote Oceania" (Figure 1.1). Near Oceania encompasses the area first settled in the Pleistocene: Greater Australia and Melanesia to the end of the main Solomon Islands chain (i.e., excluding the remote southeasterly islands encompassed by the modern state of Solomon Islands). Remote Oceania takes in all of Triangle Polynesia and all of Micronesia. Neither set of terms is entirely satisfactory, as witnessed for instance by the distribution of the Polynesian Outliers across both Near and Remote Oceania as well as both Melanesia and Micronesia. All the terms have their uses nonetheless, and so all will be used in this volume as appropriate.

Note that archipelagoes and island groups are often referred to by the plural of their name (e.g., "the Bismarcks" and "the Loyalties" for the Bismarck Archipelago and the Loyalty Islands respectively), but not when the name designates a modern state (e.g., Fiji, Samoa, Tonga).

Dates

Archaeology in Oceania is heavily reliant on absolute dating, primarily by radiocarbon, and "chronometric hygiene" – careful assessment of the technical soundness of dates themselves and of the taphonomic integrity of their stratigraphic associations with archaeological material – is a constant concern (e.g., Spriggs 2001). Here the abbreviation "B.P." ("before present," technically 1950) is used interchangeably with "years ago" to indicate generalized chronologies. The term "cal B.P." is used to signify that a radiocarbon or other absolute determination has been calibrated to calendar years and is used to indicate exact chronologies. Uncalibrated dates over about 20,000 B.P. cannot yet be reliably calibrated. To complicate matters, some contributors use A.D./B.C. dates, according to local practice. The abbreviation "AMS" refers to accelerator mass-spectrometer radiocarbon dating, which allows highly accurate determinations on minute samples.

Thematic Setting and Non-Archaeological Background

The backbone of Oceania's human history was formed by three phases of colonization. The first occurred in the late Pleistocene, when modern humans pushed out from Southeast Asia into the realm of "Greater Australia" and beyond into the Bismarck and Solomon Islands archipelagoes. Greater Australia is the continent otherwise known as Sahul, which formed when lowered sea levels joined Australia, New Guinea, and Tasmania. On the other side of the world, other modern people were edging into Ice Age Europe at about this time. The initial move into the Antipodes was a momentous shift in the course of human affairs. It saw people island-hop across a substantial sea barrier between an Old World which had been inhabited by hominids for thousands of millennia, and a truly naïve new world with an ancient marsupial fauna where there was no possibility for human progenitors to have evolved. The second foundational colonization began more than 2,000 generations later. From around 3,500 years ago, seafaring pottery-making farmers in the Bismarcks created the "Lapita phenomenon" and became the first people to occupy Remote Oceania, the last uninhabited part of the globe other than Antarctica (Figure 16.2). The final phase of colonization was signaled by the appearance of Europeans within the last 500 years. We are still in this final phase, in the sense that colonialism and its aftermath have fostered continuing large-scale migration not only to but also within and from Oceania, all of which have substantive archaeological consequences as well as profound social and political implications for archaeological praxis.

Oceanic archaeology aims to discover who was involved in these dispersals, how, where, and when they undertook their journeys, and how, where, when, and why their lives then changed through time and space. Interaction and its opposite, isolation, are core explanatory tools in this endeavor because these processes were vitally important throughout the region. When Europeans began exploring Australia, for instance, complex "chains of connection" (Mulvaney 1976) linked Aboriginal communities down-the-line from one side of the continent to the other, and joined it to Asia and the Pacific across the Arafura Sea and Torres Strait. Similarly, inter-communal links facilitated the initial colonization of the Pacific and then waxed and waned as people adjusted to the social and physical exigencies of life in their often far-flung islands. The complex maritime and highlands exchange systems of Melanesia have long compelled attention from anthropologists, as have the maritime "empires" that arose in Tonga and Yap. As Clarke and Frederickson's chapter makes clear, more recent relationships between indigenous peoples throughout Oceania and European and other non-indigenous colonizers have produced intricate patterns of cultural and biological entanglement with which we are only beginning to come to grips, in terms of their contemporary political ramifications as well as their material manifestations in the archaeological record.

Variation in the importance of interaction is one of several major strands of divergence through time and space in the economic and sociopolitical patterns of Oceania. Australia and the rest of Near Oceania started to diverge very soon after initial colonization, as revealed by O'Connor and Veth's chapter on Australia and Leavesley's contribution on the Bismarcks. The early Holocene saw agriculture arise in New Guinea but not in Australia, as Denham details below, even though the two were joined by dry land at the time. Early to mid-Holocene change in the Bismarcks is taken up by Pavlides. The mid- to late Holocene saw quite different patterns of change unfold in Australia and the Pacific. The former are described by David, Hiscock, and McDonald and Veth, while all the remaining Pacific chapters deal with such matters by definition. Toward the end of prehistory, complex state-like polities emerged in some archipelagoes in the Pacific at the same time that politically much simpler societies were being maintained elsewhere in the region. Some of the results of this process are canvassed in the contributions of Ladefoged and Graves, Millerstrom, and Rainbird.

Environmental change – including human environmental impact – threads through the other main themes as debate continues about issues such as the causal relationships between environmental and cultural variation, faunal exterminations, erosion from land-clearing and the long-term effects of regular burning-off by for-agers and agriculturalists alike (e.g., Dodson 1992). Humanly induced as well as natural environmental shifts also have an impact on the practical side of doing archaeology in a way the other themes generally do not. Past cultural variation of any sort will affect what archaeological remains are found and where, but natural events and the environmental impacts of human activity can sometimes determine whether archaeological remains can be found at all. Landforms can subside beneath the sea owing to tectonic activity, while erosion from land-clearing can deeply bury early landscapes. For these reasons, archaeologists in Oceania often have to assess very carefully whether an apparent absence of evidence for human activity really is evidence for an absence of people.

These four substantive themes are investigated in a dynamic and sometimes volatile social and political milieu. This is the flipside of one of Oceania's great methodological advantages for archaeologists: direct "ethnoarchaeological" contact with the descendants of the people who created the sites we investigate, as elabo-rated in Conte's chapter. As it should, ethically speaking, access to the archaeolog-ical record now generally requires the permission of these descendants, who remain traditional or customary landowners throughout the region, as well as approval from government authorities. Either or both can and do deny such access for a variety of reasons, not least of which is that native peoples are tired of being the focus of Western scholarly scrutiny, which is often viewed as having little or no practical benefit for the communities under the microscope. One such moratorium, cover-ing the entire archipelago of Vanuatu, lasted a decade and of course had a marked effect on the progress of archaeological research in the region.

Questions of cultural continuity and change – archaeology's "core business" – are particularly sensitive. This is especially so where they bear on identity-based access to land and other resources in contexts where vested interests seek to restrict or eliminate that access by unraveling identity claims. There is thus a swirling "pol-itics of change" in Oceania, notably but not exclusively in settler societies such as Australia, New Caledonia, and New Zealand, the ethics of which can be more difficult for archaeologists to negotiate than the matters of archaeological theory and practice that are entailed. Different facets of the scene are surveyed at the end of the volume by Sand, Bole, and Ouetcho, Smith, and a combined contribution by Cauchois, Dugay-Grist, and Mandui.

To a large extent the themes that structure archaeology in Oceania are the same as those that connect archaeology everywhere: They concern elemental issues in our global professional conversation. Indeed, in Oceania these themes encompass almost the full gamut of change witnessed by archaeologists elsewhere, excluding only the evolution of modern humans at one end of the spectrum and the advent of true states and urbanism at the other. Yet it is critical to bear in mind that investigations such as those detailed in this book show very clearly that these themes often did not play out in Oceania in the ways that Old World understandings would predict they "should" have. Thus rather than witness the adoption of agriculture following the last glaciation, as global models of cultural change suggest it ought to have done, Australia remained a "continent of hunter-gatherers" until European colonization in the 18th century A.D. owing to the continual though often subtle accommodations people made with nature and with each other to maintain their lives as foragers. While there are undoubtedly some profound differences between foragers and agriculturalists, especially in the ways in which they view their physical environments, people in Australia managed their resources in often sophisticated ways not unlike some of those used by agriculturalists. Not least amongst these mechanisms were the interaction networks mentioned above, which rivaled in complexity those in Melanesia such as the famed "*kula* ring" which so fascinated early ethnographers such as Malinowski.

In this connection, it is pertinent to point out that despite modern scholarly expectations to the contrary, the Pleistocene foragers described in Pavlides's chapter were also able to live deep within primary rain forest in Melanesia without access to agricultural produce. In a similar vein, Polynesian agriculturalists took up foraging when they settled the South Island of New Zealand, where their tropical crops could not be sustained even with the major adjustments which allowed cropping on the North Island. Just as our visions of foragers and agriculturalists are being blurred in these ways, so, too, conventional wisdom concerning variation in sociopolitical organization is being challenged. Spanning about a quarter of the Earth's circumference, the colonization of the widely spread islands of Remote Oceania was one of the truly astounding feats of human history. It ultimately resulted in the rise of the Polynesian chiefdoms, the most complex of which can properly be described as proto-states. It has conventionally been thought that Melanesia differed in kind from Polynesia in this respect, in that it had intrinsically less complex sociopolitical systems, but just as cultural anthropology has elided the boundaries between supposedly stereotypical Melanesian big-men and Polynesian chiefs, so archaeology is now finding evidence for monumental structures in Melanesia akin to those in Polynesia.

Walter and Sheppard's pivotal contribution considers the last matter at some length to set the scene for the rest of the Pacific chapters (see especially Sand et al., this volume). The point to be made here is that human history in Oceania

often took the poet Frost's "road less traveled." This is of great significance theoretically as well as practically speaking, because a good deal of the social theory underlying the interpretation of Old World archaeological patterns was founded on
prearchaeological and usually ahistorical ethnographic understandings of cultural
patterns in Oceania. This means that archaeology in Oceania is in a strong position to contribute to wider debates concerning the human condition over the
long term.

Environmental setting and history

Near Oceania exhibits considerable environmental variation through space, especially in relation to the remote Pacific. Australia is the world's largest island and
the driest and flattest continent. It has a vast arid to semi-arid core fringed by
better-watered (indeed in places extremely wet) country across the far north,
along the east and southeast coasts and in the far southwest. The north has
hot, wet summers (November through January) and cool, dry winters, while the
south has a "Mediterranean" climate with hot, dry summers and cool, wet winters.
Much of the continent comprises low plateaux, with the principal mountain range
running down the east coast. The mountains are highest in the southeast, but rise
only to about 2,000 meters. The arid and semi-arid core is characterized by shrub-
lands and grasslands merging around the edges with open woodland which in turn
merges with mostly open forest but also small areas of closed forest on the coastal
fringes. There are alpine areas in the highest mountains, which see seasonal
snowfalls.

Tasmania is like southeastern Australia but more rugged, colder, and wetter. The
west coast is windy, topographically difficult and densely forested, but the east
is more sheltered and open. New Guinea is another of the world's largest islands.
Bordering the equator, it is clothed for the most part in dense tropical rain forest,
though there are large areas of swampland associated with major river systems
flowing through low-lying coastal areas as well as extensive alpine regions and even
glaciers in the east–west trending mountain spine of the island, which rises up to
about 5,000 meters. The larger high islands of the Bismarcks and Solomons are
much like scaled-down versions of New Guinea, though without the very high
central mountains and with less abundant and varied flora and fauna. The low coral
islands differ little from those in Remote Oceania, described below, though their
marine environments are generally much richer.

Paleoenvironmental change has been substantial during the time people have
lived in Near Oceania (Dodson et al. 2004; Mulvaney and Kamminga 1999:
103–129). In brief, temperatures and sea levels were like those which obtain
today at about 120,000 years ago but then began falling. When people first settled
Sahul the sea level was perhaps 30 meters lower than today, the climate was mild
and wet, and many now-dry lakes were full. Temperatures, precipitation, and sea
levels started falling dramatically from about 35,000 years ago until the Last Glacial
Maximum (LGM) 25,000–12,000 years ago. Average sea-surface temperatures in

the LGM were up to 4°C lower than now in the tropics and up to 9°C lower in higher latitudes (Barrows and Juggins 2005), while sea levels were up to 130 meters lower.

There was little ice during the LGM, unlike the situation in the northern hemisphere, but Australia became colder and much more arid. The cold lowered the treeline, but the main environmental shift was a major expansion of the continent's arid/semi-arid core, which was accompanied by dune-building which has left a legacy still visible in now much wetter parts of the country, including Tasmania. Dust storms were frequent and severe. In addition to creating land bridges between Australia, New Guinea, and Tasmania, the lowering of sea levels as the world's water was taken up in the northern hemisphere's vast ice sheets also saw the coastline of Australia expand elsewhere to dramatically increase the size of the continent. Large brackish lakes formed in what is now the Gulf of Carpentaria in northern Australia and Bass Strait between Australia and Tasmania. Climate change and sea-level variation had relatively little impact in New Guinea/northern Sahul, though alpine areas expanded and upland vegetation communities ringing the central cordillera moved downhill.

The beginning of the end of the last glacial period was marked by a rise in temperature and sea level around 15,000 years ago, though it remained very cold and dry until perhaps 12,000 years ago. Dune-building ended and treelines began rising, but unlike sea level, which stabilized at present levels around 6,000 years ago, vegetational shifts continued until about 4,000 years ago. Sea-level rise broke up Greater Australia, with Tasmania finally separating about 14,000 years ago and New Guinea about 7,000 years ago. Australia's land area shrank considerably (Lambeck and Chappell 2001).

The nature of postglacial environmental change in the southern hemisphere remains hard to pin down. There is a well-defined series of terminal Pleistocene/ Holocene arid periods in the northern hemisphere (e.g., the Younger Dryas 12,800–11,500 cal B.P.), but no clear indication that any of them occurred in the southern hemisphere (Haberle and David 2004:166–167). Much the same can be said of the "Medieval Warm Period" between the ninth and 13th centuries A.D. and the "Little Ice Age" between the 15th and late 19th centuries A.D. (Gagan et al. 2004:131–132; Haberle and David 2004:176 though cf. Holdaway et al. 2002). Although there were various local shifts in precipitation and temperature, perhaps the greatest long-term regional change was the emergence and increasing strength and frequency of El Ninõ–Southern Oscillation (ENSO) events. Becoming established in its modern pattern between 7,000 and 5,000 years ago and with a peak between 3,000 and 1,000 years ago following an abrupt increase in event magnitude, ENSO dramatically increases climatic variability and in particular can cause prolonged periods of severe drought throughout Oceania and especially in the west (see Gagan et al. 2004 for technical details). Hiscock's chapter in this volume addresses cultural change in Australia that coincided with the onset of ENSO (see also Haberle and David 2004).

When they moved into Remote Oceania, people had to contend with even more depauperate faunas (including marine animals) and floras than those of the

Bismarcks and Solomons. While this meant, amongst other things, that there were no land mammals other than fruit bats, it also meant that beyond Vanuatu people did not have to cope with malaria-bearing *Anopheles* mosquitoes (see Sand et al., this volume). In addition, the move beyond the Solomons coincided with the dramatic increase in the frequency and intensity of ENSO events, which some scholars think assisted the colonization process. Within remote Oceania, there are considerable differences among the islands people inhabited, from tiny, low-lying coral atolls, through usually larger raised coral islands (*makatea*), to "high" and sometimes destructively active islands of volcanic origin, which are of various sizes up to the near-continental in the case of New Zealand. There is also marked divergence between windward and leeward island groups and sides of individual islands, brought about by a marked seasonal shift between the dominance of moisture-bearing southeast trade winds and dry northwesterlies which in Asia and northern Near Oceania bring the monsoon. Major variation is also evident between northern and southern hemisphere weather and ocean-current patterns and between equatorial and higher-latitude climates. In the case of New Zealand there is noticeable climatic variation from north to south and from coasts and lowlands into the uplands, some of which are glaciated on the South Island. The highest mountains in the Hawaiian chain also receive regular winter snows.

All of the foregoing patterns are periodically affected by ENSO events, which dramatically increase or decrease rainfall in different parts of the region on an irregular basis. Humanly induced changes such as deforestation, erosion, and the extinction of plant and animal species, particularly the ground-dwelling birds that proliferated in the Pacific in the absence of mammals, added to the mix of environmental shifts people had to deal with (Sand et al., this volume). More detailed information about the environment of Remote Oceania from an archaeological perspective can be found in Kirch (2000:42–62).

Language and biology

Echoing early models proposing waves of biologically distinct migrants, some biologists remain convinced that the earliest inhabitants of Near Oceania – and specifically Australia – can be sorted into groups with separate origins in Java, China, India, and elsewhere. Others propose a single original colonization by biologically diverse people followed by continual but biologically minor interchange with external source areas as well as important ongoing evolutionary modification owing to gene flow, genetic drift, and adaptation to varying environmental contexts. Skeletal characteristics such as robusticity and gracility, which are taken by the multiple-origins models as markers of separate origins, have been shown by proponents of the single-origin model to relate to sex and climatic variation (i.e., male/female, arid/non-arid). The single-origin model is based on genetic as well as skeletal evidence and accords best with the archaeological record, in which there is no evidence for multiple migrations in the form of the sudden appearance of novel items of material culture or new patterns of behavior with demonstrable external origins (see detailed discussion in Cameron and Groves 2004:251–274).

Linguistics has little to say about the initial colonization and early history of Near Oceania. Aboriginal languages in Australia differ so profoundly from those in adjacent regions that they must have been separate for a very long time. The 250 languages thought to have been spoken at European contact are classified into two main groupings: Pama-Nyungan and non-Pama-Nyungan. The former is a single language family. It covers all but the easternmost islands in Torres Strait, where Papuan languages are spoken, and the whole of the Australian mainland except the far north coast lying west of Cape York. There is too little of the Tasmanian languages left to know where they group. The far north coast is linguistically complex, being home to all 20+ language families of the non-Pama-Nyungan group as well as a handful of Pama-Nyungan tongues.

Historical linguistics is not yet well developed in Australia in general, but McConvell's controversial models see Pama-Nyungan speakers spreading from near the Gulf of Carpentaria within the past 5,000 years, to engulf a continental pattern of deep diversity like that of the current non-Pama-Nyungan group (McConvell 1996). Other linguists have strongly criticized such ideas, preferring a model of in-situ development of Pama-Nyungan through innovation and interaction, and are supported by archaeologists such as Mulvaney and Kamminga (1999:69–75). This position appears to be backed by biology as well. N. White (1994:76) notes that "currently available information from nuclear gene markers and DNA polymorphisms provides no clear evidence of migration which may have been associated with the spread of [Pama-Nyungan] speakers." Other archaeologists such as Veth (2000) argue for "convergence" of archaeological models with McConvell's propositions, at least in the Western Desert.

The languages of Oceania beyond Australia are also split into two principal classes: Austronesian and non-Austronesian (or "Papuan"). The 700+ languages in the Papuan group include most of the languages of mainland New Guinea and some of those on nearby islands to the west as well as to the east as far as New Georgia in the Solomons. They are related at the highest level only by the fact that they are not Austronesian, though a number of groupings can be discerned at lower levels of abstraction. There have been various efforts to distil historical patterns from these relationships, but they do not speak with any degree of certainty to issues concerning very early periods, except to suggest that some languages and groupings may have significant time depth, and that some in the mountainous interior of New Guinea may be distantly related to Australian languages (Foley 1986:269–283). This last suggestion finds support in biological studies which show that Aboriginal Australians have affinities with Melanesians and particularly highland New Guineans, who were isolated from major biocultural changes described below that affected the coasts and islands of Melanesia in the late Holocene (e.g., Oppenheimer 2003, 2004).

Austronesian languages were the only pre-European languages in Remote Oceania. Ultimately of Taiwanese origin, they are also spoken almost everywhere in Island Southeast Asia and, in Near Oceania, in some coastal and lowland parts of New Guinea and nearly all of the Bismarcks and main Solomons. All Austronesian languages located east of the Bird's Head in Indonesian Papua, including all but the most westerly parts of Micronesia, form a subset called Oceanic. Within Oceanic, the Austronesian languages of Melanesia separate into a number of major subgroups reflecting variation through time and space. A string of space–time shifts in an ancestral language from one of these subgroups eventually gave rise to the very closely related set of languages that spread through Polynesia. All of the islands in Micronesia except Yap, Palau, and the Marianas fall in one linguistic subgroup which originated in central Melanesia. Yap is a difficult case, but seems most closely related to Oceanic Austronesian in the Admiralty Islands of Papua New Guinea. Although Austronesian, the languages of Palau and the Marianas are not Oceanic, but rather are Western Austronesian languages of Southeast Asian type.

Although biologists and linguists (and archaeologists: see Green 2003; Smith 2002; and much of Terrell's work, e.g., 1989, 1999) continually contest the empirical and theoretical details, biology backs the overall linguistic picture concerning the colonization of Remote Oceania: The people came from Southeast Asia, via Island Melanesia, where they mixed with existing populations before moving further east. On the grounds that people in Remote Oceania share certain unique biological markers and all speak Oceanic, it is argued that their ancestors who first moved from Southeast Asia into Island Melanesia brought Austronesian tongues with them, in a well-documented form linguists call Proto Oceanic (e.g., Ross et al. 1998). Linguistics and biology agree these colonists largely avoided mainland New Guinea, though both disciplines suggest there was a pre-Oceanic Austronesian incursion along the north coast from the west (Oppenheimer 2003, 2004; cf. Green 2003).

There is growing biological evidence for sex-based differences in these patterns of movement. As Underhill et al. (2001) put it, "the Y-chromosome [male] results indicate a pattern of complex interrelationships between Southeast Asia, Melanesia and Polynesia, in contrast to the mtDNA [female] and linguistic data, which uphold a rapid and homogenous Austronesian expansion. The Y-chromosome data highlight a distinctive gender-modulated pattern of differential gene flow in the history of Polynesia." The archaeological manifestation of this movement into Near and then Remote Oceania is seen in the "Lapita cultural complex," discussed below.

Archaeological Background: Near Oceania

In the beginning

Four key questions about the Pleistocene in New Oceania need introduction: the timing of initial settlement, the pattern of continental colonization, "megafauna," and Pleistocene mainland New Guinea. There is a long chronology for the initial occupation of Near Oceania based on luminescence dating and a short one based on radiocarbon. The latter proposes that people first arrived in Greater Australia and nearby archipelagoes no more than about 45,000 years ago. Long-chronology supporters argue that this is because radiocarbon is technically unable to date anything older. They use luminescence techniques to circumvent the problem and presently date colonization at 50,000–60,000 years ago. They suggest that dates much older than 60,000 are unlikely because there is no evidence of anything like that antiquity from Tasmania, where the land bridge across Bass Strait was open between 62,000 and 70,000 B.P.

Allen and O'Connell champion the short chronology (Allen 2003; O'Connell and Allen 2004). They reject dates older than 45,000 B.P. on three main grounds. First, they argue that no dates of this antiquity are secure in their stratigraphic association with unambiguous remains of human activity. Second, they show that the long chronology does not fit with knowledge of the dispersal of modern humans elsewhere in the world. There are for instance no modern human remains in Island Southeast Asia – through which the first migrants to Australia must have passed – older than 45,000 years. Finally, they raise issues of calibration, arguing that luminescence dates are not sufficiently well understood in terms of their relationship to calendar and radiocarbon dates.

O'Connor and Chappell (2003) defend the long chronology. They believe calibration issues are well resolved in favor of accepting luminescence dates and that new discoveries in East Asia are continually pushing back the date for human occupation on this side of the world. They do not, however, address the issues of taphonomic integrity upon which Allen and O'Connell stake much of their case. Instead they go on to argue that Australia and New Guinea, though joined at the time, saw initial colonization at different times and by different ways. This is because there are no dates – luminescence or radiocarbon – older than 40,000 to 45,000 from New Guinea or the Bismarcks or Solomons (e.g., Torrence et al. 2004). In the short-chronologists' view this means that the whole of Near Oceania was effectively settled all at once, although the New Guinea highlands, the Solomons, and the Admiralty Islands in the north of the Bismarcks may not have been settled until around 10,000 years later than the rest. The highlands are remote and inaccessible, while reaching the Solomons and Admiralties requires formidable sea-crossings (see Leavesley, this volume).

O'Connor and Veth's chapter addresses aspects of Pleistocene change following the initial colonization of Australia, reflecting a relatively recent move to reassess conventional pictures of this period as one in which not much happened. Such reassessments diminish the differences previously thought to obtain between Pleistocene and Holocene; findings like theirs have important consequences for discussions of later change. This matter is taken up again below.

O'Connor and Veth deal only in passing with the occupation of the Australian landmass as a whole, mentioning Bowdler's (1977) coastal colonization hypothesis. This model states that the first arrivals were coastally oriented and initially stuck with familiar environments before moving up the major rivers and finally out into truly terrestrial habitats. Alternative models have people spreading wave-like across the whole continent, or moving first into the northern savannahs and then through the eastern woodlands and forests (Mulvaney and Kamminga 1999:130–133). O'Connor and Chappell (2003:22–26) note that while the oldest evidence from Melanesia is indeed marine oriented, that from Australia, even in coastal sites, is much more terrestrially focused. They propose that this, as well as the nature of early technology and the fact that the oldest known sites (by luminescence dating) are in savannah or woodland, supports the savannah-colonization model.

This brings us to the question of the "megafauna." Horton (1981), a proponent of savannah colonization, argued that one reason people would settle the savannahs first is that they were rich in game, including now-extinct "giant" species. Flannery's (1994) well-known popular account adopts a "blitzkreig" model in which new colonists rapidly eliminated the megafauna. There is no evidence this occurred. There are only a handful of sites in Australia and New Guinea where there is evidence for interaction between people and extinct giant fauna, and their interpretation remains the subject of passionate argument (Mulvaney and Kamminga 1999:121–129).

Leavesley's chapter covers Pleistocene developments in the Bismarcks and Solomons, but none of the contributions deal with this period on the New Guinea mainland. It was mentioned earlier that colonization of the New Guinea highlands may have occurred some 10,000 years after settlement of the island as a whole (Figure 8.1). Whenever it happened, movement into the New Guinea highlands would have seen changes in people's behavior but we know little about such shifts or developments that followed them (Kirch 2000:72–74). Work at the two most ancient highlands sites indicates amongst other things that early stone artifact assemblages included distinctive waisted tools, the "waist" being a notch for binding a handle. Similarities between such waisted tools and certain artifacts in Australia may reflect the introduction of a technological tradition of Asian origin by Sahul's first inhabitants (Golson 2001).

Only two sites with Pleistocene deposits have been excavated in Indonesian Papua (Pasveer et al. 2002). Preliminary results show that people have lived continuously in the region's lowland rain forests since at least the LGM. Pavlides's contribution to this volume takes up this question in connection with the Bismarck Archipelago. The early prehistory of coastal eastern New Guinea is also almost completely unknown (Kirch 2000:70–74). Only two Pleistocene sites are reported – the 40,000-year-old Jo's Creek site on the Huon Peninsula in northeast New Guinea and the 35,000-year-old Lachitu Cave on the north coast near the Indonesian border (Figure 9.1). No detailed reports are available for either, but the latter became the subject of renewed investigation in 2004. Most finds from Jo's Creek are waisted stone tools, broadly similar to those found in the highland sites discussed above. It has been suggested that they were used for forest clearance, thus initiating a long-term trend of change which culminated in the emergence of agriculture, but other researchers find such views unconvincing (see Denham, this volume).

Postglacial change

Background comments are needed regarding mid- to late Holocene shifts in Australia, including Tasmania and Torres Strait, and regarding Lapita and post-Lapita developments in the Pacific. Conventional views of early Holocene change in Near Oceania focused primarily on the emergence of agriculture in the New Guinea highlands, addressed here by Denham. As mentioned above, little was thought to have occurred in Australia or elsewhere in Near Oceania until the mid- to late Holocene. Pavlides's contribution to this volume shows that this was not the case in the Bismarck Archipelago. Until recently, models concerning mid-Holocene mainland Australia proposed that a package of new artifact types known as the "Small Tool Tradition" was suddenly added to the "Core Tool and Scraper Tradition" that had characterized the technology of Near Oceania since colonization. Some proposed (and periodically still propose) that the small tools were introduced from Southeast Asia, like (and perhaps with) the domestic dog, an unquestionable Holocene introduction that arrived at least 3,000–4,000 years ago. Other researchers suggested instead that the artifacts were locally invented owing either to environmental pressures or, from a theoretically different orientation, in connection with a multifaceted process of mid- to late Holocene socioeconomic intensification rooted in political competition (Lourandos 1997; Mulvaney and Kamminga 1999:223–272; O'Connor and Chappell 2003). Hiscock has shown the tools were invented early and locally. His chapter describes his efforts to completely reorient our thinking on this issue (see Mulvaney and Kamminga 1999:223–272 for more general background). Other important aspects of late Holocene change are taken up in David's and McDonald and Veth's contributions.

A number of different changes occurred in Holocene Tasmania. The most notorious is the fact that Tasmanians suddenly stopped eating fish 3,500 years ago. There were other, more gradual shifts around the same time, such as the loss of bone tools and variations in stone artifact typology and technology. Jones (e.g., 1977) characterized them all as maladaptive simplifications perhaps indicative of the negative cultural and psychological effects of long-term isolation on a relatively small island. Others (e.g., Bowdler 1980) disputed this scenario, pointing to various events and processes that compensated for any negative changes. Current models emphasize the mid- to late Holocene expansion of Tasmanian society and culture into the isolated south and west coasts and to offshore islands as well as in the more open environments of the eastern half of the island (Lourandos 1997:279–281; Mulvaney and Kamminga 1999:345–346).

Research and cultural heritage management programs have recently surged in Torres Strait, usually at the behest of local island communities (e.g., Barham et al. 2004; David and McNiven 2004; McNiven et al. 2004). The emerging picture shows that the western islands closest to Australia remained inhabited while they were being formed but were abandoned soon afterwards. Following periodic visitation from 6000 B.P. they were permanently occupied again 3,500 years ago (David et al. 2004). This ties developments in the Strait with mid- to late Holocene processes elsewhere around Australia, where offshore islands were occupied as "part of systematic territorial and sea-based expansions" (David et al. 2004:74) that some scholars link with socioeconomic intensification (but cf. Bowdler 1995). Islands close to New Guinea and in the remote east do not appear to have been occupied until 2,500, when they were settled by fisher-horticulturalists with strong links to southern New Guinea. (Barham et al. 2004; Carter et al. 2004a, b).

From about 2,000 years ago, the remote eastern islands were linked with long-distance trading systems that emerged as post-Lapita Austronesian-speakers moved west along the southeast coast of New Guinea (Carter et al. 2004a, b). This linkage joins northern Australia to the wider Pacific in a manner scarcely contemplated until Carter's discoveries. My view (Lilley 1999a; also Carter 2004) builds on Barham's (2000) insights concerning the pre-Austronesian "Torres Strait Cultural Complex" to argue that local events and processes in Torres Strait over the past 3,500 years may have been part of what drew Austronesian speakers westward along the south coast of New Guinea around 2000 B.P. rather than being the result of a Lapita-period Austronesian intervention of the sort proposed by David et al. (2004).

Walter and Sheppard's chapter explains how the Lapita phenomenon dominates the study of late Holocene prehistory in Melanesia. Other chapters dealing with Lapita-related questions include Denham, Galipaud, Leavesley, Pavlides, and Sand et al. Lapita is seen as a vast "community of culture" (Golson 1961) which, at least west of Fiji, was held together by long-distance ties through which people, ideas, and material such as obsidian moved over often vast distances. In the eyes of many researchers, this puts the phenomenon on par with the world's other major farming dispersals (Bellwood 2005; but cf. Terrell 2004). In an attempt to flesh out Lapita origins theoretically, I (1999b, 2004a) have proposed that Lapita began as a diaspora in the sociological sense, produced by processes of hybridization and creolization in the Bismarcks. These processes gave rise to a culturally distinctive social formation which allowed dispersed and highly mobile peoples to remain socially cohesive owing to a unifying ideology materialized in their elaborately decorated ceramics.

Walter and Sheppard also consider research on post-Lapita developments, including my own and many others' work in eastern New Guinea and adjacent archipelagoes on the development of long-distance maritime trading systems thought to derive from the extensive interaction systems of Lapita times (for additional background see Kirch 2000:120–130). The locality-specific models developed to describe and explain changes in these systems remain the subject of debate as to whether any of them can be generalized to explain developments in other areas. To date, only one general model has been expressly formulated to account for common characteristics in the developmental trajectories of the networks (Allen 1984). This scenario begins with an areally extensive but organizationally simple system which, through a series of systemic collapses, splits into an increasing number of more localized but organizationally more complex systems. The initial system is equated with Lapita interaction, intermediate states with the breakdown of that network, and the most localized and complex networks with ethnographic systems. Although not focused on the development of specialized long-distance maritime trade, or explicitly concerned with Allen's model, research into post-Lapita variation in Island Melanesia is feeding discussion canvassing the same general issues, as taken up next.

Archaeological Background: Remote Oceania

Melanesia

Basic chronological details of prehistory need to be sketched for most of Remote Oceania. Sand's contribution to this volume with Bole and Ouetcho details the current state of play in New Caledonia. The long-term research program in neighboring Vanuatu mentioned in chapter 7 by Walter and Sheppard has gone some way toward situating that archipelago in the broader Lapita and post-Lapita worlds. It had been hypothesized that Vanuatu was first settled by the makers of incised and applied-relief Mangaasi ceramics during the Lapita period, but before the appearance of Lapita pottery (and its makers) in those islands. Recent excavations have established that Lapita is the earliest cultural evidence, that Mangaasi developed only about 2000 B.P. out of earlier post-Lapita ceramics, and that pottery production ceased in the central islands about 1200 B.P. (Bedford and Clark 2001:66). At the time of writing, a spectacular new Lapita find on the central island of Efaté was promising to add a significant dimension to our knowledge of Vanuatu's prehistory (Bedford et al. 2004).

Fiji (Figure 17.1) is often considered together with neighboring Samoa and Tonga and nearby islands in West Polynesia, but cultural divergences emerged soon after virtually simultaneous Lapita colonization of all three island groups around 2900 B.P. by people who made what is known as Eastern Lapita, characterized by a reduced range of vessel forms and simplified decoration. Lapita evolved into Polynesian Plainware by about 2600 B.P. Although links amongst the archipelagoes were active throughout prehistory, the process of divergence soon saw western Fiji change in ways which tied it to Island Melanesia while patterns in eastern Fiji were more like those in Samoa and Tonga (Burley and J. Clark 2003). This means that in the east the evolution of Plainware also saw a diminution in the range of vessel forms, creating assemblages Kirch and Green (2001) contend were produced by an archaeologically, linguistically, and biologically well-attested "Ancestral Polynesian Society" from which all Polynesian societies sprang (Walter and Sheppard, this volume).

Whereas the earliest settlers in Fiji stuck to the coasts and were more focused on foraging than farming, in this later period settlement on larger islands expanded inland, associated with agricultural intensification. Plainware ended throughout Fiji about 1,500 years ago, to be replaced by decorated wares suggesting connections with northern Vanuatu. The chronological and technological abruptness of the replacement may indicate new people moved to Fiji with the ceramics (Burley and J. Clark 2003). Within the past 1,000 years, there was widespread agricultural intensification which coincided with the appearance of fortified villages. It is unclear whether the development of fortifications resulted from internal social processes or clashes between immigrants and locals.

Clark (2000) sees no connections at any time in the post-Lapita period between changes in Fijian ceramics and those outside the archipelago. This is important because it returns us to consideration of large-scale post-Lapita patterns in Melanesia. Spriggs (e.g., 2003, 2004) has for some time argued that there is good evidence for a "community of culture" akin to that of the Lapita period in the form of the synchronous widespread ceramic changes, and specifically the con-temporaneous appearance of applied-and-incised decoration broadly similar to Mangaasi in Vanuatu. He contends this grouping stretched from the Admiralties in the north at least as far as central Vanuatu, and perhaps also to New Caledonia and Fiji. Bedford and Clark (2001) have strongly asserted their disagreement, arguing that any widespread similarities result from shared Lapita heritage rather than continuing long-distance interaction. Spriggs (2003:207–208) responds that the connections are not just seen in pottery. Obsidian from Vanuatu has been found in Fiji, and

> many Fijians, Ni-Vanuatu, Kanaks of New Caledonia and southeast Solomons Islanders [from the Reefs/Santa Cruz] do not look Polynesian... These areas, however, like Polynesia are part of Remote Oceania... [indicating] there must have been significant post-Lapita gene flow down the chain from the main Solomons or further north into Vanuatu, New Caledonia and Fiji... We are thus still left with a need to postulate periods of post-Lapita connectedness between these various areas.

Garling (2003) takes a middle path in relation to the position of Tanga off New Ireland in the Bismarcks, suggesting there was "cultural fusion" which saw conti-nuity in vessel forms from the Lapita period overlain by incised and applied relief decoration. My own work in the West New Britain-Vitiaz Strait-North New Guinea region suggests that post-Lapita patterns there are completely different from those in contention here. (Lilley 2004b)

Clearly, much remains to be done in Melanesia to improve the resolution of our picture of the post-Lapita scene. Rock art studies are one avenue that will help that is not covered in the volume. Wilson (2003, 2004) has brought together the results of past research with the findings of her own in-depth studies in Vanuatu and explic-itly addresses the question of post-Lapita continuity in Island Melanesia. Like Garling, she (2003:280) finds her results "offer a degree of support for both argu-ments." At one level, Vanuatu "was, for the most part, following its own regional trajectory [since Lapita times] rather than participating in a broader... network." She notes for instance that the archipelago missed out on post-2000 B.P. develop-ments to the west. If Vanuatu is given less prominence, however, "then a strong argument can also be made that rock-art similarities attest to consistent inter-regional interaction... since at least Lapita times," insofar as all the traditions she identifies appeared "in some form across the entire western Pacific" (Wilson 2003:280). Wilson also delineates a "cupule-based engraving tradition" linked with the Lapita phenomenon and initial colonization in East Polynesia, tentatively tying her results with Millerstrom's findings in the Marquesas (Wilson 2003:272; see below and Millerstrom, this volume).

Polynesia

I noted above that Samoa and Tonga were settled by Lapita colonists about 2900 B.P. and that Eastern Lapita evolved into Polynesian Plainware within two centuries, heralding the advent of "Ancestral Polynesian Society." Unlike the situation in Fiji, however, pottery disappeared gradually and unevenly throughout West Polynesia by about 1500 B.P. (J. Clark 1996; also Kirch 2000:219–230). Little is known of the period directly following the end of ceramics in either Samoa or Tonga, but the past 1,000 years in both archipelagoes saw the rise of complex centralized chiefdoms governing large populations (Kirch 1984). Though low-intensity swidden gardens were maintained in Samoa throughout prehistory, the rise of the Tongan chiefdom was linked with a marked intensification of agriculture.

The advent of complex societies in West Polynesia is also linked with the appearance of monumental architecture, including various sorts of mounds and, in Samoa, fortified earthworks. All this reflects patterns common to much of Remote Oceania (Walter and Sheppard, this volume). What is unusual is that in the last few centuries before European contact, the Tongan chiefdom was positioned at the center of an extensive long-distance prestige-goods interaction sphere. Known as the "Tongan Empire," its extremities reached as far as Vanuatu and New Caledonia. The Samoan forts (and those in other archipelagoes within reach) are probably linked to Tongan expansion.

Smith (2002) has deconstructed conventional models of West Polynesian prehistory, and especially the "phylogenetic" model of Ancestral Polynesian Society promoted by Kirch and Green (2001). Her argument is that they are undermined by a growing number of empirical inconsistencies, but that this is ignored by the dominant paradigm owing to the strength of expectations generated by historical linguistics. She has proposed a hypothetical alternative sequence in West Polynesia which argues for a high degree of continuity between the Lapita and post-Lapita periods. She sees the shift as another example of the sort of post-Lapita developments discussed above in relation to Melanesia rather than as a unique cultural break, and suggests that the characteristics of Polynesian societies recorded by European observers may have arisen only within the past 1,000 years.

There have been arguments that settlement of the huge area of the Pacific beyond West Polynesia was continuous, flowing on without pause from Samoa and Tonga (Irwin 1992). At present the data support the conventional model which places a pause of at least 1,000 years in West Polynesia before people moved again after "becoming" the Polynesians ancestral to today's populations. Precisely when this dispersal occurred is debated. Spriggs and Anderson's (1993) short chronology indicates colonization of the Marquesas between 1400 and 1700 B.P., and perhaps earlier. This archipelago has long been proposed as the first part of East Polynesia to be settled. They place the settlement of the Cooks and Societies in central East Polynesia no earlier than about 1200–1400 B.P., confirming the conventional view that these archipelagoes were bypassed as people spread from West Polynesia to the Marquesas. The earliest radiocarbon date Spriggs and Anderson accept for Rapa Nui (Easter Island) is imprecise but suggests occupation toward the end of the first millennium A.D. The best-dated material in Hawai'i signals initial colonization at no more than 1400 B.P. Spriggs and Anderson accept only post-1000 BP dates in the remote eastern islands and reiterate Anderson's (1991) short chronology for New Zealand in South Polynesia. This proposes first settlement of the mainland in the past 800–1,000 years and the Kermadecs and Chathams by 800 and 700 years ago, respectively. This overall pattern accords with geological evidence concerning the emergence above sea level of habitable and/or stepping-stone islands in East Polynesia (Dickinson 2003).

The foregoing dates compress the prehistory of East and South Polynesia, and imply cultural change was faster than generally thought. Kirch and Green (2001:79 also Kirch 2000:230) contend that the short chronology excludes valid earlier dates for environmental change indicative of human activity, that there is evidence the Societies were settled as early as the Marquesas, and that by 1200 B.P. the Marquesas and central archipelagoes were all "well-populated" and linked by frequent interaction. Their long chronology dates occupation of Hawai'i to at least 1200 B.P., if not 1500–1800 B.P., and proposes that Rapa Nui was also settled from 1200–1300 B.P., but accepts the short chronology for South Polynesia.

Whichever chronology is eventually accepted, it is clear that the furthest-flung islands of Triangle Polynesia were effectively isolated not long after colonization. Hawai'i, Rapa Nui, and New Zealand may have seen occasional visits, but they were all completely cut off at the time of European contact. Interaction waned in the central islands, too, though more gradually. This process saw the societies of the Remote Pacific differentiate to a degree while remaining recognizably closely related (Walter 1996). The archaeologies of the Marquesas and especially Hawai'i are comparatively well known. Ladefoged and Graves's chapter considers aspects of their current research in Hawai'i, while Millerstrom describes some of her work in the Marquesas. Both chapters concern the situation after the appearance of complex centralized chiefdoms in those and other archipelagoes, archaeologically associated agricultural intensification and monumental architecture including the famed heads (*moai* statues) on Rapa Nui. The Hawaiian chiefdom was the most complex in the Pacific and in Kirch's (2000:289–300) view approached the status of an "archaic state."

By way of general background to these chapters, you should know that while the West Polynesian and indeed the Lapita roots of East Polynesian cultures remained apparent during the early post-colonization period, the region also witnessed the rapid materialization of a variety of distinctive traits (Walter 1996). The best known are an astonishing diversity of one-piece fishhooks and trolling lures, as well as new basalt adze forms. The latter descend from other distinctive types created in West Polynesia as colonists there adapted to crossing the "Andesite Line" separating the complex continental geology of the southwest Pacific (including Fiji) from the simplified basaltic geology of the more remote Pacific.

New Zealand stands isolated from East Polynesia, not just because it is geographically remote but also because its combined area is very large and it has a temperate rather than tropical or subtropical climate (Davidson 1984; Kirch 2000:275–283). This meant that East Polynesian colonists could grow only a restricted range of their familiar domestic plants, and then only in the North Island. Nor did domestic pigs or chickens make it: dogs alone survived the transfer. In the colder and more mountainous South Island, people gave up agriculture altogether to become full-time foragers. This process was aided by the presence throughout New Zealand of various species of flightless birds called *moa*, some of which were gigantic. All were killed off by hunting or habitat modification, mirroring a pattern of human environmental impact that is common throughout Remote Oceania and reached extremes which threatened people's capacity to cope in places such as Rapa Nui. Following this period of adaptation, societies on New Zealand's North Island began developing ranked chiefdoms based on intensive agriculture, and, in late prehistory, entailing the construction of fortified hilltop villages. Clearly, although it was isolated, cultural trends in (North Island) New Zealand were much like those elsewhere in Polynesia.

Micronesia

Historical linguistics indicate that Central and Eastern Micronesia was settled from the general area of Vanuatu or the southeast Solomons (Figure 1.1), but archaeological research has not revealed anything more specific than generalized connections dating to late or early post-Lapita times (Kirch (2000:173–174; Rainbird 2004:75–100). The high islands of the Carolines – from west to east, Chuuk, Pohnpei, and Kosrae – were aceramic at European contact but their populations made plain or minimally decorated pottery in earlier periods. Colonization occurred about 2000 B.P. None of the high islands has an archaeologically complete cultural sequence but after a series of changes including the loss of ceramics by about 500 B.P., Pohnpei and Kosrae went on to develop complex chiefdoms with astonishing monumental architecture, facets of which are discussed in Rainbird's chapter toward the end of this volume (also Rainbird 2004:168–224).

The Micronesian atolls were first occupied at the same time as the high islands. Atoll societies did not develop complex political systems and their cultural sequences reveal little change through time. They are fascinating nonetheless owing to the adaptations needed to cope with "life on the edge" (Weisler 2001) in such small, remote, and resource-poor localities. As Kirch (2000:181) puts it, "atoll islets are consummate man-made environments." Shell technology was highly developed in the absence of hard stone, and the Caroline Islanders had "the most sophisticated outrigger canoe technology and star-compass systems known in Oceania" (Kirch 2000:181–182; also Rainbird 2004:225–244).

Western Micronesia was settled directly from Southeast Asia, and/or Taiwan in the case of the Mariana Islands. There are earlier dates for environmental disturbance but reliable direct evidence for human activity in the Marianas and Palau dates to a maximum of 3300 B.P. (Clark 2004; Phear et al. 2003), and in Yap to about 2000 B.P., giving rise to the same sort of debate about short and long chronologies seen elsewhere in Oceania. The short chronology indicates initial occupation of Western Micronesia around the same time as the beginning of Lapita in the Bismarcks, but the two dispersals were probably not related. The earliest Western Micronesian ceramics, Marianas Red ware and Lime Infilled ware, are only generically similar to Lapita, suggesting a common origin in Southeast Asia.

Marianas Red evolved into Marianas Plain within the past 1,000 years, during which time monumental architecture also arose. Some scholars argue the monumental sites reflect status ranking, but others contend the sites are so common they indicate the absence of ranking (Kirch 2000:184–187; also Rainbird 2004:101–133). The Palaun sequence focuses on extensive landscape transformation in the form of monumental earthworks on the main island of Babeldaob (Kirch 2000:187–191; Rainbird 2004:135–153). The earliest date from 1600–1500 B.P. and appear to be defensive positions but those from a second building phase between 1,200 and 800 years ago are habitation sites. Other settlement pattern changes occur before and after the earthworks (Phear et al. 2003). In Yap, early pottery was replaced about 700 years ago by Yapese Laminated Ware, which lasted until after European contact. The stone architecture of the island has yet to be studied in detail, but may be linked with the elaboration of social ranking historically known as the Yapese "caste system." It may also be associated with the *sawei*, an extraordinary interaction system also known as the "Yapese Empire" which connected Yap with 14 atoll communities spread over 1,200 kilometers in the Carolines to the east (Kirch 2000:191–193; Rainbird 2004:153–163).

An Endpoint

Petersen (2000:27) compared the sawei to the Tongan "empire." He said that

> To speak of either Yap or Tonga as empires, without specifying that the term does not imply much that characterizes modern empires, may serve more to confuse than to clarify. But to deny that these complexes of economic, political, and cultural relations bore some salient similarities to other world historical empires, whether in the Americas, Africa, Asia, or Europe, would be to suggest – quite erroneously – that the indigenous societies of Oceania existed outside the realm of world historical experience.

These sentiments apply to most if not all of the matters considered in this volume. There are obvious points of comparison in the way our main themes unfolded across Oceania, whether it be processes of initial colonization of naïve new worlds in Near and Remote Oceania or the manner in which the emergence of ranked soci-

eties in geographically and historically widely separated parts of the Pacific are associated with the appearance of monumental architecture on the one hand and intensive agriculture and endemic warfare on the other. These processes echo similar
ones in many other parts of the world, placing our region well and truly inside "the
realm of world historical experience."

Other aspects of our story do not fit so readily into global scenarios, such as the
persistence of foraging in Australia and the remarkable complexity of coastal trade
in Melanesia. Instances such as these do not put Oceania or any part of it outside
global history, as Stringer recently implied they do. He (1999:876) might see this
part of the globe "as a place at the edge of the inhabited world where modern
humans arrived relatively late and then remained largely isolated from subsequent
developments." I prefer to think of such aspects of Oceania's past as telling exceptions that test supposedly universal "rules" and in doing so lead us to a richer and
more generous view of the human condition.

REFERENCES

Allen, J., 1984 Pots and Poor Princes: A Multidimensional Approach to the Role of Pottery
    Trading in Coastal Papua. *In* The Many Dimensions of Pottery: Ceramics in Archaeology
    and Anthropology. S. van der Leeuw and A. Pritchard, eds. pp. 409–473. Amsterdam: University of Amsterdam.
——2003 Discovering the Pleistocene in Island Melanesia. *In* Pacific Archaeology: Assessments and Prospects. C. Sand, ed. pp. 33–42. Les Cahiers de l'Archéologie en Nouvelle-
    Calédonie 15. Nouméa: Département Archéologie, Service des Musées et du Patrimoine
    de Nouvelle-Calédonie.
Anderson, A., 1991 The Chronology of Colonization in New Zealand. Antiquity 65:767–795.
Barham, A., 2000 Late Holocene Maritime Societies in the Torres Strait Islands, Northern
    Australia – Cultural Arrival or Cultural Emergence? *In* East of Wallace's Line. Studies of
    Past and Present Maritime Cultures of the Indo-Pacific Region. S. O'Connor and P. Veth,
    eds. pp. 223–314. Modern Quaternary Research in Southeast Asia 16. Rotterdam: A. A.
    Balkema.
Barham, A., M. Rowland and G. Hitchcock, 2004 Torres Strait Bepotaim: An Overview
    of Archaeological and Ethnoarchaeological Investigations. *In* Torres Strait Archaeology
    and Material Culture. I. McNiven and M. Quinnell, eds. pp. 1–72. Memoirs of the
    Queensland Museum Cultural Heritage Series 3(1). Brisbane: Queensland Museum.
Barrows, T., and S. Juggins, 2005 Sea-Surface Temperatures around the Australian Margin
    and Indian Ocean during the Last Glacial Maximum. Quaternary Science Reviews
    24:1017–1047.
Bedford, S., and G. Clark, 2001 The Rise and Rise of the Incised and Applied Relief
    Tradition: A Review and Reassessment. *In* The Archaeology of Lapita Dispersal in
    Oceania. G. Clark, A. Anderson and T. Vunidilo, eds. pp. 61–74. Terra Australis 17.
    Canberra: Pandanus Books.
Bedford, S., A. Hoffman, M. Kaltal, R. Regenvanu and R. Shing, 2004 Dentate-stamped
    Lapita reappears on Efaté, Central Vanuatu: A Four Decade-Long Drought is Broken.
    Archaeology in New Zealand 47:39–49.
Bellwood, P., 2005 First Farmers. The Origins of Agricultural Societies. Oxford: Blackwell.

Bowdler, S., 1977 The Coastal Colonisation of Australia. *In* Sunda and Sahul: Prehistoric Studies in Southeast Asia, Melanesia and Australia. J. Allen, J. Golson and R. Jones, eds. pp. 205–246. London: Academic Press.

——1980 Fish and Culture: A Tasmanian Polemic. Mankind 12:334–340.

——1995 Offshore Islands and Maritime Explorations in Australian Prehistory. Antiquity 69:946–958.

Burley, D., and J. Clark, 2003 The Archaeology of Fiji/Western Polynesia in the Post-Lapita Era. *In* Pacific Archaeology: Assessments and Prospects. C. Sand, ed. pp. 235–254. Les Cahiers de l'Archéologie en Nouvelle-Calédonie 15. Nouméa: Département Archéologie, Service des Musées et du Patrimoine de Nouvelle-Calédonie.

Cameron, D., and C. Groves, 2004 Bones, Stones and Molecules. "Out of Africa" and Human Origins. Amsterdam: Elsevier.

Carter, M., 2004 Between the Australian and Melanesian Realm: The Archaeology of Settlement and Subsistence in the Eastern Torres Strait Islands. Paper presented at the Global Perspectives on the Archaeology of Islands Conference, Auckland.

Carter, M., P. Veth, A. Barham, D. Bird, S. O'Connor and R. Bliege-Bird, 2004a Archaeology of the Murray Islands, Eastern Torres Strait: Implications for a Regional Prehistory. *In* Woven Histories, Dancing Lives. Torres Strait Islander Identity, Culture and History. R. Davis, ed. pp. 234–258. Canberra: Aboriginal Studies Press.

Carter, M., A. Barham, P. Veth, D. Bird, S. O'Connor and R. Bliege-Bird, 2004b The Murray Islands Archaeological Project: Excavations on Mer and Dauar, Eastern Torres Strait. *In* Torres Strait Archaeology and Material Culture. I. McNiven and M. Quinnell, eds. pp. 163–182. Memoirs of the Queensland Museum Cultural Heritage Series 3(1). Brisbane: Queensland Museum.

Clark, G., 2000 Post-Lapita Fiji: Cultural Transformation in the Mid-Sequence. Ph.D. dissertation, Australian National University.

——2004 Radiocarbon Dates from the Ulong Site in Palau and Implications for Western Micronesian Prehistory. Archaeology in Oceania 39:26–33.

Clark, J., 1996 Samoan Prehistory in Review. *In* Oceanic Culture History. Essays in Honour of Roger Green. J. Davidson, G. Irwin, F. Leach, A. Pawley and D. Brown, eds. pp. 445–460. Special Publication. Auckland: New Zealand Archaeological Association.

Clarke, A., and A. Paterson, 2003 Case Studies in the Archaeology of Cross-Cultural Interaction. Archaeology in Oceania 38.

David, B., and I. McNiven, 2004 Western Torres Strait Cultural History Project: Research Design and Initial Results. *In* Torres Strait Archaeology and Material Culture. I. McNiven and M. Quinnell, eds. pp. 199–208. Memoirs of the Queensland Museum Cultural Heritage Series 3(1). Brisbane: Queensland Museum.

David, B., I. McNiven, R. Mitchell, M. Orr, S. Haberle, L. Brady and J. Crouch, 2004 Badu 15 and the Papuan-Austronesian Settlement of Torres Strait. Archaeology in Oceania 39: 65–78.

Davidson, J., 1984 The Prehistory of New Zealand. Auckland: Longman Paul.

Dickinson, W., 2003 Impact of Mid-Holocene Hydro-Isostatic Highstand in Regional Sea Level on Habitability of Islands in Pacific Oceania. Journal of Coastal Research 19: 489–502.

Di Piazza, A., and E. Pearthree, 2001 Voyaging and Basalt Exchange in the Phoenix and Line Archipelagoes: The Viewpoint of Three Mystery Islands. Archaeology in Oceania 36: 146–152.

Dodson. J., ed., 1992 The Naïve Lands. Prehistory and Environmental Change in Australia and the South-West Pacific. Melbourne: Longman Cheshire.

Dodson, J., D. Taylor, Y. Ono and P. Wang, eds., 2004 Climate, Human, and Natural Systems of the PEPII Transect. Quaternary International 118–119:1–203.

Flannery, T., 1994 The Future Eaters: An Ecological History of the Australian Lands and People. Melbourne: Reed Books.

Foley, W., 1986 The Papuan Languages of New Guinea. Cambridge: Cambridge University Press.

Gagan, M., E. Hendy, S. Haberle and W. Hantoro, 2004 Post-Glacial Evolution of the Indo-Pacific Warm Pool and El Ninõ–Southern Oscillation. Quaternary International 118–119:127–143.

Garling, S., 2003 Tanga Takes the Stage: Another Model "Transitional" Site? New Evidence and a Contribution to the "Incised and Applied Relief Tradition" in New Ireland. *In* Pacific Archaeology: Assessments and Prospects. C. Sand, ed. pp. 213–233. Les Cahiers de l'Archéologie en Nouvelle-Calédonie 15. Nouméa: Département Archéologie, Service des Musées et du Patrimoine de Nouvelle-Calédonie.

Golson, J., 1961 Report on New Zealand, Western Polynesia, New Caledonia and Fiji. Asian Perspectives 5:166–180.

——2001 New Guinea, Australia and the Sahul Connection. *In* Histories of Old Ages: Essays in Honour of Rhys Jones. A. Anderson, I. Lilley and S. O'Connor, eds. pp. 185–210. Canberra: Pandanus Books.

Green, R., 2003 The Lapita Horizon and Traditions – Signature of One Set of Oceanic Migrations. *In* Pacific Archaeology: Assessments and Prospects. C. Sand, ed. pp. 95–120. Les Cahiers de l'Archéologie en Nouvelle-Calédonie 15. Nouméa: Département Archéologie, Service des Musées et du Patrimoine de Nouvelle-Calédonie.

Haberle, S., and B. David, 2004 Climates of Change: Human Dimensions of Holocene Environmental Change in Low Latitudes of the PEPII Transect. Quaternary International 118–119 (2004):165–179.

Holdaway, S., P. Fanning, M. Jones, J. Shiner, D. Witter and G. Nicholls, 2002 Variability in the Chronology of Late Holocene Aboriginal Occupation of the Arid Margin of Southeastern Australia. Journal of Archaeological Science 29: 351–363.

Horton, D., 1981 Water and Woodland: The Peopling of Australia. Australian Institute of Aboriginal Studies Newsletter 16:21–27.

Irwin, G., 1992 The Prehistoric Exploration and Colonization of the Pacific. Cambridge: Cambridge University Press.

Jones, R., 1977 The Tasmanian Paradox. *In* Stone Tools as Cultural Markers: Change, Evolution and Complexity. R. Wright, ed. pp.189–204. Prehistory and Material Culture Series No. 12. Canberra: Australian Institute of Aboriginal Studies.

Kirch, P., 1984 The Evolution of Polynesian Chiefdoms. Cambridge: Cambridge University Press.

——2000 On the Road of the Winds: An Archaeological History of the Pacific Islands Before European Contact. Berkeley: University of California Press.

Kirch, P., and R. Green, 2001 Hawaiki, Ancestral Polynesia. An Essay in Historical Anthropology. Cambridge: Cambridge University Press.

Kirch, P., and M. Sahlins, 1992 Anahula: The Anthropology of History in the Kingdom of Hawaii. 2 vols. Chicago: University of Chicago Press.

Lambeck, K., and J. Chappell, 2001 Sea Level Change through the Last Glacial Cycle. Science 292:679–686.

Lilley, I., 1999a Late Holocene Transformations in Eastern Torres Strait (or, the Long Arm of Lapita . . .). Paper presented at the Annual Conference of the Australian Archaeological Association, Mandurah.

——1999b Lapita as Politics. *In* Le Pacifique de 5000 à 2000 avant le Présent. Suppléments à l'Histoire d'une Colonisation. J-C. Galipaud et I. Lilley, eds. pp. 21–29. Nouméa: IRD.

——2004a Diaspora and Identity in Archaeology: Moving Beyond the Black Atlantic. *In* A Companion to Social Archaeology. L. Meskell and R. Preucel, eds. pp. 287–312. Oxford: Blackwell.

——2004b Trade and Culture History Across the Vitiaz Strait, Papua New Guinea: The Emerging Post-Lapita Coastal Sequence. *In* A Pacific Odyssey: Archaeology and Anthropology in the Western Pacific. Papers in Honour of Jim Specht, V. Attenbrow and R. Fullagar, eds. pp. 89–96. Records of the Australian Museum, Supplement 29. Sydney: Australian Museum.

Lourandos, H., 1997 Continent of Hunter Gatherers. New Perspectives in Australian Prehistory. Cambridge: Cambridge University Press.

McConvell, P., 1996 Backtracking to Babel: The Chronology of Pama-Nyungan Expansion in Australia. Archaeology in Oceania 31:125–144.

McNiven, I., J. Fitzpatrick and J. Cordell 2004 An Islander World: New Approaches to Managing the Archaeological Heritage of Torres Strait, northeast Australia. *In* Torres Strait Archaeology and Material Culture. I. McNiven and M. Quinnell, eds. pp. 73–92. Memoirs of the Queensland Museum Cultural Heritage Series 3(1). Brisbane: Queensland Museum.

Mulvaney, D. J., 1976 The Chain of Connection: The Material Evidence. *In* Tribes and Boundaries in Australia. N. Peterson (ed.), pp. 72–94. Canberra: Australian Institute of Aboriginal Studies.

Mulvaney, D. J., and J. Kamminga, 1999 Prehistory of Australia. Sydney: Allen and Unwin.

O'Connell, J., and J. Allen, 2004 Dating the Colonization of Sahul (Pleistocene Australia-New Guinea): A Review of Recent Research. Journal of Archaeological Science 31:835–853.

O'Connor, S., and J. Chappell, 2003 Colonization and Coastal Subsistence in Australia and Papua New Guinea: Different Timing, Different Modes? *In* Pacific Archaeology: Assessments and Prospects. C. Sand, ed. pp. 17–32. Les Cahiers de l'Archéologie en Nouvelle-Calédonie 15. Nouméa: Département Archéologie, Service des Musées et du Patrimoine de Nouvelle-Calédonie.

Oppenheimer, S., 2003 Austronesian Spread into Southeast Asia and Oceania: Where From and When? *In* Pacific Archaeology: Assessments and Prospects. C. Sand, ed. pp. 54–70. Les Cahiers de l'Archéologie en Nouvelle-Calédonie 15. Nouméa: Département Archéologie, Service des Musées et du Patrimoine de Nouvelle-Calédonie.

——2004 The "Express Train from Taiwan to Polynesia": On the Congruence of Proxy Lines of Evidence. World Archaeology 36:591–600.

Pasveer, J., S. Clarke and G. Miller, 2002 Late Pleistocene Occupation in Inland Rainforest, Bird's Head, Papua. Archaeology in Oceania 37:92–95.

Petersen, G., 2000 Indigenous Island Empires: Yap and Tonga Considered. Journal of Pacific History 35:5–27.

Phear, S., G. Glark and A. Anderson, 2003 A Radiocarbon Chronology for Palau. *In* Pacific Archaeology: Assessments and Prospects. C. Sand, ed. pp. 255–263. Les Cahiers de l'Archéologie en Nouvelle-Calédonie 15. Nouméa: Département Archéologie, Service des Musées et du Patrimoine de Nouvelle-Calédonie.

Rainbird, P., 2004 The Archaeology of Micronesia. Cambridge: Cambridge University Press.

Ross, M., A. Pawley and M. Osmond, eds., 1998 The Lexicon of Proto Oceanic. The Culture and Environment of Ancestral Oceanic Society. 1 Material Culture. Pacific

Linguistics C-152. Canberra: Pacific Linguistics, Research School of Pacific and Asian Studies, Australian National University.

Smith, A., 2002 An Archaeology of West Polynesian Prehistory. Terra Australis 18. Canberra: Pandanus Books.

Spriggs, M., 2001 Who Cares What Time It Is? The Importance of Chronology in Pacific Archaeology. *In* Histories of Old Ages: Essays in Honour of Rhys Jones. A. Anderson, I. Lilley and S. O'Connor, eds. pp. 237–249. Canberra: Pandanus Books.

——2003 Post-Lapita Evolutions in Island Melanesia. *In* Pacific Archaeology: Assessments and Prospects. C. Sand, ed. pp. 205–212. Les Cahiers de l'Archéologie en Nouvelle-Calédonie 15. Nouméa: Département Archéologie, Service des Musées et du Patrimoine de Nouvelle-Calédonie.

——2004 Is There Life After Lapita, and Do You Remember the 60s? The Post-Lapita Sequences of the Western Pacific. *In* A Pacific Odyssey: Archaeology and Anthropology in the Western Pacific. Papers in Honour of Jim Specht, V. Attenbrow and R. Fullagar, eds. pp. 139–144. Records of the Australian Museum, Supplement 29. Sydney: Australian Museum.

Spriggs, M., and A. Anderson, 1993 Late Colonization of East Polynesia. Antiquity 67: 200–217.

Stringer, C., 1999 Has Australia Backdated the Human Revolution? Antiquity 73:876–879.

Terrell, J., 1989 What Lapita Is and What Lapita Isn't. Antiquity 63:623–626.

——1999 Lapita for Winners. Getting off the Lapita Merry-Go-Round and Living without Compulsive Habits. *In* Le Pacifique de 5000 à 2000 avant le Présent. Suppléments à l'Histoire d'une Colonisation. J-C. Galipaud et I. Lilley, eds. pp. 49–59. Nouméa: IRD.

——2004 Introduction: 'Austronesia' and the Great Austronesian Migration. World Archaeology 36:586–590.

Torrence, R., and A. Clarke, eds., 2000 The Archaeology of Difference: Negotiating Cross-Cultural Engagements in Oceania. London: Routledge.

Torrence, R., V. Neall, T. Doelman, E. Rhodes, C. McKee, H. Davies, R. Bonetti, A. Gugliemetti, A. Manzoni, M. Oddone, J. Parr and C. Wallace, 2004 Pleistocene Colonisation of the Bismarck Archipelago: New Evidence from West New Britain. Archaeology in Oceania 39:101–130.

Underhill, P., G. Passarino, A. Lin, S. Marzuki, P. Oefner, L. Cavalli-Sforza and G. Chambers, 2001 Maori Origins, Y-Chromosome Haplotypes and Implications for Human History in the Pacific. Human Mutation 17:271–280.

Veth, P., 2000 Origins of the Western Desert Language: Convergence in Linguistic and Archaeological Space and Time Models. Archaeology in Oceania 35:11–19.

Walter, R., 1996 What is the East Polynesian 'Archaic'? A View from the Cook Islands. *In* Oceanic Culture History. Essays in Honour of Roger Green. J. Davidson, G. Irwin, F. Leach, A. Pawley and D. Brown, eds. pp. 513–529. Special Publication. Auckland: New Zealand Archaeological Association.

Weisler, M., 2001 Life on the Edge: Prehistoric Settlement and Economy on Utrōk Atoll, Northern Marshall Islands. Archaeology in Oceania 26:109–133.

White, J. P., with J. O'Connell 1982 A Prehistory of Australia, New Guinea and Sahul. Sydney: Academic Press.

White, N., 1994 Genes, Languages and Landscapes in Australia. *In* Archaeology and Linguistics: Aboriginal Australia in Global Perspective. P. McConvell and N. Evans, eds. pp. 45–81. Melbourne: Oxford University Press.

Wilson, M., 2003 Rock-Art Transformations in the Western Pacific. *In* Pacific Archaeology: Assessments and Prospects. C. Sand, ed. pp. 265–284. Les Cahiers de l'Archéologie en

Nouvelle-Calédonie 15. Nouméa: Département Archéologie, Service des Musées et du Patrimoine de Nouvelle-Calédonie.

——2004 Rethinking Regional Analyses of Western Pacific Rock Art. *In* A Pacific Odyssey: Archaeology and Anthropology in the Western Pacific. Papers in Honour of Jim Specht, V. Attenbrow and R. Fullagar, eds. pp. 173–186. Records of the Australian Museum, Supplement 29. Sydney: Australian Museum.

Part I

Australia

2

Revisiting the Past: Changing Interpretations of Pleistocene Settlement Subsistence and Demography in Northern Australia

Sue O'Connor and Peter Veth

A great deal has been written recently about the date people first arrived in Australia and the reliability of both the different radiometric methods used to achieve this end and the measurements obtained. As Lilley describes in his introduction to this volume, there is a "long chronology" of about 60,000 years based on luminescence dating techniques, and a "short chronology" of no more than 45,000 years based on traditional radiocarbon dating. In addition to concerns about luminescence techniques generally, many proponents of the short chronology doubt the archaeological association of cultural remains with the non-cultural materials these techniques actually date. Some have also argued that occupation of Australia around 60,000 years ago ignores evidence concerning the chronology of dispersal of modern humans elsewhere in the world, something the "long chronologists" argue is being or soon will be undermined by new discoveries in East Asia.

We have both been active in this debate but we want to draw attention here to the fact that far less effort has been expended on discussion of the nature of human activity following colonization and changes during the Pleistocene as the colonists began to explore the enormous and diverse landmass of Sahul (though see O'Connor and Chappell 2003; O'Connor and Veth 2000a). There are three principal reasons for this. First, the issue of chronology has taken on a life of its own and might even be seen to now lead the investigation of Pleistocene archaeology in Australia (cf. Allen 2003:38). Second, there is very little in the way of published analysis of material finds from, or following, the period of initial occupation and then on through the major environmental fluctuations of the Pleistocene (see Lilley, this volume). Third, many early sites have preserved only stone artifacts, and very small samples of stone artifacts at that, upon which it is difficult to build comprehensive interpretations of past lives. For example, at Devil's Lair, currently the oldest Australian site based on the radiocarbon chronology, a mere 15 stone artifacts occur in the earliest claimed human occupation deposits dated between 44,500 and 47,000 B.P. (Turney et al. 2001).

In recent times Australian archaeologists have increasingly turned away from earlier stereotypes which contrasted the Pleistocene as a time of relative stasis in which hunter-gatherers were few and "simple" with the Holocene as a time of rapid socioeconomic and technological change. Yet it must be admitted that it is difficult to make comparisons between the archaeological records of the first occupation period with later periods for which we have abundant material and a much richer and more diverse record. In this chapter we take a fresh look at some issues we aired in a paper written over a decade ago (O'Connor et al. 1993), which canvassed the archaeological evidence for regional settlement patterning throughout the Pleistocene and into the Holocene in western Australia. The paper advanced a number of models that might account for the patterning we observed. We suggested that marked changes occurred in settlement dynamics and demography in the Pleistocene from the time of first occupation and through the aridity that typified the Last Glacial Maximum (LGM) in Australia around 20,000 years ago. We argued that these changes were reflected in archaeological sequences as changes in intensity of occupation/number of visits and could be measured indirectly on the basis of variations in quantities of cultural materials discarded plotted against radiocarbon ages.

The issue of using numbers of stone artifacts and other culturally derived residues as a proxy for numbers of people is a complex one. However, we maintained in our earlier paper and remain convinced that questions of sample size not withstanding, "when the magnitude and direction of change . . . is internally consistent at the regional level, this must signal fundamental changes in the regional system" and must have demographic implications (O'Connor et al. 1993:101). When we wrote that paper, we had only a few sites, small excavations, and a handful of radiocarbon dates to underpin our propositions. Today our sample sizes are significantly larger, both in terms of numbers of sites within regions and numbers of radiocarbon dates from individual sites. Our understanding of the duration of the Last Glacial Maximum, the severity of aridity, and the resultant landscape changes in many regions is also far better developed.

We suggest that while increasing numbers of dates and sites have narrowed the gaps in our sequences and refined the regional patterns we identified, the changes in settlement and implied demographic variation to which we drew attention in 1991 are still evident. The following discussion (1) briefly reviews the evidence for the north of western Australia, with particular focus on the Western Desert, Kimberley, and Pilbara (Figure 2.1), (2) overviews models which have been proposed for settlement-subsistence patterns, and (3) identifies research themes that warrant future attention.

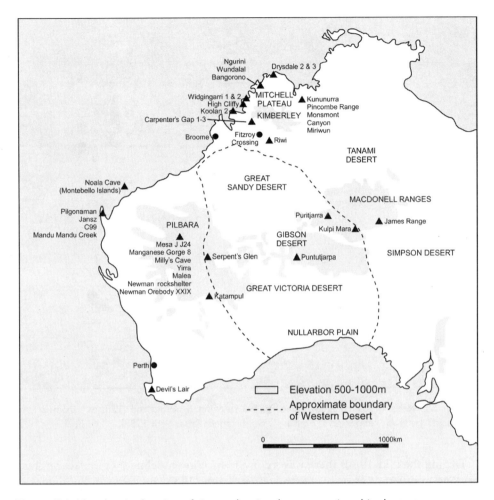

Figure 2.1 Map showing location of sites and major deserts mentioned in the text

Regional Studies

Gould's early work in the Western Desert between 1965 and 1980 was strongly influenced by his ethnoarchaeological experience. Following his excavations at Puntutjarpa and James Range rockshelters, he portrayed a uniform and conservative "Desert Culture" similar to that of the North American Great Basin (Gould 1969, 1977, 1980). The culture was Holocene in age, assumed the ethnographically described configuration of Australian desert culture, and was argued to display great uniformity in material culture, economy, and settlement patterns through time. Work in the adjacent Pilbara region by others at the same time suggested instead a deeper antiquity of occupation and greater dynamism in settlement patterns and other aspects of culture (Brown 1987; Maynard 1980; Troilett n.d.).

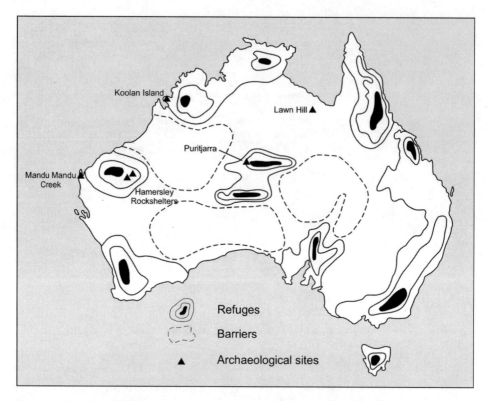

Koolan Island

Lawn Hill ▲

Puritjarra

Mandu Mandu
Creek

Hamersley
Rockshelters

◎ Refuges

⸝⸝ Barriers

▲ Archaeological sites

Figure 2.2 Veth's (1989) biogeographic model showing hypothesized "refuges" from aridity, "corridors" between refuges, and "barriers" to movement (after Veth 1989)

During the mid-1980s there was a convergence in modeling by three researchers working in different areas of the arid zone: Smith (1988) focusing on the ranges of central Australia, Hiscock (1988) studying gorge refugia in northeastern Australia, and Veth (1989) working in the Western Desert and Pilbara. In a nutshell, these studies suggested three things. First, occupation of the arid zone was Pleistocene in age. Second, there had been changes in the size of group territories in response to environmental shifts attending changes in aridity throughout the Pleistocene. People withdrew into biogeographic refuges such as permanently watered gorges in drier periods and expanded out again with climatic amelioration. Finally, significant social and economic change took place in the late Holocene. These facts constitute a very different scenario from the conservative, Holocene-aged "Desert Culture" that had been the dominant paradigm up until that time.

On the strength of these new understandings, in 1987 Veth began to look at diversity in the Australian deserts. He divided them using a biogeographic model based on the distribution of ecological "refuges" from aridity, "corridors" between refuges, and "barriers" to movement (Veth 1989, Figure 2.2). The model made a case for a delay in the occupation of linear dunefields until the mid-Holocene. Critique and empirical testing of the model's assumptions over the last 15 years have seen its core themes generally reinforced and supported. The proposal that occupation of the sandy deserts was delayed, however, has now been overturned by the discovery of Pleistocene sites such as Serpent's Glen rockshelter in these areas (Figure 2.1, O'Connor et al. 1998).

In 1986 O'Connor explored a number of large rockshelters on the Kimberley coast and offshore islands. Widgingarri 1 and 2 and Koolan 2 had evidence for occupation beginning approximately 30,000 years ago. Koolan 2 was abandoned at 24,000 B.P. and Widgingarri 1 at 19,000 B.P. (O'Connor 1999:49, 60). Both sites were reoccupied immediately following sea-level rise, as the coastline had moved close to the Koolan peninsula by 11,000 B.P. O'Connor interpreted the abandonment as the result of increased aridity and its effect on local surface-water availability in close proximity to the shelters, rather than of increased distance from the coast at a time of lowered sea levels, because by the time these sites were abandoned they would already have been several hundred kilometers inland. During the LGM these sites would have been within the continent's much-expanded arid zone (see Lilley, this volume). O'Connor hypothesized that if aridity caused these settlement shifts then the refugia model should also apply to this case, as Hiscock (1988) had shown it did at Lawn Hill in northwestern Queensland.

In 1992 O'Connor tested this proposition with an extensive excavation program in the central southern Kimberley, in an area near permanently watered gorges in the Oscar–Napier Ranges close to Fitzroy Crossing on the edge of the Western Desert. Six rockshelters were excavated. The oldest, Carpenter's Gap 1 (CG1), was dated to 42,800 B.P. (O'Connor and Fankhauser 2001; O'Connor 1995, McConnell and O'Connor 1997). Paleobotanical remains and stone artifacts occur from the basal level immediately above bedrock and while artifact numbers following first occupation are low, there is no doubt that this early cultural material is in situ and has not been vertically displaced from higher in the profile. A horizontally bedded ochre-covered limestone slab with a minimum age of ca. 40,000 B.P. was recovered. Its size and position precluded any possibility of vertical movement (O'Connor and Fankhauser 2001). Discard of stone artifacts and other cultural materials from 30,000 B.P. to 11,000 B.P. demonstrates sparse occupation during and immediately following LGM at CG1 (McConnell and O'Connor 1997). Analysis of the material from Carpenter's Gap 3 (CG3) is not yet complete but stone artifacts and faunal remains appear to occur more frequently during the LGM at this shelter than at CG1. CG3 is close to permanent freshwater in Windjana Gorge while CG1 is several kilometers from water. When pooled, the radiocarbon dates from CG1 and CG3 register a consistent human presence in the Oscar–Napier ranges from 30,000 B.P. to 11,000 cal B.P. As can be seen in Figure 2.3, there is a cluster of dates at ca. 21,000–22,000 cal B.P. This peak in occupation is also reflected in the material discard signal. Note that Figure 2.3 and the two graphs below only show determinations which fall within the range of current calibration curves (around 20,000 B.P. uncalibrated).

It should be noted, however, that other sites in this region such as Riwi in the southern Kimberley (Figure 2.1) appear to have been unoccupied during the LGM

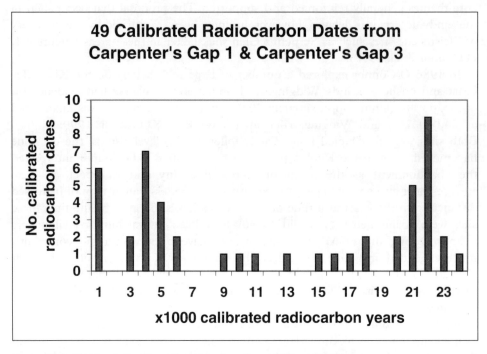

Figure 2.3 Graph of all calibrated radiocarbon dates CG1 and CG3

(Balme 2000). As at Carpenter's Gap 1, occupation is first recorded at Riwi at about 42,000 B.P. but there is a stratigraphic disconformity dating to between 30,000 B.P. and approximately 5,300 B.P. (Balme 2000:2–4). No culturally sterile sedimentary unit was recorded that could conceivably cover this "missing time," so either net sediment accumulation ceased when people ceased to visit the shelter, or one or more erosion events occurred in the past that removed a significant amount of the late Pleistocene/early Holocene deposits. Balme (2000:4) comments that the latter seems unlikely as there was no evidence at the boundary of the disconformity for a lag of artifacts or non-cultural debris. In fact the number of lithic artifacts at the juncture of the disconformity was no higher than elsewhere in the sequence, suggesting that if 25,000 years of artifact accumulation are represented, occupation must have been of a very low level throughout this time.

Balme (2000) expresses surprise that while Riwi reflects the pattern of early occupation followed by abandonment that is widely seen in northwestern Australia, abandonment appears to occur far earlier at Riwi, but perhaps this is not surprising given Riwi's location approximately 200 kilometers south east of Carpenter's Gap 1 on the northern edge of the Western Desert. Recent southern hemisphere research on the LGM and consequent landscape change indicates that the impact of the onset of aridity may have been felt far earlier and been much more severe than previously thought, especially in arid areas (Hiscock and Wallis 2004). Rainfall estimates indicate that the deserts received approximately half the current rainfall at this time (Dodson and Wright 1989). Many inland areas show pronounced reductions in surface water availability by 35,000 B.P. Some inland lakes had dried completely by 30,000 B.P. and remained so until the beginning of the Holocene. The radically "reduced precipitation/evaporation indices . . . had severe consequences for not only water availability but also for vegetation" (Hiscock and Wallis 2004). The biotic productivity of the landscape must have been dramatically reduced. The complex interaction of reduced rainfall and vegetation appears to have led to lowering of water tables and salt-crust formation in many arid areas, which at a local scale may have had an even more pronounced influence on water availability and potability (Magee et al. 1995).

Today parallel sand dunes abut the south side of the Napier Range at Carpenter's Gap 1, attesting to the major phase of dune building and sediment mobility that occurred during this time. The site has excellent paleobotanical preservation and so records the reduction in trees/shrub cover and the increase in grassland that took place (Wallis 2001). In view of its more southerly continental location, Riwi would have been rapidly engulfed within the expanding arid core and we might expect it to have registered a human response to hyperarid conditions long before more peripheral areas to the northwest, where Koolan 2 and Widgingarri 1 are located. This hiatus in occupation between 30,000 and 5,000 B.P. at Riwi may reflect a similar type of settlement retraction to that seen in the upland Pilbara ranges or more widespread abandonment such as appears to be the case for areas of the Western Desert, as reflected in shelters like Serpent's Glen, following the extreme desiccation and lowering of temperatures that occurred with the onset of the LGM as discussed below.

To the northwest, the Kimberley sites of Widgingarri 1 and Koolan 2 continued in use between 30,000 and 20,000 B.P. even when they were several hundred kilometers inland, but appear to have been abandoned between 24,000 B.P. and 20,000 B.P. (Figure 2.4). Paleobotanical material is not preserved in the archaeological sequences of these sites but the faunal remains indicate that prior to abandonment at 24,000 B.P. the local and regional environment of Koolan peninsula was significantly less arid than that hypothesized to have surrounded Riwi at 30,000 B.P. Freshwater turtle remains in the Pleistocene levels at Koolan 2 attest to the presence of a sizeable body of permanent freshwater within reach of the site and medium to large macropods and a diverse range of smaller fauna were regular prey. At Widgingarri Shelter 1, almost 100 kilometers north of Koolan Island as the crow flies, rainfall is slightly higher today than for Koolan. The more northerly location of Widgingarri may explain the slightly later date for its abandonment, as we might assume that it experienced the full impact of incorporation into the enlarged arid zone slightly later than Koolan to the south. An overview of the distribution of radiocarbon dates from the nine excavated Kimberley shelters near the coast, Widgingarri Shelters 1 and 2, Koolan 2, High Cliffy Island Shelter in the Buccaneer Archipelago (O'Connor 1999), Ngurini, Bangorono and Wundalal on the Mitchell Plateau (Veitch 1996), and Drysdale 2 and 3 in the Drysdale River area (Morwood pers. comm. 2004), shows little evidence for site use between 22,000 and 12,000 cal. years B.P.

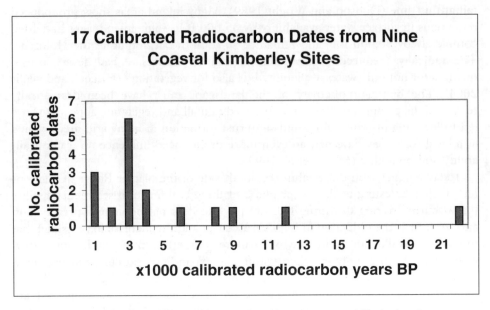

Figure 2.4 Graph of all calibrated radiocarbon dates from nine coastal Kimberley sites

In 1988, Morse (1994, 1999) returned the first Pleistocene dates for the Cape Range region in the coastal Pilbara. Dates as early as 34,000 B.P. came from rock-shelters that were uniquely positioned adjacent to the place where the edge of the continental shelf is closest to the Australian mainland. This means that these sites were always near the sea despite sometimes dramatic variation in sea levels during the LGM. Assemblages from Mandu Mandu and Pilgonaman rockshelters (Figure 2.1) contained small quantities of marine fauna as well as a variety of arid plains fauna. Sites from this area demonstrate long-term occupation from 34,000 B.P. to 17,500 B.P. and then from 12,000 B.P. to the late Holocene. Recent excavations at the northern tip of Cape Range by Pryzywolnik (2002) have reinforced Morse's findings. She notes a hiatus in deposition/occupation at two rockshelters, Jansz and C99, although the timing of this event is slightly different in the two sites. Jansz, the smaller rockshelter of the two, has no evidence for human occupation between 31,000 B.P. and 11,000 B.P. At C99 the period of occupational hiatus was consid-erably shorter, and lasted from 21,000 B.P. until 8000 B.P. Pryzywolnik (2002:300) argues that during the LGM, "sediment and artifact accumulation rates show that deposition either stopped completely, or slowed dramatically . . . This supports the conclusion that human use of the sites at this time all but ceased." The interpreta-tion she puts forward to explain the change in occupation combines changes in local movement of groups along a retreating coastline and their relocation to other areas to escape increasing aridity.

Evidence for early use of the now-drowned Northwest Shelf comes from the Montebello Islands, which were connected to the mainland until 7,500 years ago (Veth 1993a). Dates from Noala Cave (Figure 2.1) indicate first occupation at

28,000 B.P. and then from approximately 10,000 to 7,500 B.P., when the islands were abandoned as they were isolated by rising sea levels. In addition to marine species derived from reef, sand, and mangrove habitats, a rich and diverse mammalian fauna associated with now-submerged plains and dunefields of north-western Australia is present in the Montebello sites.

To recap, analysis of excavated material from coastal Pilbara lowlands and Cape Range sites produced four main findings. First, Aboriginal people used both the arid coast and adjacent plains from at least 35,000 years ago. Second, these groups were not obviously tethered to coastal resources as suggested by Bowdler's (1977, 1990) influential coastal colonization model (see also O'Connor and Chappell 2003; O'Connor and Veth 2000a, b; and Lilley, this volume). From the time of initial occupation, people relied most heavily on arid/semi-arid terrestrial faunas from sandy lowland and upland habitats. Third, there are consistent changes in occupation/deposition patterns during the LGM, with no occupation registered in the period from 17,500 B.P. to 12,000 B.P.

Turning to the Pilbara uplands, Pleistocene dates for occupation of the relatively well-watered ranges of the Pilbara have been known since the 1970s. Six sites are now dated from 20,000 B.P. up to the late Holocene, including Yirra Rockshelter (Veitch et al. n.d.), Malea (Edwards and Murphy 2003), Newman Rockshelter, Mesa J J24, Newman Orebody XXIX, and Milly's Cave (Marwick 2002). Hiscock (1988), Marwick (2002), Smith (1993), and Veth (1993b) have all proposed that the mountain and piedmont deserts of the Hamersley and Chichester uplands, with their numerous ranges, gorges, and springs, would have constituted refuges for people during the heightened aridity associated with the LGM.

Veth (1993b) predicted that there should be evidence for continuous or repeated occupation during the LGM in this area, as opposed to the lack of, or at least dimin-ished evidence for, settlement in the surrounding desert lowlands during the same time period. As Marwick (2002:24) points out, four of the key sites excavated during archaeological salvage operations, Newman Orebody XXIX, Newman rockshelter, Mesa J J24, and Malea, have poor chronological resolution, making it difficult to sustain conclusions about patterns of human occupation at these sites. However, Comtesse's (2003) recent reanalysis of these four sites argues that they display a significant decrease in occupation and sedimentation (if not abandonment) during the period between approximately 17,000 and 13,000 years ago.

The excavation of Yirra rockshelter by Veitch et al. (n.d.) and analysis of exca-vated material from Milly's Cave by Marwick (2002) have provided persuasive evi-dence for the presence of people in the Hamersley Plateau during the LGM. Milly's Cave is located on the northern edge of the Hamersley Range in a small gully that contains a permanent freshwater spring. It appears to have been first occupied around 19,000 B.P. Marwick's (2002) analysis of the stone artifacts and radio-carbon dates from Milly's Cave demonstrated that discard was highest during the period from 18,700 to 14,000 B.P., associated with peak aridity in the LGM. Marwick (2002:29) concludes that aside from the marked increase in numbers of stone artifacts the only change in the character of the assemblage during this time is a change in raw material. Between 18,000 B.P. and 14,000 B.P. there is an

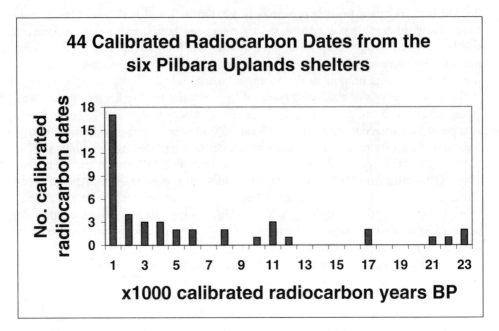

Figure 2.5 Graph of all calibrated radiocarbon dates from the Pilbara uplands

increased focus on locally available raw material to the exclusion of exotic raw materials. He interprets this change as reflecting the reduced scale of people's territorial range and notes that this pattern is similar to that observed at Lawn Hill in north Queensland by Hiscock. At the Lawn Hill shelters artifact numbers soared during the LGM but artifacts made from stone sourced more than three kilometers from the shelters are absent. Hiscock argued that Lawn Hill with its abundant permanent aquifer-fed water sources formed a refuge on which the population fell back during aridity; the focus on locally available raw material was a risk-minimizing strategy.

Figure 2.5 presents all the calibrated radiocarbon dates currently available for the Pilbara upland sites. Although there is definite evidence for occupation during the LGM, it can be seen that there are few dates between 13,000 and 20,000 calendar years. Marwick's discussion and analysis suggest that while to some extent the gaps in time in the graph may result from poor chronological resolution in several of the sites, there are grounds for believing that the spread of dates reflects real changes in territoriality and mobility. Whereas some sites like Milly's Creek with its permanent spring become a short-term focus for occupation during the LGM, others at a distance from reliable freshwater are used little if at all during this time.

Viewed collectively, results from the Pilbara sites lead to four principal conclusions. The first is that there is no evidence that people stayed on the Pilbara coastline near Cape Range during the LGM. Second, unlike the coastal situation, it appears that occupation did persist in the Pilbara uplands. Third, it seems likely

Table 2.1 Estimated artifact discard rates from Western Desert sites in pre-LGM–LGM Pleistocene levels versus late Holocene levels of deposits. (Artifact numbers summarized from a. O'Connor et al. 1998:17, b. Smith 1988:108, Table 4.4, c. Thorley 1998b:41)

Site	Pre-LGM–LGM artifacts/kyr	Late Holocene artifacts/kyr
Serpent's Glen a	37	1600
Puritjarra Pits N9 and N10 b	6	2087
Kulpi Mara c	140	250

Table 2.2 Mean weight of amorphous retouched artifacts in grams, Puritjarra (data derived from Smith 1988:108, 119, Tables 4.4, 4.9). Numbers in brackets give the numbers of artifacts in the sample that the mean weights are based on

Pit	N9	N10	QR9	Z10	Total no. artifacts
Layer Ia 650 B.P. >	6.9 (21)	8.0 (6)	37.7 (16)	14.1 (8)	51
Layer Ib 6500 B.P.–650 B.P.	18.2 (13)	8.0 (9)	10.8 (1)	8.0 (10)	33
Layer II 30,000 B.P.–6500 B.P.	17.0 (1)	75.5 (2)	691.7 (2)	104.1 (4)	9

that there was some territorial retraction into the ranges as well as within the ranges. Finally, there were different degrees of visitation to these sites owing to their different local catchments, ranging from abandonment or only episodic visits through to increased use as people became more reliant on local concentrations of resources that were increasingly scarce elsewhere.

To focus now on the edges of the Western Desert, Smith (Smith et al. 1997; Smith in press) established that occupation occurred at Puritjarra in central Australia from 30,000 years ago. He argues that shifts in residential mobility patterns and territoriality provided the appropriate mechanisms for groups to stay in the central Australian ranges during the LGM and to maintain some connection, albeit peripheral, with the arid lowlands to the west (1989, 1993, 1996). However, it can be shown that the Pleistocene assemblages from Puritjarra and the other Western Desert sites discussed below are quite different quantitatively and qualitatively from those of the Holocene.

This is most aptly demonstrated by the massive difference in numbers of artifacts discarded in three Western Desert sites, Puritjarra, Serpent's Glen, and Kulpi Mara, in the pre-LGM to LGM Pleistocene levels versus late Holocene levels (Table 2.1). It should be noted that the extremely low figure of six artifacts per thousand years at Puritjarra includes all stone artifacts dating between 30,000 B.P. and 6500 B.P. This is because Smith's (1988:108, Tables 4.3 and 4.4) presentation of the dates and artifacts within combined units does not allow the separation of Pleistocene lithics from those of the early-mid Holocene. Tables 2.2 and 2.3 show that between Layers II (dating between 30,000 B.P. and 6500 B.P.) and Ia (late Holocene) at Puritjarra the rate of artifact discard increases by a multiple of 700

Table 2.3   Mean weight of total artifacts in grams, Puritjarra, Pit
N10 (from Smith 1988:119, Table 4.10)

Pit	Local lithics	Exotic lithics
Layer Ia	2.3	0.7
Layer Ib	3.5	1.1
Layer II	24.0	15.3

(Smith 1988:108, Table 4.4). There is a tenfold increase in the rate of retouch
(Smith 1988:126, Table 4.13) and a substantial decrease in the average weight of
cores and other artifacts in the Holocene levels (Smith 1988:119).

Thorley (1998a, b) excavated Kulpi Mara rockshelter during his study of the
Palmer River catchment in the central Australian ranges, on the eastern edge of the
Western Desert. He found cultural deposits with a similar antiquity to Puritjarra,
ca. 30,000 B.P. As can be seen in Table 2.1, Kulpi Mara also has vastly fewer artifacts in the Pleistocene than the Holocene occupation levels. Thorley interprets this
lower discard signature very differently from Smith, however. He suggests that most
of the artifacts in the levels dating before 12,000 accumulated in the period following first occupation and through until about 24,000 B.P. Between 24,000 and
12,000 B.P. sediment accumulation rates were very low and artifact discard may
even have ceased entirely as humans retreated in the face of escalating aridity.

These changes suggest to Thorley and to us that land-use patterns differed significantly in the Pleistocene and Holocene in the Western Desert. He (1998b:41)
makes the important point that specialist adaptations were not necessary for this
first incursion into the center of Australia. The first occupation of Kulpi Mara and
Puritjarra "was not dependent on adjustment to aridity" but rather represents an
expansion of early colonists into the "freshwater riverine core of the central
Australian ranges and its well-watered hinterland" under conditions which were
very attractive for settlement. In contrast, the onset of the LGM provides the first
"crucial test of human adjustment to a truly arid environment" and Kulpi
Mara appears to have been completely abandoned at this time. Thorley's review of
Puritjarra led him to conclude that there was negligible evidence for occupation
through the LGM there as well (Thorley 1998a:319–324).

In this context it is telling that some 25 years after Gould's dating of Puntutjarpa
to the Holocene, the rockshelter sites of Serpent's Glen in the Little Sandy Desert
and Katampul in the semi-arid central west of western Australia (Figure 2.1) were
dated to greater than 23,500 B.P. and 21,000 B.P. respectively (O'Connor and Veth
1996; O'Connor et al. 1998), making them the first sites of undoubtedly Pleistocene
age known in the Western Desert proper. Within a few thousand years of their occupation, however, both sites ceased to be visited and contain no evidence for reuse
until the mid-Holocene. The lower levels of these sites contain very few artifacts
and no faunal or paleobotanical remains preserved beneath the late Holocene levels.
At Katampul the Pleistocene date of 21,000 from Spit 39 is located only six centimeters below the date of 4500 and only 22 stone artifacts were recovered from

Spit 39 and below, so it was uncertain if the date of 21,000 securely dated human occupation or whether the artifacts may have moved down from higher in the deposit (O'Connor and Veth 1996:47). At least episodic occupation of the Western Desert was subsequently demonstrated at Serpent's Glen, where a culturally sterile sedimentary layer effectively seals the Pleistocene assemblage (O'Connor et al. 1998).

In summary, the excavation of sites in the western Australian deserts reveals that while all desert landscape types – from mountain and piedmont deserts to arid coastal plains – have some early evidence for Pleistocene use and occupation, it was only very sporadic or intermittent. Moreover, on the basis of currently available radiocarbon dates, the first use of these regions did not occur as early as it did in better-watered northern regions such as the Kimberley. In addition, with the possible exception of Puritjarra in the Central Desert, the onset of the LGM appears to have effectively brought a stop to the exploitation of desert lowlands. There is widespread use of all desert landscapes again in the Holocene, though in many areas bordering the sandy deserts, such as at Serpent's Glen, resettlement did not take place until the mid-Holocene, with large aggregation sites focused around constructed wells appearing even later. Earlier terminal Pleistocene/early Holocene reoccupation at Kulpi Mara and Puritjarra may be explained by the fact that they are linked by continuous drainage systems into the Finke River catchment. Serpent's Glen in the smaller isolated Carnarvon Ranges of Western Australia is not linked into a larger drainage system, which probably made decolonization at the end of the Pleistocene more precarious and may explain the delay in reoccupation prior to the return to more seasonal and predictable rainfall patterns in the mid-Holocene.

Conclusion

This overview of central and northwestern Australia has described an emerging picture of regional variability in patterns of human occupation through time, with complex histories of long-term social dynamism evident in the apparent ability of groups to reconfigure their economies, mobility patterns, territorial ranges, information exchange systems, and technological organization against a backdrop of climatic oscillations of consequence to hunter-gatherers. Sites in the northwest show occupation prior to 40,000 (even using radiocarbon rather than luminescence dating), whereas those in the Pilbara and Western Desert indicate that occupation did not begin until ca. 35,000–30,000 years ago and then with only very low discard signals. The nature of early occupation at most sites seems to have been quite different from that registered after reoccupation in the Holocene. Sites in the desert that were occupied or visited at 30,000 B.P. appear to have been abandoned by 24,000 B.P. if not before. This is earlier than abandonment occurred in parts of the western Kimberley, where people appear to have held on until conditions were at their most extreme about 19,000 years ago. If the evidence for human occupation is used as a proxy for climate change, it would indicate that aridity is experienced most keenly at the local level toward the end of the LGM (i.e., after 20,000 B.P.), and that in many cases the climate across broad regions did not improve sufficiently to sustain permanent human occupation until the end of the Pleistocene or even the beginning of the Holocene. Many landscapes appear never to have returned to their pre-LGM levels in terms of vegetation cover.

In view of the widespread evidence for reduced occupation and sedimentation during the last glacial period, it is crucial that key sites are reexamined to determine why this pattern occurs. As we have argued previously (O'Connor et al. 1999), we think it unlikely that erosion events and taphonomic factors can explain the widespread gap in sedimentation and cultural material discard at this chronological juncture across different sites and regions. We know that the discovery of new sites and reworking of data can change our understandings of apparently neatly trending occupation and discard patterns at the macro-regional level. This was acknowledged in our earlier work (O'Connor et al. 1993, 1999) and is reiterated here. However, just as Clive Gamble and colleagues (2004) have been able to demonstrate major changes in population levels during the longer LGM between Northern Europe, France, and Iberia (using C14 determinations as proxies for presence and intensity of occupation), so we believe that major changes in settlement occurred in the southern hemisphere. In the face of vigorous site-focused critiques by workers such as Dortch and M. V. Smith (2001), we defend the use of pooled regional data and contend that the trends are real, despite obvious variations within and between sites and myriad taphonomic complexities. We extol the use of chronometric hygiene and believe that it is at the level of accepting occupation dates for inclusion into these pooled populations that errors can be identified and/or minimized.

We now suggest that off-site sampling is required to obtain *local* paleoclimatic records and undertake other relevant investigations of landscape and site formation processes to explain why this patterning occurs at both the local and regional level. Another primary focus of future work must be the excavation of open sites (see also Fullager 2004), which have largely been ignored by researchers because, coastal shell-middens aside, such sites rarely preserve organic material in the harsh environments of the continent's desert core and tropical north. They thus cannot be radiocarbon dated to facilitate their integration into regional archaeologies based on cave and rockshelter sequences. Recent advances in dating by methods other than radiocarbon have opened these numerically dominant sites to investigations which could add a significant dimension to our understanding of past human activity in northern Australia.

REFERENCES

Allen, J., 2003 Discovering the Pleistocene in Island Melanesia. *In* Pacific Archaeology: Assessments and Prospects. C. Sand, ed. pp. 33–42. Les Cahiers de l'Archéologie en Nouvelle-Calédonie 15. Nouméa: Département Archéologie, Service des Musées et du Patrimoine de Nouvelle-Calédonie.

Balme, J., 2000 Excavations Revealing 40,000 Years of Occupation at Mimbi Caves, South Central Kimberley, Western Australia. Australian Archaeology 51:1–5.

Bowdler, S., 1977 The Coastal Colonisation of Australia. *In* Sunda and Sahul: Prehistoric Studies in Southeast Asia, Melanesia and Australia. J. Allen, J. Golson and R. Jones, eds. pp. 205–246. London: Academic Press.

——1990 Peopling Australasia: The "Coastal Colonisation" Hypothesis Reconsidered. *In* The Emergence of Modern Humans: An Archaeological Perspective. Vol. 2. P. Mellars, ed. pp. 327–343. Edinburgh: University of Edinburgh Press.

Brown, S., 1987 Toward a Prehistory of the Hamersley Plateau, Northwest Australia. Occasional Papers in Prehistory 6, Canberra: Department of Prehistory, Research School of Pacific Studies, Australian National University.

Comtesse, S., 2003 Mt Newman Sites Re-Analysed: Newman Orebody XXIX, Newman Rockshelter and P0959. B.Sc. Honours dissertation, University of Western Australia.

Dodson, J., and R. Wright, 1989 Humid to Arid to Sub-humid Vegetation Shifts on Pilliga Sandstone, Ulungra Springs, New South Wales. Quaternary Research 32:182–92.

Dortch, C., and M. V. Smith, 2001 Grand Hypotheses: Palaeodemographic Modeling in Western Australia's South-west. Archaeology in Oceania 36:34–45.

Edwards, K., and A. Murphy, 2003 A Preliminary Report on Archaeological Investigations at Malea Rockshelter, Pilbara Region, Western Australia. Australian Archaeology. 56:44–46.

Fullager, R., 2004 Australian Prehistoric Archaeology: The Last Few Years. Before Farming 2:1–22.

Gamble, C., W. Davies, P. Pettitt and M. Richards, 2004 Climate Change and Evolving Human Diversity in Europe during the Last Glacial. Philosophical Transactions of the Royal Society of London B 359:243–254.

Gould, R., 1969 Yiwara: Foragers of the Australian Desert. London: Collins.

——1977 Puntutjarpa Rockshelter and the Australian Desert Culture. Anthropological Papers 54. New York: American Museum of Natural History.

——1980 Living Archaeology. Cambridge: Cambridge University Press.

Hiscock, P., 1988 Prehistoric Settlement Patterns and Artifact Manufacture at Lawn Hill, Northwest Queensland. Ph.D. dissertation, University of Queensland.

Hiscock, P., and L. Wallis, 2004 Pleistocene Settlements of Deserts from an Australian Perspective. *In* Desert Peoples: Archaeological Perspectives. P. Veth, M. Smith and P. Hiscock, eds. pp. 34–57. Oxford: Blackwell.

Magee, J., J. Bowler, G. Miller and D. Williams, 1995 Stratigraphy, Sedimentology, Chronology and Paleohydrology of Quaternary Lacustrine Deposits at Madigan Gulf, Lake Eyre, South Australia. Palaeogeography, Palaeoclimatology, Palaeoecology 113:3–42.

Marwick, B., 2002 Milly's Cave: Evidence for Human Occupation of the Inland Pilbara during the Last Glacial Maximum. *In* Barriers, Borders, Boundaries. S. Ulm, C. Westcott, J. Reid, A. Ross, I. Lilley, J. Prangnell and L. Kirkwood, eds. pp. 21–23. Tempus 7. Brisbane: Anthropology Museum, University of Queensland.

Maynard, L., 1980 A Pleistocene Date from an Occupation Deposit in the Pilbara Region, WA. Australian Archaeology 10:3–8.

McConnell, K., and S. O'Connor, 1997 40,000 Year Record of Food Plants in the Southern Kimberley Ranges, Western Australia. Australian Archaeology 44:20–31.

Morse, K., 1994 West Side Story: Towards a Prehistory of the Cape Range Peninsula. Ph.D. dissertation, University of Western Australia.

——1999 Coastwatch: Pleistocene Resource Use on the Cape Range Peninsula. *In* Australian Coastal Archaeology. J. Hall and I. McNiven, eds. pp. 73–78. Research

Papers in Archaeology and Natural History 31. Canberra: ANH Publications, Australian National University.

O'Connor, S., 1995 Carpenter's Gap Rockshelter 1: 40,000 Years of Aboriginal Occupation in the Napier Ranges, Kimberley, W.A. Australian Archaeology 40:58–60.

——1999 30,000 Years of Aboriginal Occupation in the Kimberley, Northwest Australia. Terra Australis 14. Canberra: ANH Publications and the Centre for Archaeological Research, Australian National University.

O'Connor, S., and J. Chappell, 2003 Colonisation and coastal subsistence in Australia and Papua New Guinea: Different timing, Different modes. In Pacific Archaeology: Assessments and Prospects. C. Sand, ed. pp. 17–32. Les Cahiers de l'Archéologie en Nouvelle-Calédonie 15. Nouméa: Département Archéologie, Service des Musées et du Patrimoine de Nouvelle-Calédonie.

O'Connor, S., and B. Fankhauser, 2001 Art at 40,000 B.P? One Step Closer, An Ochre Covered Rock from Carpenter's Gap Shelter 1, Kimberley Region, W.A. In Histories of Old Ages: Essays in Honour of Rhys Jones. A. Anderson, I. Lilley and S. O'Connor, eds. pp. 287–300. Canberra: Pandanus Books.

O'Connor, S., and P. Veth, 2000a The World's First Mariners: Savannah Dwellers in an Island Continent. In East of Wallace's Line: Studies of Past and Present Maritime Societies in the Indo-Pacific Region. S. O'Connor and P. Veth, eds. pp. 99–137. Modern Quaternary Research in Southeast Asia 16. Rotterdam: A. A. Balkema.

——2000b East of Wallace's Line. In East of Wallace's Line: Studies of Past and Present Maritime Societies in the Indo-Pacific Region. S. O'Connor and P. Veth, eds. pp. 1–9. Modern Quaternary Research in Southeast Asia 16. Rotterdam: A. A. Balkema.

——1996 A Preliminary Report on Recent Archaeological Research in the Semi-Arid/Arid Belt of Western Australia. Australian Aboriginal Studies. 2:42–50.

O'Connor, S., P. Veth and A. Barham, 1999 Cultural versus Natural Explanations for Lacunae in Aboriginal Occupation Deposits in Northern Australia. Quaternary International. 59:61–70.

O'Connor, S., P. Veth and C. Campbell, 1998 Serpent's Glen Rockshelter: Report of the First Pleistocene-Aged Occupation Sequence from the Western Desert. Australian Archaeology 46:12–21.

O'Connor, S., P. Veth and N. Hubbard, 1993 Changing Interpretations of Postglacial Human Subsistence and Demography in Sahul. In Sahul in Review: The Archaeology of Australia, New Guinea in Island Melanesia at 10–30 Kyr B.P. M. Smith, M. Spriggs and B. Fankhauser, eds. pp. 95–105. Occasional Papers in Prehistory 24. Canberra: Department of Prehistory, Research School of Pacific Studies, Australian National University.

Przywolnik, K., 2002 Patterns of Occupation in Cape Range Peninsula (WA) over the Last 36,000 years. Ph.D. dissertation, University of Western Australia.

Smith, M., 1988 The Pattern and Timing of Prehistoric Settlement in Central Australia. Ph.D. dissertation, University of New England.

——1989 The Case for a Resident Human Population in the Central Australian Ranges during Full Glacial Aridity. Archaeology in Oceania 24:93–105.

——1993 Biogeography, Human Ecology and Prehistory in the Sandridge Deserts. Australian Archaeology 37:35–50.

——1996 Prehistory and Human Ecology in Central Australia: An Archaeological Perspective. In Exploring Central Australia: Society, Environment and the 1894 Horn Expedition. S. Morton and D. J. Mulvaney, eds. pp. 61–73. Chipping Norton: Surrey Beatty and Sons.

——In press Characterising Late Pleistocene and Holocene Stone Artifact Assemblages from Puritjarra Rock-Shelter: A Long Sequence from the Australian Desert. Records of the Australian Museum.

Smith, M., J. Prescott and M. Head, 1997 Comparison of ^{14}C and Luminescence Chronologies at Puritjarra Rock Shelter, Central Australia. Quaternary Science Reviews (Quaternary Geochronology) 16:299–320.

Thorley, P., 1998a Shifting Location, Shifting Scale: A Regional Landscape Approach to the Prehistoric Archaeology of the Palmer River Catchment, Central Australia. Ph.D. dissertation, Northern Territory University.

——1998b Pleistocene Settlement in the Australian Arid Zone: Occupation of an Inland Riverine Landscape in the Central Australian Ranges. Antiquity 72:34–45.

Troilett, G., n.d. A New Radiocarbon Date from a Rockshelter Deposit Near Newman, WA. Department of Aboriginal Sites, Western Australian Museum, Perth, unpublished MS.

Turney, C., M. Bird, L. Fifield, R. Roberts, M. Smith, C. Dortch, R. Grun, E. Lawson, L. Ayliffe, G. Miller, J. Dortch and R. Cresswell, 2001 Early Human Occupation at Devil's Lair, Southwestern Australia 50,000 Years Ago. Quaternary Research 55:3–13.

Veitch, B., 1996 Evidence for Mid-Holocene Change in the Mitchell Plateau, Northwest Kimberley, Western Australia. *In* Archaeology of Northern Australia. P. Veth and P. Hiscock, eds. pp. 66–89. Tempus 4. Brisbane: Anthropology Museum, University of Queensland.

Veitch, B., F. Hook and E. Bradshaw, n.d. A Note on Radiocarbon Dates from the Paraburdoo, Mt Brockman and Yandicoogina Areas of the Hamersley Plateau, Pilbara, Western Australia. Archae-aus Pty Ltd, Perth, unpublished MS.

Veth, P., 1989 Islands in the Interior: A Model for the Colonisation of Australia's Arid Zone. Archaeology in Oceania 24:81–92.

——1993a Islands in the Interior: The Dynamics of Prehistoric Adaptations within the Arid Zone of Australia. Archaeological Series 3. Ann Arbor: International Monographs in Prehistory.

——1993b The Aboriginal Occupation of the Montebello Islands, Northwest Australia. Australian Aboriginal Studies 2:39–50.

Wallis, L.A., 2001 Environmental History of Northwest Australia based on Phytolith Analysis at Carpenter's Gap 1. Quaternary International 83–85:103–117.

3

Archaeology and the Dreaming: Toward an Archaeology of Ontology

Bruno David

What's past is prologue. (Shakespeare, *The Tempest*)

The desire to discover past meanings of things lies at the heart of much historically oriented cultural research, although in archaeology we rarely dare explicitly to venture onto those forbidden grounds. Questions of meaning are undoubtedly the hardest archaeological questions of all, but a lack of quizzical ambition, a lack of daring to address the hard questions, remains one of the most limiting and therefore unsatisfactory aspects of our disciplinary venture.

Australian archaeology is in this sense in a strange and often unwittingly compromised position. Not only do we have a rich ethnographic record to help us better understand the recent past, but in many places there are communities of indigenous peoples who have carried oral traditions and knowledges of their pasts into the present in variously transformed ways. Of course in archaeology there is a well-recognized tyranny to ethnography: While the distant past remains unknown, there is a too-easy readiness – often unstated or unrecognized – to transpose recent ethnographic details progressively deeper into history, a readiness or tendency to color the archaeological gaps with ethnographic fill. This has popular parallels in the oft-repeated assumptions of the timelessness of Aboriginal being – the "Never-Never syndrome" – a timelessness sculpted and given shape by late 19th and early 20th century ethnographic details, a literature that gave us the term "The Timeless Land" and that following the Northern Territory Tourist Commission (2002) "makes Australian Aboriginal culture the oldest living culture in the world."

Cultural researchers and historians the world over – archaeologists included – tend to be reasonably well versed in questions of epistemology, questions that concern how we construct notions and knowledges of other beings and other cultures, both past and present. Even so, in Australia to date there have been few explicit archaeological attempts to address questions of ontology, questions that concern the history of ethnographically documented Aboriginal and Torres Strait Islander ways of thinking about the world. There has been a near-total lack of enquiry into the antiquity and historical becoming of indigenous ontology, indigenous religion, and indigenous philosophy as we have come to know them from the ethnographic literature and from Aboriginal or Islander commentators themselves (for exceptions, see McNiven and Feldman 2003; Rosenfeld 2002; Taçon et al. 1996). This means there have been very few attempts to enquire into the antiquity and historical becoming of the worldviews that today give or recently gave meaning to things for Aboriginal peoples and Torres Strait Islanders. Perhaps this lack of archaeological questioning and curiosity has come from a longstanding subliminal tendency to treat the Aboriginal past in particular as a more or less ethnographic past, but this explanation is not entirely satisfactory when it is realized that it has now been over twenty years since questions of change as social process began to explicitly dominate questions of stasis in the Australian archaeological literature, taking Bowdler's (1981), Hughes and Lampert's (1982), and Lourandos's (1983) landmark papers as useful benchmarks. It is therefore questions of the archaeology of ethnography and the archaeology of Aboriginal worldviews that I would like to approach in this chapter.

Toward an Archaeology of Ontology: Place, Ritual and Symbolism

At first glance the reluctance to explicitly broach questions of meaning in Australian archaeology may appear to have been driven by a lack of methodological know-how: How can we ask questions of the intangibles of life, immaterial things that have forever disappeared? But I suggest that there is a more fundamental problem, one that has its roots in a cultural past still fundamentally approached through notions of environmental and ecological adaptation. To address the past meaningfulness of things requires a different tack, one that calls for an archaeology of ontology and that rests not so much on adaptive strategies as on the way the world is constructed in social *dwelling* – a dwelling that can usefully be approached through the work of Martin Heidegger.

A German philosopher who published his masterwork *Being and Time* (*Sein und Zeit*) in 1927 (Heidegger 1962), Heidegger wanted to explore the meaning of being, and his later work explicitly focused on the historicity of being. He framed his ideas around the notion that people do not exist in isolation from their environments. People are always situated, and being is always an expression of this embeddedness. Being can therefore be thought of more appropriately as a presence constructed through engagement in the world, rather than as an essence. Heidegger saw that subject and object are constructed each in the other and to reflect this insight used the German term *dasein* (being-there), and coined the phrase "being-in-the-world." *Dasein* is constructed as human presence emplaced in the particularities of the social and contextual situation of the time. Being is thus emergent in relation to the everyday practices in which it is embedded. So rather than timeless essence, being can be thought of as temporally emergent in relation to the world in which it dwells.

This is a world inscribed with art, with monuments – a scarification of the earth that reveals the world as socially and experientially engaged. Human dwelling is thus a situation in which people are *thrown into the world*; people are never quite apart from things, but always defined in relation to them. The way we do things defines our being, and the way we do things is constructed in the here-and-now of dwelling, as worldly engagement. Because of this, being and identity are continuously reshaped in relation to the changing world.

From this perspective we can approach an Aboriginal or Torres Strait Islander past via the way people dwelt in the world, a dwelling that is not limited to its physical or adaptive occupation but one that captures the world's meaningfulness. The world is not simply a stage onto which people superimpose their cultural ways, for it is itself a cultural artifact constructed in everyday life, a landscape of engagement. This is a world constituted as at once sentient and societal, unceasingly materializing in relations of ontology and meaning, and normatively engaged through symbolic representation, ritual, and *habitus*.

Recognizing regionally variable "Dreaming" beliefs recorded during ethnographic times to represent the ethnographically known worldviews of Aboriginal Australia positions us to track the historical emergence of recent Dreaming-mediated dwelling by tracking the archaeological emergence of its material traces. It was through the Dreaming that Aboriginal peoples dwelt in and engaged with meaningful socially constructed worlds during ethnographic times. I attempt here to undertake an archaeology of this ethnographic meaningfulness for three parts of Australia via the way Dreaming worldviews recorded during ethnographic times have become materialized in *place*, *ritual*, and *symbolism*.

The Dreaming

When Europeans first arrived in Australia, Dreaming worldviews conditioned indigenous knowledge in much, if not all, of mainland Australia and many of its offshore islands. Although little is known of Aboriginal beliefs in southeastern Australia during the early European contact period, considerable detail has been recorded elsewhere in Australia. The Dreaming is not so much a single worldview as a range of geographically and culturally varied worldviews, with a few common themes. These commonalities revolve around the widespread understanding that life essences emerge from the ground (earth and water), and around beliefs of an essential kinship between people and the ancestral beings who formed the world in a timeless age of what are nevertheless originary, creative acts.

During ethnographic times, Aboriginal peoples in different parts of Australia engaged with their worlds in ways that were structured by their Dreaming beliefs. Because of this ontologically patterned behavior, it is possible to investigate the history of ethnographically known Dreaming beliefs through archaeological research. I take my methodological lead from the view that knowledge of history is founded on a dialectic: history unfolds forward in time, while at the same time we trace the origins of what we know *back* in time. By tracking archaeological signatures of ethnographically documented worldviews back from a recent to a more distant past, the antiquity of specific archaeological details – and, by implication, of cultural practices – can be traced. At the same time, tracking the emergence of new archaeological expressions from a distant to a more recent past enables us to position cultural traits in historical perspective. Rather than jumping from one historical period of time to another, the method involves a tracing of continuity so as to identify and highlight discontinuities. I undertake this archaeology of ethnography by reference to three of its material manifestations: relations to place, as determined by specific beliefs about places, ritual practices as they relate to Dreaming beliefs, and rock art symbolism, focusing on artistic conventions known to have been undertaken in a Dreaming worldview *at the time of their creation*. My aim in each case is to identify when in the past the kinds of behaviors ethnographically known to have been associated with Dreaming worldviews first emerged in the archaeological record.

Place

Henri Lefebvre (1991:8) has noted that "spatial practice consists in a projection onto a (spatial) field of all aspects, elements and moments of social practice." It is this social projection that is touched upon in an archaeology of place. In the Dreamings of ethnographic times we see the reasons for life's spatial order, an orderliness that signals conceptualized, signified, and experienced place. Such spatial patterning can be investigated archaeologically, allowing a tracking of its historical becoming. It is the archaeological signature of the way place has been constructed in the Dreaming of ethnographic times that I wish to focus on by reference to the Dreaming mountain known as Ngarrabullgan (Mt. Mulligan).

Ngarrabullgan is an imposing, cliff-lined sandstone and conglomerate mountain located 100 kilometers northwest of Cairns in northeastern Australia. It is 18 kilometers long, 6.5 kilometers wide, and surrounded by 200–400-meter cliffs along most of its periphery. The area around the mountain, extending for tens of kilometers in all directions, consists of volcanic and metamorphic sediments. Permanent waterholes are relatively common on the mountain, and can occasionally be found interspersed along creeks and rivers near its base. Ngarrabullgan is thus a well-demarcated geological, botanical, and zoological "island" in the landscape (Figure 3.1).

When Westerners first visited the region in the late 1800s, Ngarrabullgan was – as it remains today – at the geographical and spiritual heart of Djungan country (Figure 3.2). In 1926, Francis Richards, a long-time European resident of the area, wrote of the mountain's local Dreaming significance:

> These natives were highly superstitious and had an intense fear of devils. There were
> four of these –

Figure 3.1 Ngarrabullgan, showing Initiation Cave in foreground

(1)   The Beerroo, who lived anywhere.
(2)   The Eekoo (or mountain devil), who lived on Mount Mulligan.
(3, 4)   Mooramully, Barmboo – Water devils inhabiting waterholes.

> Most sickness was attributed to the agency of these devils, the blame generally falling
> on the Beerroo or the Eekoo. These devils were able to throw hooks, stones, or pieces
> of wood into the body without leaving a mark. The Eekoo's home was a lake on Mount
> Mulligan (Lake Koongirra) . . . The Eekoo was generally held responsible for any sick-
> ness when on the mountain. (Richards 1926:256–257)

Today, the Djungan elders stress Eekoo's and Mooramully's presence on the mountain. What emerges from the early historical literature and from present-day attitudes is that Ngarrabullgan was and is a place cautiously, and rarely, approached
by Djungan people, as the mountain is the home of potentially dangerous
spirit-beings.

If the archaeological signature of ethnographic times relates to recent Aboriginal relations with place, then we may be able to trace back through time the emergence of the mountain's Eekoo-mediated Dreaming significance by tracking back
in time this recent archaeological signature. With this aim in mind, 16 rockshelters
have been excavated on or adjacent to the mountain. Eleven are on top of the moun-

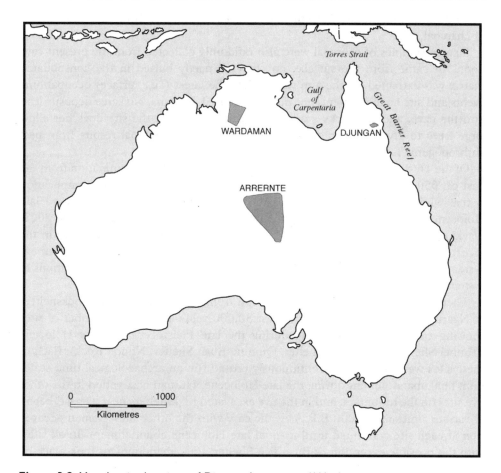

Figure 3.2 Map showing locations of Djungan, Arrernte, and Wardaman country

tain (Painted Ell, Tunnel Shelter, Bush Peg Shelter, Hand Shelter, Fig Tree Shelter, Nonda Rock, Grass Tree Shelter, Gorge Creek Shelter, Quinine Bush Shelter, Ngarrabullgan Cave, Waterhole Cave); three are immediately at the base of its cliffs (Kookaburra Rock, Courtyard Rock, Dragonfly Hollow); one is on a small, isolated detached cliff immediately west of the mountain (Lookout Shelter); and one is located on the surrounding undulating plains one kilometer to the north (Initiation Cave). All bar Waterhole Cave contain cultural materials.

Ngarrabullgan Cave is by far the largest cave or rockshelter yet recorded on the mountain. Today, the ground surface is littered with charcoal from past campfires, although their individual configurations cannot be delimited as the charcoal merges from one fireplace to another. Excavations show that a series of occupational events began shortly before 35,500 B.P., possibly continuing until around 32,000 B.P. (Bird et al. 1999; David 2002). The site was then abandoned until ca. 5400 B.P., after which it was often used until ca. 900 B.P. (ca.1,200–1,000 C.E.). Only one excavated radiocarbon date has been obtained for the past ca. 730 calendar years, despite dating more than 50 stratified charcoal samples, mainly on individual pieces of charcoal.

Sixteen samples of charcoal were also randomly collected from the present cave floor. All came from the surface; no charcoal partly buried in the consolidated matrix was extracted, as the aim was to date the latest (i.e., surface) occupational events and site abandonment, not the older buried deposits. No scree deposits lead into the cave, and the rocky surface immediately outside the site does not allow large trees to grow. We can therefore assume that the charcoal results from past anthropogenic fires within this large cave.

Of the 16 surface-samples dated, only one has revealed a determination from the past ca. 650 calendar years, reminiscent of the excavated pattern. The implication is that while human occupation was relatively intensive during the mid- to late Holocene, site abandonment was virtually complete by 650 years ago (David 2002; David and Wilson 1999). Was this abandonment an isolated case, a change in the incorporation of a particular cave in a more or less stable regional settlement system? Or does site abandonment represent broader, mountain-wide alterations in systems of land-use?

There is evidence for human occupation from the other excavated rockshelters at Ngarrabullgan dating back to at least 30,000 years ago, with a number of sites showing traces of use beginning during the late Pleistocene or early Holocene (Tunnel Shelter, Grass Tree Shelter, Quinine Bush Shelter, Nonda Rock). Each of these sites was more or less continuously reused (on an archaeological time-scale) until final abandonment during the late Holocene. Human occupation in the other five sites on the mountain, and in the five excavated rockshelters near its base, began at various times after 5000 B.P. As is the case with the other sites, human occupation at each site continued until its final late Holocene abandonment. In all sites, with the possible exception of Bush Peg Shelter, final abandonment took place by ca. 650 years ago. However, such a pattern of abandonment is not seen in the radiocarbon-dated sites located more than one kilometer from the mountain, where in nine of the ten dated sites found up to 200 kilometers from the mountain occupation continued until the advent of European colonization during the late 19th century (for details, see David 2002; David and Wilson 1999). What happened at Ngarrabullgan that led to its enigmatic pattern of abandonment? What are the implications for the history of how people related with and signified place in what we now know as Djungan country?

First, abandonment by ca. 650 years ago at Ngarrabullgan was systematic: It involved a near-total cessation of hearth construction and site use at Ngarrabullgan Cave – the largest known rockshelter on the mountain (and situated near a permanent waterhole, an uncommon environmental setting in this seasonally dry landscape) – as well as the cessation of use of the smaller sites strewn across the mountain-top and at its base. That is, changes in both individual site and regional land-use are implicated. Whatever its ultimate cause(s), abandonment by the 14th century C.E. represents changing relations to and engagement with place, mediated by a system of signification that rendered the mountain inappropriate for habitation: abandonment always involves a change in meaning relating to place. If occupational trends are grounded in relations with place, and if the world is engaged through its meaningfulness, then the archaeological changes documented at Ngarrabullgan suggest that by 650 years ago experience of place and country had changed significantly in what is now known as Djungan country. The archaeological changes suggest that Ngarrabullgan attained a new cultural significance matching the mountain's Dreaming significance as recorded by Europeans earlier this century, and reported by present-day Djungan elders. A connotation is the emergence of a new way of relating with place, akin to notions of the Dreaming as recorded ethnographically.

Rituals

Let us now turn to the archaeology of ethnographically documented Dreaming rituals from the only part of Australia where such research has been attempted, the Arrernte lands of the arid center (Figure 3.2). Peterson (1972) has noted that understanding Aboriginal relationships to place across all of Australia during the ethnographic period requires consideration of totemic classification. Totems, now more commonly referred to as Dreamings, relate people to place through the Ancestral beings and creative events of the Dreaming, and totemic affiliations are maintained and celebrated in ritual performances (see Langton 2002). Following Meyer Fortes (1967:6), Peterson (1972:13) defines totemism as "beliefs and practices in which relations of a special kind between persons and designated groups of persons, on the one hand, and natural species of animals and plants or artificial objects, on the other, are postulated." Totems, he suggests – as Spencer and Gillen (e.g., 1899) implied before him – were in the first instance attached to localities. It is by virtue of this emplacement that people gained their own Dreaming affiliations (Peterson 1972). Because people were conceived in place, were born in particular patri- or matri-estates, and died in place, they were from birth affiliated with emplaced Dreaming beings.

Every Arrernte individual belongs to a particular patriclan and recognizes the totems of this patriclan. Patriclans are of primary importance, although totemic affiliations attained via other means are also recognized, entailing a range of responsibilities and behaviors in ritual and in everyday practice. Totemic membership, for example, involves ownership of particular symbols and dances, some of great secrecy and others of public standing. They also require formal celebration and ritual maintenance.

Because some Dreaming beliefs known from ethnography involve specific ritual behaviors in specific places, it is possible to investigate their antiquity through the archaeological investigation of ritual remains. In principle this is a fairly straightforward exercise: Identify a known ritual place, determine the ritual's material manifestations, and trace its origins back in time through archaeological investigation. The only such data presently available from anywhere in Australia come from the Native Cat Dreaming place of Therreyererte, the totemic site of Kweyunpe, the Kangaroo totemic center of Keringke, and the Grass Seed totemic center of Urre.

I have elsewhere (David 2002) reviewed at some length Smith's (e.g., 1986, 1993, 1996; Smith et al. 1998) and others' (e.g., Napton and Greathouse 1985; Stockton 1971) evidence for the antiquity of occupation and Dreaming ritual at these sites, concluding that while there is fleeting evidence for a human presence at some of these sites as far back as 3,000 years ago, the earliest signs of ritual occur no more than 1,400 years ago at Kweyunpe; 1,000 to 800 years ago at Keringke and Urre; and 700 to 600 years ago at Therreyererte. In short, the archaeology shows no evidence from deep in antiquity for the kinds of ceremonial activity known from ethnography. At the Native Cat center at Therreyererte, the Kangaroo place at Keringke, Kweyunpe, and Grass Seed place at Urre, Dreaming beliefs framed ritual practices during ethnographic times. But these rituals were only performed here during the past 1,400 years, indicating cultural dynamism and changes in how belief was articulated through performance.

Yet to track the antiquity of ethnographically known Dreaming rituals is larger than a history of the rituals themselves, for it is not the outcome that is commemorated in ritual but *the ownership of process*. Christian rituals, such as Easter or Christmas, do not merely or meekly celebrate a past event such as the crucifixion or the birth of Christ, but the personal ownership of a process of identification with those events and their spiritual truths. In this sense, we celebrate our own existence as ontological beings through rituals, we celebrate the social construction of meaning. Rituals map ontology, in the sense that they concern the ways people perceive their own reality. The ritual cycles documented during ethnographic times in Arrernte country are a celebration and social reproduction of the emplacement of people as social beings through a Dreaming understanding of the world. But it is only to the past 1,400 years (and especially to the past 1,000 years) that we can trace back in time the first archaeological signs of the ritual events that Spencer and Gillen (e.g., 1899, 1927; Spencer 1896), Strehlow (e.g., 1971) and others (e.g., Kimber and Smith 1987) documented toward the end of the 19th and into the 20th centuries. As was the case at Ngarrabullgan, the Dreaming beliefs documented ethnographically cannot be traced any deeper into antiquity, implying the emergence of a new way of performing belief, perceiving the world, and relating to place late in the course of Aboriginal history.

Symbolism

Dant (1999:118) has written that "the symbolic power of the object lies in the way humans are attracted to it." We are seduced by objects, a seduction whose roots go beyond the material thing to its entanglement in a world of sociality and meaning. In this sense we are all captive, although this is not to deny our engagement as active agents. The telephone rings and we reach for the receiver (or we resist, choosing not to, in which case our captivity is in the resistance), yielding to its structured and structuring force; the telephone calls us as much as the person on the other end calls us. I am in the living room and I sit, not on the floor but on a chair; the chair beckons, guiding my experience of sitting and subsequent expectations. I do not just own, nor do I just call upon, the material world around me, for I, too, am immersed in the power of its constructiveness. This is a world not of material culture but of material behavior both engaged and engaging. It is a world of materialization and embodiment. Instead of our consciousness reaching out and grasping the material, objects themselves draw out from us a certain way of engaging with them.

Wardaman country is found some 70 kilometers southwest of the modern town of Katherine in the Northern Territory (Figure 3.2). Covering a vast expanse of land roughly quadrilateral in shape, Wardaman country is surrounded by distinctive but related language groups and territories: Jaminjung to the west, Dagoman to the north, Yangman to the east, Mudburra to the south, Ngarinyman and Ngaliwurru to the southwest (Merlan 1994). Kin, exchange, and other cultural relations were generally close between the Wardaman and members of many of these language groups during the early European contact period, especially with the west, where a number of common cultural practices were observed (e.g., subincision rites and eight-class systems of kin affiliation).

During the recent past, Wardaman country was divided into 11 totemically based territorial estates, each of which recognized a cosmological identity with specific Dreaming beings, such as *gulirrida* (peewee birds). In addition to the localized Dreamings of the various estates were also traveling beings that cut across patri-estates, such as *gorondolni*, the Rainbow Serpent. Other Dreamings were restricted to individual locations only, such as *gandawag*, the Moon, at Jalijbang. While the entire landscape gained its identity and was made discontinuous by its affiliations with disparate Dreaming beings and events, some of which identified patri-estates and others that were located on the land but did not signify patri-estates, the entire landscape was united into a cosmological whole informed by the Dreaming. In this sense the way in which the various estates were divided and interlinked at various levels reflects the pattern of Wardaman land tenure, land-use, and cosmology.

Wardaman rock art is produced in an existing system of social and territorial relations. It has, as emplaced social symbols, a role in the manifestation and maintenance of those relations. In particular, much of the rock art of Wardaman country is created and interpreted narratively via reference to the totemic landscape, and these paintings represent the Dreaming beings and events of the decorated sites. The Dreaming (*buwarraja*) "art" is a visual manifestation of the Dreaming beings. In buwarraja art the Dreaming beings place themselves in the landscape at the creative events of the beginning of time. Thus buwarraja rock paintings are the Dreaming beings "sitting" in the landscape. In the recent past people could nevertheless paint buwarraja figures as mediators of the Dreaming. Such an act should be undertaken by individuals of appropriate patri-filiation to both place and totemic beings, although others may in some circumstances also undertake such a task (Merlan 1989:17). It is only during the 20th century that Wardaman artists stopped painting Dreaming motifs in the rockshelters.

These ethnographically documented features of Wardaman Dreaming enable us to track archaeologically the antiquity of its visual symbolic expressions. If the rock

art of a kind that was painted into the ethnographic period symbolizes the Dreaming, then the art's antiquity must necessarily give a maximum age for the artistic
expression of that Dreaming belief in the site in question. Given its identity as sig-
nifier and signified of the ethnographically known Dreaming, investigations of the
rock art's antiquity may shed important light on the beginnings of Wardaman
Dreaming as we know it today. I thus begin by asking whether or not the paintings
that today express the identity of the land and the Dreaming were all initially undertaken within a relatively well-bounded and identifiable time frame.

In 1988, Flood and her co-researchers began a long-term research project on
the archaeology of rock art in Wardaman country. A series of painted rockshelters
whose ethnographic Dreaming stories were known were excavated with the above
aims in mind (e.g., Flood and David 1994). Seven painted and engraved sites were
excavated and five revealed information on the antiquity of the Dreaming paintings. At Yiwarlarlay, the Lightning Brothers site, two rockshelters were investigated
(Yiwarlarlay 1 and Delamere 3). Here the paintings relate to the Dreaming
brothers Yagjagbula and Jabirringi (see Arndt 1962 for details of the Dreaming
story) (Figure 3.3). We know from past rock art recordings and interviews that at
least some parts of the two large anthropomorphs at the site identified by Wardaman
elders as the Lightning Brothers date to the early parts of the 20th century C.E.
(Arndt 1962; Barrett and Croll 1943; Harney 1959). Archaeological investigations
confirmed that the Lightning Brothers paintings at Yiwarlarlay 1 and Delamere
3 date to the period after the arrival of Europeans (David et al. 1990; McNiven
et al. 1992).

At the rockshelter designated Garnawala 1, Dreaming beings relating to a
Rainbow Serpent/Two Sisters story sit in the rock (see David 2002 for story)
(Figure 3.4). At some 32 meters wide and 8 meters deep, the shelter is one of the
largest painted sites in Wardaman country. A series of nine adjacent 50 × 50 centimeter squares were excavated beneath the Dreaming paintings, the sediments
revealing large numbers of buried ochre pieces datable by stratigraphic association.
The Garnawala excavations revealed two major strata, an upper unit rich in cultural materials, and a lower unit dating back to about 5200 B.P., with only a few
cultural remains. The two strata are separated by a thick layer of sandstone, evidence of sheet roof-fall that took place between two radiocarbon dates of about 900
and 850 B.P. (David et al. 1994).

The implications are significant: The thickness and extent of the rocky layer imply
that a large section of the rockshelter's ceiling, if not the entire ceiling, fell around
900 B.P., exposing the present now richly decorated surface. The Dreaming paintings that today display the Rainbow Serpent/Two Sisters story cannot therefore be
older than this. This is confirmed by the presence of hundreds of ochre pieces in
the upper layer of the Garnawala deposits. The ethnographically identified Dreaming paintings at Garnawala began to be painted after 900 B.P., in calibrated terms
equivalent to some time between 1,000 and 800 years ago, despite the fact that
people first started using the site more than 5000 B.P.

In the area of Jalijbang a few kilometers away and toward the western edge
of Wardaman country, there is a small rocky gorge. Here can be found the

Figure 3.3 The Lightning Brothers, Yagjagbula and Jabirringi, at Yiwarlarlay

Figure 3.4 Garnawala, Shelter 1, showing the paintings that relate to the Rainbow Serpent/Two Sisters story

rockshelter of Mennge-ya, "at the White Cockatoo." Two large polychrome anthro-pomorphs dominate the walls. They are female White Cockatoos who gather "native cotton" (kapok) to feed their husband, old-man White Cockatoo of Winybarr, a few kilometers away. The women sit in the rock as manifestations of the Dreaming. Mennge-ya, a sandstone rockshelter 12 meters wide and 18 meters deep, was exca-vated in 1989 by Attenbrow (Attenbrow et al. 1995). The two White Cockatoos are located from near the ground level upward to about 1.5 meters above the shelter floor, on a small, localized vertical rock surface. Older, faded, and largely indeterminate paintings occur underneath and near the White Cockatoos; these are not known to be related to the White Cockatoo Dreaming story.

Six adjacent 50 centimeter × 50 centimeter squares were excavated immediately beneath the paintings. Cultural sediments began sometime shortly before a radiocarbon date of 2100 B.P. A major increase in deposition rates of cultural materials – flaked stone artifacts, bone (food remains), ochre, and charcoal – took place around 2000 B.P. (Attenbrow et al. 1995). While the number of buried ochre pieces first increases with the acceleration of stone artifact deposition rates around 2000 B.P. – that is, the evidence for painting activity increases along with other evidence for increased intensities of site use – the major increase in ochre deposition rates (including the pieces of ochre with use-wear in the form of striations and beveling) does not take place until well after, around 1400 B.P. (David et al. 1994:247). These changes can be directly related to the now-visible rock paintings. My colleagues and I (David et al. 1994) have suggested that the earliest ochre pieces probably date the paintings underlying the White Cockatoos, given patterns of superimposition, degrees of fading, and colors used. The White Cockatoos themselves have been repainted many times since their initial creation. Their first painting corresponds to a second period of increase in ochre deposition rates, shortly after a radiocarbon determination of 380 B.P. This means that the first archaeological signs of the White Cockatoo paintings appear late in the second millennium C.E.

Gordol-ya, "at the Owl," is the largest rockshelter of the sandstone outcrop known today as Jigaigarn by Wardaman elders. Located toward the western end of Wardaman country, it contains a culturally significant landmark in the form of a balancing rock placed above the rockshelter by *gordol*, the Owl, in the Dreaming. One hundred and forty-seven paintings decorate the shelter walls. The paintings are dominated by a large red and yellow striped figure, identified by Wardaman elder Tarpot Ngamunagami (pers. comm. 1991) as gordol (David et al. 1995). Little else has been recorded of the site's Dreaming significance during recent times.

Gordol-ya was excavated by Collins in 1991 (see David et al. 1995 for a brief report). Sixteen 50 × 50 centimeter squares were dug below the decorated walls, spanning the back to the center of the shelter. Human occupation began shortly before a radiocarbon date of 10,000 B.P. However, few cultural materials were deposited until the late Holocene, when quantities of charcoal, mussel shell, flaked stone artifacts, and animal bones increased noticeably. Most of the fragments of stratified earth pigment came from a buried layer that began to form shortly before 300 B.P. (David et al. 1995). My colleagues and I (David et al. 1995:5–6) thus concluded that the Gordol-ya paintings date to the late Holocene, and probably only to the past few hundred years. While our understanding of the site's chronology remains coarse-grained, there is no evidence for the presence of the paintings recently associated with the Owl Dreaming story at Gordol-ya before the second half of the second millennium C.E. As was the case at the other sites in Wardaman country, artistic expressions of the Dreaming known from ethnography at Gordol-ya emerge only during late Holocene times.

Archaeology of the Dreaming

The Djungan mountain of Ngarrabullgan was in the recent past known as a landscape meaningfully constituted in the Dreaming. But systematic archaeological research revealed its ethnographically documented sacred signification to have emerged during the course of history from dissimilar antecedents. We do not know anything definite about the mountain's signification prior to about 650 years ago, although it is clear – and contrary to the ethnographic situation – that previously the plateau and cliff bases were routinely inhabited. Ngarrabullgan reveals the ethnographically documented Djungan Dreaming construction of place, and thus Djungan worldviews, to be historically contingent and of late Holocene antiquity.

Fifteen hundred kilometers southwest of Djungan country are the arid lands of Arrernte country, where various Dreaming rituals have been documented since the end of the 19th century. These rituals performed the Dreaming as confirmation of the truth of the socially known world. But here, too, the ethnographically known Dreaming could not be traced archaeologically prior to the late Holocene.

And in signaling a Dreaming presence, the buwarraja rock paintings of Wardaman country further to the north signal a historically particular framework of meaning. In this rock art symbolism can be found visual representations – visual *proof* – of the truth of the Dreaming. But as the antiquity of buwarraja artistic representations akin to those of ethnographic times implies, such a truth appears to have a limited temporal depth. Four site complexes containing extensively decorated art panels were systematically investigated with the aim of revealing information on the antiquity of the ethnographically known Dreaming paintings. Despite some evidence of human presence going as far back as 10,000 B.P., it is only during the past 1,400 years that paintings of the ethnographically documented Dreaming beings first appear: a maximum of 1,400 years ago at Mennge-ya (and possibly considerably less), 1,000 to 800 years ago at Garnawala, and less than 400 years ago at Yiwarlarlay and Gordol-ya.

The intensification of painting activity after 1,400–800 years ago, and its continued acceleration thereafter, implicates late Holocene transformations in the way belief systems were (re)presented. It is not just the esthetic world that was altered, but the visual, symbolic manifestations of how that world was understood. After 1,400–800 years ago there emerged a new system of signs that newly divided the world symbolically, making novel structural demands on the onlooker's attention. These signs differentiated the Wardaman landscape into a network of separate but ontologically linked spaces by which people came to engage with their world. The emerging rock art conventions created new structures of difference and deference. The late Holocene antiquity of Wardaman visual symbols implies a late Holocene antiquity for the graphic presencing of the ethnographically known Wardaman Dreaming. The fact that Wardaman symbols associated with the ethnographic Dreaming cannot be tracked further back in time implies an epochal reworking of the open network of signs, as system of meaning, 1,400–800 years ago.

In each of these regional cases during ethnographic times, social behavior and worldly engagement were constructed in regionally specific Dreaming beliefs. But in each case the material traces of such engagements and beliefs could not be traced deeper than the late Holocene, leaving open to question the nature of the ethnographic Dreamings' historical antecedents. Whatever the answers to this yet-unaddressed question, it is evident that the past meaningfulness of things – past worldviews – cannot satisfactorily be revealed or answered by simply animating the material past with ethnographic details. Revealing dimensions of this meaningfulness remains a challenging disciplinary priority.

Conclusion

The influential French archaeologist and ethnologist André Leroi-Gourhan was during his lifetime renowned for his cautious approach to ethnography when interpreting the past (e.g., Leroi-Gourhan 1971; see Conte, this volume). His cautiousness stemmed from an awareness that around the globe the great diversity of present-day lifeways have history, that they are situated in present-day systems of meaning, that the cultures we know from ethnography possess their own means of explaining the world, each having emerged in the course of its own historical unfolding. Yet in one of his last books, Leroi-Gourhan noted, under the heading "Life of the Neanderthals" (*La vie des Néandertaliens*), that

> Nowhere on earth can we still find living peoples entirely comparable with Neanderthals. Yet Australian Aborigines and Tierra del Fuegans could still, but half a century ago, give us a fairly good image of the life of Neanderthals. This is particularly the case with the inhabitants of Tierra del Fuego, where the climate, in the southern extremity of the American continent, is similar to that of Europe during the last glacial: cold and humid. (1992[1983]:96–97, my translation)

Leroi-Gourhan follows this passage with a photograph of northeastern Australian Aboriginal people seated near their rain forest huts, a photograph held in the collection of the Musée de l'Homme in Paris, with the label:

> This group of Australians gives us a close image of what may have been an ancient hominid camping site. The hut made of branches, the wooden weapons, a few bags that Neanderthals may already have known how to make, some stone tools, and these totally naked men around the campfire, on a debris-strewn earth floor, give what may be a non-flattering picture of a campsite dating back to Mousterian times.

There is still in archaeology a subliminal tendency to transpose Australian Aboriginal cultural practices that we know from ethnography onto a deep human past. Such a tendency is not limited to Australian Aboriginal ethnography. It applies, rather, when and wherever convenient ethnographic examples superficially appear to suit the particular archaeological situation. Hence the latest book on archaeological research at Chauvet Cave, a 30,000-year-old site rediscovered in 1994 in the Vallon-Pont-D'Arc region of the Ardèche of south-central France – a magnificent volume exemplary for its otherwise detailed and careful treatment of the archaeological record – concludes that

> The urge to better understand Chauvet Cave by seeking comparative information and analytical details in present-day arctic cultures is all the stronger since parallels between peoples of far northern latitudes and the Aurignacians of Vallon-Pont-D'Arc are numerous. Environmental similarities between glacial-period France and modern arctic or subarctic regions (cold climates and faunas, a tundra landscape), and similarities in modes of life between the populations in question (small, mobile groups who live essentially on products of the chase complemented by fishing and gathering) are in effect strong arguments that warrant such comparisons. Everything thus lets us think that there may have existed, amongst the Paleolithic hunting societies of the Ardèche – as is the case amongst the Inuit or the northern Siberians – a perfect conjunction of everyday life, religious thought, and artistic expression. (Robert-Lamblin 2001:200, my translation)

Specific Inuit ethnographic details are then suggested for the Chauvet Cave visitors of the Aurignacian. Elsewhere, Pearson (2002:84) also legitimizes understanding the meaningfulness of Shoshonean rock art – from the Great Basin in the United States – in terms of southern African ethnography by drawing environmental and "hunter-gatherer" parallels between the two regions: "The San bushman were hunter-gatherers and were similar to the Numic-speaking people of the western Great Basin in social structure and in the kinds of environments they inhabited." What these passages reveal is an ongoing tendency to view the archaeological past not so much as a cultural past rich in historically derived systems of meaning, as an archaeological past in the first instance rendered meaningful by generalized environmental circumstances and food extraction strategies: Environmental like can be compared with environmental like – cold climate cultures can be compared with cold climate cultures – without need to invoke from the onset historically fundamental disjunctures.

Indigenous peoples around the world are regarded not in historically singular cultural terms but as cultures subject or epiphenomenal to natural circumstances useful to an illumination of the European past. Hunting or fishing or gathering in one region and period is equated with hunting or fishing or gathering in another irrespective of their social, cultural, and ontological embeddedness. Yet while there are many peoples who today, in the recent past or in the deeper past hunted and gathered, is there really such a thing as a "hunter-gatherer," a stereotypical and homogenized category of peoples whose cultures are, in the first instance, able to be understood via reference to generalized food production techniques? As the above recent associations between Neanderthals and Australian Aboriginal peoples, Chauvet Cave Aurignacians and Inuit, and recent and past Shoshonean and San illustrate, such problems of categorization and analogic reasoning remain prevalent in world archaeology today, and perhaps particularly so amongst archaeologists who do not directly confront indigenous cultures or indigenous pasts (the inadequacy of such an approach appears to be one of the lasting lessons learnt from indigenous peoples). Associations such as these between the Western past and modern indigenous peoples are also commonly found in popular general discourse, signaling a crisis of primitivist thinking as much as a problem of analytical naivety, more poignantly a social than an intellectual predicament that various authors have explored in some detail (e.g., David et al. 2002; Langton and David 2003; David 2002; McNiven and Russell 1997; Russell 2002; Russell and McNiven 1998).

What is lacking in such archaeo-ethnographic comparative discourses is not so much lip-service to but deep recognition of historical specificity. It is people's historically constructed worlds of meaning that are at stake, and it is in the history of each region that the meaningfulness of the targeted cultural worlds that archaeologists study have unfolded; environments and food procurement strategies are engaged in a process of dwelling through the meaningfulness of things, always a cultural concern. Hence the main message of this chapter has a local as well as a broader dimension: At one level, the Aboriginal Australia – or rather, the regionally varied Aboriginalities – that we know from ethnography are statements of the Australia of the last 200 years or so. Ethnographic understanding represents a historically particular set of snapshots onto Aboriginal lifeways relating to the period of European contact and interaction. As I have tried to show, ethnographic characterizations reveal recent aspects of the historical trajectories of specific Australian Aboriginal societies, but they do not necessarily indicate social or cultural circumstances for the deeper past.

The broader implications of this chapter are that not only is it invalid to impose Australian Aboriginal (or any other) ethnography onto a European or other Paleolithic past – as I once assumed most archaeologists everywhere were well aware, but recently found to be a naïve assumption on my part, especially in the case of particular popular texts by authors who have not deeply worked and lived with Aboriginal people (e.g., Anati 1995; Leroi-Gourhan 1983; Robert-Lamblin 2001) – but that it is indeed invalid to impose it onto Australia's own distant past, be it Pleistocene or even middle Holocene. If Aboriginal worldviews that we have come to know from ethnography attained their ethnographic shapes late in the Holocene, then until methodologies are refined our understanding of meaning in the deeper past may be as impoverished as or little better than an Aboriginal past without ethnography.

To understand the past meaningfulness of things requires situating objects in past worldviews, in *past* frameworks of meaning that are best approached by investigating the structural or normative contexts of past behaviors. This signals an archaeology of ontology, initial insights to which I have here tried to approach through an archaeology of ethnographically known constructions of place, ritual, and symbolism. Such an approach to the past, an approach concerned with what Clottes (2001) has termed the *"cadre explicatif"* or framework of understanding of past cultural actions, has hitherto been largely lacking in Australian archaeology. The methodological, social, and political challenge is, in this sense, an archaeology of ontology for Australia's deeper past.

ACKNOWLEDGMENTS

I thank Bill Kent, Cecilia Hewlett, and Carolyn James of the Monash University Prato Centre, and the Programme for Australian Indigenous Archaeology at the School of Geography and Environmental Science at Monash University, for institutional support, and the ARC for funding during the course of this research. Thanks also to Ian McNiven, Ian Lilley, and Marcia Langton for comments on an earlier version of this paper.

REFERENCES

Anati, E., 1995 La Religione delle Origini. Capo di Ponte: Edizioni del Centro.

Arndt, W., 1962 The Interpretation of the Delamere Lightning Paintings and Rock Engravings. Oceania 32:163–177.

Attenbrow, V., B. David and J. Flood, 1995 Mennge-ya 1 and the Origins of Points: New Insights into the Appearance of Points in the Semi-Arid Zone of the Northern Territory. Archaeology in Oceania 30:105–120.

Barrett, C., and R. Croll, 1943 The Art of the Australian Aboriginal. Melbourne: The Bread and Cheese Club.

Bird, M., L. Ayliffe, L. Fifield, C. Turney, R. Cresswell, T. Barrows and B. David, 1999 Radiocarbon Dating of "Old" Charcoal Using a Wet Oxidation, Stepped-Combustion Procedure. Radiocarbon 41:127–140.

Bowdler, S., 1981 Hunters in the Highlands: Aboriginal Adaptations in the Eastern Australian Uplands. Archaeology in Oceania 16:99–111.

Clottes, J., 2001 Conclusion. In La Grotte Chauvet: L'Art des Origines. J. Clottes, ed. pp. 210–215. Paris: Seuil.

Dant, T., 1999 Material Culture in the Social World. Buckingham: Open University Press.

David, B., 2002 Landscapes, Rock-Art and the Dreaming: An Archaeology of Preunderstanding. London: Leicester University Press.

David, B., and M. Wilson, 1999 Re-Reading the Landscape: Place and Identity in Australia during the Late Holocene. Cambridge Archaeological Journal 9:163–188.

David, B., M. Langton and I. McNiven, 2002 Re-Inventing the Wheel: Indigenous Peoples and the Master Race in Philip Ruddock's "Wheel" Comments. Philosophy, Activism, Nature 2:31–46.

David, B., I. McNiven, J. Flood and R. Frost, 1990 Yiwarlarlay 1: Archaeological Excavations at the Lightning Brothers Site, Delamere Station, Northern Territory. Archaeology in Oceania 25:79–84.

David, B., J. Collins, B. Barker, J. Flood and R. Gunn, 1995 Archaeological Research in Wardaman Country, Northern Territory: The Lightning Brothers Project 1990–91 Field Seasons. Australian Archaeology 41:1–8.

David, B., I. McNiven, V. Attenbrow, J. Flood and J. Collins, 1994 Of Lightning Brothers and White Cockatoos: Dating the Antiquity of Signifying Systems in the Northern Territory, Australia. Antiquity 68:241–251.

Flood, J., and B. David, 1994 Traditional Systems of Encoding Meaning in Wardaman Rock Art, Northern Territory, Australia. The Artifact 17:6–22.

Fortes, M., 1967 Totem and Taboo. Proceedings of the Royal Anthropological Institute 1966:5–22.

Harney, W., 1959 Tales from the Aborigines. London: Robert Hale Ltd.

Heidegger, M., 1962 Being and Time. New York: Harper and Row.

Hughes, P., and Lampert, R., 1982 Prehistoric Population Change in Southern Coastal New South Wales. In Coastal Archaeology in Eastern Australia. S. Bowdler, ed. pp. 16–28. Canberra: Department of Prehistory, Research School of Pacific Studies, Australian National University.

Kimber, R., and M. Smith, 1987 An Aranda Ceremony. In Australians to 1788. D. J. Mulvaney and J. P. White, eds. pp. 221–237. Sydney: Fairfax, Syme and Weldon Associates.

Langton, M., 2002 The Edge of the Sacred, the Edge of Death: Sensual Inscriptions. In Inscribed Landscapes: Marking and Making Place. B. David and M. Wilson, eds. pp. 253–269. Honolulu: University of Hawai'i Press.

Langton, M., and B. David, 2003 William Ricketts Sanctuary, Victoria (Australia): Sculpting Nature and Culture in a Primitivist Theme Park. Journal of Material Culture 8: 145–168.

Lefebvre, H., 1991 The Production of Space. Oxford: Blackwell.

Leroi-Gourhan, A., 1992 (1983) Les Chasseurs de la Préhistoire. Paris: A-M. Métailié.

—— 1971 Les Religions de la Préhistoire. Paris: PUF.

Lourandos, H., 1983 Intensification: A Late Pleistocene–Holocene Archaeological Sequence from Southwestern Victoria. Archaeology in Oceania 18:81–94.

McNiven, I., and R. Feldman, 2003 Ritual Orchestration of Seascapes: Hunting Magic and Dugong Bone Mounds in Torres Strait, NE Australia. Cambridge Archaeological Journal 13:169–194.

McNiven, I., and L. Russell, 1997 "Strange Paintings" and "Mystery Races": Kimberley Rock-Art, Diffusionism and Colonialist Constructions of Australia's Aboriginal Past. Antiquity 71:801–809.

McNiven, I., B. David and J. Flood, 1992 Delamere 3: Further Excavations at Yiwarlarlay (Lightning Brothers site), Northern Territory. Australian Aboriginal Studies 1992:67–73.

Merlan, F., 1989 The Interpretive Framework of Wardaman Rock Art: A Preliminary Report. Australian Aboriginal Studies 2:14–24.

—— 1994 A Grammar of Wardaman. Berlin: Mouton de Gruyter.

Napton, L., and E. Greathouse, 1985 Archaeological Investigations at Pine Gap (Kuyunba), Northern Territory. Australian Archaeology 20:90–108.

Northern Territory Tourist Commission, 2002 Aboriginal Culture. Electronic document. http://www.ntholidays.com.au/nt_mustsee_story.asp?iStoryID=1.

Pearson, J., 2002 Shamanism and the Ancient Mind: A Cognitive Approach to Archaeology. Walnut Creek, CA: AltaMira Press.

Peterson, N., 1972 Totemism Yesterday: Sentiment and Local Organization among the Australian Aborigines. Man 7:12–32.

Richards, F., 1926 Customs and Language of the Western Hodgkinson Aboriginals. Memoirs of the Queensland Museum 8:249–265.

Robert-Lamblin, J., 2001 Un Regard Anthropologique. In La Grotte Chauvet: L'Art des Origines. J. Clottes, ed. pp. 200–208. Paris: Seuil.

Rosenfeld, A., 2002 Changing Regional and Social Geographies in Central Australia. In Inscribed Landscapes: Marking and Making Place. B. David and M. Wilson, eds. pp. 61–78. Honolulu: University of Hawai'i Press.

Russell, L., 2002 Savage Imaginings: Historical and Contemporary Constructions of Aboriginalities. Melbourne: Australian Scholarly Publications.

Russell, L., and I. McNiven, 1998 Monumental Colonialism: Megaliths and the Appropriation of Australia's Aboriginal Past. Journal of Material Culture 3:283–301.

Smith, M., 1986 The Antiquity of Seedgrinding in Arid Australia. Archaeology in Oceania 21:29–39.

——1993 Biogeography, Human Ecology and Prehistory in the Sandridge Deserts. Australian Archaeology 37:35–50.

——1996 Prehistory and Human Ecology in Central Australia: An Archaeological Perspective. In Exploring Central Australia: Society, the Environment and the 1894 Horn Expedition. S. Morton and D. J. Mulvaney, eds. pp. 61–73. Chipping Norton: Surrey Beatty and Sons.

Smith, M., B. Fankhauser, and M. Jercher, 1998 The Changing Provenance of Red Ochre at Puritjarra Rock Shelter, Central Australia: Late Pleistocene to Present. Proceedings of the Prehistoric Society 64:275–292.

Spencer, B., 1896 Through Larapinta Land: A Narrative of the Horn Expedition to Central Australia. In Report on the Work of the Horn Scientific Expedition to Central Australia, Part 1. B. Spencer, ed. pp. 1–136. Melbourne: Melville, Mullin and Slade.

Spencer, B., and F. Gillen, 1899 The Native Tribes of Central Australia. London: Macmillan.

——1927 The Arunta: A Study of a Stone Age People. London: Macmillan.

Stockton, E., 1971 Investigations at Santa Teresa, Central Australia. Archaeology and Physical Anthropology in Oceania 6:44–61.

Strehlow, T., 1971 Songs of Central Australia. Sydney: Angus and Robertson.

Taçon, P., M. Wilson, and C. Chippindale, 1996 Birth of the Rainbow Serpent in Arnhem Land Rock Art and Oral History. Archaeology in Oceania 31:103–124.

4

Blunt and to the Point: Changing Technological Strategies in Holocene Australia

Peter Hiscock

All technological systems utilizing stone as tools confront the same basic issues. Stone tools can be used for only a short time before they need replacement or resharpening. This process rapidly exhausts stone and represents an economic cost to the user of the stone, who either has to transport stone from its source or pay to have this done. There may also be a risk of disruption to foraging activities if appropriate stone cannot be supplied in a timely and cost-effective way. In many situations these considerations provided the economic framework for the different strategies hunter-gatherers used to provide themselves with functioning toolkits. This principle has long been recognized by archaeologists, many of whom have explored the complex relationships between the composition of archaeological assemblages and the provisioning strategies prehistoric hunter-gatherers employed.

This chapter describes technological changes in Holocene Australia as responses to changing provisioning costs and risks. It begins with a detailed background discussion of the analytical principles entailed because a grasp of these principles is crucial to understanding the nature and the cause of the cultural changes in question. This discussion is also relevant to other chapters in this volume, especially Pavlides's consideration of Holocene change in Melanesia.

Risks and Costs

Costs are incurred because substantial amounts of rock can be consumed in tool production and use but an individual or group can transport only a limited amount of rock at any given time. Unless good quality raw material was ubiquitous, hunter-gatherers would often have been undertaking their activities in locations distant from suitable sources of replacement stone. If their supply of stone was exhausted in such a situation there could have been a substantial *provisioning cost* in terms of effort or rescheduling of activities to resupply the person or group with stone, although the magnitude of any such cost varies with available transport technology. The labor cost of the return journey to a material source has been the concern of many distance-to-source models of raw material rationing (e.g., Bamforth 1986; Hiscock 1996), while the rescheduling implications of this process have been the central issue underlying time-stress models (e.g., Torrence 1983). In reality the energetic and rescheduling costs are not separate causal factors, just different aspects of the provisioning problem. Both must be considered in evaluating the economic context of technological strategies (Jeske 1992; Torrence 1989a). Additionally these technological strategies themselves involve not only the procurement of raw material, but also the manufacture of stone artifacts, their maintenance, the construction of composite tools, and the orientation of foraging behavior to employ these artifacts. All of these activities may confer benefits but also incur a cost. The use of a technology involves both energetic and rescheduling expenses, which we term the *technological cost* of the strategies selected.

Foraging risk is the probability and cost of a failure to procure resources in a timely and cost-efficient manner (Bamforth and Bleed 1997). While these values can be hard to specify precisely using archaeological data, they are widely regarded as powerful incentives for the selection of the technological strategies emphasized by ancient foragers. In some circumstances, technology can be structured to reduce risk by providing a working toolkit that enhances resource procurement and processing, thereby lowering failure probability. It has therefore been reasoned that the level of risk and the cost of available technological strategies are key determinants of the strategies employed by any foraging group (Bamforth and Bleed 1997; Bousman 1993; Hiscock 1994a; Kelly 1988; Nelson 1996; Torrence 1989b). When the reduced risk afforded by deploying a particular technological strategy provides a benefit that outweighs the cost of employing that technology, and exceeds the relative benefit provided by available alternatives, we might predict that strategy would be used, perhaps even emphasized. Of course strategy selection is not permanent, and strategies may be replaced or switched as risks and costs change (Gould 1991).

In many situations procurement costs and risks do not exist in isolation but in relation to resource distribution and the mobility pattern and foraging strategy that groups employ. For example, extremely patchy resources, high mobility, and logistical foraging which sees people travel extended distances to obtain resources are all situations where maintaining a continuously functional toolkit could be difficult and in which the cost of stone supply and/or failure probability might increase. In many situations, risk, and perhaps procurement cost, increases as resource predictability diminishes. The likelihood of foraging risks increases as the distribution and timing of resources, including sources of replacement stone, become more difficult to anticipate.

At times and places where population density was moderate or high and hunter-gatherers lived in a known and moderately predictable environment it may have been feasible to emphasize non-technological responses to these foraging costs and risks. For example, a detailed knowledge of resource availability and terrain conformation might reduce the probability of not encountering and harvesting resources. In unfamiliar and/or highly variable environments, however, reliance on local knowledge alone is unlikely to be enough. Other examples of non-material risk-reducing behaviors are the use of storage in response to resource fluctuations or the maintenance of social networks that can provide resources, but to be successful, all such strategies also require known and predictable conditions. At times and places where there were high procurement costs and/or high foraging risk technological responses may have had substantial benefits. For instance, when sources of replacement stone are distant, when foraging patterns involve being away from sources of replacement stone for relatively long periods, or when the unknown or variable nature of resources creates high failure probabilities or costs, one effective response might be to manufacture portable and durable tools.

One model of such a technological system is what Kuhn (1995) has called *provisioning of individuals*, a tactic that involves the manufacture and maintenance of portable tools during movement across the landscape. This strategy would have been effective for mobile foragers targeting resources at a great distance from sources of replacement rock. Since it would probably be impractical to carry large volumes of rock to the distant foraging locations, a technological solution to the costs of procuring replacement stone would be to create artifacts that are small and portable and can be used for an extended period per unit weight. If this provisioning strategy also provided a toolkit that was effective for most purposes and normally ready for use it might also have reduced foraging risks.

A raw-material-conserving and risk-reducing technological strategy of this kind would have a number of characteristics. The manufacture of portable stone artifacts involves stripping as much unusable material from the object as possible before transportation and producing specimens of low weight but with high potential use-to-weight ratios. This can be accomplished in a number of ways. A common approach is to emphasize retouched flakes, but there is no reason that small, carefully shaped cores cannot be employed to the same ends (e.g., Hiscock in press a). The requirements of portability must be understood in the context of mobility and land-use, but in most situations an upper weight limit of something like 0.5–1.0 kilogram might be expected. Portability is assisted by multifunctionality inasmuch as transporting one tool, or a small number of tools, may be easier than transporting a larger number of specialized forms. Multi-functionality also has other, even more important benefits. Functionally specific tools may be effective when the nature and timing of activities are predictable, or where failure costs are low, but when foraging in uncertain environments it would reduce risk to have tools that might be adequate for almost any task. Multi-functionality may therefore act to reduce risk. Versatile tools may also contribute to raw material conservation.

Procurement costs will be reduced by obtaining relatively high returns per unit of stone material, and consequently lowering the rate at which replacement material must be supplied. Increasing returns can be obtained in a number of ways.

Regularizing production, employing manufacturing techniques that create more robust and long-lived tools, maintaining tools to prolong their use-life, and production of large numbers of relatively small items are all methods by which an artisan can enhance the use of stone material and lower procurement costs. In a sense these methods are also examples of characteristics relating to tools which are dependable and efficient to fabricate.

A useful distinction is often made between two different characteristics of tools: the speed and ease with which a tool would be repaired, with readily repairable systems being called *maintainable*; and the capacity of a tool not to break down while functioning, with robust systems termed *reliable* (Bleed 1986). These traits may co-occur and when they do they increase the duration of functionality and may therefore decrease the failure probability by increasing the readiness of the toolkit. Torrence (1989b) has suggested that maintainability is a response to the timing of risk, whereas reliability is a response to the severity of the risk. This distinction is likely to be overly precise in many instances because both traits coexist in numerous technological strategies and either trait may act to reduce the "downtime" of the toolkit.

Maintainable systems can be developed in a number of ways. In terms of the stone artifact itself, an easily maintained form usually involves shapes and dimensions that either minimize the occurrence of features such as abrupt terminations, which can limit further reduction, or increase the capacity of the knapper to remove such detrimental features. Examples of knapping strategies of this kind are numerous, with symmetrical bifaces and axes being commonly cited exemplars. A maintainable toolkit can also be constructed by facilitating the hafting and re-hafting of stone artifacts within composite tools. This may involve the techniques of attachment or specific shaping of the stone to allow efficient hafting, perhaps even creating a "modular" system in which replaceable items are of similar sizes and shapes (Nelson 1991). Uniformity of stone artifacts is likely to be advantageous in maintenance of composite tools.

Reliable systems can also be constructed in several ways. One approach that can enhance reliability is the development of redundant features. By creating a level of redundancy, such as by having multiple barbs on a spear, the likelihood that at least one will function as expected will probably increase (e.g., Myers 1987, 1989; Nelson 1991). Of course, as Jochim (1989:111) points out, the return on effort spent in adding redundancy is not always clear even though the supply of additional material incurs a cost. For that reason there are likely to be limits to how much redundancy is useful in a particular situation, and how that redundancy is organized. For instance, would it be more advantageous to have multiple spear barbs or multiple spears? The recognition of redundancy in prehistoric technologies is not simple, and a common principle is to presume that large numbers of small, regular stone implements may be a signal that several were employed in a single composite tool.

One additional characteristic that may be found in a raw-material-conserving and risk-reducing technological strategy is the standardization of implement forms.

Regularity of form, especially if combined with systematization of production, may conserve raw material by giving a high number of usable specimens per unit of rock. Production of standardized implements is also likely to increase the maintainability and reliability of tools. When employed as a component of a composite tool, standardization of the stone artifact could improve the ease and efficiency of hafting, increase the predictability of tool performance, even enhance estimates of tool longevity. Since standardizing items may imply tools that can be used in many ways, it may at first seem disadvantageous to have a toolkit which may have only average functionality for many purposes. But in uncertain environments a moderately efficient multipurpose tool will still get the job done and is a lot more useful than a tool specialized for a task other than the one at hand. When the nature of tool use cannot be predicted, a generalized rather than specialized form will return the greatest overall advantage. In such contexts the predictability of tool performance using standardized stone artifacts may outweigh the generalized performance characteristics. This is one reason why reliability is thought to be highly advantageous as a risk reduction strategy (Kelly 1988; Myers 1989; Torrence 1989b).

These characteristics may occur separately or may co-occur. There are many instances where a particular implement form contains a number of these traits. Take, for example, strategies that prolong the usefulness of each tool, as discussed earlier. They may constitute a special instance of maintainability, while at the same time being standardized in form and robust, and hence reliable. Furthermore, implements with these characteristics typically represent mechanisms that extend raw material use by creating large numbers of small, standardized items that can be intensively maintained. Consequently they can operate as technological responses to risk and high procurement costs. Such a technological response might be advantageous in some situations of heightened uncertainty and procurement cost, but because of the greater technological costs typically associated with producing these tools this response may often not be economically effective in contexts of low risk or minimal procurement costs. This principle provides the basis for a powerful model of change in archaeological artifact assemblages.

Australian artifact assemblages changed during the Holocene, and this principle is the key to understanding the nature and the cause of that change. It is thus productive to examine the characteristics of Australian implements, to describe the archaeological record of the Holocene in terms of the technological strategies that were employed, and to explore the changing emphasis on different strategies as responses to altered risks and costs. To accomplish this task briskly we focus only on the most abundant artifact classes and use case studies of assemblage change in western Arnhem Land and the Sydney region to illustrate the possible interrelationships of technology and land-use patterns. The result is an image of foraging risk and material procurement costs that are coherent explanations of the much-remarked emphasis on standardized implements at different times during the Australian Holocene.

Artifact Patterns

For many decades archaeologists have distinguished different classes of artifacts as an aid to understanding the changes in material through time and space. The process of flaking stone created two classes of artifact: the blocks of rock from which fragments were struck, called cores, and the pieces of rock detached, called flakes. Striking further flakes from a core is a common way to obtain fragments of rock that can be transported and used, and we know that throughout Australian prehistory both cores and flakes were carried and used when they were of a suitable size and shape. However, the attention of archaeologists has not often been on these items but on the way that flakes are subsequently fractured by the process of retouching. A variety of morphologies can be created by striking small flakes from the margins of larger flakes. Archaeologists have typically argued that these retouched flakes were tools, something that has never been verified by use-wear investigations (Hiscock in press b). This proposition is nevertheless accepted here for the purpose of developing the arguments that follow. Three varieties of retouched flake will be examined in this chapter: scrapers, points, and backed artifacts. These categories should be considered arbitrary and possibly artificial divisions in the diverse range of artifacts that are recovered from archaeological sites in Australia. However, such classes are a way of distinguishing kinds of artifacts that share some characteristics but are typically different in others.

Scrapers

The specimens that have conventionally been labeled "scrapers" usually have retouch forming curving edges on the margin of the flake. Such specimens are known to be morphologically variable: They are made on a great variety of flakes, the plan shape of the retouch varies between concave and convex, and the position and length of retouch differ. These variations are not simply indications that different specimens were shaped for different purposes. Studies of Australian scrapers have revealed they were employed for many cutting and scraping purposes, on both plant and animal materials. The same use can be accomplished with many sizes and shapes of scrapers, and for that reason subtle differences in the shape and length of retouched edges are not diagnostic of particular functions. The variation in scraper shapes does not reflect the *kind* of use to which the item was put, but rather the *intensity* with which it was transported, used, maintained, and recycled.

This is a critical insight. Flowing from it is the recognition that although the morphological range of scrapers can be arbitrarily separated into a number of subclasses, variation in their size and shape actually constitutes a manufacturing series which modifies the features of artifacts through resharpening and reshaping. Two detailed studies of these modifications have been published, one from Ingaladdi rockshelter in the Northern Territory (Clarkson 2002b, in press) and one from

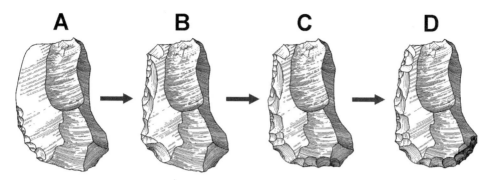

Figure 4.1 Changes in scraper morphology during reduction (after Hiscock and Attenbrow 2002)

Capertee 3 near Sydney (Hiscock and Attenbrow 2002, 2003). Although half a continent apart, these sequences of reworking display a great deal of similarity. Retouch begins at a suitable point on the margin of a flake, often toward the distal end, and gradually extends around the perimeter of the specimen as shaping and resharpening proceeds (as illustrated in Figure 4.1). In this way the dimensions of specimens are reduced and the shape of the retouched edge becomes more curved. Furthermore, as the specimens are progressively reworked the angle of the retouch often becomes steeper and step terminations on scars become more common. While some specimens were extensively retouched, others were discarded after relatively little retouch because they were too small, unsuitable in shape, or just by chance. The consequence is that while some archaeological scrapers are large with small, low-angled retouch, others are small with extensive steep retouch. Consequently, variation in the size and shape of scrapers is not so much a reflection of different tool designs as it is a consequence of a strategy to prolong the specimen in a useful state.

The extent to which scrapers were reworked depended on a number of factors. For example, raw materials were sometimes treated differently, with expensive, non-local, or better quality materials being more extensively reduced/maintained. When people were far from a quarry they often had an economic incentive to conserve material, and they typically responded to the shortage of replacement specimens by reworking the specimens they carried with them (Clarkson 2002b; Hiscock 1986, 1988a; Hiscock and Allen 2000). The extent of reduction therefore depended on the landscape context of the activity.

This context is created not only by the distribution of resources, including sources of stone, in the landscape, but also by the pattern and speed of people's movement through that landscape. For example, in situations where food and water were abundant at particular localities people often exploited these resources by spending long periods of time in those places. If abundant rock suitable for artifact manufacture was not locally available the prolonged stay would create a raw material shortage, requiring either a special resupply mission or rationing of the material already transported to the site by reducing it intensively (Hiscock 1996).

High mobility can also create conditions that trigger more intensive reduction of transported stone artifacts, including scrapers. For example, Cundy (1990) and Clarkson (2002b) have both argued that scrapers at Ingaladdi were more extensively reduced at times when people were highly mobile and therefore less familiar with local sources of rock and/or had less time to collect it. Knappers solved their mobility-induced raw material shortage by transporting artifacts with them, and reducing them extensively as a way of minimizing the risk of needing rock but not having any.

Another way of increasing the functional versatility of a stone artifact and facilitating its transportation at the same time is to haft it to another object, such as a wooden handle, by means of gum and/or twine, to create a composite tool. We know that at least some of the artifacts archaeologists classify as scrapers were hafted because they still have resin on their surfaces. Hafting scrapers may have had two effects on the morphology and size of specimens: By securing the item in a handle it is possible to resharpen it and continue using it until it is very small, and some retouching may take place to shape the specimen for placement into the haft. Both of these effects have been documented on tulas, a particular kind of scraper that is thought to have been regularly hafted (Hiscock 1988b; Hiscock and Veth 1991).

The factors producing the conditions in which scrapers are more or less extensively reduced are also present in the context of manufacturing and maintaining the other kinds of stone artifacts discussed here. These other forms, points, backed artifacts, and axes, also display patterns that reveal their users were sometimes concerned to extend the usefulness of the specimen.

Points

Points are a category of retouched flake that have converging, often straight, retouched lateral margins that produce specimens with leaf-like shapes. Most specimens are elongate and symmetrical around their long axis, increasing the superficial resemblance to a spearhead. The base of Australian points is either flat or rounded but never concave. Except in the extreme northwest of the continent, points normally exhibit only parallel percussion flake scars. The exception to this pattern is the specimens from the Kimberley and adjacent regions, where pressure flaking and serration produced distinctive forms (e.g., O'Connor 1999).

Points can be observed with different amounts of retouch. A common pattern is that some specimens were retouched on only one face ("unifacial points") while other specimens have retouch on both faces ("bifacial points"). In southern and eastern portions of the continent only unifacial points are found, sometimes with basal thinning onto a second surface but never with bifacial working of the lateral margins. Fully bifacial points, with retouch on both faces along at least one lateral margin, are restricted to northern Australia, where they co-occur with unifacial variants. While superficially similar, the northern and southern point assemblages represent different systems of manufacture, use, and repair. One way of explaining

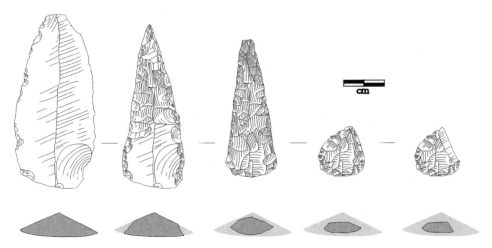

Figure 4.2 Changes in point morphology during reduction (illustration of one possible sequence as an example)

these differences is to look at the relationship of the bifacial and unifacial forms. In southern Australia it is clear that unifacial points were not converted into bifacial points, whereas in northern Australia we have a lot of evidence that the conversion of unifacial into bifacial points represents an attempt to extend artifact use-life.

In the north, the size and morphology of points is modified as unretouched flakes are manufactured into unifacial flakes, some of which are in turn converted into bifacial points. This unilinear *sequence model* generally began by retouching flakes from along one lateral margin on the dorsal surface of a flake (Hiscock 1994b, in press a). The second margin might have been flaked in a similar fashion at a later time, and eventually one or both of these margins might have been made bifacial by the removal of flakes from the ventral surface. This sequence represents a technological continuum from unifacial to bifacial points, as the former was gradually transformed into the latter (Figure 4.2).

The probability of an individual specimen being modified from a unifacial point into a bifacial point depends on a number of factors, the most important of which is the initial size of the unifacial point. Small unifacial points were normally discarded but larger unifacial points were often reworked into bifacial forms, giving an archaeological pattern in which bifacial points are sometimes larger than unifacial points (Hiscock 1994b). In many regions it is now clear that this progressive modification of points does not occur before the objects are used, but probably proceeds as a form of resharpening to extend the use-life of specimens and to standardize their shape and size.

In some regions and time periods this progressive reworking of specimens proceeded to such an extent that they no longer look like distinctive points. In Arnhem Land, for example, points were sometimes retouched until they were oval or rectangular in shape, no longer retaining their pointed ends. Such specimens illustrate that this process of retouching points to prolong their use-life was not focused exclusively on maintaining pointed artifacts but involved a variety of approaches to extending the usefulness of pieces of stone, including removing the pointed portion of a point. This observation reveals that we should not simplistically imagine points are only projectile heads, even though some specimens appear suited to that use. As I (1994b) have noted, Australian unifacial and bifacial points have properties that are shared by similar specimens in other parts of the world (Kelly 1988; Kelly and Todd 1988). These points often represent small and easily transported objects that are capable of producing large numbers of thin, sharp flakes. This means that points as well as cores could be carried around the landscape to supply the knapper with flakes as required. When points were used as tools they were not only small and transportable but were suited to multiple uses, providing stout, sharp margins as well as a pointed shape capable of penetration (Jeske 1989:36). Usewear evidence confirms that points were used on plant material, for woodworking, as well as for projectile points. While there have been insufficient wear studies to precisely define use patterns on these kinds of artifacts, it seems clear they could have been used in many ways and should not be considered to be simply "spearheads."

These qualities were enhanced by an additional characteristic: The form of the specimens, particularly bifaces, facilitates extensive resharpening and reshaping, thereby extending both their use-life as a tool and their value as a core replacement. The lenticular cross-section, resulting from and facilitating bifacial invasive flaking, often allowed reduction to be prolonged while maintaining the same general cross-section and plan shape. When the pointed shape could no longer be preserved the cross-section often lent itself to reduction in different ways. This potential stability of the bifacial form through intensive reduction is a trait that has advantages irrespective of whether any particular specimen was being used as a tool, as a transportable source of flakes or both. The multi-functionality and capacity for extended reduction of points would have been properties particularly valuable in circumstances where the specimen had been carried to a locality in which replacement raw material is rare or costly, or where the access to replacement raw material is unpredictable.

Backed artifacts

Backed artifacts are flakes with near ninety-degree retouch along one or more margins that was often accomplished with the use of bipolar techniques on an anvil. This "backed" surface may contain bidirectional scarring, and the "backing" retouch sometimes removes the platform and/or distal end of the flake. Unlike the production systems that have been recorded in other parts of the world, in which backed artifacts are typically said to be made from segments of "blades," Australian specimens were made on any flake with an appropriate cross-section and one straight or gently undulating margin of sufficient length (Figure 4.3; Hiscock 2003; Hiscock and Attenbrow 1996). This means that prehistoric manufacturing did not

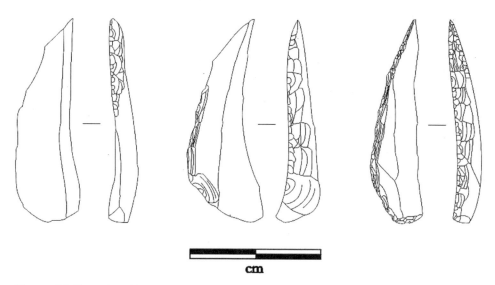

Figure 4.3 Examples of backed artifact morphology

involve mechanically applying a procedure to a uniform blank, but required the artisan to select a suitable section of each flake to retouch. Consequently, the location of the backing differs between specimens. On some specimens the unretouched portion is the lateral margin, while in others it is the distal end (e.g., Lamb 1996:154–155).

Despite the variety of flakes that were retouched, and the varied positioning of retouch, backed artifacts are extremely uniform in size and shape. Standardization of Australian backed artifacts was achieved by careful and extended retouching of flakes on an anvil, and although the process may have been assisted by the production of flakes with regular shapes it did not depend on them. Standardization of size and shape is apparent in each locality where backed artifacts are found, but there are regional differences in the format of specimens. For example, in many regions the vast majority of backed artifacts are less than 35 millimeters in length, but in the northeast of the continent there were regions in which they were up to 190 millimeters long (Hiscock 2003). In some regions the backed artifacts have asymmetrical shapes, while in other regions they are symmetrical. While intriguing and informative, these regional variations are not the subject of this discussion; what is of concern here is the general characteristic of standardization of backed artifacts and the way that characteristic is developed in the Sydney region.

Thousands of backed artifacts have been recovered from archaeological sites in eastern NSW. These specimens are usually small, 15–25 millimeters in length, and markedly asymmetrical, typically with one rounded end and one pointed end. Progressive modification of the size and morphology of backed artifacts is rarely discussed, and has not been demonstrated in Australian assemblages, but there is no

reason to think that Australian backed artifacts could not have sequences of modification similar to those inferred in other parts of the world (e.g., Neeley and Barton
1994). Some specimens retain evidence for hafting in the form of resin and resin
staining. This demonstrates that at least some backed artifacts were hafted to form
composite tools, and that this was usually done by placing the retouched edge into
the resin, leaving the sharp unretouched edge exposed. It is not clear that all backed
artifacts were used only when hafted, but although few use-residue studies have
been completed they reveal that, as a class, backed artifacts were probably used for
many tasks involving multipurpose cutting and slicing of both plant and animal
materials as well as projectile use (Robertson 2002). We can therefore infer that
backed artifacts were typically a small, standardized kind of artifact that had the
capacity to be used in many ways. They may often have been hafted for use and
perhaps the composite tool had multiple specimens hafted in it, although these
propositions are yet to be demonstrated archaeologically.

What is revealed in the archaeological material is that small individual backed
artifacts cannot have been extensively reworked in the way that points or scrapers
may have been. If backed artifacts represent a way of extending the usability of
available stone the mechanism is clearly not by prolonged reworking of specimens.
A different mechanism was proposed by Hiscock (1993a), who observed that
backed artifact manufacture often involved regular and precise knapping of small
pieces of stone, typically involving careful platform preparation and laborious controlled thermal alteration; strategies which would conserve material by extracting a
large number of specimens per unit stone.

Characterizing the relationships

The preceding discussion has explored the broad similarities between these classes
of artifacts in terms of their manufacture, multi-functionality, and potential for
maintenance. What remains to be done is to summarize the different qualities of
these forms, and to sketch the relationship between them. One approach to this
kind of task was outlined by Hayden (1989), who considered artifact morphology
to be the result of resharpening. Arguing that flaking and grinding were activities
that maintained tool edges, he hypothesized a positive relationship between the cost
of different manufacturing/resharpening techniques and their effectiveness as conservation measures. He therefore predicted that if the conservation of stone
material became a more critical concern for any group they would adopt a more
costly technique when the cost savings of raw material conservation exceeded the
added expense of the more costly resharpening technique. This prediction embodied a specific example of the principle that strategies of artifact construction and
maintenance were related to the conservation of stone material.

The usefulness of Hayden's insight can be expanded beyond its initial construction. His application of the principle was restricted to those intensively worked
stone artifacts normally thought of as "tools" in typological analysis, and his dis-

cussion presumed that these artifacts were modified to resharpen their blunted edges. However, the proposition that such objects are invariably tools and the reworked portions are their used edges is not applicable to all typological categories (such as backed artifacts). Furthermore, the suggestion that the reworking must be resharpening is typically an assumption untested by use-wear examinations and based on mentalist expectations about the goals of the prehistoric artisan (Hiscock in press b). In fact there are many possible reasons for the reworking of an artifact edge, such as the production of usable flakes, modification of the specimen for hafting, or resharpening of an edge. Hayden's focus on resharpening alone therefore directs our attention toward a single possibility and away from a comprehensive image of the function of stoneworking. By recognizing this it is possible to create a more expansive formulation of the relationship between stoneworking and conservation of stone material, namely that stoneworking strategies can be seen as different approaches to *prolonging* the usefulness of the material at hand. A strategy that prolonged the usability of a unit of rock would reduce the rate at which rock must be resupplied, and thereby reduce procurement costs, while at the same time enhancing the readiness of the toolkit. This principle would apply irrespective of whether the knapper had wanted the edge or the flakes removed from it, neither or both.

On this basis we might consider that one aspect that may vary between different technological strategies employing stone artifacts is the mechanism by which the usability of the rock is engineered. I describe this dimension of technological variation as a series of stoneworking strategies that are positioned along an *extendibility continuum*. At one end of this continuum lie attempts to maximize, or at least exaggerate, the potential use-life of specimens by manufacturing artifacts with a size and shape suitable for extended flaking, use, and resharpening. This is an investment in a small number of artifacts with the expectation that a benefit will be gained as each serves for an extended period, thereby reducing the frequency with which a replacement is needed. Some archaeologists have termed this quality "curation," but since this term has many other meanings (Bamforth 1986) I call it an *extension strategy*. At the other end are attempts to maximize, or exaggerate, the number of artifacts available for use, through a manufacturing system that has a high production rate of specimens to be used. This strategy is an investment in high artifact abundance, where the expected benefit arises from the production of a relatively large number of specimens per unit stone, providing the capacity to use several specimens at once and/or to regularly replace specimens. I call this an *abundance strategy*.

These strategies represent choices between reduction potential and production rate, a choice illustrated in Figure 4.4a. The idea is that there is a broad negative relationship between miniaturization and longer use-life, an eminently testable assertion. The proposition that there is an inverse relationship between tool size and potential utility has been the subject of vigorous debate among researchers seeking to identify the most efficient toolkit for mobile hunter-gatherers: whether it is better to transport fewer, larger artifacts or many, smaller ones (e.g., Kuhn 1994, 1996;

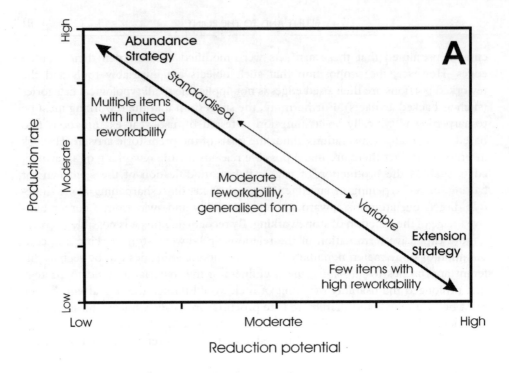

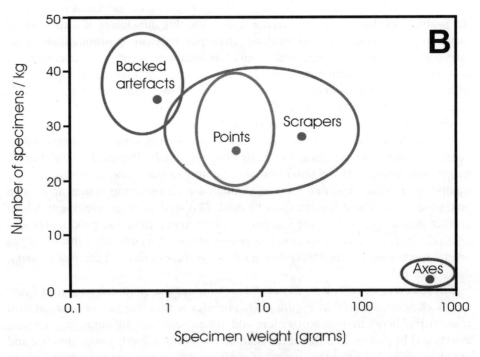

Figure 4.4 Models of the extension–abundance continuum. A) Illustration showing the continuum of possible artifact forms that play off reduction potential against production rate. B) Plot of some Australian artifact types using proxies for reduction potential (specimen weight) and production rate (number of specimens per kilogram)

Morrow 1996). Yet, as already explained, there is no single optimal solution because foragers selected their toolkits not only to be cost-effective in different environmental and social contexts but also in response to factors in addition to mobility. The extendibility continuum represents a series of non-exclusive strategic choices about how to supply stone tools at acceptable cost, each strategy containing subtly different economic advantages and costs. Explaining prehistoric changes in technology therefore requires not only information about the economic context of tool use but also recognition of the different qualities of the alternative technological strategies. For example, extension strategies typically involve medium-sized or large specimens that have moderate to high reduction potential, and consequently have low production rates per unit stone. Abundance strategies have high production rates per unit stone, often by manufacturing small and standardized items, creating multiple items each with limited capacity to be reworked. Abundance strategies typically yield more standardized implement forms than extension strategies, and this appears to be the case in the Australian context.

Showing how the Australian implements discussed above might be plotted in this way reveals the interpretative potential of this scheme (Figure 4.4b). This requires that we have measures of both production rate and reduction potential. Number of specimens per kilogram is used to express a production rate, standardized for raw material volume. Calculations of this value are not derived from the weight of the specimens but are drawn from independent technological studies of manufacturing processes (Hiscock 1993a, b; Hiscock and Attenbrow 2002, 2003). In addition to the three implement forms discussed earlier, the values for edge-ground axes have been added, since, as Hayden (1989) has noted, this artifact class is in many ways the most extendable stone implement (data from Dickson 1981). As expected, there are very few axes per unit of stone, substantially more scrapers and points, and very high numbers of backed artifacts.

Measuring reduction potential is far more difficult. Despite numerous creative attempts to define and examine the reduction, or use-life, potential, the subject is notoriously problematic (Kuhn 1994, 1996; Shott 1989, 1995). Even empirical studies of the actual amount of maintenance and reduction on prehistoric Australian artifacts have been comparatively rare (although see Clarkson 2002a, 2002b, in press; Cundy 1985, 1990; Hiscock 1988b, 1996, in press a; Hiscock and Attenbrow 2002, 2003). Quantitative statements of the different reduction capacities of these artifact forms should be revisited when more technological studies have been completed. In their absence, a proxy is used in Figure 4.4b, which has employed weight as a simple but gross indicator of reduction potential. Interpreted literally this proxy suggests that axes have a very high capacity for reduction, scrapers and points have a medium capacity, and backed artifacts a relatively low capacity. However, this measure does not incorporate the different ways each of these kinds of objects can be reworked, and it is likely that the reduction potential of bifacial points is underestimated.

Very commonly, archaeological production systems exhibit considerable variation in the success of manufacturing and maintaining artifacts, as well as differences in the forms produced, owing to variations in pieces of stone, knapper skill, economic context, and the occurrence of technical difficulties in production. This variation has two consequences for this analysis. Firstly, only data from the two case studies discussed below are plotted in Figure 4.4b: backed artifacts and scrapers from the Sydney region, and points from western Arnhem Land. At the moment these regions are two of the few regions that have adequate information on production rate and artifact size. However, not all regions have artifacts that will conform to the patterns shown in Figure 4.4b. For example, the large asymmetrical backed artifacts found in the northeast of Australia (Lamb 1996) differ from the small backed artifacts from the south which are plotted here. These large asymmetrical backed artifacts, sometimes called "Juan knives," fall in the same part of the graph as points/scrapers and share some properties with points, such as the ability to generate flakes from their retouched edges and their ability to be reworked into different forms. This indicates that on a continental scale the characteristics and role of backed artifacts are likely to be more diverse than those in the Sydney region that are the subject of this discussion.

Production rates and artifact sizes also vary within each region, and it is useful to express this variation. In Figure 4.4b this is done by plotting the arithmetic mean and standard deviation of each implement class as a dot and ellipse respectively. What becomes visible is that the three implement categories discussed here are not discrete in terms of production rate and reduction potential, but in fact overlap. Ancient technological patterns were complex and while it is reasonable to typify each class it must be acknowledged that they probably form parts of a continuum in their economic function.

Evaluating the relative emphasis on abundance versus extension strategies within the technological system of any group, or at any archaeological site, seems an appropriate way to specify the technology strategy-switching that took place as groups responded to changing levels of risk and cost. However, in practice the specification of strategy weighting in the repertoire of a group is complicated by the different archaeological measurements suited to describing the emphasis given by ancient foragers to abundance or extension strategies. For instance, while one of the most important measures of an abundance strategy is the number of specimens made and used, an extension strategy by definition yields fewer specimens and they need to be assessed for not only abundance but also for the magnitude of the extension, perhaps representing the intensity of maintenance. Unfortunately, while counts of implements are common in archaeological reports from Australia, expressions of the amount of reworking on specimens such as scrapers and points have only recently been published in Australia (e.g., Clarkson 2002a, b; Hiscock 1988b, 1994b; Hiscock and Attenbrow 2002, 2003). Consequently, quantitative expressions of the relative emphasis of abundance or extension strategies in Australian assemblages are only now becoming possible.

The advantages and disadvantages of the different technical approaches representing the extremes of the extendibility continuum have been clearly described by Kuhn (1995:33). An extension strategy, flaking a previously worked edge, perhaps to resharpen it, is often an effective way to reduce raw material expenditure and thereby transportation costs, but prevents standardization because the size and shape of the object are regularly changed by the flaking. Re-flaking may also incur additional costs in hafted specimens if the flaking damages the hafting or requires the specimen to be removed and re-hafted, which may have been the case with the percussion-flaked scrapers and points in Australia. In contrast, the abundance strategy is one that yields fresh tools rather than maintaining existing ones, given an equal consumption of raw material. Because relatively small tools may have high utility for their mass they may be a strategy that conserves material and lowers material procurement costs (Kuhn 1994). Furthermore, production of new items rather than extended maintenance of them is a strategy that facilitates the creation of standardization between specimens and can be accomplished by production at convenient locations prior to use.

This comparison reveals that while all of these retouching strategies can be responses to raw material shortages, they represent technological responses to different constructions of risk. An extreme abundance strategy, represented in this case by backed artifacts, would be advantageous in situations where uniform, multipurpose, tools of known performance were cost-effective. Such situations might typically include circumstances with low resource predictability, induced by either high mobility and/or unfamiliarity with the environment, in which systematic scheduling of activities was difficult. In such situations the added costs that might be incurred by elaborate technology would be worth while if the strategy provided reliable and maintainable toolkits that reduced foraging risk. In contrast, the moderate extension strategy of scrapers, involving larger, extendable but unstandardized forms, is suggestive of higher levels of resource predictability in which the reduction of raw material procurement costs may have been a more compelling factor than foraging risk. In many ways the characteristics of bifacial points, still standardized but small and able to be extensively reworked, represent an intermediate pattern that shares a number of the advantages of both extension and abundance strategies. Points are probably as extendable as scrapers, while being more standardized and probably more multifunctional. They can be understood as a technology suited to foraging in contexts of both high risk and high procurement costs. Interpreted in this way, technological strategies of making and reworking complex forms can be arranged along an extension–abundance continuum to measure one dimension of technological organization.

It may be that in the Australian situation all of these strategies represent versions of Kuhn's (1995) strategy of provisioning individuals, but if that is so the production of backed artifacts and points is probably a more extreme example of such a strategy than scraper manufacture. We could therefore predict that backed artifacts and points would not have been the dominant forms throughout the Holocene. Instead, it can be proposed that periods in which foragers emphasized standardized implements, involving technical strategies of moderate or extreme abundance, were times when foragers reoriented their technologies toward strategies of provisioning individuals with reliable, maintainable, and multipurpose toolkits as a means of reducing uncomfortably high levels of foraging risk. Archaeologists have begun to define the factors that may have been responsible for increasing risk and procurement costs.

Listing Risk and Cost Increasing Factors

I have proposed elsewhere that widespread similarities in the timing of the proliferation of abundance strategies probably indicate a climatic trigger (Hiscock 2003). It is likely, though, that the timing of these changes differed between regions and that increased foraging risk and procurement costs during the Holocene resulted not from a single cause but from a conjunction of a number of factors which may have been weighted differently in different regions. A non-exhaustive list of factors can be summarized as follows.

Colonization

Archaeological evidence points to a number of instances of people colonizing particular landscapes during the Holocene (summarized in Hiscock 1994a). For example, they appear to have moved into many of Australia's sandy deserts in the mid-Holocene (e.g., Veth 1989), a pattern revealed not only in many archaeological sites but also by linguistic evidence of Pama-Nyungan expansion across large tracts of the continent, particularly desert Central Australia (McConvell 1996). It seems likely that migrations/expansions of desert populations occurred several times during the Holocene, and were still occurring in the recent past (Veth 2000). The cold uplands of eastern Australia may have been occupied sporadically during earlier times but appear to have been intensively settled only in the Holocene. Similarly, many islands have archaeological material dating only from the mid- or late Holocene, indicating that niche was also only colonized in recent millennia. These examples reveal that broad changes in settlement systems took place, particularly during the past 4,000–5,000 years, at least some involving foragers moving into areas with which they were partially or entirely unfamiliar. Unfamiliarity with resources is a context in which technological strategies that reduced the chance of foraging failure would be highly advantageous.

Renegotiated territorial access

Movement of groups across the landscape would have required radical revision of inter-group social and political agreements. Even in regions in which Holocene colonization has not been detected, changes in the distribution and content of archaeological sites, including rock art, have been taken to indicate changes to social and political structure (see Macdonald and Veth, this volume). Some researchers have inferred the emergence of compartmentalized cultural landscapes, in which territorial redefinition may have created resource patchiness (e.g., David and Lourandos 1998). Group composition and the character of territorial boundaries and inter-group relationships constrain access to resources, and may be implicated in the emergence of higher procurement costs and greater uncertainty in the accessibility and predictability of resources.

Landscape change

Environments changed throughout the Holocene. In some localities there were dramatic large-scale geomorphic modifications of terrain and vegetation patterns, while in other regions more subtle alterations to the distribution of plant and animal foods stemming from climatic shifts are likely to have occurred. The effect of these changes on foraging risk and procurement costs is not simply proportional to the magnitude of landscape modification, but must be understood in relation to the structure of the environment and resource use in each location. Rapid or extensive alteration to resources, a reduction of environmental productivity, and an increase in resource patchiness are examples of the kinds of landscape changes that are likely to have increased foraging costs and risks.

Resource reductions

In many landscapes, environmental change may include the reduction of overall available resources. Employing geomorphic and palynological indicators of Effective Precipitation (EP), researchers such as Shulmeister and Lees (1995) have argued that EP increased throughout the early Holocene to plateau at a high about 5000 B.P., then declined significantly, before increasing again in the past 2,000 years (see also Clarkson and Wallis 2003; McCarthy and Head 2001). Mid-Holocene reductions in water availability are likely to have increased the patchiness of resource distribution and reduced the abundance of resources in many areas, diminishing carrying capacity. These trends affected large areas but their timing and magnitude are known to have varied regionally. One indication of human responses to resource reductions during the Holocene may be the increased foraging for foods such as moths, toxic nuts, and grass seeds, a shift in foraging strategies that can be characterized as an expansion of diet breadth (David and Lourandos 1998:212). Reduction of procurement costs and risks through an emphasis on different technological strategies would constitute a companion response.

Higher mobility

Reduced carrying capacity and unfamiliarity with the landscape may have seen groups become highly mobile for at least short periods during the Holocene.

Although changes in the level of mobility have not been systematically evaluated in most Australian regions, this possibility has been widely canvassed by archaeologists, often in conjunction with the proposition that mobile groups may have had larger territories and lower population densities than in later times.

Climatic variability

More important than the quantity and distribution of resources is their predictability through space and time. As discussed earlier, the ability to accurately anticipate resource availability is a key factor behind levels of foraging risk and procurement cost. Widespread reductions in resource predictability during different periods of the Holocene are indicated by evidence for greater climatic variability. For example, Rowland (1999) and I (Hiscock 2003) have explored the onset of a dominant Walker Circulation and El Niño–Southern Oscillation (ENSO) about 4500–5000 B.P. in southern Australia and somewhat later (4000–3800 B.P.) in northern Australia (see also Clarkson and Wallis 2003). This appears to have led not only to decreased rainfall but also a significant increase in climatic variability, and probably involved prolonged and severe droughts in patterns that were extremely variable, reducing both the availability and predictability of plant and animal foods. Extreme variability persisted until about 2,000 years ago, when variability in rainfall reduced, although it is still present. Again the timing and degree of these environmental uncertainties vary regionally.

The development of one or more of these factors may have initiated reduced, patchier, and less predictable resource bases, confronting foragers with situations in which the location and accessibility of resources were often less certain than they had been. These are precisely the conditions in which the technological costs of moderate to high abundance technological strategies that enhance versatility, reliability, and maintainability may have been outweighed by the cost and risk reduction benefits of employing such a technology. In these kinds of environmental and social contexts the production and use of implements such as backed artifacts and points could have been more advantageous than the production of other artifact forms such as scrapers. Individuals and groups employing technological strategies producing points, backed artifacts, or similar items may have been advantaged, providing a mechanism for the proliferation of those behaviors (Hiscock 2003).

Such a technological response can be predicted when any combination of risk- or cost-increasing factors reaches a threshold beyond which a shift of technological strategies returns a net benefit. This means that there is unlikely to be a single technological trend displayed in a uniform fashion across the entire Australian continent, as local differences in the nature and onset of risks and costs will be reflected in local differences in the nature and timing of change in technological strategies. Widespread coincidences in the timing of technological shifts may indicate broad triggering processes, but continental-scale uniformities are unlikely. For example, we know that backed artifacts are emphasized earlier in some regions of the northeast and later in many central desert areas than they are on the continental margin of southeastern Australia. It is predicted that these regional differences reflect both variation in the economic conditions of foraging between localities and elapsed time in the dissemination of technical approaches to creating risk- and cost-reducing toolkits. Consequently the evaluation of economic models of forager technological response should be undertaken primarily at a regional level, without presuming widespread similarities in either the context of foraging or the technological strategies that were employed. As an example of the relationship between changing foraging risk and procurement costs, and technological strategies that were favored as responses to those risks and costs, a comparison of two regions of mainland Australia is presented below. These studies not only illustrate that a consideration of foraging risks and costs is a powerful framework for explaining changing technological emphases, but also reveal that the nature and timing of changes in ancient technology vary in response to local histories and conditions rather than at a continental scale.

The Sydney Sequence

In the greater Sydney region on the eastern seaboard of Australia, scrapers and backed artifacts are found in archaeological deposits dated to before 7000–5000 B.P. (Hiscock and Attenbrow 1998). At that time scrapers were emphasized, with backed artifacts being rare. From 4000–3500 B.P. until 1500 B.P., backed artifacts were produced in immense numbers while scrapers were less frequently manufactured. Backed artifacts were still being manufactured during the last millennium, although much less frequently (Hiscock 2003). Although the relative abundance of these forms and the chronology of change vary slightly between sites, it is clear that high rates of backed artifact production occurred between 4000 B.P. and 2000–1000 B.P., while at earlier and later times production rates were substantially lower.

These patterns correspond with climatic changes that would have altered foraging risk. In particular there is a strong coincidence between the start of the period of intensive backed artifact production and the onset of an ENSO-dominated climate of reduced effective precipitation and increased climatic variability (Hiscock 2003). Between 4000 B.P. and 5000 B.P., drier and more variable climatic conditions probably created a context in which resource distribution and availability were less easily and reliably mapped or predicted. Among the adjustments to foraging practice, and perhaps social organization and interaction, which were made to reduce the increased risk attached to these new circumstances, was the greater emphasis on manufacturing a preexisting implement form, the backed artifact, which could form the basis of an abundance technological strategy providing implements that helped to reduce foraging risk by reducing raw material costs while enhancing the readiness of the toolkit. When effective precipitation increased in the past 2,000 years, backed artifact production rates declined as the technological system responded to other pressures affecting foragers.

The Kakadu Sequence

Several thousand kilometers away, in western Arnhem Land, bifacial points become archaeologically visible in low numbers between 7000 and 5000 B.P., but were only produced at high rates from 3000–3500 B.P. until 2000 B.P., after which point manufacture decreased dramatically (see Hiscock 1999 for details). This proliferation of bifacial points takes place in a context in which a number of different factors were exaggerating foraging risk and procurement costs. In this coastal region the period from 4000–2000 B.P. was one of rapid environmental change, with extensive sedimentation in lowland areas and increasing salinity creating patchy and unpredictable resources (Hiscock 1999; Hiscock and Kershaw 1992). Settlement pattern reorganization and increased foraging mobility appears to have taken place during this period. A broader climatic change was superimposed on top of these local changes. It was during this period that drier and more variable climatic conditions developed, related to the onset of ENSO, and it is likely that this also increased foraging risk (Hiscock 2003). With multiple factors creating conditions of high failure probability and cost it would have become beneficial to emphasize production of a preexisting implement form, such as the bifacial point, which reduced the required rate of raw material resupply during foraging while simultaneously providing a versatile, reliable, and maintainable toolkit.

Similar trends have been observed at a number of neighboring locations away from the coastal plains of the north. For example, in an intricate and original analysis of the assemblage at Ingaladdi, south of Arnhem Land, Cundy (1990:305–329) identified a shift from intensive flaking of local materials, which suggests relatively prolonged periods of occupation by people very familiar with local resources since the early Holocene, to a pattern initiated 3,000 years ago of rarely discarded, extensively worked small cores transported into and away from the site, which he believes indicates short visits by people with little ability to use local resources. This may represent a change toward higher mobility, with groups obtaining resources through encounter strategies, accompanied by an emphasis on a technology that reduces the rate at which suitable rock must be supplied. Clarkson and Wallis (2003) have demonstrated that these modifications of procurement and technology in the Ingaladdi region are synchronized with climatic changes.

Conclusion

Foragers in Holocene Australia, like foragers in other times and places, were confronted with basic economic concerns of supplying themselves with the necessities of life as reliably and effectively as possible. Although different paths to this goal were pursued in various parts of the continent, yielding superficially different foraging practices, the underlying principles of energy extraction and risk minimization provide a unifying framework for understanding not only spatial diversity in lifestyle but also chronological change in economies. Technology can be treated in the same way, by focusing on the properties of the technology and the relationship to foraging practice. In particular, the costs of different technological strategies and their impact on provisioning costs and foraging risk provide a model with which to explain diversity and change in ancient artifacts. In the Australian case, even a limited application to the three categories of implement discussed above provides an opportunity to understand the archaeological record. For example, in two regions it has been shown that increased emphasis on the production of backed artifacts and points during the Holocene reflects the greater benefits of extremely portable, multifunctional, maintainable and reliable, and standardized toolkits in conditions of higher risk and supply costs. The widespread shift away from generalized, moderately extension-oriented technological strategies represented by scrapers toward more standardized and abundance-oriented strategies represented by points and backed artifacts is a technological response to increased foraging risks and procurement costs in those regions. Similar technological responses by foragers are visible in many areas at times of colonization, increased group mobility, and environmental change leading to reduction of resources and resource predictability. The timing of technological change varies regionally in relation to differences in the nature, onset, and magnitude of foraging risk and procurement costs, and the nature of technological change is related not only to the economic contexts of these risks and costs but also to the technological repertoire that has developed historically in each region. Furthermore, emphasis on these technological strategies was not the only solution foragers made to the uncertain economic context emerging at that time. These technological responses probably accompanied and supplemented changes to diet breadth, group composition and residential mobility, foraging territory, and intra- and inter-group social and political dynamics.

ACKNOWLEDGMENTS

Many thanks to Ian Lilley for his invitation to write the chapter, and for his willingness to accept it in this form. The arguments presented here benefited from discussions with Chris Clarkson, Barry Cundy, Lara Lamb, Boone Law, and Robin Torrence. Thanks are also due to Brit Asmussen, Val Attenbrow, and Phil Hughes for reading drafts of this chapter. Artifacts in Figure 4.1 were drawn by Chris Clarkson.

REFERENCES

Bamforth, D., 1986 Technological Efficiency and Tool Curation. American Antiquity 51:38–50.

Bamforth, D., and P. Bleed, 1997 Technology, Flaked Stone Technology, and Risk. *In* Rediscovering Darwin: Evolutionary Theory and Archaeological Explanation. C. Barton and G.
Clarke, eds. pp. 109–139. Archaeological Papers of the American Anthropological Association 7. Washington, DC: American Anthropological Association.

Bleed, P., 1986 The Optimal Design of Hunting Weapons: Maintainability or Reliability.
American Antiquity 51:737–747.

Bousman, C., 1993 Hunter-Gatherer Adaptations, Economic Risk, and Tool Design. Lithic
Technology 18:59–86.

Clarkson, C., 2002a Holocene Scraper Reduction, Technological Organization and
Landuse at Ingaladdi Rockshelter, Northern Australia. Archaeology in Oceania 37:79–86.

——2002b An Index of Invasiveness for the Measurement of Unifacial and Bifacial Retouch:
A Theoretical, Experimental and Archaeological Verification. Journal of Archaeological
Science 29:65–76.

——In press Tenuous Types: "Scraper" Reduction Continuums in the Eastern Victoria River
Region, Northern Territory. *In* Rocking the Boat: Recent Australian Approaches to Lithic
Reduction, Use and Classification. Clarkson, C. and L. Lamb, eds. British Archaeological
Reports International Monograph Series. Oxford: Archaeopress.

Clarkson, C., and L. Wallis, 2003 The Search for El Niño/Southern Oscillation in
Archaeological Sites: Recent Results from Jugali-ya Rockshelter, Wardaman Country. *In*
Phytolith and Starch Research in the Australian-Pacific-Asian Regions: The State of the
Art. L. Wallis and D. Hart, eds. pp.137–152. Terra Australis 19. Canberra: Pandanus
Books.

Cundy, B., 1985 The Secondary Use and Reduction of Cylindro-Conical Stone Artifacts
from the Northern Territory. The Beagle 2:115–127.

——1990 An Analysis of the Ingaladdi Assemblage: Critique of the Understanding of Lithic
Technology. Ph.D. dissertation, Australian National University.

David, B., and H. Lourandos, 1998 Rock Art and Socio-Demography in Northeast
Australian Prehistory. World Archaeology 30:193–219.

Dickson, F., 1981 Australian Stone Hatchets. Sydney: Academic Press.

Gould, R., 1991 Arid-Land Foraging as Seen from Australia: Adaptive Models and
Behavioural Realities. Oceania 62:12–33.

Hayden, B., 1989 From Chopper to Celt: The Evolution of Resharpening Techniques. *In*
Time, Energy and Stone Tools. R. Torrence, ed. pp. 7–16. Cambridge: Cambridge University Press.

Hiscock, P., 1986 Raw Material Rationing as an Explanation of Assemblage Differences: A
Case Study of Lawn Hill, Northwest Queensland. *In* Archaeology at ANZAAS, Canberra.
G. Ward, ed. pp. 178–190. Canberra: Canberra Archaeological Society.

——1988a Prehistoric Settlement Patterns and Artifact Manufacture at Lawn Hill, Northwest Queensland. Ph.D. dissertation, University of Queensland.

——1988b A Cache of Tulas from the Boulia District of Western Queensland. Archaeology
in Oceania 23:60–70.

——1993a Bondaian Technology in the Hunter Valley, New South Wales. Archaeology in
Oceania 28:64–75.

——1993b The Distribution of Points within Nauwalabila 1. The Beagle 10:173–178.

——1994a Technological Responses to Risk in Holocene Australia. Journal of World
Prehistory 8:267–292.

——1994b The End of Points. *In* Archaeology in the North. M. Sullivan, S. Brockwell and
A. Webb, eds. pp.72–83. Darwin: North Australia Research Unit, Australian National
University.

—1996 Mobility and Technology in the Kakadu Coastal Wetlands. *In* Indo-Pacific Prehistory: The Chiang Mai Papers, vol. 2. I. Glover and P. Bellwood, eds. pp. 151–157. Bulletin of the Indo-Pacific Prehistory Association 15. Canberra and Jakarta: Indo-Pacific Prehistory Association and Asosiasi Prehistorisi Indonesia.

—1999 Holocene Coastal Occupation of Western Arnhem Land. *In* Australian Coastal Archaeology. J. Hall and I. McNiven, eds. pp. 91–103. Research Papers in Archaeology and Natural History 31. Canberra: ANH Publications, Australian National University.

—2003 Pattern and Context in the Holocene Proliferation of Backed Artifacts in Australia. *In* Thinking Small: Global Perspectives on Microlithization. Steven Kuhn and Robert Elston, eds. pp. 163–177. Anthropological Papers of the American Anthropological Association 12. Washington, DC: American Anthropological Association.

—In press a Australian Point and Core Reduction viewed through Refitting. *In* The Big Puzzle Revisited. M. de Bie and U. Schurman, eds. British Archaeological Reports.

—In press b Looking the Other Way. A Materialist/Technological Approach to Classifying Tools and Implements, Cores and Retouched Flakes. *In* Tools or Cores? The Identification and Study of Alternative Core Technology in Lithic Assemblages. S. McPherron and J. Lindley, eds. Philadelphia: University of Pennsylvania Museum.

Hiscock, P., and H. Allen, 2000 Assemblage Variability in the Willandra Lakes. Archaeology in Oceania 35:97–103.

Hiscock, P., and V. Attenbrow, 1996 Backed into a Corner. Australian Archaeology 42:64–65.

—1998 Early Holocene Backed Artifacts from Australia. Archaeology in Oceania 33:49–63.

—2002 Reduction Continuums in Eastern Australia: Measurement and Implications at Capertee 3. *In* Barriers, Borders, Boundaries. S. Ulm, C. Westcott, J. Reid, A. Ross, I. Lilley, J. Prangnell and L. Kirkwood, eds. pp. 167–174. Tempus 7. Brisbane: Anthropology Museum, University of Queensland.

—2003 Early Australian Implement Variation: A Reduction Model. Journal of Archaeological Science 30:239–249.

Hiscock, P., and P. Kershaw, 1992 Palaeoenvironments and Prehistory of Australia's Tropical Top End. *In* The Naive Lands. J. Dodson, ed. pp. 43–75. Melbourne: Longman Cheshire.

Hiscock, P., and P. Veth, 1991 Change in the Australian Desert Culture: A Reanalysis of Tulas from Puntutjarpa. World Archaeology 22(3):332–345.

Jeske, R., 1989 Economies in Raw Material Use by Prehistoric Hunter-Gatherers. *In* Time, Energy and Stone Tools. R. Torrence, ed. pp. 34–45. Cambridge: Cambridge University Press.

—1992 Energetic Efficiency and Lithic Technology. American Antiquity 57:467–481.

Jochim, M., 1989 Optimization and Stone Tool Studies: Problems and Potentials. *In* Time, Energy and Stone Tools. R. Torrence, ed. pp. 106–111. Cambridge: Cambridge University Press.

Kelly, R., 1988 The Three Sides of a Biface. American Antiquity 53:717–734.

Kelly, R., and L. Todd, 1988 Coming into the Country: Early Paleoindian Hunting and Mobility. American Antiquity 53:231–244.

Kuhn, S., 1994 A Formal Approach to the Design and Assembly of Mobile Tool Kits. American Antiquity 59:426–442.

—1995 Mousterian Lithic Technology. Princeton: Princeton University Press.

——1996 The Trouble with Ham Steaks: A Reply to Morrow. American Antiquity 61:591–595.

Lamb, L., 1996 A Methodology for the Analysis of Backed Artifact Production on the South Molle Island Quarry, Whitsunday Islands. *In* Australian Archaeology '95. S. Ulm, I. Lilley and A. Ross, eds. pp. 151–159. Tempus 6. Brisbane: Anthropology Museum, University of Queensland.

McCarthy, L., and L. Head, 2001 Holocene Variability in Semi-Arid Vegetation: New Evidence from *Leporillus* Middens from the Flinders Ranges, South Australia. The Holocene 11:681–689.

McConvell, P., 1996 Backtracking to Babel: The Chronology of Pama-Nyungan Expansion in Australia. Archaeology in Oceania 31:125–144.

Morrow, T., 1996 Bigger is Better: Comments on Kuhn's Formal Approach to Mobile Tool Kits. American Antiquity 61:581–590.

Myers, A., 1987 All Shot To Pieces? Inter-Assemblage Variability, Lithic Analysis and Mesolithic Assemblage 'Types': Some Preliminary Observations. *In* Lithic Analysis and Later British Prehistory. A. Brown and M. Edmonds, eds. pp. 137–153. BAR British Series 162. Oxford: British Archaeological Reports.

——1989 Reliable and Maintainable Technological Strategies in the Mesolithic of Mainland Britain. *In* Time, Energy and Stone Tools. R. Torrence, ed. pp.78–91. Cambridge: Cambridge University Press.

Neeley, M., and C. Barton, 1994 A New Approach to Interpreting Late Pleistocene Microlith Industries in Southwest Asia. Antiquity 68:275–288.

Nelson, M., 1991 The Study of Technological Organization. Archaeological Method and Theory 3:57–100.

——1996 Technological Strategies Responsive to Subsistence Stress. *In* Evolving Complexity and Environmental Risk in the Prehistoric Southwest. J. Tainter and B. Tainter, eds. pp.107–144. New York: Addison-Wesley.

O'Connor, S., 1999 30,000 Years of Aboriginal Occupation: Kimberley, North West Australia. Terra Australis 14. Canberra: ANH Publications and the Centre for Archaeological Research, Australian National University.

Robertson, G., 2002 Birds of a Feather Stick: Microscopic Feather Residues on Stone Artifacts from Deep Creek, New South Wales. *In* Barriers, Borders, Boundaries. S. Ulm, C. Westcott, J. Reid, A. Ross, I. Lilley, J. Prangnell and L. Kirkwood, eds. pp. 175–182. Tempus 7. Brisbane: Anthropology Museum, University of Queensland.

Rowland, M., 1999 Holocene Environmental Variability: Have its Impacts been Underestimated in Australian Prehistory? The Artifact 22:11–48.

——1986 Technological Organization and Settlement Mobility: An Ethnographic Examination. Journal of Anthropological Research 42:15–51.

Shott, M., 1989 On Tool-Class Use Lives and The Formation of Archaeological Assemblages. American antiquity, 54(1):9–30.

——1995 How Much is a Scraper? Curation, Use Rates, and the Formation of Scraper Assemblages. Lithic Technology 20:53–72.

Shulmeister, J., and B. Lees, 1995 Pollen Evidence from Tropical Australia for the Onset of an ENSO-Dominated Climate at c. 4000 BP. The Holocene 5:10–18.

Torrence, R., 1983 Time Budgeting and Hunter-Gatherer Technology. *In* Hunter-Gatherer Economy in Prehistory. G. Bailey, ed. pp. 11–22. Cambridge: Cambridge University Press.

——1989a Tools as Optimal Solutions. *In* Time, Energy and Stone Tools. R. Torrence, ed. pp.1–6. Cambridge: Cambridge University Press.

——1989b Retooling: Towards a Behavioural Theory of Stone Tools. *In* Time, Energy and Stone Tools. R. Torrence, ed. pp. 57–66. Cambridge: Cambridge University Press.

Veth, P., 1989 Islands in the Interior: A Model for the Colonization of Australia's Arid Zone. Archaeology in Oceania 24:81–92.

——2000 Origins of the Western Desert Language: Convergence in Linguistic and Archaeological Space and Time Models. Archaeology in Oceania 35:11–19.

5

Rock Art and Social Identity: A Comparison of Holocene Graphic Systems in Arid and Fertile Environments

Jo McDonald and Peter Veth

Evidence for the use of a referential system of symbols to mark the landscape according to a corporate system of meanings appears to have its origins during the period of rapidly changing environmental conditions of the terminal Pleistocene. (Rosenfeld 1993:77)

Rock art played a fundamental role in Aboriginal life in all parts of the country. There are major rock art provinces in every environmental zone across the continent, from the tropical north through the arid interior to the temperate south and right around the coastline. Production of rock art depends on the presence of suitable rock surfaces, and thus major style regions (e.g., Arnhem Land, the Pilbara and Kimberley regions, and the Sydney Basin: Figure 5.1) tend to be areas where the geology provides almost continuous opportunities for its creation. In other areas, such as the dunefields, gibber and sand plains of the arid zone, rock surfaces are more localized and the opportunities to produce rock art are not continuous. Sand painting evolved in such areas (forming the basis for contemporary dot paintings on canvas), demonstrating the crucial role that art played in Aboriginal society even where rock art could not be readily created. The suitable geological outcrops that do occur in the arid zone provide highly focalized opportunities for art production, often in areas that also provide other vital resources (food, permanent water) for otherwise dispersed populations.

In regions where the rock surfaces are hard and very stable (e.g., the Kimberley: Morwood 2002) there are ancient and complex rock art sequences, pointing to changes in "the natural environment, society, ideology, material culture and 'outside' contact" (Morwood 2002:144) over almost the entire period that this continent has been occupied by people. It is generally accepted, however, that while some art in Australia is of Pleistocene antiquity, most of the rock art and particu-

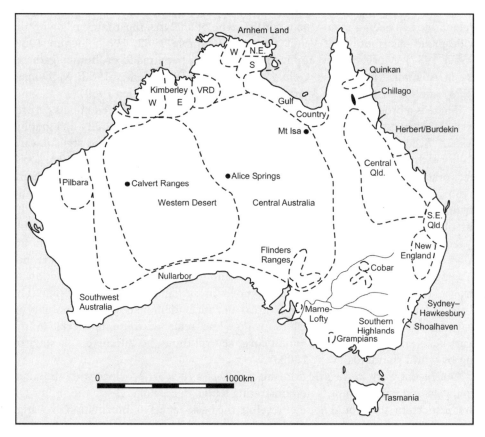

Figure 5.1 Map of Australia showing locations of Sydney–Hawkesbury Basin and Calvert Ranges in the Western Desert (after Layton 1992)

larly the development of distinct style provinces occurred during the Holocene. This phenomenon is seen to accompany a raft of social changes linked with intensification (*sensu* Lourandos 1985), most obviously marked by the widespread production and adoption of hafted stone tools in composite extractive implements such as the tula adze (cf. Hiscock and Veth 1991; also Hiscock, this volume). The development of complex art has been argued to be part of the armory of social mechanisms required to facilitate and control increasing interaction and to mark and enforce group identity in socially complex milieux (McDonald 1994; Rosenfeld 1993).

The notion of style as a social strategy is based on the work of Martin Wobst (1977). Information exchange theory has been applied to style in living societies to explain the degree of competition between groups over resources (Hodder 1978). It has also been developed to explore the maintenance of personal and social identity distinctions (Hodder 1978; Wiessner 1983, 1984, 1990). In an archaeological context, this approach has more recently been applied to relate degrees of stylistic heterogeneity to the nature of prehistoric social networks. The European Upper Paleolithic has been a major focus for this type of analysis, most famously with the widespread distribution of Venus figurines (Gamble 1982, 1983; Jochim 1983; Soffer 1987). More specific applications have also been made on hunter-gatherer art in Australia (David and Cole 1990; Godwin 1990; Lewis 1988; McDonald 1994) and on pastoralist rock art in Africa (Brandt and Carder 1989).

There is a broad assumption that different environments and their effects on pre-historic social networks will influence the amount of stylistic variability in a graphic system. Studies involving portable and fixed rock art have correlated stylistic vari-ability with the nature of prehistoric social networks. In fertile regions, where social networks are closed and kinship and territorial systems are relatively rigid (Williams 1986), rock art studies have demonstrated a high degree of social information, and distinctive group-identifying and bounding behavior. It has been argued that the distribution of stylistically homogenous traits over enormous areas of inhospitable Paleolithic Europe demonstrated widely ramified open social networks. In the Australian arid zone, where widely ramified open social networks are known ethno-graphically, it has been demonstrated that homogenous art systems function to provide broad-scale inter-group cohesion over presumably vast periods of time. The distribution of localized styles over great distances demonstrates the mobility of artists through extensive social networks. The scale of these networks in the Australian arid zone, some of which cover several thousand kilometers, is stagger-ing by world standards (Veth 2000a).

Our recent work in the arid zone has revealed a rock art province with abundant engraved and painted motifs demonstrating a high degree of stylistic variability. On first inspection, this would appear to refute the basic tenets of information exchange theory. However, when one considers the nature of social networks throughout the arid zone and the nature of aggregation behavior that constitutes part of the normal ebb and flow of social contact within the arid zone, such evidence is no mystery, as we make clear below. In the Sydney Basin on the fertile southeast coast of Australia, pigment and engraved assemblages have been compared at a regional scale (McDonald 1994). It was found that these regional assemblages had been used to demonstrate social strategies promoting larger-scale group cohesion as well as to provide mechanisms for localized-group identifying behavior. Thus Sydney Basin groups who were not in constant verbal contact with each other were able to practice important, and varying, social strategies through their use of style in dif-ferent media in different social contexts.

In this chapter we want to highlight the fact that Holocene rock art appears to have served dual functions in *both* arid and fertile environments. We would argue that the social context of rock art production provides the rationale for whether stylistic information contains traits which are significant to broad-scale or localized group identity. We will use the art provinces of the Sydney Basin and the Calvert Ranges in the Western Desert in northwestern Australia (Figure 5.1) as case studies to explore this theme. For the purposes of this discussion, "style" is defined as the particular way of doing or producing material culture which signals the activity of a particular group of people who distinguish themselves from other, similarly constituted groups. Style is non-verbal communication which negotiates identity (Wiessner 1990:107). On this basis, "stylistic heterogeneity" is perceived as the variability in style which demonstrates widely dissimilar artistic components, the end result of doing or producing material culture which signals either a less culturally fettered activity of a particular group of people, or the activity of a particular group which has less rigorous stylistic rules. In either case heterogeneity is *relative*: it can only be defined in comparison to other, more homogeneous stylistic activity.

Holocene Occupation in the Sydney Basin

The earliest occupation of the Sydney region focused on the Hawkesbury-Nepean River, a major drainage system cutting through the sandstone country. Dates suggest that this was ca. 20,000 years ago. Over the next several thousand years occupation spread, registered by evidence in rockshelters in smaller creek catchments (e.g., Mangrove Creek and the Ropesend Creek). This model has most recently been refined through open-site archaeology on the Cumberland Plain, a shale plain surrounded by sandstone country and drained by the Hawkesbury-Nepean river system (Jo McDonald Cultural Heritage Management 2001; see also Attenbrow 1987 and McDonald 1994).

During the Pleistocene, people appear to have been highly mobile, traveling considerable distances between sites. At this time, the focus of stone acquisition was on the Hawkesbury-Nepean River gravels. The cores and tools which people carried were quite large, but they used the stone sparingly, leaving few artifacts behind, and rarely discarding their cores (which acted as portable raw material supplies). With rising sea levels, stabilizing after 6000 B.P., groups occupying the drowning coastal strip would have been forced inland. The region's population gradually increased over time and by 4,000 years ago, many new sites were occupied. People took up permanent or semi-permanent residence in most parts in the region from this time. Some groups lived full-time on the Cumberland Plain, some full-time in the surrounding sandstone country. The technological strategies which people used after 4000 B.P. underwent substantial change, with an emphasis on the use of locally available stone.

Almost all stone artifacts, including most cores and tools, were small. People prepared stone at, or in close proximity to, local sources and transported small pieces of selected materials back to their residential sites. The stone was flaked until reasonably small and then discarded, along with the cores. This meant that people had to continually renew their supplies of stone. They made numerous backed artifacts; usually on bladelets and snapped portions of these where backing (assumed to be for hafting) opposes an acute angled and generally sharp chord. These were very small tools usually weighing less than one gram. Microscopic use-wear and residue studies of these tools confirm that these were small multipurpose tools, used possibly to hunt animals but also to process plant materials (see Hiscock, this volume).

Change continued. In the past 1,000 years or so ground stone implements seem to have been ubiquitous (Kohen 1986) and there is fragmentary evidence for this

at most archaeological sites. There was also increased use of bipolar flaking, probably reflecting even more intensive use of some local resources and also serving as
an economizing strategy given a greater ratio of working edges can be produced
from a given lithic mass (Hiscock 1994 and this volume). Backed artifacts declined
in frequency, possibly because there was less need for them owing to changing social
networks (Morwood 1987) or perhaps because less priority was given to their costly
bulk production (again an economizing strategy). Changing frequencies of raw
material preferences in the recent past also point to more restricted movement, and
contact via exchange networks.

Art on the fertile coast: the social context in the Sydney Basin

There are no ethnographic data concerning the function of art in Aboriginal society
prior to European contact. There is, however, the detailed context provided by four
decades of archaeological research as well as ethnohistorical literature compiled by
journalists on the First Fleet, which brought the earliest British colonists, and linguistic and ethnographic work on those pockets of the original populations which
survived into the late 19th century. The region falls within a single "culture area,"
the southeast coast (Peterson 1976). Owing to its position on the fertile coast with
numerous zones of resource distribution and its relatively high population densities
it is presumed that the region operated on the basis of local territorial affiliations.
The resulting social networks are described in other similar regions as placing a
greater emphasis on territorial boundaries with attachments, control and access to
land depending on local group membership (Sutton and Rigsby 1986:158). Extensive research suggests that environmental conditions have been relatively stable in
the region throughout the Holocene, so this general situation is likely to have existed
for millennia. Four languages were spoken across the region at contact (Capell
1970; Dawes 1790–91; Mathews 1897, 1901; Mathews and Everitt 1900): *Dark-
ingung, Guringai, Dharug*, and *Tharawal* (Figure 5.2). We do not know the antiquity
of this language system, but archaeological evidence suggests it could be at least
1,000 years old.

At European contact, residence groups consisted of named economic units
with designated tracts of land. "Tribes," as they were called by Europeans on the
colonial First Fleet to Australia from Britain, are thought to have comprised a
number of these smaller residence groups, speaking dialects of a common language.
Within the territorial range of any one linguistic group there would have been
perhaps as many as fifteen smaller, localized bands (Kohen and Lampert 1988).
These bands would have had kin and/or totemic links with people in other groups
and therefore modes of access to resources around the region. Considerable interaction within and across linguistic boundaries was observed at contact. Organized
social events (initiation ceremonies, dances and the like), as well as the exploitation
of windfall resources (such as feasts on beached whales), resulted in aggregations
of large numbers of people of mixed language groups (Collins 1975 [1798]:25;
Tench 1961 [1789]:52). It would appear that at least some forms of ritual

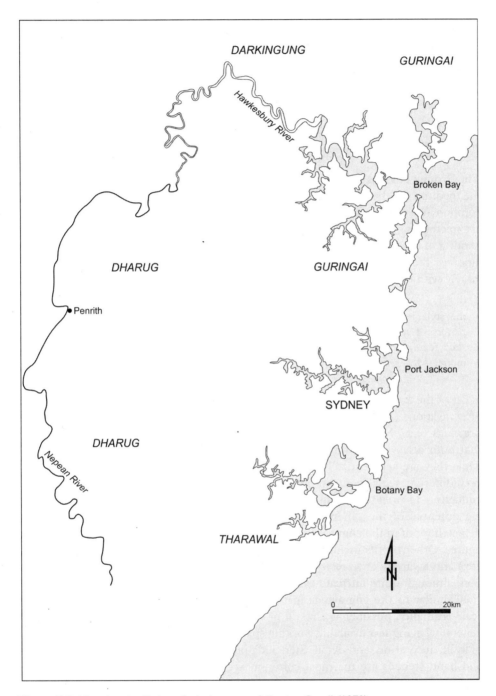

Figure 5.2 Map showing Sydney Basin languages following Capell (1970)

behavior in the region required the participation, and possibly consent, of neigh-boring tribes (Collins 1975 [1798]:486; Mathews 1897:1–2; Mathews and Everitt 1900:276). The presence of distinguishable, localized bands as well as broader lan-guage boundaries suggests that there may have been a highly complex pattern of artistic behavior and signatures within and across tribal "boundaries."

Sydney Basin rock art

The Sydney Basin is part of the Hawkesbury Sandstone Formation, which provides the medium for the region's 4,000+ art sites. They can be broadly divided into two components, open engraved (petroglyph) sites on sandstone platforms and pigment art (pictograph) sites located within sandstone shelters and overhangs. Although a handful of engraved sites are thought to be older, residual "Panaramitee"-style sites amongst the assemblage, the rest of the engravings as well as the pigment art fall largely within Maynard's (1977:200–201) Simple Figurative classification:

> the style is dominated by figurative motifs . . . the majority . . . conform[ing] to a pattern of crude naturalism. Whether the motif is engraved or painted, in outline or solid form, it usually consists of a very simplified silhouette of a human or animal model. Most portrayals are strongly standardised.

Most of the art is thought to date to the past 3,000 years on the basis of a number of excavations (McDonald 1994) and a limited number of AMS dates on charcoal drawings (e.g., McDonald 2000; McDonald et al. 1990). There is good evidence that both art systems were produced contemporaneously (McDonald 1991) but while they are schematically both part of the same stylistic art form they provide very different social contexts in terms of inferred audiences. It is these differing contexts – of private vs. public – that provide the key to interpreting the messag-ing potential of the different art forms. Human tracks are the most commonly depicted motif in the engraved assemblage, followed by fish, kangaroos, and human figures. Other motifs include items of material culture (axes, boomerangs, shields, etc.) and a variety of terrestrial animals. There is usually very little infill or decora-tion, although quite intricate examples of it do exist. The pigment art is schemati-cally similar to the engravings in terms of subject matter and general form. The scale is smaller, possibly as a result of relatively smaller "canvas" size (rockshelters generally having less available working space than open sites) and there is more use of infill, decoration, and detail. Stenciling predominates in many parts of the Basin, and hand stencils are the most common art form within this component. Of the depictive motifs, anthropomorphs are the most common, closely followed by kan-garoos, other land animals, fish, birds, and weapons. Non-figurative motifs, some quite complex, are found in localized areas of the Basin. Various analyses were undertaken to explore the different social messaging being demonstrated by the two art contexts, as outlined below.

Sampling and theoretical considerations

The two art components are roughly equal in frequency and both are found in all geographic zones across the Sydney Basin. A sample of more than thirty percent of each component was analyzed, involving 717 engraving sites and 546 rockshelter art sites. This analysis was not aimed at investigating the standardization of formal variation *per se*, but rather at the motif ranges and tendencies for motif categories to co-occur across the region, so style was investigated at a fairly general level. It is considered that cultural choices were made and indicated by the use of certain motifs, along the lines of Sackett's (1990) views on isochrestic variation (McDonald 1999). Combinations of motifs and compositional features are considered to demonstrate high levels of ethnically significant patterning. As Sackett (1990:41) states, "themes may well be the [things] that give congruence to isochrestic choices in non-material aspects of cultural life."

The potential for heterogeneity

It was necessary to consider the potential for heterogeneity in each of these two art contexts (engraved and pigment) to investigate the stylistic variability in both. This was so the significance of stylistic heterogeneity, if found, could be established. The motif classes used for the two assemblages were almost identical, with only two extra motifs being counted in the shelter art assemblage. There is little chance therefore of classification playing a role in either component's relative variability (e.g., Gamble 1982 vs. Soffer 1987; C. Smith 1989).

Several attributes were investigated, including assemblage size, motif emphasis (percentage of sites at which certain motifs are depicted), and motif occurrence (maximum number of times a motif is present at any one site). The only potential source of greater heterogeneity in the shelter art assemblage was found to be assemblage size. The variability inherent in shelter art sites according to site size is three times that of engraving sites. As this was the only area of potential bias it was dealt with by using binary data which were then double-standardized for the quantitative analysis (see Bolviken et al. 1982). This effectively removed assemblage size as a factor in the analysis.

Analyses

Correspondence analysis (CA) was used to investigate sources of variance. The advantage of this technique is that the variables, in this case *motifs*, which create the groupings can be identified. It is not so much the presence of individual motifs which create variance, but the *combination* of variables, and this of course is significant given that interpretation hinges on thematic variety (as per Sackett 1990). The

CA identified no distinctive localized variability across the region in either component. However, certain stylistic clines across the region are present and were visible when the database was subdivided into more manageable subgroups. This was done at various scales based on assorted parameters such as arbitrary map sheets, designated language boundaries, and creek catchments, the last a geographic factor relevant to language subgroup boundaries. Localized variability was demonstrated by identifying the proportion of homogenous sites in each area. The identification and distribution of outlier sites within localized areas were the answer to investigating stylistic variability across the region, since this patterning in the combinations of motifs was considered to demonstrate thematic choices (as per Sackett 1990; see McDonald 1999).

Multivariate analysis also found that both art media in the Sydney region exhibit synchronic stylistic variability on the basis of motif. In other words, style varies across the region in terms of the proportions of different motifs and themes depicted. The major finding, however, was that the degree of stylistic homogeneity is *less* in the rockshelter art component than is found in the engraved component. This was considered to be a significant result. It was proposed that these varying levels of heterogeneity revealed the pursuit of different types of social strategies. The higher level of stylistic homogeneity amongst the engravings is thought to demonstrate larger-scale group cohesion. In contrast, the more heterogeneous pigment art is seen to demonstrate localized group identifying behavior. This argument was supported by the archaeological data using the idea of audience and social context, as discussed below.

A major part of this research aimed to investigate the contemporaneity of art and occupational deposits. This was verified at all three shelter art sites investigated (Yengo I, Upside-Down-Man, and Great Mackerel), where there was a demonstrable correlation between the main phase of pigment art production and the most intensive period of shelter occupation. This, it was argued (following Wobst's 1977 prediction), was an art form viewed by a broad section of the community and thus the most susceptible to *local* group stylistic messaging. The "domestic" or public art of a region would be the most likely medium to reveal stylistic patterning to function as boundary maintenance, or at least to demonstrate localized social affiliations. Moreover, if pigment art was produced in shelters, where it would have been accessible to a wide audience, then the art *was* fulfilling a function very different from an art form which was produced "in private" or for a restricted audience. This last would appear to be the case with most engraving sites, where occupation evidence is seldom recorded. There is evidence, however, that most engraving sites are prominent on major access routes around the region, and that there are also major sites which appear, through their motif assemblages, to be depicting ceremonial or mythical beings. If these sites *did* function as ceremonial sites involving the cooperation of participating neighboring groups, it might be expected that the overriding aim of this art's production was to maintain broader-scaled group affiliation. There is no ethnohistorical evidence that engravings had a ceremonial role at European contact, but the main period of art production may have ceased by 1,000 years ago.

A more homogeneous art form is arguably more culturally fettered. If its func-tion was broad-scale social cohesion, art should be less susceptible to individuality and other forms of localized stylistic "mutation," as predicted by Polly Wiessner's work, and, therefore, more homogeneous. This result is also consistent with Wobst's prediction that art which is seen by a relatively small number of individuals will have a relatively homogeneous distribution between social units. So, information exchange theory was used to explore the relationships between particular media, style, and social strategies in the Sydney Basin. It was argued that higher levels of homogeneity amongst engravings, associated with a low incidence of occupation debris, reflect social strategies aimed at larger-scale group cohesion. Conversely, the more heterogeneous pigment art, correlated strongly with high incidences of occupation evidence, reflects social strategies aimed at localized-group identifying behavior.

The Arid Zone Context of Rock Art Production

The Western Desert covers over one-sixth of the continent and is marked by lowland sand sheets, dunefields, and gibber (stony) flats with occasional minor uplands, all marked by uncoordinated internal drainage. Resource structure is usually coarse-grained. It is generally agreed that settlement of all desert environments occurred before the Last Glacial Maximum (LGM), between 25,000 and 40,000 years ago. During at least the earliest portion of this time, conditions would generally have been better-watered than now and thus favorable to human colonization. On the edges of the Western Desert in Central Australia, Smith (1988) has established that occupation began at Puritjarra from 30,000 years ago. He sees shifts in re-sidential mobility patterns and territoriality as providing the appropriate mecha-nism for groups to persist in the Central Australian ranges during the LGM and to maintain some connection, albeit peripheral, with the arid lowlands to the west (Smith et al. 1998). The emergence of intensive seed grinding by the mid- to late Holocene is linked by Smith (1996) to a minor arid phase and population growth. A major efflorescence in artifact discard rates over the last thousand years is seen to be driven by population increase and partitioning of territory (cf. Smith 1996:68). This late phase of intensification is not explicitly linked to any ecological parameters.

Thorley (1998) has also examined a region on the eastern edge of the Western Desert, the Palmer River catchment, where the site of Kulpi Mara also dates back to 30,000 B.P. He argues that with increasing aridity from 23,000 B.P. the site was abandoned until approximately 13,000 B.P. Thorley's review of Puritjarra led him to conclude that there was negligible evidence for occupation through the LGM. Using data from more than 20 excavated sites in Central Australia, he argues that the mid- to late Holocene provides the first evidence for strategies well suited to the risks imposed by a widely fluctuating arid environment (compare Hiscock, this volume). Among these tactics are the use of low-risk seed foods and the position-ing of aggregation sites to take advantage of rich though temporary stands of

resources such as seeds near ephemeral waters. In truly interior portions of the
Western Desert, Gould (1977) had established a 10,000-year chronology at the site
of Puntutjarpa in the Gibson Desert by the late 1960s. Almost 20 years later,
Serpent's Glen rockshelter in the Little Sandy Desert was dated to greater
than 23,500 B.P., becoming the first site of substantial Pleistocene age within the
Western Desert (O'Connor et al. 1998). More recently, the Katampul site in
the Western Desert returned a Pleistocene age of 21,000 B.P. (O'Connor and
Veth 1996).

A systematic program of excavation in core and peripheral areas of the dunefields of the Little and Great Sandy Deserts has provided suites of dates from the
mid- to late Holocene (Veth 1993, 1996, 2000b; Veth and McDonald 2002; Veth
et al. 2001). Recent excavations have focused on aggregation sites in the Calvert
Ranges of the Little Sandy Desert and in the Durba Ranges. These unique spring-
watered ranges contain rockshelters with occupation evidence and very abundant
suites of rock paintings and engravings. In broader context, the Calvert Ranges are
one of a number of small isolated range systems that extend from the major desert
uplands, such as the Pilbara and Central Australian ranges, deep into the Western
Desert. While it is reasonable to argue that the paintings date to the late Holocene,
many of the engravings have been substantially weathered, chemically altered, and
in some cases covered in thick coatings of varnish and other crusts, and it is quite
likely that some date to the Pleistocene (Veth et al. 2001).

There is broad consensus that Western Desert occupation is of great antiquity
and that especially during the Holocene it was marked by periods of dynamic social
and economic transformation (cf. Gould 1996; Smith 1996; Veth et al. 2001).
These archaeological phases and social correlates are important in understanding
how the art may have functioned as a means of social identifying behavior through
time. We will begin with a brief discussion of other rock art research in the arid
zone, and describe how art is thought to have functioned in the ethnographic
present.

Rock art research in the arid zone

There has been a recent efflorescence of rock art research in the Australian arid
zone (e.g., Frederick 1997, 1999, 2000; Galt-Smith 1997; Gunn 1995; Rosenfeld
2002). While very disparate in its goals, this work has revealed an interesting trend
in the amount of localized stylistic variability apparent, particularly in the recent
past. This had not been systematically documented before and, like early European
views of Aboriginal occupation of the continent, it had been assumed that there
was little change in arid-zone art through time or space.

As regards the way(s) in which rock art functioned in Aboriginal people's lives,
art production took place in a number of contexts, from secular and casual to sacred
and ceremonial (Gunn 2000). Frederick identifies that the graphic systems of the
arid zone were important in promoting and controlling the exchange of information, functioning at a multitude of levels to identify and integrate as well as to

demarcate social boundaries (see also Galt-Smith 1997; Gould 1969; Lewis 1988; McDonald 1994, 1999).

The application of a graphic system in the production of rock art served a number of functions and operated in a variety of social contexts (Frederick 2000:5). It (1) was a way of marking place and an individual's affiliation to it, (2) had a significant storytelling or instructive context, (3) was used in initiation ceremonies, (4) provided a physical form of an ancestral being or event, and (5) was also a way of marking country to maintain longstanding links with sacred traditions.

Galt-Smith (1997) investigated aggregation locales in Central Australian rock art. He looked at both painted and engraved art. His results show distinct patterning in the assemblages, which fitted with the ethnography. The patterning among pictographs in particular correlates well with the documented clan-based totemic social system. Galt-Smith argues that the pigment art demonstrated a control of information in the local context. This was in contrast with the patterning shown by pecked engravings, which he found to be homogenous over vast areas of arid Australia.

This fits well with Smith's findings. She argues (e.g., C. Smith 1989) that art demonstrated broad-scaled group cohesion over huge areas of the arid zone. Comparing modern portable "acrylic" paintings from the Western Desert with Arnhem Land bark paintings, she tested the thesis that increased stylistic heterogeneity is correlated with more fertile environmental conditions and more closed social networks, as originally posited by Gamble (1982) and Jochim (1983). The environments of her two sample areas are as diverse as can be imagined in Australia, as were the art forms under analysis. Smith successfully demonstrated that there was greater heterogeneity amongst the secular art of the more fertile region than was found in the secular art of the arid zone. But how real is this dichotomy when rock art is considered? It has become increasing clear that the different rock art media in the arid zone present independent lines of evidence, and we propose that in fact art has a dual signaling capacity throughout the arid zone – as it did in the Sydney Basin – to demonstrate both localized group and broad-scale group cohesions. The art of the Holocene, and particularly that of the last 1,000 years, provides the clearest evidence for this proposition.

Western Desert rock art

Our arid-zone art province is a place called *Kaalpi* by the *Martu* people, and is located in the Calvert Ranges on the Canning Stock Route. This area comprises a series of well-watered gorges in a relatively small outlier of conglomerate quartz sandstone in the vast dunefields of the Little Sandy Desert. This place is typical of the more marginal landscapes to have been occupied by people in the Western Desert. The engraved art at Kaalpi is incredibly diverse in terms of its manner of execution as well as its subject matter. Obviously we are looking at an assemblage created over a very long period of time, which can account for much of the variability. There is intaglio art – the classic Panaramitee style of mainly bird and kangaroo tracks – with circles and dots, some of which have often been interpreted as animal scats. There is also a suite of very large, pecked decorative-infilled anthropomorphic figures (apparently of great antiquity), as well as smaller figures based around the theme of archaic faces (known as Cleland Hills faces after a type-site more than 1,000 kilometers to the east of our study area: see Dix 1977). As well as this, there are small infilled terrestrial animals, battered figurative motifs, pecked outline and infilled animals, and abraded outline figurative motifs. Our work in progress on initial dating of buried art in this area indicates an age greater than mid-Holocene, with several styles thought likely to be correlated with social changes at the LGM. Art has been produced in the area up to the recent past and our Aboriginal informants could tell us about pigment art being produced until the 1960s.

The first stage of our art recording has involved tracing a number of represen-tative motifs and doing counts of the various styles and site types within one valley system. To date, 44 locations have been recorded in this preliminary fashion. These were mostly in sheltered places, although art was also found on large and small boulders, horizontal platforms, and vertical walls. Most of the art is engraved. Of the 44 sites recorded, 27 have engravings only, while only three have pigment art alone. The remaining 14 sites have a combination of engraved and pigment art. The pigment art exhibits diverse subject matter: a variety of anthropomorphs, some with distinctive headdresses, and several very elongated varieties more than three meters long. Concentric circles and complex non-figurative motifs also figure strongly, as do bird tracks, snakes, and boomerangs.

The pigment art is mostly painted red and white, mostly bichrome but some monochrome. There are very few hand stencils and a lone hand print. The engrav-ings have a slightly more diverse range of motifs and a slightly different focus. This may be because the engravings represent a significantly greater time depth of exe-cution than the pigment art, though we consider there are multiple phases of pro-duction in evidence in both techniques. Bird and kangaroo tracks dominate, the former being present at more than half the sites recorded. While around two-thirds of the art sites contain small assemblages – i.e., less than 30 motifs, the other 14 shelters contained large and complex art assemblages. This is evidence of patterned behavior within the art province, which should provide evidence for changing prac-tices and foci over time.

Art and archaeology

We now return to the archaeological models for the Western Desert and what these might mean for understanding the dual rock art signaling system outlined above. Veth (2000b) has synthesized a phased occupation model for the Western Desert which argues for the initial settlement of the region before 22,000 years ago, and for the development of the types of social networks in place today after 5,000–3,000 years ago. A shift is observed at ca. 1,500 years ago, when there appears to be a major increase in site numbers and artifact densities. This timing coincides with a proposed influx of the Western Desert language, which presently is distributed across 1/6 of the continent. On the basis of McConvell's (1996) "linguistic stratigraphy," current models see the language moving from northwest to east across the arid zone. With the spread of Western Desert language came an increased intensity of site occupation, accelerated ritual and ceremonial cycles, and an increase in long-distance exchange. Indeed, if one looks at Veth's (2000b) proposed correlation of the linguistic and archaeological data, one gets a very clear indication of how the role of art within this changing social system might be modeled. It can be fairly safely assumed that the ramified social networks described by anthropological research have functioned for at least 1,000–1,500 years and possibly for as much as 5,000 years.

It is also plausible that a tightening of social and territorial organization occurred just before the LGM, following a long phase of high mobility and multivalent art. Groups could have become more tethered to uplands such as the Calvert and Carnarvon ranges (e.g., the Serpent's Glen site) owing to intensified aridity. They would then have become more mobile, with large tracts of plains and interdunal corridors being dropped from normal foraging schedules. A likely consequence of this would have been some form of intensification if continuity of occupation was maintained. This is the classic scenario for a retraction to an LGM refuge in Lawn Hill Gorge in northeastern Australia proposed by Peter Hiscock (1988). Using this model – and information exchange theory – one would expect that art would have played varying roles as a form of negotiated identity marker throughout this period.

We would argue that the initial occupation of the region may well have been accompanied by the use of rock art. Low intensity, sporadic art production at this time would have demonstrated widespread group cohesion. The engraved art, still generally called "Panaramitee," fits within this scheme, and indeed there are numerous dates around the continent supporting such a proposal (e.g., Nobbs and Dorn 1988, 1993; Watchman 1992, 1993). Similarly complex art networks functioned in the European Paleolithic at a similar time. As Veth (2000a) has suggested elsewhere, Pleistocene networks across the arid zone were probably more open and far-reaching than had been previously argued, reflecting extreme mobility. With changes in residential patterning during Phases 2 and 3 of the LGM between 22,000 and 13,000 years ago, it is likely that there was broad-scale social cohesion with perhaps increased localized identifying behavior as a result of territorial tethering to relatively favorable localities. Perhaps it was at this time that the large decorative infilled motifs – the transformation of Cleland Hills faces into large, decorated people – were developed. As indicated above, these motifs appear to be geologically old, with the tops of the heads in one art panel having weathered away. On the basis of patination and weathering, this style appears at least as old in the Calverts as the classic Panaramitee-style art.

We need to consider what sort of catalyst would create an artistic vocabulary signifying corporate identity (or identity of any kind) in the Western Desert during the Pleistocene. It is possible that the use of landscapes such as the Calvert Ranges may have intensified with the onset of heightened aridity during the LGM. In coping with increased stress and the imperative to maintain spiritual ties to country, some obvious responses would be to make shifts in residential mobility and to signal increasing boundedness as groups' ranges were reconfigured. Prior to the arrival of the Western Desert language, regional social networks which we suggest are the antecedents of current social arrangements would have developed. Art would again have been used to negotiate both broad-scale and local group identity. The art would still have been relatively homogenous, but there should have been an increased use of art to negotiate broad-scale and local group identity, with distinctive localized style regions evolving.

This pattern would have continued during the spread of the Western Desert languages in the period between 1,500 and 500 years ago and one might expect that the development of regional art provinces occurred at this time. Archaeological and anthropological evidence would suggest that art influences from the east and further afield would have been introduced into the graphic system during the last 500 years. Diachronic change is clearly evidenced in the Calvert Ranges, but so too is there evidence for amazing stylistic heterogeneity in art that is arguably recent.

So how do we explain this level of diversity in the art of the arid zone? Any model needs to consider not only residential mobility of particular groups at any one time but also the likely aggregation cycles that would have had great importance in terms of cultural/genetic/ritual flows. The "aggregation locale" concept originally developed by Conkey (1980) for Paleolithic Spain is good for describing art sites and provinces where groups from many disparate social groupings gather. The high degree of stylistic variability displayed in the abundant engraved and painted motifs in the Calverts' well-watered gorges strongly suggest that this area has acted as an aggregation locale for a long time. Such aggregation sites are believed to have served as important centers for ritual production, in the process facilitating the rapid exchange of linguistic elements, material goods, and genes. The paradox of arid-zone hunter-gatherer settlement behavior is that groups must coalesce to effectively negotiate the social contracts and relations of reciprocity that establish the conditions necessary for subsequent dispersal.

High levels of stylistic diversity are not well accommodated by the arid–fertile dichotomy and yet the optimal conditions for effective information exchange during aggregation events predict just such a configuration. In resource-poor areas aggregation locales are essentially the "engine-rooms" of information exchange and in such localities art will exhibit high stylistic diversity as an expression of contested group identities rather than bounded territoriality. Throughout the Holocene, then, rock art in the arid zone was used to communicate important social messages and demonstrate both localized identifying behavior and broad-scale group cohesion. It fulfilled a similar role to the art of the more fertile Sydney Basin, where pigment art was the preferred medium for localized group behavior.

Conclusion

This chapter shows that the arid–fertile dichotomy and the effects that environment has on social networks and the resultant stylistic diversity in their graphic systems are more complex than initially indicated by using the predictions of information exchange theory as to how style might be used in such contexts. An analysis of comparable systems operating in the two environments may well show that there is increased complexity and stylistic heterogeneity in coastal/fertile art compared to the arid-zone art. It is important, however, to investigate how style is used in a range of environments to signal between and inter-group cohesion. We argue that varying levels of stylistic heterogeneity in arid-zone and temperate coastal art assemblages demonstrate that desert and coastal peoples alike used art throughout the Holocene to signal information about themselves. Doing so made non-verbal communication less stressful and interaction more predictable during a period of substantial social change.

REFERENCES

Attenbrow, V., 1987 The Upper Mangrove Creek Catchment: A Study of Quantitative Changes in the Archaeological Record. Ph.D. dissertation, University of Sydney.

Bolviken, E., E. Helskog and H. Helskog, 1982 Correspondence Analysis: An Alternative to Principal Components. World Archaeology 14:41–60.

Brandt, S., and N. Carder, 1989 Pastoral Rock Art in the Horn of Africa: Making Sense of Udder Chaos. World Archaeology 19:194–213.

Capell, A., 1970 Aboriginal Languages in the South Central Coast, NSW: Fresh Discoveries. Oceania 41:20–27.

Collins, D., 1975 [1798] An Account of the English Colony in New South Wales, vol. 1. B. Fletcher, ed. Sydney: A.H. and A.W. Reed in association with the Royal Australian Historical Society.

Conkey, M., 1980 The Identification of Hunter-Gatherer Aggregation Sites – The Case of Altimira. Current Anthropology 21:609–630.

David, B., and N. Cole, 1990 Rock Art and Inter-Regional Interaction in Northeast Australian Prehistory. Antiquity 64:788–806.

Dawes, W., 1790–91 Vocabulary of the Language of N.S. Wales, in the Neighbourhood of Sydney, Native and English. Marsden Collection, Mitchell Library, Sydney.

Dix, W., 1977 Facial Representations in Pilbara Rock Engravings. In Form in Indigenous Art. P. Ucko, ed. pp. 277–285. Canberra: Australian Institute of Aboriginal Studies.

Frederick, U., 1997 Drawing in Differences: Changing Social Context of Rock Art Production in Watarrka (Kings Canyon) National Park, Central Australia. M.A. dissertation, Australian National University.

——1999 At the Centre of it All: Constructing Contact through the Rock Art of Watarrka National Park, Central Australia. Archaeology in Oceania 34:132–144.

——2000 Keeping the Land Alive: Changing Social Contexts of Landscape and Rock Art Production. In The Archaeology of Difference: Negotiating Cross-Cultural Engagements in Oceania. R. Torrence and A. Clarke, eds. pp. 300–330. Routledge: London and New York.

Galt-Smith, B., 1997 Motives for Motifs: Identifying Aggregation and Dispersion Settlement Patterns in the Rock Art Assemblages of Central Australia. B.A. Honours dissertation, University of New England.

Gamble, C., 1982 Interaction and Alliance in Paleolithic Society. Man 17:92–107.

——1983 Culture and Society in the Upper Paleolithic of Europe. *In* Hunter-Gatherer Economy in Prehistory: A European Perspective. G. Bailey, ed. pp. 201–211. Cambridge: Cambridge University Press.

Godwin, L., 1990 Inside Information: Settlement and Alliance in the Late Holocene of North-Eastern New South Wales. Ph.D. dissertation, University of New England.

Gould, R., 1969 Yiwara: Foragers of the Australian Desert. Sydney: Collins.

——1977 Puntutjarpa Rockshelter and the Australian Desert Culture. Anthropological Papers 54. New York: American Museum of Natural History.

——1996 Faunal Reduction at Puntutjarpa Rockshelter, Warburton Ranges, Western Australia. Archaeology in Oceania 31:72–86.

Gunn, R., 1995 Regional Patterning in the Aboriginal Rock Art of Central Australia: A Preliminary Report. Rock Art Research 12:117–127.

——2000 Spencer and Gillen's Contribution to Australian Rock Art Studies. Rock Art Research 17:56–64.

Hiscock, P., 1988 Prehistoric Settlement Patterns and Artifact Manufacture at Lawn Hill, Northwest Queensland. Ph.D. dissertation, University of Queensland.

——1994 Technological Responses to Risk in Holocene Australia. Journal of World Prehistory 8:267–292.

Hiscock, P., and P. Veth, 1991 Change in the Australian Desert Culture: A Reanalysis of Tulas from Puntutjarpa Rockshelter World Archaeology 22:332–345.

Hodder, I., 1978 The Maintenance of Group Identities in the Baringo District, West Kenya. *In* Social Organization and Settlement. D. Green, C. Haselgrove and M. Spriggs, M., eds. pp. 47–74. BAR International Series 47(i). Oxford: British Archaeological Reports.

Jo McDonald Cultural Heritage Management Pty. Ltd., 2001 Salvage Excavation of Six Sites along Caddies, Second Ponds, Smalls and Cattai Creeks in the Rouse Hill Development Area, NSW. Report to Rouse Hill Infrastructure Consortium, New South Wales Department of Environment and Conservation.

Jochim, M., 1983 Paleolithic Cave Art in Ecological Perspective. *In* Hunter-Gatherer Economy in Prehistory: A European Perspective. G. Bailey, ed. pp. 212–219. Cambridge University Press, Cambridge.

Kohen, J., 1986 Prehistoric Settlement in the Western Cumberland Plain: Resources, Environment and Technology. Ph.D. dissertation, Macquarie University.

Kohen, J., and R. Lampert, 1988 Hunters and Fishers in the Sydney Region. *In* Australians to 1788. Australians: A Historical Library. D. J. Mulvaney and J. P. White, eds. pp. 342–365. Sydney: Fairfax, Syme and Weldon Associates.

Layton, R., 1992 Australian Rock Art: A New Synthesis. Cambridge: Cambridge University Press.

Lewis, D., 1988 The Rock Paintings of Arnhem Land, Australia: Social, Ecological and Material Culture Change in the Post-Glacial Period. BAR International Series 415. Oxford: British Archaeological Reports.

Lourandos, H., 1985 Intensification and Australian Prehistory. *In* Prehistoric Hunter-Gatherer: The Emergence of Cultural Complexity. T. Price and J. Brown, eds. pp. 385–423. Academic Press, New York.

McConvell, P., 1996 Backtracking to Babel: The Chronology of Pama-Nyungan Expansion in Australia. Archaeology in Oceania 31:125–144.

McDonald, J., 1991 Archaeology and Art in the Sydney Region: Context and Theory in the Analysis of a Dual Medium Style. *In* Rock Art and Prehistory. P. Bahn and A. Rosenfeld, eds. pp. 78–85. Monograph 10. Oxford: Oxbow.

—— 1994 Dreamtime Superhighway: An Analysis of Sydney Basin Rock Art and Prehistoric Information Exchange. Ph.D. dissertation, Australian National University.

—— 1999 Bedrock Notions and Isochrestic Choice: Evidence for Localised Stylistic Patterning in the Engravings of the Sydney Region. Archaeology in Oceania 34:145–160.

—— 2000 AMS Dating Charcoal Drawings in the Sydney Region: Results and Issues. *In* Advances in Dating Australian Rock Images. G. Ward and C. Tuniz, eds. pp. 90–94. AURA Occasional Publication 10. Melbourne: Australian Rock Art Research Association, Inc.

McDonald, J., K. Officer, D. Donahue, T. Jull, J. Head and B. Ford, 1990 Investigating AMS: Dating Prehistoric Rock Art in the Sydney Sandstone Basin, NSW. Rock Art Research 7:83–92.

Mathews, R., 1897 The Burbung of the Darkinung Tribe. Proceedings of the Royal Society of Victoria 10:1–12.

—— 1901 The Thurrawal Language. Journal and Proceedings of the Royal Society of New South Wales 35:127–160.

Mathews, R., and M. Everitt, 1900 The Organization, Language and Initiation Ceremonies of the Aborigines of the South-East Coast of NSW. Journal and Proceedings of the Royal Society of NSW 34:262–281.

Maynard, L., 1977 Classification and Terminology in Australian Rock Art. *In* Form in Indigenous Art. P. Ucko, ed. pp. 385–402. Canberra: Australian Institute of Aboriginal Studies.

Morwood, M., 1987 The Archaeology of Social Complexity in South-Eastern Queensland. Proceedings of the Prehistoric Society 53:337–350.

—— 2002 Visions from the Past: The Archaeology of Australian Rock Art. Melbourne: Allen and Unwin.

Nobbs, M., and R. Dorn, 1988 Age Determinations for Rock Varnish Formation within Petroglyphs. Rock Art Research 5:108–146.

—— 1993 New Surface Exposure Ages for Petroglyphs from the Olary Province, South Australia. Archaeology in Oceania 27:199–220.

O'Connor, S., and P. Veth, 1996 A Preliminary Report on Recent Archaeological Research in the Semi-Arid/Arid Belt of Western Australia. Australian Aboriginal Studies 2:42–50.

O'Connor, S., P. Veth and C. Campbell, 1998 Serpent's Glen: Report on the First Pleistocene-Aged Occupation Sequence from the Western Desert. Australian Archaeology 46:12–22.

Peterson, N., 1976 The Natural and Cultural Areas of Aboriginal Australia: A Preliminary Analysis of Population Groupings with Adaptive Significance. *In* Tribes and Boundaries in Australia. N. Peterson, ed. pp. 50–71. Canberra and New Jersey: Australian Institute of Aboriginal Studies and Humanities Press.

Rosenfeld, A., 1993 A Review of the Evidence for the Emergence of Rock Art in Australia. *In* Sahul in Review: Pleistocene Archaeology in Australia, New Guinea and Island Melanesia at 10–30 Kyr B.P. M. Smith, M. Spriggs and B. Fankhauser, eds. pp. 71–80. Occasional Papers in Prehistory 24. Canberra: Department of Prehistory, Research School of Pacific Studies, Australian National University.

—— 2002 Rock Art as an Indicator of Changing Social Geographies in Central Australia. *In* Inscribed Landscapes: Marking and Making Places. B. David and M. Wilson, eds. pp. 61–78. Honolulu: University of Hawai'i Press.

Sackett, J., 1990 Style and Ethnicity in Archaeology: The Case for Isochrestism. *In* The Uses of Style in Archaeology. M. Conkey and C. Hastorf, eds. pp. 32–43. Cambridge: Cambridge University Press.

Smith, C., 1989 Designed Dreaming: Assessing the Relationship between Style, Social Structure and Environment in Aboriginal Australia. B.A. Honours dissertation, University of
New England.

Smith, M., 1988 The Pattern and Timing of Prehistoric Settlement in Central Australia.
Ph.D. dissertation, University of New England.

—— 1996 Prehistory and Human Ecology in Central Australia: An Archaeological Perspective. In Exploring Central Australia: Society, Environment and the 1894 Horn Expedition.
S. Morton and D. J. Mulvaney, eds. pp. 61–73. Chipping Norton: Surrey Beatty and Sons.

Smith, M., B. Fankhauser and M. Jercher, 1998 The Changing Provenance of Red Ochre at
Puritjarra Rockshelter, Central Australia: Late Pleistocene to Present. Proceedings of the
Prehistoric Society 64:275–292.

Soffer, O., 1987 Upper Palaeolithic Connubia, Refugia, and the Archaeological Record from
Eastern Europe. In The Pleistocene Old World: Regional Perspectives. O. Soffer, ed. pp.
333–348. Plenum Press, New York.

Sutton, P., and B. Rigsby, 1986 People with "Politicks": Management of Land and Person-
nel on Australia's Cape York Peninsula. In Resource Managers: North American and
Australian Hunter-Gatherers. N. Williams and E. Hunn, eds. pp. 155–172. Canberra:
Australian Institute of Aboriginal Studies.

Tench, W., 1961 [1789] A Narrative of the Expedition to Botany Bay: With an Account of
New South Wales, Its Productions, Inhabitants, &c.: to which is Subjoined, a List of the
Civil and Military Establishments at Port Jackson. London: J. Debrett.

Thorley, P., 1998 Pleistocene Settlement in the Australian Arid Zone: Occupation of an
Inland Riverine Landscape in the Central Australian Ranges. Antiquity 72:34–45.

Veth, P., 1993 Islands in the Interior: The Dynamics of Prehistoric Adaptations within the
Arid Zone of Australia. International Monographs in Prehistory 3. Ann Arbor, Michigan.

—— 1996 Current Archaeological Evidence from the Little and Great Sandy Deserts. In
Archaeology of Northern Australia: Regional Perspectives. P. Veth and P. Hiscock, eds.
pp. 50–65. Tempus 4. Brisbane: Anthropology Museum, University of Queensland.

—— 2000a Cycles of Aridity and Human Mobility: Risk-Minimization amongst Late
Pleistocene Foragers of the Western Desert, Australia. Paper presented at the Annual
Meeting of the Society for American Archaeology, Philadelphia.

—— 2000b Origins of the Western Desert Language: Convergence in Linguistic and
Archaeological Space and Time Models. Archaeology in Oceania 35:11–19.

Veth, P., and J. McDonald, 2002 Can Archaeology be used to Address the Principle of Exclusive Possession in Native Title? In After Captain Cook: The Archaeology of the Recent
Indigenous Past in Australia. R. Harrison and C. Williamson, eds. pp. 121–129. Archaeological Methods Series 8. Sydney: University of Sydney.

Veth, P., M. Smith and M. Haley, 2001 Kaalpi: The Archaeology of a Sandstone Outlier in
the Western Desert. Australian Archaeology 52:9–17.

Watchman, A., 1992 Doubtful Dates for Karolta Engravings. Australian Aboriginal Studies
92:51–55.

—— 1993 Evidence of a 25,000-Year-Old Pictograph in Northern Australia. Geoarchaeology 8:465–473.

Wiessner, P., 1983 Style and Information in Kalahari San Projectile Points. American Antiquity 48:253–76.

—— 1984 Reconsidering the Behavioral Basis for Style: A Case Study among the Kalahari
San. Journal of Anthropological Archaeology 3:190–234.

—— 1990 Is There a Unity to Style? In The Uses of Style in Archaeology., M. Conkey and
C. Hastorf, eds. pp. 105–112. Cambridge: Cambridge University Press.

Williams, N., 1986 A Boundary is to Cross: Observations on Yolgnu Boundaries and Permission. *In* Resource Managers: North American and Australian Hunter-Gatherers. N. Williams and E. Hunn, eds. pp. 131–145. Canberra: Australian Institute of Aboriginal Studies.

Wobst, H., 1977 Stylistic Behavior and Information Exchange. *In* For the Director: Research Essays in Honour of J. B. Griffen. C. Cleland, ed. pp. 317–342. Anthropological Papers 61. Ann Arbor: Museum of Anthropology, University of Michigan.

6

Closing the Distance: Interpreting Cross-Cultural Engagements through Indigenous Rock Art

Anne Clarke and Ursula Frederick

No living culture is so isolated that it does not touch another at its boundaries. No living culture is without influences from other cultures far and near. (Dening 1980:40)

"We can make any white man or Macassan," they say, "just like you take photographs. We do it by using our mind first, and then we carve." (Berndt and Berndt 1954:62)

An important and often implicit principle underpinning many contemporary interpretations in Australian archaeology is the recognition of the strength and intimacy of the attachment of Indigenous people to their land. The archaeological signatures of these ties to landscape are made tangible through the imprint of Indigenous actions on the ground through both secular and sacred activities. These relationships to land, and the associated social, moral, and spiritual geographies they shape, also incorporate the non-terrestrial environment of the sea. Seascapes, including currents, the motions of the waves, freshwater outflows from rivers, offshore islands and reefs, intertidal zones and marine life, are all places of belonging and becoming (Bradley 1998; Buku Larrngay Mulka 1999; McNiven 2004; McNiven and Feldman 2003; D. Rose 1996; N. Sharp 2002; Smyth 2001). The significance of this "saltwater country" to Indigenous people in both past and present is increasingly evident to archaeologists and anthropologists, particularly through recent research concerning systems of marine tenure (Meyers et al. 1996; Peterson and Rigsby 1998; Sharp 2002).

Unlike the land which is tangibly embedded with traces of the past, the permeable surface and fluidity of the sea wash away the actions, objects, and individuals that have passed upon it. Yet the sea also harbors a past. For Indigenous and non-Indigenous Australians alike, the sea is as significant as the land for our shared histories. It is understood as the space of arrival and departure and as a continuing source of sustenance. Indigenous Australians sing and perform the sea in ritual. In painting, sculpture, dance, and song they describe the immaterial features and the substance of its form. Seascapes are lived and depicted and the stories of the creative forces by which they were shaped are recalled in the motion, textures, and courses of the currents, waves, and flows. An Indigenous understanding of the sea is encoded visually in intimate detail, as Morphy describes for Yolngu art from northeast Arnhem Land where a particular diamond patterning may evoke equally,

> the roughness of the sea, the mixing together of salt and freshwater as the wet season floodwaters inundate the flood plains and strong currents rush out into the bay ... while the background patterns allude to the rich natural history of the landscape, to the sand crab as it scavenges on the beach removing debris before the tide wipes it clean again, the water boiling up under the swirling tail of the saltwater crocodile, the flash of the kingfisher as it dives into the water. Things seen briefly or even unseen, but that leave an impression in the eye. (2003:16)

For non-Indigenous Australians the sea also serves a central role in the foundation narratives of the colony, characterized in oceanic journeys, continental circumnavigations, and coastal explorations. The events, outcomes, and historical figures of these colonial endeavors are commemorated in song, story, and art by Indigenous and non-Indigenous Australians alike.

How can the study of rock art inform us about processes of cross-cultural interaction between indigenous people and outsiders beyond the immediate representation of the shock of the new and the unfamiliar? In this chapter we present a study of a particular rock art assemblage from Groote Eylandt in northern Australia. These paintings provide a visual narrative of how indigenous people chose to represent particular aspects of their encounters with other cultural groups, specifically Indonesian fishermen (Macassans) and European explorers and settlers. We examine the content and context of image production relating to boats to illustrate how an analysis of the design vocabulary of contact can provide access to a pictorial narrative of cross-cultural engagement beyond the documentation of the technological and biological novelties of encounter. We argue that consideration of the social, geographic, and historical contexts of rock art production as well as the content and form of the motifs can be used to examine the complexity of relationships, meanings, representations, and exchanges that formed out of the process of cross-cultural interaction between Indigenous people and outsiders in the recent past. As we illustrate through the brief study of boat paintings described in this paper, the images produced as a result of seeing, experiencing, and representing the arrival of outsiders and their watercraft form an important Indigenous archive of contact.

The Study Area

The Groote Eylandt archipelago is located about 630 kilometers east of Darwin and 43 kilometers east of the Arnhem Land coast, on the western side of the Gulf of Carpentaria (Figure 6.1). The archipelago consists of over one hundred islands,

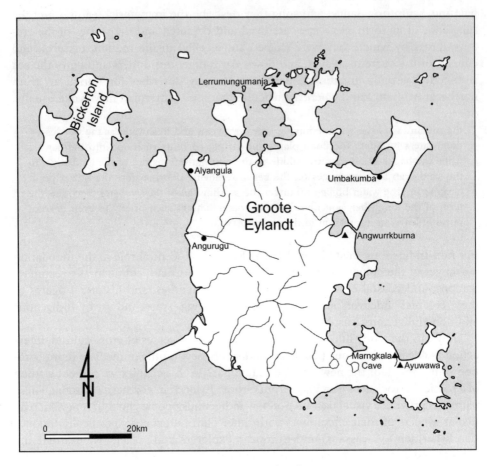

Figure 6.1 Groote Eylandt, showing places mentioned in the text

ranging in size from rocky outcrops a few tens of meters across, to substantial islands capable of sustaining permanent human populations. The complexity and extent of the marine environment and the wealth of its resources undoubtedly shaped the worldview of Indigenous people living on Groote Eylandt. Archaeological, ethnographic, and oral history sources indicate that in terms of social structure, land and sea tenure, economy, cosmology, and technology, the people of Groote Eylandt shared an intricate and intimate relationship with the sea (Clarke 1994; McCarthy 1960; Mountford 1956; Turner 1974, 1989; Tindale 1925–1926; Waddy 1988; Worsley 1954). Some of the stories linking the creation of this island landscape are significantly bound to the actions of various ancestral beings who emerged from, traveled across, or shaped the sea around them (Mountford 1956; Turner 1974, 1989). Today, the people of Groote Eylandt retain a strong relationship and living knowledge of their marine environment.

For the indigenous inhabitants of the Groote Eylandt archipelago the cross-cultural past encompassed "a multitude of experiences expressed in a variety of ways – the Aborigines' association with the Indonesian traders, their journeys to the

East India Archipelago, their intercourse with Torres Strait Islanders, Japanese, and Europeans" (Berndt and Berndt 1954:vi). Yet primarily, the people of Groote Eylandt experienced contact through two distinctive groups of outsiders, Macassan fishermen and European explorers/settlers. Both made their way into the lives and cultural consciousness of Groote Eylandt peoples via the sea.

The first series of cross-cultural encounters involved a seasonal bartering relationship with Indonesian fishing fleets from southern Sulawesi (Macknight 1976). The fishermen, often referred to as Malays in many 19th century texts, or more commonly as Macassans (Macassar was the major port of origin for many of the boats), came to northern Australia in search of commodities to sell in the marketplaces of island southeast Asia and beyond. The main focus of Asian commercial interest in the region was trepang (bêche de mer), but pearls, pearl shell, turtle shell, sandalwood, tin, manganese, and dried shark tails were also sought after by the trepangers (Berndt and Berndt 1954; Macknight 1976; Warner 1932; Worsley 1955). The archaeology, history, and operation of the trepang industry in Arnhem Land, or *marege* as it was known to the Macassans, have been described and analyzed in extensive detail by Macknight (1969a, 1972, 1976, 1986). Subsequent studies and historical accounts have broadened the geographical parameters and advanced our knowledge of the socio-cultural implications of the industry (Baker 1984; Clarke 1994, 2000a, 2000b; Mitchell 1994, 1996, 2000; Mulvaney 1975, 1989).

The advent of regular, seasonal visits by Macassan fishing fleets to the northern coast of Australia established a process of social and cultural interactions that left their mark on indigenous social institutions and practices as well as in the material record. This period of cross-cultural exchange had begun by at least A.D. 1650 and ceased in 1907 when the Australian government outlawed Macassan visits to the north Australian coast (Macknight 1976, 1986). Evidence relating to the indigenous experiences of Macassan contact exists in both material and non-material forms. Paintings of praus (Macassan boats) remain on rockshelter walls and archaeological deposits contain fragments of Indonesian and Chinese pottery, metal, glass, and other items of material culture introduced by the Macassans (Clarke 1994, 2000a, 2000b; Macknight 1976). The imprint of this cross-cultural exchange can also be traced through the subject matter of indigenous songs, stories, art, and ceremonies (Berndt and Berndt 1954; Keen 1977; Morphy 2001; Rose 1961; Tindale 1925–1926; Worsley 1955) and in the naming of local lands and places through the inclusion of Macassan loan words into Indigenous languages (Evans 1992, 1997; Urry and Walsh 1981; Walker and Zorc 1981). The adoption of Macassan items such as sails, boats, and flags as clan totems and the continuing use of Macassan personal names are all indicators of the depth of the relationships forged between Indigenous people and the Macassans.

The second series of encounters involved an initially sporadic yet intensifying engagement with European explorers which eventually saw the establishment of permanent settler societies which continue to this day. This began in A.D. 1623 when the Dutch vessels *Pera* and *Arnhem* sailed around the Arnhem Land coast (Sharp 1963; Schilder 1989). The region and its Indigenous population were first described as a result of Matthew Flinders's circumnavigation of Australia in

1802–1803. However, it was not until 1921 that there was a permanent European presence on Groote Eylandt, when the Church Missionary Society established a mission (Warren [1918] in Macknight 1969a:186–203; also Cole 1971:20–28; Dewar 1992:13; Tindale 1925–1926). Over the past century itinerant European-Australian fishermen visited Groote Eylandt for sometimes lengthy periods and the non-Indigenous population living permanently on the island swelled significantly with the establishment of a mining community in the 1960s (Cole 1971; Dewar 1992; Egan 1996). There is little material evidence relating to the earliest European encounters with Groote Eylandt's Indigenous population. The later history and anthropology concerning the socio-cultural changes brought about by the mission and mining settlement are well documented and contribute to our knowledge of the cross-cultural encounters we set out to discuss (Berndt and Berndt 1954; Kauffman 1978; Rose 1960, 1987; Tindale 1925–1926; Turner 1974, 1989; Waddy 1988; Worsley 1954).

Messing about with Boats

In the geographical context of islands, boats are the means by which outsiders arrived in Indigenous territories, visible at first on the distant horizon and then gradually coming into closer focus as they approach the shore. At face value, boats can be regarded simply as a technology invented to transport people and their products, tangible and intangible, across stretches of fresh and salt water. In the historical context of cross-cultural interactions, however, the boat becomes a site of many meanings and social interactions, some of which may be untangled from the ways in which Indigenous people chose to represent their form in rockshelters and caves around the coast of northern Australia. In the social context of the people sailing onboard, the boat is home, it becomes the entirety of their physical world, a site of cultural performance where relationships based on culturally defined social hierarchies are reenacted, reworked, and reinforced on a daily basis (Dening 1980). Once it reaches the territorial waters of a coastal community, the boat becomes a contact zone (after Clifford 1999), a place of transformation where opportunities, constraints, challenges, desires, and dangers are negotiated through the spaces in and around its physical presence.

Boats are thus vehicles of in-betweenness, mediating boundaries, forging connections, and serving to close the distance (both metaphorical and physical) between earth and water, here and there, this people and that people and, in some cosmological contexts, between being in this world and beyond being in this world. Boats can be powerful symbols that convey multi-layered meanings across time and space, between cultures, and through diverse social contexts. They are an especially appropriate metaphor for thinking about rock art production in the context of contact processes because the very act of representing outsiders, incorporating new motifs into an established visual language, bringing unfamiliar boats into their rockshelters and onto their land, are also acts of exploration, of closing distance, of voyaging and discovering. Boats are, in themselves, transitional objects and perhaps more than any other contact subject they may symbolize the material, social, and meta-physical worlds beyond our own horizon, serving to remind us that there are other places, other stories, and other people outside our own.

When we look at these images today we see, for the most part, what Indigenous people painted, and in recognizing that observation predicates description, record-ing, and communicating, we in turn experience seeing something of what they saw. By reading the content, stylistic attributes, and context of these observations we are attempting to look further into what these artists communicated about outsiders, to get a sense of what they knew and something of what they felt about having these people in their lives.

Boat images, when considered as an assemblage, may impart elements of these different kinds of observations and cross-cultural relationships. To explore the potential of boat depictions as a record of the social processes of cross-cultural inter-action, we conducted a preliminary analysis of 23 boats recorded at nine rock art sites on Groote Eylandt. We use this analysis to make a number of observations and interpretations about the contact between Groote Eylandters and outsiders.

Boats and Rock Art on Groote Eylandt

The visual culture of Groote Eylandt conveys a strong sense of the seascape and its significance is supported by the numerous marine motifs in the rock art assem-blage of the archipelago (Chaloupka 1996; McCarthy 1960; Mountford 1956; Rose 1942; Tindale 1925–1926; Turner 1973). Boats are a recurring motif in the rock art assemblage of Groote Eylandt. In the absence of other obvious representations, boats are the common denominator for picturing Macassan fishermen, European explorers, Anglo-Australian missionaries, and, quite possibly, other cultural groups. More ambiguously, it would seem that boats, in the form of bark and dugout sailing canoes, are also an important motif employed by Groote Eylandters for represent-ing themselves and/or other Indigenous Australian cultures.

Images of both praus and European sailboats may be clearly linked with their associated outsider groups because these kinds of vessels, as far as is known, were never built, owned, or operated solely by Indigenous people. Dugout canoes, although they demonstrate a technology derived from contact with Macassans, were made and used by Indigenous people and cannot be identified with certainty as visual representations of Macassans alone.

The significance of Macassan contact with Indigenous Australia is often described or framed as a technological watershed in Indigenous society which saw the introduction of new items of material culture including metal axes, knives, and fishhooks, pottery, glass, harpoon technology, and dugout canoes (see Clarke 2000b for discussion). It is not surprising then that the technological features of Macas-san sailing vessels are emphasized in the many descriptions of praus provided in eyewitness accounts, historical texts, and images. This accent on technology has extended to the study of Groote Eylandt rock art where praus have been discussed in largely descriptive accounts, identifying the technological features of the boats.

The attention to detail displayed in prau paintings has allowed authors (for example, Chaloupka 1996; Mountford 1956; Rose 1942; Tindale 1925–1926; Turner 1974) to focus on, for example, the configuration of the masts and sails, the decking, the hull structure, the rudders, and the internal storage of dugout canoes and cooking pots. While these attributes are informative, we argue that by examining these features in association with other stylistic attributes and by considering spatial patterning we may be able to move beyond technological and functional interpretations, to consider the complexity of social meaning embodied in the experiences of encountering, seeing, and depicting boats and the associated social dimensions of the cross-cultural relationships they convey.

For example, boats can be experienced from both the outside and inside. An external observational perspective will reveal features and figures both familiar and unfamiliar above the water line and in profile. An internal experience of a boat will produce a different understanding of the spatial layout of the boat, its contents, people, and the activities that took place onboard. From an inside or onboard view the boat becomes a different place. Experiencing the boat from an inside perspective will also create a different relationship with those for whom the boat is temporarily home; the people come into closer range and greater detail. Following this, we can ask whether there are observable differences in the ways that Indigenous Groote Eylandters chose to depict Macassan praus and European sailboats and what these differences might denote about the variable nature of the contact experience for Groote Eylandters.

Archaeological evidence indicates that rock paintings of Macassan praus are not unique to the Groote Eylandt archipelago (Chaloupka 1993; McCarthy 1960; Mulvaney 1989). Indeed as other scholars attest, images of praus occur in rock art sites along the coast of northern Australia (Chaloupka 1993, 1996; Mulvaney pers. comm. 2003; Taçon pers. comm. 2003), a distribution pattern broadly conforming with the geographical extent of Macassan visits to Australia. An intriguing point about the prau images of Groote Eylandt is that they are, for the most part, the *only* obvious Macassan subject consistently depicted in rock art. Despite the long history of cross-cultural engagement and material exchange, there are relatively few Macassan objects, other than praus, recorded in Groote Eylandt rock art. Of these, the majority are depicted inside praus, for example pots or dugout canoes inside the hull. Macassan material culture is literally and figuratively depicted as contained within the social space of the outsider, their praus. On the surface at least it would appear that the wealth of material culture associated with Macassans is largely under-represented in the rock art record of Groote Eylandt and that this history of interactions is communicated most consistently through the depiction of praus.

Chaloupka (1996:138) draws attention to the fact that the prau images "document in their detail the artists' intimate knowledge of the vessels' function" and show "considerable familiarity with the rigging and gear of Macassan praus." He uses these details to try to identify the particular type of prau technology in use, its time period, and its place of origin within Indonesia. While distinguishing individual details can be rewarding, it may also be misleading if due consideration is not given to the patterns of representation in the overall assemblage. As Morphy has pointed out:

In most of Australia paintings may be viewed constructively, not as individual objects, but as members of sets. Each member of the set is an instantiation of an underlying template or core structure associated with the set . . . Such sets are readily referred to by Aboriginal people and reflect indigenous conceptualizations . . . Paintings belonging to the same set may share more in common than a particular design element. Frequently they also share a common structural arrangement of elements. (1999:15)

A number of technological features of the praus have been remarked upon consistently in the literature, and to some extent we may presume that these represent the most visible or otherwise vital attributes of praus. Tindale (1925–1926:98) describes them as "the curiously shaped bow and stern, the tripod mast, the double steering paddles, and even the number and disposition of the ropes in the rigging." After concluding that there was no one standard archetype or model for a Macassan prau, Macknight (1976:25–26) identified a number of specific terms used in southern Sulawesi to describe certain kinds of praus and their distinguishing features. Chaloupka (1996:135) suggests that these variations in prau design and construction were significant enough to Macassans that they had different terms to describe them. The extent to which these variations were important to the Indigenous people who observed, encountered, and sailed upon them may be explored through a similar analysis of key attributes of the praus painted in the rock art. If the technological features of these praus were the overwhelming focus of Groote Eylandters' observations, then it would be expected that these key differences would be recorded.

An analysis of certain features in the praus, in accordance with Tindale (1925–1926), Mountford (1956), and Turner (1974), illustrates a number of interesting points. Mountford's tracing of a prau painted on a bark panel and collected by him in 1948 (Mountford 1956:99–100) points to the "names and disposition of rigging: the paddles (*miaitja*), rope (*bukuna*), rope (*panalunta*), mast (*palia*), rope (*pia pia*), rope (*lula*) and the sail (*gumbala*)." It is interesting to note that, some 20 years later, Turner's informants used many of the same words as recorded by Tindale (1925–1926) and were able to identify the same stylized features from a rock painting as those recorded by Mountford. Turner (1974:Plate 5, also pp. 54 and 180–181) distinguished additional features of the prau including bow (*andja*) anchor (*balangwa*), rudder (*gulinga*), booms (*bawa* and *bilagwanga*), and other types of ropes and rigging (*buguna, bunalunda, gandaija, lunglunga*). We analyzed the assemblage of prau paintings with regard to five of the key prau attributes identified by both Mountford (1956) and Turner (1974): sail, rudder(s), bowsprit, mast, and Y-shaped line rigging.

One of the 15 praus has deteriorated above the hull. Of the remainder we observed that eight display rudders, with all but one exhibiting double rudders. Eight praus (not the same eight) incorporate the tripod mast, one prau has four single masts while the remaining praus have no masts visible (this may be owed in part to deterioration of the rock surface). A sail is present in 11 of the praus while nine include the bowsprit. Nine show the central Y-shaped lines below the boom (although one is in a different configuration). In total, 60 percent of the praus display four or more of the five features identified while the remaining 40 percent display two or fewer of these features.

These trends suggest that praus are represented through a consistent design vocabulary. However, the manner and degree to which the different features are combined appear to be less systematic. So while there is a stylistic consistency in the use of certain design attributes they are combined in a variety of ways. The use of consistent design attributes allows the paintings to be recognized as representations of praus yet the variation in application of these features also creates unique prau depictions. This means that the prau paintings share a resemblance yet at the same time each possesses a degree of individuality. In this way the prau paintings can be seen to operate at two scales of representation. On one hand they reflect the development of a tradition that is borne out of a long-term process of interaction, while on the other hand each prau has the capacity to encode particularities which may reflect a specific event or historical encounter.

Prau Paintings

By comparison with all other boats in the rock art assemblage analyzed, representations of Macassan praus are dominant in terms of number, size, and in elaboration and attention to detail. They form 65 percent of the boat assemblage, with European sailing boats and luggers representing 26 percent and the remaining two boats identified as modern. The dominance of prau images is likely to be a reflection of the regularity of Macassan visitation and the history of interactions between Macassan fishermen and Groote Eylandt people. The repetitive use of the prau motif is particularly evocative at the coastal site of Marngkala Cave (Figure 6.2), where the superimposed layering of praus one over another creates a strong visual impression of an enduring and repeated form of cross-cultural interaction.

All of the Macassan praus in the assemblage were produced as paintings (wet pigment) while two-thirds of the European sailing vessels were drawn in dry pigment. This indicates that the praus were painted with consideration and after substantial preparation, whereas the sailboat drawings may have been a more immediate and spontaneous representation, made in response to direct observations or fleeting encounters. All of the dry-pigment drawings were produced on accessible surfaces at rockshelters adjacent to coastal waters where European boats may have been observed from some distance. This spatial patterning and the use of dry charcoal supports the idea that the European encounters elicited quick, spontaneous sketches.

Prau images also feature in coastal sites from where Macassans may have been observed at sea but they also occur inland, some at considerable distance from open water. For example, there are prau paintings at Yinumalyuwalumanja 01, a large rockshelter some 10–15 kilometers from the coast. At Angwurrkburna, over 500 meters from Salt Lake and 3 kilometers from the coast, a large, detailed prau is painted, out of hands' reach, on the ceiling of the shelter. It appears that unlike European boats these prau images were internalized within memory and carried further inland, away from the center of the cross-cultural stage. This demonstrates

Figure 6.2 The Marngkala Cave site showing superimposition of praus

a strong familiarity with Macassan praus but also symbolizes an incorporation of Macassan people deeper within the social landscape of Groote Eylandt.

The preferential use of color and stylistic use of silhouette, outline, and infill also distinguishes praus from the sailing boats. Of the total boat assemblage, 52 percent were depicted using three or more colors. All of these polychromatic paintings are praus. By contrast, only 17 percent of the boat motifs are monochromatic and all but one of these are European vessels. In terms of silhouette, outline, and infill characteristics, only the European sailing boats were produced using just one stylistic attribute, although some exhibit two. In contrast, all of the Macassan praus were painted utilizing two or more of these styles and indeed the majority 67 percent appear as a combination of silhouette, outline, and infill.

The European sailboats are generally schematic in form, displaying the prominent features of masts, sails, and occasionally a rudder. The sails are always apparent and unfurled. This could suggest that the nature of the experience with European sailing boats was largely an observational encounter made from a distance while the boat was at sea. The majority of Macassan praus also appear with open sails but the detail in form, and emphasis on rigging and internal structure together with the content of these boats, suggests a different level of experience and observation to the relatively obscure European sailboats.

While the visual record of praus reflects a certain degree of convention in terms of the relative proportions of sail to hull, there is a degree of diversity in sail shape and angle to suggest scope for individualized representations or actualized events. It is interesting to note in this context that Macknight observed that the sails of these praus were so designed that they could be "inclined in any direction – straight up, slanting or horizontal – whichever suits best for the wind" (1976:25).

There is only one prau recorded from Groote Eylandt depicted with its mast lowered (Chaloupka 1996:Figure 6d), perhaps suggesting that it was anchored for a longer stay. This may imply that the majority of prau paintings, with masts up and sails open, depict the praus as they are arriving or departing. Given that once they had arrived in a particular bay Macassans spent most of their time diving for trepang or based onshore, the praus are likely to have been moored with sails down, as shown in illustrations from the 19th century (Macknight 1969b:154–155; Mulvaney 1975:32–33 Plate 7; Westall 1781–1850). Furthermore, six of the praus in this assemblage incorporate a figure at the top of the mast. This may be significant when we consider the Berndts' observation that

> The Arnhem Land Aborigines took careful notice of some of the religious customs of these traders. When the mast of a prau was erected, as it prepared to set out on the journey to another settlement or to return to the Celebes, a prayer-man would climb the mast and chant (djelauwa) (1954:45–46).

This detail in the depictions of praus shows an intimacy with the boat and an understanding of its internal geography, and implicitly its crew. There is a focus on the human interactions, with anthropomorphic figures apparently engaged in activities in different parts of the prau.

Clearly, Groote Eylandters chose to represent Macassan boats with an open sail, in varying perspectives, as if sailing. This is interesting because we know from other archaeological evidence, oral history, and historical sources that the Macassans did engage with Aboriginal people on land, trading their material culture and spending much of their time processing trepang at their beach camps. This, in conjunction with the dominant posture (82 percent) of the anthropomorphic figures with arms stretched upwards (as Chaloupka 1996 indicates), suggests Groote Eylandters placed an obvious emphasis on the arrival and the departure of Macassan praus, and on the people and cargo they carried.

And while each prau is different, this emphasis on depicting Macassan praus at sail is one of several key conventions that seem to dictate the representation of praus. The formality of an established canon of common attributes, which includes mast, rudders, decking, rigging, sail, is again suggestive of an enduring and established set of relationships that are both recalled and recognizable. The singularity, lack of particular stylistic conventions, and the obvious absence of people, relative to the Macassan boat images, imply a social distance and a lack of understanding between Groote Eylandters and the Europeans embodied in the subject of the sailing boats.

People on Boats

As vehicles of transportation, boats have a definite social dimension. Whether this was understood and communicated by Groote Eylandt people through rock art may be explored by considering the presence/absence of people in rock art. Of the 23

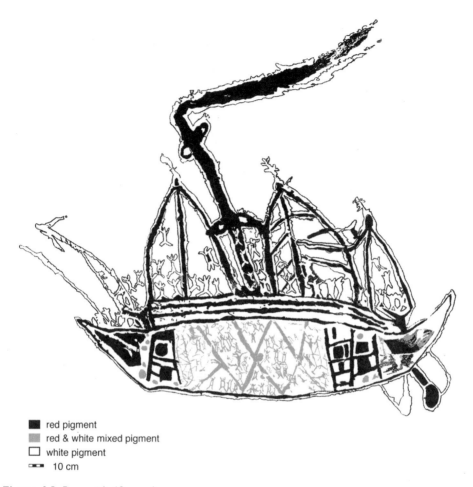

red pigment
red & white mixed pigment
white pigment
10 cm

Figure 6.3 Prau with 68 people

boats analyzed, 16 (14 praus and two European boats) include anthropomorphic figures, which we interpret to be people. Interestingly, all but one of the praus incorporate people. In comparison, only two of the European sailboats and one of the modern European boats also depict people. It is clear that people are not as strongly associated with European boats and this may suggest that the people on board these boats were either unseen or unknown. This advances the suggestion that European boats, and the peoples associated with them, were glimpsed or sighted rather than directly encountered.

In contrast to the European sailboats, praus are quite clearly socially laden. Anthropomorphic figures are dispersed throughout the internal composition of the prau, up the mast, on the top sail, in cabins, below deck, and in varied states of animation. These figures imbue the praus with a dynamism and their placement symbolically entwines the social with the technical features of the prau. Nine out of the 14 peopled praus show more than five people onboard and one prau has around 68 figures (Figure 6.3). Out of the 250 anthropomorphic figures depicted in association with boats, 95 percent occur on the praus. Anthropomorphic figures, in terms of number and composition, and in frequency of association are clearly a vital part of prau depictions. This lends support to the emphasis placed on the social aspects of Groote Eylandter and Macassan relationships.

Compositionally, the figures are an important component of the prau paintings, clearly integrated within the linear design of the praus. This compositional structure reflects that the people are an integral feature of the praus, not separate to it. The position and the gestural emphasis with which the figures are depicted highlight the significance of the people within the boats. The majority of figures are represented face on, as if directly engaging the painter and viewers of the prau. This directness implies a certain familiarity between the artist, subject, and viewers. A major proportion (82 percent) of these figures is depicted with arms upraised, as if they were waving. Another nine percent appear as if actively involved in the mechanics of sailing, several leaning in profile, arms engaged with the mast and rigging.

A major proportion (89 percent) of all anthropomorphic figures associated with the praus are painted in white silhouette, exhibited in all but one of the praus. This shows a strong preference for color selection, leading to the possibility that white anthropomorphs may have been intended to represent Macassans. The dominance of white figures in prau paintings is especially notable when considered in the context of McCarthy's (1960:398) comprehensive analysis of color frequencies of over 2,400 motifs recorded in sites across the Groote Eylandt archipelago. Overall, monochromatic red is the dominant color preference (84 percent), while monochromatic white is represented by only 0.4 percent of McCarthy's assemblage.

While white is an obvious preference in depicting anthropomorphs, it is similarly interesting that half of the praus incorporate figures of different colors within the one composition. One prau has 35 white, 12 yellow, and one red figure appearing throughout different parts of the boat. This could indicate that the Groote Eylandters were not only conscious of different ethnicities onboard the praus but, as Chaloupka (1996:139) has suggested, may also have represented this with different colored pigments. Whether they were intentionally depicting their own people amongst Macassans or the different ethnicities of the crew remains a matter of conjecture. Nevertheless, the possibility that Groote Eylandt artists may have distinguished figures on the basis of some ethnic, social, or cultural difference only highlights the artists' knowledge of and interest in conveying the social complexities of their interactions with outsiders. The possibility that they were recording and accommodating these socio-cultural differences within a single image plane adds weight to the interpretation that praus and images of praus were used as mediating devices or as visual codes, acting to close the difference and distance between the observer and the observed.

Conclusions

The collective set of features – the open sails, the animated gestures of the people, and the interior details – all give the prau paintings a dynamism that is evocative of mobility. People are depicted in various states of activity, holding onto the ropes, climbing the mast, hoisting the sail, and fishing off the back of the boat. The momentum achieved in these paintings gives each prau an astonishingly narrative dimension, leading us to conclude that these paintings may indeed reflect actual events in the artists' experiences or familiar scenes in the artists' or communities' lives. But most importantly we reiterate that these are not observational recordings alone. The location and aspect of the shelters, the detailed observations of the praus, and the preparation required for the production of these images all point to the paintings being important in the social performances of remembering and telling. The praus were a way of accessing the recollections and memories of past events in both specific and general details. If artists were depicting actual episodes in their history of Macassan interaction, it is telling that the moments they consistently chose to recall were arrivals and departures. This repetitive emphasis evokes a sense of grieving and loss, joy and welcome, and it represents an intentional choice on the part of the artist.

We argue that the boat images, praus in particular, represent not merely a fascination with new forms or introduced technology but reflect Indigenous social agency and cross-cultural relations. They represent creative and communicative acts which attempt to close the distance between one place, one group of people and another. They are images that seek to unravel difference, to distinguish but also to connect with outsiders through the shared platform of the sea. Dissimilarities in the representation of Macassan and European boats indicate further that Indigenous artists distinguished and asserted the differences in their experiences of these two groups of outsiders.

The prau paintings convey the social relationships between the Macassans and Groote Eylandters. The praus are neither wholly inside nor entirely outside the Groote Eylandt social landscape. The prau can be seen as a kind of map, an embodiment of the extent of these relationships, at times external while at others intimately knowing and part of the indigenous knowledge system. We suggest that the form of the prau has a performative force. It is a vessel and vehicle of connections and crossings, while the conventions, complexities, and details of the paintings act as both a mnemonic and a metaphorical embodiment of the Groote Eylandters' experience of contact with Macassans. This is most evident when the praus are compared to the other boat motifs.

In conjunction with the use of polychromatic wet pigments, diversity in detail and stylistic attributes, the appearance of Macassan praus in inland sites provides some indication that these boat motifs were becoming or had become a feature of the artistic tradition of Groote Eylandt people. In contrast, the cursory appearance of European sailing boats in the assemblage would seem to reflect the sporadic nature of Indigenous relations with Europeans. The singularity of each painting, the lack of detail, and the obvious absence of people relative to the Macassan boat images imply a process of contact defined more by distance than by intimacy.

Clear trends in the depiction of Macassan praus indicate that Groote Eylandters were making choices about how they saw and chose to represent Macassans. Within this framework of representation there is a considerable degree of flexibility in the expression of broadly conventionalized forms. The totality of stylistic conventions renders each prau collectively and conformably recognizable. It is the varying combination of different design elements that gives each of the praus an individuality while still conforming to a general set of stylistic conventions regarding form, content, and media. This pattern, of difference encompassed by sameness, is also reflective of the history of Groote Eylandters' interactions with Macassans. The regularity and predictability of the seasonal visits would also incorporate a degree of variation engendered by encounters with different crews and different boats over time appearing with a sense of sameness; one prau at first seems to be depicted much like any other. But the diversity with which these conventions are applied also lends the paintings individuality. Each represents perhaps a different prau, a different year, a different crew, and a different experience. The prau paintings embody the basic characteristics of the Indigenous experience of cross-cultural interactions with Macassans, that is, annual variation within a seasonal pattern of continuity.

We recognize that in making stylistic choices Indigenous artists were exposing something of their position in relation to these outsiders. And we seek to examine the rock art in the context of knowing that while people are making innovations in their artistic vocabulary, they are also reassessing their own artistic conventions for a range of reasons. While these boat images appear as new forms within the context of a longer rock art tradition, they did not retain their newness forever. The superimpositioning of praus at Marngkala rockshelter is testimony to this point (Figure 6.2). At some point these praus were no longer "new." They perhaps shifted to represent what they "knew." People paint what they know: their lives, their experiences, the world around them. Rather than representing merely the shock of the new, the incorporation of praus within the artistic traditions of Groote Eylandt suggests that what was known expanded to close the distance between different places, peoples, and possessions.

The potential for examining boat motifs as a source of information about cross-cultural interactions is much greater than the observations put forward here, and with specific regard to the rock art of Groote Eylandt the intricacy of detail on many of the boats motifs will provide a great opportunity for more in-depth analyses. What we have illustrated in this chapter is that Groote Eylandt artists not only presented their observations, but displayed preferences in the depiction of certain cross-cultural forms. The rock art exhibits conventions of cross-cultural representation some of which, in the case of Macassan praus, endure to this day in contemporary bark paintings and printed works on paper.

In representing outsiders, by figuratively drawing them into their own landscape and visual culture, Indigenous artists demonstrate acts of observation, enquiry, and also an intentionality to grapple with difference, to comprehend and communicate something of the world outside their own. Interestingly, Groote Eylandt people chose to represent outsiders through depicting their boats. This shows us something of the artists' maritime worldview and it demonstrates that the paintings themselves symbolize the performance of cross-cultural interaction. It tells us that they recognized something in common with these outsiders and in choosing to represent their boats it seems to us that they were finding some understanding of these outsiders, a common platform of connection, a shared relationship with the sea. The rock art of Groote Eylandt demonstrates that paintings themselves symbolize the performance of cross-cultural interaction.

REFERENCES

Baker, R., 1984 Macassan Site Survey Report. Report to the Northern Territory Museum and the Australian Heritage Commission.

Berndt R., and C. Berndt, 1954 Arnhem Land. Its History and Its People. Melbourne: F. W. Cheshire.

Bradley, J., 1998 "We Always Look North": Yanuwa Identity and the Maritime Environment. *In* Customary Marine Tenure in Australia. N. Peterson and B. Rigsby, eds. pp. 125–141. Sydney: Oceania Publications.

Buku Larrngay Mulka, 1999 Saltwater. Yirrkala Bark Paintings of Sea Country. Sydney: Jennifer Isaacs Publishing.

Chaloupka, G., 1993 Journey in Time. Sydney: Reed.

——1996 Praus in Marege: Makassan Subjects in Aboriginal Rock Art of Arnhem Land, Northern Territory, Australia. Anthropologie 34:131–142.

Clarke, A., 1994 Winds of Change: An Archaeology of Contact in the Groote Eylandt Archipelago, Northern Australia. Ph.D. dissertation, Australian National University.

——2000a Time, Tradition and Transformation: The Archaeology of Intercultural Encounters on Groote Eylandt, Northern Australia. *In* The Archaeology of Difference: Negotiating Cross-Cultural Engagements in Oceania. R. Torrence and A. Clarke, eds. pp. 142–181. London: Routledge.

——2000b "The Moormans Trowsers": Aboriginal and Macassan Interactions and the Changing Fabric of Indigenous Social Life. *In* East of Wallace's Line: Studies of Past and Present Maritime Cultures of the Indo-Pacific Region. S. O'Connor and P. Veth, eds. pp. 315–335. Modern Quaternary Research in Southeast Asia 16. Rotterdam: A. A. Balkema.

Clifford, J., 1999 Museums as Contact Zones. *In* Representing the Nation. A Reader. Histories, Heritage and Museums. D. Boswell and J. Evans, eds. pp. 435–458. London: Routledge.

Cole, K., 1971 Groote Eylandt Pioneer, A Biography of the Reverend Hubert Ernest de Mey Warren, Pioneer Missionary and Explorer Among the Aborigines of Arnhem Land. Melbourne: Church Missionary Historical Publications Trust.

Dening, G., 1980 Islands and Beaches: Discourse on a Silent Land Marquesas 1174–1880. Honolulu: University of Hawai'i Press.

Dewar, M., 1992 The "Black War" in Arnhem Land. Missionaries and the Yolngu 1908–1940. Darwin: North Australian Research Unit.

Egan, T., 1996 Justice All Their Own: the Caledon Bay and Woodah Island Killings 1932–1933. Melbourne: Melbourne University Press.

Evans, N., 1992 Macassan Loanwords in Top End Languages. Australian Journal of Linguistics 12:45–91.

——1997 Macassan Loanwords and Linguistic Stratification in Western Arnhem Land. *In* Archaeology and Linguistics: Aboriginal Australia in Global Perspective. P. McConvell and N. Evans, eds. pp. 237–260. Oxford: Oxford University Press.

Kauffman, P., 1978 The New Aborigines: The Politics of Tradition in the Groote Eylandt Area of Arnhem Land. M.A. dissertation, Australian National University.

Keen, I., 1977 Sand Sculptures in Context from Arnhem Land. *In* Form in Indigenous Art. Ucko, P., ed. pp. 165–183. Canberra: Australian Institute of Aboriginal Studies.

Macknight, C., 1969a The Farthest Coast. A Selection of Writings Relating to the History of the Northern Coast of Australia. Melbourne: Melbourne University Press.

——1969b The Macassans: A Study of the Early Trepang Industry Along the Northern Territory Coast. Ph.D. dissertation, Australian National University.

——1972 Macassans and Aborigines. Oceania 42:283–319.

——1976 The Voyage to Marege. Macassan Trepangers in Northern Australia. Melbourne: Melbourne University Press.

——1986 Aborigines and Macassans. Archaeology in Oceania 21:69–75.

McCarthy, F., 1960 The Cave Paintings of Groote Eylandt and Chasm Island. *In* Anthropology and Nutrition. C. Mountford, ed. pp. 297–414. The American–Australian Scientific Expedition to Arnhem Land 1948, vol. 2. Melbourne: Melbourne University Press.

McNiven, I., 2004 Saltwater People: Spiritscapes, Maritime Rituals and the Archaeology of Australian Indigenous Seascapes. World Archaeology 35:329–349.

McNiven, I., and R. Feldman, 2003 Ritually Orchestrated Seascapes: Hunting Magic and Dugong Bone Mounds in Torres Strait, NE Australia. Cambridge Archaeological Journal 13:169–194.

Meyers, G., M. O'Dell, G. Wright and S. Muller, 1996. A Sea Change in Land Rights Law: The Extension of Native Title to Australia's Offshore Areas. Native Title Research Unit Legal Research Monograph. Canberra: Aboriginal Studies Press.

Mitchell, S., 1994 Culture Contact and Indigenous Economies on the Cobourg Peninsula Northwestern Arnhem Land. Ph.D. dissertation, Northern Territory University.

——1996 Dugongs and Dugouts, Sharp Tacks and Shellbacks: Macassan Contact and Aboriginal Marine Hunting on the Cobourg Peninsula, Northwestern Arnhem Land. *In* Indo-Pacific Prehistory: The Chiang Mai Papers, vol. 2. I. Glover and P. Bellwood, eds. pp. 181–191. Bulletin of the Indo-Pacific Prehistory Association 15. Canberra and Jakarta: Indo-Pacific Prehistory Association and Asosiasi Prehistorisi Indonesia.

——2000 Guns or Barter? Indigenous Exchange Networks and the Mediation of Conflict in Post-Contact Western Arnhem Land. *In* The Archaeology of Difference: Negotiating Cross-Cultural Engagements in Oceania. R. Torrence and A. Clarke, eds. pp. 182–214. London: Routledge.

Morphy, H., 1999 Encoding the Dreaming – A Theoretical Framework for the Analysis of Representational Processes in Australian Aboriginal Art. Australian Archaeology, 49:13–22.

——2001 Ancestral Connections: Art and an Aboriginal System of Knowledge. Chicago: University of Chicago Press.

——2003 Buwayak: Surface and Inner Form. *In* Buwayak Invisibility. Exhibition Catalogue 16–17, Sydney: Annandale Galleries.

Mountford, C., 1956 The Art of Groote Eylandt. *In* Art, Myth and Symbolism. C. Mountford, ed. pp.19–106. Records of the American–Australian Arnhem Land Expedition to Arnhem Land, vol. 1. Melbourne: Melbourne University Press.

Mulvaney, D., 1975 The Prehistory of Australia. Melbourne: Penguin.

——1989 Encounters in Place. Outsiders and Aboriginal Australians 1606–1985. St Lucia: University of Queensland Press.

Peterson, N., and B. Rigsby, eds., 1998 Customary Marine Tenure in Australia. Oceania Monograph 48. Sydney: Oceania Publications.

Rose, F., 1942 Paintings of the Groote Eylandt Aborigines. Oceania 13:170–176.

——1960 Classification of Kin, Age Structure and Marriage amongst the Groote Eylandt Aborigines. Berlin: Akadmeie Verlag.

——1961 The Indonesians and the Genesis of Groote Eylandt Society, Northern Australia. Beitrage zur Volkerforschung, Veröffentlichungen des Museums fur Volkerkunde zu Leipzig, heft II.

——1987 The Traditional Mode of Production of the Australian Aborigines. Sydney: Angus and Robertson.

Rose, D., 1996 Nourishing Terrains. Australian Aboriginal Views of Landscape and Wilderness. Canberra: Australian Heritage Commission.

Schilder, G., 1989 From Secret to Common Knowledge – the Dutch Discoveries. *In* Studies from Terra Australis to Australia. J. Hardy and A. Frost, eds. pp. 71–86. Canberra: Highland Press.

Sharp, A., 1963 The Discovery of Australia. Oxford: Oxford University Press.

Sharp, N., 2002 Saltwater People. The Waves of Memory. Sydney: Allen and Unwin.

Smyth, D., 2001 Management of Sea Country: Indigenous People's Use and Management of Marine Environments. *In* Working on Country. Contemporary Indigenous Management of Australia's Lands and Coastal Regions. R. Baker, J. Davies and E. Young, eds. pp. 60–74. Oxford: Oxford University Press.

Tindale, N., 1925–1926 Natives of Groote Eylandt and of the West Coast of the Gulf of Carpentaria, Parts 1–2. Records of the South Australian Museum 3:61–143.

Turner, D., 1973 The Rock Art of Bickerton Island in Comparative Perspective. Oceania 43:286–325.

——1974 Tradition and Transformation. A Study of Aborigines in the Groote Eylandt Area, Northern Australia. Australian Aboriginal Studies 53. Canberra: Australian Institute of Aboriginal Studies.

——1989 Return to Eden. A Journey through the Promised Landscape of Amagalyuagba. New York: Peter Lang Publishing.

Urry, J., and M. Walsh, 1981 The Lost "Macassar Language" of Northern Australia. Aboriginal History 5:91–108.

Waddy, J., 1988 Classification of Plants and Animals from a Groote Eylandt Point of View, vols. 1 & 2. North Australia Research Unit Monograph. Darwin: Australian National University.

Walker, A., and D. Zorc, 1981 Austronesian Loanwords in Yolngu-Matha of Northeast Arnhem Land. Aboriginal History 5:109–134.

Warner, W., 1932 Malay Influence on Aboriginal Cultures of North-eastern Arnhem Land. Oceania II:476–495.

Westall, W., 1781–1850 The Malay fleet [picture]. *In* Drawings by William Westall. Canberra: National Library of Australia collection.

Worsley, P., 1954 The Changing Social Structure of the Wanindiljaugwa. Ph.D. dissertation, Australian National University.

——1955 Early Asian Contacts with Australia. Past and Present 7:1–11.

Part II
The Pacific

7

Archaeology in Melanesia: A Case Study from the Western Province of the Solomon Islands

Richard Walter and Peter Sheppard

In 1991 Roger Green introduced the concepts of Near and Remote Oceania into the literature of Pacific anthropology (Green 1991a). His aim was twofold: first, to discourage the comparative use of the terms "Melanesia" and "Polynesia" in Oceanic culture history, and second, to highlight the environmental differences between the two regions and the implications of these for human colonization and economic adaptation (see Figure 1.1). In culture-historical terms Polynesia is a phylogenetic unit: All daughter communities descend from a small founder population that settled the core region of Fiji–West Polynesia some three millennia ago. From there, and following a period of formative social and linguistic development in relative isolation, the archipelagoes of Polynesia were colonized in a series of generally eastward-trending migrations. This historical reality is expressed in the unity of Polynesian language, biology, and socio-cultural practices (Kirch and Green 1987, 2001). Melanesia, on the other hand, has no such historical unity. Instead it is inhabited by a mosaic of culturally and linguistically diverse peoples with various historical relations and complex patterns of social and political interaction. Thus "Melanesia" remains a purely geographic term, while Polynesia conveys both geographic and culture-historical meaning.

Archaeology in Melanesia and Polynesia

We accept the arguments put forward by Green that "Melanesia" and "Polynesia" are not equivalent typological units and that the terms "Near" and "Remote" Oceania convey a more meaningful historical division of Oceanic island geography than that implied by the classical terminologies. But we are concerned not to lose sight of the meaningful differences that exist between the archaeology of these two geographic regions: Melanesia and Polynesia. Our contention is that there are environmental and cultural differences between Melanesia and Polynesia which have had a profound influence on the course of Pacific archaeology. Archaeology has to a large extent followed different paths in the two regions, leading to big differences in the relative quality and quantity of archaeological knowledge. In this chapter we begin with a brief comparative overview of Pacific archaeology in which we point to one or two salient areas where the archaeologies of Melanesia and Polynesia have differed. We then discuss an archaeological sequence from the Western Province of the Solomon Islands that addresses some of the points we raise, and highlights some of the issues in working on late-period Melanesian prehistory.

We use the terms "Melanesia" and "Polynesia" in the strictly geographic sense. Our discussion of Melanesian archaeology thus includes Green's Near Oceania except that, in terms of the issues in question, it is more meaningful to group Vanuatu and New Caledonia with the islands to the west rather than with Polynesia. Fiji, as usual, occupies a somewhat ambiguous "in-between" position (Kirch 2000:155).

The most obvious difference between the archaeology of Melanesia and Polynesia is the relative extent of archaeological coverage. In comparison with Polynesia the archaeological record of Melanesia is less comprehensively described and far less well understood. Much of this disparity can be attributed to logistical issues such as proximity to institutional bases, funding differences, and the relative complexity of political and social conditions affecting fieldwork in Melanesia. Furthermore, Melanesia has a much greater combined landmass, a far more complex and diverse geography and, in most areas (i.e., in Near Oceania), a much longer time-depth of human occupation. Nevertheless, it is worth comparing the type of archaeological information that is available from the two regions.

The quality of the geographic sample in Polynesia is impressive given the vastness of the Polynesian world. Major fieldwork initiatives since the 1920s have resulted in the publication of archaeological surveys spanning all the major Polynesian archipelagoes (Kirch 2000; see also Cauchois, this volume). In some places, such as Hawai'i, New Zealand, areas of French Polynesia, and Rapa Nui (Easter Island), there have been continuous research efforts over many decades which are now targeting very fine-grained research questions (e.g., Ladefoged and Graves, this volume). But even the small equatorial islands and those of marginal East Polynesia have received quite high levels of archaeological attention. This has resulted in a good understanding of dynamic landscape interactions and long-term adaptive processes on each of the major island types.

By way of contrast, the archaeology of Melanesia is extremely patchy. As Lilley points out in his introduction, almost nothing is known of the western (Indonesian) half of mainland New Guinea. There has been a steady stream of research along parts of the south coast of mainland Papua New Guinea since the 1960s but the rest of the coast and the islands of the Massim are little explored (Lilley 1998 and this volume; also Burenhult 2002). Moving east, there has been some recent major attention paid to the archaeology of the Bismarck Archipelago, much of it under the auspices of the Lapita Homeland Project (Allen and Gosden 1991; also

Galipaud, Leavesley, and Pavlides, this volume; see Figure 9.1) or one of a number of important follow-up projects (e.g., Kirch 2001; Wickler 1995). While work continues to advance in parts of Vanuatu and New Caledonia (e.g., papers in Bedford et al. 2002 and Clark et al. 2001; Galipaud, Sand et al., this volume) areas of Island Melanesia still remain archaeological terra incognita or very poorly reported, including most of the main Solomon Islands chain. Melanesian survey has also often been concentrated along the coastal fringes of the larger islands and, outside the New Guinea highlands (Denham, this volume; see Figure 8.1), comparatively little is known of the archaeology of inland areas (but see Anderson et al. 2000; Pasveer et al. 2002; Pavlides, this volume). The distinction between coastal and inland is of minor significance in Polynesia, where the islands are usually too small for the difference to matter much. On larger Polynesian islands it is the distinction between the windward (wet) and leeward (dry) sides of islands that is important (Lilley, this volume).

The temporal coverage of Melanesian archaeology is also uneven compared to that of Polynesia. In the latter region archaeologists have been largely successful in delineating full island sequences. Melanesian archaeology, however, has produced few published sequences, even for places that have attracted more than the average amount of archaeological attention (Kirch 2000:117; Lilley, this volume). Polynesian archaeology has very well-defined beginning points. In West Polynesia the colonization date of around 3000 B.P. is uncontroversial and even in East Polynesia, where there is still some debate over the dates of island settlement (e.g., Kirch and Ellison 1994; Lilley, this volume), there are well-defined horizons of archaeological visibility and a continuous archaeological record from that point through to the historic period. Even if the date of East Polynesian settlement is pushed back it will not radically alter our basic understanding of the archaeological sequences.

In contrast, the beginnings of the Melanesian sequences are poorly resolved, except in Melanesian Remote Oceania (Galipaud 1996 and this volume; Garanger 1972; Green 1988; Green and Mitchell 1984; Sand 1995, 1996, and Sand et al., this volume). A lot of attention has been paid to the Pleistocene end of sequences in the far west, especially in the Bismarcks (Leavesley, this volume) and on the north coast of mainland New Guinea (a major project began in 2004 to build upon the results of Gorecki et al. 1991) and throughout Melanesia a great deal of effort has gone into exploring the Austronesian/Lapita baseline that came some 30,000 years later. The rest of the archaeological record has received far less scrutiny. In large part this is the result of the absence of Holocene occupation in the caves and rockshelters which have provided the Pleistocene record and the difficulty of finding the ephemeral archaeological signature of non-ceramic peoples in tropical rain forests (though see Pasveer et al. 2002; Pavlides, this volume). But perhaps the most significant problem with the Melanesian sequences is the almost complete lack of information about the post-Lapita phases of prehistory. In fact there are only a few places in Melanesia where the late-period archaeological record, especially of the past 1,000 years (cf. Spriggs 1997:193, 196, 202), is known in any detail at all. As Lilley indicates in his introduction, much of the primary reporting that is available is still to be found in unpublished Ph.D. dissertations (e.g., Bedford 2000; Lilley 1986; Roe 1993; Sand 1995; Specht 1969; Spriggs 1981; Terrell 1976; Ward 1979; Wickler 1995), although preliminary reports for the Southeast Solomons Project led by Green (Green and Cresswell 1976) contain baseline data for that region which in the case of the Polynesian Outlier of Tikopia led to publication of a full sequence (Kirch and Yen 1982). This is a critical problem but one that offers enormous potential for future research because recent prehistory represents the formative period in which the rich and diverse cultural landscape of historical Melanesia was forged.

As well as differences in the scale of coverage, the archaeologies of Melanesia and Polynesia have tended to be driven by different research objectives. Polynesian archaeology, especially in the past decade and a half, has seen a major focus on issues of colonization including voyaging and chronology (Anderson 1991, 1995; Black 1980; Green 1995; Irwin 1980, 1989, 1992; Kirch 1986; Kirch and Ellison 1994; Spriggs and Anderson 1993; Sutton 1987). Some of these discussions focus on what could be seen as the minutiae of archaeological interpretation: discussions about what is meant by colonization and settlement (Graves and Addison 1995), about how to identify the presence of humans in a pristine landscape, about alternative voyaging strategies, and low-level controversies surrounding dating.

These detailed and highly theoretical debates have little relevance to island Melanesian colonization issues. As Lilley mentions at the beginning of the volume, two principal colonization events/processes are recognized in Melanesian prehistory. There is a Pleistocene colonization phase represented in northern Sahul/New Guinea, the Bismarck Archipelago, and Bougainville which has pushed the lower boundary of human arrival beyond New Guinea back to at least 35,000 B.P. (Spriggs 1997:35; also Lilley, this volume). The second major colonization event occurred some time after 4000 B.P. with the arrival of Austronesian settlers (Kirch 1997; Spriggs 1997:96–98; also Galipaud, Sand et al., this volume) and the timing and geographic extent of this event is much better defined, especially in its Lapita manifestation. There has been debate, however, about whether the Lapita cultural complex does in fact represent indigenous developments in the region of the Bismarck Archipelago or whether it represents intrusive cultures and peoples from Southeast Asia or a mix of both (Green 1991b, 1992, 2003; Spriggs 1997:67–107; also Galipaud, Sand et al., this volume). This issue, which might be described as asking "How Lapita-like are the people before Lapita in Near Oceania?," has served as the focus for most of the discussion of pre-Lapita sequences in Near Oceania (see Denham, Leavesley, Pavlides, this volume). Beyond these two "events," colonization of particular landmasses where the colonizing event founds a new society is not really an issue in Melanesian archaeology, largely because there has been constant movement to and fro of people, ideas, and things across the close-knit Melanesian island world since first human arrival. In this context, the archaeology of interaction, social mobility, and exchange is more relevant than colonization (see Lilley, this volume).

Instead of colonization, the overwhelming research effort outside of New Guinea has gone into the study of Lapita. The bias toward Lapita in Melanesian research agendas is reflected in the publication record, not only in the sheer number of volumes dedicated solely to Lapita archaeology but also in the way Melanesian archaeology is presented in synthetic treatments of Pacific prehistory (cf. Galipaud, this volume). In his recent archaeological history of the Pacific Islands, for example, Kirch (2000) organizes the Melanesian sections around the concepts of "old" and "new" Melanesia, terms used "to speak of the periods prior to and after the emergence of Lapita" (2000:117). Spriggs takes a similar approach in his (1997) *Island Melanesians*. In that volume the three chapters that deal with the past 6,000 years revolve around the introduction of Lapita ("The World Turned Upside Down"), then its decline (the "Success and Failure of Lapita"), and finally "The Making of Traditional Island Melanesian Cultures."

Neither Kirch nor Spriggs implies that Melanesian archaeology is all about Lapita and both note the unfortunate paucity of knowledge of the post-Lapita phases (see Kirch 2000:117–120), but many archaeologists tend to discuss late Melanesian prehistory in terms of Lapita transformations. Thus Lapita has become a fundamental organizing principle around which we build our understanding of Melanesian prehistory. Of course, one could hardly argue against the significance of Lapita, especially from the Remote Oceanic standpoint, but one could also argue that this perspective is somewhat self-fulfilling in that the focus on Lapita has left so little known about other aspects of the Melanesian record.

Another difference between Melanesian and Polynesian archaeology is the relative importance of pottery (see Figure 16.2). Polynesian ceramic sequences are limited in duration and distribution and, with the exception of a handful of sherds from the Marquesas and Cook Islands, are confined to West Polynesia. This part of the archaeological record is still the subject of interest, but on the whole the pottery sequences are reasonably well understood and do not figure largely in ongoing research agendas. This is far from the case in Melanesia, where the pottery record is complex, has wide regional variability, and takes up a large part of the research effort. There is debate about claims for pre-Lapita pottery on north coast New Guinea and its relationship with Lapita (e.g., Gorecki et al. 1991; see Galipaud, this volume), but the earliest pottery recorded so far in Island Melanesia is Lapita while on the south coast of New Guinea, with no Lapita record, the earliest ceramics are Lapita-derived (Allen 1972; Kirch 2000:122).

Throughout Melanesia pottery is discontinuous in its distribution, both spatially and temporally, but in many parts of Near and Remote Oceania there is up to a 3,000-year ceramic record. This is a mixed blessing for Melanesian archaeology. Above all, pottery sherds are durable cultural items which generate a strong archaeological signature in the field while ceramic analysis provides some of the most powerful interpretative tools in the archaeological inventory. In Melanesia the pottery record has served as the vehicle for a large and diverse range of archaeological studies. But the basic chronological and typological configuration of Melanesian ceramic assemblages is proving very difficult to unravel and seems to be taking up a disproportionate amount of research time. This is deemed necessary, of course, because pottery sequences are the stable infrastructure around which fine-grained archaeological inquiries will be built in the future.

Once the basic ceramic work is complete, Melanesian archaeologists expect to have available to them powerful relative chronologies for which there will never be any equivalent in Polynesia. Similarly, pottery analysis can support exchange studies and other investigations of social interactions that cannot be carried out with anything like the same power using the stone and shell tool traditions of Polynesia (e.g., Hunt 1989; Irwin 1978; Lilley 1986; Summerhayes 1997, 2000). Unfortunately, at present the research commitment involved in carrying out the basic comparative and typological work is in part holding up the investigation of late-period social and political change. In Vanuatu, for example, there has been a major effort over the past few years to sort out the ceramic record, especially that component with incised-and-applied decoration. This has involved the painstaking construction of typologies and their detailed comparisons with pottery from other parts of Melanesia and Fiji (Bedford 2001; Bedford and Clark 2001). While these efforts are undoubtedly paying off, "the archaeology of the last 1,000 years in Vanuatu, a period that has witnessed significant cultural change, remains one of the least well-defined periods" (Bedford 2001:112). Lilley discusses this matter further in his introduction.

In Polynesia, where pottery has a less dominant influence, archaeologists have tended to take a much broader approach to the archaeological record. In both places there is a rich surface record which includes religious and secular architecture, fortifications, agricultural systems, and other classes of modified landscapes. In Polynesia these features have been the focus of intense archaeological inquiry, which has contributed to a diverse archaeology dealing with economic and demographic transformation, social change, and political centralization (see Ladefoged and Graves, Millerstrom, this volume). In Melanesia the surface archaeological landscape has received more meager attention. New Caledonia, for example, contains what are perhaps the largest and most spectacular agricultural systems in Oceania, yet these have not yet received the comprehensive reporting and archaeological analysis they deserve. New Caledonian archaeologists are fully aware of the significance of the agricultural systems and monumental architecture and Sand (1995 and Sand et al., this volume) has discussed their implications for understanding prehistoric sociopolitical and demographic change on Grande Terre and Maré. Again, however, the emphasis on Lapita and on unraveling the complex ceramic record of New Caledonia, something which has been done with spectacular success (e.g., Sand 2001 and Sand et al., this volume), has meant that these other projects have perhaps not received the attention or publicity they deserve. A similar case can be made for the rich record of stone structures, shrines, house platforms, and other features, which have a wide distribution across Island Melanesia.

The particular research objectives summarized above, and especially the relative lack of knowledge of the recent record and of its non-ceramic components in particular, have led to a situation in Melanesia where, compared to Polynesia, there has been very little emphasis on the archaeology of social change. In fact archaeology has not been very widely used to study the development of historic Melanesian societies at all, that is, to provide a time perspective to the rich ethnographic record. As Kirch (2000:164) put it, "our knowledge of prehistoric social formations [in post-Lapita Melanesia] remains for the most part rudimentary" and thus "a sophisticated 'social archaeology' that can tease out the evidence [of] social-political transformation is barely nascent in Melanesia at present." We have already suggested that part of the reason for this lack of research is the emphasis that has been placed on Lapita and the Melanesian ceramic record more generally, especially its decorated elements. But equally important is the very nature of Polynesian versus Melanesian sociopolitical history and geography.

Two features of the Polynesian situation are particularly pertinent to the emergence of a well-developed social archaeology. The first is the phylogenetic relationships that have been stressed by Kirch (1984) and Kirch and Green (1987) and which allow the development of particular socio-political configurations to be conceived of in terms of "evolutionary" transformations and change within the context of specific environmental and historical situations. The second factor is the circumscribed nature of Polynesian geopolitical units. For the most part, archaeologists can investigate social change within the context of a well-defined and tightly bounded physical and social landscape. Polynesian polities did not, despite the evidence of long-distance interaction (Weisler 1997), engage in the complex and intensive types of social interactions amongst ethnically distinct groups that occurred in Melanesia.

In the Polynesian chiefdom setting there is a wealth of anthropological theory that can provide models for social-archaeological inquiry. These range from the classic works of Carneiro, Service, Sahlins, and Wittfogel, through a range of demographic, neo-Marxist, and evolutionary approaches. Although these models vary in their orientation and emphasis, all stress processes of social change that leave fairly specific archaeological traces, often in the form of major landscape transformations including architectural ones. Thus a type of social archaeology has developed in Polynesia that has tended to be environmentally oriented (though not necessarily determinist) and which emphasizes processes such as demographic growth, intensification of production, and the development of "landesque capital" (long-term investment in land). Particular attention is paid to identifying and dating transformations in the landscape because these are associated with demographic shifts and changes in production systems which are in turn associated with the growth of political hierarchies.

While it is possible that aspects of these types of model may also be appropriate in parts of Melanesia once the archaeological record is further developed (see Sand 1995; Spriggs 1981, 1986), in many places political history has been more complex, or is simply unknown (see Spriggs 1997:161). Melanesian political systems frequently articulate around exchange cycles, rounds of competitive feasting, the circulation of shell valuables, cults of the dead, ritual and secular violence, and other phenomena occurring at both the local and regional (inter-ethnic) scale that must be understood within specific geographic settings. It is our view that the broad processual and environmentalist models which have been so useful in Polynesia are going to be less powerful in understanding Melanesian sociopolitical change than ones that emphasize highly localized historical trajectories.

The purpose of the foregoing brief review has been to show how the archaeologies of Melanesia and Polynesia have diverged and to advance an argument that

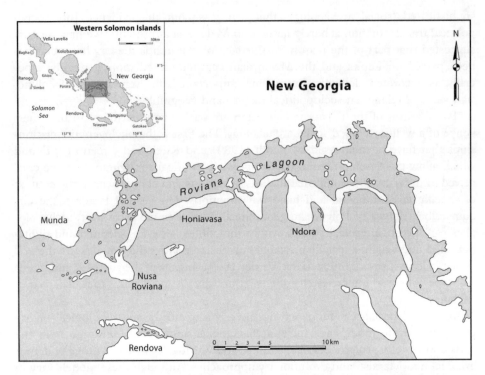

Figure 7.1 Roviana Lagoon, New Georgia Island, Western Province of the Solomon Islands

this divergence stems from essential differences in the geographic and culture historical particulars, including colonial histories, of the two regions. In relation to Melanesia we have noted problems in the scope of the geographic sample, of which the Solomon Islands stands out, and a lack of detailed knowledge of late prehistory with particular reference to the non-ceramic record and the archaeology of social change. In the next part of the chapter, we present an archaeological sequence from the Solomon Islands based on recent research in the Western Province. This sequence contributes to the goal of filling in some of the regional gaps in Island Melanesian archaeology. It also focuses explicitly on the archaeology of the recent past, on late-prehistoric social change, and on some of the problems in working with the recent record in Island Melanesian archaeology.

Roviana: People, Place, and History

New Georgia is a mountainous volcanic island with extensive inshore lagoons around most of its coastline. One of the largest of these is Roviana Lagoon which is about 50 kilometers long and up to three kilometers wide. Roviana Lagoon is bounded on one side by the mainland and along its seaward margin by a string of upraised coral islands on a barrier reef (Figure 7.1). The reef is cut in places by deep narrow passages that pass from the sea into the sheltered lagoon waters. The

Roviana coast of the New Georgia mainland consists of a narrow strip of land that rises steeply to a rugged interior cut by river systems that run into the lagoon opposite the major reef passages. Until the early Holocene these rivers flowed over a low coastal plain which is now flooded. The forested interior of New Georgia is no longer inhabited but oral traditions trace the origins of the contemporary polities of Roviana to inland tribal groups who migrated to the coast some 12–15 generations ago.

New Georgia is linguistically diverse, with both Austronesian and non-Austronesian languages spoken, often in communities separated by only a few kilometers. The contemporary inhabitants live in small villages and hamlets strung out along the barrier island and mainland coasts. Their economy is strongly oriented toward the sea and its products, and the lagoon, the passages, and the open waters beyond the barrier islands provide a rich and diverse range of resources. The limestone soils of Roviana are low in nutrients but support a shifting cultivation system centered around sweet potato, cassava, taro, yam, banana, and sago. The first two of these crops are the most intensively cultivated today but are European introductions arriving in New Georgia in the mid-19th century. Wet-field taro is produced in only a few locations in Roviana but oral traditions and archaeological survey show that taro production was practiced more intensively in parts of New Georgia in the past (Sheppard et al. 1998; Tedder and Barrus 1976).

When Roviana Lagoon was first visited by Europeans they encountered a powerful chiefdom, the leaders of which controlled an exchange and raiding network that spanned the Western Province (Dureau 1994; Hocart n.d.; Jackson 1975; McKinnon 1975; Miller 1978; Walter and Sheppard 2001; White 1979; Zelenietz 1979). Within the Roviana exchange system, food and manufactured items changed hands in transactions that ranged from ritual exchange to commodity purchase. Pivotal to these extensive networks was the circulation of shell valuables, known generically as *poata*. These items had a variety of social and economic roles: Sometimes they appear to have been used as a currency for the purchase of goods or services while in other contexts they took on the properties of "inalienable objects" (Weiner 1992) and were used to mark social transactions (Aswani and Sheppard 2004) or to finance or reward headhunting which was the activity around which the Roviana political economy articulated (Sheppard et al. 1999; Walter and Sheppard 2001).

The political structure of Roviana was based on hereditary social ranking (Aswani 2000; Goldie 1909; Schneider 1997) but power was ultimately bestowed by the ancestors whose skulls were deposited on the ancestral skull shrines or *hope* along with votive offerings of poata. Ceremonial acts carried out on these shrines by priests channeled power from the ancestors to the living, where it was expressed as *mana*, the lifeblood of political efficacy (Codrington 1891:118; Walter and Sheppard 2001). Thus all acts, political, economic, and ceremonial, required sanction from the ancestors. This sanction was demonstrated by success in headhunting raids and thus the power and authority of chiefdomship depended on the ability of chiefs and potential chiefs to organize headhunting expeditions and to return with bounties of trophy skulls. These skulls were deposited in the canoe houses

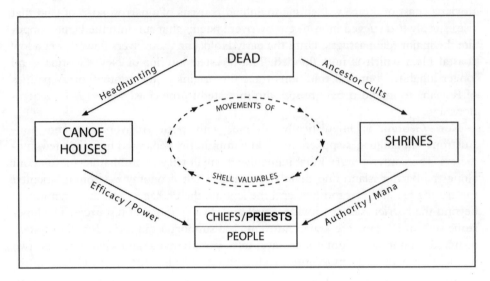

Figure 7.2 A model of the flow of power in the late period Roviana Chiefdom

which housed the *tomoko* war canoes, which were the most potent symbol of Roviana political power. A simple model of the networks linking headhunting, ancestor cults, and the circulation of shell valuables with the generation and flow of power in the Roviana politico-economic system is shown in Figure 7.2.

European traders found the Roviana chiefs willing to participate in commerce and Western and indigenous exchange systems were soon successfully integrated, at least from the Roviana standpoint. By the late 19th century the power of the Roviana chiefs had grown to the point where certain individuals were able to finance and control large forces in long-distance expeditions to acquire heads, slaves to work the local plantations, and turtle shell to exchange for weapons and other commodities (Elkington 1907:99–100; Somerville 1897:399; Walter and Sheppard 2001). The center of power had shifted by the late 19th century to the offshore barrier island of Nusa Roviana and the adjacent mainland coast around the settlement of Munda (Figure 7.1). In 1891 the British attacked the headhunting strongholds of Nusa Roviana and Munda as part of a general attempt to curtail headhunting in the Western Province, which had now grown to the point where it was causing severe deprivation in the target communities, and interfering with the commercial activities of white traders. Despite a reported loss of up to 150 canoes and the destruction of most of the skull shrines and houses in the western part of the lagoon (Davis 1892), headhunting continued well into the first decade of the 20th century.

The Archaeological Record

When we commenced work in Roviana Lagoon in 1996 our first objective was to outline a broad archaeological sequence that would serve to situate the region, previously unknown archaeologically, within the broader picture of Melanesian pre-history, particularly in regard to Lapita. As the survey work continued we realized that the archaeological landscape contained a rich record, in the form of surface monumental architecture and material culture, pertaining to the development of the social systems that were encountered by the first Western visitors. Below we present an archaeological sequence for Roviana Lagoon which addresses the first of these issues, and also provides a case study of sociopolitical change in a late pre-historic Melanesian society.

The early record

Although first human intrusion into the Solomon Islands could conceivably have occurred in the Upper Pleistocene, the earliest dated sites are found in Guadalcanal at around 6000 B.P. (Roe 1992). At that time sea levels were stabilizing in the Western Province and growing reef platforms would have created coastal landscapes increasingly attractive to human settlement. Lateral erosion in Roviana had created large coastal plains and it is probable that at this time settlers were moving into the Roviana coastlands. By 4000 B.P. the lagoon was certainly extant with water levels higher than they are at present, and pollen cores taken from a series of sites along the shores of the barrier islands and mainland coastal swamps show evidence for firing and vegetation change by 3200 B.P. This includes an increase in grasses, fern growth, and the appearance of breadfruit.

These changes represent an increase in shifting horticulture along the Roviana coasts which may be associated with an Austronesian expansion. Sites of this period are located in the inter-tidal zone. Only one site (Hoghoi) displays the characteristic ceramic signature of a Lapita settlement, containing some classic Lapita dentate sherds and complex carinated pot forms (Felgate 2001, 2003). Others such as the Panaivili site produced a range of sherds of which the decorated component included incised, pinched, fingernail impressed, punctuate, and applied-relief wares (Reeve 1989; Spriggs 1997:172). Several *Tridacna* adzes, a *Cassis* shell chisel, a *Tridacna* arm-ring, and a range of *Conus* shell rings and bracelets which are conceivably but not necessarily contemporary with the ceramics were also recovered from the inter-tidal zone, along with some polished adzes of characteristic Lapita form (Reeve 1989:55). About 20 similar sites have now been recorded along the lagoon edges and these might represent stilt-house settlements like those reported in Lapita contexts on Mussau (Kirch 1988), Buka (Wickler 2001), and Nissan (Spriggs 2000:355). Although the evidence for Lapita occupation in Roviana is thin, Lapita or closely related cultures represent the baseline for Western Province archaeology at present (Sheppard et al. 1999; Felgate 2003). Most of the decorated sherds, however, fall within a fairly characteristic post-Lapita Melanesian decoration system which includes incision, pinching, impressing, and applied-relief work. A similar ceramic series is poorly known from Choisel, and it perhaps has more distant connections to those of the Shortland Islands, Bougainville, and Buka to the north.

Munda Tradition (700–100 B.P.)

The late-period archaeological landscape of Roviana Lagoon is dominated by sets of stone and coral monumental structures. Many of these are shrines but there is also an assortment of residential complexes and associated material culture. Although we have shown that these sites span at least 700 years of prehistory, they are recognized by the people of Roviana as part of their cultural heritage in that they relate directly to the histories, genealogies, and traditions of their own ancestors. For this reason we treat these sites as components of a single tradition which we call the Munda Tradition after one of the key settlement areas of the late 19th century. The archaeological record of the Munda Tradition traces the development of the political, economic, religious, and ceremonial complex known historically as the Roviana chiefdom.

The shrines of the Munda Tradition are extremely varied in form and in the range of ritual items they contain. The people of Roviana classify them according to function and chronology, but these classifications are difficult to systematize. In order to provide some control over chronology we developed a simple seriation model which identifies two shrine classes and divides the Munda Tradition into two periods, an early Bao Period and a later Roviana Period. The shrine seriation was supplemented with information from oral tradition in order to develop an account of social, political, and ideological change within the Munda Tradition (Sheppard et al. 2000; Walter and Sheppard 2001). The chronology below is based on radio-carbon dating of selected shrines and associated features, the details of which are discussed elsewhere (Sheppard et al. 2000; Walter and Sheppard 2001). Most of what we know of the Munda Tradition archaeology is via the extensive monumental record, of which we have recorded and mapped more than 1,000 sites. Ceramic production (or use since much of the latter pottery is probably non-local) continued for most of the Munda Tradition and is represented by a thin, undecorated ware found scattered through the gardening soils and around the habitation zones. Pottery was not being manufactured in Roviana in the historic period, but was still made on nearby Choisel into the early 20th century.

Bao Period (700–400 B.P.)

Bao Period shrines are constructed of basalt or coral slab walls and unlike later sites do not contain any human bone, shell valuables, or ovens. Additional features include basalt "table-stones" (sometimes described locally as "stone altars") and stone-lined cists on the main platform mound. The sites are found principally on the mainland but there are several clusters on the barrier islands. All feature the use of basalt in the form of uprights, table stones, cobble flooring, or wall components. On the barrier islands this had to be carried several kilometers or more from the mainland. The walls of the mainland shrines are also made of basalt obtained from nearby rivers while those of the barrier islands often have walls made of cut coral blocks. According to oral traditions the Roviana people originated from Bao in the interior of New Georgia, an area that is currently uninhabited. Our survey of the Bao region located a group of 18 basalt shrines spread out along 500 meters of ridgeline. No additional features, middens, or signs of occupation other than the shrines were located within a kilometer of these sites.

Excavation of the largest structure provided a date indicating construction in the early 13th century (Sheppard et al. 2000). This is the earliest date obtained from any Munda Tradition sites. This date is consistent with oral histories that associate the Bao area with the first ancestors of the Roviana people. The Bao shrines are the most tightly aggregated set located on the mainland but small clusters of sites located along a ridge parallel to Bao suggest that there may have been a number of ridge-line shrine clusters in this region, though Bao was clearly the most important. Elsewhere on the mainland, Bao Period shrines are located in isolated positions no closer than 170 meters and usually a kilometer or more from any other recorded structure. So far no habitation complexes have been recorded, although taro terracing or *ruta* have been found high in some of the valleys. The settlement pattern inferred by this site distribution is one of small inland settlements, based on the production of irrigated taro and the harvesting of nut trees, near the headwaters of larger streams with the shrines located at some distance away, often on the first coastal ridge.

The barrier island of Nusa Roviana became the center of the ancestor and headhunting cults by the 19th century and there the vast majority of the shrines present on the landscape date to the later Roviana Period. But there are also several examples of Bao Period structures. One of these, Kogu, is associated with the chief Ididubangara. According to tradition, it was he who came to Nusa Roviana from Bao and established the Roviana chiefdom (Nagaoka 1999:111). Excavations at Kogu produced radiocarbon dates indicating construction in the 14th century A.D. This is consistent with genealogical accounts which place Ididubangara some time prior to A.D. 1600. A second Bao Period site located on the central ridge of the island also provided a date suggesting a construction age early in the 14th century (Sheppard et al. 2000:Table 2).

Further southeast, in the inner lagoon, Bao Period sites are found in at least two other locations. On the barrier island of Honiavasa there is a cluster of 34 platforms and associated features located in a 150-meter band running parallel to the coast. Most of these structures have all the characteristics of the later Roviana Period structures, but there are several which have sections of well-built slab walling and are associated with basalt features including table stones and these have produced dates indicating construction in the late 14th century A.D. Another cluster of Bao Period sites is located at Kekehe further into the inner lagoon. The Kekehe complex consists of about 20 major structures and a number of ancillary features within an area measuring about 200 meters by 150 meters. All the structures are slab-faced platforms with basalt and coral paving, many of which contain basalt uprights. The oral accounts from nearby Patmos Village provide no indication of connections between the contemporary communities and the people who once occupied Kekehe. In Roviana historiography this usually indicates time depth rather than cultural discontinuity. In fact the Kekehe structures, while typologically of Bao

Period form, have several features which show strong connections with the shrines and monuments of the later Roviana period and on this basis we consider it likely that they fall late within the Bao Period.

None of the Bao sites contained stone ovens (*opotu*), skull houses, or evidence for sacrificial offerings. At Honiavasa several of the sites contained a small number of weathered shell rings, and this is the only example of votive offerings found on any Bao Period sites. However, these were found at a very low density (mean = 0.22 per shrine) compared to those of the Roviana Period (mean = 10.39).

Roviana Period (400–100 B.P.)

The Roviana Period shrines are constructed of coral rubble and are strongly associated with human bone and artifacts, which range from shell valuables and debris resulting from their manufacture, to historic artifacts such as ceramics, trade axes, and muskets. Skull houses made of sheet coral containing skulls and associated votive offerings are often built on top of the main shrine mound. The shrines of this period are more varied in form than those of the Bao Period and often occur in aggregations with other shrines or structure classes. Each shrine or shrine cluster relates to the people in whose area it lies, to the individuals who made it and whose ancestors' skulls may be contained within it, and to those who make use of it in ritual fashion. The archaeological landscape of the Roviana Period is characterized by the sheer quantity and density of archaeological remains; in some areas the ground surface is literally carpeted with portable artifacts and stone constructions. Sites of this period are found all along the lagoon coasts but there are several places where the features are particularly dense. One of these places, the small barrier island of Nusa Roviana, was a particularly important settlement area of late prehistory and about which there are abundant traditions, myths, legends, and genealogical records. In combination with the archaeological record, these provide a rich source of understanding about the last centuries of socio-political and economic development in the Roviana polity.

By the late 18th century Nusa Roviana and the adjacent mainland coast had become the political center of the Roviana chiefdom, although first shrine construction occurred in the Bao Period (see above). The Roviana Period features on Nusa Roviana consist of a dense cluster of shrines, wharves, and stone platforms that once supported dwellings and canoe houses along two coasts, and a fortification along the central ridge of the island.

The coastal features are distributed along the flat and gently sloping land that encircles the central ridge and run in a continuous strip for 700–800 meters. During our first surveys along the coast we recorded each of the monumental sites as we encountered them, but as we cleared the scrub for mapping it became apparent that we were dealing with a continuous, dense scatter of midden shell, artifacts, and structures extending from the hill slopes into the inter-tidal zone and sometimes beyond. These habitation zones were intensely occupied with the structures piling up against one another in a manner that suggests the constant rebuilding and reorganization of space. Many of the structures are composite features; shrines and house platforms adjoining small walled compounds and all containing votive caches of shell arm rings and a wide variety of other items. Wharves of coral rubble extend out into the mangrove swamps and some of these support small shrines or caches of skull fragments and shell valuables. Throughout the entire complex, shell valuables, stone bowls, stone carvings, and human skulls are scattered amongst domestic refuse or cached in the platform walls, giving the impression of a ritually charged social landscape (Sheppard et al. 2000).

The central ridge of Nusa Roviana contains a hill fort and some of the most important shrines of the Roviana chiefdom. The fort consists of a series of transverse ditches and banks which divide the ridge into sections. Within each section are named shrines which are associated with particular ancestors, spiritual beings (*mateana*), and important events in the history of the Roviana people. Thus a journey along the ridge in the company of an elder from Nusa Roviana, who can tell the stories of each feature as it is encountered, effectively recapitulates the social and political history of the Roviana chiefdom (Thomas et al. 2001). Oral tradition indicates the first section of the fort is the most powerful and sacred area of Roviana Lagoon. Here chiefs and priests could call on the most powerful ancestors through the use of magic which referenced their descent from mateana (human ancestors with supernatural associations). This first (northernmost) cluster contains the most important ancestral skull shrines and these are followed, as one moves south along the ridge, by shrines that are associated with warfare, and where rituals were carried out to disrupt the enemy or improve the fighting ability of the Roviana warriors. The last two shrines in this first section consist of small coral mounds with shell rings and other artifacts, and are associated with the men who became mateana ancestors of all Roviana chiefs. There is a powerful symbolic association between these shrines and the ancestral homeland of the Roviana peoples in the mainland forests of Bao (Thomas et al. 2001). For example, two of the shrines in this area are named Lio and Lio Zuzulongo respectively, which are names of areas on the mainland coast to the east of Bao. Informants from Nusa Roviana tell us that these shrines were transferred from there and represent a connection to the mainland.

The next section of the fort is the most heavily fortified part of the ridge and contains shrines associated not with supernatural links, but with the earthly powers of chiefs to defend Nusa Roviana from its enemies. The shrines in this area contain human skulls and shell valuables and one is said to have been a place where rituals were carried out by warriors prior to combat. On either side of the ridge at this point a series of 24 terraces have been cut back into the slopes and may have supported housing. Beyond the southern defensive wall there is a cluster of terraces and platforms but no clearly defined shrines or living terraces. This part of the fort terminates in a cobble wall over 3 meters in height and 2 meters wide which isolates the highest and narrowest part of the ridge. Here there is a small paved and terraced area supporting the shrine of Tiola, one of the most important ancestral figures in Roviana mythology. Tiola assumed the form of a dog and some accounts say that it was he who taught the people of Roviana how to make war canoes (tomoko). Tiola is also associated with the genesis of the ancestor cults and with headhunting. Today a small statue of a dog's head sits amongst a pile of shell valuables on the highest point of the island. From here Tiola was said to bark out warnings when Roviana was under threat. The dog's head figure of Tiola is obviously related to the dog-like *nuzunuzu* figure, which is one of the best known symbols and art motifs of the Western Province, and which was rendered as a wooden carving and used to adorn the bow of the tomoko.

Late Prehistory and the Growth of the Roviana Chiefdom

The archaeological landscape of Roviana Lagoon contains a continuous record of human occupation spanning 3,500 years, the last 700 of which trace the development of the Roviana chiefdom which was encountered and described by the first Western visitors to New Georgia. Central to our understanding of the growth of the Roviana polity is the structural connection between ancestral skull shrines and the canoe houses where the skulls of the slain enemy were put on display. Ancestor veneration and headhunting mediate between the worlds of life and death and provide the paths through which mana and efficacy flow from the dead to the living (Sheppard et al. 2000). Shell valuables circulated along the same paths linking the living and the dead. After passing through networks of human exchange they ultimately end up on the shrines, as part of the ritual landscape of Roviana Lagoon. In the Roviana world the outcome of all acts depended on ancestral intercession and the mana of any individual thus depended on his or her being able to demonstrate ancestral sanction through efficacy in temporal action. At some point in the history of Roviana the key to chiefly and corporate mana became invested in the ability to acquire human heads in headhunting raids. In Roviana tradition this is associated with Tiola, and it coincided with the construction of skull shrines, or, more probably, the incorporation of skull houses into an existing shrine tradition.

As in many Pacific Island societies, the Roviana traditions are clear about origin points. The Roviana polity formed through a fusion of several different tribes after a movement to the coast and barrier islands by ancestral groups formerly resident in Bao. This movement is also associated with the transfer of shrine traditions from the mainland but skull veneration and the circulation of shell ornaments were incorporated into the political economy sometime later. The archaeological evidence coincides strongly with the oral accounts and provides further insight into the process of socio-political growth in Roviana Lagoon. Although we are unable at this point to provide a detailed chronology for the Munda Tradition, essential processes of change are already quite well defined. Central amongst these is a process of intensification whereby the worlds of the living and the dead gradually merged and ritual and symbolic structures, once located in separate domains, encroached on the domestic realm and came to dominate every aspect of daily life (Sheppard et al. 2000). This is documented in changes in shrine form, content, and the organization of social space.

The oldest shrines recorded are the Bao Period shrines located in the forests at Bao on the New Georgia mainland. Although these shrines were simple in form and did not contain skull houses or deposits of shell valuables, they did involve a great deal of labor in their construction. Bao Period shrines on the barrier islands were more varied in form but they too did not contain skull houses, although a few artifacts on the Honiavasa shrines suggest the beginnings of an association between shell valuables and ritual life. All Bao Period shrines on the barrier islands use basalt, which is a symbolic reference to the origin point of the Roviana peoples and of their religion in the forests of the New Georgia mainland (Thomas et al. 2001). By the Roviana Period the shrines reached their greatest complexity and most contained internal features including skull houses and an abundance of shell valuables and other items left as votive caches. By the early historic period, muskets and trade axes were also being placed on the ancestor shrines, which indicates that material culture could pass from commodity to ritual status in the Roviana system. Human bone was ubiquitous and ovens for the preparation of burnt offerings were located in close proximity to many shrines. As shrines changed in form and content, changes also occurred in their spatial patterning within the Roviana landscape.

On the mainland the settlement patterns were highly dispersed. Although we have not located any habitation complexes, oral accounts suggest that they were located adjacent to the taro systems at the headwaters of larger streams. The shrines, however, were located far away on ridges a few kilometers from the coast. Associated with the dead, the shrines were kept apart from the habitation zones, indicating the importance in the Bao Period of maintaining a separation between sacred and secular space. The barrier island sites of the Bao Period were more clustered, with both domestic and religious structures spread out along the peripheries of the horticultural land. In some places shrines are located a few meters from house platforms but in most places each structure is located up to 50 meters or more from the next one. By contrast, in the Roviana Period a very nucleated settlement pattern had emerged in which sacred and secular space had become fully integrated. The shrines, covered in human bone and ritual paraphernalia, are scattered amongst the house platforms and often share one or more walls. The structures are clustered enough around the flat coastal lands of Nusa Roviana to interpret these places as villages and on the planting lands above, isolated shrines are associated with the rituals of production and first fruits. The space around and between the shrines and house platforms is littered with domestic waste in the form of midden shell and the debris of tool and ornament production. On Nusa Roviana we see the complete fusion of the domestic and sacred components of village life and, via the ancestral shrine and canoe houses, a merging of the worlds of the living and the dead (Sheppard et al. 2000).

The process of religious intensification documented in the archaeological record and the growth of the chiefdom itself can be understood in terms of basic structures that exist within the Roviana political economy. The key element is the relationship between temporal efficacy and the supernatural world of the ancestors. Before they could enjoy power, a Roviana chief had to demonstrate ancestral blessing in the form of mana, by success in large-scale temporal endeavors, particularly headhunting. With constant competition amongst would-be leaders, this system contains the potential to develop into an ever-increasing competitive cycle. Each time a chief succeeds in validating their status the stakes are raised in future social enterprise, both for them and for their competitors. Pressure is placed not only on the chiefs but also on the entire religious system. The outcome in Roviana was an acceleration in the construction of shrines to facilitate the successful initiation of new events, and an increase in the intensity and frequency of headhunting. This process was clearly accelerated by the arrival of Europeans, but the Roviana chiefdom with its attendant headhunting and ancestor cults was an indigenous tradition which had developed over many centuries in the Roviana region.

Conclusions

The Roviana sequence makes some contribution to the problems of regional archaeological coverage in Island Melanesia, although not as much as we might have hoped, and the Solomon chain is still a significant gray area archaeologically. We have shown that the continuous archaeological record in the Western Province begins with Lapita but unlike other parts of Island Melanesia (such as the Bismarcks, the southeast Solomons, Vanuatu, or New Caledonia), the Lapita presence there so far is quite ephemeral. Roe (1993) has already suggested that Lapita peoples failed to settle Guadalcanal and it is possible that the main Lapita colonization mostly bypassed the larger islands in the Solomons. One possibility is that the first Lapita settlers in the Reef and Santa Cruz islands deliberately leapfrogged established cultures and exchange networks in the rest of the Solomons (Sheppard et al. 2000:321).

Returning to some of the issues raised in our opening discussion, the Roviana sequence highlights some of the problems in the archaeology of late Melanesian prehistory. One of these is the problem of defining the regional unit in Island Melanesia. In Polynesia the unit of analysis is usually a single island or at most an archipelago occupied by a single ethnic or linguistic group. In contrast, in Melanesia large islands are home to a multitude of linguistic and ethnic groups, the identities and histories of whom are bound up in complex networks of movement and interaction. In this study we focused on Roviana Lagoon as the unit of inquiry because we had access to a body of ethnographic and historical data that showed Roviana to have had a coherent social configuration at the time of European contact. But if we had carried out our work on the adjacent lagoon of Morovo or elsewhere in the Western Province the nature of the archaeological sequence would have been quite different. It may well be the case that further archaeological inquiry in the Western Province will simply uncover different perspectives on the growth of the Roviana chiefdom. However, we suspect that this is not the case, and that to present the Roviana sequence as a general model of social change in late Solomon Island prehistory would be to impose a highly Roviana-centric slant on what is in fact a very diverse archaeological record. The problem, then, of developing a regional sequence for a large island like New Georgia or for the Western Province is one of piecing together and synthesizing a number of very localized sequences.

In Roviana we relied very heavily on the use of oral tradition and on the ethnohistoric record in site interpretation as well as in the development of the research design (cf. Conte, this volume). The key to this is that the archaeological landscape of Roviana, including its material culture and architectural components, is very much a part of the modern cultural landscape. While the context may have changed, the shrines and other structural remains still have meaning in contemporary polit- ical and social settings and, drawing on traditional histories and genealogy, they are manipulated in disputes and negotiations relating to political succession and access to land and resources, including royalties from logging and commercial fishing. Where processual models linking social change with environmental variables have proved successful in Polynesia, we suggest that in Island Melanesia the archaeol- ogy of the recent past, say the past 1,000 years, will need to draw heavily on the rich ethnographic and traditional record. In this case a multidisciplinary archaeol- ogy will rely as much on input from oral history, history, and ethnography as on the environmental sciences. While we have suggested that the delineation of archae- ological sequences may be more difficult in Melanesia than in Polynesia, the pres- ence of a strong living tradition linking the past to the present offers enormous opportunity for the development of a rich historical anthropology dealing with the recent past.

REFERENCES

Allen, J., 1972 The First Decade in New Guinea Archaeology. Antiquity 46:180–190.

Allen, J., and C. Gosden, eds., 1991 Report of the Lapita Homeland Project. Occasional Papers in Prehistory 20. Canberra: Department of Prehistory, Research School of Pacific Studies, Australian National University.

Anderson, A., 1991 The Chronology of Colonization in New Zealand. Antiquity 65:767–795.

——1995 Current Approaches in East Polynesian Colonization Research. Journal of the Polynesian Society 104:110–132.

Anderson, A., G. Clark and T. Worthy, 2000 An Inland Lapita Site in Fiji. Journal of the Polynesian Society 109:311–316.

Aswani, S., 2000 Changing Identities: The Ethno-History of Roviana Predatory Headhunt- ing. Journal of the Polynesian Society 109:39–70.

Aswani, S., and P. Sheppard, 2003 The Archaeology and Ethnohistory of Exchange in Pre- colonial and Colonial Roviana: Gifts, Commodities and Inalienable Possessions. Current Anthropology 44 (supplement):S51–S78.

Bedford, S., 2000 Pieces of the Vanuatu Puzzle: Archaeology of the North, South and Centre. Ph.D. dissertation, Australian National University.

——2001 Ceramics from Malekula, Northern Vanuatu: Two Ends of a Potential 3000-Year Sequence. In The Archaeology of Lapita Dispersal in Oceania. G. Clark, A. Anderson and T. Vunidilo, eds. pp. 105–114. Terra Australis 17. Canberra: Pandanus Books.

Bedford, S., and G. Clark, 2001 The Rise and Rise of the Incised and Applied Relief. In The Archaeology of Lapita Dispersal in Oceania. G. Clark, A. Anderson and T. Vunidilo, eds. pp. 61–74. Terra Australis 17. Canberra: Pandanus Books.

Bedford, S., D. Burley and C. Sand, eds., 2002 Fifty Years in the Field: Papers in Honour of Richard Shutler. Monograph 25. Auckland: New Zealand Archaeological Association.

Black, S., 1980 Demographic Models and Island Colonization. New Zealand Journal of Archaeology 2:51–64.

Burenhult, G., ed., 2002 The Archaeology of the Trobriand Islands, Milne Bay Province, Papua New Guinea: Excavation Season 1999. British Archaeological Report S1080. Oxford: Archaeopress.

Clark, G., A. Anderson and T. Vunidilo, eds., 2001 The Archaeology of Lapita Dispersal in Oceania. Terra Australis 17. Canberra: Pandanus Books.

Codrington, R., 1891 The Melanesians: Studies in their Anthropology and Folk-Lore. Oxford: Clarendon Press.

Davis, C., 1892 Australian Station, Solomon Islands, 1891: Correspondence Respecting Outrages by Natives on British Subjects and Other Matters, which have been Under Inquiry during the Year 1891, being Continuation of Reports of Cases dealt with in Former Years, together with Other Cases which have Since Arisen. Government Printer.

Dureau, C., 1994 Mixed Blessings: Christianity and History in Women's Lives on Simbo, Western Solomon Islands. Ph.D. dissertation, Macquarie University.

Elkington, E., 1907 The Savage South Seas. London: A. and C. Black.

Felgate, M., 2001 A Roviana Ceramic Sequence and the Prehistory of Near Oceania: Work in Progress. In The Archaeology of Lapita Dispersal in Oceania. G. Clark, A. Anderson and T. Vunidilo, eds. pp. 39–60. Terra Australis 17. Canberra: Pandanus Books.

——2003 Reading Lapita in Near Oceania: Intertidal Shallow-water Pottery Scatters, Roviana Lagoon, New Georgia, Solomon Islands. Ph.D. dissertation, University of Auckland.

Galipaud, J-C., 1996 New Caledonia: Some Recent Archaeological Perspectives. In Oceanic Culture History: Essays in Honour of Roger Green. J. Davidson, G. Irwin, F. Leach, A. Pawley, and D. Brown, eds. pp. 297–305. Special Publication. Dunedin: New Zealand Journal of Archaeology.

Garanger, J., 1972 Archéologie des Nouvelles Hébrides. Publications de la Société des Océanistes 30. Paris: Musée de l'Homme.

Goldie, J., 1909 The People of New Georgia. Their Manners and Customs, and Religious Beliefs. Proceedings of the Royal Society of Queensland 22:23–30.

Gorecki, P., M. Mabin and J. Campbell, 1991 Archaeology and Geomorphology of the Vanimo Coast, Papua New Guinea: Preliminary Results. Archaeology in Oceania 26:119–122.

Graves, M., and D. Addison, 1995 The Polynesian Settlement of the Hawai'ian Archipelago: Integrating Models and Methods in Archaeological Interpretation. World Archaeology 26:257–282.

Green, R., 1988 Those Mysterious Mounds are for the Birds. Archaeology in New Zealand 31:153–158.

——1991a Near and Remote Oceania: Disestablishing "Melanesia" in Culture History. In Man and a Half: Essays in Pacific Anthropology and Ethnobiology in Honour of Ralph Bulmer. A. Pawley, ed. pp. 491–502. Auckland: The Polynesian Society.

——1991b The Lapita Cultural Complex: Current Evidence and Proposed Models. In Indo-Pacific Prehistory 1990, vol. 2. P. Bellwood, ed. pp. 295–305. Bulletin of the Indo-Pacific Prehistory Association 11. Canberra and Jakarta: Indo-Pacific Prehistory Association and Asosiasi Prehistorisi Indonesia.

——1992 Definitions of the Lapita Cultural Complex and its Non-Ceramic Component. In Poterie Lapita et Peuplement. J-C. Galipaud, ed. pp. 7–20. Nouméa: ORSTOM.

——1995 Linguistic, Biological and Cultural Origins of the Initial Inhabitants of Remote Oceania. New Zealand Journal of Archaeology 17:5–27.

——2003 The Lapita Horizon and Traditions – Signature of One Set of Oceanic Migrations. *In* Pacific Archaeology: Assessments and Prospects. C. Sand, ed. pp. 95–120. Les Cahiers de l'Archéologie en Nouvelle-Calédonie 15. Nouméa: Département Archéologie, Service des Musées et du Patrimoine de Nouvelle-Calédonie.

Green, R., and J. Mitchell, 1984 New Caledonian Culture History: A Review of the Archaeological Sequence. New Zealand Journal of Archaeology 5:19–67.

Green, R., and M. Cresswell, eds., 1976 Southeast Solomon Islands Cultural History: A Preliminary Report. Bulletin 11. Wellington: The Royal Society of New Zealand.

Hocart, M., n.d. Chieftainship. Hocart Papers, MSS 22–7. Alexander Turnbull Library, Wellington, unpublished MS.

Hunt, T., 1989 Lapita Ceramic Exchange in the Mussau Islands. Ph.D. dissertation, University of Washington.

Irwin, G., 1978 The Development of Mailu as a Specialized Trading and Manufacturing Center in Papuan Prehistory: The Causes and the Implications. Mankind 11:406–415.

——1980 The Prehistory of Oceania: Colonization and Cultural Change. *In* The Cambridge Encyclopedia of Archaeology. A. Sherratt, ed. pp. 325–332. Cambridge: Cambridge University Press.

——1989 Against, Across and Down the Wind: A Case for the Systematic Exploration of the Pacific Islands. Journal of the Polynesian Society 98:167–206.

——1992 The Prehistoric Exploration and Colonization of the Pacific. Cambridge: Cambridge University Press.

Jackson, K., 1975 Head-Hunting in the Christianization of Bugotu 1861–1900. Journal of Pacific History 10:65–78.

Kirch, P., 1984 The Evolution of the Polynesian Chiefdoms. Cambridge: Cambridge University Press.

——1986 Rethinking East Polynesian Prehistory. Journal of the Polynesian Society 95:9–40.

——1988 The Talepakemalai Site and Oceanic Prehistory. National Geographic Research and Exploration 4:328–342.

——1997 The Lapita Peoples. Oxford: Blackwell.

——2000 On the Road of the Winds: An Archaeological History of the Pacific Islands before European Contact. Berkeley: University of California Press.

——ed., 2001 Lapita and its Transformations in Near Oceania. Archaeological Investigations in the Mussau Islands, Papua New Guinea, 1985–88, vol. 1. Introduction, Excavations, Chronology. Contribution 59. Berkeley: Archaeological Research Facility, University of California at Berkeley.

Kirch, P., and J. Ellison, 1994 Palaeoenvironmental Evidence for Human Colonization of Remote Oceanic Islands. Antiquity 68:310–321.

Kirch, P., and R. Green, 1987 History, Phylogeny, and Evolution in Polynesia. Current Anthropology 28:431–456.

——2001 Hawaiki, Ancestral Polynesia. An Essay in Historical Anthropology. Cambridge: Cambridge University Press.

Kirch, P., and D. Yen, 1982 Tikopia: The Prehistory and Ecology of a Polynesian Outlier. Bernice P. Bishop Museum Bulletin 238. Honolulu: Bishop Museum Press.

Lilley, I., 1986 Prehistoric Exchange in the Vitiaz Strait, Papua New Guinea. Ph.D. dissertation, Australian National University.

——1998 East of Irian: Archaeology in Papua New Guinea. *In* Bird's Head Approaches. Irian Jaya Studies – A Programme for Interdisciplinary Research. G-J. Barstra, ed. pp. 135–156. Modern Quaternary Research in Southeast Asia 15. Rotterdam: A. A. Balkema.

McKinnon, J., 1975 Tomahawks, Turtles and Traders: A Reconstruction of the Circular Causation of Warfare in the New Georgia Group. Oceania 45:290–307.

Miller, D., 1978 An Organisational Approach to Exchange Media: An Example from the Western Solomons. Mankind 11:288–295.

Nagaoka, T., 1999 Hope Pukerane: A Study of Religious Sites in Roviana, New Georgia, Solomon Islands. M.A. dissertation, University of Auckland.

Pasveer, J., S. Clarke and G. Miller, 2002 Late Pleistocene Occupation in Inland Rainforest, Bird's Head, Papua. Archaeology in Oceania 37:92–95.

Reeve, R., 1989 Recent Work on the Prehistory of the Western Solomons, Melanesia. Bulletin of the Indo-Pacific Prehistory Association 9:46–67.

Roe, D., 1992 Investigations into the Prehistory of the Central Solomons: Some Old and Some New Data from Northwest Guadalcanal. In Poterie Lapita et Peuplement. J.-C. Galipaud, ed. pp. 91–102. Nouméa: ORSTOM.

——1993 Prehistory Without Pots: Prehistoric Settlement and Economy of North-West Guadalcanal, Solomon Islands. Ph.D. dissertation, Australian National University.

Sand, C., 1995 "Le Temps d'Avant": La Préhistoire de la Nouvelle-Calédonie. Paris: L'Harmattan.

——1996 Recent Developments in the Study of New Caledonia's Prehistory. Archaeology in Oceania 31:45–71.

——2001 Evolutions in the Lapita Cultural Complex: A View from the Southern Lapita Province. Archaeology in Oceania 36:65–76.

Schneider, G., 1997 Land Dispute and Tradition in Munda, Roviana Lagoon, New Georgia Island, Solomon Islands: From Headhunting to the Quest for the Control of Land. Ph.D. dissertation, Cambridge University.

Sheppard, P., M. Felgate, K. Roga, J. Keopo and R. Walter, 1999 A Ceramic Sequence from Roviana Lagoon, (New Georgia, Solomon Islands). In Le Pacifique de 5000 à 2000 avant le Présent. Suppléments à l'Histoire d'une Colonisation. J-C. Galipaud et I. Lilley, eds. pp. 313–322. Nouméa: IRD.

Sheppard, P., R. Walter and T. Nagaoka, 2000 The Archaeology of Head-Hunting in Roviana Lagoon, New Georgia, Solomon Islands. Journal of the Polynesian Society 109:9–37.

Sheppard, P., S. Aswani, M. Felgate, T. Nagaoka, R. Walter, J. Dodson and S. Grimes, 1998 New Georgia Archaeological Survey (NGAS) Roviana Lagoon Year 3. Annual Report (1998). Auckland: Department of Anthropology, University of Auckland.

Somerville, B., 1897 Ethnographical Notes in New Georgia, Solomon Islands. Journal of the Royal Anthropological Institute 26:357–413.

Specht, J., 1969 Prehistoric and Modern Pottery Industries of Buka Island, T.P.N.G. Ph.D. dissertation, Australian National University.

Spriggs, M., 1981 Vegetable Kingdoms: Taro Irrigation and Pacific Prehistory. Ph.D. dissertation, Australian National University.

——1986 Landscape, Land Use and Political Transformation in Southern Melanesia. In Island Societies: Archaeological Approaches to Evolution and Transformation. P. Kirch, ed. pp. 10–19. Cambridge: Cambridge University Press.

——1997 The Island Melanesians. The Peoples of South-East Asia and the Pacific. Oxford: Blackwell.

——2000 The Solomon Islands as a Bridge and Barrier in the Settlement of the Pacific. In Australian Archaeologist: Collected Papers in Honour of Jim Allen. A. Anderson and T. Murray, eds. pp. 348–364. Canberra: Coombs Academic Publishing.

Spriggs, M., and A. Anderson, 1993 Late Colonization of East Polynesia. Antiquity 67: 200–217.

Summerhayes, G., 1997 Interaction in Pacific Prehistory: An Approach Based on the Production, Distribution and Use of Pottery. Ph.D. dissertation, Australian National University.

——2000 Lapita Interaction. Terra Australis 15. Canberra: ANH Publications.

Sutton, D., 1987 A Paradigmatic Shift in Polynesian Prehistory: Implications for New Zealand. New Zealand Journal of Archaeology 19:135–155.

Tedder, M., and S. Barrus, 1976 Old Kusaghe. Journal of the Solomon Islands Cultural Association 4:41–95.

Terrell, J., 1976 Perspectives on the Prehistory of Bougainville Island, Papua New Guinea: A Study in the Human Biogeography of the Southwestern Pacific. Ph.D. dissertation, Harvard.

Thomas, T., P. Sheppard and R. Walter, 2001 Landscape, Violence and Social Bodies: Ritualized Architecture in a Solomon Islands Society. Journal of Royal Anthropological Institute 7:545–572.

Walter, R., and P. Sheppard, 2001 Nusa Roviana. The Archaeology of a Melanesian Chiefdom. Journal of Field Archaeology 27:295–318.

Ward, G., 1979 Prehistoric Settlement and Economy in a Tropical Small Island Environment: The Banks Islands, Insular Melanesia. Ph.D. dissertation, Australian National University.

Weiner, A., 1992 Inalienable Possessions: The Paradox of Keeping-While-Giving. Berkeley: University of California Press.

Weisler, M., ed., 1997 Prehistoric Long-Distance Interaction in Oceania: An Interdisciplinary Approach. Monograph 21. Auckland: New Zealand Archaeological Association.

White, G., 1979 War, Peace, and Piety in Santa Isabel, Solomon Islands. In The Pacification of Melanesia. M. Rodman and M. Cooper, eds. pp. 109–139. Association for Social Anthropology in Oceania Monograph 7. Lanham, MD: University Press of America.

Wickler, S., 1995 Twenty-Nine Thousand Years on Buka: Long-Term Cultural Change in the Northern Solomon Islands. Ph.D. dissertation, University of Hawai'i.

——2001 The Prehistory of Buka: A Stepping Stone Island in the Northern Solomons. Terra Australis 16. Canberra, ANH Publications and Centre for Archaeological Research, The Australian National University.

Zelenietz, M., 1979 The End of Head Hunting in New Georgia. In The Pacification of Melanesia. M. Rodman and M. Cooper, eds. pp. 91–108. Association for Social Anthropology in Oceania Monograph 7. Lanham, MD: University Press of America.

8

Envisaging Early Agriculture in the Highlands of New Guinea

Tim Denham

Prejudices are not necessarily unjustified and erroneous, so that they inevitably distort the truth. In fact, the historicity of our existence entails that prejudices, in the literal sense of the word, constitute the initial directedness of our whole ability to experience. Prejudices are biases of our openness to the world. They are simply conditions whereby we experience something – whereby what we encounter says something to us. (Gadamer 1976:9)

Why is it difficult to accept that agriculture developed independently in New Guinea? What co-intended presuppositions about agriculture, its origins and social forms come to mind when this question is asked? Are these assumptions relevant to understanding subsistence in New Guinea during prehistory or the recent past?

Traced historically, conceptions of agriculture persistently draw on packages of accompanying traits that include cereals, domesticated animals, settlements and sedentism, pottery, the emergence of socio-political hierarchies and "high" civilizations (Childe 1936; Diamond 2002; Piggott 1954; Vavilov 1992 [1926]; Zvelebil 1989). Such proxy traits reflect little about agriculture and much about the cultural traditions, education, and experiences of those who study it. None of these traits is necessary to understanding the emergence of agricultural practices in the highlands of New Guinea in the early to mid-Holocene.

The aim of this chapter is to consider how the origins of prehistoric agricultural practices in New Guinea are envisaged. Three conceptions of agriculture relevant to the New Guinean context are assessed and evaluated against corresponding lines of evidence. The intention is to be critical, foster reflection and stimulate debate, and not to prescribe yet another inclusive and absolute definition of agriculture.

Inherited Interpretations

Historical context

On March 8, 1933, the first Europeans flew over the Wahgi Valley, one of the largest inter-montane valleys in New Guinea. The following description encapsulates their view:

> Spread out for a hundred miles between the high mountains was the green, sunlit immensity of the Wahgi. A big river fed by innumerable streams ran through its centre, and oblong houses in homestead groups of four or five dotted across a continuous patchwork of neat, square gardens. The Wahgi, enormous, fertile and heavily popu- lated, greatest of New Guinea's highland valleys, had been "discovered." (Connolly and Anderson 1987:79)

At that time, the antiquity of agriculture in the highlands, or those areas of New Guinea above 1,200 meters, was unknown. From the late 1950s onward, archaeo- logical and paleoecological investigations were conducted with the intention of determining the antiquity of agriculture in the highlands (e.g., Bulmer 1966; Bulmer and Bulmer 1964).

By 1970, a provisional antiquity of prehistoric cultivation in New Guinea was established following archaeological and paleoecological investigations at several sites in the Wahgi Valley. These sites were Warrawau (formerly Manton's) Planta- tion in 1966 (Golson et al. 1967; Lampert 1967), Minjigina in 1967 (Lampert 1970; Powell 1970a), Kindeng in 1968 (unpublished) and Kuk in 1969 (Allen 1970). From the record of vegetation clearance at Warrawau and Draepi-Minjigina (Powell 1970a), agriculture was inferred to be of greater antiquity than the provi- sional time depth of 2300 B.P. obtained for a wooden digging stick at Warrawau (Golson et al. 1967).

Following Allen's reconnaissance, multidisciplinary investigations commenced at Kuk Swamp (hereafter referred to as Kuk) in 1970. These investigations were intended to "confirm and extend . . . the antiquity of agriculture in the New Guinea highlands; the age and circumstances of the move of cultivation into the swamp- lands; the nature and organization of agricultural activities there and associated set- tlement; and the date, causes and extent of their abandonment" (Golson 1976:209).

In part, the aims of the Kuk project changed as the increasing antiquity of the evidence at the site became apparent. The aims also changed as the results of botanical and ethnobotanical research suggested the increasing significance of New Guinea to understanding the origins of Pacific agriculture (Powell 1976; Yen 1973, 1985). Initially, the project was intended to establish the antiquity of pre-Ipomoean (sweet potato) agriculture in the highlands (e.g., Golson 1976, 1977), and was couched in terms of ultimate Southeast Asian origins (e.g., Golson 1976, 1985; Golson and Hughes 1980). As fieldwork neared completion, the interpretative emphasis shifted to highlight the independent origins of agriculture in New Guinea (e.g., Golson 1989, 1990, 1991a).

Origins of agriculture in New Guinea: indigenous or introduced?

The findings from Kuk initiated an unresolved debate concerning the antiquity and origins of agriculture in New Guinea. Golson, Yen, and others proposed that the archaeological and paleoenvironmental data from Kuk and other wetland sites in the interior provide convincing evidence for agriculture from ca. 10,200 cal B.P. (Golson 1977, 1991a; Golson and Hughes 1980; Gorecki 1986; Yen 1991). Most of these authors conceive agriculture as originating in the lowlands and being brought to the highlands as people migrated with the mixed oak forests following post-glacial climatic amelioration (e.g., Golson 1991a; Hope and Golson 1995). In contrast, Haberle (1993:299–306) proposed the mid-altitude, inter-montane valleys to be the locus of agricultural development from preexisting subsistence practices in the terminal Pleistocene.

The claims for independent agricultural origins from at least ca. 10,200 cal B.P. have not received universal acceptance. Doubts were fostered by substantive and conceptual problems with previous portrayals of indigenous agricultural development (see below). Alternative chronologies propose fully blown agriculture, domesticated crops, and techniques diffused to New Guinea with Austronesian dispersal (Spriggs 1996) as marked by the Lapita cultural complex at 3300–3100 cal B.P., or slightly earlier (Spriggs 2001:240; see also Galipaud, Lilley, Pavlides, Sand et al., and Walter and Sheppard, this volume). Austronesian influence on mainland New Guinea occurred perhaps 1,000 years later (Spriggs 1995; cf. Terrell and Welsch 1997 for reference to Lapita sherds from the north coast). From this position, preexisting indigenous practices represent forms of "cultivation or hunter-horticulturalism" (Spriggs 1996:533). Taking into account the possibilities of earlier Austronesian influence through western New Guinea and potential trade with Lapita peoples in the Bismarck Archipelago, evidence for independent agricultural origins on mainland New Guinea would pre-date at least 3500 cal B.P., and possibly ca. 3800 cal B.P.

The indigenist versus introduced debate may be a false dichotomy between early, independent agricultural origins and later Austronesian or Lapita introduction. The dichotomy rests on two assumptions. Firstly, after initial settlement of New Guinea by at least 40,000 B.P. (Groube et al. 1986), there was no pre-Lapita contact or sphere of exchange between Melanesia, Indo-Malaysia, and ultimately Southeast Asia. However, faunal translocation (Spriggs 1997:53–54) and plant movement (Yen 1998) suggest there was earlier, Pleistocene interaction between these regions. The ease of navigation and lines of sight between and within these regions, especially during periods of lower sea level in the Late Pleistocene and Early Holocene, make this proposition plausible (Irwin 1992). Secondly, the Lapita cultural complex was intrusive and not an indigenous development. Although there is now widespread agreement that Lapita was intrusive (e.g., Kirch 1997; Spriggs 1997), this position is not universally accepted (e.g., Allen and Gosden 1996; Terrell and Welsch 1997). If Lapita was an indigenous cultural efflorescence, then it need not mark or be contemporaneous with the diffusion of Austronesian or other Southeast Asian influences. If either assumption is erroneous, the terms of debate for the origins of agriculture in New Guinea shift. There is greater potential for more continuous and fluid exchange between Melanesia and Southeast Asia, with the likelihood of earlier introductions of crops and techniques (Denham 2004a). Any such, pre-Lapita introductions to New Guinea from mainland Southeast Asia probably occurred along localized exchange pathways as opposed to by long-distance voyaging and were possibly transmitted independently of other material cultural traits.

Conceptual and substantive problems

Previous attempts to critically assess the veracity of claims for independent origins in New Guinea were hindered by Golson's lack of an explicit conception of agriculture and lacunae in the lines of evidence presented. These inherited problems structured my ongoing investigation of early agriculture in New Guinea. Both conceptual and evidential lacunae are addressed in this chapter.

Golson envisaged early agriculture to have emerged from preexisting subsistence activities associated with arboriculture and the exploitation of other plants including numerous green vegetables and major sources of starch (Golson 1991a; Hope and Golson 1995). Major starch sources potentially indigenous to New Guinea and present for human exploitation include taro (*Colocasia esculenta*), yams (*Dioscorea* spp.), Australimusa and Eumusa bananas (*Musa* spp.), and sago (*Metroxylon sagu*) (see De Langhe and de Maret 1999; Lebot 1999; Matthews 1995; Mitsuru 2002; Yen 1995, 1998). However, Golson never developed a clear definition of agriculture vis-à-vis other subsistence activities and against which the prehistoric evidence could be measured (cf. Golson 1997a:44–46). Terms such as agriculture, horticulture, and cultivation were used without clear definition and almost interchangeably to refer to the same things at different times. For Golson, although there can be cultivation without horticulture or agriculture, the reverse does not hold, i.e., there is no horticulture and agriculture without cultivation (Golson pers. comm. 2003).

Golson's interpretations reflect dualistic thinking about the character of the archaeological remains at Kuk. The earlier three phases (1–3, ca. 10,000–4000 B.P.) are horticultural in that "each is structurally diversified in ways suggesting that provision was being made for crops of different edaphic and hydrologic requirements growing side-by-side in the same plantings" (Golson 1997a:45). The later three phases (4–6, ca. 2000–100 B.P.) are agricultural in the sense that they "exhibit standardized patterns based on long, straight ditches parallel and at right angles to each other that enclosed square to rectangular plots, thought to be planting areas for a single crop" (Golson 1997a:45). Golson envisages all these practices (Phases 1–6) to be agricultural and to be located along a gradient of intensification (Golson pers. comm. 2003). Although explicitly the phases through time represent an intensification of agricultural practices and a greater cultural imprint on the landscape, implicitly the earlier phases are conceived as being more natural than later forms. Similar views are implicit to many classifications of agricultural–nonagricultural practices (Terrell et al. 2003). In actuality, both sets of practices are socially contingent, involve a range of human–environment interactions, and arise out of *different* ways of living in the world.

Several substantive problems undermined acceptance of claims for the independent origins of agriculture in New Guinea by the broader archaeological community. First, only limited archaeological evidence associated with Phases 1–3 was published (Bayliss-Smith 1996:508; exceptions being Golson 1976, 1977, 1991b, 2000; Golson and Hughes 1980). Second, interpretations of the evidence, especially for Phase 1, changed through time (Bayliss-Smith 1996:508–509). Consequently, the mode of formation and function of constituent features on the Phase 1 and 2 paleosurfaces are uncertain (Smith 1998:142–143; Spriggs 1996:528). Third, there is a near-absence of published archaeobotanical evidence for former crop plants (Bayliss-Smith 1996:508; Spriggs 1996:528). *Musa* phytoliths (Wilson 1985) and seeds of useful plants (Powell 1982a) are associated with early phases at Kuk, but their significance is unclear because they need not represent deliberate, human dispersal. Fourth, the extent of landscape change coincident with the early phases is not known (Spriggs 1996:528).

Envisioning Agriculture: Three Approximations

How are agriculture and its origins in New Guinea to be conceived? Three alternative conceptions, or approximations, of agriculture are considered below to illuminate some definitional problems. These conceptions are presented within a narrative sketching the chronological unfolding of different views on Pacific agriculture and its origins.

The search for terminological clarity

A vast array of terminology and identifying characteristics has been proposed to differentiate agricultural from hunter-gatherer subsistence practices in the present and the past. Several terms connote strategies situated between these poles including "domiculture" (Hynes and Chase 1982), "incipient agriculture" (Ford 1985), "complex hunter-gatherers" (Zvelebil 1986), "transitional" and "proto-agriculture" (Yen 1989), "hunter-horticulturalism" (Guddemi 1992), and "low-level food production" (Smith 2001). As Harris stated:

> The published literature on "agricultural origins" is characterized by a confusing multiplicity of terms for the conceptual categories that define our discourse. There is little agreement about what precisely is meant by such terms as agriculture, horticulture,

cultivation, domestication and husbandry. This semantic confusion militates against clear thinking about the phenomena we investigate, leads to misunderstanding, and can provoke unnecessary disputes over interpretation of the evidence. (1996a:3)

To overcome this semantic confusion, Harris proposed terminology and a con-tinuum of human–environment interactions for subsistence (Harris 1989, modified in Harris 1996a:3–5). These were based on ethnographic and historical accounts of the exploitation of plants and animals for food (Harris 1989:18). Although Harris claimed the model to be purely descriptive and nondirectional, there are correspondences between ecological effects, socio-economic trends, and food yielding systems through time (Harris 1989:17; 1996a:4). The continuum is based on two entwined processes: the manipulation of biotic resources leading to their eventual domestication and the transformation of natural to artificial ecosystems (Harris 1989). Harris's schema has an implicit unilinear interpretation of human subsistence strategies with episodic intensification across developmental thresholds.

Approximation 1.   Domestication as marker

The most significant energetic threshold within Harris's original schema is the emergence of agriculture. From this perspective, agriculture is the propagation and cultivation of genotypic and phenotypic variants, i.e., domesticated crops, and the establishment of agro-ecosystems. Agriculture is associated with "such activities as soil preparation, the maintenance of soil fertility, weeding, seed selection and storage, and the exclusion of potential predators attracted by the enlarged food-storage organs of domesticated plants" (Harris 1989:21–22).

For Harris, the cultivation of domesticated crops is the key identifying criterion of agriculture. Domesticated species require sustained human intervention, or selec-tion, for their development and "have become dependent upon human assistance for their survival" (Harris 1989:19). These human interventions produce beneficial morphogenetic transformations in plants and animals that increase productivity, ease of processing, and so on. Morphogenetic transformations in plant macrofossils and microfossils, as well as animal bones, are used to trace domestication and the antiquity of agriculture in various parts of the globe, such as lowland neotropics (e.g., Piperno and Pearsall 1998).

Approximation 2.   Toward social definitions of agriculture

The use of morphogenetic markers and domestication as identifying characteristics of agriculture has been criticized. Jones et al. (1996:93) do not consider domesti-cation to be a major evolutionary threshold but a minor genetic transforma-tion. With respect to vegeculture, Hather (1996:548) rejected the concept of

domestication as a meaningful marker of agriculture because genetic transformations in plants begin once selective pressure is exerted, a process that potentially
commences with the earliest food production strategies (cf. Mitsuru 2002:18).
Additionally, most cultivated plants are not dependent on people for their survival,
but are able to reproduce independently of deliberate human intervention.

Developing these themes, Spriggs modified Harris's schema for application
to the Pacific context (Spriggs 1996:524–526). Spriggs proposed a continuum
between foraging, wild-food production, and cultivation, with a dramatic disjunc-
ture to agriculture. For him, it was not relevant whether a cultivated plant was
domesticated, but when dependence on agriculture began. Agriculture was defined
as "the creation of agro-ecosystems that limit subsistence choice because of environmental transformation or labour demands" (Spriggs 1996:525). Others have
also defined agriculture in increasingly social terms, e.g., "the relative scope of
human involvement in establishing the conditions for growth" (Ingold 1996:
21) and "a strategy that people have come to rely on for subsistence" (Hather
1996:548). These perspectives decouple the emergence of agriculture from
domestication. Harris (1996b:553) has partially accepted these modifications
(1995:849–850) and stated that "'agriculture' . . . differs in spatial scale, in labour
demands/energy input, and in environmental impact from the procurement and
small-scale production/protection of (mainly) wild plants and animals." However,
problems of archaeological visibility and the definition of agricultural thresholds
remain (Harris 1995:850; Yen 1998:164).

Approximation 3.   Ambiguity of practice

The wide range of subsistence practices in contemporary New Guinea includes
intensive wetland, semi-permanent and swidden agriculture (Brookfield with Hart
1971:92–124), and hunting and gathering (Roscoe 2002). Most groups are dependent to varying degrees on major starch staples including sweet potato (*Ipomoea
batatas*), *Colocasia* taro, *Musa* bananas, yams, and *Metroxylon* sago. There is considerable variability among agricultural practices, with marked differences between
the densely populated inter-montane valleys in the highlands (e.g., Brookfield and
Brown 1963) and more sparsely populated highland fringe and lowlands (e.g.,
Clarke 1971).

In the New Guinea context, there is considerable conceptual uncertainty in
classifying some practices as agricultural. Some fringe and lowland groups are
heavily reliant on a single staple. The Kubo, for instance, obtain over fifty percent
of their energy from *Musa* bananas, but obtain a large proportion of their diet from
hunting and gathering a broad range of food sources including *Metroxylon* sago
(Dwyer and Minnegal 1991). Some lowland groups are classified as hunter-
gatherers even though they are heavily reliant on managed stands of *Metroxylon*
sago (see Roscoe 2002). The definition of other lowland groups is similarly
"ambiguous," because their reliance on cultivated plots is variable and periodic
(Terrell 2002).

From the foregoing, how does the diversity and conceptual ambiguity of con-temporary subsistence practices map onto interpretations of prehistoric agriculture in New Guinea? In what sense are definitions of agriculture accurate representa-tions of fundamental differences in the way people live(d), as opposed to being rel-atively arbitrary impositions of an artificial framework to delimit the present or past? On a general level, Hodder has criticized attempts to provide inclusive, ahistoric definitions and to determine "origins." He claims (1999:175) that "in all . . . cases the claim for origin is part of a wider narrative which ends with ourselves. Indeed, it could be said that it is the end point which has led to the focus on a particular starting point." Following Hodder, the definition of agriculture determines the timing and location of its origins. In place of attempts to find ultimate origins, and *causa efficiens* to drive such inclusive narratives, Hodder states:

> Contextual emphases on diversity, meaning, agency and contingency undermine any notions of "the origin". In a multivalent world, past and present, it becomes difficult to separate out a fixed "thing" for which an origin can be found. Rather than focus-ing on major transformations, it is possible to use archaeological data to gain an under-standing of the indeterminate relations between large-scale processes and individual lives. (1999:175)

Taking Hodder's criticisms into account, we need to focus on the "indeterminate relations between large-scale processes and individual lives." Only once these inde-terminate relations are clarified, through understanding past practices, can we then go on to develop an historically contingent idea of "agriculture" relevant to the New Guinean context.

Subsistence Practices in the Early to Mid-Holocene

Given the absence of an agreed definition for agriculture, how are subsistence practices to be envisaged in the New Guinea highlands during the early to mid-Holocene? Three different approaches to the question of agriculture were reviewed above: the cultivation of domesticated plants (Harris 1989); a dependence on agro-ecosystems within a highly altered environment (Spriggs 1996); and a refocusing on practices (after Hodder 1999). Lines of evidence corresponding to each of these approximations are evaluated below: archaeobotanical remains, potential agricul-tural signatures in material culture and landscape change, and the archaeological remains of former subsistence practices at Kuk, respectively.

Archaeobotanical remains and visibility

The archaeobotanical visibility of New Guinea agriculture, and particularly vege-culture, is poor (Golson and Ucko 1994). Most tubers, which function as staples in the highlands, do not produce phytoliths and rarely produce pollen and seeds (after Powell 1970b; also Maloney 1994). Recent advances in the identification of tubers in the Pacific were made using preserved parenchymatous tissues (Hather 1994) and starch grains on stone tools (Barton and White 1993; Loy et al. 1992) and in sediments (Barton et al. 1998; Therin et al. 1999). These findings have greatly augmented our understanding of late Pleistocene to mid-Holocene subsistence in Melanesia and, more recently, the highlands of New Guinea.

Arboriculture

Substantial evidence for the exploitation of fruit-, nut- and starch-bearing trees dates to at least the early to mid-Holocene in lowland Melanesia (Gorecki 1992; Hayes 1992; Kirch 1989; Swadling et al. 1991; Yen 1998) and highland New Guinea (Donoghue 1988). Using macrobotanical collections from lowland sites in Melanesia, Yen proposed *Canarium* spp. were indigenous to New Guinea (1990:262) and *C. indicum* was subject to selection, inter-island transportation, and domestication from the late Pleistocene (Yen 1996:41). For the highlands, Haberle (1995) proposed domestication of *Pandanus brosimos* (wild form) to *P. julianettii* (domesticated form) commencing in the late Pleistocene.

By the early Holocene, the availability of arboreal resources on the valley floors in the highlands greatly increased with post-glacial climatic amelioration. Advancing mixed-oak forests contained several fruit- and nut-bearing species including *Castanopsis-Lithocarpus* spp., *Elaeocarpus* spp. and *Ficus* spp. (Golson 1991a; Hope and Golson 1995). Although these tree species are well represented in pollen diagrams across the highlands at this time, archaeobotanical collections from contemporary occupation sites are sparse, largely unexamined, and have yet to provide direct evidence for broad-spectrum plant use.

Starch staples

Stone-tool residues from Pleistocene contexts in lowland Melanesia include aroids (*Colocasia esculenta* and *Alocasia macrorrhiza*), a yam (*Dioscorea* sp.), and *Cyrtosperma* spp. (Barton and White 1993; Loy et al. 1992). These findings are augmented by recent discoveries at Kuk including *Colocasia* taro starch grains and probable ginger (Zingiberaceae) or possible palm phytoliths on tools from early Holocene contexts (Denham et al. 2003; Fullagar et al. 2002). Phytoliths of cf. *Setaria palmifolia* and bananas, including Eumusa morphotypes, were documented from 10,000-year-old contexts at Kuk (Denham et al. 2003; Lentfer 2002; cf. Wilson 1985). In addition to these finds, the remains of sugarcane (*Saccharum officinarum*) were found in a mid-Holocene context at Yuku rockshelter (Bulmer 1975:31), although the basis for this identification is unknown (Yen 1998:168).

The presence of Eumusa bananas, *Colocasia* taro, probable *Setaria palmifolia*, and probable *Zingiber* gingers from the early Holocene, and probable sugarcane by the mid-Holocene, are highly significant and open up new interpretative possibilities for the prehistory of agriculture in New Guinea. These plants could have functioned as high caloric staples in prehistoric diets, even though they were probably low-yielding in comparison to contemporary varieties. The exploitation of starch-rich plants, in conjunction with deliberate environmental modification and translocation of species, enabled people to permanently inhabit the interior rain forests and were instrumental to the emergence of agriculture in New Guinea (Denham and Barton in press; also Pavlides, this volume).

Other vegetables

A vast array of plants is used in the highlands for food, construction, medicines, and ritual (Powell 1976; Powell et al. 1975). In contrast to starchy plants, some vegetables yield readily identifiable phytoliths, pollen, and seeds. Fragments of gourd exocarp were collected from a mid-Holocene context at Warrawau, although the species represented is uncertain and variously reported as *Lagenaria siceraria* (Powell 1970a:145); *Lagenaria* (cf.) *siceraria* (Powell 1970b:199), or *Benincasa hispida* (Golson 2002). Extensive seed assemblages of utilized plants and corroborating pollen data were collected at several wetland sites in the highlands (Powell 1970a, 1982a; Powell et al. 1975).

The seeds and wood of several cultivated and wild-food plants were collected from archaeological contexts associated with Phases 1, 2, and 3 at Kuk. During Phase 1 only two species utilized in a wild form were present (*Pouzolzia hirta* and *Rubus rosifolius*), with the possible cultivation of *Pandanus* spp. During Phase 2 a much greater range of presently cultivated species is recorded, although many were probably wild at that time. The interpretation of seed data in highland New Guinea is problematic because most species are not diagnostic of specific habitats and probably colonized wetland margins independently of, or after, anthropogenic disturbance (Powell 1982a:32). However, many species represented in the seed assemblages are commonly found in gardens, fallow and secondary regrowth today and are indicative of the range of plants available for human exploitation at various times in the past (Powell 1982a:32).

Revised scenarios

The "floristic and structural complexity" of the mixed oak forests, which were established on the floors of the main inter-montane valleys by the early Holocene, greatly increased the range of available arboreal resources (after Hope et al. 1988:603). As well as nut- and fruit-bearing trees (especially *Castanopsis-Lithocarpus* spp., *Elaeocarpus* spp., *Ficus* spp., and *Pandanus* spp.), there were numerous under-storey and epiphytic plants such as fruit-bearing vines, vegetables (e.g., *Rungia klossii*, *Oenanthe javanica*), shade-tolerant species (e.g., "yam-like tubers, apparently of the genus *Dioscorea*" [Golson 1991a:87]), likely ecotone, edge and gap colonizers (e.g., *Colocasia* taro, *Musa* bananas, and sugarcane), and fungi (after Golson 1991a; Hope and Golson 1995). There is now archaeobotanical evidence for the availability and/or use of most of these species from the early to mid-Holocene. The plant resources could have supported broad-spectrum exploitation based around high caloric, starch staples.

At present it is not possible to determine if these archaeobotanical finds are domesticated or wild varieties. Lebot (1999) reviewed the biomolecular signatures for important vegetables, e.g., *aibika* (*Abelmoschus manihot*) and most of the major Pacific staples including *Colocasia* taro, *Musa* bananas, the greater yam (*Dioscorea alata*), giant taro (*Alocasia macrorrhiza*), breadfruit (*Artocarpus altilis*), and sugarcane (*Saccharum officinarum*). Lebot claims these plants were all domesticated in "New Guinea and some parts of Melanesia" which "have been important centers of diversity for species that also exist in Asia" (Lebot 1999:626).

Archaeobotany and biomolecular analysis are mutually supporting lines of evidence for an ancient reliance on plant resources in the interior rain forests of New Guinea. Archaeobotany has shown the presence and/or use of a whole range of plants in highland New Guinea by the early to mid-Holocene and prior to any known contact with Southeast Asia. These same species were subject to anthropogenic selection evidenced from present-day biomolecular composition and reproductive strategies, e.g., parthenocarpy in *Musa* bananas. Additionally, the presence of *Colocasia* taro at Kuk by ca.10,200 cal B.P. (Fullagar et al. 2002) and in contemporary and earlier contexts in lowland Melanesia (Haberle 1995; Loy et al. 1992) lends credence to suggestions of the deliberate movement of this plant into the highlands (after Yen 1995:835).

In summary, definite evidence for domesticated plant use in the early to mid-Holocene has yet to be obtained. However, the presence, use, and movement at this time of species including starch staples claimed to be Melanesian domesticates are highly significant. These archaeobotanical finds provide evidence for a trajectory of indigenous plant use in the highlands from at least the early Holocene. Later cultivated varieties of Southeast Asian origin were introduced in the mid- to late Holocene and supplemented an indigenous, domesticated gene pool of the same species, e.g., *Colocasia* taro and Eumusa bananas (after Yen 1998). Future macrobotanical, phytolith, and starch grain analyses will enable anthropogenic dispersal and morphogenetic transformations of plant species to be traced across space and through time, as has been successfully undertaken for several crop plants in the neotropics (Piperno and Pearsall 1998).

An agricultural package

Interpretations of agriculture in Europe and Southwest Asia have attempted to identify a "Neolithic package" of associated cultural traits (e.g., Piggott 1954; Zvelebil 1989). The idea of a "Neolithic package" underpins conceptualizations of Austronesian dispersal through Indo-Malaysia (Bellwood 1997:201–254) and the Lapita cultural complex in island Melanesia (Green 1991; Spriggs 1989, 1995). In the highlands, several agricultural signatures were similarly proposed to accompany agriculture and be present by 6800–5700 cal B.P., including the pig, ground stone axes/adzes, and widespread forest clearance (Bulmer 1975:45; Christensen 1975:34; White 1972:147). The antiquity and significance of these putative elements of an agricultural package are unclear, e.g., the pig (Harris 1996b:568), and some are briefly reviewed here.

Signatures in material culture

New Guinea is the second largest island in the world, and relatively few sites in its interior have been excavated and reported in full. The archaeological record from the highlands can be characterized as spatially and historically fragmented. Excavations at Kosipe (White et al. 1970) and Nombe (Mountain 1991) suggested human presence in the mountainous interior by at least 30,000 cal B.P. (Lilley, this volume).

No clear signatures of a transition to agriculture were identified in lithic, faunal, and macrobotanical assemblages recovered from caves, open sites, and rockshelters in the highlands (see Denham 2003a:21–93; see Figure 8.1). The most plausible agricultural signature is a change in stone-tool technology at or before ca. 6800–5700 cal B.P. with the presence of the ground axe/adze (Christensen 1975:33). This technological shift is not well dated and need not mark the advent of agriculture, although these tools would have greatly facilitated forest clearance.

Two reported settlements of Pleistocene age, NFX (Watson and Cole 1977) and Wañlek (Bulmer 1973, 1977, 1991), are potentially significant indicators of sedentism. The claimed antiquity at each site is, however, based on a single radio-carbon date and is unreliable. No structural remains at open sites in the highlands date to the early to mid-Holocene. Although "five stratified occupation horizons" from the late Pleistocene through the Holocene were claimed for Wañlek (Bulmer 1991:471), the published evidence indicates the earliest Holocene occupation dates to 2840–3430 cal B.P., is associated with pottery, and could potentially be Austronesian-influenced (Denham 2003a; cf. Bulmer 1991). The structural remains documented in the highlands need not signify anything significant about agriculture, as they could represent temporary or seasonal shelters made by foraging groups.

Anthropogenic clearance of the rain forest

The earliest anthropogenic disturbances of vegetation in the highlands are con-temporary with earliest settlement and date to at least 30,000 cal B.P. (Haberle et al. 1991; Hope 1998; Hope and Golson 1995:822; Lilley, this volume). These burning events were interpreted to represent crop-procurement practices intended to enhance the productivity of seasonally exploited *Pandanus* spp. (Hope and Golson 1985:822–823; also see White et al. 1970). Based on the ecology of *Nothofagus* spp. forests, Golson has suggested that human use of the highlands as a whole during the Pleistocene focused on *Pandanus* spp. (Golson 1991a:86–88).

In the late Pleistocene and early Holocene, the rain forests on the floors of several large inter-montane valleys at 1,400–1,650 meters+ were subject to more extensive disturbance. These clearances were spatially limited, asynchronous, and mostly non-cumulative. For example, two early episodes of prolonged clearance followed by

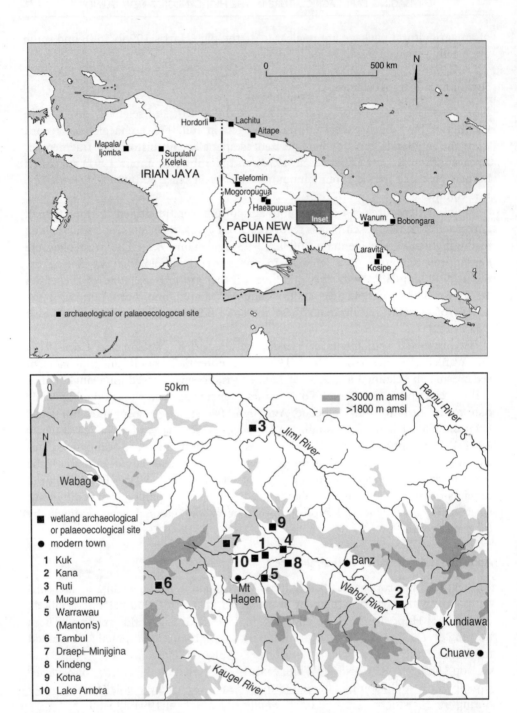

Figure 8.1 Map showing location of archaeological sites in the Highlands of New Guinea. Inset depicts wetland sites

forest recovery occurred at Telefomin (Hope 1983). In contrast, the records for Kelela Swamp in the Baliem Valley and Kuk Swamp in the Wahgi Valley show cumulative disturbance from before ca. 7800 cal B.P. to the present and between 10,200 and 6800 cal B.P., respectively (Haberle et al. 1991 and Haberle 2002, respectively). From 10,200 cal B.P. at Kuk, there is a marked decline in primary forest species and replacement by a mosaic of secondary forest, swamp forest, and open grassland. A coincident peak in charcoal particle frequencies suggests vegetation clearance using fire was the cause of vegetation change. These clearances are not climate-induced because they occurred during a period of warmer and wetter climates (after Brookfield 1989). The record of vegetation clearance accords with previous interpretations of increased erosion rates from the Kuk catchment (Golson and Hughes 1980:296–298; Hughes et al. 1991).

By the mid-Holocene (6100–5700 cal B.P.), anthropogenic degradation of primary forest had occurred across the Upper Wahgi Valley, although it was not ubiquitous (Powell 1982b:218). Several sites signal a change from undisturbed primary forest in the Late Pleistocene to a disturbed environment by the mid-Holocene (6800–5700 cal B.P.) with the establishment of grasslands (Kuk), higher percentages of woody non-forest species (Draepi-Minjigina, Lake Ambra), or the establishment of secondary forest (Warrawau) (after Haberle 2002; Denham, Haberle, and Lentfer 2004; Powell 1970a, 1981; Powell et al. 1975:43–48). Most sites record a further decline in forest cover up to 4500 cal B.P. with concomitant rises in grass frequencies (Powell 1982b:218).

By 4500 cal B.P., "considerable areas of forest had been cleared throughout the highlands" (Powell 1982b:224). The disturbance of forest and establishment of anthropogenic landscapes occurred throughout the main inter-montane valleys and spread to adjacent higher and lower altitudes (Walker and Flenley 1979 and Gillieson et al. 1989, respectively). Although a recovery of forests occurred in parts of the Wahgi Valley after 4500 cal B.P. (i.e., Warrawau; Powell 1982b:218), it was not dramatic and the following 1,800–2,400-year period represents stabilization of a disturbed environment. The scale of environmental change by the mid-Holocene was considerable, with some inter-montane valleys denuded to grassland by this time.

Is there an "agricultural package" for the highlands?

Asynchronies between material culture and land clearance are visible in the prehistory of southwest Asia, a region in which the antiquity of agriculture is often assumed to be clearly demonstrable. Several authors have noted the delay of almost 4,000 years after the putative origins of agriculture before vegetation clearance on a regional or continental scale becomes visible (Jones et al. 1996:94–95). Inspired by these asynchronies, Hodder (1999:175) has stated: "It is increasingly difficult to identify any point within a 4,000-year period at which agriculture 'began' in the Near East."

Similarly, in reviewing the origins and spread of agriculture in northern Europe and the British Isles, Thomas questioned the relevance of agricultural packages:

"there was no point at which an homogeneous 'Neolithic' package of economic practice and material culture ever existed" (Thomas 1999:14, also see Thomas 1996a:141–149; 1996b:311–313). In contrast to such totalizing conceptions, Thomas demonstrated the differential and asynchronous diffusion of traits, explicated their individual trajectories, and emphasized the social and cultural complexity, diversity, and idiosyncrasy of the "British Neolithic." A similar scenario applies to highlands' prehistory, in which no clear signatures of an "agricultural package" are visible.

Thomas discussed the spatial and temporal variability of land clearance in Britain to criticize depictions of uniform, demographically driven, agricultural expansion (Thomas 1999:29–32). This image resonates with the asynchronous, non-cumulative, and non-ubiquitous records of Early Holocene clearance in the New Guinea highlands, and contrasts with the more synchronous and extensive degradation to grassland and secondary regrowth that occurred in several inter-montane valleys by the mid-Holocene. Following Spriggs (1996), land-use practices from at least the mid-Holocene appear to be "agricultural" as they severely degraded the environment to grassland and restricted subsequent subsistence choice.

Subsistence activities on wetland margins

Six sequential, prehistoric phases of wetland drainage were identified during multidisciplinary investigations at Kuk (Golson 1977). Kuk is the type-site for the investigation of prehistoric agriculture in the interior of New Guinea against which the evidence from other sites was compared and cross-correlated (see Figure 8.1). As noted earlier, the earlier drainage networks of Phases 1–3 were morphologically distinct from the later (Phases 4–6) (e.g., Golson 1982a:300–301; 1990:145; Golson and Gardner 1990:405). The more recent Phases 4–6 "exhibit[ed] standardized patterns based on long, straight ditches parallel and at right angles to each other that enclosed square to rectangular plots, thought to be planting areas for a single crop" (Golson 1997a:45). Only Phases 1–3 are significant in terms of determining early and independent agricultural origins in New Guinea.

The Phase 1 paleosurface dates to approximately 10,220–9910 cal B.P. and comprises irregularly distributed features (Figure 8.2). Some are probably natural and may be associated with rill erosion on an exposed ground surface, while others are more plausibly anthropogenic and interpreted as stake and post holes, pits, and complexes of inter-cut features (Denham, Golson, and Hughes 2004; Golson 1977, 1991b; Golson and Hughes 1980). These latter features may represent digging, planting, and tethering activities within a cultivated plot, possibly on higher and episodically drier ground adjacent to a paleochannel. The presence of residues of *Colocasia* taro starch (Fullagar et al. 2002), *Eumusa* banana phytoliths (Lentfer 2002), and a few artifacts, including a pestle, from broadly contemporary contexts supports this interpretation. New lines of archaeobotanical evidence support earlier interpretations that Phase 1 represents experimental cultivation of indigenous plants (Golson 1977:614; 1991b:484–485; Yen 1990:262–263). Palynological and

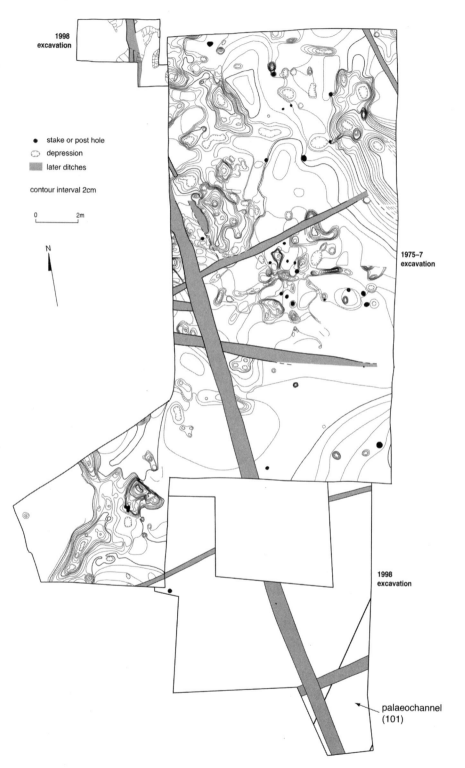

1998 excavation

- stake or post hole
- depression
- later ditches

contour interval 2cm

0   2m

N

1975–7 excavation

1998 excavation

palaeochannel (101)

Figure 8.2 Composite plan of 1975–1977 and 1998 excavations at Kuk Swamp showing Phase 1 paleosurface adjacent to paleochannel (101; modified version of Denham 2004, Fig. 7)

geomorphological evidence for forest clearance within the catchment (Haberle 2002; Hughes et al. 1991) indicates that the plot on the wetland margin, represented by Phase 1 at Kuk, is the visible remnant of a much broader land-use strategy.

The Phase 2 paleosurface at Kuk dates to 6950–6440 cal B.P. and occurs as integrated and less integrated types (Figure 8.3). The integrated form consists of "a web of short [runnels], so disposed as to define roughly circular clay islands of about one meter diameter" (Golson 1977:616). This paleosurface was interpreted to retain water during periods of low runoff and drain water through the system and into an associated paleochannel during high runoff (Golson 1977:616). The less integrated paleosurface type consists of more dispersed features that lacked an overall pattern (Golson 1977:616–617). Similar, but slightly later, integrated paleosurfaces were recorded in the Upper Wahgi Valley at Mugumamp (Harris and Hughes 1978) and Warrawau Plantation (Golson 1982b:121) with more equivocal evidence being documented at Ruti, Lower Jimi Valley (Gillieson et al. 1985), and Kana, Mid-Wahgi Valley (Muke and Mandui 2003; see Denham 2003b for a review).

The anthropogenesis of the integrated paleosurface is suggested by the regularity of mound morphology and distribution, the associations between stake and post holes and deeper depressions, and the presence of artifacts, charcoal, and manuports in feature fills. This paleosurface represents small-scale micro-topographical manipulation of the wetland to enable the multi-cropping of plants with different edaphic requirements (Golson 1977:617). Water-tolerant plants, e.g., *Colocasia* taro, were potentially planted along the edges and in the bases of the runnels, and water-intolerant plants, e.g., sugarcanes (*Saccharum* spp.), edible *pitpit* (*Setaria palmifolia*), *Musa* bananas, and mixed vegetables, were planted on the raised "beds" (Golson 1977:616; 1981:57–58; Powell et al. 1975:42). Archaeobotanical remains from feature fills, associated contexts, and stone-tool residues are consistent with this interpretation. The Phase 2 paleosurfaces represent mounded cultivation on a wetland margin within a landscape heavily degraded to grassland.

Major paleochannels were originally interpreted to be artificial, to divert runoff from the southern catchment across and away from the wetland margin, and to articulate with the Phase 1 and 2 paleosurfaces (Golson 1977; Golson and Hughes 1980). However, the artificiality of the paleochannel associated with Phase 1 is doubtful (Denham 2004b). Similarly, the artificial construction of Phase 2 paleochannels is unverified and their previously reported associations between paleochannels and paleosurfaces for Phase 2 at Kuk, Mugumamp, and Warrawau are unsubstantiated (Denham 2003b).

Phase 3 drainage networks at Kuk represent the advent of intensive forms of wetland management and drainage. Phase 3 ditches and ditch networks group into three sub-phases based on stratigraphic and tephrachronological correlations (Denham in press; Figure 8.4): three early, rectilinear ditch complexes date to approximately 4350–3980 cal B.P.; mid–late, unarticulated ditches and ditch pairs (poorly dated); and two late ditch complexes with dendritic, rectilinear, and triangular components pre-date 3260–2800 cal B.P.

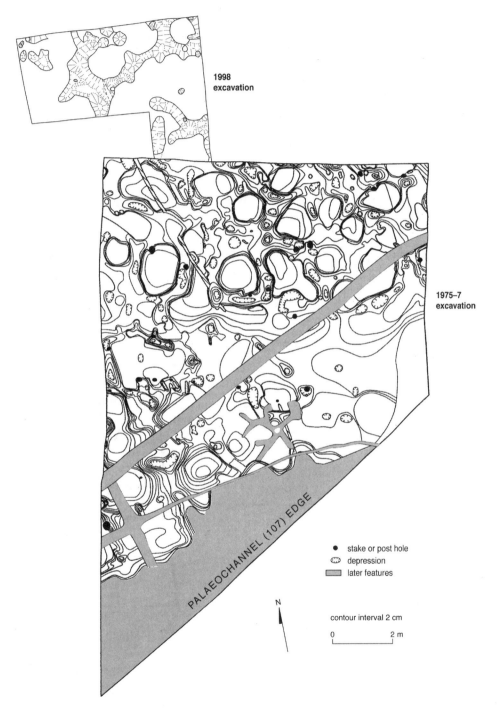

1998
excavation

1975–7
excavation

PALAEOCHANNEL (107) EDGE

● stake or post hole
⬭ depression
▨ later features

N

contour interval 2 cm

0 — — — — 2 m

Figure 8.3 Composite plan of 1975–1977 and 1998 excavations at Kuk Swamp showing Phase 2 paleosurface cut by later paleochannel (107)

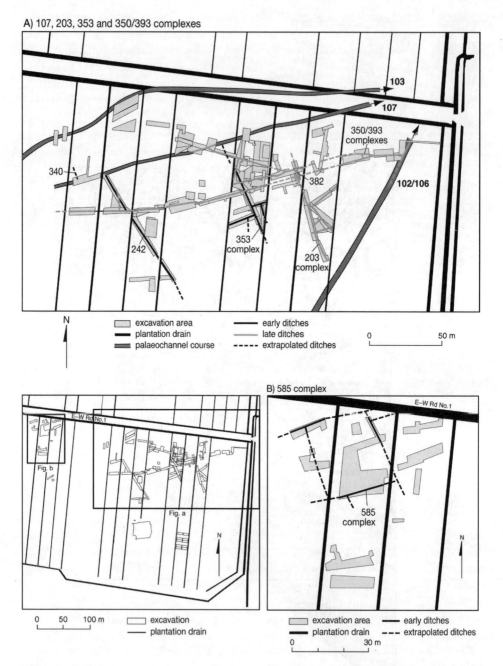

A) 107, 203, 353 and 350/393 complexes

103
107
350/393
complexes
102/106
340
382
242
353
complex
203
complex

N

excavation area   early ditches
plantation drain   late ditches
palaeochannel course   extrapolated ditches

0   50 m

B) 585 complex

E–W Rd No.1

Fig. b

Fig. a

E–W Rd No.1

585
complex

N

N

0   50   100 m   excavation
                   plantation drain

excavation area   early ditches
plantation drain   extrapolated ditches
0   30 m

Figure 8.4 Summary plan of Phase 3 ditch networks and contemporary paleochannels (102, 103, 106, and 107) at Kuk Swamp. Inset A depicts early and late sub-phase ditch complexes and Inset B depicts an early Phase 3 ditched enclosure (reproduced with permission from Denham, Golson, and Hughes 2004, Fig. 16)

Ditch-digging was an indigenous innovation that may reflect an increased reliance on relatively productive wetlands within a grassed landscape. Contemporary ditching was documented for several other wetlands in the highlands. A wooden spade from a ditch at Tambul at 2,170 meters altitude is contemporary with early Phase 3 at Kuk (Golson 1997b). Ditch networks at Warrawau (Golson 1982b:121) and Kana (Muke and Mandui 2003) in the Wahgi Valley and Haeapugua in the Tari Basin (Ballard 1995, 2001) are contemporary with late Phase 3 at Kuk. The archaeological evidence for Phase 3 reflects the spatial expansion of ditching through the Wahgi Valley and other inter-montane valleys. Although late Phase 3 ditch networks are within an Austronesian or Lapita time-frame, the early Phase 3 evidence at Kuk and Tambul pre-dates any likely influence on mainland New Guinea by several hundred years.

Burden of proof

Spriggs questioned whether agricultural development in New Guinea was an inevitable development from preexisting subsistence strategies given the lack of plant remains, lack of evidence for landscape transformation, and uncertain archaeological evidence (Spriggs 1996:528–529; 1997:62). These three lacunae are reviewed here with the intention of clarifying the prehistory of subsistence, and in particular the antiquity of agriculture, in the highlands. The review has found evidence for the presence and use of several food plants including major starch staples, for extensive landscape transformation, and for likely subsistence practices along wetland margins from the early Holocene. Cumulative environmental degradation occurred until the mid-Holocene, with more intensive manipulation of the wetland margins from that time. All these lines of evidence conform to ideas of agriculture widely applied to contemporary practices in New Guinea.

For example, the Phase 1 paleosurface at Kuk is consistent with a garden or swidden plot cleared on a wetland margin for plant cultivation. This plot was situated in a catchment subject to extensive clearance using fire, with resultant floral degradation and soil erosion. Several feature types within the plot are suggestive of plant cultivation, with the remains of utilized plants being found in associated sediments and on stone tools, particularly *Colocasia* taro and Eumusa bananas. Greater detail is still required to determine the range of plants used, but a more coherent picture of early Holocene activities and associated impacts is emerging.

The development of agriculture in New Guinea was certainly not an inexorable unfolding from preexisting subsistence strategies. The causes and nature of these early agricultural activities are uncertain. The locus of agricultural development, whether in the lowlands or highlands, and its geographical and historical dispersal are unknown. These issues will remain opaque given the lack of archaeological and archaeobotanical information for the interior. Without additional investigations, the prehistories of plant use, environmental manipulation, resource exploitation, and subsistence practices presented here will remain glimpses of a complex, differenti-ated, and idiosyncratic past.

Living with Uncertainty

How is the emergence of agriculture in the highlands of New Guinea to be under-stood? Origins-of-agriculture debates are largely projections of categories and con-cepts derived from European and Southwest Asian experience. Concepts such as domestication, landscape change, and agricultural packages are not necessary, value-free, or to be uncritically accepted. These concepts are essentially arbitrary projections from specific historical contexts. These demarcations constitute teleo-logical arguments that place agriculture within broader historical processes, e.g., the spread of Neolithic cultures and rise of "civilizations." As such, origin-of-agriculture debates exemplify neo-colonialist attitudes that are embedded at the heart of much archaeological practice. In this light, it is not surprising that New Guinea is often omitted or receives cursory discussion in presentations of early and independent agriculture.

The early to mid-Holocene evidence for the origins of agriculture in the high-lands of New Guinea is relatively robust for all three approximations. In terms of plant domestication (Harris), there is early Holocene evidence for the presence, use, and movement of plants that were subsequently domesticated in New Guinea. In terms of landscape transformation and a dependence on agro-ecosystems (Spriggs), clearances of vegetation accelerated in the early Holocene at Kuk with the resul-tant need of people to obtain their subsistence in a highly degraded grassland envi-ronment by the mid-Holocene. In terms of past practices (after Hodder), wetland archaeological sites provide direct evidence for anthropogenic alteration and plant use from the early Holocene. The nature of prehistoric activities and agricultural denotation require further clarification, but similar ambiguities cloud the classifi-cation of contemporary subsistence practices in New Guinea and of prehistoric practices elsewhere in the world.

ACKNOWLEDGMENTS

This chapter was written during 2002. The author is grateful to Jack Golson for his permission to use the archive of previous investigations at Kuk including excavation plans by Art and Cherie Rohn (incorporated into Figures 8.2 and 8.3). Richard Fullagar, Simon Haberle, and Carol Lentfer permitted reference to unpub-lished work. Mary-Jane Mountain permitted the reproduction of Win Mumford's map of archaeological sites in the highlands (presented in amended form in Figure 8.1). Julie Gardiner, *Proceedings of the Prehistoric Society*, granted permission for the reproduction of Figure 8.4. The figures were drafted by Kay Dancey and Rob Patat.

REFERENCES

Allen, J., 1970 Prehistoric Agricultural Systems in the Wahgi Valley – A Further Note. Mankind 7:177–183.

Allen, J., and C. Gosden, 1996 Spheres of Interaction and Integration: Modelling the Culture History of the Bismarck Archipelago. In Oceanic Culture History: Essays in Honour of Roger Green. J. Davison, G. Irwin, F. Leach, A. Pawley and D. Brown, eds. pp. 183–197. Special Publication. Dunedin: New Zealand Journal of Archaeology.

Ballard, C., 1995 The Death of a Great Land: Ritual, History and Subsistence Revolution in the Southern Highlands of Papua New Guinea. Ph.D. dissertation, Australian National University.

——2001 Wetland Drainage and Agricultural Transformations in the Southern Highlands of Papua New Guinea. Asia Pacific Viewpoint 42:287–304.

Barton, H., and J. P. White, 1993 Use of Stone and Shell Artifacts at Balof 2, New Ireland, Papua New Guinea. Asian Perspectives 32:169–181.

Barton, H., R. Torrence and R. Fullagar, 1998 Clues to Stone Tool Function Re-Examined: Comparing Starch Grain Frequencies on Used and Unused Obsidian Artifacts. Journal of Archaeological Science 25:1231–1238.

Bayliss-Smith, T., 1996 People–Plant Interactions in the New Guinea Highlands: Agricultural Hearthland or Horticultural Backwater? In The Origins and Spread of Agriculture and Pastoralism in Eurasia. D. Harris, ed. pp. 499–452. London: University College London Press.

Bellwood, P., 1997 Prehistory of the Indo-Malaysian Archipelago. Honolulu: University of Hawai'i Press.

Brookfield, H., 1989 Frost and Drought through Time and Space, Part III: What were Conditions like when the High Valleys were First Settled? Mountain Research and Development 9:306–321.

Brookfield, H., and P. Brown, 1963 Struggle for Land. Melbourne: Oxford University Press.

Brookfield, H., with D. Hart, 1971 Melanesia. London: Methuen.

Bulmer, S., 1966 The Prehistory of the Australian New Guinea Highlands: A Discussion of Archaeological Field Survey and Excavations, 1959–60. M.A. dissertation, University of Auckland.

——1973 Notes on 1972 Excavations at Wañlek, an Open Settlement Site in the Kaironk Valley, Papua New Guinea. Working Paper 29. Auckland: Department of Anthropology, University of Auckland.

——1975 Settlement and Economy in Prehistoric Papua New Guinea: A Review of the Archaeological Evidence. Journal de la Société des Océanistes 31:7–75.

——1977 Between the Mountain and the Plain: Prehistoric Settlement and Environment in the Kaironk Valley. In The Melanesian Environment. J. Winslow, ed. pp. 61–73. Canberra: Australian National University Press.

——1991 Variation and Change in Stone Tools in the Highlands of Papua New Guinea: The Witness of Wañelek. In Man and a Half: Essays in Pacific Anthropology and Ethnobiology in Honour of Ralph Bulmer. A. Pawley, ed. pp. 470–478. Auckland: The Polynesian Society.

Bulmer, S., and R. Bulmer, 1964 The Prehistory of the Australian New Guinea Highlands. American Anthropologist 66:39–76.

Childe, V. G., 1936 Man makes Himself. London: Watts.

Christensen, O., 1975 Hunters and Horticulturalists: A Preliminary Report of the 1972–4 Excavations in the Manim Valley, Papua New Guinea. Mankind 10:24–36.

Clarke, W., 1971 Place and People: An Ecology of a New Guinea Community. Berkeley, CA: University of California Press.

Connolly, B., and R. Anderson, 1987 First Contact: New Guinea's Highlanders Encounter the Outside World. New York: Viking Penguin.

De Langhe, E., and P. de Maret, 1999 Tracking the Banana: Its Significance in Early Agriculture. In The Prehistory of Food. C. Gosden and J. Hather, eds. pp. 377–396. London: Routledge.

Denham, T., 2003a The Kuk Morass: Multi-Disciplinary Investigations of Early to Mid Holocene Plant Exploitation at Kuk Swamp, Wahgi Valley, Papua New Guinea. Ph.D. dissertation, Australian National University.

——2003b Archaeological Evidence for Mid-Holocene Agriculture in the Interior of New Guinea: A Critical Review. Archaeology in Oceania 38:159–176.

——2004a The Roots of Agriculture and Arboriculture in New Guinea: Looking Beyond Austronesian Expansion, Neolithic Packages and Indigenous Origins. World Archaeology 36:610–620.

——2004b Early Agriculture in the Highlands of New Guinea: An Assessment of Phase 1 at Kuk Swamp. In A Pacific Odyssey: Essays in Archaeology and Anthropology in Honour of Jim Specht. V. Attenbrow and R. Fullagar, eds. pp. 47–58. Records of the Australian Museum Supplement 29. Sydney: Australian Museum.

——In press Agricultural Origins and the Emergence of Rectilinear Ditch Networks in the Highlands. In A. Pawley, R. Attenbrough, J. Golson and R. Hide, eds. Papuan Pasts: Studies in the Cultural, Linguistic and Biological Diversity of the Papuan-Speaking Peoples. Adelaide: Crawford House.

Denham, T., and H. Barton, In press The Emergence of Agriculture in New Guinea: Continuity from Pre-Existing Foraging Practices. In Human Behavioral Ecology and the Origins of Food Production. D. Kennett and B. Winterhalder, eds., Washington, DC: Smithsonian Institution Press.

Denham, T., J. Golson and P. Hughes, 2004 Reading Early Agriculture at Kuk Swamp, Wahgi Valley, Papua New Guinea: The Archaeological Features (Phases 1–3). Proceedings of the Prehistoric Society 70:259–297.

Denham, T., S. Haberle and C. Lentfer, 2004 New Evidence and Revised Interpretations of Early Agriculture in Highland New Guinea. Antiquity 78:839–857.

Denham, T., S. Haberle, C. Lentfer, R. Fullagar, J. Field, M. Therin, N. Porch and B. Winsborough, 2003 Origins of Agriculture at Kuk Swamp in the Highlands of New Guinea. Science 301:189–193.

Diamond, J., 2002 Evolution, Consequences and Future of Animal and Plant Domestication. Nature 418:700–707.

Donoghue, D., 1988 Pandanus and Changing Site Use: A Study from Manim Valley, Papua New Guinea. B.A. Honours dissertation, University of Queensland.

Dwyer, P., and M. Minnegal, 1991 Hunting in Lowland, Tropical Rain Forest: Towards a Model of Non-Agricultural Subsistence. Human Ecology 19:187–212.

Ford, R., 1985 The Processes of Plant Production in Prehistoric North America. In Prehistoric Plant Production in North America. R. Ford, ed. pp. 1–18. Anthropological Paper 75. Ann Arbor, MI: Museum of Anthropology, University of Michigan.

Fullagar, R., M. Therin, C. Lentfer and J. Field, 2002 Tool-Use and Plant Processing: Stone Artifacts and Sediments from Kuk, Papua New Guinea. Paper presented at the Annual Meeting of the Society for American Archaeology, Denver.

Gadamer, H-G., 1976 Philosophical Hermeneutics. D. Binge, trans. and ed. Berkeley, CA: University of California Press.

Gillieson, D., P. Gorecki and G. Hope, 1985 Prehistoric Agricultural Systems in a Lowland Swamp, Papua New Guinea. Archaeology in Oceania 20:32–37.

Gillieson, D., G. Hope and J. Luly, 1989 Environmental Change in the Jimi Valley. *In* A Crack in the Spine: Prehistory and Ecology of the Jimi-Yuat River, Papua New Guinea. P. Gorecki and D. Gillieson, eds. pp. 103–122. Queensland: James Cook University.

Golson, J., 1976 Archaeology and Agricultural History in the New Guinea Highlands. *In* Problems in Economic and Social Archaeology. G. de G. Sieveking, I. Longworth and K. Wilson, eds. pp. 201–220. London: Duckworth.

—— 1977 No Room at the Top: Agricultural Intensification in the New Guinea Highlands. *In* Sunda and Sahul: Prehistoric Studies in Southeast Asia, Melanesia and Australia. J. Allen, J. Golson and R. Jones, eds. pp. 601–638. London: Academic Press.

—— 1981 New Guinea Agricultural History: A Case Study. *In* A Time to Plant and a Time to Uproot. D. Denoon and C. Snowden, eds. pp. 55–64. Port Moresby: Institute of Papua New Guinea Studies.

—— 1982a Kuk and the History of Agriculture in the New Guinea Highlands. *In* Melanesia: Beyond Diversity. R. May and H. Nelson, eds. pp. 297–307. Canberra: Research School of Pacific and Asian Studies, Australian National University.

—— 1982b The Ipomoean Revolution Revisited: Society and Sweet Potato in the Upper Wahgi Valley. *In* Inequality in New Guinea Highland Societies. A. Strathern, ed. pp. 109–136. Cambridge: Cambridge University Press.

—— 1985 Agricultural Origins in Southeast Asia: A View from the East. *In* Recent Advances in Indo-Pacific Prehistory. V. Misra and P. Bellwood, eds. pp. 307–314. Leiden: E. J. Brill.

—— 1989 The Origins and Development of New Guinea Agriculture. *In* Foraging and Farming: The Evolution of Plant Exploitation. D. Harris and G. Hillman, eds. pp. 678–687. London: Unwin Hyman.

—— 1990 Kuk and the Development of Agriculture in New Guinea: Retrospection and Introspection. *In* Pacific Production Systems: Approaches to Economic Prehistory. D. Yen and J. Mummery, eds. pp. 139–147. Occasional Papers in Prehistory 18. Canberra: Australian National University.

—— 1991a The New Guinea Highlands On the Eve of Agriculture. *In* Indo-Pacific Prehistory 1990, vol. 2. P. Bellwood, ed. pp. 48–53. Bulletin of the Indo-Pacific Prehistory Association 11. Canberra and Jakarta: Indo-Pacific Prehistory Association and Asosiasi Prehistorisi Indonesia.

—— 1991b Bulmer Phase II: Early Agriculture in the New Guinea Highlands. *In* Man and a Half: Essays in Pacific Anthropology and Ethnobiology in Honour of Ralph Bulmer. A. Pawley, ed. pp. 484–491. Auckland: The Polynesian Society.

—— 1997a From Horticulture to Agriculture in the New Guinea Highlands. *In* Historical Ecology in the Pacific Islands: Prehistoric Environmental and Landscape Change. P. Kirch and T. Hunt, eds. pp. 39–50. New Haven, CT: Yale University Press.

—— 1997b The Tambul Spade. *In* Work in Progress: Essays in New Guinea Highlands Ethnography in Honour of Paula Brown Glick. H. Levine and A. Ploeg, eds. pp. 142–171. Frankfurt: Peter Lang.

—— 2000 A Stone Bowl Fragment from the Early Middle Holocene of the Upper Wahgi Valley, Western Highlands Province, Papua New Guinea. *In* Australian Archaeologist: Collected Papers in Honour of Jim Allen. A. Anderson and T. Murray, eds. pp. 231–248. Canberra: Coombs Academic Publishing.

—— 2002 Gourds in New Guinea, Asia and the Pacific. *In* Fifty Years in the Field. Essays in Honour and Celebration of Richard Shutler Jr.'s Archaeological Career. S. Bedford, C.

Sand and D. Burley, eds. pp. 69–78. New Zealand Archaeological Journal Monograph 25. Auckland: Auckland Museum.

Golson, J., and D. Gardner, 1990 Agriculture and Sociopolitical Organisation in New Guinea Highlands Prehistory. Annual Review of Anthropology 19:395–417.

Golson, J., and P. Hughes, 1980 The Appearance of Plant and Animal Domestication in New Guinea. Journal de la Société des Océanistes 36:294–303.

Golson, J., R. Lampert, J. Wheeler and W. Ambrose, 1967 A Note on Carbon Dates for Horticulture in the New Guinea Highlands. Journal of the Polynesian Society 76:369–371.

Golson, J. and P. Ucko, 1994 Foreword. *In* Tropical Archaeobotany: Applications and New Developments. J. G. Hather, ed. pp. xiv–xix. London: Routledge.

Gorecki, P., 1986 Human Occupation and Agricultural Development in the Papua New Guinea Highlands. Mountain Research and Development 6:159–66.

——1992 A Lapita Smoke Screen? *In* Poterie Lapita et Peuplement. J-C. Galipaud, ed. pp. 27–47. Nouméa: ORSTOM.

Green, R., 1991 The Lapita Cultural Complex: Current Evidence and Proposed Models. *In* Indo-Pacific Prehistory 1990, vol. 2. P. Bellwood, ed. pp. 295–305. Bulletin of the Indo-Pacific Prehistory Association 11. Canberra and Jakarta: Indo-Pacific Prehistory Association and Asosiasi Prehistorisi Indonesia.

Groube, L., J. Chappell, J. Muke and D. Price, 1986 A 40,000 Year-Old Human Occupation Site at Huon Peninsula, Papua New Guinea. Nature 324:453–455.

Guddemi, P., 1992 When Horticulturalists are like Hunter-Gatherers: The Sawiyano of Papua New Guinea. Ethnology 31:303–314.

Haberle, S., 1993 Late Quaternary Environmental History of the Tari Basin, Papua New Guinea. Ph.D. dissertation, Australian National University.

——1995 Identification of Cultivated *Pandanus* and *Colocasia* in Pollen Records and the Implications for the Study of Early Agriculture in New Guinea. Vegetation History and Archaeobotany 4:195–210.

——2002 The Emergence of an Agricultural Landscape in the Highlands of New Guinea: The Palynological Record from Kuk Swamp. Paper presented at the Annual Meeting of the Society for American Archaeology, Denver.

Haberle, S., G. Hope and Y. de Fretes, 1991 Environmental Change in the Baliem Valley, Montane Irian Jaya, Republic of Indonesia. Journal of Biogeography 18:25–40.

Harris, D., 1989 An Evolutionary Continuum of People–Plant Interaction. *In* Foraging And Farming: The Evolution of Plant Exploitation. D. Harris and G. Hillman, eds. pp. 11–26. London: Unwin Hyman.

——1995 Early Agriculture in New Guinea and the Torres Strait Divide. *In* Transitions: Pleistocene to Holocene in Australia and Papua New Guinea. J. Allen, and J. O'Connell, eds. pp. 848–854. Antiquity 69 Special Number 265. Oxford: Antiquity Publications.

——1996a Introduction: Themes and Concepts in the Study of Early Agriculture. *In* The Origins and Spread of Agriculture and Pastoralism in Eurasia. D. Harris, ed. pp. 1–9. London: University College London Press.

——1996b The Origins And Spread of Agriculture and Pastoralism in Eurasia: An Overview. *In* The Origins and Spread of Agriculture and Pastoralism in Eurasia. D. Harris, ed. pp. 552–573. London: University College London Press.

Harris, E. and P. Hughes, 1978 An Early Agricultural System at Mugumamp Ridge, Western Highlands Province, Papua New Guinea. Mankind 11:437–445.

Hather, J., 1994 The Identification of Charred Root and Tuber Crops from Archaeological Sites in the Pacific. *In* Tropical Archaeobotany: Applications and New Developments. J. Hather, ed. pp. 51–64. London: Routledge.

—— 1996 The Origins of Tropical Vegeculture: Zingiberaceae, Araceae and Dioscoreaceae in Southeast Asia. *In* The Origins and Spread of Agriculture and Pastoralism in Eurasia. D. Harris, ed. pp. 538–550. London: University College London Press.

Hayes, T., 1992 Plant Macrofossils from Archaeological Sites in the Arawe Islands, Papua New Guinea. B.A. Honours dissertation, La Trobe University.

Hodder, I., 1999 The Archaeological Process: An Introduction. Oxford: Blackwell.

Hope, G., 1983 The Vegetational Changes of the Last 20,000 Years at Telefomin, Papua New Guinea. Singapore Journal of Tropical Geography 4:25–33.

—— 1998 Early Fire and Forest Change in the Baliem Valley, Irian Jaya, Indonesia. Journal of Biogeography 25:453–461.

Hope, G., D. Gillieson and J. Head, 1988 A Comparison of Sedimentation and Environmental Change in New Guinea Shallow Lakes. Journal of Biogeography 15:603–618.

Hope, G., and J. Golson, 1995 Late Quaternary Change in the Mountains of New Guinea. *In* Transitions: Pleistocene to Holocene in Australia and Papua New Guinea. J. Allen, and J. O'Connell, eds. pp. 818–830. Antiquity 69 Special Number 265. Oxford: Antiquity Publications.

Hughes, P., M. Sullivan and D. Yok, 1991 Human Induced Erosion in a Highlands Catchment in Papua New Guinea: The Prehistoric and Contemporary Records. Zeitschrift für Geomorphologie Suppl. 83:227–239.

Hynes, R. and A. Chase, 1982 Plants, Sites and Domiculture: Aboriginal Influence on Plant Communities. Archaeology in Oceania 17:138–150.

Ingold, T., 1996 Growing Plants and Raising Animals: An Anthropological Perspective on Domestication. *In* The Origins and Spread of Agriculture and Pastoralism in Eurasia. D. Harris, ed. pp. 12–24. London: University College London Press.

Irwin, G., 1992 The Prehistoric Exploration and Colonisation of the Pacific. Cambridge: Cambridge University Press.

Jones, M., T. Brown and R. Allaby, 1996 Tracking Early Crops and Early Farmers: The Potential of Biomolecular Archaeology. *In* The Origins and Spread of Agriculture and Pastoralism in Eurasia. D. Harris, ed. pp. 93–100. London: University College London Press.

Kirch, P., 1989 Second Millennium B.C. Arboriculture in Melanesia: Archaeological Evidence from the Mussau Islands. Economic Botany 43:225–240.

—— 1997 The Lapita Peoples. Oxford: Blackwell.

Lampert, R., 1967 Horticulture in the New Guinea Highlands – C14 dating. Antiquity 41:307–309.

—— 1970 Appendix 5. Archaeological Report of the Minjigina site. *In* The Impact of Man on the Vegetation of the Mount Hagen Region, New Guinea. J. Powell. Ph.D. dissertation, Australian National University.

Lebot, V., 1999 Biomolecular Evidence for Plant Domestication in Sahul. Genetic Resources and Crop Evolution 46:619–628.

Lentfer, C., 2002 Phytolith Analysis of Sediments from Kundil's Sections at Kuk, Papua New Guinea and Evidence of Early Holocene Banana Cultivation. Paper presented at the Annual Meeting of the Society for American Archaeology, Denver.

Loy, T., M. Spriggs and S. Wickler, 1992 Direct Evidence for Human Use of Plants 28,000 Years Ago: Starch Residues on Stone Artifacts from Northern Solomon Islands. Antiquity 66:898–912.

Maloney, B., 1994 The Prospects and Problems of Using Palynology to Trace Origins of Tropical Agriculture: The Case of Southeast Asia. *In* Tropical Archaeobotany: Applications and New Developments. J. Hather, ed. pp. 139–171. London: Routledge.

Matthews, P., 1995 Aroids and Austronesians. Tropics 4:105–126.

Mitsuru, H., 2002 The Origins and Spread of Tuber Crops (Imo). *In* Proceedings of the International Area Studies Conference VII: Vegeculture in Eastern Asia and Oceania. Y. Shuji, and P. Matthews, eds. pp. 17–30. Osaka: National Museum of Ethnology.

Mountain, M-J., 1991 Highland New Guinea Hunter-Gatherers: The Evidence of Nombe Rockshelter, Simbu, with Emphasis on the Pleistocene. Ph.D. dissertation, Australian National University.

Muke, J., and H. Mandui, 2003 Shadows of Kuk: Evidence for Prehistoric Agriculture at Kana, Wahgi Valley, Papua New Guinea. Archaeology in Oceania 38:177–185.

Piggott, S., 1954 The Neolithic Cultures of the British Isles. Cambridge: Cambridge University Press.

Piperno, D., and D. Pearsall, 1998 The Origins of Agriculture in the Lowland Neotropics. San Diego, CA: Academic Press.

Powell, J., 1970a The Impact of Man on the Vegetation of the Mount Hagen Region, New Guinea. Ph.D. dissertation, Australian National University.

——1970b The History of Agriculture in the New Guinea Highlands. Search 1:199–200.

——1976 Ethnobotany. *In* New Guinea Vegetation. K. Paijmans, ed. pp. 106–183. Canberra: Commonwealth Scientific and Industrial Research Organization and Australian National University Press.

——1981 The Origins of Agriculture in New Guinea. Proceedings of the IVth International Palynology Conference, Lucknow (1976–77) 3:295–310.

——1982a Plant Resources and Palaeobotanical Evidence for Plant Use in the Papua New Guinea Highlands. Archaeology in Oceania 17:28–37.

——1982b The History of Plant Use and Man's Impact on the Vegetation. *In* Biogeography and Ecology of New Guinea, vol. 1. J. Gressitt, ed. pp. 207–227. The Hague: Junk.

Powell, J., A. Kulunga, R. Moge, C. Pono, F. Zimike and J. Golson, 1975 Agricultural Traditions in the Mount Hagen Area. Occasional Paper No. 12. Port Moresby: Department of Geography, University of Papua New Guinea.

Roscoe, P., 2002 The Hunters and Gatherers of New Guinea. Current Anthropology 43:153–162.

Smith, B., 1998 The Emergence of Agriculture. New York: Scientific American Library.

——2001 Low-Level Food Production. Journal of Archaeological Research 9:1–43.

Spriggs, M., 1989 The Dating of the Island Southeast Asian Neolithic: An Attempt at Chronometric Hygiene and Linguistic Correlation. Antiquity 63:587–613.

——1995 The Lapita Culture and Austronesian Prehistory in Oceania. *In* The Austronesians: Historical and Comparative Perspectives. P. Bellwood, J. Fox and D. Tryon, eds. pp. 112–133. Canberra: Research School of Pacific Studies, Australian National University.

——1996 Early Agriculture and What Went Before in Island Melanesia: Continuity or Intrusion? *In* The Origins and Spread of Agriculture and Pastoralism in Eurasia. D. Harris, ed. pp. 524–537. London: University College London Press.

——1997 The Island Melanesians. Oxford: Blackwell.

——2001 Who Cares What Time It Is? The Importance of Chronology in Pacific Archaeology. *In* Histories of Old Ages: Essays in Honour of Rhys Jones. A. Anderson, I. Lilley and S. O'Connor, eds. pp. 237–249. Canberra: Pandanus Books.

Swadling, P., N. Araho and B. Ivuyo, 1991 Settlements Associated with the Inland Sepik-Ramu Sea. *In* Indo-Pacific Prehistory 1990, vol. 2. P. Bellwood, ed. pp. 92–112. Bulletin of the Indo-Pacific Prehistory Association 11. Canberra and Jakarta: Indo-Pacific Prehistory Association and Asosiasi Prehistorisi Indonesia.

Terrell, J., 2002 Tropical Agroforestry, Coastal Lagoons and Holocene Prehistory in Greater Near Oceania. *In* Proceedings of the International Area Studies Conference VII: Vegeculture in Eastern Asia and Oceania. Y. Shuji, and P. Matthews, eds. pp. 195–216. Osaka: National Museum of Ethnology.

Terrell, J., and R. Welsch, 1997 Lapita and the Temporal Geography of Prehistory. Antiquity 71:548–572.

Terrell, J., J. Hart, S. Barut, N. Cellinese, A. Curet, T. Denham, C. Kusimba, K. Latinis, R. Oka, J. Palka, M. Pohl, K. Pope, P. Williams, H. Haines and J. Staller, 2003 Domesticated Landscapes: The Subsistence Ecology of Plant and Animal Domestication. Journal of Archaeological Theory and Method 10:323–368.

Therin, M., R. Fullagar and R. Torrence, 1999 Starch in Sediments: A New Approach to the Study of Subsistence and Land Use in Papua New Guinea. In The Prehistory of Food. C. Gosden, and J. Hather, eds. pp. 438–462. London: Routledge.

Thomas, J., 1996a Time, Culture and Identity: An Interpretive Archaeology. London: Routledge.

——1996b The Cultural Context of the First Use of Domesticates in Continental Central and Northwest Europe. In The Origins and Spread of Agriculture and Pastoralism in Eurasia. D. Harris, ed. pp. 310–322. London: University College London Press.

Thomas, J., 1999 Understanding the Neolithic. London: Routledge.

Vavilov, N., 1992 [1926] Centers of Origin of Cultivated Plants. In Origin and Geography of Cultivated Plants. D. Löve, trans. and ed. pp. 22–135. Cambridge: Cambridge University Press.

Walker, D., and J. Flenley, 1979 Late Quaternary Vegetational History of the Enga Province of Upland Papua New Guinea. Philosophical Transactions of the Royal Society of London 286:265–344.

Watson, V., and J. Cole, 1977 Prehistory of the Eastern Highlands of New Guinea. Seattle, WA: University of Washington Press.

White, J. P., 1972 Ol Tumbuna: Archaeological Excavations in the Eastern Central Highlands, Papua New Guinea. Terra Australis 2. Canberra: Research School of Pacific Studies, Australian National University.

White, J. P., K. Crook and B. Ruxton, 1970 Kosipe: A Late Pleistocene Site in the Papua Highlands. Proceedings of the Prehistoric Society 36:152–170.

Wilson, S., 1985 Phytolith Evidence from Kuk, an Early Agricultural Site in New Guinea. Archaeology in Oceania 20:90–97.

Yen, D., 1973 The Origins of Oceanic Agriculture. Archaeology and Physical Anthropology in Oceania 8:68–85.

——1985 Wild Plants and Domestication in Pacific Islands. In Recent Advances in Indo-Pacific Prehistory. V. Misra, and P. Bellwood, eds. pp. 315–326. New Delhi: Oxford University Press and IBH Publishing.

——1989 The Domestication of Environment. In Foraging and Farming: The Evolution of Plant Exploitation. D. Harris, and G. Hillman, eds. pp. 55–75. London: Unwin Hyman.

——1990 Environment, Agriculture and the Colonisation of the Pacific. In Pacific Production Systems: Approaches to Economic Prehistory. D. Yen, and J. Mummery, eds. pp. 258–277. Occasional Papers in Prehistory 18. Canberra: Research School of Pacific Studies, Australian National University.

——1991 Domestication: The Lessons from New Guinea. In Man and a Half: Essays in Pacific Anthropology and Ethnobiology in Honour of Ralph Bulmer. A. Pawley, ed. pp. 558–569. Auckland: The Polynesian Society.

——1995 The Development of Sahul Agriculture with Australia as Bystander. In Transitions: Pleistocene to Holocene in Australia and Papua New Guinea. J. Allen, and J. O'Connell, eds. pp. 831–847. Antiquity 69 Special Number 265. Oxford: Antiquity Publications.

—— 1996 Melanesian Arboriculture: Historical Perspectives with an Emphasis on the Genus *Canarium. In* South Pacific Indigenous Nuts. M. Stevens, R. Bourke and B. Evans, eds. pp. 36–44. Canberra: Australian Centre for International Agricultural Research.

—— 1998 Subsistence to Commerce in Pacific Agriculture: Some Four Thousand Years of Plant Exchange. *In* Plants for Food and Medicine. H. Pendergast, N. Etkin, D. Harris and P. Houghton, eds. pp. 161–183. Kew: Royal Botanic Gardens.

Zvelebil, M., 1986 Hunters in Transition: Mesolithic Societies of Temperate Eurasia and the Transition to Farming. Cambridge: Cambridge University Press.

—— 1989 On the Transition to Farming in Europe, or What was Spreading with the Neolithic: A reply to Ammerman (1989). Antiquity 63:379–383.

9
Late Pleistocene Complexities in the Bismarck Archipelago

Matthew Leavesley

Behavioral complexity can be defined in a number of ways. It can be defined in linear terms, as a trajectory, process, or progression. In this context the zenith of complexity is the present, with decreasing degrees of complexity receding into the past. This can be regarded as the received view of long-term cultural variation. Alternatively, complexity may be considered in terms of a process of adaptation that is responsive to local conditions but is not inevitably unidirectional (Rowley-Conwy 2001). From the latter perspective, complex behavior is as likely to have occurred in the Pleistocene as in more recent times. This position is a quite radical departure from conventional social theory regarding long-term trajectories of cultural change, but one that is gaining substantial support from current research in Oceania. The obvious difficulty for archaeologists in dealing with behavioral complexity in either framework, however, is that not all aspects of human behavior have a physical manifestation. Archaeological investigation relies on material evidence and so some aspects of human complexity, such as cognitive processes, must to some degree be considered archaeologically epiphenomenal unless they have a demonstrable material connection. In an archaeological framework, complexity might thus best be considered a reflection of the number of steps or stages in a process that leads to a given material outcome: More steps produce greater complexity.

This chapter will consider the economic, technological, and social complexities of life in the Bismarck and Solomon archipelagoes during the Pleistocene (Figure 9.1), with particular emphasis on the fit between different models of Pleistocene behavior and the evidence upon which they rest. Discussion begins with a general description of the study area and an overview of regional archaeological patterns.

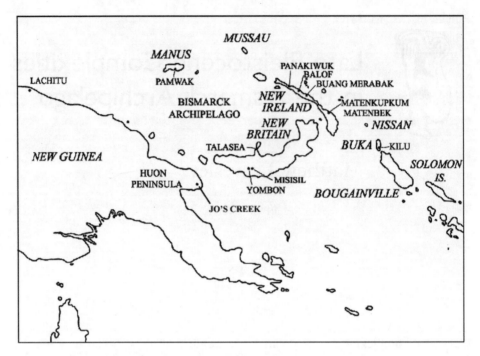

Figure 9.1 New Guinea, the Bismarck Archipelago, and the Solomon Islands, showing places mentioned in the text (derived from Allen and Gosden 1996)

Geographical Background

The Bismarck Archipelago is located off the northeastern coast of New Guinea, to which it has never been connected by land. It consists of three large islands and hundreds of smaller ones (Mayr and Diamond 2001). The three large islands, New Britain, New Ireland, and Manus, were also never joined to each other in the past. The first two consist of basal volcanic rock overlaid by limestone and sandstone. Manus consists primarily of volcanics, small quantities of limestone, and coastal alluvium. All are covered with dense tropical rain forest. Most of the Pleistocene archaeological data for the Bismarck Archipelago come from a series of caves located along the east coast of New Ireland (Allen and Gosden 1991). Two additional Pleistocene sites are located in the New Britain interior (Pavlides 1999; Specht et al. 1981).

The main Solomon Islands chain includes seven large and about 1,000 small islands. The Solomons volcanic basement is variously overlain within sandstone and limestone. The archipelago changed significantly during the late Pleistocene, with the islands of Buka, Bougainville, the Shortlands, Choiseul, Santa Isabel, and Nggela being connected at times of low sea level to form "Greater Bougainville" (Spriggs 1997:28). Like the Bismarcks, the main Solomons Archipelago is covered in tropical rain forest. The single Pleistocene site known in the Solomons, on Buka Island (Wickler 2001), is discussed below.

Pulses of Deposition

Our understanding of the regional archaeology is limited by the very small number of sites representing any given period, but some broad trends are becoming apparent. Allen and I (Leavesley and Allen 1998) have identified six "pulses" of deposition representing shifts in human behavior in the New Ireland sites. Four of these pulses are relevant to the Pleistocene. They can illuminate specific aspects of behavioral complexity through broad comparisons with patterns in the Holocene.

Pulse I

The first pulse represents initial human colonization of the region and is intimately associated with the colonization of Sahul, the continent formed when low sea levels joined Australia, New Guinea, and Tasmania (Birdsell 1977; Lilley, this volume). There are two likely routes into "Greater Australia" from Southeast Asia, a northern route via Sulawesi and a southern route via Timor, and compelling arguments have been made for the use of both (Allen and Gosden 1996:184; Chappell 2000; Lilley, this volume). The earliest evidence for colonization of the Bismarcks comes from the cave site of Buang Merabak in central New Ireland (Leavesley et al. 2002), which indicates that humans may have reached the island by 39,500 B.P. In addition, there are dates of at least the same magnitude from Matenkupkum cave in southern New Ireland (Leavesley and Allen 1998) and from open sites around Yombon in interior New Britain (Pavlides 1999 and this volume). The passage from northern Sahul (i.e., New Guinea) to New Britain signals the beginning of a learning process, of adaptation to biotically increasingly-depauperate islands and, with the colonization of the Solomons, to lengthening sea-crossings, a process that ultimately led to the colonization of Polynesia (Allen and Gosden 1996:185).

There is comparatively little evidence from the Bismarcks for the period following the initial incursion of people until about 20,000 B.P. This sparseness is taken as the signature of the activities of small, highly mobile groups of hunter-gatherers who moved to find the resources they required (Allen and Gosden 1991). On the basis of continuing work in western New Britain, however, Torrence et al. (2004) argue that this pattern may be peculiar to New Ireland, as they have evidence that resources were moved over reasonable distances to people, rather than the reverse. As they suggest, such regional variation is to be expected, and we are likely to see more of it as research in the region progresses. Be that as it may, a significant movement of people occurred by 28,000 B.P., in the form of the colonization of the main Solomons chain. This evidence comes from Kilu Cave on Buka (Wickler 2001) and represents a sea-crossing from New Ireland of 180 kilometers (Allen and Gosden 1996:186). This event stands apart from others in the region because there is little evidence for continuing communication between Buka and the Bismarck

Archipelago (Spriggs 1997). The colonization of Buka, then northern "Greater Bougainville," represents an important phase of human adaptation in Oceania because the environment is even more depauperate of terrestrial human prey than the Bismarcks. During the Pleistocene, the Solomons had only a limited range of bats, rats, and reptiles including the large and now-extinct rats *Solomys spriggsarum* and *Melomys spechti*. The cuscus *Phalanger orientalis*, which is an important part of the Pleistocene diet in the Bismarcks, is absent in the Solomons until after 3300 B.P. Moreover, although the variety of pelagic fish in the Indo-Pacific region is presumed to have been relatively constant, the reefs of the Solomons have a lower coral biodiversity than the Bismarcks (Veron 1995). This may imply a more general reduction in reef-based marine life. In this context the large rats are likely to have played an important role in human subsistence.

Pulse 2

The second pulse in archaeological deposition occurred at the Last Glacial Maximum (LGM) about 22,000–20,000 B.P., when a series of significant behavioral changes occurred in the Bismarck Archipelago. People occupied Manus for the first time by at least 20,000 B.P. (Minol 2000:25). The journey was probably made either by island-hopping from New Ireland via New Hanover and Mussau, or from the north coast of Sahul/New Guinea (Spriggs 1997:29–30). Both routes were used in the ethnographic period and both potential source-regions have later archaeological connections with Manus. The colonization of Manus required an open-sea crossing of over 200 kilometers, about 75 kilometers of which would have been out of the sight of land (Allen and Gosden 1996:188; Irwin 1992). This makes it the longest sea journey up to this time anywhere in the world and the only known Pleistocene voyage beyond the limits of one-way island intervisibility. It implies capable marine craft and considerable navigational ability, even by modern standards. Today, journeys of this distance are rarely attempted by anyone but the people who reside on remote islands such as Wuvulu or Nugaria between Manus and New Guinea, who use modern navigational equipment. In other words, the colonization of Manus entailed extensive planning and great skill in execution.

New Ireland also saw an increase in communication with New Britain at this time. Prior to 20,000 B.P., people moved to the resources they required. After 20,000 B.P., Matenkupkum and Buang Merabak contain cuscus bones and obsidian, intimating the movement of exotic wild animals and stone into New Ireland and thus reflecting an increase in the complexity of human behavior in the region (Allen et al. 1989; Flannery and White 1991; Gosden and Robertson 1989; Summerhayes and Allen 1993). The introduction of *P. orientalis* entails the manipulation of the environment through the addition of a new prey taxon to provide an extra protein source. This indicates increased awareness of the rain forest and its resources and how they might be altered to better sustain human life (Gosden and Robertson 1991). The presence of obsidian from Mopir in central north-coast New Britain signifies an awareness of its superior flaking properties and perhaps recognition of its potential social value. It is also an expression of the presence of an expansive interaction sphere in which obsidian was exchanged down-the-line across more than 350 kilometers to southern and central New Ireland (Summerhayes and Allen 1993). Those who worked the quarry presumably knew at the very least that the people they gave it to valued it, but need not have had any idea of the geographical spread of its distribution.

The second phase is followed by a gap in the evidence for occupation in New Ireland between the LGM and 15,000 B.P. which is broadly mirrored elsewhere. In the rain forests of interior western New Britain, Yombon was occupied until 17,000 B.P. with a hiatus until 12,000 B.P. (Pavlides 1999 and this volume), and Kilu in Buka has a gap from 20,000 to 10,000 B.P. (Wickler 2001). In New Ireland the hiatus is signaled by a reduction in the number of sites with evidence for human occupation. This shift may indicate a reduction of occupation or even regional abandonment. Alternatively, it may result from a change in the focus of landscape use away from cave sites or a destruction of archaeological deposits by non-human taphonomic processes (Specht in press).

Pulses 3 and 4

The third pulse, beginning around 15,000 B.P., sees the reoccupation of the cave sites in central and southern New Ireland and the first evidence for occupation in northern New Ireland sites, with similar processes evident in western New Britain and Buka at slightly later dates. In particular, we see the reuse of Matenkupkum at 16,000 B.P., Buang Merabak at 14,000 B.P., and Yombon at 12,000 B.P. (Pavlides 1999). In northern New Ireland, Panakiwuk was first occupied at 13,000–15,000 B.P. and Balof at 12,000 B.P. This pulse represents the greatest density of deposition of any period in the New Ireland sites, which suggests that regional populations had grown substantially.

The fourth pulse occurred at about 12,000–10,000 B.P., when all the New Ireland sites show their highest rates of cultural deposition (Allen and Gosden 1996:189). This change may represent some form of intensification (Spriggs 1993:190). It is paralleled in New Britain by the first use of Misisil Cave (Specht et al. 1981; see Figure 10.1) and the re-occupation of the Yombon area (Pavlides 1999 and this volume), while Kilu in Buka is reoccupied at 10,000 B.P. (Wickler 2001). In New Ireland, the fourth pulse was followed by the abandonment of all the sites at about 8000 B.P.

The four pulses of deposition provide a broad framework in which to consider notions of complex human behavior in the Bismarcks and Solomons during the Pleistocene. What follows is a more detailed discussion of specific aspects of economic, technological, or social complexity, including some thoughts on ways in which our understanding of these matters could be enhanced.

Economy

Economic complexity is measured by the number of steps undertaken to acquire a resource, primarily raw materials and food. The following discussion focuses on such matters but also considers broader economic strategies associated with particular periods of time or environmental contexts.

While the Wallace Line marks the divide between the placental fauna of Asia and the marsupials of Australia and New Guinea, no such divide occurs between the marine faunas of the two regions (Allen 2000:144). There is also a direct relationship between the size of a given landmass and its biotic diversity. Thus people became dependent upon a restricted range of terrestrial resources for subsistence when they crossed the Vitiaz Strait to move from New Guinea, the second largest island in the world, out into the Bismarck Archipelago and Solomon Islands. In order to exploit these taxa, high mobility predicated on watercraft was essential (Allen 2000:144–145). Before the discovery of Pleistocene evidence from the inland site of Yombon (Pavlides 1999; Pavlides and Gosden 1994; also Pavlides, this volume) it was suggested that the first colonists of the Bismarck Archipelago and other parts of the Pacific employed a "strandlooper" strategy of resource procurement and exploitation (Groube 1971). Strandloopers were small, transient groups of hunter-gatherers predominantly using reef and coastal resources (Spriggs 1997:37; cf. Galipaud, this volume, regarding much later Pacific strandloopers).

There are four converging lines of archaeological data in support of the strandlooper model. First, in order to colonize an island from the sea, one must land at the coast. Secondly, all the earliest sites with the exception of Yombon (Pavlides 1993) are coastal sites. Thirdly, there are more Pleistocene coastal sites than inland sites overall, and fourthly, the coastal sites all contain shell middens (Allen 2000:144–146). However, the earliest sites do not contain large quantities of fish and their capture would not have required any specialized technology beyond the "fortuitous accidental or deliberate trapping or spearing on reefs on outgoing tides" (Allen 1993:144). With the discovery of evidence for the human exploitation of resources deep in the rainforest at Yombon during the Pleistocene, the strandlooper model has been scaled back to apply perhaps only to the initial colonization phase. Evidence from the New Guinea highlands clearly shows that settlers on mainland Sahul had adapted to non-coastal environments by at least 25,000 B.P. and probably before (Allen 1993:141; Denham, Lilley, this volume). Moreover, although Buang Merabak and Matenkupkum in New Ireland are coastal sites, their faunal assemblages include extinct forest birds, consistent with the use of the forests for hunting (Steadman et al. 1999). They also contain large quantities of bat remains, confirming that people targeted a variety of bush animals. In Buka, the Kilu evidence shows the exploitation of two large rodent species and reptiles, both of which may indicate the use of inland resources (Wickler 2001). Thus present results suggest that while the exploitation of coastal resources was extremely important to the Pleistocene colonists of the Bismarcks and Solomons, they also exploited inland resources from soon after their arrival. As an adaptation to depauperate island environments, this multifaceted foraging strategy clearly entails increased behavioral complexity.

New Ireland has an even more depauperate fauna than New Britain. The first colonists undoubtedly had to adjust their behavior in order to survive in an environment with a different range of taxa from their place of origin. The focus of hunting and gathering may have become skewed, if not specialized, toward the taxa known previously from New Britain, although there is very little evidence as to what these taxa might have been. A case in point is the shell midden at Matenkupkum. After the initial colonization of New Ireland, people selected larger individual shell specimens from a narrow range of the larger available taxa. The pattern subsequently alters to the selection of smaller specimens from a wider range of taxa. This pattern has a number of implications. First, it suggests selective shellfish gathering, requiring knowledge of the range of taxa available and a view about which taxa are most desirable. Second, Gosden and Robertson (1991) interpret the data as an indication that shellfish resources in the vicinity of the cave were "over-predated" in the pre-20,000 B.P. period because people continually selected the biggest shellfish. Subsequently, a general diminution in size of the largest individuals is interpreted as representing the human response to diminishing shellfish stocks.

Our understanding of the situation at Matenkupkum could be strengthened in three ways. First, the archaeological sample for the earliest time unit could be increased to provide a more secure basis for interpretation. Although the excavation trench was 9 meters × 1 meter, the earliest stratigraphic unit contains only a small quantity of specimens (Robertson 1986:66–67). Secondly, the site's chronology could be investigated further, with the aim of refining its temporal resolution. Presently the chronological units span 10,000, 6,000, and 2,000 years respectively. In a best-case scenario, chronological resolution would mirror the life cycle of the taxa in question. Thirdly, more malacological research on the relevant taxa in the region would facilitate a more informed consideration of the environmental effects of the human collection on shellfish populations (Spriggs 1993:190).

Other interesting examples of people moving into new islands with low levels of taxonomic diversity come from Buka and Manus. Buka had none of the varieties of cuscus or pademelon (small wallabies) of New Britain and also had a reduced range of bats and birds. However, Buka did have the two large species of rat mentioned earlier (Flannery and Wickler 1990), which appear to have made up a large percentage of the terrestrial component of the Pleistocene diet prior to their extinction somewhere between 20,000 and 5000 B.P. (Wickler 2001). Manus also had a restricted range of fauna primarily consisting of bats, rats, and birds prior to the introduction of the spotted cuscus *Spilocuscus kraemeri* and spiny bandicoot *Echymipera kalubu* at 13,000 B.P. (Spriggs 1997:54).

Environmental Manipulation

Discussion of the human translocation of animals between islands in the Indo-Pacific is not new (Wallace 1869). The cuscus *P. orientalis* first appears in New

Ireland at 19,000–20,000 B.P. and is thought to be the product of possibly deliberate but probably accidental human behavior (Flannery and White 1991; White
1993:174). Flannery and White (1991) list four criteria on which they base their
proposal concerning human rather than natural translocation. First, cuscuses have
been moved extensively elsewhere in Melanesia (see also Grayson 2001). Second,
its prospects of successful establishment on previously uninhabited islands are good
because it was known to regularly produce twins. Third, *P. orientalis* can inhabit a
range of environments. It is a lowland species with broad ecological tolerance,
its generalized diet enabling it to survive in secondary as well as primary forest
(Flannery 1993:175). Finally, the natural translocation of *P. orientalis* appears
unlikely because it does not seem to occur in New Ireland for at least one million
years prior to human occupation (Flannery and White 1991:108). Flannery
(1993:175) subsequently added that the New Ireland *P. orientalis* colonists were
probably "back young," that is, young animals that have developed beyond dependence upon their mothers' milk but remain with them, on their backs, for about a
month after weaning. "Back young" are considered to be the optimum age for transfer because younger animals can easily succumb to illness and older animals are
less tractable and more likely to be injured during capture or suffer from "capture
myopia."

Specht (in press) questions animal translocation in general on two grounds. First,
terrestrial animal protein remains very limited in the Bismarcks even today (Allen
2000:144–145), so if human translocation of animals was undertaken as a strategy
to increase the availability of prey it was not very successful. Second, the appearance of taxa in an archaeological deposit represents their first inclusion in the
human diet, and perhaps only in the archaeological record, not necessarily their
introduction into the wider environment. A natural bone-trap such as a sink-hole
in limestone would be the ideal context in which to determine when a species first
entered a given environment (Heinsohn 1998:77; Specht in press). In the absence
of any systematic paleontological studies in New Ireland there is no pre-20,000 B.P.
natural material with which to compare the archaeological assemblages. In addition, "recent natural range extensions and human-assisted dispersals may mimic
each other in effect and . . . zoogeographic evidence may be inconclusive"
(Heinsohn 1998:76). Although the case for the human translocation of *P. orientalis*
is strong, the limitations listed above suggest that a number of lines of scientific
enquiry remain to be pursued before we understand the processes that brought the
cuscus to New Ireland. Irrespective of the answer, however, the phalanger's appearance coincides with the aforementioned change in shellfish selection at Matenkupkum and Buang Merabak. The cuscus may have taken pressure off existing prey,
moving the focus of protein procurement from the rocky shore to the adjacent
forests. If these two events can be demonstrably linked in this way, more light
will be cast on the complexities of people's response to the changing availability
of prey.

While protein acquisition is an important part of subsistence strategies, plants
would have provided the bulk of the carbohydrate. The development of agriculture
in the Bismarck Archipelago may have occurred through a series of phases starting

with arboriculture amongst foragers (Gosden 1995; Yen 1995). Arboriculture is orchard-based tree cropping (Kirch 2000:82). A vast array of botanical remains have been collected from the Pleistocene deposits and identified to taxon. Edible types include *Canarium indicum*, coconut, *Aleurites*, *Terminalia*, *Panadanus*, *Pangium*, *Spondias*, and *Dracontomelon* (Spriggs 1997:79). Starch residues on stone artifacts from Kilu indicate the use of both *Alocasia* and *Colocasia* taro in Buka during the Pleistocene (Loy et al. 1992). Plant residues have also been identified on the Balof 2 stone artifacts (Barton and White 1993) from New Ireland, representing local-ized and short-term vegetation clearance of a sort that might be expected with small-scale cultivation or forest-edge manipulation (Spriggs 1997:85). Gosden (1995) has suggested that this evidence supports the case for Pleistocene arbori-culture, which in turn reflects substantial behavioral complexity in a number of ways. First, it indicates intimate knowledge of New Ireland's flora. Second, it reflects the process of differentiating those plants that have value to humans from those that do not. Third, it adds a significant dimension to the region's Pleistocene hunter-gatherer economy, one more usually associated with more recent periods.

The quest for sustenance is a driving force of all life on earth, but only humans engage in the complex deployment of tools as capital equipment for the acquisition and processing of food. The redistribution of valuable raw materials for the pro-duction of capital equipment is commonly exemplified by the prehistoric exploita-tion of high-quality flaking stone such as obsidian. Obsidian appears in the New Ireland assemblages from 20,000 B.P. (Rosenfeld 1997; Summerhayes and Allen 1993). As obsidian occurs naturally in only a few places in the Bismarck Archipel-ago – and nowhere in New Ireland – its dispersal away from the sources implies the movement of resources to people (Gosden and Robertson 1991). From a micro-economic perspective, the most important items attract the highest input of resources in their acquisition and maintenance. In a highly mobile society with limited transport capacity, items which are either renewable or of lesser value would be disposed of first and those that are considered to be difficult to replace or impor-tant will be carried for longer. The identification of obsidian in central New Ireland over 350 kilometers from its sources in western New Britain signifies the prehistoric identification of a resource with intrinsic value. Noteworthy behavioral complexity is also indicated by the various stages of quarrying, distribution, and modification entailed prior to the obsidian's end use.

Technology

The late Pleistocene sites of the Bismarcks and Solomons contain evidence for technological complexity previously thought to have occurred only during the Holocene. As described above, early mariners developed the technology to cross wide water-gaps and, in cases such as Manus, may have deliberately sought out unoccupied islands. In addition, people selected between different raw materials for the production of stone tools and distributed obsidian across vast distances (Pavlides 1999 and this volume; Summerhayes and Allen 1993).

In relation to the first matter, Allen and Gosden (1996:184) propose a method of distinguishing between the deliberate and accidental colonization of the Bismarck Archipelago from northern Sahul/New Guinea. Colonization might have been deliberate if New Britain was settled via the Vitiaz Strait and both sides of the Strait were first settled at roughly the same time. Alternatively, if colonization east of the Vitiaz Strait significantly postdates that of northern Sahul/New Guinea it may imply an accidental crossing. Evidence from the Huon Peninsula indicates colonization by at least 40,000 B.P. (Groube et al. 1986). Leavesley et al. (2002) report that central New Ireland was occupied at 39,500 B.P., indicating that both sides of the Vitiaz Strait were occupied at approximately the same time at an archaeological scale. The rapid crossing into the Bismarcks suggests that it was colonized as part of a deliberate strategy of exploration. In this context, substantial behavioral complexity is evident in the process of purposeful migration requiring sailing technology, maintenance of watercraft, and the organization of populations large enough to sustain colonization.

Upon arrival in the Bismarck Archipelago there is evidence from both New Britain and New Ireland that people distinguished between stone raw materials on the basis of quality. Judgments about quality require in-depth knowledge of available resources and their suitability for particular processes of reduction. The human settlement of Yombon at 35,500 B.P. is associated with the exploitation of local outcrops of high-quality chert (Pavlides 1999 and this volume; Pavlides and Gosden 1994). At the same time, the southern New Ireland assemblages consist of a wide variety of material including small quantities of high-quality local chert (Allen and Gosden 1996:186; Allen et al. 1989). The presence of the chert artifacts at Yombon indicates deliberate exploration of the rugged rain-forest interior of New Britain and the repeated systematic exploitation of a valuable resource (Allen and Gosden 1996:186). In New Ireland it reflects a process of discrimination amongst local sources. In addition there is evidence for variation through time in patterns of source selection (Allen et al. 1989). Before 20,000 B.P., the high-quality stone in the assemblages consists solely of local chert (Allen et al. 1989:554). Obsidian occurs from 20,000 B.P. and increases through time as a proportion to other types of stone, seeing the use of chert diminish significantly.

Accepting that both resources remained available throughout the period of human occupation, the foregoing trend indicates a cultural change in preference for exotic obsidian over local chert as a raw material for the production of artifacts. In utilitarian terms, it is hard to judge why this may have occurred. Obsidian is a volcanic rock containing more than eighty percent glass. The glass content gives it exceptional flaking qualities, enabling the production of very sharp edges and making obsidian highly desirable for stone artifact production. For most purposes, however, there would be little if any discernible difference between the ease of flaking or the sharpness of the edges of obsidian and high-quality chert. Moreover, there would have been much greater costs involved in obtaining obsidian from far distant sources than there would have been in using local chert sources. These factors suggest there may have been additional dimensions to the acquisition and use of obsidian, similar perhaps to the sociopolitical characteristics of obsidian trade in ethnographic times, which saw tiny pieces of obsidian given great social value when traded from a great distance (e.g., Harding 1967).

The acquisition of specific raw materials for artifact production also extended to marine mollusk shell. Shell artifact manufacture involved a range of technologies applied to specific taxa (Leavesley and Allen 1998; Smith and Allen 1999; Wickler 1990:140). Smith and Allen (1999:293) identified a pattern of "tab" removal from the medial whorl of the turban shell *Turbo argyrostroma*. In some instances the tab was removed by drilling a sequence of holes to weaken the shell before separating the tab. For those shells without drill holes it appears that there is little to distinguish between tab removal and meat extraction as the cause of observed breakage patterns. The production of shellfish hooks on the top shell *Trochus niloticus* has also been posited for the Pleistocene (Smith and Allen 1999:293–294). While such shell industries were not as developed as the shell technologies of the mid- to late Holocene (Green 2000), the fact that shell artifacts were made at all during the Pleistocene greatly diminishes the technological distance conventionally thought to exist between that period and more recent times.

Society

While the movement of artifacts across the landscape is commonly described in economic terms it also inevitably entails social interaction (Gosden 1993). In an attempt to elucidate the "social" in Pleistocene Melanesia, Allen and Gosden (1996:184) drew on Caldwell's (1964) idea of interaction spheres to propose that "social, ideological and trade connections between different populations in different places ... [were vital for] locally specific forms of change." Such interaction spheres encompass local and regional change as equally important causal processes and there are no hierarchical distinctions between the regions involved. A variety of evidence indicates there may have been a series of such spheres in Melanesia from the Pleistocene onward. Normally archaeological interpretations of information exchange rely on the demonstration of the two-way movement of material goods, but one-way movement of material such as New Britain obsidian to New Ireland is also indicative of communication. In the absence of any direct evidence, Allen (2000:142) has also suggested that the presence of shell ornaments may also reflect social as well as economic behavior, on the basis of ethnographic reports of the use of shell ornaments in ceremonies and for exchange.

Discussion

Archaeologists have spent a great deal of time contemplating the many issues that arise in the Pleistocene prehistory of the Bismarck Archipelago and Solomon Islands. While much important research has been completed, many tantalizing gaps remain. One curious aspect of the southern New Ireland Pleistocene sites stems from differences between Matenbek and Matenkupkum (Gosden 1995:811). The sites are located on the same cliff-line only 70 meters apart, with no evidence for any past barrier between them. While it is easy to imagine the two sites constituted a single unit of behavior, they have remarkably different contents. It is not clear why. Matenbek has abundant evidence for human behavior during the height of the LGM while Matenkupkum does not. The lack of deposit at Matenkupkum is difficult to understand given its proximity to Matenbek and the lack of an obvious physical barrier between them. Matenbek contains significant difference in content to Matenkupkum (Allen 2000:152). Matenbek contained 435 fragments of obsidian from a 1 meter × 1 meter test-pit including only deposits dated from 8000 to 6000 B.P., while Matenkupkum has a total of 106 fragments from a 10 meter × 1 meter trench (Robertson 1986:102) which spans the entire period that the site was occupied. Why should Matenbek contain so much less obsidian? Allen proposes that the variation results in part from sampling error at Matenbek. Roof-fall at some time in the past has partially closed the mouth of cave, restricting archaeological access to some of the deposit. It is also possible that the two sites were used in different periods (Allen 2000:152), but that begs the question of why only one was used at a time.

Another more fundamental question concerns the development of agriculture. This is an extremely important issue for the region because agriculture provided the economic basis of the late Holocene Lapita expansion into the biotically extremely depauperate islands of Remote Oceania (see Denham, Galipaud, Lilley, Pavlides, Sand et al., and Walter and Sheppard, this volume). A crucial concern is whether agriculture as we understand it today existed in the region prior to 3500 B.P. (Denham, this volume). One way to approach this question might be to accept the argument that humans required agriculture to colonize very small, very remote islands and then survey Pleistocene and pre-Lapita Holocene landforms on small islands in the Bismarck Archipelago and Solomons. One such small island with pre-Lapita Holocene evidence is Nissan, between New Ireland and Bougainville. A reduction in density of shellfish after Spriggs's Halikan Phase is consistent with a switch from subsistence strategies based on foraging and arboriculture before 3500 B.P. to a greater reliance on agriculture (Spriggs 1997:80; 1991:240). While Gosden (1995) has addressed the issue of early agriculture in the Bismarcks, no pre-Lapita agricultural sites in the region have been identified, much less intensively investigated after the fashion of the Kuk site in the New Guinea highlands (Denham, this volume). Plainly, research of this kind would help determine the role, if any, of agriculture in the Bismarcks and Solomons before Lapita and the colonization of the remote Pacific.

Conclusion

The purpose of this chapter has been to emphasize the economic, technological, and social complexities of human behavior during the Pleistocene in Near Oceania, and how received wisdom regarding directionality in long-term patterns of cultural change is undermined by the evidence emerging from the Bismarcks and Solomons.

In doing so, it has summarized some of the major interpretations while also drawing attention to a number of questions yet to be resolved. It is hoped that it has in this way highlighted the importance of the matters that have been comparatively well researched and placed them within the overall context of archaeology in Oceania, but at the same time shown that much remains to be done. The Pleistocene archaeology of Near Oceania is nothing if not a work in progress!

ACKNOWLEDGMENTS

Thanks to Glenn Summerhayes, Matthew Spriggs, Peter Hiscock (Australian National University), and Christina Pavlides (La Trobe University) for their comments on various drafts.

REFERENCES

Allen, J., 1993 Notions of the Pleistocene in Greater Australia. *In* A Community of Culture: The People and Prehistory of the Pacific. M. Spriggs, D. Yen, W. Ambrose, R. Jones, A. Thorne and A. Andrews, eds. pp. 139–151. Occasional Papers in Prehistory 21. Canberra: Department of Prehistory, Australian National University.

——2000 From Beach to Beach: The Development of Maritime Economies in Prehistoric Melanesia. *In* East of Wallace's Line: Studies of Past and Present Maritime Cultures of the Indo-Pacific Region. Modern Quaternary Research in Southeast Asia 16. S. O'Connor and P. Veth, eds. pp. 139–177. Rotterdam: A. A. Balkema.

Allen, J., and C. Gosden, eds., 1991 Report of the Lapita Homeland Project. Occasional Papers in Prehistory 20. Canberra: Department of Prehistory, Research School of Pacific Studies, Australian National University.

——1996 Spheres of Interaction and Integration: Modeling the Culture History of the Bismarck Archipelago. *In* Oceanic Culture History: Essays in Honour of Roger Green. J. Davidson, G. Irwin, B. Leach, A. Pawley and D. Brown, eds. pp. 183–197. Special Publication. Auckland: New Zealand Journal of Archaeology.

Allen, J., C. Gosden and J. P. White, 1989 Human Pleistocene Adaptations in the Tropical Island Pacific: Recent Evidence from New Ireland, a Greater Australian Outlier. Antiquity 63:548–561.

Barton, H., and J. P. White, 1993 Use of Stone and Shell Artifacts at Balof 2, New Ireland, Papua New Guinea. Asian Perspectives 32:169–181.

Birdsell, J., 1977 The Recalibration of the Paradigm for the First Peopling of Greater Australia. *In* Sunda and Sahul: Prehistoric Studies in Southeast Asia, Melanesia and Australia. J. Allen, J. Golson and R. Jones, eds. pp. 113–167. London: Academic Press.

Caldwell, J., 1964 Interaction Spheres in Prehistory. *In* Hopewellian Studies. J. Caldwell, and R. Hall, eds. pp. 133–143. Scientific Papers 12. Springfield, IL: Illinois State Museum.

Chappell, J., 2000 Pleistocene Seedbeds of Western Pacific Maritime Cultures and the Importance of Chronology. *In* East of Wallace's Line: Studies of Past and Present

Maritime Cultures of the Indo-Pacific Region. S. O'Connor and P. Veth, eds. pp. 77–98. Modern Quaternary Research in Southeast Asia 16. Rotterdam: A. A. Balkema.

Flannery, T., 1993 Moving Animals from Place to Place. *In* The First Humans: Human Origin and History to 10,000 B.C. G. Burenhult, ed. p. 175. The Illustrated History of Humankind. Brisbane: University of Queensland Press.

Flannery, T., and S. Wickler, 1990 Quaternary Murids (Rodentia: Muridae) From Buka Island, Papua New Guinea with Descriptions of Two New Species Australian Mammalogy 13:127–139.

Flannery, T., and J. P. White, 1991 Animal Translocation. National Geographic Research and Exploration 7:96–113.

Gosden, C., 1993 Understanding the Settlement of Pacific Islands in the Pleistocene. *In* Sahul in Review: Pleistocene Archaeology in Australia, New Guinea and Island Melanesia at 10–30 Kyr B.P. M. Smith, M. Spriggs and B. Fankhauser, eds. pp. 131–136. Occasional Papers in Prehistory 24. Canberra: Department of Prehistory, Research School of Pacific Studies, Australian National University.

———1995 Arboriculture and Agriculture in Coastal Papua New Guinea. *In* Transitions: Pleistocene to Holocene in Australia and Papua New Guinea. J. Allen and J. O'Connell, eds. pp. 807–817. Antiquity 69 Special Number 265. Oxford: Antiquity Publications.

Gosden, C., and N. Robertson, 1991 Models for Matenkupkum: Interpreting a Late-Pleistocene Site from Southern New Ireland. J. Allen and C. Gosden, eds. pp. 20–45. Report of the Lapita Homeland Project. Occasional Papers in Prehistory 20. Canberra: Department of Prehistory, Research School of Pacific Studies, Australian National University.

Grayson, D., 2001 The Archaeological Record of Human Impacts on Animal Populations. Journal of World Prehistory 15:1–68.

Green, R., 2000 Lapita and the Cultural Model for Intrusion, Integration and Innovation. *In* Australian Archaeologist. Collected Papers in Honour of Jim Allen. A. Anderson and T. Murray, eds. pp. 372–392. Canberra: Coombs Academic Publishing, Australian National University.

Groube, L., 1971 Tonga, Lapita Pottery and Polynesian Origins. Journal of the Polynesian Society 80:278–316.

Groube, L., J. Chappell, J. Muke and D. Price, 1986 A 40,000 Year Old Human Occupation Site at Huon Peninsula, Papua New Guinea. Nature 324:453–455.

Harding, T., 1967 Voyagers of the Vitiaz Strait. Seattle, WA: University of Washington Press.

Heinsohn, T., 1998 The Realm of the Cuscus: Animal Translocation and Biological Invasions to the East of Wallace's Line. M.Sc. dissertation, Australian National University.

Irwin, G., 1992 The Prehistoric Exploration and Colonization of the Pacific. Cambridge: Cambridge University Press.

Kirch, P., 2000 On the Road of the Winds: An Archaeological History of the Pacific Islands before European Contact. Berkeley, CA: University of California Press.

Leavesley, M., and J. Allen, 1998 Dates, Disturbance and Artifact Distributions: Another Analysis of Buang Merabak, a Pleistocene Site on New Ireland, Papua New Guinea. Archaeology in Oceania 33:63–82.

Leavesley, M., M. Bird, L. Fifield, P. Hausladen, G. Santos and M. di Tada, 2002 Buang Merabak: Early Evidence for Human Occupation in the Bismarck Archipelago, Papua New Guinea. Australian Archaeology 54:55–56.

Loy, T., M. Spriggs and S. Wickler, 1992 Direct Evidence for Human Use of Plants 28,000 Years Ago: Starch Residues on Stone Artifacts from the Northern Solomon Islands. Antiquity 66:898–912.

Mayr, E., and J. Diamond, 2001 The Birds of Northern Melanesia: Speciation, Ecology, and Biogeography. Oxford: Oxford University Press.

Minol, B., 2000 Manus from the Legends to Year 2000. Port Moresby: University of Papua New Guinea Press.

Pavlides, C., 1993 New Archaeological Research in Yombon, West New Britain, Papua New Guinea. Archaeology in Oceania 28:55–59.

——1999 The Story of Imlo: The Organisation of Flaked Stone Technologies from the Lowland Tropical Rainforest of West New Britain, Papua New Guinea. Ph.D. dissertation, La Trobe University.

Pavlides, C., and C. Gosden, 1994 35,000 Year Old Sites in the Rainforests of West New Britain, Papua New Guinea. Antiquity 68:604–610.

Robertson, N., 1986 Matenkupkum: A Late Pleistocene Cave on New Ireland, Papua New Guinea. B.A. Honours dissertation, La Trobe University.

Rosenfeld, A., 1997 Excavations at Buang Merabak, central New Ireland. Bulletin of the Indo-Pacific Prehistory Association 16:213–224.

Rowley-Conwy, P., 2001 Time, Change and the Archaeology of Hunter-Gatherers: How Original is the "Original Affluent Society"? In Hunter-Gatherers: An Interdisciplinary Perspective. C. Panter-Brick, R. Layton and P. Rowley-Conwy, eds. pp. 39–72. Cambridge: Cambridge University Press.

Smith, A., and J. Allen, 1999 Pleistocene Shell Technologies: Evidence from Island Melanesia. In Australian Coastal Archaeology. J. Hall and I. McNiven, eds. pp. 291–297. Research Papers in Archaeology and Natural History 31. Canberra: Division of Archaeology and Natural History, Research School of Pacific Studies, Australian National University.

Specht J., I. Lilley and J. Normu, 1981 Radiocarbon Dates From West New Britain, Papua New Guinea. Australian Archaeology 16:92–95.

Specht, J., In press Revisiting the Bismarcks: Some Alternative Views. In Papuan Pasts: Studies in the Cultural, Linguistic and Biological History of the Papuan Speaking Peoples. A. Pawley, R. Attenborough, J. Golson and R. Hide, eds. Canberra: Pandanus Books.

Spriggs, M., 1993 Island Melanesia: The Last 10,000 years. In A Community of Culture: The People and Prehistory. M. Spriggs, D. Yen, W. Ambrose, R. Jones, A. Thorne and A. Andrews, eds. pp. 187–205. Occasional Papers in Prehistory 21. Canberra Department of Prehistory. Research School of Pacific Studies, Australian National University.

——1997 The Island Melanesians. Oxford: Blackwell.

Steadman, D., J. P. White and J. Allen, 1999 Prehistoric Birds from New Ireland, Papua New Guinea: Extinctions on a Large Melanesian Island. Proceedings of the National Academy of Science 96:2563–2568.

Summerhayes, G., and J. Allen, 1993 The Transport of Mopir Obsidian to Late Pleistocene New Ireland. Archaeology in Oceania 29:144–148.

Torrence, R., V. Neall, T. Doelman, E. Rhodes, C. McKee, H. Davies, R. Bonetti, A. Gugliemetti, A. Manzoni, M. Oddone, J. Parr and C. Wallace, 2004 Pleistocene Colonisation of the Bismarck Archipelago: New Evidence from West New Britain. Archaeology in Oceania 39:101–130.

Veron, J., 1995 Corals in Space and Time: The Biogeography and Evolution of the Scleractinea. Sydney: University of New South Wales Press.

Wallace, A., 1869 The Malay Archipelago: The Land of the Orang-Utan and the Bird of Paradise. A Narrative of Travel with Studies of Man and Nature. 2 vols. London: Macmillan and Co.

White, J. P., 1993 The First Pacific Islanders: 30,000 Years Ago–10,000 Years Ago. *In* The First Humans: Human Origin and History to 10,000 BC. G. Burenhult, ed. pp. 171–182. The Illustrated History of Humankind. Brisbane: University of Queensland Press.

Wickler, S., 1990 Prehistoric Melanesian Exchange and Interaction: Recent Evidence From the Northern Solomon Islands Asian Perspectives 29:135–154.

——2001 The Prehistory of Buka: A Stepping Stone Island in the Northern Solomons. Terra Australis 16. Canberra: Division of Natural History, Research School of Pacific and Asian Studies, Australian National University.

Yen, D., 1995 The Development of Sahul Agriculture with Australia as Bystander. *In* Transitions: Pleistocene to Holocene in Australia and Papua New Guinea. J. Allen and J. O'Connell, eds. pp. 831–847. Antiquity 69 Special Number 265. Oxford: Antiquity Publications.

10

Life before Lapita: New Developments in Melanesia's Long-Term History

Christina Pavlides

The early and mid-Holocene in Melanesia is known through a series of mostly small sites in Near Oceania. Two larger sites centered around West New Britain's chert and obsidian outcrops stand out as different from other contemporary Melanesian sites in terms of their structure and contents. A detailed examination of the data from one of these areas, situated deep in the tropical rain forest, reveals much about culture process and social change during this dynamic period in Oceania's prehistory. There is strong evidence at these sites to suggest that society was radically transformed between 10,000 and 3,600 years ago, and that the main elements of social and economic organization more usually associated with later Lapita settlements were already in place by about 4,000 years ago. Holocene change was directional, moving toward more organized and intensive patterns of economy, seemingly uninterrupted by New Britain's explosive volcanic history. Using evidence from flaked stone artifacts, this chapter explores both the configuration and direction of this change in the wider context of Oceania's long-term history. For a comprehensive understanding of the issues involved, and especially the principles underlying the stone-tool analysis, it should be read in conjunction with Hiscock's chapter on Australia as well as the other chapters on Melanesia, especially Walter and Sheppard.

The Early Holocene: 10,000 to 5000 B.P.

The early Holocene was a time of considerable change in Near Oceania (see Figure 9.1). Population densities were greater than at any time previously, as witnessed by the establishment of many new sites, the reuse of previously occupied sites, and higher discard rates in all sites. A wider range of site types and a greater diversity of settings were occupied than during the Pleistocene (see Leavesley, this volume). Greater numbers and varieties of artifacts and faunal remains including those of introduced species at sites in New Ireland and the Solomons (Allen and Gosden 1996; Marshall and Allen 1991; White et al. 1991; Wickler 1990), as well as the discovery of dense quarries at inland chert sources (Pavlides 1993, 1999) and north-coast obsidian sources in New Britain (Torrence 1992; Torrence et al. 2000), point to a more varied range of activities.

Economic tree crops such as *Canarium* in New Ireland, Manus, the Solomons, and north-coast New Guinea (Fredericksen et al. 1993; Marshall and Allen 1991; Swadling et al. 1991; Wickler 1990; Yen 1990), root-crop residues on artifacts from the Solomons, New Ireland, and New Britain (Barton and White 1993; Fullagar 1993; Loy et al. 1992), structural evidence for swamp drainage in highland and highland-fringe New Guinea (Gillieson et al. 1985; Golson 1991a, 1991b; Gorecki 1989), and the discovery of earth ovens in New Ireland (Allen and Gosden 1996) indicate other new subsistence practices at this time. New shell ornaments and tool types occur in Manus, New Britain, New Ireland, the Solomons, and north-coast New Guinea (Allen and Gosden 1996; Fredericksen 1994; Gosden et al. 1994; Marshall and Allen 1991; Roe 1992; Smith and Allen 1999; Swadling et al. 1991; White et al. 1991; Wickler 1990). Although some of these items are not new to the region, they have not previously been found together in the same assemblage. Allen and Gosden (1996) describe such assemblages as having a familiar Oceanic Melanesian character.

Various models have been put forward to explain this evidence. For example, Marshall and Allen (1991) argue that the artifactually denser early Holocene phase at Panakiwuk indicates more constant use of the cave, over a shorter period of time, associated with changes in subsistence orientation and mobility. Similar changes are suggested by White et al. (1991:57), who state that targeting of particular animals such as phalangers indicates increased sedentism. The argument here is that because phalangers favor certain locations as resting places, human use of the same areas assures "a continuous 'take' over the medium term." In contrast, Torrence (1992; Torrence et al. 2000) argues that the organization of stone procurement and production around the Talasea obsidian sources indicates quite extensive patterns of mobility, linked to non-intensive food management strategies. She interprets the targeting of reliable tool-stone, a higher level of planning, and the production of finished multipurpose tools as evidence for far-reaching foraging ranges and relatively casual plant-resource management. I (Pavlides 1999) have raised similar arguments in relation to the rain forest sites around the Yombon chert sources of West New Britain. These opinions conform with arguments that there is no direct evidence for organized agriculture in the early Holocene, but rather evidence for some other form of economic intensification as discussed in Denham's chapter.

Analyses of flaked stone assemblages have rarely been involved in assessing these models. Assemblages from the early Holocene are usually described as being infrequent, dominated by small unretouched flakes with few instances of formal tools. Exceptions are waisted blades and adzes from the New Guinea highlands (Bulmer 1964; Christensen 1975), stemmed tools from New Britain (Pavlides 1993; Torrence et al. 2000), and possibly some "discoids" from Manus (Fredericksen

1994). Polished and edge-ground axes are present in early Holocene assemblages from north-coast and highland New Guinea (Bulmer 1966, 1975; Gorecki 1992; Gorecki et al. 1991) and New Ireland (Allen and Gosden 1996). One artifact from north-coast New Guinea is also described as a possible tanged form (Gorecki et al. 1991). At many sites, stone-procurement strategies involved local material, often extracted from secondary sources such as stream beds, although extraction of material from sedimentary sources is indicated at a handful of sites.

Studies of debitage are rare but have found a range of different approaches to artifact manufacture. For example, the Panakiwuk assemblage has a wide range of industrial components (Marshall and Allen 1991). At Matenbek, imported obsidian occurs much more frequently than in the Pleistocene strata and almost replaced local raw materials (Allen and Gosden 1996). The replacement of local stone by obsidian is a feature repeated at many other New Ireland sites.

These stone artifact analyses have been used to suggest frequent and broad-ranging mobility during the Holocene. However, other explanations are possible. Combined, there appears to be little cohesion amongst these various assemblages in terms of the amounts of planning or the organization of technology more generally. Instead, lithic extraction is expedient and production relatively unsystematic, revealing a series of localized responses to resource distribution and availability. The only significant difference to this pattern is the organized targeting of key stone resources in New Britain: chert at Yombon and obsidian at Talasea.

The production of formal, stemmed tools around Talasea certainly indicates something new. However, there is little movement of material between the New Britain chert and obsidian source areas. This may indicate that the mobility range of early Holocene people in New Britain only rarely included the north and south coasts together. Whether this, in itself, can be equated with Gosden's (1995) notion of decreasing mobility since the Pleistocene requires further consideration.

The Mid-Holocene: 5000 to 3600 B.P.

The mid-Holocene is perhaps the most elusive phase in Melanesian prehistory. Many cave sites go out of use in the early Holocene, with occupation only recommencing 3,000 years ago (Allen et al. 1989). This hiatus in activity is important because it may reflect a shift to more organized and intensive plant-management (Pavlides 1999). The general absence of evidence from the mid-Holocene does, however, pose problems for the development of models of change during the Holocene as a whole because the former period is followed by the widespread introduction of decorated Lapita pottery (see Denham, Galipaud, Leavesley, Lilley, Sand et al., and Walter and Sheppard, this volume).

Continuity of occupation between the early and mid-Holocene is noted at many cave and open sites in Near Oceania (Gosden 1991; Gosden et al. 1994; Kennedy 1979, 1983; Pavlides 1993, 1999; Pavlides and Gosden 1994; Roe 1992; Specht and Gosden 1997; Specht et al. 1983; Spriggs 1991, 1993; Torrence et al. 2000;

Vanderwal 1973; Wickler 1990). This pattern is similar to the early Holocene. Mainland New Guinea lowland open sites exhibit agricultural sequences starting at approximately 5,100 years ago (e.g., Gillieson et al. 1985; Gorecki 1989; Gorecki and Gillieson 1984), indicating that plant manipulation is not a late Holocene phenomenon in this region. Furthermore, pollen cores and other environmental evidence point to humanly associated forest clearance and burning from about 7,000 years ago at several locations in New Guinea (Haberle 1993, 1998; Haberle et al. 1991; Hope 1983). The New Ireland site of Balof 2 also reveals evidence for short-term local clearance during the early Holocene (Allen et al. 1989).

The structure and organization of mid-Holocene flaked stone technology is unknown apart from data collected at the New Britain chert and obsidian sources (Pavlides 1993, 1999; Torrence et al. 2000). At these sites there is a clear indication of a major reorganization of stone-working activities between the early and mid-Holocene: there is no continuity with the Pleistocene – early Holocene pattern of non-intensive hunting and gathering. Furthermore, when the organization of flaked stone technology during the early, mid-, and late Holocene is compared, the profile of the late Holocene Lapita discontinuity, conventionally argued to be the major Holocene cultural change in Melanesia, is reduced. This is because the organization of technology, and by extension settlement patterns, resource use, and economy, is similar during the mid- and late Holocene. The major points of variation occur between the early Holocene and these later periods. The New Britain sites reveal complex patterns of behavior during the mid-Holocene. Unfortunately, similar changes are not apparent at other sites because the early and mid-Holocene periods are often absent or combined during analysis, before being contrasted as a whole with the late Holocene/Lapita phase.

An exceptional feature of the sites at the New Britain stone sources during the mid-Holocene is the production of formally shaped composite tools. Although the production of stemmed obsidian tools is not new around Talasea (Torrence 1992), where they first appear during the early Holocene, formal tools with stems and waists are only found in mid-Holocene assemblages in the rain forest chert sources (Pavlides 1999). The manufacture of formal tools in these two areas is marked by radically different patterns of production. Perhaps surprisingly, equivalent tool forms and production strategies have not been identified in other locations around Near Oceania. This may be because of the strategic location of the New Britain sites (situated at high-quality stone sources), and/or the absence of detailed technological studies of artifacts from other sites. Other mid-Holocene flaked stone assemblages from coastal New Britain are most often just ephemeral scatters rather than large production sites (e.g., Gosden 1991; Gosden and Webb 1994; Gosden et al. 1994).

Discussion

In general, models of early and mid-Holocene settlement and economy in Near Oceania are largely undeveloped and *ad hoc*. The paucity of archaeological data

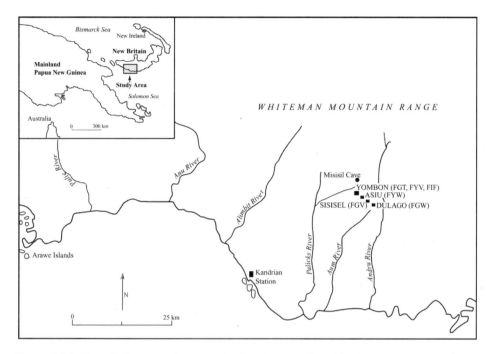

Figure 10.1 The rain forest study area and other sites mentioned in the text

dating to these critical phases, especially the mid-Holocene, has severely affected the formulation of hypotheses and models concerning change through time. However, a clearer picture of social evolution for sites in New Britain has recently been presented (Pavlides 1999; Torrence et al. 2000). My work entailed techno-logical analyses of flaked stone artifacts from the sites around the Yombon chert sources in the island's southern rain forests (Figure 10.1). These data have been used to examine the structure and direction of change in economy and settlement before the appearance of Lapita pottery. Gradual changes can be discerned in the way people utilized their environment, culminating in more intensive resource man-agement in the mid-Holocene. The second part of this chapter presents some new technological data from the Yombon sites to further develop this alternative view of change during the Holocene.

The Chronology of the New Britain Rain Forest Sites

The problem of tracking change during the Holocene has as much to do with taphonomy and site location as it does with the limitations of current analytical techniques. As mentioned before, early and mid-Holocene deposits are often absent or missed by excavators at most Melanesian sites or combined during analysis, before being contrasted with the late Holocene/Lapita phase. The sites in New

Table 10.1   Archaeological units and known tephras at the Yombon rain forest sites (Pavlides 1999)

Analytical unit	Chronological unit	Estimated age range (cal. B.P.)
Unit 1	Recent contexts	1300 B.P. to the present
	Witori-Kimbe 3–4 & Dakataua	1700–1400–1000
Unit 2	Late Holocene contexts	1400 to 3400
	Witori-Kimbe 2	3600
Unit 3	Mid-Holocene contexts	3600 to 5900
	Witori-Kimbe 1 & Witori-Rikau	5900
Unit 4	Early Holocene contexts	5900 to 12,400
	Unidentified tephra & Pleistocene tephra	12,400, 17,000
Unit 5	Pleistocene contexts	17,000 to 35,000

Britain do not suffer these limitations because of their exceptional preservation, which results from the catastrophic volcanism that has affected the island throughout its entire 35,000-year history (Pavlides 2004; Torrence et al. 2004). While volcanic instability would have had dire consequences for local communities, the huge volumes of tephra (ash) ejected during eruptions sealed and preserved entire cultural landscapes. The sequence of eruptions and associated tephras (tephrostratigraphy) has been combined with radiocarbon dates from intervening cultural layers to construct a tephrochronological sequence that uses the presence of geochemically "fingerprinted" tephra beds as chronological indicators. These markers can be traced over most of western New Britain, providing a robust island-wide chronostratigraphy. The envelopes of time encompassed by these tephra markers at the rain forest sites are listed in Table 10.1.

Each analytical unit is separated from the next by a layer of tephra derived from the Mt. Witori volcano inland of Cape Hoskins or the Dakataua volcano on the tip of the Willaumez Peninsula (Pavlides 1999; Machida et al. 1996). Two distinct archaeological units (4 and 3) cover the early and mid-Holocene at the rain forest sites. The same two units have been observed around Talasea at the base of the Willaumez Peninsula (Torrence 1992; Torrence et al. 2000). Evidence for the early and mid-Holocene eruptions (W-1 and W-K2) is also present in the Arawe Islands, approximately 180 kilometers southwest of Mt. Witori (Gosden et al. 1994).

The Early Holocene around Yombon

The early Holocene is represented at Yombon and nearby Asiu village by occupation dating from about 6800 to 5900 cal. B.P., at which time the W-K1 tephra from Mt. Witori ended this phase of deposition in the rain forest (Pavlides 1993, 1999). Analysis of early Holocene flaked stone artifacts reveals a spatially organized pattern of procurement arranged around central nodes characterized by key resources such as high-quality chert with production and use occurring at other distant locations. The chert at one location, Auwa hamlet, was targeted repeatedly, possibly via a large sinkhole in the local limestone bedrock. Away from this location, assemblages consist of low-density scatters of flakes and tools made from the same kind of stone. The technological characteristics of the two sets of assemblages, the quarry at Auwa hamlet and non-quarry sites at the other locations, also set them apart.

Quarrying

Only one excavated early Holocene assemblage other than the Auwa quarry contains more than 200 artifacts. This uneven spread of flaked stone around the rain forest sites is directly related to flaking activities occurring in the proximity of the chert-bearing sinkhole. There is about 30 times more non-artifactual rubble at Auwa site than at other sites, as well as significantly more artifacts with cortical surfaces. High proportions of artifacts with unaltered chalky limestone cortex and the proportion of artifacts with fresh unaltered flaked surfaces indicate that most raw material was acquired from primary geological sources. There are also proportionally more complete and broken cortical flakes at the Auwa site than at all the other sites combined. These patterns are consistent with a pattern of primary reduction at a quarry and/or primary knapping site (Hiscock and Mitchell 1993).

Production technology

The spatial organization of technology demonstrates clear differences in the nature of production activities at quarry and non-quarry sites during the early Holocene. While data from the quarry indicate early-stage reduction, flaking away from this locality was primarily restricted to the later stages of reduction. The quarry assemblage also has a significantly higher proportion of flakes with cortical platforms than non-quarry assemblages. This suggests that early stage reduction occurred at the quarry while the later stages of reduction occurred elsewhere. Similarly, the proportion of chert flakes indicating intensive platform preparation is much higher at non-quarry sites, as is that of unmodified flakes with proximal dorsal trimming indicative of intensive core platform preparation and maintenance. These details are matched by the high ratio of tools to unmodified flakes at non-quarry sites, revealing a greater focus on artifact use as opposed to production. All the chert cores that were found came from the quarry, a spatial dichotomy which may reflect high production rates and discard of exhausted cores around the main source (see Torrence 1984).

Tool production

Early Holocene assemblages from Yombon reflect the production and selection of both early and late stage artifacts for modification. The spatial organization of technology, however, exhibits little difference between the quarry and non-quarry assemblages apart from the frequency of tools exhibiting cortex. This result is opposite to the organization of flake production at this time, indicating that away from the main quarry, non-cortical flakes were primarily produced and selected for further modification. The non-quarry sites do, however, have a higher proportion of modified artifacts than the quarry assemblage.

Tool types and the morphology of retouch

Early Holocene tool types include simple flake tools and notched flake tools, a double-notch tool (which has opposing notches that form a constriction or stem on the flake), a bifacial scraper, and a unifacial ovoid scraper. These tools exhibit only low-intensity retouching and edge-use. Edge-damage is characterized by light, scaled retouch or quite small notches, and high-magnification examination revealed edge modification and residues consistent with soft plant and woodworking. The double-notch tool is a flat flake with two large invasive notches opposite each other, flaked onto the ventral surface. Microscopic examination of this artifact discerned polishes, masses of organic residues and starch grains within the notches, and striations running perpendicular to the notch edges.

The unifacial ovoid scraper and bifacial scraper have retouch characterized by steep flaking on the dorsal surface and steep bifacial flaking. The ovoid is a large, totally cortical flake with steep, unifacial denticulate flaking along both margins. The technology and general pattern of retouch are like that of a Pleistocene unifacial ovoid scraper from Yombon, but the Pleistocene tool is more carefully retouched and has quite obviously been used (Pavlides 1999, 2004). The bifacial scraper is a large outrepassé flake with flat, invasive bifacial retouch along three edges and more than fifty percent dorsal cortex.

In summary, early Holocene tools lack heavy retouch and there is little evidence for repeated retouching and rotation of tools involving more than two edges. Tool production is restricted to a few formal and informal types. The Auwa quarry assemblage yielded two different scraper forms. One, the unifacial ovoid scraper, has been shaped to some degree through retouching. Along with the double-notch tool and possibly one other large broken notched flake tool, these artifacts are the only identifiable morphological types in the early Holocene assemblage.

Early Holocene settlement and economy

The spatial differentiation of different reduction stages, such as initial reduction at the quarry and later stages of flaking at other locations, is more obvious at this time than it was in the Pleistocene (Pavlides 2004). This suggests that the collection of material from a known, reliable source was important for people exploiting the rain forests of western New Britain in the early Holocene. Yet production at the quarry cannot be described as systematic. The explanation is probably direct access to the quarry by different groups and *ad hoc* production. Away from the sinkhole there is not much differentiation in stone working intensity or variation in tool discard.

This early Holocene pattern is similar to that at the obsidian sources around Talasea on New Britain's north coast (Torrence 1992; Torrence et al. 2000): In both regions there is technological evidence for source targeting which does not continue into later times. In the rain forest, both bedrock and creek-bed deposits provide abundant and accessible sources of raw material. The repeated selection of particular sources could have incurred greater costs than using the closest and most accessible sources. In this context, one way of explaining such a procurement strategy is that the acquisition of stone was embedded in other activities rather than a specially scheduled task (Binford 1979). Torrence (1992) has suggested that this strategy was adopted along the north coast during the early Holocene. A land-use pattern involving high residential mobility that incorporates scheduled visits to sources of quality stone is also consistent with the observed pattern. The types of flaked stone assemblages recovered from the non-quarry sites in the rain forest, as well as from contemporaneous sites in other parts of Melanesia, indicate low-intensity short-term occupation by small groups of people. High residential mobility is almost certainly associated with movement over a large area. The presence of obsidian in the rain forest assemblages, whether acquired directly from the source or indirectly, reveals an island-wide pattern of communication and resource use.

One major difference between the artifact production systems of the rain forest and those at the north-coast obsidian sources is the manufacture of highly retouched forms such as stemmed tools. Very few heavily retouched artifacts were deposited in the rain forest sites during the early Holocene phase. Only one artifact, the unifacial ovoid scraper, is heavily retouched and even this artifact is not formally shaped and may in fact be unfinished. If it is a tool preform produced at the quarry, it is the only one of its kind in the assemblage. Contemporaneous assemblages from the north-coast obsidian sources contain many highly retouched tools, characterized by finely worked stems. Torrence (1992) has argued that these tools solved the problems faced by forest foragers in that they were a buffer against the risks associated with high mobility. The potential problems faced by early Holocene societies included a generalist economy, high transport costs, and raw material availability. In this case, high residential mobility may have increased the risks associated with raw material availability rather than the short-term risk associated with food capture. This pattern of settlement mobility and economy required strategic technological solutions, such as increased planning and targeting of reliable raw material. In the rain forest study area, only the difference between the raw material source at Auwa hamlet and the non-quarry sites points to a strategy of increased planning.

The absence of composite stemmed tools from the early Holocene rain forest assemblages is odd. Two possibilities may be considered. Firstly, tools similar to those from the north coast may have been produced at the rain forest chert sources but did not make their way to the sites that were excavated because they were used up and/or recycled prior to return trips to the area. High residential mobility and a large foraging range could keep people away from the chert sources long enough to exhaust tools. Also, quick trips to the chert sources would limit the time spent in this part of the rain forest, perhaps to the extent that used or broken tools were not deposited close to the source. A more plausible scenario, however, is that the costs of procuring fresh material were sufficiently low for the southern rain forest groups that advanced planning, involving the production and maintenance of composite tools, was not needed during the early Holocene. This is because of the way in which stone procurement was integrated or embedded with other aspects of settlement organization and subsistence strategies and the impact this had on the organization of technology and the production of tools. A land-use pattern of high residential mobility may in fact mitigate the costs otherwise associated with the use of particular resources. In this sense, the situation in the lowland rain forest differs from that around the north-coast obsidian sources. There is little evidence at the rain forest sites to support the model of tools as mobile sources of raw material during the early Holocene.

Even if embedded procurement best describes the way that the rain forest chert and north-coast obsidian sources were exploited, it may not be the only factor contributing to the cost of acquiring raw materials or to the structure of tool assemblages. It is possible that differences in social organization between the two regions may also be contributing to differences in flaked stone technology. For example, Talasea obsidian has a history of movement around Near Oceania spanning at least 20,000 years (Summerhayes and Allen 1993), whereas the rain forest chert was only ever used locally. This difference between the two regions is likely to have had an impact on flaked stone technology. Intra-group social tensions arising out of prestige, exchange, and communication relationships involving the long-established movement of north-coast obsidian were probably not part of the Pleistocene and early Holocene social landscape of the southern rain forests. A comparison of the production and circulation of rain forest chert and obsidian in contemporary networks suggests an extremely low level of social organization associated with the production and use of the chert sources (Summerhayes and Allen 1993; Summerhayes et al. 1993; Torrence et al. 1996; White 1996; White and Harris 1997). Instead, a model of low-intensity resource management, including direct access to resources and unsystematic quarry-based production, is suggested for the early Holocene.

The Mid-Holocene around Yombon

Mid-Holocene assemblages from the New Britain rain forest were deposited between 5,900 and 3600 cal. B.P. (Pavlides 1999; Machida et al. 1996), when the cataclysmic W-K2 eruption occurred at Mt. Witori. Layers dating to the mid-Holocene are thus sandwiched between the W-K1 and W-K2 tephras. Radiocarbon assays on excavated archaeological charcoal from this period currently fall between about 4800 and 4100 cal. B.P. (Pavlides 1993, 1999; Specht et al. 1981). During this time the organization of stone procurement and artifact production shifted away from activities that are easily defined as quarry or non-quarry. Instead, reduction took place across a wide area and thus does not suggest the targeting of an identifiable primary source such as the Auwa sinkhole. Mid-Holocene stone assemblages are mixtures of early- and late-stage flaking products and reflect non-intensive flaking. However, an innovation at this time was the production of a sophisticated toolkit including stemmed unifacial and stemmed and waisted bifacial tools. Thought to be restricted to the southern rain forest region of western New Britain (the *Passismanua* tools) (Bulmer 1977; Chowning and Goodale 1966; White 1982), the stemmed unifacial and stemmed and waisted bifacial tools are present as finished tools only during the mid-Holocene phase. They are part of a hafted composite tool assemblage and may be interpreted as multipurpose tools that also served as a source of usable flakes in a technological strategy geared toward curation (Binford 1973; Kelly 1988; Shott 1986, 1996).

Quarrying

Unlike the early Holocene, there is no mid-Holocene evidence for high-intensity quarrying and primary knapping at Auwa. However, several other sites in the Yombon area contain large quantities of flaked chert. There is also a substantial expansion of the area utilized for artifact production, with reduction being less staged or differentiated between sites, including the Auwa source. Furthermore, there is no correlation between high artifact frequencies and an abundance of non-artifactual rubble at any one location. Cortex is present on artifacts from all sites, with many assemblages revealing almost equal proportions of cortical and non-cortical artifacts. These data are consistent with a picture of shifting procurement and production activities away from the Auwa source, although some flaking and procurement activities continued in the vicinity of the sinkhole. The extraction of material from *in situ* sedimentary deposits rather than secondary contexts such as stream or riverbeds does, however, persist during the mid-Holocene, as witnessed by the type and condition of cortex on artifacts and the selection of chert blocks and nodules as core blanks.

Production technology

Unlike the early Holocene pattern of segregated and staged reduction, the structure of mid-Holocene assemblages indicates a mixture of both early- and late-stage reduction across the rain forest sites. For example, high frequencies of complete and broken flakes and tools along with low frequencies of other flaking debris and core rejuvenation flakes characterize assemblages found throughout the area. In fact, high proportions of early-stage debris are the most common element of assemblages at most sites. Assemblages from sites situated both close to and distant from Auwa hamlet display quite high ratios of tools to unmodified flakes.

Nearly all assemblages are dominated by flakes with simple platform treatments. Only one assemblage has a high proportion of flakes with complex platforms and a few assemblages have relatively even proportions of simple and complex platforms. Similarly, relatively equal amounts of core trimming and maintenance are noted at many sites, regardless of proximity to the raw material source at Auwa hamlet. The distribution of discarded chert cores largely follows the same pattern. In short, the spatial organization of mid-Holocene assemblages does not reflect a structured pattern of reduction intensity and core platform preparation related to the Auwa raw material source.

The foregoing evidence indicates there was a major change in stone artifact manufacturing strategies during the mid-Holocene. Flaking was not centered solely on the Auwa source or any other single location: stone was extracted from multiple *in situ* sources. Primary production activities also shifted from one main site to multiple locations around the rain forest. Furthermore, production was more evenly spread around the rain forest, with many assemblages revealing either low-intensity early-stage reduction or a mixture of early- and late-stage flaking. The distribution of equivalent reduction stages across most sampling locations is consistent with a more generalized pattern of procurement and production during the mid-Holocene. This pattern of technological organization is different from the early Holocene pattern.

Tool production

Mid-Holocene tool assemblages consistently reveal the preferential production and selection of non-cortical tool blanks for modification. This result is consistent with the organization of flake production at this time.

Tool types and the morphology of retouch

Several new tool types are noted within the mid-Holocene assemblages. These include flake tools, notched flake tools, unifacial scrapers, a scalar core, bifacial scrapers, bifacial stemmed tools, a bifacial waisted tool, and unifacial stemmed tools (Figure 10.2). The pattern of deposition of these tools is consistent with a shift in the focus of flaking, tool-using, and artifact deposition away from the Auwa source. All of the highly retouched forms were deposited at a distance from this quarry.

The number of utilized edges on chert tools reveals a pattern of low-intensity retouching and modification, with the majority of tools having only one or two modified edges. More than half of the tool assemblage exhibits dorsal retouch, with only

Figure 10.2 The bifacial stemmed and waisted and unifacial stemmed tools (dorsal view)

moderate amounts of ventral retouching and bifacial modification. Dorsal flaking also dominated in the early Holocene, but many of the mid-Holocene tools are more heavily retouched. Use-wear and residue analyses revealed edge modification consistent with low-angled scraping of medium-density wood and plant material, grass cutting, and bamboo working, including scraping, sawing, and slicing. Residues resembling blood were identified on two tools, and a mammalian hair on one.

The reduction sequence for the stemmed unifacial and stemmed and waisted bifacial tools is like that of the unifacial ovoid scrapers from the Pleistocene and early Holocene. All were produced on primary flakes detached from large boulders or partially prepared cores. All are steeply retouched and most retain at least some dorsal cortex but none displays invasive flaking on the ventral surface only. Despite early claims to the contrary (Shutler and Kess 1969), there is no evidence that anything other than primary source material was used in the production of these tools. Microscopic patterns of wear and polish around the stems and dorsal ridges of the complete stemmed and waisted bifacial tools and stemmed unifacial tools are consistent with lashing or hafting in an organic handle fashioned from rattan or bamboo.

In summary, the analysis of tool edges indicates low-intensity tool retouching and utilization. This pattern of edge modification is not very different from that noted for the early Holocene, indicating a similar type and direction of retouching activity. What is different from the early Holocene phase is the production of repeated highly specific tool forms with a stem or waist for hafting.

Mid-Holocene settlement and economy

The mid-Holocene pattern conforms to longstanding expectations about the way stone resources are used in areas where they are abundant and accessible (Andrefsky 1994a, 1994b; Bamforth 1986, 1990). No single source is targeted and the products of stone working are spread around the landscape. Raw material is not intensively worked and tools are not carefully maintained. The exception to this rule in New Britain is the production of stemmed and waisted tools. The production and use of a variety of formal types, including composite tools which may have acted as core tools, indicates a more complex and organized reduction sequence for chert. The production of composite core tools during the mid-Holocene provided both useful cutting edges and raw material for the production of smaller tool blanks, within a curated technological strategy. Their production and use did not, however, necessitate repeated exclusive use of one particular high-quality stone source such as that at Auwa hamlet. Nor is it associated with spatially organized production. This suggests that this aspect of the mid-Holocene stone technology did not involve tight scheduling of activities. The appearance of these tools in the rain-forest sites must therefore indicate a shift in the scheduling of activities around the chert sources, perhaps indicating a set of problem-solving strategies differing from those of the early Holocene.

One interpretation of these composite tools is that they reduced the risks associated with accessing material of uncertain, or unsatisfactory, quality from untested locations. This type of problem would not arise, though, unless the mid-Holocene settlement pattern was in some way different from that of the early Holocene. Following the arguments presented earlier, a reduction in mobility might have been associated with an increase in the costs of procuring raw material if procurement then had to be undertaken as a special activity outside the regular subsistence schedule (Binford 1979). In other words, changes in the character of mid-Holocene artifact assemblages may result from changes in procurement strategies associated with a reduction in settlement mobility.

Following Binford (1979), Lurie (1989) associates the production of a greater number of hafted tools, highly modified tools, and more intensively used and reworked artifacts, with logistically organized strategies during the middle Archaic at the Koster site in the USA. Her argument is that there was a change from high residential mobility to semi-sedentism in multi-seasonal camps. This reorganization changed the costs of raw material procurement and tool production. Following the same logic, the mid-Holocene rain forest sites, for which procurement and transport costs are high, should contain tools used in a range of tasks, i.e., unspecialized, multifunctional tools (see also Shott 1986; Torrence 1983). The stemmed and waisted bifacial tools and stemmed unifacial tools can be seen as versatile and maintainable multipurpose tools in the terms defined by Bleed (1986) and Nelson (1991). In short, these tools are modular, portable, generalized, and designed for partial function in the case of breakage. Such artifacts would be effective in a wide range of situations, an obvious advantage in rain forest environments characterized by a great variety of low-density resources. Bleed (1986) argues that the timing of risk determines the need for maintainability as it extends tool use-life and is sufficiently versatile to be useful in a wide range of situations which have low failure costs (see also Shott 1986). The composite and maintainable form of the rain forest tools were designed for unpredictable schedules, unpredictable situations, and continuous use. The absence of obvious reliable design features associated with time-limited, high-stress hunting (Bleed 1986; Torrence 1983, 1989) also indicates that the risks associated with hunting mobile, migratory game were not relevant in the rain forest, especially given that plant manipulation and maintenance of organic tools were the primary functions of the tools in question.

The production of stemmed and waisted tools does not suggest that good-quality chert was no longer accessible after W-K1. Rather, the movement and curation of these tools probably provided a ready source of high-quality material, in the form of both a prepared core and a tool with usable edges (Kelly 1988). These traits would be advantageous if extended periods of time were spent away from known raw material sources. Arguments suggesting increased sedentism and a new focus on lowland plants are consistent with the production of these new composite tool types. By increasing the level of planning in relation to tool design and production, the costs of procurement could be reduced without compromising the efficiency of the tool or its maintenance.

Discussion

The models presented here invoke broad changes in the organization of resource exploitation, mobility patterns, and subsistence activities. Changes between early and mid-Holocene approaches to stone artifact production indicate a shift in the factors structuring technology in the rain forest. The most notable difference is a shift from embedded procurement, centered around a few high-quality chert sources visited infrequently as part of wide-reaching patterns of settlement mobility, to a more generalized production system incorporating many small multi-component sites. The appearance of new composite tool forms also suggests a novel approach to problems of changing mobility and resource availability. One explanation is that there was a new concentration of land-use in the mid-Holocene. In this scenario, greater sedentism would allow a greater number of resources to be harnessed more efficiently from a smaller range. In addition, longer periods of time spent away from key resources would require more planning. The manufacture of composite tools, prepared in advance of use, was scheduled into activities in the same way that regular trips to a particular quarry can be said to be embedded in other activities within a broader economic system (Binford 1977, 1979, 1980). In this sense people occupying the rain forest after the deposition of the W-K1 tephra were involved in a more intensive system of land management and economy which necessitated the development of new technological strategies and solutions. To conclude: The early Holocene pattern of technology and land-use had many parallels with Pleistocene patterns but mid-Holocene data reflect a new approach to the landscape and economy. This new approach continued into the late Holocene in western New Britain despite the devastating impact of the W-K2 eruption around 3600 cal. B.P.

So, What's New with Lapita?

In contrast to my suggestions concerning the redirection of activities during the mid-Holocene, it is generally argued by Lapita scholars that there is no evidence for settled villages before the late Holocene. Yet it is clear from the New Britain rain forest sites that the organization of flaked stone technologies following the deposition of the W-K2 tephra about 3,600 years ago was similar to that noted for the mid-Holocene. The approach to raw material acquisition and selection was more relaxed than in earlier periods but there was no return to the pattern of procurement witnessed in the early Holocene. Similarly, while many late Holocene sites are ephemeral artifact scatters dominated by late-stage flakes and tools, production was distributed uniformly around the rain forest area, indicating no substantial break with the mid-Holocene. The critical difference between the middle and late Holocene is the presence of composite tools in the former and their absence from the latter, but new tool types were produced during the late Holocene.

The flaked stone assemblages from New Britain's coastal fringes and from other Lapita sites in island Melanesia are similar to those found in the rain forest at this time. This observation does not support the idea that coastal lithic resources had replaced the rain forest chert sources in some sort of island-wide reorganization of activities away from the interior regions. Technological evidence from coastal Lapita sites around the north-coast obsidian sources (Torrence 1992), consumer settlements in the Arawe Islands (Halsey 1995) and the more distant Reefs/Santa Cruz Islands beyond the main Solomons archipelago (Sheppard 1993) all reflect patterns of stone use and tool production similar to those described for the rain forest. More significantly, these studies reveal that the organization of flaked stone technology during the late Holocene had very little to do with being in a location of stone resource abundance or poverty. This result is unexpected in view of current theories regarding technology and resource availability, indicating that neither raw material availability nor proximity to source was the major influence on these late Holocene assemblages. The same appears to be true of the rain forest assemblages from this period. On this basis it appears that these changes in technology are more likely to represent changes in the way resources were used, and thus changes in subsistence and settlement patterns. Increased sedentism linked with more intensive exploitation of smaller territories may explain the features of the late Holocene artifact assemblages. These hypothesized changes in mobility would significantly alter the costs and benefits associated with acquiring raw material and manufacturing tools. Increased sedentism confers a benefit in terms of reduced pro-curement costs: Large amounts of material can be stockpiled at settlements fol-lowing special-purpose trips to the source (Binford 1979; Parry and Kelly 1987) or through exchange (Torrence 1992). Increased sedentism, combined with special-purpose trips to retrieve material and resource stockpiling, effectively makes the process of tool manufacture highly predictable. As a consequence, the proximity of settlements to stone sources such as the rain forest chert quarry is irrelevant. In this context, neither the procurement of high-quality material nor the production of composite tools is a necessary risk-minimizing strategy. Semi-sedentism and regular returns to critical resource patches are more consistent with late Holocene data (Gosden 1994; Gosden and Pavlides 1994).

Directional Change in Western New Britain

The changes in technology noted in the early and mid-Holocene rain forest assem-blages point to significant organizational changes in land-use and economy. When these two periods are compared with the late Holocene it appears that approaches to stone use and technology continue in the same way as they had during the mid-Holocene even though one group of tools disappears. The change from the early to mid-Holocene occurred against a backdrop of catastrophic volcanism, but this is also true of the continuities between the mid- and late Holocene. Thus while it is tempting to point to drastic short-term events such as volcanic eruptions to explain the changes in procurement observed between the early and mid-Holocene phases, how can one then explain the organizational similarity in resource use and tech-nology between the mid- and late Holocene? The blanketing of large areas of the rain forest with dense tephra had little effect on resource availability over time. Instead, the switch from targeted procurement and production in the early Holocene to the generalized use of multiple locations in the mid- and late Holocene appears more deliberate and strategic. This must result from changes in broader social processes. I contend that the pre-Lapita mid-Holocene switch in technology heralds a major shift involving a steady decrease in settlement mobility and, by implication, an increase in land management, culminating in the late Holocene landscape pattern which encompasses a limited territorial range and almost total reliance on plant foods. This set of changes is directional and points to a concen-tration and contraction of land-use beginning in the mid-Holocene and continuing into the late Holocene.

A Regional Perspective

The interpretations offered in this chapter have significant implications for the way in which larger-scale changes in Melanesia are understood. As other chapters make clear, it has been argued that the late Holocene social and economic changes asso-ciated with the Lapita phenomenon were unique. However, changing procurement strategies and production systems in the rain forest suggest increased sedentism, and by inference, changes in the subsistence base, well before Lapita appeared. Furthermore, the rain forest data show quite clearly that the behavioral changes that took place there during the Lapita period are not the only, or even the most marked, changes in past subsistence and settlement activities in the region. Rather, a long-term trend toward decreased mobility, decreased home range, and intensified land management can be postulated.

The reorganization of subsistence and settlement as a result of migration or the importation of entire suites of cultural practices, including flaked stone technology, are not necessary in this scenario. The evidence from the rain forest sites clearly indicates that it is premature to assume either long-term continuity of settlement and economic organization throughout the Holocene until the past few thousand years, or a drastic break from the past with the introduction of new late-Holocene technologies, economy, and social organization associated with Lapita. The stone assemblages from the rain forests of New Britain hint at internal local developments consistent with many of the traits ascribed to much later forms of socioeconomic organization. In this view, Lapita merely represents one late Holocene expression of the adjustments in resource use, settlement mobility, land-use, and trade that have characterized the region since it was first settled.

REFERENCES

Allen, J., and C. Gosden, 1996 Spheres of Interaction: Modelling the Culture History of the Bismarck Archipelago. *In* Oceanic Culture History: Essays in Honour of Roger Green. J. Davidson, G. Irwin, F. Leach, A. Pawley and D. Brown, eds. pp. 183–197. Special Publication. Dunedin: New Zealand Journal of Archaeology.

Allen, J., C. Gosden and J. P. White, 1989 Human Pleistocene Adaptations in the Tropical Island Pacific: Recent Evidence from New Ireland, a Greater Australian Outlier. Antiquity 63:548–561.

Andrefsky, W. Jr., 1994a. Raw-Material Availability and the Organization of Technology. American Antiquity 59:21–34.

——1994b The Geological Occurrence of Lithic Material and Stone Tool Production Strategies. Geoarchaeology 9:375–391.

Bamforth, D., 1986 Technological Efficiency and Tool Curation. American Antiquity 51:38–50.

——1990 Settlement, Raw Material and Lithic Procurement in the Central Mojave Desert. Journal of Anthropological Archaeology 9:70–104.

Barton, H., and J. P. White, 1993 Use of Stone and Shell Artifacts at Balof 2, New Ireland, Papua New Guinea. Asian Perspectives 32:169–181.

Binford, L., 1973 Inter Assemblage Variability: The Mousterian and the 'Functional' Argument. *In* The Explanation of Culture Change. C. Renfrew, ed. pp. 227–254. London: Duckworth Press.

——1977 Forty-Seven Trips: A Case Study in the Character of Archaeological Formation Processes. *In* Stone Tools as Cultural Markers: Change, Evolution and Complexity. R. Wright, ed. pp. 40–59. Canberra: Australian Institute of Aboriginal Studies.

—— 1979 Organization and Formation Processes: Looking at Curated Technologies. Journal of Anthropological Research 35:255–273.

—— 1980 Willow Smoke and Dogs' Tails: Hunter-Gatherer Settlement Systems and Archaeological Site Formation. American Antiquity 45:4–20.

Bleed, P., 1986 The Optimal Design for Hunting Weapons: Maintainability or Reliability. American Antiquity 51:737–747.

Bulmer, S., 1964 Prehistoric Stone Implements from the New Guinea Highlands. Oceania 34:246–268.

—— 1966 The Prehistory of the Australian New Guinea Highlands: A Discussion of Archaeological Field Survey and Excavations 1959–1960. M.A. dissertation, University of Auckland.

—— 1975 Settlement and Economy in Prehistoric Papua New Guinea: A Review of the Archaeological Evidence. Journal de la Société des Océanistes 31:7–75.

—— 1977 Waisted Blades and Axes: A Functional Interpretation of Some Early Stone Tools from Papua New Guinea. In Stone Tools as Cultural Markers: Change, Evolution and Complexity. R. Wright, ed. pp. 178–188. Canberra: Australian Institute of Aboriginal Studies.

Chowning, A., and J. Goodale, 1966 A Flint Industry from Southwest New Britain, Territory of New Guinea. Asian Perspectives 9:150–153.

Christensen, O., 1975 A Tanged Blade from the New Guinea Highlands. Mankind 10:37–39.

Fredericksen, C., 1994 Patterns in Glass: Obsidian and Economic Specialisation in the Admiralty Islands. Ph.D. dissertation, Australian National University.

Fredericksen, C., M. Spriggs and W. Ambrose, 1993 Pamwak Rockshelter: A Pleistocene Site on Manus Island, Papua New Guinea. In Sahul in Review: Pleistocene Archaeology in Australia, New Guinea and Island Melanesia at 10–30 Kyr B.P. M. Smith, M. Spriggs and B. Fankhauser, eds. pp. 144–154. Occasional Papers in Prehistory 24. Canberra: Department of Prehistory, Research School of Pacific Studies, Australian National University.

Fullagar, R., 1993 Flaked Stone Tools and Plant Food Production: A Preliminary Report On Obsidian Tools From Talasea, West New Britain, PNG. In Traces et Fonction : les Gestes Retrouvés. 2 vols. P. Anderson, S. Beyries, M. Otte and H. Plisson, eds. pp. 331–337. Etudes et Recherches Archéologiques de l'Université de Liège 50. Liège: Université de Liège.

Gillieson, D., P. Gorecki and G. Hope, 1985 Prehistoric Agricultural Systems in a Lowland Swamp, Papua New Guinea. Archaeology in Oceania 20:32–37.

Golson, J., 1991a The New Guinea Highlands on the Eve of Agriculture. In Indo-Pacific Prehistory 1990, vol. 2. P. Bellwood, ed. pp. 48–53. Bulletin of the Indo-Pacific Prehistory Association 11. Canberra and Jakarta: Indo-Pacific Prehistory Association and Asosiasi Prehistorisi Indonesia.

—— 1991b Bulmer Phase II: Early Agriculture in the New Guinea Highlands. In Man and a Half: Essays in Pacific Anthropology and Ethnobotany in Honour of Ralph Bulmer. A. Pawley, ed. pp. 484–491. Memoir 48. Auckland: The Polynesian Society.

Gorecki, P., 1989 Prehistory of the Jimi Valley. In A Crack in the Spine: Prehistory and Ecology of the Jimi-Yuat Valley, Papua New Guinea, P. Gorecki and D. Gillieson, eds. pp. 130–188. Townsville: Division of Anthropology and Archaeology, School of Behavioral Sciences, James Cook University of North Queensland.

—— 1992 A Lapita Smoke Screen? In Poterie Lapita et Peuplement: J-C. Galipaud, ed. pp. 27–47. Nouméa: ORSTROM.

Gorecki, P., and D. Gillieson, 1984 The Highland Fringes as a Key Zone for Prehistoric Developments in Papua New Guinea: A Progress Report. Bulletin of the Indo-Pacific Prehistory Association 5:93–103.

Gorecki, P., M. Mabin and J. Campbell, 1991 Archaeology and Geomorphology of the Vanimo Coast, Papua New Guinea: Preliminary Results. Archaeology in Oceania 26:119–122.

Gosden, C., 1991 Towards an Understanding of the Regional Record from the Arawe Islands, West New Britain, Papua New Guinea. In Report of the Lapita Homeland Project. J. Allen and C. Gosden, eds. pp. 205–216. Occasional Papers in Prehistory 20. Canberra: Department of Prehistory, Research School of Pacific Studies, Australian National University.

——1994 Social Being and Time. Oxford: Blackwell.

——1995 Arboriculture and Agriculture. In Transitions: Pleistocene to Holocene in Australia and Papua New Guinea. J. Allen, and J. O'Connell, eds. pp. 807–817. Antiquity 69 Special Number 265. Oxford: Antiquity Publications.

Gosden, C., and C. Pavlides, 1994 Are Islands Insular? Landscape vs. Seascape in the Case of the Arawe Islands, Papua New Guinea. Archaeology in Oceania 29:162–171.

Gosden, C., and J. Webb, 1994 The Creation of a Papua New Guinean Landscape: Archaeological and Geomorphological Evidence. Journal of Field Archaeology 21:29–51.

Gosden, C., J. Webb, B. Marshall and G. Summerhayes, 1994 Lolmo Cave: A Mid to Late Holocene Site, the Arawe Islands, West New Britain, Papua New Guinea. Asian Perspectives 33:98–119.

Haberle, S., 1993 Pleistocene Vegetation Change and Early Human Occupation of a Tropical Mountainous Environment. In Sahul in Review: Pleistocene Archaeology in Australia, New Guinea and Island Melanesia at 10–30 Kyr B.P. M. Smith, M. Spriggs and B. Fankhauser, eds. pp. 109–122. Occasional Papers in Prehistory 24. Canberra: Department of Prehistory, Research School of Pacific Studies, Australian National University.

——1998 Late Quaternary Vegetation Change in the Tari Basin, Papua New Guinea. Palaeogeography, Palaeoclimatology, Palaeoecology 137:1–24.

Haberle, S., G. Hope and Y. De Fretes, 1991 Environmental Changes in the Baliem Valley, Montane Irian Jaya, Republic of Indonesia. Journal of Biogeography 18:25–40.

Halsey, A., 1995 Obsidian Resource Maximisation: A Comparison of Two Lapita Assemblages. B.A. Honours dissertation, La Trobe University.

Harris, D., 1989 An Evolutionary Continuum of People–Plant Interactions. In Foraging and Farming: The Evolution of Plant Exploitation. D. Harris and G. Hillman, eds. pp. 11–26. London: Unwin Hyman.

Hiscock, P., and S. Mitchell, 1993 Stone Artifacts Quarries and Reduction Sites in Australia: Towards a Type Profile. Australian Heritage Commission Technical Publications 4. Canberra: Australian Government Publishing Service.

Hope, G., 1983 The Vegetational Changes of the Last 20,000 years at Telefomin, Papua New Guinea. Singapore Journal of Tropical Geography 4:25–33.

Kelly, R., 1988 The Three Sides of a Biface. American Antiquity 53:717–734.

Kennedy, J., 1979 Recent Archaeological Work in the Admiralty Islands. Mankind 12:72–73.

——1983 On the Prehistory of Western Melanesia: The Significance of New Data from the Admiralty Islands. Australian Archaeology 16:115–122.

Loy, T., M. Spriggs and S. Wickler, 1992 Direct Evidence for Human Use of Plants 28,000 Years Ago: Starch Residues on Stone Artifacts from the Northern Solomon Islands. Antiquity 66:898–912.

Lurie, R., 1989 Lithic Technology and Mobility Strategies: The Koster Site Middle Archaic. *In* Time, Energy and Stone Tools. R. Torrence, ed. pp. 46–56. Cambridge University Press, Cambridge.

Machida, H., R. Blong, J. Specht, J. H. Moriwaki, R. Torrence, Y. Hayakawa, B. Talai, D. Lolok and C. Pain, 1996 Holocene Explosive Eruptions of Witori and Dakataua Caldera Volcanoes in West New Britain, Papua New Guinea. Quaternary International 34–36:65–78.

Marshall, B., and J. Allen, 1991 Excavations at Panakiwuk Cave, New Ireland. *In* Report of the Lapita Homeland Project. J. Allen and C. Gosden, eds. pp. 59–91. Occasional Papers in Prehistory 20. Canberra: Department of Prehistory, Research School of Pacific Studies, Australian National University.

Nelson, M., 1991 The Study of Technological Organization. Method and Theory in Archaeology 3:57–100.

Parry, W., and R. Kelly, 1987 Expedient Core Technology and Sedentism. *In* The Organization of Core Technology. J. Johnson and C. Morrow, eds. pp. 285–305. Boulder: Westview Press.

Pavlides, C., 1993 New Archaeological Research at Yombon, West New Britain, Papua New Guinea. Archaeology in Oceania 28:55–59.

——1999 The Story of Imlo: The Organization of Flaked Stone Technologies from the Lowland Tropical Rainforest of West New Britain, Papua New Guinea. Ph.D. dissertation, La Trobe University.

——2004 From Misisil Cave to Eliva Hamlet: Rediscovering the Pleistocene in Interior West New Britain. *In* A Pacific Odyssey: Archaeology and Anthropology in the Western Pacific. Papers in Honour of Jim Specht. V. Attenbrow and R. Fullagar, eds. pp. 97–108. Records of the Australian Museum, Supplement 29. Sydney: Australian Museum.

Pavlides, C., and C. Gosden, 1994 35,000 Year-Old Sites in the Rainforests of West New Britain, Papua New Guinea. Antiquity 68:604–610.

Roe, D., 1992 Investigations into the Prehistory of the Central Solomons: Some Old and Some New Data from Northwest Guadalcanal. *In* Poterie Lapita et Peuplement: J-C. Galipaud, ed. pp. 91–101. Nouméa: ORSTROM.

Sheppard, P., 1993 Lapita Lithics: Trade/Exchange and Technology. A View from the Reefs/Santa Cruz. Archaeology in Oceania 28:121–137.

Shott, M., 1986 Technological Organization and Settlement Mobility: An Ethnographic Examination. Journal of Anthropological Research 42:15–51.

Shott, M., 1996 An Exegesis of the Curation Concept. Journal of Anthropological Research 52:259–280.

Shutler, R. Jr., and C. Kess, 1969 A Lithic Industry from New Britain, Territory of New Guinea, with Possible Areal and Chronological Relationships. Bulletin of the Institute of Ethnology, Academia Sinica 27:129–140.

Smith, A., and J. Allen, 1999 Pleistocene Shell Technologies: Evidence from Island Melanesia. *In* Australian Coastal Archaeology. J. Hall and I. McNiven, eds. pp. 291–297. Research Papers in Archaeology and Natural History 31. Canberra: Division of Archaeology and Natural History, Research School of Pacific Studies, Australian National University.

Specht, J., and C. Gosden, 1997 Dating Lapita Pottery in the Bismarck Archipelago, Papua New Guinea. Asian Perspectives 36:175–199.

Specht, J., I. Lilley and J. Normu, 1981 Radiocarbon Dates from West New Britain, Papua New Guinea. Australian Archaeology 12:13–15.

——1983 More on Radiocarbon Dates from West New Britain, Papua New Guinea. Australian Archaeology 16:92–95.

Spriggs, M., 1991 Nissan: The Island in the Middle. Report of the Lapita Homeland Project. J. Allen and C. Gosden, eds. pp. 222–243. Occasional Papers in Prehistory 20. Canberra: Department of Prehistory, Research School of Pacific Studies, Australian National University.

——1993 Island Melanesia: The Last 10,000 years. *In* A Community of Culture: The People and Prehistory of the Pacific. M. Spriggs, D. Yen, W. Ambrose, R. Jones, A. Thorne and A. Andrews, eds. pp. 187–205. Occasional Papers in Prehistory 21. Canberra: Department of Prehistory, Research School of Pacific Studies, Australian National University.

Summerhayes, G., and J. Allen, 1993 The Transport of Mopir Obsidian to Late Pleistocene New Ireland. Archaeology in Oceania 28:144–148.

Summerhayes, G., C. Gosden, R. Fullagar, J. Specht, R. Torrence, J. Bird, N. Shahgoli and A. Katsaros, 1993 West New Britain Obsidian: Production and Consumption Patterns. *In* Archaeometry: Current Australasian Research. B. Fankhauser and R. Bird, eds. pp. 57–68. Canberra: Division of Archaeology and Natural History, Research School of Pacific and Asian Studies, Australian National University.

Swadling, P., N. Araho and B. Ivuyo, 1991 Settlements Associated with the Inland Sepik-Ramu Sea. *In* Indo-Pacific Prehistory 1990, vol. 2. P. Bellwood, ed. pp. 92–112. Bulletin of the Indo-Pacific Prehistory Association 11. Canberra and Jakarta: Indo-Pacific Prehistory Association and Asosiasi Prehistorisi Indonesia.

Torrence, R., 1983 Time Budgeting and Hunter-Gather Technology. *In* Hunter-Gatherer Economy in Prehistory: A European Perspective. G. Bailey, ed. pp. 11–22. Cambridge: Cambridge University Press.

——1984 Monopoly of Direct Access: Industrial Organization at the Melos Quarries. *In* Prehistoric Quarries and Lithic Production. J. Ericson and B. Purdy, eds. pp. 49–64. Cambridge: Cambridge University Press.

——1989 Retooling: Towards a Behavioral Theory of Stone Tools. *In* Time, Energy and Stone Tools. R. Torrence, ed. pp. 92–105. Cambridge: Cambridge University Press.

——1992 What is Lapita about Obsidian? A View from the Talasea Sources. *In* Poterie Lapita et Peuplement. J-C. Galipaud, ed. pp. 111–126. Nouméa: ORSTROM.

Torrence, R., J. Specht, R. Fullagar and G. Summerhayes, 1996 Which Obsidian is Worth It? A View from the West New Britain Sources. *In* Oceanic Culture History: Essays in Honour of Roger Green. J. Davidson, G. Irwin, F. Leach, A. Pawley and D. Brown, eds. pp. 211–224. Special Publication. Dunedin: New Zealand Journal of Archaeology.

Torrence, R., C. Pavlides, P. Jackson and J. Webb, 2000 Volcanic Disasters and Cultural Discontinuities in Holocene Time, West New Britain, Papua New Guinea. *In* The Archaeology of Geological Catastrophes. W. McGuire, D. Griffiths, P. Hancock and I. Stewart, eds. pp. 225–244. Special Publications 171. London: The Geological Society.

Torrence, R., V. Neall, T. Doelman, E. Rhodes, C. McKee, H. Davies, R. Bonetti, A. Guglielmetti, A. Manzoni, M. Oddone, J. Parr and C. Wallace, 2004 Pleistocene Colonisation of the Bismarck Archipelago: New Evidence from West New Britain. Archaeology in Oceania 39:101–130.

Vanderwal, R., 1973 Prehistoric Studies in Central Papua. Ph.D. dissertation, Australian National University.

White, J. P., 1982 Notes on Some Stone Tools from Passismanua, New Britain. Bulletin of the Indo-Pacific Prehistory Association 3:44–46.

——1996 Rocks in the Head: Thinking About the Distribution of Obsidian in Near Oceania. *In* Oceanic Culture History: Essays in Honour of Roger Green. J. Davidson, G. Irwin, F. Leach, A. Pawley and D. Brown, eds. pp. 199–209. Special Publication. Dunedin: New Zealand Journal of Archaeology.

White, J. P., T. Flannery, R. O'Brian, R. Hancock and L. Pavlish, 1991 The Balof Shelters, New Ireland. *In* Report of the Lapita Homeland Project. J. Allen and C. Gosden, eds. pp. 46–58. Occasional Papers in Prehistory 20. Canberra: Department of Prehistory, Research School of Pacific Studies, Australian National University.

White, J. P., and M-N. Harris, 1997 Changing Source: Early Lapita Period Obsidian in the Bismarck Archipelago. Archaeology in Oceania 32:97–107.

Wickler, S., 1990 Prehistoric Melanesian Exchange and Interaction: Recent Evidence from the Northern Solomon Islands. Asian Perspectives 29:136–154.

Yen, D., 1990 Environment, Agriculture and the Colonisation of the Pacific. *In* Pacific Production Systems: Approaches to Economic Prehistory, D. Yen and J. Mummery, eds. pp. 258–277. Occasional Papers in Prehistory 18. Canberra: Department of Prehistory, Research School of Pacific Studies, Australian National University.

11
The First Millennium B.C. in Remote Oceania: An Alternative Perspective on Lapita

Jean-Christophe Galipaud

The first millennium B.C. in Near and Remote Oceania is largely the story of Lapita. There is now general agreement that Lapita, understood as an archaeological culture rather than just the distinctive pottery of the same name, triggered a vast dynamic which in a few centuries saw the discovery and colonization of most of Melanesia and western Polynesia. In this chapter, I discuss the nature of Lapita in the light of the past 20 years of research and propose an alternative view which integrates the different models and data available today. This view is premised on a skeptical approach to the ease with which Lapita researchers often seem to "jump" from pottery to potters and from potters to culture. Does Lapita pottery represent a potters' diaspora or unaccompanied cultural diffusion? It is important to consider the people behind the pottery (Best 2002; Galipaud 1997) and realize that the artifact known as "Lapita" only partly represents the people who created "Lapita sites," first in the Bismarcks and later elsewhere as they settled the islands of Remote Oceania. This chapter should be read in conjunction with those of Denham, Lilley, Pavlides, Sand et al., and Walter and Sheppard.

The Lapita Culture and the Lapita Cultural Complex

Following extensive work in the Santa Cruz Islands, Green (1979, 1982) developed the concept of the "Lapita Cultural Complex" (LCC) to describe an immense cultural network extending east as far as Samoa from a "homeland" in the Bismarck Archipelago. He saw the original far-flung settlers slowly becoming isolated in their archipelagoes and, after a millennium, those in Samoa and Tonga becoming culturally and biologically identifiable as the ancestors of present-day Polynesians. In Green's model, Lapita ceramics and associated artifacts in early sites are evidence for a large diaspora of Austronesian-speakers which ultimately originated in South-east Asia and arrived in western Melanesia about 3500 B.P. to give rise to the Lapita phenomenon (Spriggs 1984).

Our knowledge of the Lapita expansion increased rapidly during the 1980s following the Lapita Homeland Project and its spin-offs (Allen and Gosden 1991; Walter and Sheppard, this volume). Its objectives were to test an alternative, "indigenist" model of Lapita origins, which posited the local development of the Lapita culture in the Bismarcks in continuity with earlier trajectories of cultural change in the region and with minimal input from Southeast Asia (Allen and White 1989). The project greatly increased the number of well-dated sites in the Bismarcks, which helped refine Lapita chronology, but the archaeological results did not in general support the indigenist model.

Both the LCC and the indigenist models agree that the development of the Lapita Culture coincides with the arrival in Near Oceania of a few innovations, the most prominent being (1) Lapita pottery and its distinctive decorative system using dentate-stamping (i.e., using a toothed tool), incising, and probably painting (Galipaud n.d.), (2) a distinctive stone-adze kit not known in earlier assemblages from the Bismarcks, (3) a distinctive range of shell ornaments, and, to a lesser extent, (4) the spread of Bismarcks obsidian east into Remote Oceania and back west into Southeast Asia.

Spriggs (1995) has tried to determine the origin of these innovations. He concludes that the intrusive elements far outweigh local ones and he rejects as unconvincing the idea of a predominantly Melanesian origin for Lapita. Others have used the possible pre-Lapita antiquity of pottery on mainland New Guinea proposed by Gorecki and Swadling (Gorecki et al. 1991; Swadling et al. 1989) as an argument in favor of a local origin for Lapita ceramics. This has led archaeologists defending the orthodox "out of Asia" model to strongly reject old, pre-Lapita dates for ceramics. One should bear in mind that the proposition of a "Papuan" (i.e., non-Austronesian) pottery tradition earlier than Lapita is not new. It was proposed years ago by Christian Kauffmann (for a recent synthesis see Kauffmann 1999) following a thorough study of Austronesian and non-Austronesian pottery technologies in New Guinea, and his more recent hypotheses concerning the introduction to New Guinea of an Austronesian pottery technology earlier than Lapita should probably be considered more seriously. After all, pottery made by Austronesian-speakers is present in the Marianas in Micronesia at least as early as it is in the Bismarcks, without a direct link with Lapita (Rainbird 2004; see Rainbird, this volume, for discussion of other aspects of Micronesian prehistory).

Many new sites have been discovered in the past 20 years of Lapita research, underpinning a more accurate image of the Lapita diaspora. The increasing use of AMS dating has enabled further refinement of the chronology of dispersal and duration (Anderson et al. 1999; Burley et al. 1999; Specht and Gosden 1997; Spriggs 1990), greatly aided by the re-excavation of key sites in Tonga, Fiji, Vanuatu, New Caledonia as well as the much-anticipated publication of the Watom excavation (Green and Anson 1998). Nevertheless, our vision of Lapita is to some degree still balanced between the LCC model and the minimalist strandlooper hypothesis

Groube (1971) proposed decades ago, which posited colonization by beach-dwelling fisherfolk with a very faint "footprint" on the landscape. On one hand, Lapita, although short-lived as a form of pottery, must be understood as a long-term process with an evolutionary trajectory through time and space, as evidenced in the space–time "provinces" being delineated in different parts of the Lapita sphere (Kirch 1997; cf. Summerhayes 2000 and Sand et al., this volume) and the recognition that incised and applied pottery comprises part of the Lapita tradition (see below). On the other hand, Lapita, recognized primarily as a form of pottery, appears on beaches on previously uninhabited islands and represents the sailors who first visited those islands in search of marine products for their living and probably trade (Burley and Dickinson 2004). These two visions of Lapita culture contrast sea gypsies with horticulturists and raise the question of the duration of those initial occupations.

At first, the limited number of known sites and sparse material remains as well as the difficulty of precisely dating Lapita contexts led to the hypothesis that the Lapita period was long and that Lapita culture expanded gradually from west to east, on the way losing part of its stylistic character to become, in the east, ancestral Polynesian culture. Later, a more thorough focus on Lapita ceramic designs led to the definition of the previously mentioned "stylistic provinces," smaller stylistic areas or cultural spheres, linked in a vast maritime network. These provincial divisions somewhat contradict the LCC model both because they challenge the homogeneity of Lapita culture and because they limit the gradient of any west-to-east evolutionary process. Summerhayes (2000) brings us back to firmer ground in proposing to replace the time–space provincial division by a simpler time division (i.e., early, middle, and late periods). There is definitely a relationship between style and antiquity of settlement and because early as well as late Lapita (although in differing proportions) occurs in most areas, why should we not consider that there were several processes of colonization rather than just one, a network with more mobile elements than can be seen at the moment from current studies? General support for this proposition is provided by a recent genetic study of the distribution of the commensal Polynesian rat *Rattus exulans* (Matisoo-Smith and Robins 2004), which suggests that at least two populations were introduced by human migrants into Oceania. On this basis, the researchers argue for "multifaceted models incorporating a more complex view of the Lapita intrusion" (Matisoo-Smith and Robins 2004:9167).

There is no doubt that Lapita, seen as a period of rapid human expansion into the uninhabited islands of Remote Oceania, is a complicated cultural phenomenon which goes beyond the occurrence of its decorated pottery component. The probable diversity of origins of the actors in this large migration can only be recognized, however, if sufficient attention is paid to *difference*. By its nature, the LCC model necessarily promotes cultural homogeneity and simplification that may be leading us to overlook the richness of local adaptive strategies or developments. The study of Lapita pottery is critical here because it is the most abundant and distinctive artifact of this period, but for the same reason it is necessary to keep in mind the difficulty in linking the pottery with the wider culture and we should recall that the study of ceramics will illuminate only a small part of a vastly more complex phenomenon.

Lapita Pottery and Lapita Potters

Green (e.g., 1992) has in several instances strongly defended the fact that Lapita is not "just pots." Even so, Lapita as pottery is the most visible part of, and often the only artifactual evidence for, Lapita history. Luckily for Pacific archaeologists, however, Lapita remains a rich domain of study because the material culture, and especially the pottery, with its elaborate forms and intricate designs, allows them to go further into the reconstruction of history than any later assemblage does.

The complex design system used by Lapita potters has been intensively studied and the occurrence of recurring motifs has allowed several models to infer the nature of the "Lapita phenomenon" itself. Depending on the scale of the analysis, it has been argued that stylistic similarities demonstrate that Lapita culture was very homogenous over a large geographical area or, using the same criteria at a different scale, that the diversity and degree of abstraction of some motifs could be linked with the movement of Lapita people into Remote Oceania. Later, the time–space "provinces" began to be tentatively identified, from a "Far Western Province" in the Bismarcks where it may have all begun, through "Western" and "Southern" provinces to an "Eastern Province" where abstract and simplified designs became predominant.

The thorough study of a highly visible but not necessarily prominent part of what the Lapita culture might have been could be misleading. Apart from anything else, we should never forget that pottery is primarily a *potter's* art, and thus that its stylistic properties might have as much to do with potters' or potters' clans' choices than with the culture as a whole (Galipaud 1997). In many traditional societies, styles have a general cultural meaning but specific designs are owned by a potter or a family who has "copyright" on them. In this connection, a good example of the limitation of the "stylistic provinces" approach is found on Tikopia (Kirch and Yen 1982). The few decorated Lapita sherds found on the island were initially classified into the Eastern Province stylistic group, which is well represented in Tonga, Samoa, and some Fijian sites. However, Tikopia lies geographically in the Western Province, among the Santa Cruz Islands in the Solomon Islands. The occurrence there of an easterly style was interpreted as a late settlement from the east. Twenty years later and after some new discoveries of sites in the Bismarcks, we now know that these supposedly Eastern motifs are also present in the Bismarcks, in the Far Western Province of the Lapita distribution (Summerhayes 2000).

Another example of the difficulty in using style analysis to explain broad cultural behaviors is given by Summerhayes (2000:119), who shows that the decrease in fine dentate decoration from adjacent sites in the Bismarcks is correlated with decreases in bowls and vessel stands. This again points to a cultural usage or potters' technical choices rather than to a chronological decline in decoration *per se*, as it has often been perceived. The complex shapes and designs, as well as localization of decorated assemblages in well-documented sites, encourage the hypothesis that decorated Lapita had a religious or ritual function (Best 2002; Lilley 1999, 2004, this volume). We know, however, that the richly decorated ceramics are not the only ceramic component of the Lapita Cultural Complex and that plainware pottery in particular is slowly becoming recognized as a key constituent of Lapita assemblages (see Green 2003 for detailed discussion of such issues).

Lapita Potters and Plainware

Having discussed the limits of an approach focusing on pottery, we need to ask how we should define the Lapita period: as a horizon or a tradition (Anderson 2001)? Considering it as a horizon means that only sites with classic Lapita dentate-stamped decorated ceramics can be considered Lapita. Accepting it as a tradition implies that all pottery types and artifacts related in time or present in Lapita sites belong to the same cultural context. In the first case, we come back to the idea that the Lapita culture is primarily defined by its ceramics, and indeed a very particular element of those ceramics, whereas in the second case, we open Lapita culture to encompass all or most of what is contemporaneous with dentate-stamped pottery and can be somehow associated with it. Archaeologically, the limits of a Lapita horizon are easier to delineate than the limits of a Lapita tradition. Many archaeologists agree today that Podtanéan pottery from New Caledonia, Buka-style pottery from the North Solomons, and Arapus pottery from Vanuatu, to cite only a few examples, belong to the Lapita tradition despite not being dentate-stamped (Bedford 2000; Galipaud 1999; Specht 1969; also Sand et al., this volume). In agreeing to this, we extend the frame of the Lapita tradition, introduce a notion of continuity in evolution, and at the same time challenge the concept of persistence which is implied by dentate-stamped Lapita pottery. To suggest that such non-dentate pottery is culturally related to Lapita, which except for Podtanéan ware has yet to be experimentally demonstrated (see below), might mislead in that it promotes a false sense of cultural continuity when that might in fact not always be the case.

In this context, it is useful to consider the case in New Caledonia, where dentate-stamped Lapita ceramics are always associated with paddle-impressed Podtanéan material (but not the reverse). Mineralogical analysis has confirmed that the two wares were made from the same clay (Galipaud 1990). However, Lapita ceramics do not last very long in the archaeological record while Podtanéan ceramics were widely used for nearly a millennium. Thus in many respects the number and distribution of Podtanéan sites in New Caledonia have more to tell us about the colonization of this large island than does Lapita (Galipaud 2000; for another perspective, see Sand et al., this volume).

I have proposed associating Lapita and Podtanéan in a cultural phase or tradition I call the Koné period (Galipaud 1992), keeping in mind that Podtanéan ceramics sometimes occur in contexts where Lapita does not (e.g., caves) and that the duration of Podtanéan ceramics does not obviously indicate that "Lapita" as a horizon was long-lasting. Considering the evident temporal and geographical relationships of Lapita and Podtanéan pottery, one could speak of them both as belonging to the Lapita tradition. I strongly believe, however, that the complexity and diversity of this period of initial colonization are better preserved by linking these pottery styles as I have done rather than merging them into a single tradition named after only one (and the archaeologically more ephemeral) of the two, which gives a false impression of dominance (Galipaud 1999:539–540). Sand (Sand et al. 2000:105, also this volume) has recently hypothesized from my work that the occurrence of two pottery types could be interpreted as evidence for population replacement in New Caledonia, but that was not a conclusion I drew. The view that a type of pottery, defined by a set of physical and stylistic characteristics, should directly correspond to a discrete and identifiable population is obsolete. It is now widely understood that pottery styles are only an indirect marker of cultural changes and as such cannot be a good indicator of population replacement (Arnold 1984).

In New Caledonia, the two types of pottery are constituents of the same tradition or culture and the early disappearance of one of them is an important sign of the evolution of this tradition. In this instance it has been indirectly demonstrated that people are the same, whether they made dentate-stamped Lapita or paddle-impressed Podtanéan pottery. On Watom, similarity in pottery raw material and technology has also been demonstrated by Anson (1983:263, 278–279) between dentate-stamped Lapita on one hand and applied-relief and fingernail-incised on the other. The inferences drawn from the New Caledonian and Watom examples can be extended to include the pottery styles generally referred to as "plainwares," which usually occur in the Lapita sites of Near and Remote Oceania within the time frame of dentate-stamped Lapita, the distinctions between the pottery styles probably reflecting functional and perhaps social differences (Galipaud 1999:540; Kirch 1997:146).

The definition of "plainware" needs some attention as the term has been used in diverse situations over the past 25 years, even for decorated pottery. It was initially used instead of "lapitoid" to describe simple Lapita forms present in western Polynesia. It was later extended to the non-decorated component present in all Lapita sites but only recognized when data from larger excavations became available (Green 1979). It has recently been associated with incised pottery styles thought to represent an evolution of Lapita in some islands (Bedford 2000). Study of the Lapita decorative system in the late 1970s suggested "an overall west to east trend indicative of distance decay in the Lapita design system, from the rather ornate curvilinear and fairly elaborate rectilinear design patterns of the western Lapita to the more simplified and generally rectilinear forms of the eastern Lapita" (Green 1979:42). The end product of this evolutionary process, called Polynesian Plainware, has been dated to around 500 B.C. in western Polynesia. It is characterized by its simple forms, which unlike "classic" Lapita are devoid of any shoulder or carination, and without any decoration except for simple dentate stamping on flat rims. As its description suggests, it is an integral part of Lapita in western Polynesia.

Much earlier in time and present in "Far Western" as well as "Eastern" Lapita assemblages is another simple plain pottery which fully deserves the label

"Plainware." Its usual form is a large globular jar with flaring notched rim and its presence is attested in early Lapita contexts as well as later ones without the dentate pottery component. It is difficult to decide at the moment whether these two types of Plainware, which appear at opposite ends of the Lapita tradition, should be considered the same thing.

To summarize the argument thus far, decorated Lapita pottery is part of a tradition that comprises several other pottery types and related artifacts. Plainware ceramics are now attested in early contexts with and without "classic" Lapita and its study will enhance our understanding of the whole Lapita tradition in the years to come. When dating the Lapita phenomenon we need to take into account the recognized diversity of the pottery component.

Chronology and Continuity

For many years, the few radiocarbon dates from a limited number of sites that were available and the apparent homogeneity of Lapita ceramics were good reasons to see it as a long-lasting cultural development in the islands of Remote Oceania. The increase in excavation and dating with more accurate methods starting in the mid-1990s has led us to revise the chronology for the Lapita period as a whole.

Initial settlement dates differ in Near and Remote Oceania, confirming a west-to-east migration front. The pace of dispersal through the islands of Remote Oceania was very quick: 1300 B.C. in the Bismarcks, 1200 B.C. in Vanuatu and Fiji, and 1100 B.C. in New Caledonia. The speed of the spread of Lapita pottery implies either a rapid rate of initial colonization of the uninhabited islands of Remote Oceania or the rapid diffusion of a cultural item in an already-discovered island world. But what are we really dating when trying to set out a chronological framework for Lapita? We are dating a context in which decorated Lapita pottery is predominant, taking for granted that other cultural items are just additions to this prominent feature of the Lapita tradition. Looking at early non-decorated ceramics can increase the precision of our analysis.

Early Plainware as identified above has been recently found in the Bismarcks, Solomons, Vanuatu, New Caledonia, and Samoa. It is dated to 1550 B.C. at Balof rockshelter in New Ireland and to 900 B.C. at Feru rockshelter in Santa Ana (Spriggs 1997:25). In the Talepakemalai site in the Mussau Islands near New Ireland, a red-slipped Plainware was concentrated on the beach terrace and recently dated to at least 1200 B.C. (Kirch 1997:147). In Vanuatu, the recently identified Arapus Ware on Efate Island is dated to 1100 B.C. as well (Bedford 2000), while a red-slipped ware dated to 1150 B.C. is characteristic of the earliest Lapita level in the newly discovered Makue site on Aore Island, near Santo (Galipaud 2001). Although it can be described as decorated, paddle-impressed Podtanéan pottery from New Caledonia is comparable to Plainware ceramics in other archipelagoes because the paddle impressions are simply manufacturing marks that are wiped off to make the other wares plain. It has been dated to about 1100 B.C. in several sites and I suggested some years ago that Podtanéan pottery might represent the earliest arrival on the island (Galipaud 1999). Plainware sites contemporary with the earliest Lapita are known in Samoa (Smith 2002), while data from the To'aga site in that same archipelago (Kirch 1997:148) suggest a continuity in Plainware pottery from as early as 1100 B.C. up to A.D. 300–400, with gradual change from a thin, fine ware to a thick, coarse-tempered one.

This issue of the antiquity of Plainware ceramics should be seriously considered because it has important implications for our understanding of the dynamics of the initial colonization of Remote Oceania. Plainware pottery is easily traceable to Southeast Asian Neolithic cultures and its early appearance in Oceania could be an indication that "the elaborate and extensive decoration of Lapita ceramic wares in Near Oceania are not brought in by migrants from elsewhere, rather they developed out of a largely Southeast Asian Neolithic red slipped plain ware assemblage in situ" (Burley, 2003:180). Alternatively we could hypothesize that these first migrants to Oceania had diverse origins in Southeast Asia and that the appearance of decorated Lapita at one stage in the early prehistory of the remote Pacific is an indication of a migration which followed the tracks of earlier ones still unknown, one of which entailed the spread of Plainware pottery. If debate on the origin of the Lapita ceramics is not yet closed off, the early presence of plain, red-slipped pottery in a few key sites of Remote Oceania indicates to my mind that the early process of colonization stems quite directly from Southeast Asia rather than indirectly with a formative stage in the Bismarcks of the sort initially proposed by Green (1979) and accepted by most Lapita scholars today.

The end of Lapita is difficult to establish. Firstly, when does the Lapita pottery cease to be manufactured? To answer this question we need well-dated contexts with clear relationships between dated material (charcoal, usually) and decorated pottery. Such contexts are rarely found. Because most are close to the sea, Lapita sites have often been eroded or re-deposited and dated material provides only a snapshot of what might have been. On the island of Malo in Vanuatu, for instance, the Atanoasao site yielded several charcoal samples dated from 2800 B.P. from a horizon containing decorated Lapita pottery as well as a few plain sherds. There is no indication in this site of prolonged use or later occupation with decorated Lapita and so I have hypothesized that it was occupied only once, for a very short period, probably as a fishing or harvesting camp (Galipaud 2000). An accumulation of pumice and gravel suggests that what was a sand beach during the Lapita occupation was rapidly covered by the sea at some time afterwards, perhaps even forcing people to leave. This could be an indication that eustatic or tectonic instability played a role in the initial colonization process. A period of eustatic instability might have contributed to the rapid disappearance of the decorated Lapita component of the colonizers' material culture owing to the fact that it was generally used in vulnerable littoral zones. If these localities disappeared, the activities involving dentate pottery that were carried out in such places may simply have ceased, eliminating the need for "classic" Lapita. More local case-studies in different parts of the Pacific are needed to model the natural changes which occurred during this period before we can take such suggestions very far.

In other islands, the taphonomic impact of long-term human occupation makes it difficult to specifically date individual levels in sites. When we precisely date two overlying layers, can we automatically infer that there was continuous occupation between those two dates? This has been done often by archaeologists everywhere and the Lapita *tradition* is no exception, because it encompasses many different features and characteristic artifacts in different locations during the course of the first millennium B.C., all of which are considered to be part of a single, continuous tradition. The Lapita *horizon*, however, is definitely very short-lived and this alone is good reason to question the use and importance of the decorated Lapita pottery in the construction of social identities in Remote Oceania. The more dynamic and longer-lived part of the Lapita tradition lies more in the non-Lapita ceramic component (Plainware, Podtanéan, and so on) and the very early dates recently obtained from Plainware contexts in the Talepakemalai site (Kirch 1997:147) and the Arapus site (Bedford 2000) support my hypothesis that these Plainwares represent the active part of the initial settlement dynamic (Galipaud 1999). That said, there seems to be a clear difference between sites in Near Oceania and sites in Remote Oceania. Lapita as a pottery might have been very short-lived in the latter while it started earlier and might have lasted longer in the former. Regional differences are perhaps more important than the relative homogeneity in ceramics tends to show.

Conclusion

For a long time we have considered that decorated Lapita ceramics were the main feature and are now the best witness of the Lapita tradition. This tradition has recently been extended to encompass all other ceramic types found during that same period, reinforcing the idea of a homogenous, long-lasting tradition and promoting a sense of continuity in the development of Oceanic cultures over the millennia. We have been focusing too much on decorated Lapita, which has blinded us to other possibilities. These possibilities are best exemplified by Podtanéan ware in New Caledonia, which is evidently related to but different from "classic" decorated Lapita. The fact that we have Plainware at the beginning and end of our sequences should direct us to look more closely at it as a whole and try to understand its place and role in sites which also have an important decorated Lapita assemblage.

The origin of the Lapita style is still a matter of debate, but the origin of paddle-impressed and Plainware styles is less problematic because both are widely distributed in Southeast Asia. While research in western Micronesia has not yet allowed us to draw any direct link to Lapita, Micronesian ceramics are closely related to the Plainware component of the Lapita tradition and one should consider that some of the cultural shifts which led to Lapita played out in these latter islands. Research in the years to come will have to focus more on the less visible part of this early tradition. Plainwares do have a real homogeneity in time and space, draw a clear link between Southeast Asia and Oceania, and seem to last for a long time.

Plainware has been better dated in recent years and is now securely associated with the earliest part of the colonization process linked to Lapita. This recent advance in our understanding poses anew the question of the role of decorated Lapita ceramics in this initial dispersal. Rather than using pottery typologies to highlight cultural differences, we need to enlarge our understanding of the Lapita tradition. This will probably give us a more accurate perception of the diversity of origins of these early Oceanians and a better comprehension of the later changes leading to the emergence of the traditional societies of the Pacific.

REFERENCES

Anson, D., 1983 Lapita Pottery of the Bismarck Archipelago and its Affinities. Ph.D. dissertation, University of Sydney.

Allen, J., and J. P. White, 1989 The Lapita Homeland. Journal of the Polynesian Society 98:129–146.

Allen, J., and C. Gosden, 1991 Report of the Lapita Homeland Project. Canberra: Department of Prehistory, Research School of Pacific Studies, Australian National University.

Arnold, D., 1984 Ceramic Theory and Cultural Process. Cambridge: Cambridge University Press.

Anderson, A., 2001 Mobility Models of Lapita migration. In The Archaeology of Lapita Dispersal in Oceania. G. Clark, A. Anderson and T. Vunidilo, eds. pp. 15–23. Terra Australis 17. Canberra: Pandanus Books.

Anderson, A., S. Bedford, G. Clark. I. Lilley, C. Sand, G. Summerhayes and R. Torrence, 1999 In The Archaeology of Lapita Dispersal in Oceania. G. Clark, A. Anderson and T. Vunidilo, eds. pp. 1–13. Terra Australis 17. Canberra: Pandanus Books.

Best, S., 2002 Lapita: A View from the East. Special Publication. Auckland: New Zealand Journal of Archaeology.

Bedford, S., 2000 Pieces of the Vanuatu Puzzle: Archaeology of the North, South and Centre. Ph.D. dissertation, Australian National University.

Burley, D., 2003 Review of Lapita and its Transformations in the Mussau Islands, Papua New Guinea, 1985–1988: Volume 1, Introduction, Excavations and Chronology. P. Kirch, ed. Asian Perspectives 42:178–181.

Burley, D., D. Nelson and R. Shutler, 1999 A Radiocarbon Chronology for the Eastern Lapita Frontier in Tonga. Archaeology in Oceania 34:59–72.

Burley, D., and W. Dickinson, 2004 Late Lapita Occupation and its Ceramic Assemblage at the Sigatoka Sand Dune Site, Fiji, and their Place in Oceanic Prehistory. Archaeology in Oceania 39:12–25.

Galipaud, J-C., 1990 The Physico-Chemical Analysis of Ancient Pottery from New Caledonia. In Lapita Design, Form and Composition. M. Spriggs, ed. pp. 134–142. Occasional Papers in Prehistory 18. Canberra: Department of Prehistory, Research School of Pacific Studies, Australian National University.

——1992 Un ou Plusieurs Peuples Potiers en Nouvelle-Calédonie. Journal de la Société des Océanistes. 95:185–200.

——1997 A Revision of the Southern New Caledonia Archaeological Sequence. New Zealand Journal of Archaeology. 17:77–109.

——1999 De Quelques Impressions. L'Exemple de la Poterie Imprimée au Battoir en Océanie Lointaine. *In* Le Pacifique de 5000 à 2000 avant le Présent. Suppléments à l'Histoire d'une Colonisation. J-C. Galipaud et I. Lilley, eds. pp. 531–541. Paris: IRD.

——2000 The Lapita Site of Atanoasao, Malo, Vanuatu. World Archaeological Bulletin 12:41–55.

——2001 The Aore Resort Lapita Site, a Preliminary Assessment. Technical Report. Nouméa: Laboratoire d'Archéologie, IRD, Centre de Nouméa.

——n.d. Surprising Lapita: Painted Lapita ware from Vanuatu and New Caledonia. Laboratoire d'Archéologie, IRD, Centre de Nouméa, unpublished MS.

Gorecki, P., M. Mabin and J. Campbell, 1991 Archaeology and Geomorphology of the Vanimo Coast, Papua New Guinea: Preliminary Results. Archaeology in Oceania 26:119–122.

Green, R., 1979 Lapita. *In* The Prehistory of Polynesia. J. Jennings, ed. pp. 27–60. Canberra: Australian National University Press.

——1982 Models for the Lapita Cultural Complex: An Evaluation of Some Current Proposals. New Zealand Journal of Archaeology. 4:7–20.

——1992 Definition of the Lapita Cultural Complex and its Non Ceramic Component. *In* Poterie Lapita et Peuplement : J-C. Galipaud, ed. pp. 7–20. Nouméa: ORSTOM.

——2003 The Lapita Horizon and Tradition–Signature for One Set of Oceanic Migrations. *In* Pacific Archaeology: Assessments and Prospects. C. Sand, ed. pp. 95–120. Les Cahiers de l'Archéologie en Nouvelle-Calédonie 15. Nouméa: Service des Musées et du Patrimoine de Nouvelle-Calédonie.

Green, R., and D. Anson, 1998 Archaeological Investigations on Watom Island: Early Work, Outcomes of Recent Investigations and Future Prospects. New Zealand Journal of Archaeology. 20:183–197.

Groube, L., 1971 Tonga, Lapita Pottery and Polynesian Origins. Journal of the Polynesian Society 80:278–316.

Kauffmann, C., 1999 Research on Sepik Pottery Traditions and its Implications for Melanesian Prehistory. *In* Le Pacifique de 5000 à 2000 avant le Présent. Suppléments à l'Histoire d'une Colonization J-C. Galipaud et I. Lilley, eds. pp. 31–47. Paris: IRD.

Kirch, P., 1997 The Lapita Peoples: Ancestors of the Oceanic World. Oxford: Blackwell.

Kirch, P., and D. Yen, 1982 Tikopia: The Prehistory and Ecology of a Polynesian Outlier. Bernice P. Bishop Museum Bulletin 238. Honolulu: Bishop Museum Press.

Lilley, I., 1999 Lapita as Politics. *In* Le Pacifique de 5000 à 2000 avant le Présent. Suppléments à l'Histoire d'une Colonization. J-C. Galipaud et I. Lilley, eds. pp. 21–30. Paris: IRD.

——2004 Diaspora and Identity in Archaeology: Moving Beyond the Black Atlantic. *In* A Companion to Social Archaeology. L. Meskell and R. Preucel, eds. pp. 287–312. Oxford: Blackwell.

Matisoo-Smith, E., and J. Robins, 2004 Origins and Dispersals of Pacific Peoples: Evidence from mtDNA Phylogenies of the Pacific Rat. Proceedings of the National Academy of Sciences 101:9167–9172.

Rainbird, P., 2004 The Archaeology of Micronesia. Cambridge: Cambridge University Press.

Sand, C., A. Ouetcho, J. Bole and D. Barret, 2000 Evaluating the "Lapita Smoke Screen." Site SGO015 of Goro, an Early Austronesian Settlement on the South-East Coast of New Caledonia's Grande Terre. New Zealand Journal of Archaeology 22:91–111.

Smith, A., 2002 An Archaeology of West Polynesian Prehistory. Terra Australis 18. Canberra: Pandanus Books.

Specht, J., 1969 Prehistoric and Modern Pottery Industries of Buka island, Territory of Papua New Guinea. Ph.D. dissertation, Australian National University.

Specht, J., and C. Gosden, 1997 Dating Lapita pottery in the Bismarck Archipelago, Papua New Guinea. Asian Perspectives 36:175–189.

Spriggs, M., 1984 The Lapita Cultural Complex: Origins, Distribution, Contemporaries and Successors. Journal of Pacific History 19:202–223.

——1990 Dating Lapita: Another View. *In* Lapita Design, Form and Composition. M. Spriggs, ed. pp 6–27. Occasional Papers in Prehistory 18. Canberra: Department of Prehistory, Research School of Pacific Studies, Australian National University.

——1995 What is Southeast Asian about Lapita? *In* Prehistoric Mongoloid Dispersals. T. Akazawa and E. Szathmary, eds. pp. 324–348. Oxford: Oxford University Press.

——1997 The Island Melanesians. Oxford: Blackwell.

Summerhayes, G., 2000 Far Western, Western, and Eastern Lapita: A Re-Evaluation. Asian Perspectives, 39:109–138.

Swadling, P., J. Chappell, G. Francis, N. Araho and B. Ivuyo, 1989 A Late Quaternary Inland Sea and Early Pottery in Papua New Guinea. Archaeology in Oceania 24:106–9.

12
Ethnoarchaeology in Polynesia

Eric Conte

There is no simplified version of social reality for archaeologists to use. (Coudart and Lemonnier 1984:167)

To write about past societies in both diachronic and the synchronic dimensions, archaeology must move beyond the description and classification that, according to Chang (1967:71), occupy 90 percent of archaeologists' time, in order to favor explanation (i.e., the "how" but also the "why"). To achieve this objective, information other than that derived from excavation and routine analysis is needed to interpret our discoveries. Our needs, stemming from the material sources we deal with, may appear simplistic from the perspective of the living societies that produced them: to find out about the whole from just one part (reconstructing the binding of an adze, for example), to determine not only the exact function of a tool, but also the process of its manufacture, its manner of use, its efficiency, and so on. On a larger scale, that of a site for example, we can try to interpret the remains we discover in relation to the society that produced them, through the study of dumping strategies, for instance, in an effort to reconstruct life in a habitation area or activity zones. Taking matters one step further, we could insert the site into a much larger space, natural or socio-cultural, a resource-exploitation area, reconstruct inter-site exchange networks and interregional contact spheres, demonstrate seasonal movements of populations, and so on. Of course, all information on the sociopolitical organization of the groups in focus, their religious universe and the like, would be welcome for our purpose of producing an ethnography of the past.

On the other hand, the greater the geographic scale, the more complex the interrogation of the archaeological sources becomes if one wishes to tackle an understanding of structural mechanisms and the like, and the more such sources show their own limits. As this critique has already been made in sufficient detail in relation to living societies (e.g., Gallay 1986:126), this problem – perhaps the most fundamental in archaeology – is not developed further here. Even if every vestige of archaeological material carries information, in what Gardin (1979) calls its "intrinsic characteristics" (the chemical composition of a rock, for instance, can indicate provenience and thus allow us to trace exchange networks), most interpretations must still use external references. Indeed, this is the basis of all interpretative reasoning in archaeology. Thus, as Moberg (1976) indicates, archaeological traces are compared with those of known meaning and, taking into account natural alteration, it is possible to deduce the past activity that led to the archaeological trace on the assumption that the same causes produce the same effects. In this way, analogy, which as we will see is the basis of the ethnoarchaeological approach, is inherent in *all* archaeological interpretation. Moreover, understanding the formation of the archaeological record has an important place in ethnoarchaeological work. Indeed, for some scholars understanding formation processes is the principal justification for taking an ethnoarchaeological approach.

There are of course two ways to acquire the external references needed for archaeological interpretation, not including the excavator's imagination, which I contend has been and continues to be drawn upon more than is reasonable. First, there is experimentation. This approach has demonstrated its worth but can only be applied in the technological domain (in flaking lithic material, for example), and has limitations that include, amongst others, the aptitude of the experimenter. Even if the reconstructed techniques include a technological dimension which approaches the knowledge of prehistoric people owing to long-term practice with the experimental methods, such knowledge cannot include the socio-cultural milieu, ritual, and so on that underpinned and justified the techniques used in the past. The second solution consists of searching for parallels in historical descriptions of past societies – with all the limitations of this type of information – and in the present-day or recently past societies studied by ethnographers.

Use of Ethnographic Information in Archaeology

The temptation to use ethnographic information in archaeology (these two terms being understood here in their widest meanings) retraces in some sense the "prehistory" of the two disciplines. As far back as 1723, for example, Jussieu (1723:6 cited by Stiles 1977:88) used information about stone tools from the New World to explain the use of "thunder stones" found in France. Throughout the 19th century, ethnographic analogy was routinely used in the nascent field of prehistory hand-in-hand with the emergence of ethnography as a discipline and the development of field techniques for the observation of so-called "primitive" societies. This search for ethnographic parallels was structured by a cultural-evolutionary schema which considered that contemporary "primitive" societies remained conceptually fixed in prior stages of human history. On that basis, these societies were judged to be comparable to the prehistoric societies which produced archaeological remains revealed by excavation. Although the roots of this approach were misguided from a scientific perspective (not to mention their philosophical and moral implications),

it possessed a narrow practical value. To understand the functioning of a Mag-
dalenian spear-thrower, for instance, by reference to a similar tool known from the
Inuit or Australian Aborigines is both possible and reasonable. (Many consider
Thomson's (1939) study of the Wik-Munkan Aborigines in northeastern Australia
as the first true ethnoarchaeological study, that is, an ethnographic enquiry conducted from an archaeological perspective.) The recourse to ethnography would
not have been open to much criticism had it remained focused on specific, one-to-
one analogies and limited to the technological sphere where the physical constraints
of raw materials and the human body impose a restricted number of possible solutions and thus produce convergent technologies. Indeed, it even corresponds to the
direction of some recent research (e.g., Pétrequin and Pétrequin 1992, 1993). Yet
the recourse to "ethnographic comparison" regards ethnographic data – often badly
collected and interpreted in the 19th and early 20th centuries – as a great reservoir
of ideas to be used to give shape to hypotheses, if not fantasies, owing to a concern
to make archaeological remains "speak" about sociopolitical organization, beliefs,
magical practices, and so on.

However, when prehistorians want to go beyond mere ethnographic description
of the past to explanation, the "why," especially in the socio-cultural domain, they
must be able to grasp the internal logic of the society that produced the traces and
remains in question. It is at this level that ethnographic comparison becomes most
questionable, because it considers that the social or ritual logics of "primitive" societies, taken randomly depending on the chance finds of ethnographic references
and superficial similarities between certain material items, are comparable (that is
to say, of the same order) to those of prehistoric societies separated from the "ethnographic present" by thousands of years and without any cultural or biological connection to the ethnographic group. In the end it is a racist conception that places
present-day peoples at an earlier stage of a unilinear evolutionary pathway. Moreover, the random character of the choice of references means that all the societies
being classed as "primitive" are judged to be the same, lumped in an undifferenti-
ated category from which it is possible to take what one needs, without discrimi-
nating. However, if archaeology wants to be ethnography and history it must, at the
level of explanation, resolve the question of the cultural significance of the remains
in their specific socio-cultural context, not merely by reference to some undiffer-
entiated category of behavior. This can only be done by rediscovering the actual
values of individual past societies. This is without doubt impossible for prehistorians studying the remote past. Here the ethnographic literature can certainly provide
a corpus of possibilities, though without much more value than the products of the
imagination of this or that prehistorian, each source of possibilities being historically unrelated to the past societies in question.

In France, Leroi-Gourhan (1990) amongst others made an unreserved critique
of this sort of practice (see also David, this volume). He nevertheless specified in
an earlier joint paper that his critique should not be interpreted as an attack on the
use of ethnographic sources *per se*, with a view to using only excavated information.
Rather, his objective was to establish a hierarchy of interpretation, beginning with
natural and technological explanations before social and religious factors because
the former have "greater probability and because mechanical contingencies and

technological determinants are easier to detect" (Audouze and Leroi-Gourhan 1981:172). In the USA, where prehistoric archaeology has never been separated from anthropology from an institutional or scientific point of view, researchers interested in Native American societies from a Boasian historical perspective first studied them in the ethnographic present before working on their prehistoric pasts. (Hence the term "ethnoarchaeology" was first proposed in 1900, by Fewkes [1900:579, cited by Stiles 1977:89] of the Smithsonian Institution.) They therefore employed a "retrodictive" procedure that is one of the possible avenues of ethnoarchaeological research. As I will show was also the case in Polynesia, this procedure found fertile ground when it was applied to the archaeological remains of Native American societies of the recent past possessing historical and cultural continuity with those observed ethnographically.

Questions about the validity of ethnographic analogy in archaeology have been posed repeatedly during the second part of the 20th century. As just mentioned, in France Leroi-Gourhan fought strongly against the abuse of ethnography, his training in this discipline making him particularly sensitive to the complexity and diversity of human societies, which preclude the simplistic comparison of material facts from two utterly different cultural universes to identify general behavioral laws. The increase in explicitly ethnoarchaeological approaches during the 1970s was part of an attempt to rethink archaeology by attending to its epistemological aspects and modes of archaeological reasoning. This tendency was particularly clear in the "New Archaeology," which exercised a direct influence on the constitution of ethnoarchaeology.

Today, work following a variety of approaches claims to be ethnoarchaeology. The more modest – or more realistic – proposes to contribute to the resolution of specific questions, especially in relation to technological issues, by drawing analogies between cultural traits observable in archaeological and ethnographic contexts. This procedure is entirely justified, and is comparable to that established by earlier writers, with the difference that the collection of information is now oriented toward the resolution of specifically *archaeological* problems, increasing in general the quality of usable data and the pertinence of ethnoarchaeological procedures. It is even possible to extend such technological analogies to the social domain, and in this regard, ethnographic mapping (like that used in archaeology) of technological or social activities (e.g., cooking, the spatial structure of camp sites, etc.) is most interesting (see Binford 1978). From there, if we take the risky path used by some authors (e.g., Gould 1980a, 1980b) to research and formulate cross-cultural laws of behavior conditioning relationships between archaeological traces and social practices, in my view we would venture into a territory of evidence equally trivial and deceptive when one attempts to interpret concrete situations. The only laws that appear strong, and that do not involve this problem, are those elaborated on ethnographic observations concerning the physical constitution of archaeological remains, as they refer to intrinsic characteristics of the materials studied and allow quantification by procedures comparable to the ones used experimentally by scholars of use-wear.

If ethnology teaches us anything about human societies, it is that the anticipated does not always occur. Certainly, some constants can be observed at the level of cultural or behavioral tendencies, because there are not an infinite number of responses to the constraints of similar materials, environments, and the like. This leads to an acceptance under certain conditions of the principle of uniformitarianism alluded to earlier. Borrowed from the natural sciences, it proposes that "certain phenomena . . . are identical in the present and in the past" (Coudart and Lemonnier 1984:157–158). But this level is far too broad to allow the formation of anything but the most banal "laws." These would include, for example, the "law" announced by Gould (1980b) relating the degree of fracturing of faunal remains found in excavations with the difficulties of food collection encountered by the related population, or the postulate concerning the displacement of camping rubbish toward the edges of living areas.

In reality, the "facts," like the multiple empirical versions of laws of that kind, are extremely variable. They stem from the cultural domain in the broadest and most complex sense, where an infinity of possibilities emerge and crystallize, the products of the individual history of each group and its choices (symbolic representations, contacts, innovations, and so on). But for prehistory to be ethnography, it must interpret those facts with which it is confronted in their own ecological and cultural context, even if later they can be reinserted in a larger picture accommodating cultural affinities between groups, indications of chronology, and so on.

In light of the above, if we stay at what in my view is the more realistic level of analogy, it is certain that the more that present-day observation is done in societies evolving in an ecological environment and a cultural context close to the group that produced the archaeological traces we seek to understand, the more the analogy will be pertinent. The ideal situation (cf. Hodder 1980) is to observe a single society at two different moments in its history, if possible not too far apart in time (i.e., "direct analogy"). This was recognized by 20th-century American archaeologists through the use of the "direct historical approach," recently revitalized by Lightfoot (1995) in his study of culture-contact situations. The role of direct analogy was similarly recognized by Schiffer (1978) even when arguing for research on general laws: Inferences obtained from the observation of groups descended from the ones studied possess a higher degree of archaeological probability than would be the case otherwise. No society is static, however. Thus even in situations of direct historical continuity, models based in the present only offer one of a range of possibilities, albeit very strong ones.

A number of favorable conditions combine to make the Pacific a particularly propitious place for ethnoarchaeological studies. The foregoing introduction puts into perspective the different ways ethnographic information is used to answer particular questions in Oceanic archaeology. The next part of the chapter will discuss some of these questions, especially in relation to the Polynesians. In the discussion that follows, ethnoarchaeology is seen primarily as a strategy which guides interpretative choices between possibilities. Associated with experimentation and archaeometry, it can also help control archaeological inferences (cf. Coudart and Lemonnier 1984:159). This latter aspect, which must form part of our interpretative procedures, is only mentioned here as a reminder and is not discussed further.

Ethnoarchaeological Approaches in Polynesia

The islands of the Pacific are an exceptional place to carry out several approaches that can be grouped under the term ethnoarchaeology and which illustrate the diversity of information that archaeology and ethnography share in this region of the world. Let us rapidly examine these different approaches, illustrating them with examples taken from work carried out in the Pacific. Note that we are concerned solely with applications *in* the Pacific. We will not evoke cases where ethnographic observations *of* the Pacific are used for ethnoarchaeological models for other regions of the world or other periods, such as studies carried out in New Guinea to shed light on problems in Neolithic Europe (Coudart 1992).

The researches grouped here as ethnoarchaeology are all pursued in a context of historical and cultural continuity. Human arrival is recent in Polynesia (see Lilley, this volume), and the societies in focus have experienced slow rhythms of cultural evolution in ecological contexts that, while not static, nevertheless witnessed a limited scale of variation that can be readily integrated into our models. The lifestyles reported by the first European observers and, in some cases (under conditions that we have to define) more recent or even contemporary observations, can yield information applicable to the most remote periods. At present, even the longest of the chronologies proposed for Polynesia provide for no more than 2,000 years of human occupation and much less for those located on the margins, such as New Zealand. When we hazard to formulate models, we do not aim to develop cross-cultural behavioral laws which can be transposed to radically different situations. In that respect, our models need not be audacious, because the *direct* analogies permitted by Polynesia's unique conditions preclude high theoretical risks. This gives more value to our use of ethnoarchaeological approaches – without casting any doubts about those developed in other regions – and limits the criticism that is generally attracted by this type of research.

Different works styled as ethnoarchaeology in the Pacific proceed from quite distinct foundations, the diversity of which will be portrayed here in the widest sense. This risks an overly systematic presentation which weakens the individuality of each approach to some extent. To limit this possibility, I consider them in order of increasing analytical complexity. This is not an order of value, as each approach is pertinent to different archaeological and ethnographic situations. This chapter should be read in conjunction with that of Millerstrom, who provides an example of ethnoarchaeology in action in the Marquesas.

Direct use of ethnohistorical sources and continuing cultural traditions

This approach is only possible for relatively recent periods. In the Pacific, one always uses informants, guides, and narratives to locate sites: information that is ethnographic in its broadest sense. The best example of this use of ethnography to orient the archaeologist is incontestably the discovery of the burial of Roy Mata by José

Garanger in Vanuatu (1976), a case unfortunately too brilliant to correspond to normal reality!

Another orientation in the direct use of ethnographic sources by archaeologists is to assist in the interpretation of discovered remains. Here also, at least for the material evidence of recent periods, researchers commonly work with informants and the ethnohistoric and ethnographic sources to determine the function of particular monuments, their names, genealogies, and narratives pertaining to them. Such a combination of oral and ethnohistorical information and archaeological study has been used to interpret horticultural pits in the Tuamotu Archipelago, permitting the reconstruction of planting practices and their social and economic contexts (Chazine 1985a, 1985b). There are many similar examples of the use of people's memories and continuities in present-day practices of activities or knowledge dating from before the arrival of Europeans (e.g., Conte and Kape 1983a, 1983b; Ghasarian 2004; Sand and Valentin 1990). Of course, the more isolated a study area is from Western influences, the more likely one will encounter such continuities, the value of which is evident even if they can only allow very specific case-to-case comparisons with archaeological data.

It is from the same perspective that ethnohistorical sources such as descriptions by the first European navigators or missionaries are mobilized to shed direct light on certain archaeological discoveries and indeed sometimes replace or substitute for them. In a less narrow sense than in the strictly technological domain, but based on the same principle, attempts have been made to write down the history of an island community by drawing together ethnographic sources (e.g., traditional stories, genealogies) and archaeological sources. The work of Frimigacci and Vienne (1990) on Futuna, for instance, illustrates this type of approach, which we would like to attempt in other isolated parts of French Polynesia such as the Austral and Tuamotu archipelagoes. However, my 1996 study of the *marae* Te Tahata on Tepoto Island in the Tuamotus shows amongst other things the difficulty of aligning archaeology's material facts with ethnohistorical information. Regarding the function of this site, we possessed rich ethnographic information, in particular concerning the ritual consumption of turtles which were displayed there (see Emory 1947). However, excavation revealed 32 human skeletons, mostly recent, of which the oral traditions retained no recollection.

This research provides a useful caveat concerning the capacity of oral sources to orient archaeological fieldwork and interpretation. It underlines the fact that the integrity of an oral tradition, or of collective memories more generally, is not necessarily guaranteed by the recency with which the events in question occurred. Other factors – in this case a determination to conceal certain particularly sensitive information about burials – can rapidly lead to the loss of accurate knowledge about major elements of the past life of a community. In other words, although cultural and social factors *may* lead to the persistence over many centuries of precise oral traditions such as the one concerning Roy Mata, similar factors can rapidly erode collective memory and encourage the reformulation of oral traditions, genealogies, and so on. This fact enjoins caution in the use of oral and ethnographic sources for historical purposes. The same can be said about attempts to use recent land divisions to reconstruct past patterns of occupation. This method, which so far has been published only in preliminary form (Orliac and Orliac, 1996), may be justified in those islands where social structures and control of the land were not too disrupted by the Western influence before the establishment of the *tomite* system (individual land claiming) at the end of the 19th and the beginning of the 20th centuries. An alternative approach to this general question is outlined in the present volume by Ladefoged and Graves.

Using contemporary information to interpret the archaeology of the ancient past

The previous section of the chapter considered the use of early historical records, collective and individual memories, and continuities in social and technological (or even religious) practices to guide archaeological description and interpretation. As noted, these direct contributions, and especially those of oral traditions, which can have greater historical depth than ethnohistorical data, are especially applicable for recent prehistory (some centuries before contact). Some researchers, however, try to integrate these sorts of sources into their interpretations of archaeological remains from the more ancient past. I refer here to proper ethnoarchaeological study, namely ethnographic enquiries being conducted in the same locations as the archaeological information we seek to illuminate. This necessitates the construction of a model, mediating between present and past, to assist interpretation. A good example of this approach in the Pacific is illustrated by the work of Kirch and Dye (1979) on Niuatoputapu in Tonga, concerning the reconstruction of Lapita fishing strategies. To summarize, their study can be divided into three steps. First, the study of present-day fishing strategies allowed a survey of the main animal species present in the four principal biotopes of the island and the study of all the techniques used for their exploitation. The second step saw the excavation of Lapita sites covering a time depth of around 1,000 years between 800 B.C. and A.D. 200, which allowed a diachronic view of the exploitation of marine resources. Bone identification showed that the species of fish and the fishing zones in which they were caught were identical to those of the present day. On this basis, Kirch and Dye related the ichthyological remains found in the excavations with present-day techniques in order to deduce those in use in Lapita times. It is this third step that permits us to document the array of methods employed by the ancient occupants of the sites we examine, in much more detail than is usually possible on the basis of archaeological fishing gear alone, which is generally only found in small quantities, and to interpret apparent changes from a diachronic perspective.

This procedure, which uses cultural continuity and ecological coherence between societies and environments in the present and the past, appears especially pertinent, not only because it aids in the interpretation of archaeological remains, but also because it gives a certain time depth to information gathered through ethnographic observation. Archaeologists often forget (and ethnographers neglect) that while useful in comprehending the past, archaeological remains are no less important for understanding the history of the technological, social, and other structures that ethnography describes in the present. One need but note, in a domain vaster than that of techniques, the debate stirred up by the archaeological contestation of

certain ethnographic models, to judge that this diachronic perspective is as interesting as it is difficult to concede. Thus, for example, archaeological study of the
remains of settlements and horticultural systems in New Caledonia led Sand (1995)
to hypothesize that the image of Kanak society conveyed by ethnographic tradition
is more a reflection of significant recent demographic collapse than a reality trans-
posable to the pre-European period. His proposition was violently criticized by the
ethnographer Guiart (1996).

To return to the specific subject, even if such studies are stimulating, they cannot
be conducted systematically everywhere archaeological work is done nor necessarily cover everything one may wish to document, even if one limits oneself to the
technological domain (e.g., fishing, horticulture, cooking practices). Not all communities have retained the sort of structured, traditional exploitation of resources
found in Niuatoputapu: Some islands or portions of islands where we study
archaeological sites are now uninhabited and constraints of time as well as variations in the nature of archaeological training do not always permit ethnographic
studies of the required detail and rigor. However, there are many ways to escape
the need to produce new ethnographic observations every time one finds archaeological remains in a previously unresearched locality. This leads us to consider establishing ethnoarchaeological models that are widely applicable through space
and time.

Widely applicable models: the example of pre-European fishing techniques

Models of broad utility are especially pertinent in the technological domain, owing
to the constraints imposed by raw materials, the environment, and the physical
needs and capacities of human beings. Even here, however, the role of cultural
choice is essential and only plausible models, the credibility of which varies with
their distance in time and space from the places in which they were constructed,
can be reliably transferred to new situations. We certainly cannot advance models
concerning the social, ideological, or similar domains of culture with the same kind
of assurance as those dealing with technological matters. Rather, we must be
content with credible analogies which allow at least some play of the "imagination"
(Garanger 1979).

I can illustrate this process through the study I (Conte 1988) carried out on
ancient fishing strategies in French Polynesia on the basis of contemporary cultural
continuities. To understand this major activity of Polynesian societies, archaeology
gives us, in the best of cases, only two types of remains: faunal bone and shell that
allow the identification of part of the catch, and the tools of fishing such as hooks,
mostly in pearl shell, net weights, and, more rarely, items such as harpoon heads.
We could add coral traps, the traces of which are still observable in lagoons and
which, although usually recent, are in technological continuity with past practices.
These remains represent only part of the ancient material culture, the vegetal side
of which has generally disappeared, and they do not allow any detailed knowledge
of the technology associated with fishing. And yet one would wish to go far beyond

just technology to reconstruct at least capture strategies, the organization of fishing activities, and modes of distribution and consumption of the catch. For a fully ethnographic level of reconstruction which accords pre-European fishing its true complexity as a major social fact, we would also need to have a better knowledge of the way humans represented their natural environment and tackle the beliefs and ritual practices implicated in fishing.

The ethnoarchaeological analysis I carried out on these questions does not pretend to have met all these expectations in any final or infallible manner. What it allowed, though, is an advancement of knowledge far beyond what had been formulated on the subject beforehand, at least in ethnographic terms. While papers by Nordhoff (1930) and Ottino (1965) and to a lesser extent the work of Handy (1932) are exceptions, this progress can easily be gauged by examining most publications treating the ethnography of fishing in French Polynesia. These are usually compilations of ethnohistorical documents with some archaeological data appended, or descriptions of fishing gear presented as culturally decontextualized museum objects (e.g., Beasley 1928; Anell 1955; Emory et al. 1968; Emory 1975). In addition, as we shall see, my work has established the basis of radically different interpretations of fishing material and archaeological faunal remains.

It has been said above that reconstruction of even the simplest facets of ancient Polynesian fishing strategies was not possible using only archaeological evidence. Even with the best evidence, such as the examination of the many and formally highly varied sorts of hooks we have recovered from excavations as well as surface contexts, it was thought they would not tell us with any precision what prey they caught and with what methods (apart from bonito caught with trolling lures like those still in use). Indeed, hooks had previously not been used to reconstruct fishing techniques at all, but simply as "*fossiles directeurs*" for the definition of cultural sequences or the demonstration of settlement scenarios (e.g., Sinoto 1970, 1984). One of the most interesting aspects of this study was having the opportunity to confer on the hooks' role in the reconstruction of ancient technologies by the restitution of their functional value as fishing gear.

In the early contact period in Polynesia, Europeans recorded certain fishing activities, established an iconography, and collected hooks, thus providing quite vivid information on the technological, social, and even ritual aspects of fishing. However, this information cannot be used to make precise functional interpretations of archaeological material because the data are very uneven from one archipelago to the next. Indeed, even for recent periods and in well-documented areas such as the Society Islands, it appears that the first observers, wishing to please their readers, insisted above all on recording the most spectacular methods, such as fishing for sharks and turtles (cf. Elliott 1997). A study on the fishing strategies of past Polynesians, those of the contact period as well as of more distant times, was therefore ultimately not feasible until the archaeological remains, and especially fishhooks and bone remains, could be made to "speak" more. It was also important to fill gaps in the archaeological information resulting from low or non-existent archaeological visibility, from the past use of techniques with no material component or employing tools made of perishable materials, or of past patterns of prey consumption or waste discard which left no discoverable remains. The first priority is to resolve these problems at a purely technological or technical level (determining, for example, for which fish and with which strategies a certain type of archaeological hook was employed). Beyond this, however, we would wish to obtain information concerning all the cultural domains where fishing is implicated. It is in this arena that ethnoarchaeology is the only approach that allows us to move beyond the limits imposed by the historical sources and the way in which they are conventionally employed in archaeological description, analysis, and interpretation.

I initially took this approach to identify the relations between the conditions of the maritime environment, the nature and distribution of prey, and forms of fishing technology, so that I might interpret archaeological material culture and bone remains in terms of fishing strategies. As noted earlier, Polynesia presents researchers with optimal conditions in which to pursue such matters. First, the natural environment – the tide, currents, moon, and so on – has remained stable at the temporal scale in question, as have the fish and shell populations. Moreover, the species fished today are identical to those captured by the occupants of the oldest known sites. Present-day fishers are thus confronted by the same problems as those of yesterday and they resolved these problems in the same way despite certain changes in the materials they used. In the end, the transmission of knowledge has remained relatively uninterrupted from generation to generation, guaranteeing cultural continuity through time. Contemporary fishers are, to put it simply, the heirs of those whose sites we study.

On this basis, the study entailed going to the most isolated islands I could find that were representative of the archipelagoes of French Polynesia in all their varied ecological and cultural conditions, and where the cultural conditions remain as close as possible to the pre-European situation. My intention was to collect the most detailed information possible concerning the cultural domains encompassed by fishing. First, I considered the physical environment and the implications for fishing conditions in the way it is represented by Polynesians. Next, I examined prey species and their representation, trying to identify the logic of traditional classification schemes and behavioral descriptions and how they might influence fishing strategies. A central place was reserved in the study for fishing techniques, or more precisely, an analysis of how fishing gear and techniques were chosen in relation to the prey to be caught and the conditions in which these prey would be found (depending on their behavior or some independent factors). The idea was to start from environmental constraints, including those introduced by the prey itself, to reconstruct the process of technological adaptation. Demonstrating the logic which ordered these elements would help achieve the major goals of the research concerning the study of the archaeological material, namely, to provide a key to the functional interpretation of the remains, especially the fishhooks, out of any ethnographic or even archaeological context in the case of surface collections; to allow the formulation of credible hypotheses regarding past techniques used to capture different marine species, the skeletal remains of which are found in excavation; and to compensate for gaps in the record owing to taphonomic processes, in the interpretation of fishing gear as well as faunal remains.

Even after an extensive phase of research in 1981 in diverse island groups I was unable to produce wholly satisfactory findings. Indeed, because they occur infrequently and are dispersed across Polynesia, continuing traditional fishing techniques did not offer the anticipated potential in terms of technological systems, or allow me to build an analytically useful corpus of data. It appeared that because of massive adaptation of imported techniques (spear fishing, trolling from motor boats, etc.) demanding less observation of the environment and prey, the information collected from most fishermen was too imprecise and too far from prehistoric reality to be of much use. Apart from the technological questions forming the core of the enquiry, data concerning social conditions, beliefs, rituals, and the like associated with fishing were represented only by fragments of knowledge or practice, hearsay, and stories, reformulated to greater or lesser degrees under missionary influence. This made it impossible to relate such matters with techniques in any systemic way.

I was lucky enough to find an area – the atolls of Napuka and Tepoto in the northeast of the Tuamotus (Figure 12.1) – where particular historical conditions had maintained until recently, and in some cases until today, a technological and social milieu in cultural continuity with the pre-European period. This situation allowed me to establish a solid factual substrate upon which to apply my ethnoarchaeological procedures. I have to acknowledge that the conditions of enquiry were ideal because these studies were conducted at the request of the inhabitants of these atolls and with the support of the local *Tamariki Te Puka Maruia* association. It is not my intention to detail the methods employed or the results obtained; these matters have been published elsewhere (Conte 1985, 1988, 1994). It is enough to note that the exceptional circumstances allowed me to study 103 fishing techniques forming a real technological system, and to collect extremely detailed information concerning local knowledge of the environment and fish behavior. This has led to the development of a new database on the functions of fishing gear (use of direct or indirect hooks, for example) and technological choices, as required by my approach. In addition to fulfilling the primary objectives of the research, observations were also made on the treatment of prey after capture (e.g., cleaning, scaling), and on cooking methods. These data are very useful for archaeologically defining past refuse disposal strategies. Moreover, precise information has been gathered on the social organization of fishing (e.g., division of labor by sex and age), as well as on the beliefs, taboos, and rituals of the pre-missionary period which are still practiced by some.

Alone or in concert with observations made in other archipelagoes, the study carried out on Napuka and Tepoto illustrates some of the different ways to use ethnographical information in Polynesia. Primarily, it exploits an exceptional degree of cultural continuity between the pre-European past and the present. This aspect of the research comprises a monographic study that is justified in and of itself because anthropological works on the Tuamotus are rare and those concerning traditional fishing in the region even more so. Moreover, just as this type of observation was probably not possible in parts of the archipelago at that time, it might not be possible now even on Napuka and Tepoto owing to the death of most of my

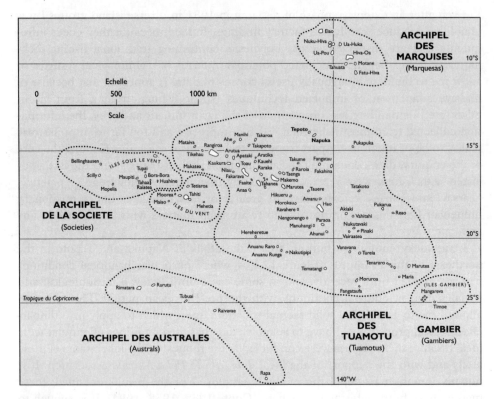

Figure 12.1 French Polynesia (Conte, 1988)

elderly informants. We can also say that the remarkable cultural continuity makes the picture obtained through the ethnography pertinent over many centuries prior to the missionary period, which began around 1880 and saw the first noticeable European influence. It is, in a way, a visit to the past that allows one to document aspects of culture such as beliefs which are difficult if not impossible to reach through archaeology. It is also reasonable to apply the findings from Napuka and Tepoto more widely through space and time. We can take these results to be representative of pre-contact reality on all 76 atolls of the Tuamotus, allowing for variations in the size of the atolls, the extent of their lagoons, the existence of passes through the reefs, and the like. Prehistoric fishing in the entire archipelago is thus illuminated in a very detailed manner by research in one privileged place.

As certain techniques observed on Napuka and Tepoto were also used outside the archipelago, we can gain more complete knowledge of fishing methods known only incompletely from less detailed sources: for instance, bonito fishing practiced everywhere, or fishing using hand nets on the reef observed being used by a single fisherman on Rurutu in the Australs. This last has been the subject of a documentary made in collaboration with Patrick Auzépy (*Pêches sur le récif à Rurutu, Australes*, 10 minutes, Département Archéologie du Centre Polynésien des Sciences Humaines). It is also remarkable that some of the prehistoric fishing techniques in the Marquesas can be described in detail because of the data collected on Napuka and Tepoto. In his doctoral thesis, Rolett (1998) surveyed Marquesan fishing techniques described in the ethnohistoric sources. Of the 26 techniques discussed, 11 have equivalents on Napuka and Tepoto and another six are very close to techniques for which we have detailed information. Thus 17 of the 26 known pre-European Marquesan fishing techniques can be precisely known through information from the Tuamotus even though the Marquesan ethnohistory concerning these techniques is limited. Clearly, if one wanted to use the ethnographic data to understand the full range of sites that might eventually be found in the Tuamotus, following Kirch and Dye's approach on Niuatoputapu, the Napuka and Tepoto data set would offer a solid basis for doing so.

I said above that the first major aim of this work was to move beyond the simple direct use of cultural continuities or the localized use of ethnographic information and towards the development of models which can be applied widely through time as well as space. I have just given some examples of applying the information synchronically to different localities. Let us now imagine how the project's findings might be used diachronically, in the study of archaeological material. The study of ethnohistorical sources and an extensive survey of techniques used in the various Polynesian archipelagoes indicate that the ancient Polynesians used three major methods to capture fish: fishhooks, spears, and traps, although there were special procedures for animals with particular behavior patterns (e.g., turtle, octopus, crayfish). The studies reveal that the choice of method depended on two series of factors: those related to the type of prey (e.g., size, weight, number, behavior) and those related to the fishing conditions (e.g., night or day, tide, phase of the moon) which usually affect the behavior of the fish. For prey like bonito, which has a very regular pattern of behavior, the number of alternative methods and techniques is limited – in fact, there may only be one. On the other hand, fishing for species with variable habits entailed the use of different methods in different conditions. Whatever the case, it can be shown that there are a finite number of technological choices to take a particular species of prey. It is here that the database produced for Napuka and Tepoto really comes into its own, as the 103 techniques it describes can illuminate the optimal choices for the capture of around 100 types of prey. The number is even greater when the extensive observations done in the other archipelagoes are added to the equation.

In addition, bone identification allows hypotheses to be formulated about the procedures used to capture the species concerned, though to provide more than just an indication of the procedure requires the integration of information regarding marine environmental parameters in the place of capture, such as the presence of a lagoon or reef. Whatever the site, very reliable deductions can be made concerning the techniques and strategies used to capture the fish whose remains have been excavated. The same type of reasoning can even be applied to species not covered by ethnographic observations. Owing to the adaptive relationship between natural conditions, species-specific prey behavior, and fishing procedures, knowledge concerning the first two factors permits one to make predictions concerning the third.

The second major aim of my study was to contribute to the functional interpretation of archaeological material, and especially the hooks that are the most
common items of fishing gear found in excavations. In other publications (Conte
1988, 1994), I demonstrate how, starting with a hook, one can deduce different
techniques that are implicated, the categories of prey which are susceptible to being
caught, and even certain social information (sexual division of labor, for example).
For example, a large indirect hook is used for prey of a large size (tuna, say) which
one encounters offshore. This type of fishing is practiced from a canoe. One knows
that with such a fishhook it is necessary to fish at depth, perpendicular to the canoe.
For the hook to be able to attain a certain depth, it is necessary to make use of a
disposable weight (fishing weight, cobble, . . .). In addition, in the case of open-sea
fishing it is virtually certain, given what one knows about Polynesian practices, that
it is a man who uses the hook.

Beyond the interpretation of excavated evidence, the study allows us to envisage
the use of technological procedures that leave no material traces (such as net fishing,
hand fishing, or poisoning). The same approach is possible for prey species that
cannot be readily identified from the osteological remains and/or whose method of
capture would not leave any traces, starting from present-day prey populations, and
the uniformitarian hypothesis that they were exploited in the past.

In addition to research dealing strictly with fishing, it is worth noting that observations made on the treatment of prey after their capture (e.g., cleaning, cooking,
preservation, disposal of bones) may be directly used in interpreting archaeological remains in the Tuamotus. One example would be cooking structures, whose differences can be attributed to the food that was cooked in them. This work can also
inform us how different modes of consumption and disposal might influence the
archaeological remains produced by the society in question.

Turning to the social and ideological dimensions of fishing, the sexual division
of labor, for example, and fishing rituals, the very detailed observations conducted
on Napuka and Tepoto cannot be transferred entirely through space or deep time.
Nevertheless, they find numerous resonances in the writings of the first European
observers, whatever little was recorded in their surveys, or in the analyses of other
anthropologists, such as the existence of *tapu* in relation to "the ideology of blood"
(Testart, 1986). This indicates that this type of information, which is usually difficult to gain, can serve to enrich archaeological data when proper precautions are
taken. We should note that when this model was first conceived as an aid to the
interpretation of archaeological remains, there were few good quality data related
to fishing.

Conclusion

To conclude, let us note that some data, especially the laws of technological adaptation to fishing conditions and prey, can be used outside the area of the archipelagoes of present-day French Polynesia. The parallels mentioned earlier with
Niuatoputapu and Tonga (Kirch and Dye, 1979) and others with Hawai'i (Kirch

1979) for instance, seem to show that my database, without equivalent in the Pacific but certainly open to improvement, could serve as a foundation for the creation of an ethnoarchaeological reconstruction of Polynesian fishing strategies, and more broadly of relationships between people and their marine environments in the whole region. The study of fishing techniques has shown how present-day ethnographic information can effectively enrich excavated archaeological data by using not only cultural continuities that can be directly projected into the past in the location of collection, but also of lessons from these analyses which can be abstracted from specific local and historical conditions to be used outside the observation area for remains from other regions or from remote periods in Polynesian prehistory. This procedure can be compared with broader ethnoarchaeological approaches used elsewhere (Gould 1980a). However, even allowing for some loss of information content related to the distance from the central area of ethnographic observation, the interpretative quality of such analogies remains far stronger than the process of transferring information from Africa or New Guinea to Europe, though these latter analogies can have heuristic value if applied in an appropriately cautious manner.

From a purely technical point of view, ethnoarchaeological research is becoming increasingly urgent as ways of life change and the elders from whom it is still possible to obtain firsthand information on traditional practices, or even to carry out replicative construction projects, progressively disappear. Thus in addition to some highly focused observations of bird hunting, I have undertaken work on food-cooking techniques in the Tuamotus in a manner similar to that described above (Conte 1986), while Ghasarian (2004) has done the same in the Marquesas, the Society Islands, and the Australs. More recently an ethnoarchaeological approach has been applied to the study of dry horticulture practiced on hillsides on the island of Maupiti in the Leeward Islands (Cauchois 2002), following the model which Kirch (1994) developed in Futuna. At the time of writing, a survey is under way on the consumption of seaweed in French Polynesia (Conte and Payri 2002). As regards fishing, various works incorporating material about fishing and/or ichthyological remains have recently begun to be published (e.g., Allen 1992, 1996; P. R. Ottino 1992a, 1992b; Rolett 1998; Walter 1991), some taking my study into account.

The approach described in this chapter primarily concerns technological domains that have been maintained with sufficient continuity to allow fruitful ethnographic enquiry regarding traditional practices. When questions arise regarding the social and religious context of a technological activity such as fishing, I suggest that it is not the technical "facts" themselves that make ethnographic analogies through time and space conceivable, but rather the nature of the internal logics that sustain the cultural contexts in question. This approach to ethnoarchaeology allows one to tackle the reconstruction and understanding of social and ideological issues, the material traces of which are particularly ambiguous. In doing so, we must seek assistance in the categories and values of Polynesian societies themselves, reconstructed from linguistic, ethnohistorical, and ethnographic information in a process of reconstitution of the cultural context that is indispensable in historical work to avoid the traps of anachronism which can be set for us by a tenacious ethnocentrism.

ACKNOWLEDGMENTS

Thanks to Christophe Sand and Ian Lilley for translating this chapter from French, and to Pat Kirch for his additional editing.

REFERENCES

Allen, M., 1992 Temporal Variation in Polynesian Fishing Strategies: The Southern Cook Islands in Regional Perspective. Asian Perspectives 31:183–204.

——Allen, M., 1996 Style and Function in East Polynesian Fish-Hooks. Antiquity 70:97–116.

Anell, B., 1955 Contribution to the History of Fishing in the Southern Seas. Uppsala: Almqvist and Wiksell.

Audouze, F., and A. Leroi-Gourhan, 1981 France: A Continental Insularity. World Archaeology 13:170–189.

Beasley, H., 1928 Pacific Island Records. Fish Hooks. London: Service and Co.

Binford, L., 1978 Dimensional Analysis of Behavior and Site Structure: Learning from an Eskimo Hunting Stand. American Antiquity 43:330–361.

Cauchois, H., 2002 Dryland Horticulture in Maupiti: An Ethnoarchaeological Study. Asian Perspectives 41:269–283.

Chang, K-C., 1967 Rethinking Archaeology. New York: Random House.

Chazine, J-M., 1985a Du Présent au Passé: Questions d'Ethnoarchéologie. Les Fosses de Culture des Tuamotu. Techniques et Culture 6:85–98.

——1985b Les Fosses de Culture dans les Tuamotu. Travaux en Cours et Perspectives. Journal de la Société des Océanistes 80:25–32.

Conte, E., 1985 Recherches Ethno-Archéologiques sur l'Exploitation du Milieu Marin à Napuka (Tuamotu). Journal de la Société des Océanistes 80:51–56.

——1986 Techniques de Cuisson et de Conservation de la Nourriture aux Tuamotu, Polynésie Française. Goûts Culinaires et Procédés Techniques. Papeete: Service de la Culture et du Patrimoine, Département Archéologie.

——1988 La Pêche Pré-Européenne et ses Survivances. L'Exploitation Traditionnelle des Ressources Marines à Napuka (Tuamotu-Polynésie Française). Thèse pour le Doctorat, Université Paris I.

——1994 L'Ethnoarchéologie: Pour que le Présent Éclaire le Passé. Bulletin de la Société des Etudes Océaniennes 263–264:51–64.

——1996 Un Cas de Mémoire Tronquée: Les Sépultures du Marae Te Tahata de Tepoto (Archipel des Tuamotu, Polynésie Française) In Mémoire de Pierre, Mémoire d'Homme. Tradition et Archéologie en Océanie. Hommage à José Garanger. M. Julien, M. Orliac et C. Orliac, eds. pp. 75–94. Paris: Publication de la Sorbonne.

Conte, E., and J. Kape, 1983a La Production du Feu par Friction, Éléments d'Observation et d'Analyse. Bulletin de la Société des Etudes Océaniennes 222:1272–1282.

——1983b La Conservation du Feu: Description d'une Méthode Ancienne. Bulletin de la Société des Etudes Océaniennes 225:1450–1453.

Conte, E., and C. Payri, 2002 La Consommation des Algues en Polynésie Française: Premiers Résultats d'une Enquête. Journal de la Société des Océanistes 114–115:165–172.

Coudart, A., 1992 Entre Nouvelle-Guinée et Néolithique Européen. De la Correspondance entre les Variations de l'Architecture Domestique, la Durabilité Culturelle et la Cohésion Sociale du Groupe. In Ethnoarchéologie. Justification, Problèmes, Limites. XIIe Rencontres Internationales d'Archéologie et d'Histoire d'Antibes. F. Audouze, ed. pp. 409–446. Actes des Rencontres, 17–18–19 Octobre 1991. Juan-Les-Pins: APDCA.

Coudart, A., and P. Lemonnier, 1984 Ethnoarchéologie et Ethnologie des Techniques. Techniques et Culture 3:157–169.

Elliott, J., 1997 The Choosers or the Dispossessed? Oceania 67:234–256.

Emory, K., 1947 Tuamotuan Religious Structures and Ceremonies, Bernice P. Bishop Museum Bulletin 191. Honolulu: Bishop Museum Press.

——1975 Material Culture of the Tuamotu Archipelago. Pacific Anthropological Records 22. Honolulu: Department of Anthropology, Bernice P. Bishop Museum.

Emory, K., W. Bonk and Y. Sinoto, 1968 Hawaiian Archaeology Fishhooks. Bernice P. Bishop Museum Special Publication 47. Honolulu: Bishop Museum Press.

Frimigacci, D., and B. Vienne, 1990 Aux Temps de la Terre Noire. Ethno-Archéologie des Îles Futuna et Alofi. Paris-Louvain: Peeters-SELAF.

Gallay, A., 1986 L'Archéologie Demain. Paris: Belfond.

Garanger, J., 1976 Tradition Orale et Préhistoire en Océanie. Cahiers de l'ORSTOM, Série Sciences Humaines 8(2):147–161.

——1979 Archéologie et Anthropologie. In L'Anthropologie en France. Situation Actuelle et Avenir. G. Condominas and S. Dreyfus-Gamelon, eds. pp. 83–103. Colloques Internationaux du CNRS 573. Paris: CNRS.

Gardin, J-C., 1979 Une Archéologie Théorique. Paris: Hachette.

Ghasarian, C., 2004 La Cuisson au Four de Terre en Polynésie Française. Une Technique Traditionnelle dans une Société en Mutation. Cahiers du Patrimoine (Savoirs et traditions). Puta Tumu, Tahiti: Ministère de la Culture de Polynésie française.

Gould, R., 1980a Living Archaeology. New York: Cambridge University Press.

——1980b Quatre-Vingt Années d'Ethnoarchéologie. Les Nouvelles de l'Archéologie 4:11–16.

Guiart, J., 1996 Archéologie et Ethnologie. In Mémoire de Pierre, Mémoire d'Homme, Tradition et Archéologie en Océanie. Hommage à J. Garanger. M. Julien, M. Orliac et C. Orliac, eds. pp. 31–63. Paris: Publications de la Sorbonne.

Handy, E., 1932 Houses, Boats and Fishing, Bernice P. Bishop Museum Bulletin 90. Honolulu: Bishop Museum Press.

Hodder, I., 1980 L'Ethnoarchéologie: Une Approche Contextuelle. Les Nouvelles de l'Archéologie 4:24–33.

Kirch, P., 1979 Marine Exploitation in Prehistoric Hawaii: Archaeological Investigation at Kalahuipua'a, Hawaii Island. Pacific Anthropological Records 29. Honolulu: Department of Anthropology, Bernice P. Bishop Museum.

——1994 The Wet and the Dry: Irrigation and Agricultural Intensification in Polynesia. Chicago: University Of Chicago Press.

Kirch, P., and T. Dye, 1979 Ethno-Archaeology and the Development of Polynesian Fishing Strategies. Journal of the Polynesian Society 88:53–76.

Leroi-Gourhan, A., 1990 [1964] Les Religions de la Préhistoire. Paris: Quadrige, PUF.

Lightfoot, K., 1995 Culture Contact Studies: Redefining the Relationship between Prehistoric and Historical Archaeology. American Antiquity 60:199–217.

Moberg, C., 1976 Introduction à l'Archéologie. Paris: François Maspero.

Nordhoff, C., 1930 Notes on the Off-Shore Fishing in the Society Islands. Journal of the Polynesian Society 39:137–173, 221–262.

Orliac, C., and M. Orliac, 1996 L'Écrit, le Dit et l'Enfoui. Considérations sur l'Histoire d'une Vallée de Tahiti. In Mémoire de Pierre, Mémoire d'Homme. Tradition et Archéologie en Océanie. Hommage à José Garanger. M. Julien, M. Orliac et C. Orliac, eds. pp. 230–243. Paris: Publications de la Sorbonne.

Ottino, P., 1965. La Pêche au Grand Filet à Tahiti. Cahiers de l'ORSTOM, Série Sciences Humaines 2(2). Paris: ORSTOM.

Ottino, P. R. 1992a Anapua: Abri-sous-roche de Pêcheurs. Étude des Hameçons (1re Partie). Journal de la Société des Océanistes 94:57–79.

——1992b Anapua: Abri-sous-roche de Pêcheurs. Étude des Hameçons (2è Partie). Journal de la Société des Océanistes 95:201–226.

Pétrequin, A., and P. Pétrequin, 1992 De l'Espace Actuel au Temps Archéologique ou les Mythes d'un Préhistorien. In Ethnoarchéologie: Justification, Problèmes, Limites. XIIe Rencontres Internationales d'Archéologie et d'Histoire d'Antibes. F. Audouze, ed. pp. 211–238. Juan-Les-Pins: APDCA.

——1993 Écologie d'un Outil: La Hache de Pierre en Irian Jaya (Indonésie). Monographie du CRA 12. Paris: CNRS.

Rolett, B., 1998 Hanamiai: Prehistoric Colonization and Cultural Change in the Marquesas Islands (East Polynesia). Publications in Anthropology 81. New Haven: Yale.

Sand, C., 1995 "Le Temps d'Avant." La Préhistoire de la Nouvelle-Calédonie. Paris: l'Harmattan.

Sand, C., and F. Valentin, 1990 The Excavation of the Faitoka of Petania, Uvea: Stratigraphy, Mortuary Practices and Biological Anthropology. Paper presented at the 14th Indo-Pacific Prehistory Association Congress, Jogyakarta.

Schiffer, M., 1978 Methodological Issues in Ethnoarchaeology. In Explorations in Ethnoarchaeology. R. Gould, ed. pp. 229–247. Albuquerque: University of New Mexico Press.

Sinoto, Y., 1970 An Archaeologically Based Assessment of the Marquesas Islands as a Dispersal Center in East Polynesia. In Studies in Oceanic Culture History, vol. 1. R. Green and M. Kelly, eds. pp. 105–132. Pacific Anthropological Records 11. Honolulu: Department of Anthropology, Bernice P. Bishop Museum.

——1984 An Analysis of Polynesian Migrations based on the Archaeological Assessments. Journal de la Société des Océanistes 76:57–67.

Stiles, D., 1977 Ethnoarcheology: A Discussion of Methods and Applications. Man. 12:87–103.

Testart, A., 1986 Essai sur les Fondements de la Division Sexuelle du Travail chez les Chasseurs-Cueilleurs. Paris: Éditions de l'École des Hautes Etudes en Sciences Sociales.

Thomson, D., 1939 The Seasonal Factor in Human Culture. Proceedings of the Prehistoric Society 5:209–221.

Walter, R., 1991 Fishing on Ma'uke. An Archaeological and Ethnographic Study of Fishing Strategies on a Makatea Island. New Zealand Journal of Archaeology 13:41–58.

13

The Formation of Hawaiian Territories

Thegn Ladefoged and Michael Graves

One of the hallmarks of behavioral ecology is the study of community interactions, particularly the establishment and maintenance of territories, among populations of the same species (Adams 2001; Morrell and Kokko 2003). Ecological anthropologists have pursued this topic among contemporary groups (Borgerhoff Mulder 1991; Dyson-Hudson and Smith 1978). Archaeologists, too, are interested in understanding the history and functioning of community interactions or territories among humans. For instance, humans can be organized into spatio-temporal groups of different spatial scales, sometimes hierarchically structured and highly territorial (e.g., see Field 2004). Archaeologists have also developed the means and labels for recognizing distinctive social units or groups (e.g., Lipo et al. 1997). In fact, virtually all archaeological data must be organized into units that reflect the products of multiple individuals or groups and building such units is a cornerstone of traditional and contemporary archaeological research (Lyman et al. 1997; Teltser 1995; Tschauner 1994).

In Oceania, archaeologically based social units have been bounded in space by island archipelagoes (e.g., the Hawaiian Islands), or as individual islands (e.g., Rapa Nui). In this context, physical distance and its subsequent limiting effects on interaction between many archipelagoes and islands are the bases for recognizing different societies. In Hawai'i, when archaeologists do not treat the entire archipelagoes or an individual island as a single entity, two cultural units dominate our study: the *ahupua'a* (community) and the *moku'āina* (district). Many ahupua'a or moku'āina have distinctive names associated with particular locations; all were marked by boundaries, sometimes with physical manifestations, and were associated with demarcated territories corresponding in scale to the unit of organization. Ahupua'a represent the territories associated with individual communities, comprising a population of interacting individuals, most of whom would be more closely related to each other than to other individuals living elsewhere. Ahupua'a territories typically, although not always, extended across a series of ecological zones from the coast to the uplands and mountains of the Hawaiian Islands.

Mokuʻāina (or *moku*) represent named political territories comprising multiple contiguous ahupuaʻa and are often glossed by the term "district." Mokuʻāina are also associated with Hawaiian chiefdoms. As Kirch (1985:2) observes, "Whole islands or parts of large islands constituted moku, independent chiefdoms." As they included multiple ahupuaʻa, moku covered larger areas, and extended from the coast to the mountains. At the time of European contact in the late 18th century, there were about thirty recognized districts on the islands of Hawaiʻi, Maui, Molokaʻi, Oʻahu, and Kauaʻi.

Students of traditional Hawaiian culture have long speculated on the nature and the timing of the formation of these two units of social and political organization. They have increasingly sought archaeological data that would pertain to these issues. We present here some background for understanding how mokuʻāina and ahupuaʻa were organized in traditional Hawaiian culture, and then we turn to hypotheses that attempt to account for some of their similarities and differences. Drawing on a variety of evidence we illustrate how the social groups comprising these units may have interacted, developed, and evolved in relation to each other and the natural environment of Hawaiʻi. We argue that the formation of social units at different scales remains a significant research topic for archaeologists here and elsewhere in Polynesia.

Hawaiian Political and Social Organization

At the time of European contact in the late 18th century, Hawaiian society included at least four complex chiefdoms vying with each other for power and prestige (Figure 13.1). These chiefdoms were centered on the islands of Kauaʻi, Oʻahu, Maui, and Hawaiʻi (Tuggle 1979). The areas encompassed by these complex chiefdoms in Hawaiʻi had been and were, at that time, dynamic, either increasing or decreasing in line with the successes and failures of political strategies (see Cachola-Abad 2000 for analyses based on oral traditions). By the early part of the 19th century, Kamehameha I had integrated much of the islands, conquering the Maui and Oʻahu chiefdoms and receiving tacit fealty from the Kauaʻi paramount chief.

At this highest level, portions of an island, an entire island, or even a group of islands were ruled by paramount chiefs. Each of these chiefdoms, then, was associated with multiple territories or moku and these provided the base for extensive production of agricultural and animal foods, construction of and worship at ritual sites (*heiau*), and the hierarchical integration of numerous communities. Mokuʻāina represent the territorial building blocks by which Hawaiian chiefdoms were organized and, at times, integrated. As the statement by Kirch reveals, most archaeologists believe that individual moku constituted independent chiefdoms at some point in Hawaiian history. As more complex chiefdoms emerged in Hawaiʻi with

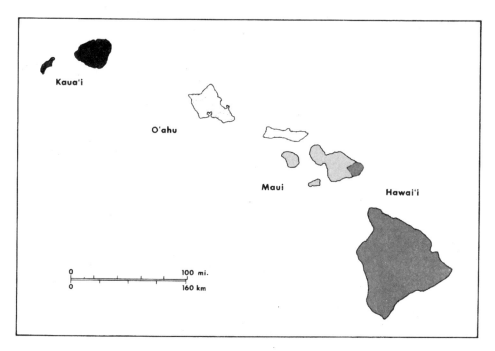

Figure 13.1 The four Hawaiian chiefdoms at European contact (after Cordy 1981)

paramount chiefs integrating multiple moku, district chiefs would be assigned by the paramount to manage the affairs of individual moku.

This territorial system is thought (see Kirch 1984) to have emerged from an earlier land-tenure system in which lineage-based corporate descent groups controlled sections of land and their members were provided access to lands for agriculture and with other resources (Hommon 1986). One model of Hawaiian settlement suggests that these descent groups originally occupied localities containing more optimal resources, with unoccupied buffer zones between lineage territories. These original lineage territories are likely visible as the traditional moku or districts on the major Hawaiian Islands. Through time, as population increased, people moved into the buffer zones, creating a more fully utilized and territorially defined landscape. During the late phase of prehistory, ownership of land was vested in the paramount chiefs and separated from corporate descent groups.

Individual districts were divided into a number of ahupua'a or community territories. The ideal ahupua'a extended from the mountains to the sea, cross-cutting a range of environmental zones. Again in the ideal, ahupua'a would have access to a variety of resources necessary to maintain the human population of each community. Ahupua'a in turn were divided into *'ili*, smaller territorial units associated with family groups, and 'ili were divided into *mo'o*, smaller plots of land worked by households. Traditionally in Hawai'i, ownership of land within each ahupua'a was not vested in the individuals or groups who produced its foods or lived within its boundaries. Rather, land was held by *ali'i* or chiefs, usually paramount chiefs, and managed by a hierarchy of lesser chiefs.

The communities associated with individual ahupua'a are generally represented as being mostly autonomous, self-sufficient in critical resources (Earle 1977), and largely endogamous (Earle 1978:14–15). *Maka'āinana* (or commoner) populations of about 100–200 individuals, on average, are suggested for most communities (Cordy 2000:50) on Hawai'i Island. These communities would have been composed of a number of extended families, which are thought to have been organized as kindreds sharing a common social identity based on their residence within the ahupua'a (Sahlins 1958). Unlike moku boundaries, which are often viewed as developing quite early and being relatively static, it has been suggested that ahupua'a territories changed through time, first developing in the 13th to 14th century A.D. (Hommon 1986), and generally subdividing into smaller and smaller administrative units.

Spatial Evidence Documenting Hawaiian Territorial Boundaries

In the following analysis we present two related approaches suggesting how moku and ahupua'a boundaries might be analyzed from a spatial perspective which provides a hierarchical and possibly historical sequence of land division. For moku we work from larger to smaller geographic units, hypothesizing how islands may have been sequentially divided. We also consider evidence suggesting moku boundaries that were imposed/redrawn relatively late in time. For ahupua'a, we work in the opposite direction, showing how these territories might be joined at successively larger geographic scales. Again, we also illustrate cases where ahupua'a territories may have either been formed relatively contemporaneously or where boundaries were redrawn late in time. Other sources of information from both archaeology and oral history are used to assess the spatial analysis.

Moku territories

A number of hypotheses have been presented to account for the formation of moku territories. Still other propositions are embedded in statements about the islands' history. The "wet and dry" dichotomy forwarded by Kirch (1994) and others (Hommon 1986; Hunt 1990) suggests that district boundaries might be aligned with the division between wet (windward) and dry (leeward) sides of an island. The peaks of mountains or summits of mountain ranges which created the rainshadows would be the natural topographic corollary to this (see Hommon 1986:61). Tuggle (1979) notes that district boundaries were defined, in part, by resource distributions with the boundaries between districts usually occurring in areas of lower productivity. Hommon (1986:61) seconds this: "It is reasonable to infer that sparse rainfall, absence of permanent water courses, and a general lack of conditions conducive to agriculture were in large part responsible for the absence of settlements in these [district boundaries]." Tuggle also infers that the centers of districts were located in higher productivity areas and these were likely settled first with the margins of districts often serving as sparsely populated buffer zones. Buffer zones at this level are likely to be larger than those that might reflect community boundaries (Cordy 1981). If the foregoing is true, we might expect evidence for the most ancient or oldest district boundaries to correspond to natural features or long-term properties of the physical environment. We also anticipate that the very oldest district boundaries would have been drawn along the division between windward and leeward zones. These earliest boundaries we will label as primary. Where boundaries are also functioning as buffers between groups, there should be little evidence for early human occupation in these zones. Permanent human occupation along district peripheries would be later and probably would be associated with processes of ahupua'a formation.

While little mention of it has been found in the literature, we ask whether districts have been partitioned over time, with subdivision of larger districts into smaller districts. This might have occurred when there were multiple individuals who claimed to be the paramount chief of a given district, or where collateral chiefly lines sought and received areas in which to establish their sovereignty. Or, a larger district may have been subdivided when it was conquered by a new paramount chief who chose to divide its management between two allies. Subsequent partitioning of larger into smaller districts would be evident when one boundary joins or intersects another, primary boundary. Successive partitioning would be indicated by boundaries that join to secondary (or lower order) boundaries. The names of the individual districts also provide clues into the history of changing boundaries. Contiguous districts that share a common name were probably joined together at one time as a single district. Inspection of their common boundary may suggest how to identify partitioning.

Partitioning is not the only possible outcome of competitive interaction between chiefs. Districts may have been merged or portions of one district may have been incorporated into another's territory. Evidence for portions of moku being appropriated by adjacent districts might be seen when moku boundaries diverge from or no longer follow natural features.

The moku boundaries of O'ahu, Moloka'i, Kaua'i, Maui, and Hawai'i

These principles can be used to develop possible scenarios of moku definition and development for the larger Hawaiian islands. The use of natural topographic features to define moku boundaries, especially mountain ridges, cliffs, and mountain tops, is evident on all of the Hawaiian Islands but is especially clear on Moloka'i and O'ahu. On Moloka'i (Figure 13.2a) the boundary between the Ko'olau and Kona districts conforms to the ridgeline of the mountains from Pu'u 'Ōlelo on the

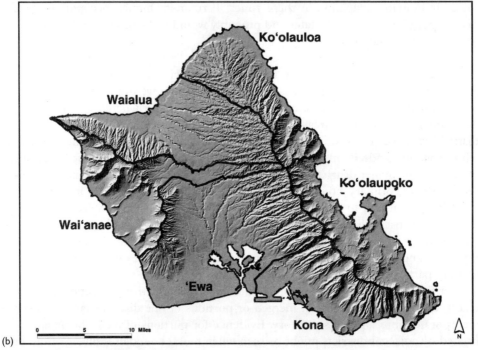

Figure 13.2 The districts of Moloka'i, O'ahu, Kaua'i, Maui, and Hawai'i Island

west to Kamakou (the highest point on the island) to Pu'u Hoku on the east. On O'ahu, the Ko'olau Mountains serve as a primary division between the windward and leeward districts (Figure 13.2b). All other moku boundaries intersect this boundary, suggesting that at one time the island may have comprised a windward moku (Ko'olau) and a leeward moku (perhaps referred to as Kona, and made up of Kona 'Ewa, Wai'anae, and Waialua).

O'ahu probably best illustrates a possible sequence of moku subdivision. The original single Ko'olau district was divided into two (Ko'olaupoko and Ko'olauloa).

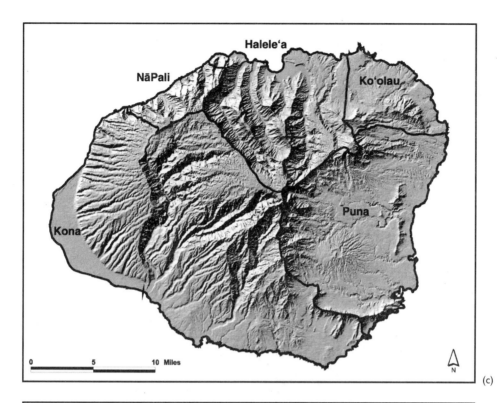

(c)

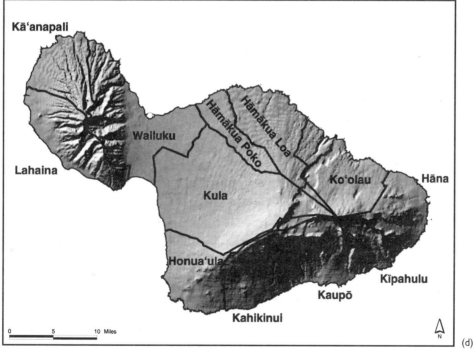

(d)

Figure 13.2 *Continued*

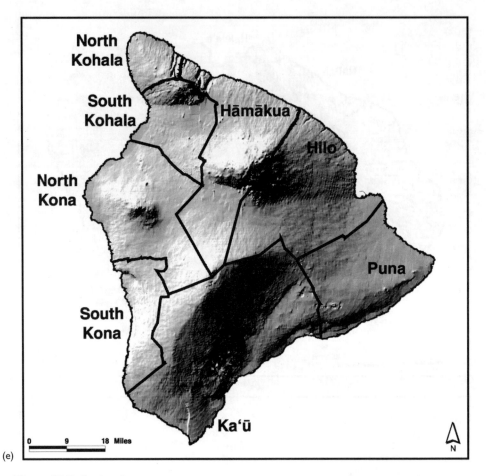

(e)

Figure 13.2 *Continued*

It seems that the large Kona district (consisting of Kona 'Ewa, Wai'anae, and Waialua) was separated at some point into two leeward zones along the boundary between 'Ewa and Wai'anae. This boundary lines up perfectly with the boundary separating the two windward Ko'olau districts, and suggests that at some time there was also a north–south division on O'ahu. The larger leeward units of Wai'anae/Waialua and Kona/'Ewa were apparently subdivided, with 'Ewa being separated out from Kona in the south, and Waialua and Wai'anae being divided in the north. Oral traditions provide some support for these divisions (see Cachola-Abad 2000; Kikiloi n.d.). There is an early divide between paramount chiefs who ruled either in windward or leeward districts. Later there are paramount chiefs on O'ahu who ruled either the three northern districts (Wai'anae/Waialua/Ko'olauloa) or the three southern districts ('Ewa/Kona/Ko'olaupoko). It may be at this time that the boundary separating these two sets of districts was placed so as to create an unbroken line across windward to leeward zones. Kikiloi's (n.d.) seriation of O'ahu heiau using construction design attributes also shows a similar shift in interaction from a windward/leeward division of the island's districts to a north–south division of districts.

On Kaua'i, three district boundaries converge near the center of the island, at Wai'ale'ale, adjacent to Kawaikini, the highest point on the island (Figure 13.2c). There appears to have been an early division between the Kona (leeward) districts (Kona and NāPali) and the windward districts (Halele'a, Ko'olau, and Puna); the boundary line follows a series of topographic features, including the Wahina Pali, and the Pali 'Ele'ele north of Kawaikini and, then southward along the ridgeline associated with Hā'upu to Pu'u Pihakapu near Kawelikoa Point. There are indications that larger districts on Kaua'i were subdivided into smaller ones. The NāPali moku is clearly a division cut out of the large Kona moku and it also follows an important landform. On the windward side of Kaua'i, the sequence is more ambiguous; perhaps it involved first a division into two windward districts, one comprising Halele'a and the other consisting of Ko'olau and Puna. Subsequently it appears that the Ko'olau and Puna area was divided into the two individual areas of Ko'olau and Puna moku.

On both Maui and Hawai'i it is much more difficult to identify a complete sequence of political division based on district boundaries. On Maui, moku boundaries converge on mountaintops: Haleakalā in east Maui and Pu'u Kukui in west Maui (Figure 13.2d). It is possible to place the districts from Kipahulu to Hāmākua poko in an eastern zone and the rest from Kaupō through Kula, Wailuku, and Ka'anapali into a western zone. This roughly corresponds to a windward and leeward division of the island and it is represented in oral traditions from the island (Cachola-Abad 2000; Kolb 1994). Seriation of heiau from Maui consistently divide into two geographic groups that include this windward/leeward divide of districts (Graves and Cachola-Abad 1996; n.d.). Further subdivision is much less certain, but based on the intersection of the boundaries the two Hāmākua districts are likely aligned with Ko'olau; Hāna and Kīpahulu may be combined, as were likely Kahikinui and Kaupō. Honua'ula and Kula are also a plausible earlier unit. Lahaina and Ka'anapali form a single unit in west Maui that may have been joined with Wailuku at one point.

Hawai'i Island offers the most difficult set of moku boundaries to sequence (Figure 13.2e). The three moku whose boundaries converge on Mauna Loa would have included a large western (or leeward) district (consisting of the Kohala and Kona districts), a southern district (consisting of Ka'ū), and an eastern (windward) district (consisting of Hāmākua, Hilo, and Puna). This early tripartite division of the island is suggestive of the pattern on Kaua'i, and reminiscent of what has been reported for O'ahu. Later divisions include the separation of Kona and Kohala on the west side of Hawai'i; the boundary which separates them demarcates one of those zones of relatively low productivity referred to by Tuggle (1979). The moku of Puna also represents a subdivision, apparently from a region that at one time consisted of Hilo and Puna. Oral traditions, however, do not support this interpretation and are clear that Puna is consistently associated with Ka'ū. The two latest sub-divisions include those of North and South Kona and North and South Kohala.

Note that the northeast boundary of North Kohala diverges from the mountains' ridgeline to include several of the larger, permanently watered valleys. As this division of Kohala and Hāmākua has a long history in oral traditions (Cachola-Abad pers. comm. 2004), it may be that the boundary demarcates a zone of lowered resource productivity.

The boundary evidence from extant maps and the limited evidence from oral traditions and archaeology support the proposition that moku territories changed over time on the four largest islands (Kauaʻi, Oʻahu, Maui, and Hawaiʻi), with larger units, often based on a windward/leeward divide, dominating an earlier period of history. These larger units were subsequently subdivided into smaller moku. And even after the time when complex, multi-district chiefdoms emerged in the archipelagoes, moku boundaries may have been altered or additional subdivisions may have developed.

Ahupuaʻa-level boundaries

Like moku, several lines of evidence document ahupuaʻa territorial boundaries. Ahupuaʻa boundaries were surveyed in the mid-19th century, and are currently depicted on US Geological Survey (USGS) topographic maps. In addition to these documentary sources, ahupuaʻa boundaries are often defined by archaeological remains, including walls, trails, and even sacrificial pig burials.

Although moku territories are treated as relatively stable over time, most archaeologists envision ahupuaʻa territories as more dynamic. Following Hommon's lead we suggest the organization of prehistoric Hawaiian society into an ahupuaʻa model of community territories that would occur first in those areas with abundant or predictable resources and that had critical upland or inland resources. This, in part, reflects the hypothesis offered by Tuggle regarding resource productivity within moku, there being some locations with greater or lesser abundances of resources or with greater or lesser predictability of resources. That being the case, a locality with abundant resources would not only be settled first but would be most likely to undergo division into separate communities if resource productivity could have been increased to support larger populations. Furthermore, it has been suggested that the size of ahupuaʻa territories within individual districts was negatively correlated with productivity so that as productivity increases, ahupuaʻa area decreases. This needs to be tempered, however, with the potential dynamic of ahupuaʻa subdivision, a feature that is often missing from archaeological analyses.

As with the earliest or most persistent moku boundaries, it may be that the oldest ahupuaʻa boundaries will be associated with significant and mostly contiguous topographic features but that over time, subdivision will have partitioned these original units on the basis of less obvious (or spatially discontinuous) physical features. The most recently formed ahupuaʻa, in fact, may have few or no topographic features that define them. Rather, other features of these boundaries (e.g., branching) may help to identify their relative position in a sequence of subdivision.

This does not exhaust the possibilities, as Cordy (1981) suggests that ahupua'a communities may have been initially distributed spatially to provide buffers between groups. Again, these buffers may take advantage of less productive locations. Under this hypothesis, evidence for early ahupua'a boundaries should be consistent with dispersion of these units across the landscape within a district.

The division of one community into multiple units can be summarized by two general models: (1) where increases in production lead to an increase in population beyond some threshold for effective community functioning (Hommon 1986:65); and (2) where new communities are imposed, i.e., created, by political decision making at higher levels. Here, we argue that the former is more likely to be evidenced by the successive division of land via a branching process that adheres to or mirrors features of the landscape. The latter, we suspect, is indicated when land division is more arbitrarily applied and new units are "cut out" of larger units or the landscape itself.

Leeward North Kohala ahupua'a

Archaeologists have had some limited success in documenting the chronological development of ahupua'a. Most of these studies, however, have been impressionistic; here we present the results of a more rigorous analysis based on several criteria for sequencing ahupua'a formation and which allow us to hypothesize about historical territorial trends within the moku of North Kohala. Our analysis begins with the boundaries of the 35 leeward North Kohala ahupua'a depicted on USGS maps (Figure 13.3), and again we also include archaeological evidence that supports this sequence. The analytical strategy here departs from that of the moku study, by grouping contiguous ahupua'a into increasingly larger geographic units. This inverts the likely historical sequence, moving from the most recent to older divisions of land. Upon completing the analysis, we will return to the issue of historically ordering the formation of these community territories.

It is possible to order the 35 ahupua'a into groups on the basis of a number of explicit criteria. We hypothesize that at some point in time the ahupua'a that share common names were originally part of the same territorial unit. For example, it seems likely that Kapa'a and Kapa'anui were originally part of a single territorial unit (Figure 13.4), as were Kehena 1 and Kehena 2. In our data there are six instances where adjacent ahupua'a have common names (Pu'uepa 1 and Pu'uepa 2; Kapaa 1–2 and Kapaanui; Kehena 2 and Kehena 1; Pohakulua and Pohakulua Ahula; Puanui and Puaili; and Kahua 1 and Kahua 2), and combining these results in a reduction of the original 35 ahupua'a into 29 groups. There are also instances where it is apparent that one of the last divisions cut one ahupua'a out from another. There are three instances where this relationship between units appears (Figure 13.5). Kokoili was cut out from Pu'uepa 2, Kapunapuna was cut out from Haena, and Puaili was cut out from Ki'iokalani. The relationship between the ahupua'a of Kehena 2, Puaili, Puanui, and Ki'iokalani is interesting. On the basis of a common

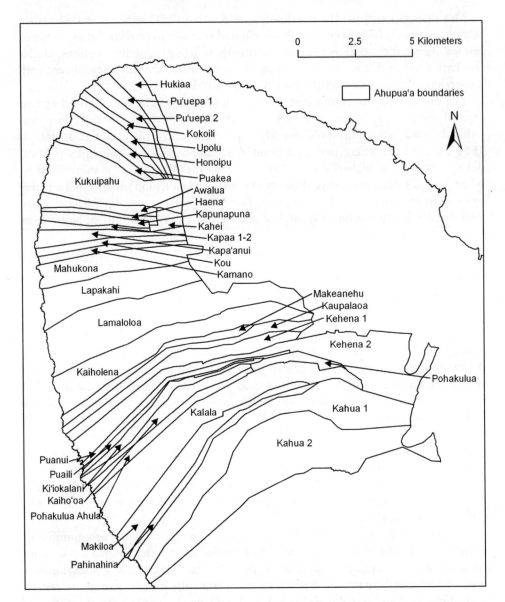

Figure 13.3 The ahupua'a of North Kohala with labels on the 35 ahupua'a that are analyzed

name, Puaili is grouped with Puanui, but on the basis of an area being cut out from another area, Puaili is grouped with Ki'iokalani, and Puanui is grouped with Kehena 2. Joining ahupua'a that share common names and cutout relationships results in 25 groups being formed. Note that most of these combinations involve the smallest ahupua'a in leeward North Kohala.

In a number of locations it is clear that ahupua'a share a common bifurcation point. There are two types of bifurcation points: joins that occur close to the

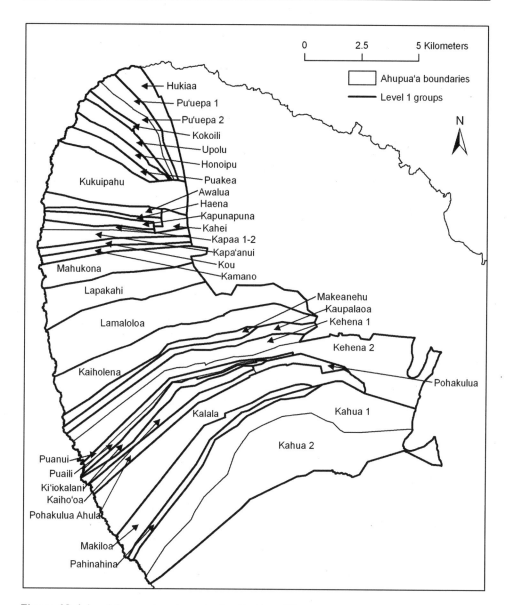

Figure 13.4 Level 1 grouping, ahupua'a classified into 29 groups

most inland extent of an ahupua'a boundary, and joins that occur part way down the long axis of an ahupua'a boundary. The former we refer to as "full" bifurcation points, and the latter as "partial" bifurcation points. We assume that partial bifurcations postdate full bifurcations. Grouping ahupua'a with partial bifurcation joins Puakea, Honoipu, and 'Upolu with Kokoili, Pu'uepa 2, and Pu'uepa 1. It also joins the boundary linking Makeanehu to Kaupalaoa; Makiloa with Kalala; and Pahinahina with Kahua 1. If we join all the ahupua'a that have

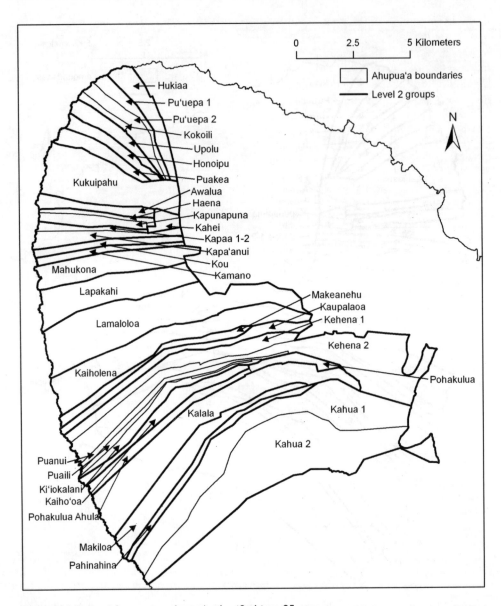

Figure 13.5 Level 2 grouping, ahupua'a classified into 25 groups

partial bifurcation points, the number of groups is reduced from 25 to 19 (Figure 13.6).

In two instances an ahupua'a caps or bounds the inland side of another ahupua'a. This occurs where Kahei caps the ahupua'a of Awalua, Haena, Kapunapuna, and Kapa'a 1–2; and where Pohakulua caps Pohakulua Ahula and Kaiho'oa (Figure 13.7). If the ahupua'a bounded by a cap are grouped together, the number of groups decreases to 15. Further joining all of the ahupua'a that have common full bifur-

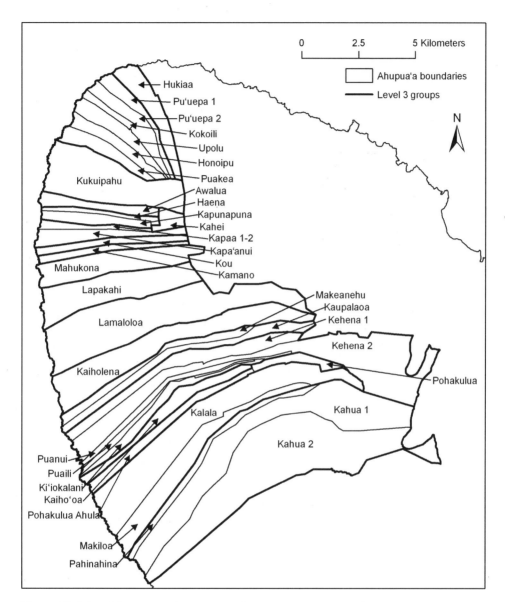

Figure 13.6 Level 3 grouping, ahupua'a classified into 19 groups

cation points further reduces the number of groups to 11 (Figure 13.8). In the north, Hukiaa is joined with the grouping of Pu'uepa 1, Pu'uepa 2, Kokoili, 'Upolu, Honoipu, and Puakea. In the south, the grouping of Pohakulua, Pohakulua Ahula, and Kaiho'oa is joined with the grouping of Makiloa and Kalala. This group is then joined with the grouping of Kehena 1, Kehena 2, Ki'iokalani, Puaili, and Puanui. Note that at this level of inclusion all of the 11 groups have boundaries that extend fully from coastline to the upper reaches of the Kohala mountains' ridgeline.

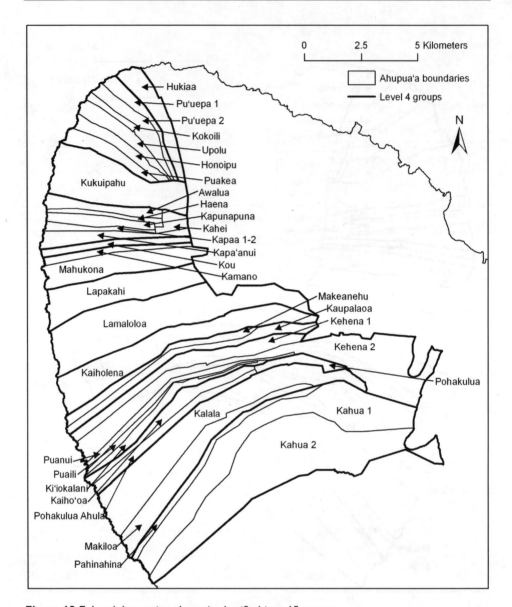

Figure 13.7 Level 4 grouping, ahupua'a classified into 15 groups

Finally, and we must admit to being a little less sure of applying the following procedure, if ahupua'a that have similar boundary orientations are grouped together, the number of groupings is reduced to nine (Figure 13.9). This last procedure is only applied in one place, where Kou and Kamano are joined with Mahukona, although this criterion could also be used to group the northernmost ahupua'a, as well as the sets comprising the Kehena grouping and the Kalala group-

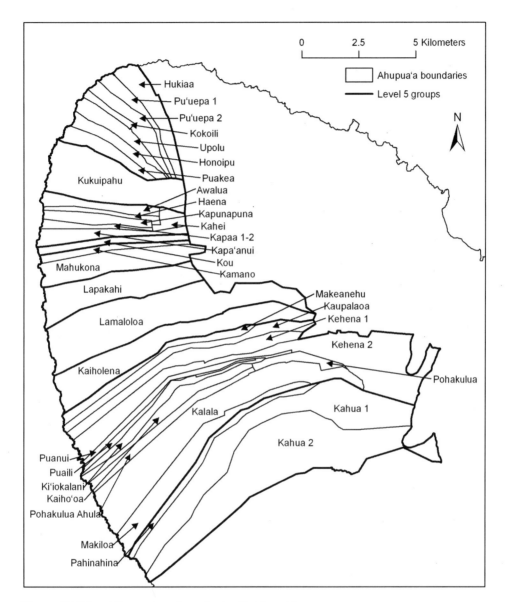

Figure 13.8 Level 5 grouping, ahupua'a classified into 11 groups

ing. These latter two sets are grouped together based on other criteria as well, e.g., partial bifurcation points, and cutouts.

The application of the rules has allowed us to identify six levels of ahupua'a groupings. The question that must be asked, however, is whether these groupings somehow reflect a chronological development. We do believe that levels 5 and 6 possibly reflect the earlier-established community territories for the leeward section

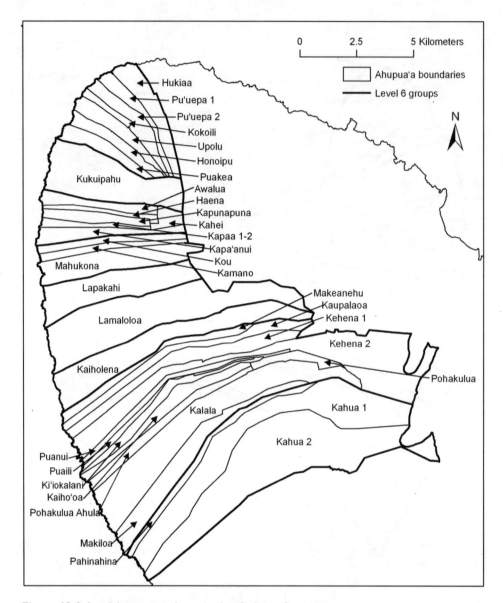

Figure 13.9 Level 6 grouping, ahupua'a classified into 9 groups.

of North Kohala. Levels 3 and 4 produce a middle array of territories, showing possible territorial divisions but with most community boundaries reaching up to or near the ridgeline. Finally, levels 1 and 2 appear to be the most recent set of community territorial divisions, resulting in some very small units as well as units whose territories do not reach the Kohala mountains' ridgeline. Additional archaeological evidence supports the notion that the groupings reflect chronological development.

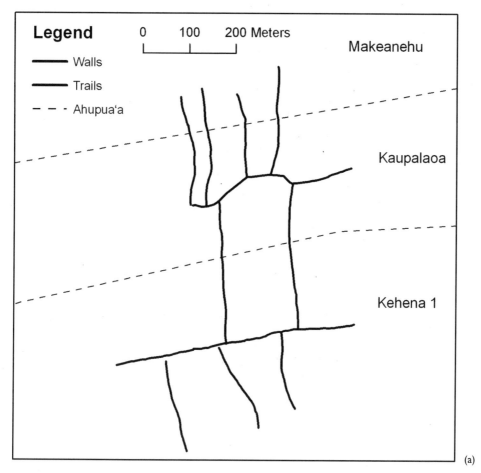

(a)

Figure 13.10 GPS data depicting suspected early, intermediate, and late phase walls and trails in the Kehena I, Kaupalaoa, and Makeanehu area

We have proposed a chronology for the development of dry-land agriculture in the North Kohala area (Ladefoged and Graves 2000; Ladefoged et al. 2003). The Kohala Field System is located in this region (Newman 1970; Rosendahl 1994), and consists of a series of field border walls and trails that extend over an area of about nineteen by four kilometers. In a separate analysis (Ladefoged et al. 2003) we elaborated a model developed by McCoy (1999) to order the construction phases of walls and trails within the Field System. Our analysis of data derived from a GPS survey of the trails and walls in the area suggests that not all ahupua'a boundaries were constructed at the same time. Specifically, if we examine the boundaries between Kehena 1, Kaupalaoa, and Makeanehu, we can document a historical pattern of their respective development. Using information on the spatial relationships between the walls and trails we suggest that during the earliest phases of

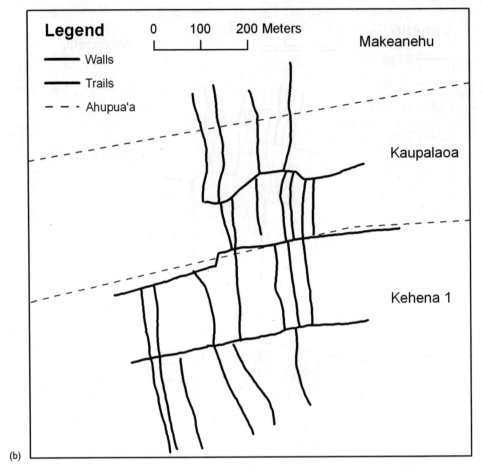

(b)

Figure 13.10 *Continued*

occupation in the area, none of the boundaries separating these ahupua'a was yet
in existence (Figure 13.10a). There were agricultural walls and trails in the area,
but none aligns with the historically documented ahupua'a territories. This temporal interval would correspond to our earliest grouping (levels 5 and 6) of
ahupua'a. Following this, a trail was constructed and this feature lines up perfectly
with the historically documented boundary between Kehena 1 and Kaupalaoa
(Figure 13.10b). It was apparently one of the first ahupua'a boundaries to be constructed in the area, and this boundary corresponds to the level 4 grouping. At some
later point, the boundary between Kaupalaoa and Makeanehu was established, and
this corresponds to a recent grouping of community subdivision (level 2) (Figure
13.10c). In sum, the ahupua'a groupings based on the boundary relationships
depicted on USGS maps coincide with the relative chronological development of
ahupua'a suggested by the GPS survey of archaeological trails and walls.

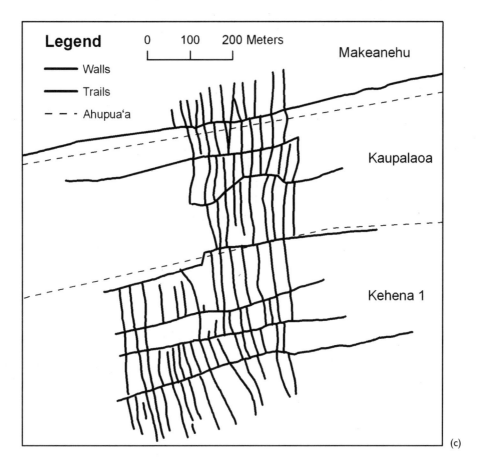

Figure 13.10 *Continued*

We have presented a methodology for identifying at least three intervals of temporal patterning in Hawaiian community territorial units. The primary data are the 35 ahupua'a in North Kohala depicted on the USGS maps. At issue are the processes by which these ahupua'a have come to be located where they are and to have acquired their dimensions and sizes. Perhaps the simplest alternative is that the ahupua'a are located where they are and as they are depicted as a result of a historical trend involving the differential subdividing of originally a small number of larger units into a larger number of smaller units through time. In this case, the higher-level groupings, such as those depicted at levels 5 or 6 (see Figures 13.8 and 13.9), might reflect earlier territorial units that were later subdivided. While the GPS data support this notion, we would conclude that additional research, including the absolute dating of archaeological material associated with territorial boundaries, is needed.

A second alternative is that ahupua'a variability, particularly the different sizes represented during the most recent temporal interval, might reflect the expansion out of one or more originally occupied areas into unoccupied buffer zones during relatively short periods of time. We think that the relatively larger southern ahupua'a of Kahua 1 and Kahua 2 may represent an area that was developed relatively quickly during the final intervals of prehistory in Hawai'i (see Ladefoged and Graves 2000). As such there has been insufficient time for these relatively large ahupua'a to undergo further subdivision.

Finally, the ahupua'a variability depicted on the USGS maps could be the result of surveying bias, with some named ahupua'a actually being 'ili or subdivisions of the real ahupua'a territories. Alternatively, in some areas communities may have divided but these were not represented on the USGS maps. For instance, there are several named divisions in Lapakahi (see Newman 1970) that are treated as 'ili but most of these are named as well. These units would have been approximately the same size as some of the other ahupua'a in North Kohala included on the USGS maps.

Conclusion

The methodology we have presented here may be applicable elsewhere in Oceania where comparable units occur. While community-scale territories are less often described, politically organized units at the scale of districts are common throughout Oceania, being reported for instance on Tahiti (Goldman 1970; Henry 1928), Mangaia (Goldman 1970; Kirch 2000), Aneityum (Spriggs 1986), Rotuma (Ladefoged 1993, 1995), Kosrae (Cordy 1993), Pohnpei (Hanlon 1988; Riesenberg 1968). Both Kosrae and Pohnpei, for example, are characterized by district-scale land units very similar in shape to those described in Hawai'i, especially Kaua'i. The kind of research described here – investigating the material and spatial expressions of human territories at different scales – promises to be a valuable means for reconstructing the history of islands and archipelagoes in the region. The research of Stevenson (2002) on Rapa Nui, and more recently by Shepardson (2005) where a set of inland *moai* "heads" are interpreted as territory boundary-markers, suggests that we are only beginning to understand the ways in which prehistoric groups were organized with respect to one another. Our analyses here do highlight the fact that the formation of Hawaiian political and community territories was complex, where in many instances larger units were divided into smaller units and this may have occurred in successive phases. It is also likely that the development of the ahupua'a that were physically mapped after European contact was not a simultaneous phenomenon, but occurred in different places at different times and over a duration of some centuries. While our methodology can help us depict different models of community and political formation, explaining these patterns of spatial and temporal variation will still require independent sets of large-scale archaeological data conjoined with interpretive frameworks that can accommodate the dynamic social and political landscape of complex Hawaiian chiefdoms.

ACKNOWLEDGMENTS

Our research was funded by a National Science Foundation biocomplexity grant (BCS-0119819), a grant from Wenner-Gren, and grants from the University of Hawai'i and the University of Auckland. The research was enhanced through discussions with Melinda Allen, Roger Green, Stephanie Jolivette, Patrick Kirch, Peter Ladefoged, Chris Lockwood, Sarina Pearson, Matthew Spriggs, Julie Stein, and Peter Vitousek. Permission to conduct fieldwork was provided by the State of Hawai'i, Department of Land and Natural Resources, and by Monty Richards (Kahua Ranch), Pono Van Holt (Ponoholo Ranch), and David Ramos (Parker Ranch).

REFERENCES

Adams, E., 2001 Approaches to the Study of Territory Size and Shape. Annual Review of Ecology and Systematics 32:277–303.

Borgerhoff Mulder, M., 1991 Human Behavioral Ecology. *In* Behavioral Ecology: An Evolutionary Approach, 3rd edition. J. Krebs and N. Davis, eds. pp. 69–98. Oxford: Blackwell Scientific.

Cachola-Abad, K., 2000 An Analysis of Hawaiian Oral Traditions: Descriptions and Explanations of the Evolution of Hawaiian Socio-Political Complexity. Ann Arbor, MI: University Microfilms.

Cordy, R., 1981 A Study of Prehistoric Social Change. New York: Academic Press.

——1993 The Lelu Stone Ruins (Kosrae, Micronesia) 1978–1981 Historical and Archaeological Research. Asian and Pacific Archaeology Series, 10. Honolulu: Social Science Research Institute, University of Hawai'i.

——2000 Exalted Sits the Chief: The Ancient History of Hawai'i Island. Honolulu: Mutual Publishing.

Dyson-Hudson, R. and E. Smith, 1978 Human Territoriality: An Ecological Assessment. American Anthropologist 80:21–41.

Earle, T., 1977 A Reappraisal of Redistribution: Complex Hawaiian Chiefdoms. *In* Exchange Systems in Prehistory. T. Earle and J. Ericson, eds. pp. 213–229. New York: Academic Press.

——1978 Economic and Social Organization of a Complex Chiefdom: The Halele'a District, Kaua'i, Hawai'i. Papers 63. Ann Arbor. MI: Museum of Anthropology, University of Michigan.

Field, J., 2004 Environment and Climatic Considerations: A Hypothesis for Conflict and the Emergence of Social Complexity in Fijian Prehistory. Journal of Anthropological Archaeology 23:79–99.

Graves, M., and K. Cachola-Abad, 1996 Seriation as a Method of Chronologically Ordering Architectural Design Traits: An Example from Hawai'i. Archaeology in Oceania 31:19–32.

——n.d. The Evolution of Social Groups in Hawai'i. Department of Anthropology, University of Hawai'i, unpublished MS.

Goldman, I., 1970 Ancient Polynesian Society. Chicago: University of Chicago Press.

Hanlon, D., 1988 Upon a Stone Altar: A History of the Island of Pohnpei to 1890. Honolulu: University of Hawaii Press.

Henry, T., 1928 Ancient Tahiti. Bernice P. Bishop Museum Bulletin 148. Honolulu: Bishop Museum Press.

Hommon, R., 1986 Social Evolution in Ancient Hawaii. *In* Island Societies: Archaeological Approaches to Evolution and Transformation. P. Kirch, ed. pp. 55–68. Cambridge: Cambridge University Press.

Hunt, T., 1990 Variation in Agricultural Production and Evolution of Socio-Political Complexity in the Hawaiian Islands. Paper presented at the Annual Meeting of the Society for American Archaeology, Las Vegas.

Kikiloi, S., n.d. The Evolution of Complex Polities in Pre-Contact Oʻahu: Measuring Social Differentiation through Heiau Architecture Variability and Oral Traditions. Unpublished MS.

Kirch, P., 1984 The Evolution of Polynesian Chiefdoms. Cambridge: Cambridge University Press.

——1985 Feathered Gods and Fishhooks: An Introduction to Hawaiian Archaeology and Prehistory. Honolulu: University of Hawaiʻi Press.

——1994 The Wet and the Dry: Irrigation and Agricultural Intensification in Polynesia. Chicago: University of Chicago Press.

——2000 On the Road of the Winds: An Archaeological History of the Pacific Islands before European Contact. Berkeley, CA: University of California Press.

Kolb, M., 1994 Monumentality and the Rise of Religious Authority in Precontact Hawaiʻi. Current Anthropology 35:521–547.

Ladefoged, T., 1993 Evolutionary Process in an Oceanic Chiefdom: Inter-group Aggression and Political Integration in Traditional Rotuman Society. Ann Arbor, MI: University Microfilms.

——1995 The Evolutionary Ecology of Rotuman Political Integration. Journal of Anthropological Archaeology 14:341–358.

Ladefoged, T., and M. Graves, 2000 Evolutionary Theory and the Historical Development of Dry Land Agriculture in North Kohala, Hawaiʻi. American Antiquity 65:423–448.

Ladefoged, T., M. Graves and M. McCoy, 2003 Archaeological Evidence for Agricultural Development in Kohala, Island of Hawaiʻi. Journal of Archaeological Science. 30:923–940.

Lipo, C., M. Madsen, R. Dunnell and T. Hunt, 1997 Population Structure, Cultural Transmission, and Frequency Seriation. Journal of Anthropological Archaeology 16:301–333.

Lyman, R., M. O'Brien and R. Dunnell, 1997 The Rise and Fall of Culture History New York: Plenum Press.

McCoy, M., 1999 Agricultural Intensification and Land Tenure in Prehistoric Hawaiʻi. M.A. dissertation. University of Auckland.

Morrell, L., and H. Kokko, 2003 Adaptive Strategies of Territory Formation. Behavioral Ecology and Sociobiology 54:385–395.

Newman, T., ed., 1970 Hawaiian Fishing and Fanning on the Island of Hawaii in A.D. 1778. Honolulu: Division of State Parks, Department of Land and Natural Resources.

Riesenberg, S., 1968 The Native Polity of Ponape. Washington, DC: Smithsonian Institution Press.

Rosendahl, P., 1994 Aboriginal Hawaiian Structural Remains and Settlement Patterns in the Upland Agricultural Zone at Lapakahi, Island of Hawaii. Hawaiian Archaeology 3:14–70.

Sahlins, M., 1958 Social Stratification in Polynesia. Seattle, WA: University of Washington Press.

Shepardson, B., 2005 The Role of Rapa Nui (Easter Island) Statuary as Territorial Boundary Markers. Antiquity 79:169–178.

Spriggs, M., 1986 Landscape, Land Use and Political Transformation in Southern Melanesia. *In* Island Societies: Archaeological Approaches to Evolution and Transformation. P. Kirch, ed. pp. 6–19. Cambridge: Cambridge University Press.

Stevenson, C., 2002 Territorial Divisions on Easter Island in the Sixteenth Century: Evidence from the Distribution of Ceremonial Architecture. *In* Pacific Landscapes: Archaeological Approaches. T. N. Ladefoged and M. W. Graves, eds. pp. 213–229. Los Osos: Easter Island Foundation.

Teltser, P., 1995 Culture History, Evolutionary Theory, and Frequency Seriation. *In* Evolutionary Archaeology: Methodological Issues. P. Teltser, ed. pp. 51–68. Tucson, AZ: University of Arizona Press.

Tschauner, H., 1994 Archaeological systematics and cultural evolution: Retrieving the honour of culture history. Man 29:77–93.

Tuggle, D., 1979 Hawaii. *In* The Prehistory of Polynesia. J. Jennings, ed. pp. 167–199. Cambridge, MA: Harvard University Press.

14

Ritual and Domestic Architecture, Sacred Places, and Images: Archaeology in the Marquesas Archipelago, French Polynesia

Sidsel Millerstrom

Launched by the former Department of Archaeology in Tahiti, a long-term Marquesas Rock Art Project commenced on the islands in 1984 (Figure 14.1). The results were astonishing (Edwards and Millerstrom 1995; Millerstrom 1985a, 1985b, 1988, 1989, 1990, 1992, 1997, 2001, 2003; Millerstrom and Edwards 1998). Approximately 6,500 individual design elements (petroglyphs), 110 wall paintings (pictographs), and 91 anthropomorphic stone sculptures were located and documented. Recently, archaeological research on rock art was carried out on the north coast of Nuku Hiva, specifically in the western section of Hatiheu Valley (Millerstrom 2001, 2003; also Ottino 2002).

When completed, the investigations will yield a great deal of information on spatial and temporal sociopolitical variation. Results to hand show that many of the images are associated with what were tentatively interpreted as ritual sites. Many of these sites are both extensive and complex but Marquesan ritual complexes (*ahu* or *me'ae*) are among the most difficult prehistoric architecture in the archipelago to identify. In part this is because they differ considerably in placement, size, and architectural components. Despite ethnohistoric accounts and previous archaeological study of ritual architecture, this research problem has only been highlighted lately (Kellum-Ottino 1971; Millerstrom 2001; Rolett 1998). One of the reasons for this is that Polynesian archaeologists have in the past focused largely on monumental structures such as tribal ceremonial complexes (cf. Walter and Sheppard, this volume).

It is critical to address the question of ritual architecture because archaeological interpretation of rock art, one of the most challenging cultural records of the past

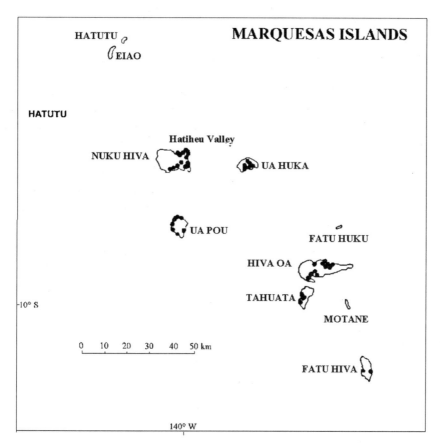

Figure 14.1 Marquesas Islands, French Polynesia

to understand, depends to a significant degree on being able to associate the images with archaeological structures, features, and artifacts (Millerstrom and Kirch 2002, 2004). How then can archaeological methods and theories help to establish the past functions of these structures? What constitutes a sacred, ritual, or taboo (*tapu*) site? For instance, how does ritual architecture differ from that of a chiefly household unit? Can we expect variations in ritual architecture according to the status of the people associated with the various places? Finally, what is the spatial relationship between archaeological art and architecture and how did it vary through time? In this chapter I first give an overview of previous archaeological (including ethnoarchaeological) research in the Marquesas and then discuss recent archaeological field surveys of domestic and ritual complexes. The results of this current fieldwork are tentative as the data are culled from the first year of a three-year field study.

Archaeological Art

Petroglyphs and pictographs

The terms "archaeological art" and "rock art" refer here to anthropomorphic sculptures (*tiki*), images carved on boulders (petroglyphs), and painted figures on walls of rockshelters (pictographs). I use the term "rock art" provisionally as it is imbued with Western connotations that in my view have little to do with Marquesan perspectives. Marquesan rock art sorts into five distinct categories: anthropomorphs, zoomorphs, material objects, geometric design, and plant forms. Human figures occur in several different subclasses, with numerous variations in each category. However, contrary to what is generally assumed (Linton 1925; Suggs 1961), circular geometric motifs, not human figures, constitute the largest category. Numerically, geometrics represent 66 percent of the total motifs recorded for the archipelago whereas anthropomorphs make up only 23 percent (Millerstrom 1997, 2001). Among the anthropomorphs the most prevalent types are stick figures and faces or *mata kome* (Figures 14.2 and 14.3). Along with combinations of curvilinear geometrics, these figures are also seen in other cultural materials such as tattoos and objects carved in bone and wood.

Overall, the Marquesan motif repertoire is limited in its range of types; it is repetitive and remarkably homogeneous. Although attribute variations do occur, the same motifs can be found on all the islands in the archipelago. This homogeneity in archaeological art and decoration on cultural objects collected in the early historic period suggests that Marquesan decorative organization embodied a collective belief system and that a great amount of inter-island contact occurred in the past to maintain inter-island cohesiveness. The archaeological art appears to be associated with shrines, chiefs' platforms, and temples within the public tribal complexes. Petroglyphs that occur on public me'ae are placed on the facing stones, on the top surface of the platform, or in some cases around the upper part of stone-lined sunken pits. Images were also placed on large boulders incorporated into the me'ae complexes (Millerstrom 1997). As I will discuss later, however, the majority of the images in the Hatiheu Valley on Nuku Hiva are not associated with ritual places but rather with high-status architecture.

Although the petroglyphs may date back to the settlement period, this is largely speculation. The earliest relative date is from Ha'ata'ive'a Valley, Nuku Hiva. A petroglyph slab with a human face was excavated from a stratigraphic layer between two earth ovens. The upper oven was in use sometime between A.D. 1100 and A.D. 1400 (Suggs 1961:66–67). The petroglyphs are perhaps a precursor to the human sculptures that developed in several stages. It is clear, though, that petroglyphs and human sculptures overlap in time and space.

Anthropomorphic sculptures (tiki)

Ninety-one tiki were documented during my field research in the islands. Elsewhere four anthropomorphic heads were uncovered during excavation of a me'ae in

Anaho
331 ANA 3b

To scale

Figure 14.2 Anthropomorphic stick figure, Anaho, Nuku Hiva

Vaitahu, Tahuata in 1900 (Rolett n.d.:1–5). Several sculptures also have been recently discovered on Hiva Oa (Olivier pers. comm. 2002, 2003). Thirty-seven of the 91 tiki are carved of basalt and another 37 are carved of red volcanic tuff (*ke'etu*, solidified ash). The remaining 16 are cut from gray or yellow tuff. Traces of red pigment were noticed on one of the images on me'ae Iopona, Puamau Valley, Hiva Oa (Linton1925:162; Millerstrom and Edwards 1998) and on one statue on the

TAIPIVAI

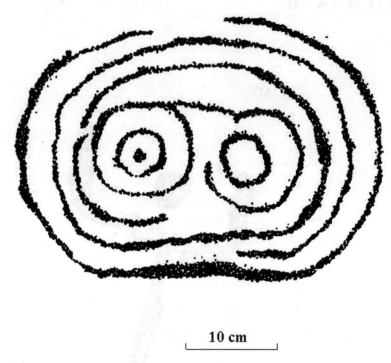

10 cm

Figure 14.3 Anthropomorphic face (*mata komoe*), Taipivai Valley, Nuku Hiva

me'ae of a tribal ceremonial complex in Punai Valley, Hiva Oa (Millerstrom and Edwards 1998). Dating the statues is problematic and their age is still uncertain. It appears, however, that they were developed in the late prehistoric period and continued to be carved into the historical era (Millerstrom and Edwards 1998; Suggs 1961). The majority of the Marquesan stone sculptures recorded in situ were linked to me'ae.

Linton (1925:70–95) correctly observed that, in general, Marquesan tiki can depict either males or females. However, taking into account all the sculptures, heads, and torsos, 75 percent of known tiki are genderless. About 18 percent are male and about seven percent female. Linton (1925:116) claimed that at the site of Paeke, in Taipivai, all the human stone sculptures represent females. This position is not supported by recent archaeological research. Of the 12 statues, four represent females and four represent males. The sex of the remaining sculptures remains undetermined.

The pervasive geometric and human motifs, especially the face motifs, expressed on the surface in most media collected at the time of Western contact, including images on calabashes, canoes, house posts, bone, and human skin as well as stone, identify and intensify the ideology of the Marquesans in the past. A pervasive art system can help promote and reinforce social solidarity in order to maintain belief systems that bolster the political position of hereditary chiefs, priests, or warriors. Pervasive decorative organization experiences a much lower rate of change than, for example, an opposing partitive art system which displays no uniform decorative organization in different media (DeBoer 1991:157). DeBoer's theoretical perspective has important implications regarding changes in the Marquesan art system and how these changes reflect social transformation.

In general, the archaeological art lacks cultural context and the extent of its spatial and temporal diversity is largely unknown. However, recent archaeological research on both the regional and individual site levels has shed considerable light on the images' spatial distribution, socio-political context, and architectural associations. The next part of the chapter discusses what we know about Marquesan architecture.

Domestic and Ritual Architecture

Three major types of architectural sites have been defined in the Marquesas on the basis of variations in form and function among the various architectural stone remains described in ethnohistoric and ethnographic accounts (e.g., Crook n.d. [1790]; Delmas 1927; Handy 1923; Linton 1925; Porter 1970 [1822]; Tautain 1897) and more recent archaeological work (e.g., Bellwood 1972; Kellum-Ottino 1971; Millerstrom 2001; Ottino 1990; Rolett 1998; Suggs 1961). They include (1) residential sleeping platforms (*paepae hiamoe*), (2) sacred structures (ahu or me'ae), and (3) tribal ceremonial complexes (*tohua*). While the residential platforms and ceremonial complexes are relatively easy to identify, the category of sacred structures is problematic.

Residential sleeping platforms (paepae hiamoe)

Sleeping platforms are the most common structures observed and their overall morphology is relatively standardized throughout the archipelago (Bellwood 1972; Crook n.d.[1790]:cxxxii; Handy 1923; Kellum-Ottino 1971; Krusenstern 1968 [1813]:159; Linton 1923, 1925; Melville 1964 [1846]:98–99; Ottino 1990; Porter 1970 [1822]:39). According to Crook (n.d. [1790]:cxxxii), all Marquesan houses were of similar construction and building material, but differed in size. Every family had a house where they slept, but only the women and children would cook and eat there. While size and associated features differ, a paepae hiamoe was typically a single-terraced rectangular structure. Owing to the often rugged topography, most platforms were terraced on hillsides. The height of the facing wall generally signified the status of the occupants. All sides were faced with roughly fitted boulders while the interior was earth- and rubble-filled. The top surface consisted of two parts. The front part or terrace was paved with water-worn river stones (*kiva*) or irregular stones set in mud during construction. The other half, a raised sleeping area, was mostly unpaved. Sometimes a small part of the sleeping area was paved and served as a storage place for special objects (Lisiansky 1968:72).

A dividing wall separated the sleeping space and the terrace. It consisted of fitted basalt boulders sometimes intermixed with rectangular slabs of red volcanic tuff. In Hatiheu Valley some of the slabs were cut beach-rock (*papatea*, "white rock"). A structure of perishable material (e.g., bamboo poles, pandanus and breadfruit leaves, coconut trunks and fronds) was constructed over the sleeping section (Handy 1923; Linton 1925; Porter 1970 [1822]:39–40; Von den Steinen 1969 [1925]; Tautain 1897).

Sacred structures (me'ae or ahu)

Linton (1925:31) writes that the term "me'ae" was used in the southern Marquesas and in Ua Huka to designate a sacred place while in Nuku Hiva and Ua Pou the term "ahu" was used. However, both terms mean a sacred place for Dordillon (1931) and Le Cléac'h (1997). I use me'ae to designate any sacred tribal place. These sites are similar to residential house platforms in their construction (Linton 1925:34), but are highly variable and so can be difficult to identify. Thus Kellum-Ottino (1971) questioned some previous identifications of me'ae in Hane Valley, while Rolett (1998:119) was unable to identify the me'ae part of tohua Aimaha in Hanamiai, Tahuata. One of the main reasons me'ae are difficult to define may be that a chief's paepae hiamoe sometimes became a me'ae after his death (Millerstrom 2001).

The first Westerners to the Marquesas observed that me'ae were located apart from villages, surrounded by palisades. A house with wooden tiki was located in the center (Markham 1904:27). In other early accounts me'ae were described as consisting of one or two houses built on a square raised stone platform. Tall drums were stored inside and life-sized wooden or stone tiki were placed outside (Radiguet 1978 [1860]; Tautain 1897; Wilson 1997 [1797]:110). Wilson (1997 [1797]:110) described an ornamental shield-shaped surface with a pyramid-like side "wrought with small reeds" stained in different colors with the figure of a bird placed on the top. Linton (1925) distinguished between public me'ae linked to tohua and separate mortuary me'ae. A me'ae could also be a fisherman's shrine located near the sea, or it could be a household me'ae. Generally, me'ae were more complex in the southern islands than in Nuku Hiva (Linton 1925). This was confirmed by Bellwood (1972) in one southern locality, Hanatekua, where the me'ae consisted of several terraces, enclosures, and sunken areas. Me'ae were universally associated with special trees or sacred groves. Banyan trees (*aoa*; *Ficus* sp.) were considered to be more sacred than all other trees and would grow on or near the platform (Handy 1923:119).

While a chief resided over the tohua, the me'ae was the domain of the priestly establishment. The priestly establishment consisted of an inspirational priest or priestess, and their attendants. The temple was considered a place for the gods and tapu for the general population, so such places were greatly feared. Me'ae were always tapu to women other than inspirational priestesses, but during certain ceremonies, no one, not even the chief, could enter (Linton 1923:120).

Tribal ceremonial complexes (tohua)

A tohua or *taha ko'ina* served as a tribal assembly place where feasts (*ko'ina*) and certain ceremonies took place. Although they differ greatly in size, in the number of surrounding platforms, and in attached architectural components, these sites are generally easy to recognize archaeologically. Typically they consisted of a complex of paepae, raised platforms for spectators and visitors, terraces, pavements, alignments, and enclosures surrounding a large rectangular unpaved court (Krusenstern 1968 1813]:133; Porter 1970 [1822]:105; Handy 1923; Linton 1925). The French sandalwood trader Camille de Roquefeuil (1823:48–49) reported that the rectangular section was some 30 meters long and a quarter of that wide. Unlike the me'ae in the northern Marquesas, the tohua in Nuku Hiva were enclosed and were larger, better constructed, and more complex compared to the tohua in the rest of the Marquesas. The structures were constructed of massive basaltic stones (*ke'etu*), and located in elevated (up to three meters high) and prominent positions.

Frequently, large communal subterranean silos for storing fermented breadfruit (*ma*) were located nearby. However, in the western section of Hatiheu Valley, breadfruit silos were associated not only with the tribal community complexes but also linked to elite households (Millerstrom 2001). One tohua, Porter (1970 [1822]:39) wrote, was located high up in a valley, next to a river at the foot of a mountain. It consisted of 16 houses around a public square. The open space was shaded by special trees (Melville 1964 [1846]) such as breadfruit, coconut, and *toa* trees (*Casuarina equisetifolia*). Porter (1970 [1822]:39) noted that the houses on the tohua platforms were unoccupied except during periods of feasting.

In general, each Marquesan valley was occupied by one or several related social groups (*mata'eina'a*), each with their own public ceremonial center (Handy 1923; Linton 1925:24; compare Ladefoged and Graves, this volume, regarding such territorial divisions in Hawai'i). In a few instances two related tribes shared one tohua. Although in one recorded case a tohua had no chief (Linton 1925), these sites were the domain of the hereditary tribal *haka'iki* or in some cases a chiefess (*ha'atepei'u*). All social functions related to the chief and his family took place on the tohua. For instance, the death of an important chief, which created a great deal of social stress, was followed by a series of ritual activities, many of which took several years to complete (Handy 1923). The tohua formed the center of the community where social activities that concerned the whole tribe took place, including commemorative feasts (*mau*) for important persons other than the chiefs.

During feasts, ritual activities were performed by the priests (*tuhuna o'ono*) at one end of the tohua, while musicians, women, children, dancers, drummers, and visiting tribes occupied other platforms. It is unclear whether inspirational priestesses played any part at all in ritual activities on the tohua. It is also hard to identify which social groups normally occupied precisely which of the various platforms in any particular tohua. Linton (1925), who recorded numerous structures and features, did not, in general, specify the function of individual structures. Thus it is unclear which structures on the tohua were used by the priests/priestesses, the chiefs/chiefesses, the warriors, women and children, and spectators during ceremonies. It is known that certain parts of the dance floor were forbidden to women and children (Linton 1925:25) but that they occupied special platforms on the tohua (Handy 1923:36; Lawson n.d. [1861–1867]; Linton 1925:25). At tohua Nanauhi, Hatiheu Valley, for instance, a platform which formed part of the spectators' area was reserved for women and children (Linton 1925:118, Figure 6, nos. 31 and 32). It is also known that the haka'iki and his warriors regularly occupied separate platforms within the tohua even though they lived in the vicinity of the ceremonial complex.

The chief's residential unit was usually placed along one of the long sides of the dance floor, from where the chief could overlook festivities taking place (Handy 1923; Linton 1925). However, the chief's paepae did not always overlook the dance space, as was the case at tohua Tekeia, Hanapaoa Valley, Hiva Oa, where the chief and the chiefess occupied two paepae upstream from the dance floor (Linton 1925:171). According to Krusenstern (1968 [1813]:159), the chief's residence was similar to the other structures but was larger, better built, and appears to have been 60 centimeters higher. At tohua Tamaeka, Hakamoui Valley (Ua Pou), the chief's paepae measured 5 meters × 8 meters and 3 meters high and was situated on a hill (Linton 1925:135). Different platforms of the tohua were assigned for visiting tribes where they could build houses in which to live during the festivities. At such times the visiting chief sat in front of the house of the local chief (Handy 1923; Linton 1925:25). The chief's establishment could also be placed at the short end of the dance floor. At tohua Ponaouoho on Nuku Hiva, for instance, the chief's residence occupied the whole northern end of the tohua with an establishment consisting of a sleeping house, another small house, and a cookhouse (Linton 1925:108, 114, 117, 135). The wall facing the dance floor measured 1.8 meters in height (Linton 1925:109, Figure 3).

Many of the chiefs' paepae, whether part of a tohua proper or located in other areas of the valley, appeared to contain well-carved house posts (Linton 1925:175). Placement of structure, height of wall, the type of stones used, and the amount of decoration signify high status in Oceania. An early description of Pohnepeian houses in Micronesia provided by James F. O'Connell, a Western resident who lived on Pohnpei from approximately 1828 until 1833, states that "dwelling houses seldom exceed forty feet by twenty . . ." while commoners' houses were even smaller. But ceremonial houses were often 30 meters in length and 15 meters wide (Morgan 1988:79; cf. Rainbird, this volume).

Warriors' platform (the tapu house)

The hereditary chief was often also the chief warrior (Handy 1923), but he was obliged to house and feed his men to assure their loyalty (Krusenstern 1968 [1813]:160). Crook (n.d. [1790]) referred to the warriors' house as the "tabbu" house. The men ate their meals and consumed kava, made weapons, ornaments, and drums on the platform, and stored tapu objects such as war paraphernalia in the thatch of the sleeping area, the tapu place. During warfare, when the men were considered tapu and could not be in contact with women, they also slept on the tohua (Handy 1923).

This sacred place was marked with white bark-cloth (*tapa*) banners and women and commoners were forbidden to walk past it (Crook n.d. [1790]; Porter 1970 [1822]). Some men, of the Kiao or Kioe class, could eat with women (Crook n.d. [1790]:cxvi), but most men were tapu (sacred), lived at the warriors' house near the ceremonial place, and had little to do with the opposite sex. Said Crook, "the tabbu house is usually situated upon a raised pavement made of large stones, the bounds of which cannot be passed by women; nor, even, if it belongs to any person of a superior class, by men of the general tabbu class" (Crook n.d. [1790]:cxxvi).

In the southern Marquesas the warriors often had a separate structure (Linton 1925), but on Nuku Hiva the warriors' platforms appear to have been part of the tohua. The warriors' house tended to be long, with narrow bed spaces, and, like the chief's house, built of massive stones and located at the outer edge of the dance floor (Linton 1925:117, 172; 1923). Melville (1964 [1846]:110) described a long warrior platform measuring more than 60 meters in length and 6 meters in width. Porter (1970 [1822]:38) reported that some "tabbooed" houses measured 30 meters in length and 12 meters in width:

> The whole front of this latter structure was completely open, and from one end to the other ran a narrow veranda, fenced in on the edge of the pi-pi [paepae] with a picket of canes. Its interior presented the appearance of an immense lounging place, the entire floor being strewn with successive layers of mats, lying between parallel trunks of coconut trees, selected for the purpose from the straightest and most symmetrical the vale afforded. (Porter [1822] 1970:38)

Were women allowed on the tribal ceremonial complexes?

As mentioned earlier, there is little in the literature concerning the place of priests, warriors, and particularly the women on the tohua. This last is not surprising, considering that almost all observers – from explorers to missionaries to archaeologists – were men. Willowdean Chatterson Handy accompanied her husband, the ethnologist E. S. Craighill Handy, as a volunteer associate on the Bayard Dominick Expedition to the Marquesas in 1920. She published several academic books and novels based on her experiences in the islands, but unfortunately had little to say about Marquesan women. However, a beachcomber named Robarts, who lived in the islands for several years, called the tribal ceremonial place a "play-ground" or "dancing ground." He claims to have taken part on several occasions in festivities with females of high rank and their attendants on the play-ground, but the women he describes appear to be of the tapu class because elsewhere he says women were not permitted in tapu areas (Dening 1974:89, 100, 111, 155).

Porter, on the other hand, had this to say about women and the public ceremonial places:

> The women are, on no occasions whatever, allowed to enter their places of feasting, which are houses raised, to the height of six or eight feet on a platform of large stones, neatly hewn and fitted together, with as much skill and exactness, as would be done by our most expert masons: and some of them are one hundred yards [91.5 m] in length and forty yards [36.5 m] in width, surrounded by a square of buildings executed in a style of elegance, which is calculated to inspire us with the most exalted opinion of the ingenuity, taste, and perseverance of a people, who have hitherto remained unnoticed, and unknown to the rest of mankind. (Porter 1970 [1822]:38)

Elsewhere he wrote that all sacred places and places that were tapu for women were marked with "a bundle of long sticks, about half the size of the wrist, with the bark stripped off and placed on end" (Porter 1970 [1822]:116).

Four years after Captain Porter's departure in 1817, de Roquefeuil spent several weeks in the islands on the ship Le Bordelais. He wrote that in Taiohae both men and women met at a feasting place (Roquefeuil 1823:48–49). It is uncertain whether the discrepancies between his account and Porter's result from regional or temporal cultural changes or to status variations. Like Porter and Robarts, Crook (n.d. [1790]) and Kabris (Terrell 1982:110) wrote that ordinary females were not allowed to come near the altars or enter sacred places. There is no doubt that what Kabris referred to as a "maraie" was the sacred part of the tribal ceremonial place: "these temples are sacred, and each one takes three to four thousand heads to bring it to perfection. Entry is forbidden to women, children and men who have not yet been to war" (Terrell 1982:110).

In short, while it is clear that a woman could not go near the me'ae unless she was involved in religious ceremonies as a spiritual priestess, the historical sources disagree on the presence or absence of women on the tribal ceremonial complexes. Following Tautain (1897), it seems reasonable to propose that women were allowed on certain parts of the tohua at certain times. If religious and secular rites were being performed, access depended on where the tapu men's house and the me'ae were situated on the tohua. Women were allowed on certain platforms and on parts of the dance floor, perhaps near the chief's residence, but could not enter or be close to the me'ae and the warriors' house. Access also depended on the personal status of the woman. Inspirational priestesses and high-ranking women were exempt from restrictions put on the men and the women from the mata'hina'a class.

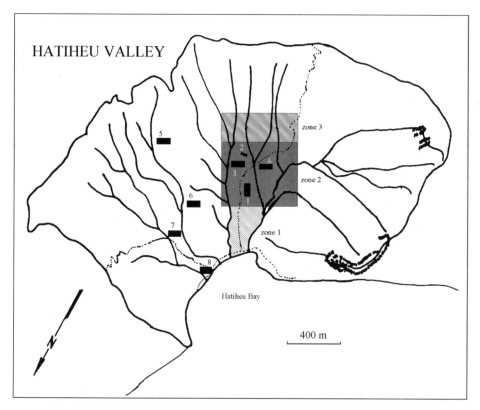

Figure 14.4 Map of Hatiheu Valley showing zones I–III and Tohua Hikoku'a (1), Tohua Kamuihei II (2), Tohua Kamuihei I (3), Tohua Tahakia (4), Tohua Maikuku (5), Tohua Pa'aha'ua (6), Tohua Ninauhi (7), and Tohua Pahumano (8)

The foregoing suggests that the tohua was divided into a strict tapu place and a more communal or public space. Perhaps the women's presence and absence on the tohua, as variously described by the early visitors, changed according to the seasons and the different ceremonies that were performed during the year.

Settlement Patterns in the Hatiheu Valley, Nuku Hiva

Because a large amount of archaeological art is located on the north coast of Nuku Hiva, specifically in Hatiheu Valley, a settlement pattern study was conducted in the western section of the valley in the 1990s (Millerstrom 1991, 2001). Archaeological survey was undertaken between Vaiu'ua and Puhi'oho, two of the four major rivers dissecting the valley (Figure 14.4). All surface structures and above-ground features were mapped and recorded. Three distinct settlement zones were evident. Architectural remains in the coastal area, Zone I, were sparsely distributed for the first 200 meters inland from the beach. Not surprisingly, archaeological remains were intermixed with modern structures. The greatest concentration of archaeological remains was located in the central section, Zone II, approximately 50 meters above sea level. Five test excavations were undertaken at various elevations in Zone II. Zone III, at the head of the valley, contains few above-surface archaeological remains and no visible rock art.

A total of 158 structures, including those incorporated in the Hikoku'a–Kamuihei–Tahakia ceremonial cluster, were recorded and mapped. Thirty-one of the 78 sleeping houses (paepae hiamoe) were located on the tohua. At least four structures among the total number were me'ae; several others may have been temples or shrines but for the time being they remain unidentified. The remaining architecture consisted of platforms and terraces (Millerstrom 2001). Megalithic underground breadfruit pits (*ua ma*) are linked to many of the high-status residential units (Figure 14.5). The spatial distribution of petroglyphs and sculptures, tribal ceremonial complexes, and domestic architecture and features demonstrated that the area had been divided into two separate settlements. While the elite occupied the eastern parts, including four public tribal ceremonial complexes situated in close proximity to each other (tohua Hikoku'a, Kamuihei I, II, and Tahakia), the elite residential units extended behind the tohua to the steep and narrow Ototemoui ridge to the south and southeast, and to Kahuvai, located southwest and adjacent to Puhi'oho River. The ordinary people, the mata'eina'a, lived in the agricultural sector to the west.

The majority of the rock art was not found on the tohua but on and around high-status residential units. Indeed, there are significant increases in motif frequency, complexity, and variability away from the ceremonial complexes. Of the total of 1,282 figures, only about 12 percent occur on the tohua, while 85 percent are found in the Hikoku'a-Kamuihei-Tahakia, Ototemoui, and Kahuvai elite residential regions. Of this total number, about 57 percent are geometrics and 31 percent depict anthropomorphs. The other images that are represented are zoomorphs. In descending order of frequency they include dog, turtle, fish, bird, lizard, octopus, and unidentified creatures.

Images in the Niuamapu-Tauehua agricultural area to the west, below Kahuvai near Puhi'oho River, comprise a mere three sites with a total of 30 figures, or around two percent of the total number of images in Zone II. Geometric motifs comprise less than one percent and anthropomorphs less than two percent. Cultural remains consist mostly of terraces and extensive irrigated taro fields. Domestic house sites and associated ma pits are small and less complex. The prevalence of geometric and anthropomorphic figures reflects personal status and prestige. These figures, associated with late-period architecture, correspond with historic tattoo designs and carved decorative motifs on elite regalia such as bone fan handles, war clubs, stilt foot-holders, carved turtle-shell head pieces, and so on. The remarkable similarities between archaeological images and the motifs on historic material objects suggest that, while emphasis and distribution of motifs changed according to time and place, the fundamental principles regarding the symbolic repertoire remained basically intact after European contact.

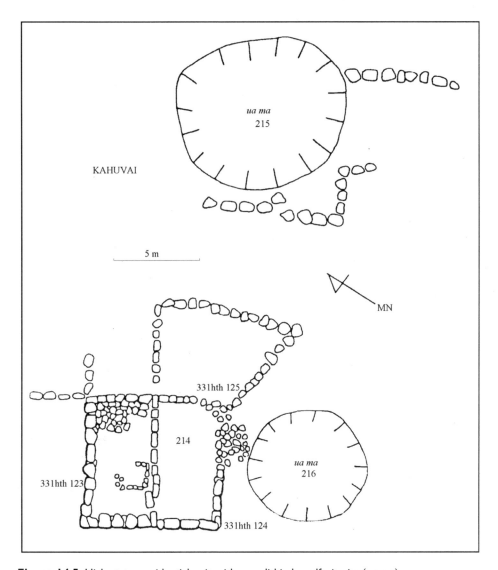

Figure 14.5 High-status residential unit with megalithic breadfruit pits (*ua ma*)

Tentative Results of the 2002 Archaeological Field Survey

In total, 15 ritual complexes, 11 petroglyph boulders, and four tiki were documented in the field in 2002. In addition, I documented another 12 tiki in the Kaikahanui Museum in Taiohae on Nuku Hiva (Millerstrom 2003). The identifications of some of the architecture remain uncertain pending further investigation. The archaeological survey was mainly a reconnaissance to understand the general distribution of ahu/me'ae architecture on the northern coast of Nuku Hiva, an area with which I am familiar from my extensive rock art research in the region (Millerstrom 2001). The project began in Taiohae Valley. Field investigation also took place in the valleys of Taipivai, Hakapa'a, Hatiheu, and Anaho.

My research on ritual architecture is incomplete and as description and analysis proceed, a pattern will emerge that will help identify the ambiguous structures. However, there are some general characteristics that appear to be associated with most of the ritual architectural complexes mapped to date. They are often placed on narrow ridges. Almost without exception, one or more banyan *Ficus* (sp.) or kamanu (*Calophyllum inophyllum*) trees grow on or next to each structure. Most of the mapped me'ae are extensive and complex. They have multiple terraces partly paved with smooth river stones (kiva), and numerous polished boulders. At some sites petroglyphs were positioned on a boulder in the facing walls, and some structures have one or more tiki. Pieces of branch coral and *Murex* and oyster shells were sometimes placed in one wall, or on a platform or pavement. This placement had ritual significance: at prehistoric sites at Ha'atuatua and Ue'a on Nuku Hiva similar shells were associated with ceremonial sites (Humphrey and Suggs 1995; Suggs 1961). Building materials sometimes consisted of megalithic boulders but more often walls were built of small stones. Rectangular-cut stones of red volcanic tuff (ke'etu) were incorporated into only one of the 15 structures I examined. The names of the me'ae, as recorded by early missionaries, are problematic. Few names are remembered today, but sites known to local residents as tapu structures are perhaps ahu/me'ae complexes.

Although much remains to be done, the results indicate that a settlement pattern approach of the sort I have pursued can generate the sort of data required to shed light on questions of cultural change and is particularly well suited to the study of archaeological art in the Marquesas Islands. While we will never be able to fully understand each individual Marquesan image and its use, examining the spatial relationship of images at the site level as well as at intertribal and regional scales can help us understand some of the significance of images in the lives of the Marquesans. When combined with archaeological excavation, this type of investigation will enable us to place the Marquesan images in their proper cultural time-frame.

ACKNOWLEDGMENTS

I wish to thank the government of French Polynesia, Dr. Priscille Tea Frogier, Director of Service de la Culture et du Patrimoine, and Dr. Henri Marchesi for granting me a permit to continue to conduct research in the Marquesas Islands. No doubt I would have been less successful without information and generous assistance provided by the people of the Marquesas. Field research is never done in isolation. Edmundo Edwards, various volunteers, field assistants, and I worked together in the Marquesas from 1984 to 1989. I thank them for friendship and support. While a considerable amount of work on rock art has taken place in the archipelago in the 1990s, especially on Nuku Hiva, much of my work is based on those first field seasons. I especially wish to acknowledge Heidy Baumgartner Lesage for assistance in the field as well as in helping in many other capacities. Once again I am indebted to my daughter Jessica Gypsy Millerstrom for finding more mistakes than I care to think about.

REFERENCES

Bellwood, P., 1972 A Settlement Pattern Survey, Hanatekua Valley, Hiva Oa, Marquesas Islands. Pacific Anthropological Records 17. Honolulu: Department of Anthropology, Bernice P. Bishop Museum.

Crook, W., n.d. [1790] Account of the Marquesas Islands. In Marquesan Source Materials 1952. G. Sheahan, ed. The Mitchell Library, Sydney, unpublished MS.

DeBoer, W., 1991 The Decorative Burden: Design, Medium, and Change. In Ceramic Ethnoarchaeology. W. Longacre, ed. pp. 144–161. Tucson, AZ: The University of Arizona Press.

Delmas, S., 1927 La Religion ou Le Paganisme des Marquisiens. Paris: Gabriel Beauchesne.

Dening, G., ed., 1974 The Marquesan Journal of Edward Robarts 1797–1824. Honolulu: University Press of Hawai'i.

Dordillon, M., 1931 Grammaire et Dictionnaire de la Langue des Iles Marquises. Paris: Marquisien-Français.

Edwards, E., and S. Millerstrom, 1995 Peintures Rupestres de la Vallée de Eiaone a Hiva Oa. Bulletin de la Société des Etudes Océaniennes 267:5–17.

Handy, E., 1923 The Native Culture in the Marquesas. Bernice P. Bishop Museum Bulletin 9. Honolulu: Bishop Museum Press.

Humphrey, L., and R. Suggs, 1995 Mata Peto: An Unusual Marquesan Tiki. Pacific Arts 11–12:10–19.

Kellum-Ottino, M., 1971 Archéologie d'une Vallée des Iles Marquises. Publications de la Société des Océanistes 26. Paris: Musée de l'Homme.

Krusenstern, A., 1968 [1813] Voyage Round the World in the Years 1803, 1804, 1805, and 1806, vol. 1. Bibliotheca Australiana 38. New York: Da Capo Press.

Lawson, T., n.d. [1861–1867] Manuscripts, Letters, and Notes. Honolulu: Bernice P. Bishop Museum, unpublished MS.

Le Cléac'h, H., 1997 Pona Te'ao Tapapatina. Lexique Marquisien-Français. Papeete: L'Harmattan.

Linton, R., 1923 The Material Culture of the Marquesas Islands, vol. VIII(5). Memoirs of the Bernice P. Bishop Museum. Honolulu: Bishop Museum Press.

——1925 Archaeology of the Marquesas Islands. Bernice P. Bishop Museum Bulletin 23. Honolulu: Bishop Museum Press.

Lisiansky, U., 1968 [1814] A Voyage Round the World in the Years 1803, 4, 5, and 6. New York: Da Capo Press.

Markham, S., 1904 The Voyages of Pedro Fernandez de Quiros, 1595 to 1606, 2 vols. London: The Hakluyt Society.

Melville, H., 1964 [1846] Typee. New York: Signet Classic.

Millerstrom, S., 1985a Rock Art in the Marquesas Islands: A Preliminary Report. La Pintura 12(1):7.

——1985b Up-Date on Marquesan Rock Art. La Pintura 12(2):5–6.

——1988 Rock Art in the Marquesas Islands. Rapa Nui Journal 2(2):1–3.

——1989 Experimental Archaeology in Rock Art. Rapa Nui Journal 3(2):1.

——1990 Marquesas Rock Art Project. Rapa Nui Journal 4(1):4–6.

——1992 Report on the Marquesas Islands Rock Art Project. Pacific Arts 6:19–25.

——1997 Carved and Painted Rock Images in the Marquesas Islands, French Polynesia. Archaeology in Oceania 32:181–196.

——2001 Images Carved in Stones and Settlement Patterns Archaeology in Hatiheu Valley, Nuku Hiva, the Marquesas Islands, French Polynesia. Ph.D. dissertation, University of California, Berkeley.

——2003 Ritual Architecture in the Northern Marquesas Archipelago. Bilan de la Recherche Archéologique en Polynésie Française 2001–2002. Punaauia, Tahiti: Service de la Culture et du Patrimoine.

Millerstrom, S., and E. Edwards, 1998 Stone Sculptures of the Marquesas Islands (French Polynesia). *In* Easter Island in Pacific Context, South Seas Symposium. C. Stevenson, ed. pp. 55–62. Los Osos, CA: The Easter Island Foundation.

Millerstrom, S., and P. Kirch, 2002 History on Stones: A Newly-Discovered Petroglyph Site at Kahikinui, Maui. Hawai'ian Archaeology 8. Honolulu: The Society for Hawai'ian Archaeology.

——2004 Petroglyphs of Kahikinui, Maui, Hawaiian Islands: Rock Images within a Polynesian Settlement Landscape. Proceedings of the Prehistoric Society 70:107–127.

Morgan, W., 1988 Prehistoric Architecture in Micronesia. Austin, TX: University of Texas Press.

Ottino, P., 1990 L'Habitat des Anciens Marquisiens: Architecture des Maisons, Evolution et Symbolisme des Formes. Journal de la Sociéte des Océanistes 90:3–15.

——2002 Pétroglyphes Marquisiens: Images Brouillées du Passé et Mémoire Transmise. Bulletin du LARSH 1: De l'Ecriture au Corps. Tahiti: Au Vent des Iles.

Porter, C., 1970 [1822] Journal of a Cruise made in the Pacific Ocean by David Porter, in the United States Frigate *Essex*, in the Years 1812, 1813, and 1814, vol. 2. New York: The Free Press.

Radiguet, M., 1978 [1860] Derniers Sauvages: La Vie et Les Meurs aux Iles Marquises (1842–1859). Papeete: Les Editions du Pacifique.

Rolett, B., 1998 Hanamiai. Prehistoric Colonization and Cultural Change in the Marquesas Islands (East Polynesia). Yale University Publications in Anthropology 81. New Haven, CT: Department of Anthropology and the Peabody Museum, Yale.

——n.d. Marquesan Prehistory and the East Polynesian Homeland. Fourth Interim Report: Marquesan Chiefdoms and the Emergence of Monumental Architecture. Department of Anthropology, University of Hawai'i, unpublished MS.

Roquefeuil, C. de, 1823 Voyage Round the World, Between the Years 1816–1819. London: Richard Phillips and Co.

Steinen, K. von den, 1969 [1925] Die Marquesaner und ihre Kunst, 3 vols. Berlin: D. Reimer.

Suggs, R., 1961 The Archaeology of Nuku Hiva, Marquesas Islands, French Polynesia. Anthropological Papers 49(1). New York: American Museum of Natural History.

Tautain, M., 1897 Notes sur les Constructions et Monuments des Marquises. L'Anthropologie 8:538–558, 667–678.

Terrell, J., 1982 Joseph Kabris and his Notes on Marquesas. Journal of Pacific History 17:101–112.

Wilson, J., 1997 [1797] A Missionary Voyage in the Ship *Duff*. Papeete: Société des Etudes Océaniennes, Haere Po No Tahiti.

15

The Archaeology of
the Conical Clan
in Micronesia

Paul Rainbird

My aim as an archaeologist is to construct what anthropologists describe as an ethnography, a detailed account of aspects of a community's social life, through the material traces left from previous times. I prefer to call the process of research and construction an archaeological anthropology, and in doing this I do not only utilize the material remains, but also knowledge of the different ways that people have lived in historical and modern times. This knowledge of history, anthropology, sociology, and social theory, in association with the material remains drawn from the variety of evidence available to the archaeologist to contextualize the environment of specific times in the past, makes possible the development of holistic and sometimes radically different understandings of the traces of past lives. This approach derives from what became known in Anglo-American archaeology as post-processual or interpretative archaeology, and so differs from the culture-historical and processual approaches that have more typically characterized archaeological interpretation in Micronesia and indeed Oceania more generally, especially when used to explicate processes of perceived social change (see also Conte, and Walter and Sheppard, this volume).

A tenet of processualist (including neo-evolutionary) theories is that culture is an adaptive response to alterations in the natural environment or in adjacent and competing societies. That is, all change in society must be a response to external pressure otherwise the social "system" would retain its equilibrium. The environmentally deterministic element of this approach has been favored in interpretations of island societies that were, and often still are, considered isolated and restricted to the resources available in the bounded island environment. This approach spawned the concept of "islands as laboratories" in which human adaptations to the island "ecosystem" could be tested with little fear of influence from external sources.

In Marshall Sahlins's (1958) influential early work *Social Stratification in Polynesia*, generalizations about social forms could not begin without a consideration of adaptation to the environment. Energy from the environmental context was seen to determine the possibilities for the evolution of social stratification, so that "impoverished" environments, such as atolls, would have low social differentiation, while large, fertile islands would develop complex social hierarchies. In the region generally known as Micronesia (see Lilley, this volume), where both the "low" atolls and the larger "high" island-types exist, such approaches to reconstructing past social structure have often been adopted by archaeologists based on the environment and material indicators.

The material indicators that have been identified as having the potential to provide evidence for past sociopolitical organization include the *latte* stone structures of the Mariana Archipelago in western Micronesia, the monumental-scale terracing on the larger islands of the Palau Archipelago in the western Caroline Islands, and the stone-built hilltop enclosures in Chuuk Lagoon and monumental stone architecture on Pohnpei and Kosrae in the eastern Carolines. In this chapter the focus will be on these last two islands, although it might be possible to apply a similar argument to the other localities. I will return to this issue briefly in the discussion.

For anthropologist Glenn Petersen (1999), all Micronesian societies, with the possible exception of Yap and modern Kosrae, are based on the conical clan realized unilineally through the matriline. The conical clan should establish for every member of society a ranking based on closeness to the founding ancestor. Following studies of historical linguistics and concurring with Hage (1998), Petersen finds that the conical clan was the sociopolitical organizing principle that was used at first settlement of Pacific Islands by the speakers of the Proto-Oceanic (POc) subgroup of the Austronesian language family (which excludes the original settlers of the Palau and Mariana Archipelagoes, whose settlers appear to have spoken an earlier, non-Oceanic form of Austronesian; see Lilley, this volume). Kirch (2000), who like many Oceanic scholars equates POc-speakers with users of Lapita pottery (see Denham, Galipaud, Lilley, Pavlides, Sand et al., and Walter and Sheppard, this volume), believes that the conical clan system at this stage was heterarchical, meaning that ranking was spread laterally, but as people moved out through time to settle the previously uninhabited islands of Remote Oceania the organizing principles of society became more hierarchical. This led to the development of hereditary chiefs and, although there are many variations on the theme, the classic pyramidal structure of the "complex chiefdoms." The clans themselves are ranked in relation to order of settlement, with the clan regarded as the first on the island having the highest rank. According to Bellwood's (1996) model of "founder rank enhancement," this landholding and ranking system is in itself a consequence of island colonization, allowing for social mobility through island exploration and initial settlement.

In the past, matrilineal systems of social organization have often been considered by anthropologists to be inherently unstable and thus baffling in their ability to survive in the long term, leading to debate over the "matrilineal puzzle." However, it has been noted that in relation to systems of descent from a common ancestor, the unilineal form following the matriline is the only one where the biological parent is without possibility of contradiction "provable." If this was the organizing social principle 3,500 to 3,000 years ago in parts of Near Oceania, we might ask why the matrilineal form has been maintained in the majority of the Caroline and Marshall Islands while it has been substantially modified elsewhere. Polynesian systems, for example, are generally regarded as non-unilineal, with a person able to choose to affiliate with the descent unit of either parent or both (Kirch and Green 2001). Bellwood (1996) has proposed that opportunities for the establishment of a strong unilineal tendency are possible through the self-aggrandizement available to a new community that is separated from its homeland after colonizing a new island. Here, the effect of becoming the founding clan, with an originary female or male (in patrilineal cases) ancestor, allows a new mythohistory of rank and primogeniture to be established each time.

More recently, and perhaps in a sense taking a different tack by being concerned about maintenance rather than origins (but nevertheless in an argument that can be regarded as contradictory to that proposed by Bellwood), Hage and Marck (2002) find that the success of the maintenance of the matrilineal conical clan in the Carolines and Marshalls is owed to lack of separation or isolation. They argue that in fact such a system ought to be regarded as typical of neighboring societies in constant contact, in this case by seafaring, especially where a gender divide separates male travelers from female gardeners and homemakers. In such cases it makes sense, they argue, that ties to the land should be held in the female line so that they will remain unchallenged while the male is away or does not return. This scenario makes a good argument both for the maintenance of such a system and for its presence in seafaring communities from the very beginning of human settlement of these islands some 2,000 years ago.

According to Petersen, however, the matrilineal conical clan system is an ideal, the way people *say* they are organized, but in reality ranking is related to the contemporary context of politics rather than a simple reading of genealogy. The mythohistory of the clans can be (and is) reworked by those in power. Thus the sociopolitical arena is dynamic and constantly negotiated within the supposed stability of the clan system. This keeps a cap on absolute power, as no one can be sure of achieving power. This results in significant competition because upward social mobility through good deeds is possible and restricts centralization through fragmentation, as exemplified in the Pohnpeian maxim, "one man cannot rule a thousand." The ambiguity of succession leads to competition, but Hage (2000) has warned that we should not stray too far from Petersen's basic understanding of how this works and has worked in Pohnpei and neighboring islands rather than extrapolate beyond these communities.

Accepting that Petersen's detailed understanding of sociopolitical organization in the Pohnpeian region is right, I want to explore the possibility that the material record may indicate that the matrilineal conical clan has formed the basic structuring principle of society for a significant portion of the human history of these islands, if not since people first arrived there. In this connection, how would we explain the sociopolitical motivations behind the construction of the eastern Carolinian monumental sites of Nan Madol on Pohnpei and Leluh on Kosrae? I

Figure 15.1 Entrance to Nan Douwas Islet, Nan Madol, Pohnpei

will deal with the archaeology and interpretations of these sites separately, starting with Nan Madol.

Nan Madol, Pohnpei

Nan Madol is a famous site created from 92 artificial islets separated by canals and situated upon a tidal fringing reef. The sandy substrate was occupied earlier, with the artificially raised islets being built starting around 1,500 years ago and islet construction slowly moving outwards toward the reef edge. The site developed into a complex of monumental architecture probably serving secular, mortuary, and, perhaps, other non-secular functions (Figure 15.1). Radiocarbon dates derived from archaeological excavations directed by Ayres (1993) suggest that the outer area of Nan Madol was not constructed before 800 years ago, suggesting that the site developed over a period of at least 700 years.

Archaeological investigations at Nan Madol have led to the recovery of a wide range of artifacts including pottery, bone, and shell. Some of the earliest explorations report the recovery of human remains including within the central tomb of Nan Douwas. More recent research has uncovered other remains of the probable inhabitants of Nan Madol. Ayres and his team explored Pahnwi, a massively constructed enclosure with a tomb and other features on the southeast corner of the sea wall. The large tomb is constructed in the typical header and stretcher method of Pohnpei. Such construction utilizes columnar basalt, with each layer at right angles to the last, as in the construction of log cabins, but using stone rather than timber. The tomb contained the remains of a minimum of six adults as well as at least two children aged between two and four years. Another area contained the fragmentary remains of two children aged between three and five years.

In association with the human skeletal remains, the Pahnwi tomb also contained approximately 10,000 artifacts, 9,000 of which are shell beads (Tasa 1988). These and the other artifacts collected fall into the categories recovered by earlier excavators from other tombs around the site. They include pearl shell fishing-lure shanks, *Tridacna* shell adzes, perforated shark teeth, shell pendants and/or needles, and armbands or rings manufactured from both *Conus* and *Tridacna* shell. Rare basalt stone adzes and imported obsidian flakes have also been reported from mortuary contexts. The stone adzes appear to be important artifacts, perhaps prestige objects, and have been found in tombs outside of the Nan Madol complex and on the island proper, but the occasional flaking of basalt to provide basic cutting tools is also known.

The apparently specific spatial distribution of formal stone artifacts can be matched at Nan Madol by the spatial distribution of mortuary architecture. In Figure 15.2 it can be observed that the islets that show some indication of mortuary activity are, with one exception that I will return to below, constructed on the seaward side of the site. Many are actually on the sea wall itself, and this spatial location indicates that they are some of the last stone structures to have been constructed at Nan Madol. The only tomb within the core area of Nan Madol that does not fit this pattern is that on the islet of Peinkitel. As Ayres (1993) has previously observed, the islet of Peinkitel is noteworthy for two reasons. First, it is the only islet that appears to have been built half on the dry land of Temwen Island and half on the fringing reef. Second, the tomb on Peinkitel is reputed in oral history to be the burial place of Isohkelekel.

Isohkelekel is the man reputed to have freed Pohnpeians from a long history of evil dictatorship by defeating the last of the Saudeleur dynasty. The Saudeleur dynasty is regarded as able to trace a direct ancestry to the brothers Olsipha and Olsopha, who are regarded locally as the founders of Nan Madol. The Saudeleurs are reputed to have ruled Pohnpei through a harsh regime that involved taking massive tribute from the rest of the population, in order to be maintained on their reef of islands. They were reputed to have been able to observe all of their subjects all of the time, and terrible retribution would follow any transgression of their law. If we can today find any material links between the oral history and archaeology, then the period of tomb construction on the seaward side of Nan Madol may be linked to the Saudeleur hegemony, and the greater expression of their power connected not only to locals, but also to visitors. The only entrance available to long-distance visitors is through the sea wall at a point adjacent to the greatest mortuary expression at Nan Douwas (see Figure 15.2).

The burial of Isohkelekel on the islet of Peinkitel may be seen to formally link the man with his political history after death. Here, the architecture links the fringing reef with the dry land and, according to Hanlon (1988), metaphorically draws

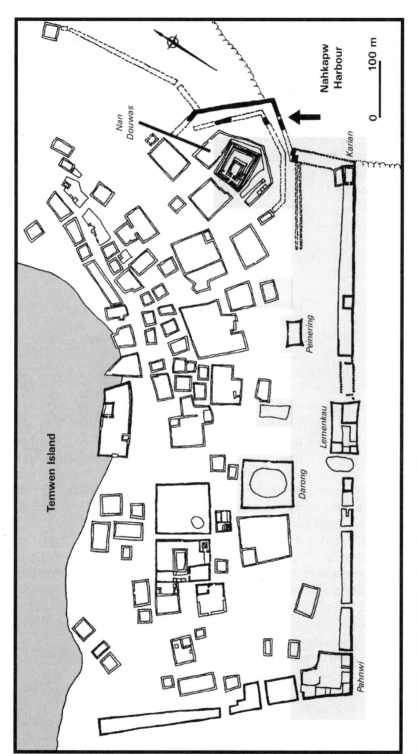

Figure 15.2 Plan of Nan Madol indicating "mortuary area"

Isohkelekel in from the sea, whence he came, and on to the dry land of which he became a part as a popular hero or "stranger king." Petersen (1990a) observes that Isohkelekel had his origins in Pohnpei and therefore cannot be considered a stranger king, but we might nevertheless consider that no longer was elite power separated from the land by being situated on the reef.

Ayres (1990: 89), utilizing a blend of written history, oral history, and archaeology, divides the history of Pohnpei into six "culture-historical phases":

(1) *Settlement and Adaptive Integration Phase* (pre-500 B.C.–A.D. 1) – inland forest clearance; pottery in use.
(2) *Peinais Phase* (A.D. 1–1000) – stone house foundations, breadfruit storage pits, pottery with rim notching, rare punctate and incised line designs; Nan Madol islets with some columnar basalt construction as early as A.D. 500–600.
(3) *Nan Madol Phase* – expansion and formalization of Nan Madol complex and associated sociopolitical aspects (Deleur "empire"), chiefly residential architecture, stylized tombs (*lolong*), pottery declining in use (increasingly plainware or absent).
(4) *Isohkelekel Phase* – disintegration of the Deleur polity, Nahnmwarki title in use, chiefly complexes and new style meeting houses (*nahs*), post-pottery.
(5) *Early Contact Phase* – Western contact; Nan Madol occupation continues but in non-center role.
(6) *Historic Phase* – Western contact and colonial governments.

The first two of these phases are defined by archaeological and proxy environmental indicators. The next two phases (3 and 4) are defined almost wholly by oral-historical accounts which for the most part the archaeology merely serves to illustrate. For example, in Phase 3 the archaeology of Nan Madol cannot be considered an entity worthy of consideration detached from its presumed "sociopolitical aspects," which are derived from oral accounts relating the site with the "Deleur Empire." Phase 4 goes one step further in actually naming this period after a mythological (or mythologized) figure named in traditional stories.

It appears as if the archaeology in the more recent pre-contact phases is of secondary importance to Ayres in comparison with the "primary" source of oral history. He makes sense of this history by including it in an overarching but implicit social-evolutionary perspective. This is evident in statements such as "the primary hypothesis is that Nan Madol's development as a chiefly and priestly center reflects an *evolving chiefdom* that controlled a Pohnpei polity from c. A.D. 1000 to 1500" (Ayres 1990:202, my emphasis).

Archaeologists and others have at times been guilty of not taking a critical stance in relation to historical and oral sources. In an assessment of the early Euro-American accounts of Nan Madol, many of which are taken to reflect an "end-point" by archaeologists, Hanlon (1988:109) found them to be full of "presumptions, ignorance, racism, self-justification, exploitation and factual errors." In another paper addressing one of the major published records of Pohnpeian oral history, *The Book of Luelen* (Luelen 1977), Hanlon (1992:20) accepts that while there is unease about such things, Luelen Bernart's book, and oral history more generally, can "provide precious glimpses of a deeper, more distant past." He nonetheless expresses the need for understanding the context of its production and the localized and personal nature of its content. For Hanlon discrepancies should be expected and where they occur they provide a sense of the complexities of life in the past (see also Conte, this volume).

Petersen has also pursued the issue of the value of oral history in reconstructions of Pohnpei history, and especially to archaeology. He (Petersen 1990b:149) makes the point that "sociopolitical organization was in considerable flux in the early nineteenth century." Further, owing to this flux "we cannot use modern images . . . as indicative of what Pohnpei life was like at the time of contact, nor can we use such an image of that period to explain what had been taking place 400 years earlier." Petersen concludes his paper by requesting that archaeologists stop relying on the historical sources and utilize the archaeological record to provide evidence to elucidate the complexities of Pohnpeian social organization through time (cf. Conte, this volume).

The complexity of Pohnpei's traditional social structure is not to be doubted. Matrilineality is the basis for title achievement in many ranking systems, but as Petersen has shown, the "matrilineal puzzle" of the apparent growing separation of descent and authority in such a system, the puzzle that caused consternation to a generation of anthropologists such as Schneider (1961), who worked in the Carolines, was maintained and still exists owing to its flexibility. For Petersen the stories of the evil Saudeleur hegemony are not to be taken as a direct historical account, but rather are moral directives issued as warnings regarding the containing of political and ritual authority in a single center.

Leluh, Kosrae

As at Nan Madol, the site at Leluh is constructed on artificial ground, on the fringing reef of a small island on the eastern coast of the main island (Figure 15.3). Leluh has walls up to 6.4 meters in height constructed of basalt, some of it columnar and in header and stretcher style, and coral rubble. Unlike Nan Madol, the majority of these compounds are not separated by water, but can be approached along coral paved paths. A tidal canal runs as a central artery through the complex. Cordy (1993) and Athens (1995) have established a chronology for the development of the site.

Although later developments have removed much of the site, in final form, perhaps only 200 years ago, the fringing reef was covered by more than 100 compounds. The whole area measured approximately 800 meters by 500 meters, with coral-paved "streets" up to 6 meters wide connecting the compounds. All of the compounds appear to have been separated by walls constructed of basalt and coral, but they were modest in comparison to the ones constructed in the core area. Historical accounts and the compounds that remain now indicate that the largest and

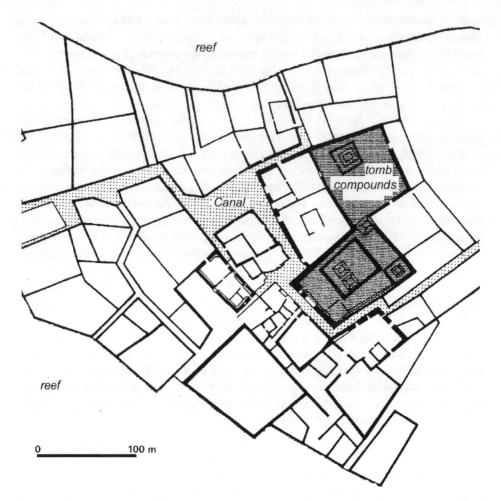

Figure 15.3 Plan of Leluh, Kosrae

most impressive of the compound walls were located in the early eastern area of the complex.

The archaeological remains indicate that the construction of Leluh was a massive undertaking which required much labor and planning. Unlike Nan Madol, at the time of European visits in the nineteenth century, Leluh was a flourishing settlement and was recorded in a number of journals. Dumont d'Urville, who was second-in-command of an 1824 expedition, described Leluh as having "beautiful huts surrounded by high walls, [and] well paved streets" (Ritter and Ritter 1982:29).

The historical records, supported by archaeological and ethnographic studies, indicate that there were three types of compound. The first, defined by the largest walls, were habitations of "high chiefs" and Cordy believes that there were about ten of these. One was apparently the paramount ruler (*Tokosra*), and resided in the compound named *Posral*, but Lütke found in 1827 that "we could not recognize in any way Togoja [Tokosra] as king of all the island" (Ritter and Ritter 1982:133). Each of these compounds had a feasting/meeting house at the main entrance and behind this, hidden by bamboo screens, were houses for the wives, children, servants, and the chief's sleeping house. Within the compound were also a garden area for trees and a place for burials. The Tokosra, however, had a particular form of burial, and this involves the second compound type.

Neighboring the high-status residences are mortuary and ritual enclosures and their associated tombs. What eventually became the central area of Leluh, where the tombs are located, is accessible from the open sea through the arterial canal. The tomb architecture is standardized, with the five tombs constructed in the style of a truncated pyramid, with a crypt in the center, only accessible from the top. Investigations by Cordy found that the central Insru compound tombs are the earliest, built between 600 and 400 years ago, with the "wall tomb" in the north corner of the Insru compound constructed most recently, at approximately 200 years ago. Each of the tomb compounds appears to have had a large feasting house next to its main entrance.

The core of the tomb is constructed using quarried columnar basalt, and is covered by a layer of coral rubble collected from the reef. Similarly, the boundary walls of the mortuary compounds, unlike other walls at Leluh, are constructed of basalt capped with coral rubble. Excavations in the Inol tomb compound by Athens also show that unlike the deposits in other excavated compounds, there is no evidence for domestic use or the presence of vegetation in the mortuary precinct. It is possible to infer from the clean soils in this compound that there is something different about its use compared with the others.

The third type of compound is undistinguished in comparison, and most are located in the western section of the site. According to Cordy these formed the residences of the servants/retainers of the chiefs and contained two or three houses, but no meeting or feasting structure. These compounds, being more ephemeral, are the least well known of the types.

The range of artifacts collected from Leluh includes pounding stones, adzes of *Tridacna*, *Terebra* shell, and basalt. The most common portable artifacts collected during Cordy's project were *Anadara* shell "peelers," usually thought to be related to breadfruit processing.

According to Cordy, Leluh represents the dwelling place of the two highest strata of the four-stratum Kosraean society that developed after about A.D. 1400. Other than those members of lower strata who were required to serve the needs of the high chiefs, the rest of the population lived on the main island, which was separated into some fifty or so sections (*facl*). The sections were managed by a stratum of lower chiefs, and labor for agricultural production was provided by the lowest and most populous level of society, the "commoners." Each of the sections was linked to a specific high chief and provided food tribute to sustain him and his retinue at Leluh. Once again, although other historical commentators agree with the presence of highly differentiated class-based strata, Lütke finds that Lesson, a chronicler of Duperrey's visit three years previous, was wrong. He says (Ritter and Ritter 1982:133) that "we did not notice this rigorous distinction between the various classes, nor the striking difference between the exterior of the chiefs and that of the common people of which Mr Lesson speaks."

A second level of sites dating to this period are the relatively large multi-compound enclosures located on the coast of the main island, and Cordy regards these as the residences of the lower chiefs. These sites are less architecturally impressive than Leluh, but still represent a major investment in the establishment of significant places. They each have high walls and revetments, often have boat docks, and contain material evidence for basic domestic settlement activities. A third level of settlement type consists of a smaller and much more diverse range of sites that may have been inhabited by the lowest strata of society.

A three-tier settlement hierarchy model for Kosrae may be too simple and not able to portray the different functions of enclosure sites. The settlements on the main island show a clear division between the coastal complexes and the scattered individual dwelling units, which are located from the coast up to 150 meters above sea level in upland river valleys. This perhaps indicates a two-tier habitation model that excludes Leluh as quite different, but also interconnected, as a simple mundane and sacred functional model is not likely to be appropriate either.

In further attempting to elucidate the role of Leluh, Cordy takes as his starting point the "historic baseline" which for him is the record provided by the early European visitors to the site. These 19th-century visitors, on scientific expeditions, presented the occupied site as "the capital of Kosrae, a feudal society . . . [and] the hub of this society . . . [as] it was here that the king and nobility lived" (Cordy 1993:1). He accepts that massive changes occurred in Kosraean society as a consequence of the European encounters, but argues that these did not occur until after A.D. 1850, more than 25 years after the first recorded European visit to the island.

In addition to data collected from mainland sites, Cordy concludes that the "four strata feudal society" recorded in the historical documents can be traced back to at least A.D. 1400. The "ethnographic present" (the "endpoint") is used to explain as much of the archaeology as possible. In an evolutionary framework such as Cordy's, all understanding of the archaeology prior to the "development" of the recorded "traditional" society is based on the notion that incremental social evolution took place in Kosraean society, starting at initial colonization and continuing until the supposed endpoint.

By the 1850s, when missionaries arrived, the glowing accounts of Leluh by members of the Duperrey and Lütke expeditions a generation earlier were ridiculed as outdated. Gulick reported that (Damon 1861, pp. 36–37):

> from M. D'Urville's reports and from the accounts of sea captains we had received glowing ideas of the architectural exhibitions at Lila [Leluh]; we were to find a native city handsomely laid out, with paved streets, and at frequent intervals handsome piles of stone-cut masonry. On the contrary, we found nothing but muddy paths, zigzagging hither and thither over rubbish and stones.

Discussion

How then are we to interpret the monumental material remains of Nan Madol and Leluh? If we follow the archaeologists who have worked in these places, the sites represent local social evolution constrained by the environmental parameters of high islands. In the case of Nan Madol, devolution occurred when what is believed to have been a centralized society based at Nan Madol was destroyed and replaced by a system of five independent polities that became fossilized shortly after prolonged contact with Euro-Americans. If Petersen is right, however, sociopolitical organization should have been resistant to any form of centralized or feudal control. Indeed, his research on Pohnpei underlines the long-term resilience of the conical clan system, a politically manipulated system based on both genealogy and competition. How could we envisage Nan Madol and Leluh operating under such conditions? Do we need to get away from reading these monuments in the Giddensian sense as "containers of power"? How is labor mobilized for such projects when there are only "chiefs among chiefs"?

Perhaps we should be looking at the role of ancestry, given that the overriding ideal principle of the conical clan, whether it is reckoned through the female or male line, is the identification of links to the ancestors and through this the kinship ties that bind individuals and clans to the land. In this connection there is a telling report from missionaries who said that according to informants each wall at Leluh was built in honor of the dead and that "one of their most decisive evidences of public grief is to rebuild the wall about the premises of a bereaved chief" (Damon 1861:37). Further evidence for the importance placed on honoring and commemorating the ancestors can be seen in the tombs of both Leluh and Nan Madol. If then we can conceive of these places as the stages for maintaining the ancestors, something that became solidified in stone over the past 500 to 1,500 years, then competition for worthy deeds could have led to the gradual accretion of structures at a specific locale. This would be a manifestation of competitive emulation occurring internally, as I am suggesting here, but there is also evidence that this is also occurring externally and leading to the structures that were built at a later date at Leluh. In both these places we may be observing manifestations of ancestry and the maintenance of genealogical ties. The tombs, walls, and platforms are perhaps all acting as mnemonics in the recounting of genealogies. Access to the recounting of genealogies is manifested as competition for the creation of goodly works that would allow people greater opportunity to gain higher titles.

Given such a scenario, we may have envisaged Nan Madol in completely the wrong way in the expectation that this was some sort of urban center, with the multitude of roles that this term implies. Rather, parts may have been more or less permanently occupied, with perhaps a chief in residence whose status was heightened by physical and mythical closeness to the ancestors, and within whom sacredness was embodied, but who had nothing like absolute power. The other islets and tombs may have acted as sepulchers where occasional ceremonies were enacted. Depending on which ancestor was being referred to at any particular time for politically expedient reasons, some islet or tombs would have become more important than others: some may have been left to overgrow while others were cleared and the ancestor revered. At Leluh we may be observing the expected material variations on the unilineal conical clan theme. The emulation of Nan Madol, in at least some small way, cannot, I think, be doubted. On the other hand, Cordy, as a necessary corollary of maintaining his "founder effect" propositions regarding social evolution on Kosrae, argues that no links can be observed.

Of course, the particular manifestations of eastern Carolinian high-island-style conical clanship still require explaining: Why did this happen here and not elsewhere in the region? In answering this and part of the related question of mobilization of labor, it can be noted that owing to superior resource availability, Pohnpei and Kosrae had large and probably stable populations compared with neighboring atoll populations. It is also the case that material manifestations of conical clanship can only be realized through available materials; in some circumstances this may have been of wood, which has not survived. Elsewhere on the high islands, monumental and prestige elements can be identified in the large stone-built hilltop enclosures and platforms of Chuuk Lagoon, the terraces of Palau, the stone money of Yap, and the latte stones of the Marianas, but these cases need to be understood in their specific contexts if they are also to be seen as manifestations of unilineal conical clan organization. What I have illustrated here, however, is that contrary to conventional expectations, unilineal and probably matrilineal conical clan systems that are basically heterarchical in organization can lead to monumental architecture and complex settlement types. This eliminates the necessity of trying to find social-evolutionary arguments for social change in order to explain material traces from the past. Equally there is no need for devolution: As Petersen has shown and the archaeological remains may attest, long-term stability and flux are not antithetical. Clearly, if hierarchical pyramidal systems are not needed to explain the presence of dual chieftainship, ranked clans, complex individual title system, and multiple polities in the eastern Carolines, then a closer look at other places where the conventional interpretation has been applied, such as some Polynesian societies, might lead to some radical rethinking of how these societies should be understood in historical perspective.

Nan Madol and Leluh may be regarded as places where power was negotiated through genealogy and competition. It may be no surprise that these locales were chosen, given the importance of primary domain in the conical clan system, as they are archaeologically amongst the earliest dated settlement sites on their islands. So rather than being individual containers of power in centralized hierarchical systems, they may actually have been central to negotiation in dynamic systems of fragmentation and fusion, each pulling in opposite directions and creating the multiple polities as witnessed on Pohnpei historically.

Conclusion

Through the 1980s and 1990s archaeologists have interpreted Nan Madol and Leluh as urban centers in centralized political systems led by a single ruler in a pyramidal hierarchy with three or four basic levels of social stratification. These were seen to have evolved and in the case of Nan Madol, eventually devolved, in their bounded island environments, with little notion of outside contact or a prior history of social organization possessed by the settlers. Although substantial differences in sociopolitical organization are exhibited across the region, underlying basic similarities do suggest, in much the same way as linguistic patterns, that there is some shared history among these island communities. It is clear that these communities did not need to evolve socially; they were already organized by historical understandings.

As the communities settled into and adapted their new islands they also varied their sociopolitical organization around the themes they had inherited. As I have argued elsewhere (Rainbird 1999), at some point in the first millennium of settlement, ancestors stopped being regarded as situated overseas and became related to the island itself. Once this occurred, local ancestors could be celebrated and commemorated and maintained as central to community organization as they always had been. In this sense, if we return to Bellwood's argument for "founder rank enhancement," it is not necessary to invoke local ancestry except in terms of clan ranking, as members of the "first" clan are able to choose to locate their ancestry overseas as they see fit in order to legitimate power. As Petersen argues, the mytho-history of the Saudeleurs is one that warns of the evils of absolute power, a power that within the contradictions of the matrilineal conical clan system is impossible to achieve.

What Leluh and Nan Madol, in their monumental glory, are most likely to represent is the importance of ancestry and place in the past negotiation of sociopolitical organization. They are not, as is so commonly insisted, the apogee of sociopolitical systems in their social evolutionary march toward supposedly more complex levels of social hierarchy. The organization of society in these islands was already complex, negotiated, contingent, and thoroughly historical. These places do not need to be interpreted as representing entirely new forms of sociopolitical organization, derived from isolation or separation. Rather, they are manifestations of an old but very resilient system that is antithetical to the type of distinct hierarchical structure that archaeologists attempt to apply to them.

ACKNOWLEDGMENTS

I would like to thank participants of a Sydney University seminar, in particular Roland Fletcher, Robin Torrence, and Peter White, for comments on an earlier version of this chapter. I would also like to acknowledge that the manuscript was prepared while in residence in the Department of Archaeology and Natural History, Research School of Pacific and Asian Studies, The Australian National University, as a Visiting Fellow in the Centre for Archaeological Research.

316

PAUL RAINBIRD

REFERENCES

Athens, J., 1995 Landscape Archaeology: Prehistoric Settlement, Subsistence, and Environment of Kosrae, Eastern Caroline Islands, Micronesia. Honolulu: International Archaeological Research Institute, Inc.

Ayres, W., 1990 Pohnpei's Position in Eastern Micronesian Prehistory. *In* Recent Advances
in Micronesian Archaeology. R. Hunter-Anderson, ed. pp. 187–212. Micronesica Supplement 2. Mangilao: University of Guam.

—— 1993 Nan Madol Archaeological Fieldwork: Final Report. Historic Preservation Office,
Pohnpei State, Federated States of Micronesia.

Bellwood, P., 1996 Hierarchy, Founder Ideology and Austronesian Expansion. *In* Origins,
Ancestry and Alliance. J. Fox and C. Sather, eds. pp. 18–40. Canberra: The Australian
National University.

Cordy, R., 1993 The Lelu Stone Ruins (Kosrae, Micronesia): 1978–1981 Historical and
Archaeological Research. Asian and Pacific Archaeology Series 10. Honolulu: Social
Science Research Institute, University of Hawai'i.

Damon, S., 1861 Morning Star Papers (Supplement to The Friend). Honolulu: Hawaiian
Missionary Society.

Hage, P., 1998 Was Proto-Oceanic Society Matrilineal? Journal of the Polynesian Society,
107:365–379.

—— 2000 The Conical Clan in Micronesia: The Marshall Islands. Journal of the Polynesian
Society, 109:295–309.

Hage, P., and J. Marck, 2002 Proto-Micronesian Kin Terms, Descent Groups, and Inter-
island Voyaging. Oceanic Linguistics 41:159–170.

Hanlon, D., 1988 Upon a Stone Altar: A History of the Island of Pohnpei to 1890.
Honolulu: University of Hawai'i Press.

—— 1992 The Path Back to Pohnsakar: Luelen Bernart, His Book, and the Practice of
History on Pohnpei. Isla: A Journal of Micronesian Studies 1:13–35.

Kirch, P., 2000 On the Road of the Winds: An Archaeological History of the Pacific Islands
Before European Contact. Berkeley, CA: University of California Press.

Kirch, P., and R. Green, 2001 Hawaiki, Ancestral Polynesia: An Essay in Historical Anthropology. Cambridge: Cambridge University Press.

Luelen, B., 1977 The Book of Luelen. J. Fisher, S. Riesenberg and M. Whiting, trans. and
eds. Canberra: Australian National University Press.

Petersen, G., 1990a Lost in the Weeds: Theme and Variation in Pohnpei Political Mythology. Occasional Paper 35. Honolulu: Center for Pacific Island Studies, University of
Hawai'i.

—— 1990b Some Overlooked Complexities in the Study of Pohnpei Social Complexity. *In*
Recent Advances in Micronesian Archaeology. R. Hunter-Anderson, ed. pp. 137–152.
Micronesica Supplement 2. Mangilao: University of Guam.

—— 1999 Sociopolitical Rank and Conical Clanship in the Caroline Islands, Journal of the
Polynesian Society 108:367–410.

Rainbird, P., 1999 Entangled Biographies: Western Pacific Ceramics and the Tombs of
Pohnpei. World Archaeology 31:214–224.

Ritter, L., and P. Ritter, 1982 The European Discovery of Kosrae Island. Accounts by Louis
Isidore Duperrey, Jules-Sébastien-César Dumont d'Urville, René Primevère Lesson,
Fyedor Lütke and Friedrich Heinrich von Kittlitz. Micronesian Archaeological Survey
Reports 13. Saipan: Historic Preservation Office.

Sahlins, M., 1958 Social Stratification in Polynesia. Seattle, WA: University of Washington Press.

Schneider, D., 1961 The Distinctive Features of Matrilineal Descent Groups. *In* Matrilineal Kinship. D. Schneider and K. Gough, eds. pp. 1–35. Berkeley, CA: University of California Press.

Tasa, G., 1988 Report of the Human Skeletal Remains from Pahnwi and Wasau, Nan Madol, Pohnpei. Historic Preservation Office, Pohnpei State, Federated States of Micronesia.

Part III

Politics

16

What is Archaeology for in the Pacific? History and Politics in New Caledonia

Christophe Sand, Jacques Bole, and André Ouetcho

In an island world, where control over limited land has always been a source of conflict, human history has probably always been manipulated. Far from being closed, isolated entities separated by wide and dangerous waters, the islands of Melanesia, Polynesia, and Micronesia have regularly seen arrivals of new canoes, for trading, social exchange, or new settlement (Kirch 2000). To account for progressive transformations in cultural traditions as well as to help establish new settlers, oral traditions had to manipulate historical processes and events to provide evolving societies with identifiable foundations.

Depending on one's perspective, the intrusion of Western colonists into the Pacific from the 18th century can be placed anywhere along a spectrum ranging from an "invasion" of foreigners to just the arrival of more new canoes. European influence on indigenous societies has been very different from one archipelago to another, depending on local circumstances. Situations range from permanent self-government in the Kingdom of Tonga to overthrowing the indigenous government in Hawai'i , and from "terra nullius" in Australia to the Treaty of Waitangi in New Zealand-Aotearoa. Yet in all these settings, Europeans tried to understand the indigenous societies they were facing, often in a very basic opposition of "savage: civilized," with the explicit intention to bring "undeveloped" cultures to "modernity." It is clear, though, that early researchers working in the western Pacific were confronted with a far more complex picture than they expected when they first began recording oral traditions and writing histories of the islands to incorporate them into "World History" (Oliver 1988).

Indigenous histories were rapidly obscured by the increasing use of archaeology from the second half of the 19th century. Archaeological objectives and methods are directly linked to the evolution of European science during the 17th and 18th centuries. No earlier society ever advanced so distinctively the idea that studying the material remains of past societies was useful. However, attempts to reconcile archaeological findings with local histories transmitted by oral traditions – as most local histories were until the early 20th century – led in most cases to divergent conclusions, simply because the two approaches to the past are so different. In all colonial situations, archaeology was a political tool in the hands of the ruling foreign elite. Consciously or otherwise, researchers using archaeology in the Pacific during the first part of the 20th century (and sometimes still) often tried to minimize the historical rights of indigenous populations by "demonstrating" the presence of "older" cultures in the islands that had been "invaded" by the forefathers of the modern indigenous groups, just as the Europeans had later done to them. Selectively using oral traditions to support such notions, researchers proposed, for example, the invasion of Island Melanesia by "black Papuans" who destroyed a highly developed civilization of "white Ainu" (Avias 1950), and the invasion of New Zealand by the Maori, who overthrew the Moriori (Trotter and McCulloch 1971:60). Similarly, Windshuttle and Gillin (2002) recently argued that the ancestors of modern Aborigines extinguished earlier populations of "Australian pygmies."

This classic process of colonial analysis, serving in its first stage as a means to justify historically the invasion of the Pacific by European newcomers and to deny Pacific peoples their rights to the land, shrank back with the rise of a new generation of professional archaeologists in the Pacific after World War II. Over the past half century, new scientific findings have encouraged a new perspective on Oceanic history and prehistory, particularly in relation to the abandonment of any cultural hierarchy between human societies (for a review, see Kirch 2000: chapter 1). Pushed by global processes, this period has also seen the rise of claims for indigenous self-determination, leading to political independence for most Pacific archipelagoes. The advent of new nations politically controlled by indigenous leaders has brought about a shift in archaeological policies, with the creation of local research institutions and the promotion of "indigenous archaeologies." In Vanuatu this led to a ten-year ban on archaeological excavations between 1984 and 1993 (Bedford et al. 1998), but there are many examples from the past few decades of the diverse uses that can be made of archaeological results, from supporting land-claims in the Solomons and encouraging protests against site destruction by developers in Hawai'i and Tahiti, to resistance against archaeological research in Fiji (Crosby 2002) and manipulation of archaeological writings in Australia (e.g., Dortch 1998; Smith 1998).

In this chapter we present a case study from New Caledonia (Figure 16.1) which outlines the politics of doing archaeology in Oceania today. New Caledonia is the southernmost archipelago in Island Melanesia and comprises a long, narrow island called Grande Terre, of continental origin, surrounded by a set of smaller uplifted limestone formations. Settled by Austronesian-speakers about 3,000 years ago, the country is now a decolonizing Pacific nation with a multicultural society of just over 200,000 people. Doing archaeology and writing about the history of the archipelago has become a complex business, complicated over the past decade by an explicit political project to "create a unified nation." We will try to show this complexity by first sketching the history of archaeological research in New Caledonia, identifying the major trends that the local context can impose on the reconstruction of the

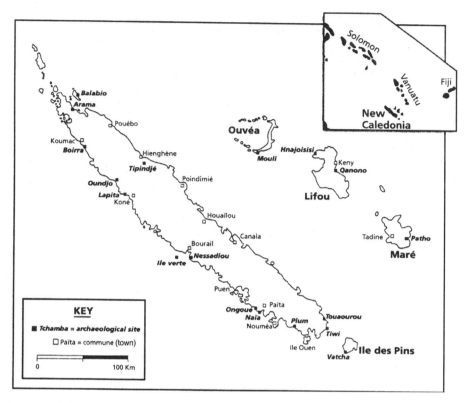

Figure 16.1 New Caledonia

past. We will then provide a summary of the archipelago's prehistoric chronology as we understand it today, to highlight the complexity of pre-European cultural change in Island Melanesia and the impossibility of taking a simplistic approach to historical diversity. This discussion underpins consideration in the final part of the chapter of the difficulty of addressing a nuanced picture of the past in a multi-cultural society whose representatives do not necessarily share the same origins or political beliefs and projects for the future.

The History of Prehistory: Archaeological Research in a Colonial Context

In every colonial history, researchers can identify different "periods," each charac-terized by a particular political environment. "Orthodox thinking" during these successive phases can change profoundly, depending on the local as well as the international context. But as we discuss below, often this does not prevent local people from being far slower to accept changes in thinking or ideas. In New Caledonia, three major periods can be identified in the history of the past 150

Figure 16.2 Examples of reconstructed Lapita pottery

years: (1) French colonization, (2) the entrenchment of the colonial system, and (3) indigenous revival.

From the seizure of New Caledonia by France in 1853 for use as a convict settlement until the beginning of the 20th century, all writers who discussed the Kanaks considered them to be the first people of the archipelago, though usually not in a positive light. The Kanaks were mostly seen as "part of the landscape," occupying land that would be "much better used" by Western settlers. Things changed markedly at the beginning of the 20th century. The end of convict settlement stopped the regular influx of newcomers and interest in the colony began to fade in metropolitan France. The small-scale arrival of free settlers made for a continuing rise in European numbers though, and political control fell into the hands of a few colonial families. The changing social structure gave rise to the first claims for local but non-indigenous roots. Contrary to expectations, however, the Kanaks had not disappeared in the face of European superiority. In these times of building a local colonial society, which granted civil rights to the Kanaks only after WWII, one of the dangers confronting colonial leaders was the possible emergence of political claims from indigenous groups.

In a period which saw the full development of racist theories about biological differences and human evolution, when a well-respected anthropologist such as Fritz Sarazin (1924) could publish papers on the relationships between the Kanaks and Neanderthals, it is not surprising to see researchers of this time such as Archambault (1901) deny the Kanaks any relationship with New Caledonian rock art, which he supposed to be too sophisticated for "Papuan races." Similar analyses concerning intricately decorated Lapita pottery (Figure 16.2), complex adze forms, and extensive terraces for wet taro horticulture were published at the end of the period by geologist Avias (1949, 1950, 1953), who related all the "civilized" components he recognized in prehistoric New Caledonia to a society of probably Japanese Ainu origin, who had the advantage of being "white-skinned."

The repeatedly published idea that there were "pre-Kanak civilizations" in the islands slowly became historical truth, even for Kanaks. Taught in schools, the concept of successions of races and cultures in the human history of the archipelago (Le Borgne 1959) promoted a positive image of European colonization, which was presented as bringing morally as well as intellectually advanced civilization to the Pacific. The unsavory side of colonial history, such as the alienation of Kanak land, was presented as morally superior to supposed earlier invasions, which were said to have seen the forefathers of the Kanaks commit the "uncivilized" crime of exterminating the members of older cultures through cannibalism (see Trotter and McCulloch 1971:60 for a similar case in New Zealand). At the same time, the descendants of convicts voluntarily destroyed most of the architectural and written witnesses to their own forefathers' origins, in order to foster a positive picture of European origins in New Caledonia.

This description of history was strongly attacked by indigenous leaders following the revival of the Kanak culture and the emergence of land claims and calls for self-determination from the 1970s. Knowing intuitively the danger posed by history for the unity of "the people," Kanak thinkers criticized the overall concept of "history," decrying it as a colonial construct used by Westerners to deny indigenous rights (Collective 1983). In opposition they proposed that the Kanak people were the "first occupants" of the archipelago and on that basis held all rights to land. This clear-cut political division of New Caledonia's society, from the late 1970s, between "the indigenous first occupants" claiming all the rights, and all other communities of later arrivals identified as "invaders," led to a profound civil crisis in the archipelago.

Aside from the political consequences of the division, which ultimately led to periods of undeclared civil war, the whole concept of history had to be reanalyzed. Interestingly, this was first done by left-wing French anthropologists supporting Kanak claims. Their writings transformed New Caledonia's history into a simplistic two-step scenario beginning with a monolithic Kanak prehistory where everything was peaceful and well organized, much like European misconceptions of the Australian "Dreamtime" (see David, this volume). This state of natural grace was suddenly destroyed by the irruption of Western invasion (e.g., Bensa 1990). This "Kanak-centric" history, promoting a timeless, idealized pre-European society which was able to remain unchanged indefinitely even when absorbing groups from elsewhere in the Pacific, became the new orthodoxy in the 1980s. For some writers, even the colonial period was to be analyzed only in terms of the resistance of indigenous people to their domination by intruders (e.g., Guiart 1983).

No one anticipated the enormous demand that this complete shift in New Caledonia's received history would create for historical reconnaissance among the other cultural communities of the archipelago, which were frustrated at being marginalized in what they consider their own country. Since the end of the 1980s, numerous local non-Kanak historians have conducted high-level university research on convict settlement (Barbançon 2003), free settlers (Terrier 2000), the history of the Japanese in New Caledonia (Palombo 2002), the contribution of the archipelago to WWI (Boutin-Boyer 2003), post-WWII political changes (Kurtovitch 1999), and so on. The New Caledonia Department of Archaeology has even been able to start archaeological excavations on historical sites such as convict settlements, something that was unthinkable 20 years ago. The complete absence of equivalent research conducted by Kanaks on their history (apart from our archaeological team) reveals how difficult the indigenous community finds it to replace a simple account with a more complex version of the nearly 3,000 years of human history in the archipelago (Angleviel 2003:244).

Faced with the very real dilemma of having to navigate between opposing claims presenting cultural changes as either successions of people or Western colonial scientific constructs, archaeologists working in New Caledonia tried until the late 1980s not to engage in the political debate, focusing mostly on the reconstruction of a ceramic chronology, seen as a simple "archaeological artifact" (Frimigacci and Maitre 1981; Galipaud 1992). When we three local archaeologists created the Department of Archaeology in the early 1990s, we thought it time to propose a more complete analysis of the prehistoric sequence of New Caledonia, by taking into account cultural dynamics, political transformation, and landscape intensification processes, as well as historical archaeology (Sand 1995, 1996a). The sharing of work, information, and analysis among the members of our team, comprising two Kanaks and one Caldoche (European of local descent) of different cultural and political backgrounds, facilitates the presentation of conclusions that take into account, as much as possible, the sensibilities of each major community. This has led to the integrated historical chronology presented in the next section.

The Prehistoric Chronology of New Caledonia: An Integrated Synthesis

The "first settlers": Lapita and its evolutions

Like all the other islands of the world, New Caledonia was discovered by navigators. This means that the first settlers arrived with cultural baggage conceptualized in a point of origin elsewhere in the region. First discovery of the archipelago appears to be related to the spread of people of the "Lapita Cultural Complex" at the end of the second millennium B.C. (Green 2003; Kirch 1997; Spriggs 1997; see also Denham, Galipaud, Leavesley, Lilley, Pavlides, and Walter and Sheppard, this volume). The immediate origin of the navigators was probably Vanuatu, but on archaeological grounds the spread of people was very rapid across the New Caledonian archipelago, with all the major settlements founded in just one century (Sand 1997a, 2001).

At the very beginning, the cultural characteristics of the first settlers were very close to those of other Lapita groups living elsewhere in the region. The existence of some form of regional interaction can be identified on the one hand by the early import of obsidian sourced to the region of Talasea in New Britain, nearly 3,000 kilometers to the north (Sand and Sheppard 2000; also Pavlides, this volume) and on the other by the export of dentate-stamped pots produced in New Caledonia to localities at least as far as Malo Island in northern Vanuatu (Dickinson 1971). In this early period, it is not surprising to see close relationships in pottery form and design motifs in the ceramics produced throughout the newly discovered and hitherto uninhabited region of southern Melanesia, from the Reefs/Santa Cruz Islands near the main Solomons to the Isle of Pines off southern Grande Terre. Very rapidly, however, probably only a few generations, the Austronesian-speakers of New Caledonia started to diversify their traditions, boosting the production of some pottery forms and decorative motifs, nearly abandoning others, and developing a whole range of specific characteristics that allow us to identify the emergence of a distinctive "Southern Lapita Province" (Sand 2000a).

This process led to the local development alongside classical Lapita of paddle-impressed utilitarian ceramics known as Podtanéan ware (Sand 1999a; cf. Galipaud, this volume). Other changes did not take exactly the same path across the whole archipelago. This can be seen, for example, in the divergence of Lapita motifs between Grande Terre and the Loyalty Islands immediately to the east. In the first region, we clearly see the maintenance for more than 200 years of a predominantly dentate-stamped set of designs, while the second region sees the rapid appearance of a whole series of non-dentate-stamped motifs (Sand et al. 2002). These changes, which clearly do not relate to any decline of inter-site contact, are vivid testimony to the processes of cultural diversification at work in the first centuries of Austronesian settlement in southern Melanesia. This divergence of cultures, also evident in nearby Vanuatu (Bedford 2000), stands in marked contrast to the regionally integrated transformations that can be identified in the Fiji–West Polynesian region further east (Burley and Clark 2003).

"Transforming the landscape": Austronesian settlers take root

Internal cultural change saw Lapita pottery slowly drop out of the ceramic kit between 850 and 750 B.C., along with a whole series of distinctive shell ornaments. In the meantime, the descendants of the first settlers started to move inland. Archaeological data show that first exploration of some of the major inland valleys was conducted during the initial discovery period, but the first substantial inland settlement was probably delayed in most places for a number of generations. Although it appears that Austronesians had an impact on the flora in the first generations of their presence in some low-elevation valleys near the shore (Stevenson 1998), the start of forest clearance in the inner valleys, more than 10 kilometers from the coast, seems to have started only at the very end of the Lapita period and to have developed on a large scale mostly during the second half of the first millennium B.C. (Sand 1999b).

The slow spread of people into the different environments of Grande Terre and the Loyalties was probably related primarily to natural demographic increase. But it was also linked, in social terms, to the cultural diversification which attended the gradual transformation of navigators into horticulturists. Although population densities in a landmass as large as Grande Terre was probably never high during the first millennium B.C., the distances separating different groups certainly encouraged the eventual diversification of languages and the ever-greater differentiation of regional cultures. This can, for example, be seen in the emergence of two major types of ceramics on Grande Terre during this time (Sand 1995, 1999a), in parallel with the complete abandonment of pottery-making in the Loyalties. In the south, the development of post-Lapita ceramics led to the appearance of mostly small, incised globular pots of the Puen tradition, and the apparent abandonment of relations with the Loyalties. In the north, Podtanéan paddle-impressed pots – some traded with the Loyalty Islands – seem to have been more prolific, with the gradual advent of new forms of incurved pots of the Pindai tradition by the end of the millennium (Sand et al. 2001).

The progressive diversification of local cultures had a massive impact on the local environment. The landscape of Grande Terre is an old and fragile ecosystem of Gondwanaland origin, which developed strong local endemism in its flora and fauna over millions of years. The appearance of small groups of hunters, but certainly even more the introduction of pests such as the Pacific rat and the increasing use of fire to clean the forested landscape, led to an identifiable loss in species diversity as well as a change in landscape characteristics during the first millennium of human presence. Important endemic animals which encountered the first Austronesian settlers, including the megapode fowl *Sylviornis neocaledoniae*, the land crocodile *Mekosuchus inexpectatus*, and the horned turtle *Meilania mackayi*, along with a monitor lizard (*Varanus* sp.) and various species of birds, had almost completely disappeared less than a millennium later (Balouet and Olson 1989). Landslides and erosion, linked to forest destruction and cleaning of hillsides for cultivation, led to the progressive loss of fertile soils on upper hills, and the infilling with alluvial deposits of lower plains and parts of swampy seashores. In some areas, several meters of alluvium built up over the centuries, profoundly changing the characteristics of the local landscape (Sand 1999b).

"Times of conflict": socio-cultural diversification

As long as population numbers remained low, the development of field systems using simple but destructive slash-and-burn horticultural techniques was not much of a problem. The area of arable land was effectively unlimited, and there was plenty of time for environmental recovery in long fallow cycles after a planting season. But New Caledonia is outside the range of the deadly malaria which limits population growth further north in Melanesia, so natural demographic expansion over the centuries eventually led to unprecedented stress on the landscape.

Tensions over the control of limited land probably began first in the smallest islands. In the Loyalties, excavated layers dating from around A.D. 200–300 to the end of that millennium contain almost nothing from Grande Terre, unlike the preceding as well as the following millennium (Sand 1998). This indicates a breakdown in exchange relations for hundreds of years. Tensions among the islanders are also illustrated by the construction of massive stone fortifications (Sand and Ouetcho 1993). But it is probably not correct to reduce the rationale for these great forts simply to episodic warfare. Such sites also signal the development of strong political entities on islands such as Maré and Lifou, leading to the appearance of prestige rivalries (Sand 1996b). It is probably in that direction that we must seek the reason for raising such massive walls rather than narrower ones which would have been just as efficient in war.

Friction over the control of land, in what was probably the worst period of landscape change owing to the impact of slash-and-burn agriculture, certainly also led to episodes of stress on Grande Terre. Apart from the patterns of change in ceramic chronology (Sand et al. 2002), this part of the chronology is poorly known at present, but it appears that a need for better boundary identification led to an explosion of petroglyph production on the large island, with engraving being concentrated on natural frontiers like riverbanks, hilltops, and watershed divides between valleys (Monnin 1986; Monnin and Sand 2004). Increasing isolation allowed the diversification of languages and other cultural characteristics, already started in the preceding millennium, to advance further. It also led to the differentiation of local phenotypes between island populations and socio-cultural groups, distinctions which survived until European contact. Studies of human remains indicate the presence of physiological stresses, testimony to a period of episodic food shortages and limited life expectancy (Valentin and Sand 2003).

"The Kanak path": the rise of Kanak societies

Archaeologists have long debated the causes and dynamics of socioeconomic intensification in the Pacific (see Kirch 1984 for a review). For New Caledonia, it appears from modern data that a combination of high population density and landscape exhaustion owing to excessive burning, as well as the rise of stronger political systems, led to a gradual intensification of activity (Sand 1995). On horticultural grounds, intensification is at first characterized by the use of walls and mounds to protect fertile soils from erosion. The two major techniques developed from the end of the first millennium A.D. on the Grande Terre of New Caledonia were irrigated terraces – mainly for wet taro – and long, high mounds for dry yams (Figures 16.3 and 16.4) (Sand 1999b). In an archipelago located on the southern edge limit of the tropics and subject to droughts as well as long periods of rain, these two developments attained a level of complexity unprecedented in Oceania (Kirch and Lepofsky 1993; Walter and Sheppard this volume).

Over the next millennium, hundreds of hills became transformed by tens of thousands of taro terraces, flushed with fresh water by numerous artificial water

Figure 16.3 Abandoned taro terraces, La Grande Terre

Figure 16.4 Abandoned raised yam fields, La Grande Terre

channels, some several kilometers long. This massive restructuring of the landscape, through a highly demanding horticultural system needing control, repair, and attention every day, indicates the presence of a large population during this last millennium before first European contact (Sand et al. 2000). A similar conclusion can be reached when studying the extensive dry-land systems developed on the flat plains of Grande Terre, as well as the numerous raised horticultural mounds built in the hills. In the Loyalty Islands, which lack hills and regular water sources, it was the development of varieties of large yams, sometimes over two meters long, that characterized intensification. Only on Ouvea were people able to develop wetland planting, by removing thousands of cubic meters of sand to reach the water lens at the back of the sand dunes, in which they raised their wet taro in artificial compost (Sand 1995).

The gradual emergence of these intensified horticultural techniques led to different sociocultural groups becoming progressively more closely tied to particular landscapes, leading to what ethnobotanist Barrau (1956:56) called "agricultural sedentism." Increased sedentism fostered the emergence of more permanent settlements, characterized by elevated round house-mounds often organized in precise patterns around a central alley (Sand 1997b). Political structures also changed, with the advent of chiefdoms which controlled large regions, though without functioning as pyramidal hierarchies (Sand 1999b). Changes in material culture occurred as well, with the appearance of new pottery traditions, new ceremonial adze types, particular forms of traditional shell money, and so on. All these new objects continued to develop until the advent of the Europeans, and characterize what the present-day indigenous societies of New Caledonia consider to represent "Kanak culture." It was from the end of the first millennium A.D., though, about two-thirds of the way through the prehistoric chronology, that the cultural, social, and political specificities that are characteristic of the "indigenous" societies of the archipelago appeared. These new developments are clearly not related to the massive arrival of new populations, but merely to the gradual transformation of island societies over the preceding millennia, leading to adjustments and shifts that created the "Traditional Kanak Cultural Complex" (Sand 2002a).

The development of intensified horticultural techniques, the settlement of the population in permanent villages through a process of sedentarization, and the advent of new types of chiefdoms developing more ritualized wars to prevent massive field destruction led to the reopening of regular contacts between different parts of the archipelago. Interestingly, the new trading routes developed in completely different directions from those which existed one millennium before, supporting our hypothesis that there was a moderately long period in the chronology without exchange. During the second millennium A.D., the south of Grande Terre was in contact with Maré and Lifou, the island of Ouvea being a gateway to the northern part of Grande Terre (Sand 1998). Specific objects, like the rounded ceremonial *ostensoir*-axe in nephrite, were traded and exchanged between these islands in a "Kula-like" circle (Kasarherou 1990). The new ties created by these exchanges, and reinforced by marriage between chiefdoms, led to the creation of an archipelago-wide set of cultural traditions and customs, without seeing the disappearance of local cultural characteristics and languages. This opening-up to others, which can be identified throughout the southwestern Pacific during this period, led to the periodic arrival of new groups, mainly from Vanuatu, Fiji, and West Polynesia. The newcomers often put down roots in existing political systems and over the generations lost their cultural specificities. Only some Polynesians retained their languages until the end of the millennium (Carson 2002).

"New boats on old shores": European arrival and its consequences

New Caledonia was one of the last large archipelagoes in the western Pacific to be put on a map by Europeans. Captain Cook "discovered" northern Grande Terre in September 1774. Unfortunately, the second ship on the voyage was waiting for him in New Zealand, so he stayed only briefly in the archipelago. We thus have far less information on the indigenous societies at the time of first European contact than is the case in other places where Cook stopped (Beaglehole 1961). Over the next three decades, New Caledonia was irregularly visited by other European ships. It was only with the development of Sydney Harbour in Australia from the end of the 18th century and the emergence of the China trade that contacts multiplied, the archipelago being located directly on the sailing route to Asia. The advent of whaling, and then of the sandalwood trade, led to the first long-term Western settlements in the region, and with them the introduction of iron adzes, glass, new trading items, and finally firearms, alcohol, and tobacco (e.g., Shineberg 1967).

Until very recently, historians considered that these irregular early encounters with Europeans led to very few changes in indigenous societies prior to the appearance of Christian missionaries in the 1840s and France's takeover in 1853 (e.g., Doumenge 1994). The "traditional" Kanak societies described in the second half of the 19th century were seen as the direct descendants of the "prehistoric" societies seen by Cook nearly a century before, with fewer than 50,000 people living at low density in small semi-nomadic clans directed by low-level chiefs (Guiart 1983). For a century, these characteristics were considered to be the basis of "traditional" Kanak social and political organization. But such descriptions are now strongly criticized by archaeologists, who can clearly identify through field surveys the existence, during the last millennium before European contact, of a densely populated landscape based on labor-intensive horticulture (e.g., Sand 2000b).

This latter image of "traditional pre-contact" Kanak societies contrasts strongly with the situation witnessed by the French during the second part of the 19th century, and leads us to suspect that there was massive demographic and cultural disruption between first contact and the French takeover nearly 80 years later (Sand et al. 2000). We believe that in New Caledonia, like everywhere else in the Pacific (e.g., Miles 1997), Europeans introduced – mostly unwittingly – new diseases such as tuberculosis, smallpox, and dysentery. These diseases became deadly epidemics in Oceanic populations, which had no immunity to these scourges. Massive population collapse in the generations after Cook led to the failure of the large, strong chiefdoms, the rise of endemic warfare and cannibalism, and the rapid trans-formation of large sedentary clans into small semi-nomadic family groups regularly changing their habitation sites (Sand 1995).

It was these much-diminished Kanak societies, profoundly affected by decades of population decline, demographic restructuring, and political stress, that wit-nessed the arrival of missionaries in the 1840s and the progressive expansion of the first French settlers across Kanak lands during the late 1850s. The creation in 1864 of a penal colony on Grande Terre changed the situation dramatically. Aiming to copy the Australian example, Paris decided to create an Antipodean convict colony. Over the succeeding 35 years, more than 30,000 French, Italian, Spanish, and North African prisoners were sent to New Caledonia. Agricultural land had to be taken from the Kanaks of Grande Terre, who defended their settlements and field systems from spoliation in several episodes of war against French soldiers. Con-vinced that the Kanaks were going to disappear altogether in the succeeding decades owing to continuing demographic collapse, colonial officials moved indigenous clans from their land and placed them on reservations, mostly located on poor soils (Saussol 1979). The settling in New Caledonia of Europeans (Merle 1995) but also of Asian, Melanesian, and Polynesian workers over the following century created an ethnic melting pot in the archipelago, structured around a basically Western society.

It was not until the end of World War II that the Kanaks were given free move-ment and voting rights, leading to a period of apparent shared development toward an autonomous polity (Kurtovitch 2000). But it was only in the 1970s that lands began to be given back to indigenous people. By that late stage, the Kanaks had started demanding independence and rejecting claims for rights on the part of more recently settled groups. The political upheaval led to a period of undeclared civil war in the mid-1980s, until the signing of what can be called a peace treaty in 1988. This brought strong autonomy to the three provinces of New Caledonia, balanced to a degree by the political desire to create a common future for all the different cultural groups living in the archipelago. Today the provinces decide what archae-ological projects they want conducted on their land, as per their differing political agendas.

Archaeology and Contemporary Politics: What Written Past for a Common Future?

Finding common trends to build a peaceful future is a real challenge in an archi-pelago with such a complex history and such a diversified cultural as well as ethnic background. But the challenge has been dictated by the particular political future imagined by local political parties and the French government since 1988 (Mohamed-Gaillard 2003). To win the battle against cultural, ethnic, and political partition, the children of New Caledonia need to share a set of common principles as well as traditions and roots. The way history is constructed and taught is today one of the cornerstones of the integrative process that is under way (Collective 1992). History has always been about politics, and the writing of historical facts is linked to a larger understanding of the way a society needs to perceive its past. New Caledonia, like the rest of the Pacific, is no exception to this rule. What differentiates the inhabitants of our archipelago from the surrounding countries, however, is the multiplicity of their origins and cultures, with different groups promoting different agendas for the future. It is therefore not surprising that perspectives on history as a whole, as well as on specific points in the chronology, depend upon the group(s) or people(s) concerned (Sand et al. 2003a, 2003b).

Differences in historical perspectives between modern archaeology and indigenous traditions

Modern archaeology is about dates, chronologies, cultural evolution, and social transformation. What it tries to achieve above all is an understanding of the dynamics of history (Renfrew and Bahn 1996). This vision of the past, stemming from Judeo-Christian tradition and structured over the past three centuries by Western philosophical developments, looks for "facts," for "truth," for "testimonies" or "witnesses" in each period and culture. Conceptually far distant from this perspective, most non-Western and traditional societies around the globe have seen history – or millennia – as a means to validate contemporaneous situations and to root political, social, and cultural systems in the medium of "tradition." The intellectual scope is different from the very beginning, so it is to be expected that modern archaeologists in different parts of the world come into conflict with indigenous societies about the way to construct and write indigenous history (e.g., Nicholas and Andrews 1997; Watkins 2000). The main criticism of archaeologists in this context is that they do not take into account the "indigeneity" of the people they are studying, putting too much emphasis on historicizing the past through the identification of "changes" and "transformations" in the "stable" structures that in indigenous perspectives provide the basis for historical rights.

Although partly linked to a real difference in the way in which history is conceived in the Western world and in non-Western societies, these divergent perspectives have been profoundly deepened by the way Western ethnographers – followed today by indigenous leaders – have presented a lot of indigenous societies over the past 100 years. Mistakenly believing that "traditional" societies were stable, "cold" systems, trapped in their customs without any chance to change and thus doomed to remain "without history," ethnographic writings have led to a synchronic vision of indigenous histories (e.g., Kirch 1990). Because archaeology today underwrites a diachronic view of indigenous histories, some indigenous people feel very strongly that this "return to history" betrays their past and undermines their historical rights. Political considerations are thus a central issue in this debate, as oral traditions in every non-literate society tell of stories of fights, changes of chiefs, shifts in residence patterns and alliances, all clearly illustrating the dynamic nature of all past cultures (e.g., Bensa 2000).

The Lapita problem: accepting the evolution of prehistoric cultural traditions in Oceania

In the western Pacific, one of the major points of contention in the pre-European chronology concerns descriptions of first settlement and its consequences. As mentioned earlier, colonial discourse, here like elsewhere, has identified pre-traditional archaeological remains as testimony to other "races" which came before the traditional indigenous occupants (e.g., Avias 1949, 1950). These "former occupants" have been depicted with far more pleasant characteristics than the inhabitants encountered by European colonists. This colonial construction of history, based on the idea that indigenous societies do not change and that every observable cultural shift is the sign of a new "invasion," was regularly echoed in local oral traditions concerning "mythical" pasts peopled by all sorts of individuals: small or large, dark or pale-skinned, with long or very short hair, and so on. But what oral traditions justify most of the time through references to such "aliens" are complex sets of creation myths. In the western Pacific, most of these myths tell of the creation of the "first man" in situ on the island or archipelago. This is clear in an anecdote described by noted Polynesian scholar Te Rangi Hiroa (Sir Peter Buck) in the 1930s, on the day Hiroa presented the concept of a migration of Asians into the Pacific to a local community:

> Influenced by mythology and local legends, the Samoan regards himself as truly autochthonous. At a kava ceremony in Tau, I was welcomed by a talking chief in the stilted phrases of his office. In my reply, I alluded to the common origin of the Polynesians somewhere in Asia and the wonderful voyages our ancestors had made in peopling Polynesia. The talking chief replied, "We thank you for your interesting speech. The Polynesians may have come from Asia, but the Samoans, no. We originated in Samoa." He looked around with an air of infallibility, and his fellow scholars grunted their approval. In self-defense, I became a fundamentalist. I said, "The good book that I have seen you carrying to church three times on Sundays says that the first parents of mankind were Adam and Eve, who were created in the Garden of Eden." In no way disturbed, the oracle replied, "That may be, but the Samoans were created here in Manu'a." A trifle exasperated, I said, "Ah, I must be in the Garden of Eden." I took the silence which followed to be a sign of affirmation (Buck 1938: 286-87).

It is with some difficulty in this context that indigenous people hear archaeologists today speaking about "first settlement" and the arrival, in empty islands, of sailors who had other cultural backgrounds but who at the same time are said to be their ancestors (see also Cauchois, this volume). The discovery of Lapita sites dated around 3,000 years ago in the whole southwestern Pacific, crossing the cultural boundary between "Melanesia" and "Polynesia," and characterized by types of finely decorated pots (Kirch 1997) different from everything produced in the region over the past 200–300 years, has created over the past 30 years a contentious debate about the concept of origins (Sorovi-Vunidilo 2003). The questions that invariably arise can be labeled as "Were these our ancestors?" and "Why didn't our ancestors continue to produce these beautiful pots instead of replacing them with coarser ones?"

Although never clearly expressed, the main question that these discoveries raise in indigenous people's minds is: "How can we correlate scientific discoveries with the origin myths that justify our local societies?" The question is important, but it certainly cannot be resolved by archaeologists alone. The identification through excavation of changes in pottery types, of a human impact on local fauna and flora leading to ecological transformations, of evolutions in the settlement of a landscape through time, of the creation of localized languages, political systems, and cultural traditions, are topics unrelated to what most indigenous societies feel is their own history. As told by Fijian archaeologist Tarisi Sorovi-Vunidilo after confronting her chiefs: "They challenged me more on the fact that our social structure in Fiji is based on the Kaunitoni Migration. Meaning that if the archaeological research contradicts with the migration story, then our social structure will collapse or will be of no use" (Sorovi-Vunidilo 2003; see also Cauchois, this volume).

But the integration of a dynamic history into modern Pacific societies is also a way for present-day Oceanians to demonstrate that they have not been "outside history" and that their ancestors have played a part in the great history of humanity (see Lilley, this volume). Everything depends on the way this history is related through archaeological action and writings to contemporary indigenous groups. By identifying and recognizing clear historical links between past cultures and modern societies, archaeologists can create conceptual ties with this distant past for indigenous groups, securing a feeling of relationship which can bypass culture-historical differences. This type of linkage was felt in August 2002 on the eponymous site WKO013A at Lapita in New Caledonia, when representatives from all the nations of the southwest Pacific gathered for a customary ceremony celebrating their shared Austronesian origins, while at the same time recognizing their present-day differences (Sand 2003).

Kanak indigenous societies and archaeology: historical perspectives

As we have noted, ethnographic data appeared to provide in-depth knowledge of the Kanak societies observed by Europeans from 1774 onward (e.g., Guiart 1963, 1992), but the intrusion of archaeological knowledge concerning the late prehistoric period has recently made the picture more complex (Sand 1995). Proper ethnographic studies of the indigenous societies of New Caledonia started at the very end of the 19th century, over a century after the first encounters, leading to profoundly stereotyped reconstructions of "traditional" Kanak culture trapped in a never-changing customary world (e.g., Collective 1990). By not taking into account the very particular historical context in which their information was collected, namely one marked by oppressive Western colonial rule, ethnographers created a model which over the past century became the orthodox picture of pre-colonial Kanak society. It was toward this historically ill-founded model that Kanak leaders turned in the 1960s and 70s, to support claims for the restitution of their ancestral rights and lands (e.g., Tjibaou 1976; Tjibaou and Missotte 1976).

Unexpectedly in New Caledonia as in all the other Melanesian islands where late prehistory has been studied in some depth, archaeological researches have shown that far more complex societies existed before first European contact than was hitherto believed. Probably the most important differences with the orthodox model flow from the reconstruction of intensified landscape use and complex political systems, illustrating the existence of large populations with highly diversified patterns of sociopolitical organization. In other words, the whole picture of "simple Melanesian societies" has been turned on its head by archaeology (Sand 2002b; see also Walter and Sheppard this volume), necessitating a complete rethinking, by the modern-day indigenous groups, of what their "traditional" societies might have been like.

It is in this connection that divergence is most apparent between the historical perspectives of scientists – acknowledging that no society has ever stopped its development at one particular stage to become "traditional" – and islanders trying to reconstruct their past. Elements of a cultural tradition, like rituals, craft production and technology, are maintained in societies over long periods of time and form the core of distinctive "cultural complexes," while other elements, such as settlement rights, political positions and alliances, are far more volatile and normally change at a faster rate. It is the subtle difference between these two sides of culture that allows us to place a clearly existing "Traditional Kanak Cultural Complex" in an appropriate historical perspective.

This type of analysis (Sand et al. 1998) leads to a profound dilemma in modern Kanak society, as it requires people to accept that there were shifting political structures over the centuries, changing chiefdoms and alliances, and episodes of indigenous war, destruction, and despoliation, all of which created renewed competition amongst different clans over land. These conflicts inside the community are a far cry from the political ideals of the Kanak freedom movement, which seeks to create a unified "Kanak people." It is thus not surprising that the archaeological model of a dynamic pre-colonial Kanak society, which takes into account field data as well as oral traditions, is rejected by some cultural and political leaders, who prefer to develop a postmodernist approach to "traditional" Kanak history. This approach is identifiable in the New Caledonia Museum in Nouméa, where Kanak objects from the 18th and 19th centuries are presented without chronological background, as well as in the Tjibaou Cultural Centre, where no "Kanak history" is put forward at all.

From "first discovery" to new religions:
19th-century transformations and their present-day consequences

The marked differences observed by archaeologists between the late prehistoric situation and the simple "traditional" Kanak societies of the colonial era are directly related to changes caused by European contact. Contrary to what has been written on the subject for generations, there appears to have been a drastic change between the end of the 18th century and the middle of the 19th century, primarily owing to the demographic impact of introduced diseases. We will probably never know the precise number of Kanaks in New Caledonia in 1774, but the population was certainly far larger than the 50,000 people acknowledged by history (Kasarherou 1992; Rallu 1990). This means that the currently accepted demographic decline of around forty-three percent by the beginning of the 20th century (Shineberg 1983) has to be increased by a substantial degree, as it must have been more like the eighty to ninety-five percent reported elsewhere in the Pacific (e.g., Miles 1997; Stannard 1989).

This adjustment means that indigenous societies had lost nearly all of their members by the time the first detailed ethnographic studies were conducted. The effect of this central point cannot be overemphasized. It means that the indigenous societies of New Caledonia at the time of the first permanent settlement of some Europeans in the early to mid-1840s were not in their "prehistoric" condition, but rather had changed profoundly, losing most of their sophisticated high chiefdoms, leading to the progressive abandonment of the most complex intensified horticultural systems, with the development of warfare, cannibalism, and the constant movement of people through landscapes that were slowly being emptied of human life (Sand et al. 2000).

The Kanaks clearly understood the links between the development of new diseases, the rapid disappearance of a large part of the indigenous population, and sporadic contacts with Westerners. In a revealing work, the anthropologist Illouz (2000) has shown how the new Christian God brought by the Catholic and Protestant missionaries was soon raised on Maré Island to the title of *Hma-kaze*, the "big killing dead body." It was not in a move toward an enlightening new religion that most islanders converted to Christianity, but rather traditional alliance-seeking, aimed in a customary way to slow down the effects of the epidemics.

While their numbers were being so massively diminished, the Kanaks of Grande Terre from 1855 onward had also to confront occupation by the French colonial army, which was sent into the valleys and hills to push back the villages and planting grounds to gain land for European colonists (Dauphiné 1989). The process was a long and devastating succession of low-level ambushes, the torching of Kanak houses, and random shootings, sometimes leading to organized Kanak rebellion resulting in the killing of Europeans and the destruction of their houses before the colonial army was sent back in to reestablish order (Saussol 1979). When the clans were put onto small reservations, the complex historical processes experienced by the Kanaks over the preceding century had already led to confusion about indigenous land rights amongst conflicting chiefdoms. Over the succeeding three generations, this confusion was deepened by the development of diverging oral traditions between separated groups claiming the same land. At the same time, the colonial power officially named new high chiefs in opposition to the customary chiefs, and, through a subtle system of forced labor, made the traditional chiefs nominate the people in their villages who would be forced to work for the Europeans (Mohamed-Gaillard 2003:174). This destruction of customary sociopolitical relations led to a perverse situation based upon the manipulation of tradition and reality in most aspects of indigenous society.

This construction of the early "post-contact" and colonial periods explains the historical processes that have led to the major issue facing Kanak society today: the legitimation of clan-based land claims and the representativeness of the chiefs. Unfortunately, although they demonstrably explain the present situation, the historical dynamics we have described are not usually accepted because the identification of manipulation of traditional land and political claims conflicts directly, in New Caledonia like everywhere else, with contemporary belief in the unassailable primal "truth" of indigenous oral traditions. Although an apparent unity joins the Kanak claims in parts of Grande Terre where land has not been given back, community conflict has emerged everywhere that restitution has been made over the past 30 years. This position is exacerbated by the fact that the descendants of European colonists and convicts feel legitimately that the land they inherited from their parents is theirs, legally bought from recognized government institutions and cultivated over the generations with no small sacrifice (e.g., Brou 1973).

Conclusion: What is Archaeology for in the Pacific?

How do we reconcile different cultural and ethnic groups, each with its specific understanding and perception of history and historical processes, in a political project to create a nation? How do we write a balanced history acknowledging the contributions of each community, the positive and negative side of each period, without favoring one group against the others? How are we to conduct rigorous archaeology in an archipelago such as New Caledonia, when each conclusion brought forward, whether concerned with ancient or more recent history, has immediate consequences for the people whose past is in focus as well as for those who live around them?

These questions, which confront the archaeological community throughout Oceania with increasing intensity, are most directly of concern to the indigenous and non-indigenous native archaeologists working in their own lands. Local archaeologists are today in the uncomfortable position of being between two extremes, two opposing political projects, each of which needs to write history in a particular way. In New Caledonia, promoters of a future limited to the "indigenous" groups want to promote an idealized vision of "traditional times" and a simplistic one-dimensional picture of the massive disruption and pain of the colonial era. Promoters of permanent French control of the archipelago, on the other hand, emphasize the benefits of European colonization and the "progress" it brought to the islands over the past 150 years. Much the same situation obtains in many other parts of Oceania.

As their results demonstrate time and again, archaeologists know that historical reality lies between these two poles (Sand et al. 2003a). But in writing about their homeland, about their own history, they have to deal directly with criticisms of their own cultural and ethnic groups, as they appear to develop concepts and ideas at odds with majority opinion in those communities. Putting forward, on the basis, for example, of oral tradition, the idea that different clans settled a particular place at different times, appears to resurrect internal conflicts about the historical rights of each family on the land (Mapou 2003). At the other end of the spectrum, excavating historical sites from the convict period can be perceived by some people of non-Western origin to glorify the non-indigenous past and the depth of European roots in the archipelago, with archaeologists appearing in this case to promote non-indigenous rights (see also Smith this volume). It is thus not surprising that local archaeologists are often criticized for expressing non-orthodox ideas which are considered to be subversive by political leaders of all stripes (Sand et al. 2003b).

Such perceptions of archaeological research show how much each result gained from the past can become a contentious contemporary issue and on that basis in danger of being politically manipulated by non-archaeological vested interests. Although an impossible goal, we often wish we could disconnect archaeology and politics. This was certainly the case recently in relation to our use of the term "Kanak." The term, derived from a Polynesian loan introduced by the missionaries to mean "working boy" when in fact referring to men, became an insult, but since the 1960s has been used by indigenous political leaders to mean "man." Today, the term is synonymous with "the indigenous Melanesians of New Caledonia" (Angleviel 2002). Culturally, the roots of traditional Kanak societies developed from the end of the first millennium A.D., building on transformations throughout the preceding millennia. In historical terms, the advent of the "Traditional Kanak Cultural Complex," that is, the emergence of cultural traits that the indigenous populations of New Caledonia identify today as their own, demonstrably started around 1,000 years before first European encounter (Sand et al. 2000).

Although in archaeological terms this point is readily understandable, the simple use of the term "Kanak" to name this period of time implies for some that indigenous people "were not Kanaks" in earlier times. This idea is totally unacceptable in today's political climate (Sand 2003), underlining the difficulty of relating culture-historical facts, which are necessarily dynamic over the entire span of human history, with political claims based on totally different worldviews. The term "Kanak," applied to a specific historical trajectory unfolding over millennia, takes a different meaning from that attached to the same term by an ethnic group claiming control as indigenous inhabitants of their political rights while confronted by the presence of other cultural and ethnic groups on their soil.

To help resolve such misunderstandings between archaeology and politics, it seems obvious that we need to encourage and support the emergence of new generations of indigenous archaeologists conducting scientific research on their own past (see Cauchois, Dugay-Grist, and Mandui, this volume). The creation of local archaeological institutions in different archipelagoes of the Pacific has shown that it is not only necessary to provide physical infrastructure: It is also vital to have well-trained scientists who are given the financial, legal, and technical tools to do archaeology properly. Although times are currently hard for locally conducted archaeology in the Pacific, with great political pressure in every archipelago to prevent development of locally constructed dynamic historical models, we hope the time will soon come when the voices of local archaeologists in Oceania will be strong and they will be able to write the past history of our region in their own words.

REFERENCES

Angleviel, F., 2002 De Kanaka à Kanak: L'Appropriation d'un Terme Générique au Profit de la Revendication Identitaire. Hermès, Cognition, Communication, Politique 32–33: 191–196.

——2003 Historiographie de la Nouvelle-Calédonie. Paris: Publibook.

Archambault, M., 1901 Les Mégalithes Néo-Calédoniens. L'Anthropologie 12:257–268.

Avias, J., 1949 Contribution à la Préhistoire de l'Océanie: Les Tumulis des Plateaux de Fer en Nouvelle-Calédonie. Journal de la Société des Océanistes 5:15–50.

——1950 Poteries Canaques et Poteries Préhistoriques en Nouvelle-Calédonie. Contribution à l'Archéologie et à la Préhistoire Océanienne. Journal de la Société des Océanistes 6:11–139.

——1953. La Préhistoire Néo-Calédonienne. Journal de la Société des Océanistes 9:55–63.

Balouet, J-C., and S. Olson, 1989 Fossil Birds from Late Quaternary Deposits in New Caledonia. Smithsonian Contributions to Zoology 469. Washington, DC: Smithsonian Institution Press.

Barbançon, J., 2003 L'Archipel des Forçats. Histoire du Bagne de Nouvelle-Calédonie de 1863 à 1931. Paris: Septentrion.

Barrau, J., 1956 L'Agriculture Vivrière Autochtone de la Nouvelle-Calédonie. Nouméa: Commission du Pacifique Sud.

Beaglehole, J., 1961 The Journal of Captain James Cook on his Voyages of Discovery. The Voyage of the *Resolution* and *Adventure* 1772–1775. Cambridge: Cambridge University Press.

Bedford, S., 2000 Pieces of the Vanuatu Puzzle: Archaeology of the North, South and Centre. Ph.D. dissertation, Australian National University.

Bedford, S., M. Spriggs, M. Wilson and R. Regenvanu, 1998 The Australian National University-National Museum of Vanuatu Archaeology Project 1994–97: A Preliminary Report on the Establishment of Cultural Sequences and Rock Art Research. Asian Perspectives 37:165–193.

Bensa, A., 1990 Nouvelle-Calédonie, un Paradis dans la Tourmente. Paris: Découvertes Gallimard.

——2000 Le Chef Kanak. Les Modèles et l'Histoire, *In* En Pays Kanak. Ethnologie, Linguistique, Archéologie, Histoire de la Nouvelle-Calédonie. A. Bensa et I. Leblic, eds. pp. 9–48. Collection Ethnologie de la France 14. Paris, Éditions de la Maison des Sciences de l'Homme.

Boutin-Boyer, S., 2003 De la Première Guerre Mondiale en Océanie. Les Guerres de tous les Calédoniens, 1914–1919. Paris: Septentrion, Presses Universitaires.

Brou, B., 1973 Histoire de la Nouvelle-Calédonie, les Temps Modernes, 1774–1925. Société d'Etudes Historiques de la Nouvelle-Calédonie 4.

Buck, P. (Te Rangi Hiroa), 1938 Vikings of the Sunrise. New York: Frederick Stokes.

Burley, D., and J. Clark, 2003 The Archaeology of Fiji/Western Polynesia in the Post-Lapita Era. *In* Pacific Archaeology: Assessments and Prospects. C. Sand, ed. pp. 235–254. Les

Cahiers de l'Archéologie en Nouvelle-Calédonie 15. Nouméa: Département Archéologie, Service des Musées et du Patrimoine de Nouvelle-Calédonie.

Carson, M., 2002 Inter-Cultural Contact and Exchange in Ouvea (Loyalty Islands, New Caledonia). Ph.D. dissertation, University of Hawai'i at Manoa.

Collective, 1983 Contribution à l'Histoire du Pays Kanak. Nouméa: IKS.

——1990 De Jade et de Nacre. Patrimoine Artistique Kanak. Paris: Réunion des Musées Nationaux.

——1992 La Nouvelle-Calédonie. Histoire-CM. Nouméa: CTRDP-Hachette.

Crosby, A., 2002 Archaeology and *Vanua* Development in Fiji. World Archaeology 34:363–378.

Cugola, U., 2003 Perspectives pour une Décolonisation en Nouvelle-Calédonie. Journal de la Société des Océanistes 117:273–280.

Dauphiné, J., 1989 Les Spoliations Foncières en Nouvelle-Calédonie (1853–1913). Paris: L'Harmattan.

Dickinson, W., 1971 Temper Sands in Lapita-Style Potsherds in Malo. Journal of the Polynesian Society 80:244–246.

Dortch, C., 1998 Cultural Sensibilities and Archaeological Actualities. Australian Archaeology 47:66–67.

Doumenge, J-P., 1994 La Nouvelle-Calédonie au Plan Humain. Approche Géographique et Historique des Réalités Culturelles, Démographiques, Economiques et Politiques. *In* Géo-Pacifique des Espaces Français. P. Le Bourdiec, C. Jost et F. Angleviel, eds. pp. 63–105. Nouméa: CTRDP Nouvelle-Calédonie/Université Française du Pacifique.

Frimigacci, D., and J-P. Maitre, 1981 Archéologie et Préhistoire (planche 16). Atlas de la Nouvelle-Calédonie et Dépendances. Paris: ORSTOM.

Galipaud, J-C., 1992 Un ou Plusieurs Peuples Potiers en Nouvelle-Calédonie. Journal de la Société des Océanistes 95:185–200.

Green, R., 2003 The Lapita Horizon and Tradition – Signature for One Set of Oceanic Migrations. *In* Pacific Archaeology: Assessments and Prospects. C. Sand, ed. pp. 95–120. Les Cahiers de l'Archéologie en Nouvelle-Calédonie 15. Nouméa: Département Archéologie, Service des Musées et du Patrimoine de Nouvelle-Calédonie.

Guiart, J., 1963 La Chefferie en Mélanésie du Sud. Paris: Institut d'Ethnologie, Musée de l'Homme.

——1983 La Terre est le Sang des Morts. Paris: Editions Anthropos.

——1992 Structure de la Chefferie en Mélanésie du sud. Paris: Institut d'Ethnologie, Musée de l'Homme.

Illouz, C., 2000 Chronique Meurtrière d'une Mutation Théologique. Maré (Îles Loyauté). *In* En Pays Kanak. A. Bensa et I. Leblic, eds. pp. 195–216. Paris: Editions de la Maison des Sciences de l'Homme.

Kasarherou, C., 1992 Histoire Démographique de la Population Mélanésienne de la Nouvelle-Calédonie entre 1840 et 1950. Thèse de Doctorat, Université Paris I.

Kasarherou, E., 1990 La Hache Ostensoir. De Jade et de Nacre. Patrimoine Artistique Kanak. Paris: Réunion des Musées Nationaux.

Kirch, P., 1984 The Evolution of the Polynesian Chiefdoms. Cambridge: Cambridge University Press.

——1990 The Evolution of Sociopolitical Complexity in Prehistoric Hawaii: An Assessment of the Archaeological Evidence. Journal of World Archaeology 4:311–345.

——1997 The Lapita Peoples. Oxford: Blackwell.

——2000 On the Road of the Winds: An Archaeological History of the Pacific Islands before European Contact. Berkeley, CA: University of California Press.

Kirch, P., and D. Lepofsky, 1993 Polynesian Irrigation: Archaeological and Linguistic Evidence for Origins and Development. Asian Perspectives 32:183–204.

Kurtovitch, I., 2000 La Vie Politique en Nouvelle-Calédonie 1940–1953. Paris: Septentrion, Presses Universitaires.

Le Borgne, J., 1959 Géographie de la Nouvelle-Calédonie et des Îles Loyauté. Paris: Gaillard.

Mapou, L., 2003 Sur le Terrain de la Recherche. Mwà Véé 40:5–10.

Merle, I., 1995 Expérience Coloniales. La Nouvelle-Calédonie (1853–1920). Paris: Belin.

Miles, J., 1997 Infectious Diseases: Colonising the Pacific? Dunedin: University of Otago Press.

Mohamed-Gaillard, S., 2003 150 Ans de Liens Institutionnels et Politiques entre la France et la Nouvelle-Calédonie. Journal de la Société des Océanistes 117:171–186.

Monnin, J., 1986 Les Pétroglyphes de Nouvelle-Calédonie. Nouméa: Office Culturel Scientifique et Technique Canaque.

Monnin, J., et C. Sand, 2004 Kibo, le Serment Gravé. Essai de Synthèse sur les Pétroglyphes Calédoniens. Les Cahiers de l'Archéologie en Nouvelle-Calédonie 16. Nouméa: Département Archéologie, Service des Musées et du Patrimoine de Nouvelle-Calédonie.

Nicholas, G., and T. Andrews, 1997 At a Crossroads. Archaeology and First Peoples in Canada. Burnaby, BC: Archaeology Press, Simon Fraser University.

Oliver, D., 1988 Oceania. The Native Cultures of Australia and the Pacific Islands. Honolulu: University of Hawai'i Press.

Palombo, P., 2002 La Présence Japonaise en Nouvelle-Calédonie (1890–1960). Les Relations Economiques entre le Japon et la Nouvelle-Calédonie à travers l'Immigration et l'Industrie Minière. Thèse d'Histoire, Université de la Nouvelle-Calédonie.

Rallu, J-P., 1990 Les Populations Océaniennes aux XIXe et XXe Siècles. Institut d'Etudes Démographiques. Travaux et Documents, Cahier 128. Paris: Presses Universitaires de France.

Renfrew, C., and P. Bahn, 1996 Archaeology. Theories, Methods and Practice. London: Thames and Hudson.

Sand, C., 1995 "Le Temps d'Avant." La Préhistoire de la Nouvelle-Calédonie. Paris: L'Harmattan.

——1996a Recent Developments in the Study of New Caledonia's Prehistory. Archaeology of Oceania 31:45–71.

——1996b Structural Remains as Markers of Complex Societies in Southern Melanesia during Prehistory: The Case of the Monumental Forts of Maré Island (New Caledonia). In Indo-Pacific Prehistory: The Chiang Mai Papers, vol. 2. I. Glover and P. Bellwood, eds. pp. 37–44. Bulletin of the Indo-Pacific Prehistory Association 15. Canberra: Indo-Pacific Prehistory Association.

——1997a The Chronology of Lapita Ware in New Caledonia. Antiquity 71:539–547.

——1997b Variété de l'Habitat Ancien en Nouvelle-Calédonie. Journal de la Société des Océanistes 104:39–66.

——1998 Recent Archaeological Research in the Loyalty Islands of New Caledonia. Asian Perspectives 37:194–223.

——1999a Lapita and Non-Lapita Ware during New Caledonia's First Millennium of Austronesian Settlement. In Le Pacifique de 5000 à 2000 avant le Présent. Suppléments à l'Histoire d'une Colonization. J-C. Galipaud et I. Lilley, eds. pp. 139–159. Nouméa: IRD.

——1999b From the Swamp to the Terrace: Intensification of Horticultural Practices in New Caledonia, from First Settlement to European Contact. In The Prehistory of Food. C. Gosden and J. Hather, eds. pp. 252–269. London: Routledge.

——2000a The Specificities of the "Southern Lapita Province": the New Caledonian Case. Archaeology in Oceania 35:20–33.

——2000b Reconstructing "Traditional" Kanak Society in New Caledonia: The Role of Archaeology in the Study of European Contact. In The Archaeology of Difference: Negotiating Cross-Cultural Engagements in Oceania. R. Torrence and A. Clarke, eds. pp. 51–78. London: Routledge.

——2001 Evolutions in the Lapita Cultural Complex: A View from the Southern Lapita Province. Archaeology in Oceania 36:65–76.

——2002a Creations and Transformations of Prehistoric Landscapes in New Caledonia. In Pacific Landscapes. Archaeological Approaches. T. Ladefoged and M. Graves, eds. pp. 13–34. Los Osos, CA: Bearsville Press.

——2002b Melanesian Tribes vs. Polynesian Chiefdoms: Recent Archaeological Assessment of a Classic Model of Sociopolitical Types in Oceania, Asian Perspectives 41:284–296.

——2003 Introduction to the Conference: Commemorating the First Excavation at Lapita. In Pacific Archaeology: Assessments and Prospects. C. Sand, ed. pp. 1–10. Les Cahiers de l'Archéologie en Nouvelle-Calédonie 15. Nouméa: Département Archéologie, Service des Musées et du Patrimoine de Nouvelle-Calédonie.

Sand, C., J. Bole and A. Ouetcho, 1998 Traces. 3000 Ans de Patrimoine Archéologique Calédonien. Les Cahiers de l'Archéologie en Nouvelle-Calédonie 8. Nouméa: Département Archéologie, Service des Musées et du Patrimoine de Nouvelle-Calédonie.

——2000 Les Sociétés Préeuropéennes de Nouvelle-Calédonie et leur Transformation Historique: L'Apport de l'Archéologie. In En Pays Kanak. A. Bensa et I. Leblic, eds. pp. 171–194. Paris: Editions de la Maison des Sciences de l'Homme.

——2001 Tiouandé. Archéologie d'un Massif de Karst du Nord-Est de la Grande Terre (Nouvelle-Calédonie). Les Cahiers de l'Archéologie en Nouvelle-Calédonie 12. Nouméa: Département Archéologie, Service des Musées et du Patrimoine de Nouvelle-Calédonie.

——2002 Site LPO023 of Kurin: Characteristics of a Lapita Settlement in the Loyalty Islands (New Caledonia). Asian Perspectives 41:129–147.

——2003a Prehistory and its Perception in a Melanesian Archipelago: The New Caledonia Example. Antiquity 77:505–519.

——2003b Les Aléas de la Construction Identitaire Multi-Ethnique en Nouvelle-Calédonie: Quel Passé pour un Avenir Commun? Journal de la Société des Océanistes 117:147–169.

Sand, C., and A. Ouetcho, 1993 Etudes Archéologiques sur les Îles Loyauté. Les Cahiers de l'Archéologie en Nouvelle-Calédonie 3. Nouméa: Département Archéologie, Service des Musées et du Patrimoine de Nouvelle-Calédonie.

Sand, C., and P. Sheppard, 2000 Long Distance Prehistoric Obsidian Imports in New Caledonia: Characteristics and Meaning. Comptes-rendus de l'Académie des Sciences de Paris. Sciences de la Terre et des Planètes 331:235–243.

Sarazin, F., 1924 Sur les Relations des Néo-Calédoniens avec le Groupe de l'Homonéanderthalensis. L'Anthropologie 34:193–227.

Saussol, A., 1979 L'Héritage. Essai sur le Problème Foncier Mélanésien en Nouvelle-Calédonie. Publication de la Société des Océanistes 40.

Shineberg, D., 1967 They Came for Sandalwood. A Study of the Sandalwood Trade in the South-West Pacific, 1830–1865. Melbourne: Melbourne University Press.

——1983 Un Nouveau Regard sur la Démographie Historique de la Nouvelle-Calédonie. Journal de la Société des Océanistes 76:33–43.

Smith, C., 1998 Editorial. Australian Archaeology 47:iii–iv.

Sorovi-Vunidilo, T., 2003 Developing Better Relationships between Researchers and Local Pacific Communities: The Way Forward. In Pacific Archaeology: Assessments and

Prospects. C. Sand, ed. pp. 371–374. Les Cahiers de l'Archéologie en Nouvelle-Calédonie 15. Nouméa: Département Archéologie, Service des Musées et du Patrimoine de Nouvelle-Calédonie.

Spriggs, M., 1997 The Island Melanesians. Oxford: Blackwell.

Stannard, D., 1989 Before the Horror. The Population of Hawai'i on the Eve of Western Contact. Honolulu: Social Science Research Institute.

Stevenson, J., 1998 Late Quaternary Environmental Change and the Impact of Melanesian Colonization in New Caledonia. Ph.D. dissertation, Australian National University.

Terrier, C., 2000 La Colonization de Peuplement Libre en Nouvelle-Calédonie (1889–1909) ou des Conséquences de la Confrontation entre Intérêts Métropolitains et Insulaires dans l'Évolution d'une Utopie Française en Océanie vers un Type Colonial Spécifique. Thèse d'Histoire, Université de la Nouvelle-Calédonie.

Tjibaou, J-M., 1976 Recherche d'Identité Mélanésienne et Société Traditionnelle. Journal de la Société des Océanistes 53:281–292.

Tjibaou, J-M., and P. Missotte, 1976 Kanaké, Mélanésien de Nouvelle-Calédonie. Nouméa: Société Nouvelle des Editions du Pacifique.

Trotter, M., and B. McCulloch, 1971 Prehistoric Rock Art of New Zealand. Wellington: A. H. & W. Reed.

Valentin, F., and C. Sand, 2003 Squelettes de Nouvelle-Calédonie et Sociétés Préhistoriques Océaniennes. In Archéologie en Océanie Insulaire. Peuplement, Sociétés et Paysages. C. Orliac, ed. pp. 10–27. Paris: Artcom.

Watkins, J., 2000 Indigenous Archaeology. Walnut Creek, CA: AltaMira Press.

Windshuttle, K., and T. Gillin, 2002 The Extinction of the Australian Pygmies. Quadrant June: 7–18.

17

Levuka, Fiji: A Case Study in Pacific Islands Heritage Management

Anita Smith

Levuka, Fiji's first colonial capital, is located on the island of Ovalau to the east of Viti Levu, the largest island in Fiji (Figure 17.1). The heritage values of Levuka and its potential as a tourist destination have been internationally recognized since the early 1970s but conservation of the town's unique cultural landscape has to date been limited. Although the Fijian government registered the town as the nation's premier historic site in 1989, this has not yet translated into a systematic or inclusive heritage management plan despite Levuka being mooted as Fiji's first nomination for inscription on the UNESCO World Heritage List.

This chapter looks at various factors contributing to the town's standing as a heritage place worthy of conserving and those that have made limited practical advances toward achieving this. Many of these issues affect the conservation of heritage sites in the Pacific Islands in general. In Levuka they are exacerbated because the town's heritage values have been associated with processes of European colonization in the Pacific, posing questions as to whose values are represented by Levuka's heritage and whether conservation programs in the town should be a government priority in post-colonial Fiji. As is argued in this chapter, a narrow focus on conservation of the town's architectural heritage has contributed to perceptions of Levuka as simply a "heritage of colonialism," limiting recognition of the significance of the place as a cultural landscape. The aim of the chapter is to explore issues to be resolved in the development of a long-term conservation strategy for Levuka and, perhaps more importantly in the context of this volume, to provide a case study of heritage management in the Pacific.

When the deed of cession that handed the Fiji Islands to the British was signed in Levuka in 1874, the town had been providing a safe harbor for European vessels for over fifty years. Until this time, Levuka's development in many respects mirrored that of other European ports of call in the Pacific such as Apia in Samoa (Ralston 1977). Unlike these other Pacific ports, however, development in Levuka was truncated by the moving of the colonial capital to Suva in 1882. By the

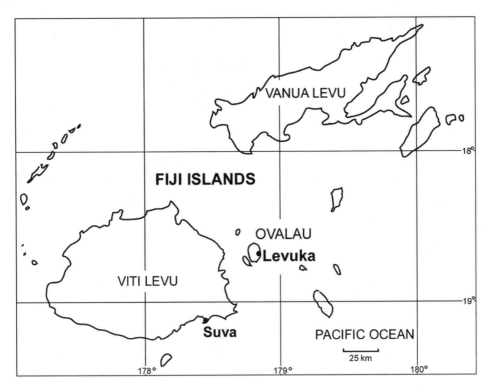

Figure 17.1 Location of Levuka and Ovalau in relation to the principal Fiji Islands

mid-20th century the town was very much a backwater in Fijian economy and politics. Much of the town's streetscape of Victorian shop-fronts, bungalow-style houses, churches, and public buildings has remained largely unchanged since the early 20th century (Figure 17.2). Levuka's potential as a heritage tourism attraction was recognized in the early 1970s and so too the need to conserve the town's built colonial heritage.

Issues in Pacific Island Heritage Management

As in other post-colonial Pacific Island nations, the management and the conservation of Fiji's heritage are constrained by several interrelated factors. Primary amongst these is limited resources, both human and economic. Most Pacific Island countries are struggling to build and maintain economic independence and to provide basic infrastructure and heritage conservation may be "an ill-afforded luxury" (Crosby 2002:364). O'Neill and Spennemann (2001:47) found the people of the Marshall Islands in Micronesia "generally feel that satisfying present-day community and family needs is more important than preserving a disused building."

Figure 17.2 Beach Street, Levuka

When Pacific nations do allocate scarce resources to heritage conservation, local expertise is often lacking. Despite international agencies having funded heritage management training programs in the Pacific, especially since the early 1990s (Smith n.d.), few Pacific Islanders have skills they feel would enable them to make informed decisions about conservation policy and practice, leading to a continuing reliance on foreign expertise. This further drains scarce resources but more importantly, foreign experts may lack experience in working with Pacific Island communities and an understanding of the traditional systems of authority and land tenure that will be central to long-term conservation management strategies in Pacific states (Hooper 2000).

Lack of consideration of these issues is also apparent in the heritage legislation of independent Pacific nations that was developed during their colonial period. In this legislation, models of heritage significance and management were commonly adopted directly from those of the colonizing countries and are therefore unlikely to recognize traditional cultural practices of Pacific Islanders, especially in regard to decision-making processes. Roe et al. (1994:128) found the Vanuatu Cultural and Historical Sites Survey to be underlain by Eurocentric concepts limiting recognition of the significance of less tangible aspects of heritage. Conservation of the intangible heritage of traditional knowledge and skills, storytelling, dance, and song is a priority for many Pacific nations, but existing legislation primarily protects the tangible heritage mirroring Western values and priorities (Qoro 2000). As a consequence, much of this legislation and policy is limited in its strength and application. This is the case in post-colonial Fiji, where, in Crosby's (2002:364) opinion, the "departing [British] colonial administration bequeathed a toothless and ill-funded heritage management structure to an apathetic and near-destitute beneficiary."

Fiji does not yet have any comprehensive legislation for legal protection of cultural heritage (Nawalowalo 2002:4). Various laws for the protection of sites of national significance were in place prior to independence but they were not under the jurisdiction of a single government ministry, making coordination of conservation efforts difficult and hindering the development of comprehensive legislation. In 2002 the ministries were realigned to form an umbrella body, the Department of Culture and Heritage, which will coordinate arts and cultural programs through the Fiji Museum, National Trust of Fiji, and the Fiji Arts Council. The immediate priorities of the Ministry include the development and implementation of a cultural policy framework and overarching legislation (Nawalowalo 2002:5).

Several pieces of legislation, all initially a product of the British colonial administration, protect different aspects of Fiji's tangible heritage and reflect distinctions and priorities of European heritage management in the early to mid-20th century. The *National Trust of Fiji Act (1970)* aims to promote the preservation of lands, built heritage, and movable heritage having national, historic, architectural, or natural interest or beauty. The *National Trust for Fiji (Amendment) Act (1998)* established a National Heritage Register. The Trust has acquired five natural and cultural sites including the historic Morris Headstrom Building and Old Bond Store in Levuka. The Fiji Museum is responsible for the *Fiji Museum Act (1929)* and the *Preservation of Objects of Archaeological and Palaeontological Interest Act (1940)*, which charges the Museum with protection of archaeological heritage. This is one of the earliest pieces of legislation protecting archaeological material in the Pacific. Under the Act, the Fiji Museum is required to issue permits for archaeological excavation and surface operations. The Museum also has responsibility for the Archaeological Site Register and storage and curation of excavated material.

Town-planning schemes are developed under the *Fiji Town Planning Act (1946)*. The *General Provisions of the Act (1980)* consider protection of cultural heritage, focusing on built heritage of "historic or architectural merit" and "sites, objects and areas of natural beauty" when drawing up local planning schemes. The Levuka Town Planning Scheme protects Levuka's built heritage and it was under this Act that Levuka was declared Fiji's first Historic Town.

In a recent paper on the management of Fiji's archaeological heritage, Crosby (2002:394) argued that the *Fiji Town Planning Act* is a structure of colonialism and as such is "most effective in protecting its own [colonial] architectural edifice." Although the degree of protection afforded to Levuka's heritage under this Act is debatable, Crosby's conclusion is important in drawing attention to what many have seen as an inconsistency in Fiji's national recognition of Levuka as a heritage place, namely whether conservation of this heritage of colonialism should be a priority.

Heritage of the colonial period poses a particular dilemma for heritage management in the Pacific. Many Pacific Island states have achieved independence only since the 1970s and in building their national cultural identities these emerging post-colonial states commonly emphasize their indigenous and pre-colonial culture (see Cauchois, Dugay-Grist, Mandui, and Sand et al., this volume). In this context, colonial heritage, in particular built heritage, is unlikely to be highly valued and its conservation may even be actively discouraged.

O'Neill and Spennemann (2001:47) observe that in recently independent Micronesian states, there is a "passionate interest in what Micronesians perceive to be their 'real' heritage . . . together with the realization that they must now manage their past on their own terms." This was evident in a Micronesian survey of stakeholders in the tourism industry who ranked tangible heritage places associated with the colonial administration of lowest priority in tourism development after indigenous and natural heritage sites (Spennemann et al. 2001:16). As a consequence, preservation of the German colonial heritage in Micronesia depends for the most part on these small nation-states receiving sufficient resources from outside (O'Neill and Spennemann 2001:47). This is also the case for World War II sites in Melanesia (White 1995) and special interest sites such "Vailima," the author Robert Louis Stevenson's house in Samoa, which was extensively restored in the 1990s by the Robert Louis Stevenson Museum Foundation using mainly US funding (Murtagh and Lightner 1996:44).

Colonial heritage is usually associated with built heritage, with structures of architectural and/or historical significance constructed and used during the colonial period. As such, it can be argued to express colonial power relations and the dominance of colonial society and economy. When considered from this perspective, the conservation of such structures by post-colonial nations may easily be seen as valuing and celebrating the ideology of the colonizer rather than the culture and values of the independent nation-state. As Yeoh (1996) argues of colonial Singapore, though, "the colonial landscape . . . not only articulates the ideological intent of the powerful who plan and shape the landscape in a particular way but also reflects the everyday meanings implicit in the daily routines of ordinary people associated with the landscape." The physical fabric of place gains its significance from a much larger body of discursive meaning that includes not only multiple and often disparate voices of the colonizer but also the multiple voices and histories of the colonized. Yet the motivation for much of the conservation of colonial architecture in Southeast Asia came from tourism, especially international tourism, rather than any recognition of the multiple histories and values the architecture reflects. This has drawn criticism that the conservation of colonial built-heritage is a form of neo-colonialism driven by foreign tourists' desires to experience their nation's colonial past (see Henderson 2002).

Conservation in Levuka was also initially motivated by the "discovery" of the town's unique heritage by European tourists and Europeans working in Fiji in the 1970s and 1980s. However, in Levuka visitor numbers remain low. Levuka, and indeed Ovalau in general, is not a major tourist destination in Fiji principally because the island lacks the white sandy beaches and associated resorts that draw most international tourists. In 1999, 7,639 people visited Levuka, of which nearly 5,000 were international visitors (Local Case Study Team 2000). Like elsewhere in

Fiji, visitor numbers fell dramatically during and following an attempted coup against the Fiji Government in 2000. While it is the case that Fijian heritage agencies support conservation in Levuka because they consider the heritage values of the town warrant this, local people, although undoubtedly proud of their heritage, look to the conservation of the town as a means to ensure their economical and social survival through tourism.

In this context, heritage conservation priorities may be determined by economic factors rather than community consensus about which tangible expressions of their cultural identity are worthy of conservation. The revenue generated by tourism is insufficient to fund conservation efforts in the town and is unlikely to do so in future (Local Case Study Team 2000). At present, the town lacks the infrastructure to support growth in visitor numbers and a major increase would inevitably detract from the quaint charm of the town that tourists come to experience.

A Brief History of Levuka

Histories of Levuka commonly divide the period from initial settlement to the 1920s into four stages of the town's development, beginning with the "beachcomber period." Levuka hosted a beachcomber population in the early 19th century, beginning around the mid-1820s. "Beachcombers," white men who spent various periods of time living with indigenous communities in the Pacific prior to the establishment of permanent European settlements, were a phenomenon of early European contact in many Pacific Islands. Often they acted as intermediaries between European ships' crews and indigenous leaders (Ralston 1977:20). American shipwright David Whippy and two other Europeans settled in the Fijian village of Levuka in the 1820s with the permission of the Tui Levuka (the Chief or King of Levuka) (Ralston 1977:54). The fringing reef at Levuka provided a safe harbor and easy anchorage for sailing ships, especially those harvesting bêche-de-mer or sea slug, the dominant industry in the region between about 1828 and 1840. The industry supported the beachcomber population through their direct participation in harvesting and indirectly through their skills in ship building and repair.

By the mid-19th century, the site of Levuka had become a major port in the southwest Pacific. In 1845, Lieutenant Wilkes of the United States Exploring Expedition reported a Levuka community "living in traditional houses under the protection of the Tui Levuka" (cited in Burley and Chatan 2002:3). Calvert, a British missionary, described the town in 1850 as "a peaceful and industrious community where men lived with native women while developing trade and piloting businesses" (cited in Samson 1996:26), although the image appears at odds with Calvert's allegations that Fijian women were enslaved by white men (Samson 1996).

The bêche-de-mer industry had collapsed by 1850 and commerce at Levuka waned in the ensuing decade (Burley and Chatan 2002:4). A Roman Catholic mission was established in 1851, followed by the Wesleyans in 1852 (Ralston 1977:71). In 1850, alcohol became freely available in the town and from this time Levuka gained a reputation for drunkenness (Derrick 1950:195). Between 1852 and 1865, the town's foreign population grew from around 50 to over 80 (Ralston 1977:103).

The Levuka of 1860–1874 has been described as a "Port of Call and *entrepôt*" (Burley and Chatan 2002:5). Foreign immigration rapidly increased during this period, "establishing an agrarian based plantation economy with Levuka as its trans-shipment port" (Burley and Chatan 2002:5). This was aided by cotton shortages in Europe resulting from the American civil war in the 1860s, as planters in Fiji attempted to fill the gap by establishing cotton plantations (Knapman 1987:48). In the 1860s Levuka was also a center for the importation of Melanesian villagers as labor on Fijian plantations, a widespread practice known as "blackbirding." Some of the villagers, primarily from the Solomon Islands, subsequently settled on Ovalau (People of Levuka 2001:53).

The first British consul in Levuka, W. T. Pritchard, arrived in 1858 (Ralston 1977:103). The possibility of British annexation of Fiji was mooted from this time, but a first offer of cession was rejected by the British in 1861 (Burley and Chatan 2002:5). The town continued to grow with settlers from various European countries and other Pacific islands, creating a fluid and culturally diverse population. By 1870 the white population numbered over 2,000 (Derrick 1950:184).

Levuka's white settlers were occasionally caught up in political struggles between indigenous villages on Ovalau and between the Fijian chiefs, most notably in 1844 when Levuka's white population was temporarily banished from Ovalau by Chakobau, the high chief of Bau on Viti Levu's east coast (Derrick 1950:93). It was at Levuka in 1865 that the high chiefs of Fiji met to establish a confederacy and form a national government with Chakobau as its president. The confederacy was short-lived and the Fijian chiefs made a second offer of annexation of Fiji to Great Britain as a Crown Colony (Burley and Chatan 2002:7). This time the British accepted. A Deed of Cession was signed in Levuka in 1874 and the town became the colonial capital from 1874 to 1882, heralding its third period of development.

In 1874 the town was a thriving center. The British established the colonial government at Nasova, converting the Chakobau Government Building into the Government House for the first Governor, Sir Arthur Hamilton Gordon, who stayed from 1875 to 1880 (Burley and Chatan 2002:10). The 6th Company of the British Royal Engineers arrived in Levuka in 1875 to survey the town and construct a sea wall, canals where the creeks had flowed, and other drainage systems and sanitation facilities plus the Queen's Wharf and Customs House. European women arrived in numbers in the 1870s and social life in the town became more ordered (Ralston 1977:180–183). Stores along Beach Street expanded and the development of the port facilities consolidated Levuka's regional commercial importance. The Town of Levuka was created in 1877, making it the oldest municipality in Fiji (HJM Consultants and Timothy Hubbard Pty. Ltd. 1994:24).

In 1879 Levuka was the first port of call in the Fiji Islands for the first boat carrying indentured laborers from India bound for Fiji's emerging sugar industry (Lal 2000:5). Few of the laborers stayed on in Levuka or Ovalau as the cane plantations were principally located on Fiji's two largest islands, Viti Levu and Vanua Levu. However, subsequent arrivals from India have settled in the town along with people of Chinese descent. The first Chinese merchant settled in Levuka around the beginning of the 20th century (People of Levuka 2001:47).

Burley et al. (2002:13) describe the fourth period of Levuka's history from the 1880s to the 1920s as "post-capital development." The colonial capital was moved to Suva in 1882, principally because the topography of Levuka – a narrow strip of land between the sea and steep slopes behind – did not permit further expansion of the town. Despite this change, Levuka continued to develop, especially through the copra (dried coconut) trade, and many of the extant administrative and civic buildings were constructed during this period (HJM Consultants and Timothy Hubbard Pty. Ltd. 1994).

Industry in the town diversified in the early 20th century to include a shell-button factory. Levuka remained Fiji's central copra collection point until 1957 (HJM Consultants and Timothy Hubbard Pty. Ltd. 1994:21). Commercial fishing was also important throughout the 20th century and the PAFCO fish cannery, located adjacent to the port, remains Ovalau's major employer. In 1997 almost half the 8,625 residents of Ovalau lived in Levuka (Local Case Study Team 2000).

Levuka's history has given the town a higher percentage of residents of mixed descent than many other places in Fiji. This includes people with Indian, Chinese, European, Japanese, and other Pacific Island heritage as well as Indigenous Fijian heritage, whose ancestors or they themselves came to Levuka variously through choice, indenture, or force.

Levuka as a Heritage Place

The heritage site of Levuka incorporates remnant colonial architecture, numerous archaeological remains, and a townscape without extensive modern disturbance (Levuka Case Study Team 2000:7). The town consists of Beach Street along the sea front and several adjoining streets and laneways running up into the hills behind. These are associated with creek lines that run down from the interior of the island, alongside which are paths that now and in the pre-contact past connected the inland villages to the coastal village of Levuka.

Levuka's built heritage consists of structures in the town itself and a number of historic buildings and monuments outside the town's perimeter, including the cemetery. Many buildings retain their original function, including administrative buildings, schools, churches, residences, shops, and other workplaces. Some churches, the school, and government buildings were the first of their kind in Fiji. There are various important features in the town plan including drainage systems, stepped pathways, and the sea wall. There is also industrial and maritime movable cultural heritage visible as rusting iron debris scattered along the high tide mark and around the town. Several shipwrecks lie in the harbor.

The link between Levuka's heritage and tourism was first made in the early 1970s in a national study of newly independent Fiji's tourism industry. The study by

Belt Collins and Associates (1973:155) found that the town's historical charm, reflected in its "unspoiled nineteenth century building styles" would be of interest to foreign tourists and the key to tourism development was the town's historical preservation. The study recommended Levuka become Fiji's first historical district with associated land use and development controls to ensure its preservation (1973:156).

The study stressed the need for local resident involvement in conservation programs, perhaps reflecting the United Nations Development Program's funding of the study, recommending the establishment of an advisory board of local residents "to ensure local participation and interest in matters that affect the site" (1973:158). Yet involvement of the community in conservation did not include any process by which the community could identify the heritage of significance to them. The study assumed Levuka's built heritage is what should be conserved because it is the historic and architectural qualities of the town that tourists would wish to experience. In response, residents of Levuka formed the Ovalau Tourism and Promotion Committee in 1977. The committee subsequently became the Levuka Historical and Cultural Society and despite some commentators expressing concern that the society had a narrow base, consisting primarily of "part-Europeans" (Harrison 2002), it continued to provide a forum for local residents' voice to express opinions about heritage matters in the town until the early 1990s.

The conservation model outlined by Belt Collins and Associates (1973) was not implemented but the findings were taken up in 1985 by a Pacific Area Travel Association (PATA) task force investigating the tourism potential of Levuka and Ovalau. Unlike the previous study, PATA considered the town's heritage values in their own right. It concluded that conservation of the town was not only in the interest of tourism but also Fiji's national interest, stating "Levuka is the cradle of modern Fiji. It has the potential to focus the attention of all Fiji's disparate community groups on a common national identity, thus emphasizing their shared heritage" (PATA 1985:3).

This located the significance of the town's colonial heritage in Fiji's present, perceiving it as a shared heritage rather than the heritage of "outsiders." With regard to conservation of those values, however, the report considers only the deterioration of the town's built heritage. The study recommended that conservation be part of the town planning process (1985:12), proposing that Levuka become a conservation zone and that a legislative/regulatory framework be created to assess any development proposals or changes to existing buildings. Like the Belt Collins (1973) study, PATA (1985) also emphasized that "the citizens themselves must be part of the preservation process. It is only with their consent and their involvement that Levuka can continue to be both a living town and a place to which tourists can go" (PATA 1985:40). Again no consideration was given to community assessment of heritage significance. The program for "community restoration" focused exclusively on buildings in the town, the only exception being beautification of the beach front through tree planting.

Following the PATA study, the Levuka Town Planning Scheme was created in 1987 under the *Fiji Town Planning Act* (1946) and in 1989, Levuka was declared Fiji's first "Historic Town" by the Director of Town and Country Planning. This provided for the preservation and protection of historic buildings, objects, and places of historic interest although no systematic survey of the town's heritage had been undertaken. The Planning Scheme continues to be the primary means of protection for Levuka's tangible heritage. Under the Scheme, Levuka Town is declared a conservation zone and new developments have to be compatible with existing architectural styles, so too repairs or alterations. The Scheme provides some detail guiding conservation of individual buildings or types of buildings but pays almost no attention to conserving the integrity of the town as a whole. For example, only 66 percent of Levuka's houses are identified as worthy of conservation but the criteria for this assessment are not detailed (Fiji Department of Town and Country Planning 1987). Under the Scheme, the streetscape of Beach Street is to be conserved but guidelines are at best minimal and no consideration is given to other vistas in the town. The scheme does not consider industrial movable heritage or maritime heritage in the town. The statement calls for a landscape plan to be prepared as part of the overall process of restoring the town's existing buildings and precincts but no such plan has been developed.

In 1992 the Levuka Conservation Committee was formed to provide technical expertise for conservation of the town's heritage buildings. The Committee included Levuka's Mayor and representatives of the Town Council, representatives of the various government heritage agencies, and the Department of Tourism. A full survey of Levuka's built heritage was finally carried out in 1993–1994 by Australian heritage consultants (HJM Consultants and Timothy Hubbard Pty. Ltd. 1994), funded by the Fijian Government and PATA. The consultants recorded over 120 individual places of heritage value and wrote the town's first "Statement of Heritage Significance." It identified Levuka's national and regional (South Pacific) cultural significance as:

(1) the seat of Fiji's first capital from the 1860s
(2) the focus for most British, Australian, German and American commercial activity in the South Pacific until the early 1880s
(3) the site of the Cession of Fiji to the British Crown in 1972
(4) one of the best remaining examples of a town or settlement which reflects the European exploitation and colonization in the South Pacific
(5) it retains its pattern of inter-cultural relationships, urban forms and layers of successive development until the post World War II period
(6) it retains key buildings which reflect the introduction of European education and religion including some of the first sites in the region such as the Levuka School, various churches, the Town Hall and Hospital.
(7) it retains key buildings that reflect the introduction of European administration and social development including some of the first such sites in the region
(8) it is important for the range of its building types, their architectural style and very high integrity

The statement principally identifies the tangible built heritage as significant, reflecting the history of the town in the mid- to late 19th century and especially the period when the town served as the colonial capital. Although Levuka's "pattern of inter-cultural relationships, urban forms and layers of successive development" are also seen as significant, they are not discussed in relation to specific evidence in the survey of individual structures. Unlike the earlier reports, no mention is made of community consultation or involvement in the conservation process.

The consultants reviewed the heritage protection afforded by the Levuka Town Planning Scheme and found that "defects in the legislation [the *Town Planning Act 1946*] under which the Levuka Planning Scheme is made . . . preclude any real con-trols from being imposed" (HJM Consultants and Timothy Hubbard Pty. Ltd. 1994:68). These include lack of any real penalties for breaches of the Act and lack of any control over demolition. The consultants also found the Levuka Town Council and residents lacked understanding of the Scheme and the Council lacked resources and expertise meaning no effective conservation measures could be imple-mented (1994:72). To remedy this situation, PATA subsequently funded three Heritage Advisors for the town between 1994 and 2001 (see Takano 1996).

The PATA study in 1985 found that despite Levuka having some architecturally significant buildings "it is the totality of the place, the continuity of new and old which captures the eye and would delight any visitor" (PATA 1985:39). Similarly, HJM Consultants and Timothy Hubbard (1994) recommended "retention of inter-cultural relationships – the urban forms and expressions of the layers of successive development of the town." Neither of these studies moved beyond built heritage of the late 19th century to encompass other kinds of heritage places or movable cul-tural heritage which could provide the basis on which various cultural layers and patterns of inter-cultural relationships could be identified and included in conservation planning. In the late 1990s, such a shift in conservation priorities enabled the significance of successive stages in the town's development – from pre-European contact to the present – to be recognized. This permitted a greater range of tangible heritage to be considered in conservation programs and the diversity of community values and attitudes toward heritage to be accommodated.

In 1999, Levuka provided a case study for a UNESCO project to develop models of consultation between various stakeholders in the management of heritage tourism sites in the Asia-Pacific region (UNESCO 2000). The project team for the Levuka case study included representatives of the National Trust of Fiji, the Fiji Museum, Department of Town and Country Planning, the Levuka Town Council, various Levuka business people, and the Levuka Heritage Officer. Responses to the project were sought from the wider Levuka/Ovalau community. The study found that the tourism attraction of Ovalau is not limited to the historic town of Levuka but includes the island as a whole, in particular the rich and diverse cultural record of the prehistory of Fiji in the areas adjacent to the town (Local Case Study Team 2000:8). In reference to claims of tensions between pre-colonial or indigenous values and the colonial heritage values of the town, the project team found that "Levuka and Ovalau do not represent conflicting aspects of Fiji's history and culture, simply different aspects that now live in harmony (2000:53)." Interpreting Levuka's heritage values in the context of Ovalau's cultural landscape enabled the people throughout the island to articulate their heritage priorities during the project's consultation process.

Recent research has also begun to record the diversity of Levuka's tangible cultural heritage. In 2000, archaeological investigations were carried out in the grounds of Nasova House on the site of Chakobau's Government House and the British administration's parade ground (Chatan 2002) and in the vicinity of the Totaga Creek in the town's center where an indigenous village was located in the early 19th century. The site of the village is visible in the present street plan. Also in 2000, marine archaeologists from the Fiji Museum and National Maritime Museum of Australia recorded a number of the shipwrecks in the harbor. The Fiji Museum has registered several pre-contact sites on Ovalau, including a historically important hill fort. A survey of the town's industrial and movable heritage is still lacking.

In the same year, the significance of the time depth of Levuka's settlement pattern and land use practices was identified in an initial landscape and architectural study (Purser 2003), in which a range of features and structures in the town, relating to successive stages in the town's development, were identified for future research.

Levuka as World Heritage

Identification of Levuka's heritage values has been given a global dimension through the Fijian Government's decision to nominate Levuka for inscription on the UNESCO World Heritage List. Fiji became a signatory to the UNESCO *World Heritage Convention (1972)* in 1990, enabling the country to make such nominations. To be inscribed as World Heritage, a site must be successfully argued to represent particular universally significant values and to be the outstanding example of sites that reflect such values.

The Pacific Islands are greatly under-represented on the World Heritage List. Rennell Island in the Solomon Islands has been inscribed for its natural values, but no Pacific Island nation has nominated a cultural site. To redress this imbalance the UNESCO World Heritage Committee organized a UNESCO World Heritage Global Strategy Meeting in Suva in 1997. A subsequent meeting was held in Vanuatu in 1999. The aim of the Suva meeting was to promote the *World Heritage Convention* to Pacific states and to ascertain Pacific heritage priorities and the kinds of sites Pacific peoples consider important. Representatives of the Pacific nations at the meeting put a series of recommendations to the World Heritage Committee in which they reinforced the inseparable connection between the outstanding seascapes and landscapes of the Pacific region "woven together by the rich histories, oral and life traditions of the Pacific Island peoples and comprise the cultural heritage of the region that is bound through voyaging, kinship, trade and other relationships" (UNESCO 1997). Their recommendations emphasized the significance of traditional sites and storied landscapes to Pacific people.

In light of this, the Fiji Government's decision to put forward Levuka as the first cultural site to be nominated by a Pacific nation appears somewhat contradictory. However, in 1997 when the Fiji Government proposed and endorsed the nomination of Levuka/Ovalau to the World Heritage List the proposed site included not only Levuka town but the entire island. This was to include selected pre-colonial hill forts and forested areas of the island: "the listing of Levuka/Ovalau as a World Heritage Site will allow traditional Fijian people and other cultural and natural values to be understood, preserved, respected and shared for all time by all peoples" (Fiji Ministry of Women and Culture et al. n.d.).

Nomination of Levuka/Ovalau enabled pre- and post-contact cultural heritage to be recognized along with the natural heritage of the island. The values of Levuka's "colonial" heritage would be contextualized within the longer history of the island and broader cultural and natural heritage of the landscape in line with the emphasis given to traditional sites and storied landscapes in the recommendations of the Global Strategy meeting.

In 2001, however, the World Heritage Officer for the Pacific Region found that broadening the nomination beyond Levuka Town would make nomination a more difficult and lengthy process requiring consultations with customary leaders and landowners regarding customary ownership and a flora and fauna survey to select the best area for a nature reserve (Wingham n.d.). In consultation with stakeholders including the Levuka Heritage Committee, it was decided to proceed with the nomination of Levuka Township only because it has a clear boundary (although the boundary for the proposed conservation zone is yet to be agreed) and is well documented. The other sites on Ovalau, and especially the hill forts, would then be reexamined for possible inclusion in the World Heritage listing at a later date.

This returned the focus of the nomination to the "colonial" heritage and an emphasis on Levuka Town's "universal" values as a tangible expression of processes of European colonization in the Pacific. The evolution of the town in the 19th century reflects a pattern of development evident in other ports in the Pacific but the built heritage of these other ports has changed markedly since the 19th century as they continued to grow as national capitals or major towns. Some retain outstanding examples of 19th century colonial architecture but none has the integrity of the 19th and early 20th century streetscape found in Levuka.

This makes Levuka the outstanding example of such a site, but nomination on this basis tends to reinforce the idea of the heritage value of the town being "European" or "non-indigenous." While from the perspective of built heritage it is true that the town has value as a unique example of Pacific Island towns of the late 19th and early 20th centuries, Levuka's cultural landscape includes much that transpired since many of the buildings were built as well as much that was there prior to their construction. Like all heritage, Levuka is not a snapshot of a particular period but a palimpsest of cultural layers and interactions from pre-European contact to the present. Although this was acknowledged in the PATA study in 1985, locating these values in the tangible heritage of the town has been limited by the focus of conservation efforts on the built heritage of the town dating to the late 19th and early 20th centuries. Further, the assessment of the significance of these structures in architectural or historic terms has not recognized their continuing social significance as places of long-term cultural interaction. Nominating Levuka

Town to the World Heritage List should emphasize the town's "colonial" heritage in arguments for the site's outstanding universal value. However, this emphasis should not preclude recognition of the town's heritage significance as a place of cultural contact and diversity. Interestingly, the community of Levuka, which some argue has been marginalized in plans to nominate the town for World Heritage listing (Harrison 2002), see their town as important precisely for these reasons.

Local Community Attitudes to Levuka's Heritage

In 2001, members of the Levuka community published a collection of histories and oral histories entitled *Levuka: Living Heritage* (People of Levuka 2001). It presents the histories of various family and cultural groups in the town, the Tui Levuka, and various institutions including the church, hospital, and school. The town's cultural diversity and history are reflected in the stories of families of Chinese, Indian, indigenous Fijian and Solomon Islands, and European ancestry. An aim of the book is to argue that "the historical aspects of the old capital Levuka pale in comparison to its living heritage: its people . . . Their stories reflect daily life within a context of multicultural and multiracial history" (2001:i). George Gibson, Levuka's mayor, notes that "no other community of this size in the Pacific has such diverse background or such a high degree of interaction and integration. This has led not only to inevitable tensions, but also to many achievements" (2001:9). The book celebrates the cultural diversity and relative harmony of the town in light of recent ethnic tensions between Fiji's indigenous and Indo-Fijian communities.

Fiji's heritage agencies have sought to assess the attitudes of the Levuka/Ovalau community toward conservation and to engage them in heritage and tourism planning through a number of stakeholder workshops since 1999. The participants include representatives of national and local government, the Levuka and Ovalau community, and business. The workshops were part of the UNESCO tourism and heritage management project (Local Case Study Team 2000) discussed above, and aimed to raise awareness of World Heritage and the potential impacts of a nomination on the island's culture and economy (Fiji Ministry of Women and Culture et al. n.d.; Erasito et al. n.d.).

A workshop in 2002 reinforced the notion that aspects of Levuka's heritage considered culturally important to stakeholders are diverse and include layered sites, monuments, buildings and pre-colonial cultural sites. Participants identified several key issues in identifying the values and management of Levuka's heritage that still need to be addressed:

(1)   a need to clarify people's confusion over their understanding of Fiji's indigenous cultural heritage, Levuka's heritage and their relation to World Heritage,

(2)   the lack of cooperation between relevant government authorities over their responsibilities towards Levuka as a national heritage site, and

(3)   the lack of a policy document that defines the Fiji Government's role in meeting its obligations to the *World Heritage Convention* (1972).

Discussion

Recent realignment of Fiji's heritage agencies under one Department of Culture and Heritage provides an opportunity for a coordinated approach to heritage planning for Levuka and Ovalau and the development of legislation enabling Fiji to meet its obligations under the *World Heritage Convention (1972)*. This will provide comprehensive protection of Fiji's national heritage. Even with its recent amendment, the outdated current legislation does not permit an inclusive approach for assessing the significance of tangible heritage. The separation of protection of archaeological from other tangible heritage and the emphasis in the *Provisions of the Town Planning Act (1980)* on preserving individual buildings is not conducive to developing management plans that recognize cultural landscapes and the historic, cultural, and social relationships that created them. Further, separation of the protection of archaeological sites from built or post-contact sites reinforces a distinction between "indigenous" and "non-indigenous" heritage that is based on the anachronistic concept that indigenous culture disappeared upon European contact. This is patently untrue in Levuka's past, as elsewhere (Chapman 1996; Smith and Beck 2003), and is strikingly evident in Chakobau's establishment of his government at Levuka in 1866. The present Tui Levuka retains traditional authority over the town. To narrowly define the town's heritage values as "European" also disregards the diverse identities and heritage of the people who now reside in Levuka (and Fiji in general).

The successful inscription of Levuka Town on the World Heritage List would inevitably increase tourist interest in the town. However, a substantial increase in visitor numbers is unlikely without substantial investment in the infrastructure of the town and in transport from Suva. Even if visitor numbers do increase, the income they will generate is unlikely to be enough to fund ongoing conservation of the town's heritage. Increased numbers would also be unsustainable in terms of its disruption of the social and cultural life of the present Levuka/Ovalau community. Thus inscription will require an ongoing commitment from the Fiji Government and the people of Levuka. It should be emphasized that priorities for heritage management in the town need to be established regardless of the World Heritage nomination process. The basis for this must be comprehensive assessment of the town's heritage significance that considers the diverse expressions of the Levuka's tangible heritage and their interrelationships.

Although the town of Levuka is not representative of cultural heritage sites in the Pacific Islands, which are more commonly storied landscapes or archaeological sites, the core issues for successful management of the town's heritage values are similar to those which arise at many different kinds of sites. Most importantly there is a need to engage local people or traditional owners of the heritage in the management process. This is not simply a matter of having them assist as volunteers or even rank-and-file employees in conservation projects or tourism. Rather, they should be centrally involved in the identification of what is significant heritage and why. In the words of Gerald Takano (1996:17), Levuka's Heritage Advisor from 1994 to 1996, "South Pacific preservation is not just about pretty buildings and pristine symbols of the elite. Instead, it is about vernacular settings of the countless, unnamed individuals who now inhabit places like Levuka."

REFERENCES

Belt Collins and Associates, 1973 Tourism Development Program for Fiji. Suva: United Nations Development Programme, Government of Fiji.

Burley, D., and R. Chatan, 2002 Context and History for the Levuka Project. *In* Historic Levuka Archaeological Project. D. Burley, R. Chatan and M. Purser, eds. pp. 1–15. Suva: Fiji Museum and National Trust of Fiji.

Burley, D., R. Chatan and M. Purser, eds., 2002 Archaeological Investigations: Totoga Creek and Vicinity. *In* Historic Levuka Archaeological Project. Suva: Fiji Museum and National Trust of Fiji.

Chapman, W., 1996 Hawaiian Perspectives on Historic Preservation and Cultural Resource Management. *Cultural Resource Management* 19:4–7.

Chatan, R., 2002 Archaeological Investigations at Nasova House. *In* Historic Levuka Archaeological Project. D. Burley, R. Chatan and M. Purser, eds. pp. 36–57. Suva: Fiji Museum and National Trust of Fiji.

Crosby, A., 2002 Archaeology and *Vanua* Development in Fiji. World Archaeology 34:363–378.

Derrick, R., 1950 History of Fiji, vol. 1. 2nd edition. Suva: Government of Fiji.

Erasito, E., S. Pene and R. Avisaki, n.d. Report of the 1st Levuka Heritage Workshop (Levuka, March 12, 2002), unpublished MS.

Fiji Department of Town and Country Planning, 1987 The Levuka Town Planning Scheme (1987). Suva: Government of Fiji.

Fiji Ministry of Women and Culture, National Trust of Fiji, Fiji Museum and Levuka Town Council, n.d. Report of Stakeholder Workshop, Levuka World Heritage Site (Levuka, Fiji, January 27–28, 1999), unpublished MS.

Harrison, D., 2002 Levuka: Whose Heritage? Paper presented at the Politics of World Heritage Conference, International Institute for Culture, Tourism and Development, London Metropolitan University.

Henderson, J., 2002 Built Heritage and Colonial Cities. Annals of Tourism Research 29:254–257.

HJM Consultants and Timothy Hubbard Pty. Ltd., 1994 Town of Levuka Heritage Study, vol. 1. Report to the Fiji Ministry of Housing, Urban Development and Environment and the Pacific Asia Travel Association. Canberra: HJM Consultants and Timothy Hubbard Pty Ltd.

Hooper, A., 2000 Introduction. *In* Culture and Sustainable Development in the Pacific. A. Hooper, ed. pp. 1–21. Canberra: Asia Pacific Press, Australian National University.

Knapman, B., 1987 Fiji's Economic History 1974–1939. Studies of Capitalist Colonial Development. Pacific Research Monograph 15. Canberra: Australian National University.

Lal, B., 2000 Chalo Jahaji. A Journey through Indenture in Fiji. Suva: Fiji Museum and Canberra: Research School of Pacific and Asian Studies, Australian National University, with the Fiji Museum.

Local Case Study Team, 2000 A Case Study on Levuka, Fiji Islands. Paper presented to UNESCO Cultural Heritage and Tourism: Models for Cooperation among Stakeholders Workshop, Bhaktapur.

Murtagh, W., and D. Lightner, 1996 Robert Louis Stevenson in the Pacific. Cultural Resource Management 19:44.

Nawalowalo, R., 2002 Status of Tangible Cultural Heritage Protection. Fiji Country Report. Paper presented at the Meeting of Experts on Regional Cooperation for the Development of Asia-Pacific Cultural Heritage Website, Suva, March 7–9.

O'Neill, J., and D. Spennemann, 2001 German Colonial Heritage in Micronesia. Cultural Resource Management 24:46–47.

Pacific Area Travel Association, 1985 Levuka and Ovalau. Tourism Development through Community Restoration. Sydney: PATA.

People of Levuka, 2001 Levuka: Living Heritage. Suva: Institute of Pacific Studies, University of the South Pacific.

Purser, M., 2003 The View From the Verandah: Levuka Bungalows and the Transformation of Settler Identities in Later Colonialism. International Journal of Historical Archaeology. 7(4):293–314.

Qoro, S., 2000 Report on the Pacific Regional Seminar. *In* Safeguarding Traditional Cultures. A Global Assessment of the 1989 UNESCO Recommendation on the Safeguarding of Traditional Culture and Folklore. Paris: UNESCO.

Ralston, C., 1977 Grass Huts and Warehouses. Pacific Beach Communities in the 19th Century. Canberra: Australian National University Press.

Roe, D., R. Regenvanu, F. Wadra and N. Araho, 1994 Working with Cultural Landscapes in Melanesia. *In* Culture Kastom Tradition. L. Lindstrom and G. White, eds. pp. 115–129. Suva: University of the South Pacific.

Samson, J., 1996 Rescuing Fijian Women? Journal of Pacific History 30:22–38.

Smith, A., n.d. Local and Global Heritage Priorities in the Pacific. Submitted for publication in Diasporas and Contested Cultural Heritage, Centre for Cross Cultural Research, Australian National University, Canberra, unpublished MS.

Smith, A., and W. Beck, 2003 The Archaeology of No-Man's-Land: Indigenous Camps at Corindi Beach, Mid-North Coast NSW. Archaeology in Oceania 38:63–74.

Spennemann, D., D. Look and K. Graham, 2001 Perceptions of Heritage Ecotourism by Micronesian Decision Makers. Albury: Johnstone Research Centre, Charles Sturt University.

Takano, G., 1996 Learning from Levuka: Fiji Preservation in the First Colonial Capital. Cultural Resource Management 19:15–17.

UNESCO, 2000 Cultural Heritage Management and Tourism: Models for Co-operation amongst Stakeholders. Electronic document. http//www.unescobkk.org/culture/norad-tourism/index.html.

UNESCO, 1997 Report of 3rd Global Strategy Meeting Identification of World Heritage Properties in the Pacific. Paris and Suva: UNESCO World Heritage Centre and Fiji Museum.

White, G., 1995 Remembering Guadacanal; National Identity and Transnational Memory-Making. Public Culture 7:529–555.

Wingham, E., n.d. World Heritage Mission to Fiji, 1–5 May 2001. National Trust of Fiji, unpublished MS.

Yeoh, B., 1996 Contesting Space: Power Relations and the Urban Built Environment in Colonial Singapore. Kuala Lumpur: Oxford University Press.

18
Last Words

Mickaelle-Hinanui Cauchois, Mark Dugay-Grist, and Herman Mandui

This chapter combines contributions from three indigenous archaeologists, one from Tahiti, one from Australia, and one from Papua New Guinea. Their perspectives complement those raised by Sand, Bole, and Ouetcho concerning New Caledonia and Smith regarding Fiji. Each piece is presented complete with its own notes and references.

A Few Words about Archaeology in French Polynesia

Mickaelle-Hinanui Cauchois

Despite an impressive archaeological heritage and a key location in the Pacific, archaeology in French Polynesia is not as well promoted as it is in its neighbors such as Hawai'i, New Zealand, or New Caledonia. However, it has undergone several changes recently, which promise a better promotion of archaeological research amongst the public in general, and the *ma'ohi* (Polynesian) community in particular. The purpose of this piece is to provide an overview of archaeology today in French Polynesia and its future perspectives by a young native archaeologist. Overall, it seeks to give a personal viewpoint about being a native archaeologist.

Archaeological investigations in French Polynesia began in the 1920s under the direction of Kenneth Emory, archaeologist at the Bishop Museum in Honolulu. He carried out an impressive project of archaeological survey throughout the Society Islands. Though he was essentially documenting the *marae* (temples) as surface remains, he also provided interesting data about house and agricultural sites. His work in the Societies was followed by different projects carried out throughout the Tuamotu Islands and the Gambier Archipelago during the 1930s (Emory 1934, 1939, 1965). In 1977, the Service of Urbanism used Emory's famous 1933 monograph *Stone Remains in the Society Islands* as the basis for the first archaeological inventory in French Polynesia, and in 1984 the Department of Archaeology of Tahiti used the same work as the basis of the first inventory there.

The early 1960s saw the beginning of important archaeological projects seeking to document the prehistory of our country in both synchronic and diachronic perspectives. The work of Roger Green and his colleagues in the Opunohu valley, Mo'orea, between 1960 and 1964 provided a preliminary chronology and preliminary models of prehistoric settlement patterns (Green et al. 1967). Meanwhile, projects managed under the joint auspices of ORSTOM[1] and the Bishop Museum marked the beginning of Yoshi Sinoto's pioneering work with Emory. Several sites were recorded and excavated in various parts of the Society Islands and the Marquesas, providing material and chronological data of great importance. The Marquesas were soon recognized as the place in which to search for the beginnings of Polynesian colonization of the eastern Pacific.

While the Bishop Museum was the main institution carrying out projects in French Polynesia until the beginning of the 1960s, from that time its domination was challenged by a French team headed by José Garanger of the Centre National Recherche Scientifique (CNRS). His influence on local archaeology was to become strong through his management of several important projects in Tahiti and Rangiroa (Tuamotus) (e.g., Garanger 1964, 1975, 1980; Garanger and Lavondés 1966). He also played an important role in the creation of a local archaeological institution in Tahiti, with the Department of Archaeology created under his influence in 1979. The Department's main purpose was to contribute to the recording, documentation, and protection of the country's rich archaeological heritage. Since its creation, the Department of Archaeology has completed a lot of important archaeological projects. The Department has conducted not only archaeological surveys and excavations but also more ethnographically oriented projects such as studies of traditional fishing techniques. Unfortunately, too few publications were made available to the public despite the quality and the diversity of the work carried out. The department was restructured in January 2001 and changed its name to the *Service de la Culture et du Patrimoine* (Office of Cultural Heritage). It is now under the direct control of the Ministry of Culture and deals with cultural heritage in a broad sense (including archaeology, history, and oral tradition), but it is now independent of the Museum of Tahiti even though it is located in the same place. The archaeological staff of five are managed by a French archaeologist hired for a four-year period. As yet, French Polynesia lacks trained Polynesian archaeologists. It is anticipated that this situation will be resolved over the next few years as several Tahitian undergraduate students have shown interest in specializing in that area. We can only hope that there will be employment opportunities for them. For now, I am the only Tahitian student undertaking postgraduate studies in archaeology in a US university. I am currently enrolled in a Masters degree, and I look forward to also completing a Ph.D.

Being a native archaeologist and willing to do a good job is not an easy task. Why? Probably because being from here, intellectually trained from there and emotionally woven throughout here and there, now and yesterday, is a fascinating but complex process to live through. It is not just an intellectual game, it is our daily reality. Being a native archaeologist means having a strong responsibility as a mediator between our whole community and the scientific public. It is an honor but do not believe that it goes without any difficulty on the way. Indeed, before the archaeologist, I am a human being. A part of that experience belongs to an area that the Western scientific approach does not care about: What scientific language will help me out when it comes to explaining to my cousins the little knowledge we have about our past? How will I translate the scientific jargon into a comprehensible language to someone who lives surrounded by these stone remains in his taro plantation? And how will I respond to the elder who asks me why archaeologists make up stories about things that our *tupuna* (ancestors) probably did not want us to know? How can I explain to the scientific community that I respond to that elder "me neither, I don't really believe us when we build up models with so few data and pretend to explain what happened in the past"? What I say to that elder, in the privacy of his house, I cannot tell my whole community. I cannot tell them about that terrible frustration and dryness of the silent dialogue between stones and charcoal. This is because most non-archaeologists do not really care about the reality of archaeological challenges, about ancient settlement patterns, carrying capacity, and artifact typologies. All that people want to know is where we are from, when we first arrived, and how and where we lived at different times. Above all, people want archaeologists to confirm that we Polynesians have a great history to be proud of. They will not ask straight out but that is what they want to hear.

That is part of why being a native archaeologist is not an easy task: because I have to talk about and for my tupuna, forgive me, but I lie sometimes. Because I have to give knowledge back to my community, don't blame me, I am just trying to understand more but I cannot know everything. Because I have to publish something scientifically correct, please indulge my long descriptions that diplomatically hide my skepticism. You do not need to be a native to feel all these contradictions; I guess a lot of archaeologists know what I am talking about. However, being from here makes it harder because people expect a lot from you. On the other hand, that is probably why being a native archaeologist can also be an exciting task, because you have no choice but to overcome your skepticism and try to brighten the flickering light of knowledge rather than submit to the static chaos of "no-archaeology land." It is just that we sometimes feel discouraged by the magnitude of the task, especially when our country lacks well-trained Polynesian archaeologists and when so few of us seem crazy enough to devote our lives to chasing after the remains of the past. Being a responsible native archaeologist means being honest about the situation, humble but firm about our capacity to achieve such a huge goal.

It means also being aware of the traps that can wait for us because we also work with people who are not natives and our intellectual tools are essentially Western. Being from here allows me to study my own ancestors; that is my privilege, my honor, and my pride. I have these terrible words from Tipene O'Regan from New Zealand in mind: "my tupuna may be dead but they are also in me and I am alive. To know them, you must know me! In order to deal with them, you must deal with me!" (O'Regan 1987:142).

Because I am from here, I have that chance of working on a land I belong to. You are a visiting specialist and I am a child of the country. It makes a difference but it never, ever allows me to take things for granted. Those of us who claim that they have nothing to learn from the others lie and I refuse to trust them. Yes, it is irritating to listen to someone from outside pretend to teach you what your country is all about but it is more irritating to find out that without help and direction, you will not get anywhere. So I am thankful for all the scholars who have helped me shape my archaeological intellect. I am also grateful for belonging to my country, which obliges me to challenge that knowledge in order to serve it in a better way.

We can talk for hours about the history of colonization, the one of the land and the one of the mind as well. However, always coming back to that point seems to be a dead-end street. Whatever kind of knowledge helps me to do my job as best as I can is fine. As long as it allows me to know a little bit more every day than I knew yesterday, it is never too late to challenge any intellectual approach regularly and add my own voice. That is what I mean by being aware of the traps that lie around a native archaeologist: if we let our voice of legitimate resentment talk too loudly, we might not hear the appealing richness of working together for the benefit of all. Of course, we have universal examples of archaeologists who work for themselves and never give anything back to the community, whether it is knowledge or artifacts, However, I prefer to look at the others, those who have a sincere interest in the communities they work with and give something back when they leave.

Maybe one day we will reach a point where we will feel obliged to establish an ethical code for archaeologists who come to work in our country. We will probably become more explicit about how archaeologists can contribute more to education programs. Perhaps some of these brilliant scientific articles that almost no non-archaeologists read will be translated into plain language for the general public. Meanwhile, being protective and severe when it is necessary does not mean being an obstacle to the investigation of the past. Every archaeological contribution is welcomed as long as it benefits the whole community. I truly believe that step by step, we can contribute to filling in the huge blanks of our history and add more material to the education package that kids receive at school. One small site recorded is one less source of information gone forever in the silent night of ignorance as one more site erased by the bulldozers becomes one more house for those in need today. I hope that, one day, we will have a lot more native archaeologists in French Polynesia. I also hope that the current geopolitical boundaries will be crossed throughout Polynesia and that there will be more interaction and exchange between archaeologists. Since our ancestors seem to have practiced long-distance inter-island voyages, why should we not do the same thing with our ideas that need to be shared?

NOTES

1 Office de la Recherche Scientifique et Technique Outre-Mer, now known as l'Institut de Recherche pour le Developpement (IRD).

REFERENCES

Emory, K., 1933 Stone Remains in the Society Islands. Bernice P. Bishop Museum Bulletin 53. Honolulu: Bishop Museum Press.
—— 1934 Tuamotuan Stone Structures. Bernice P. Bishop Museum Bulletin 118. Honolulu: Bishop Museum Press.
—— 1939 Archaeology of Mangareva and Neighboring Atolls. Bernice P. Bishop Museum Bulletin 163. Honolulu: Bishop Museum Press.
—— 1965 Preliminary Report on the Archaeological Investigations in Polynesia. Honolulu: Bernice P. Bishop Museum.
Garanger, J., 1964 Recherches Archéologiques dans le District de Tautira, Tahiti, Polynésie Française. Journal de la Société des Océanistes 20:5–22.
—— 1975 Marae Ta'ata. Travaux Effectués par la Mission Archéologique ORSTOM-CNRS en 1973 et en 1974. CNRS RCP 259.
—— 1980 Prospections Archéologiques de l'Îlot Fenuaino et des Vallées Polynésie et Vaiote à Tahiti. Journal de la Société des Océanistes 35:77–104.
Garanger, J., and A. Lavondès, 1966 Recherches archéologiques à Rangiroa. Journal de la Société des Océanistes 22:23–36.
Green, R., K. Green, R. Rappaport, A. Rappaport and J. Davidson, 1967 Archaeology on the Island of Mo'orea, French Polynesia. Anthropological Papers, American Museum of Natural History 51(2).
O'Regan, T., 1987 Who Owns the Past? Change in Maori Perceptions of the Past. In From the Beginning: The Archaeology of the Maori. J. Wilson, ed. pp. 41–45. Auckland: Penguin.

Shaking the Pillars

Mark Dugay-Grist

I am of the attitude that science can open up the minds and enhance the capacities of Indigenous Australians to function in heritage-related issues in much the same way it opened my own mind. I have titled this paper "Shaking the Pillars" because I believe that there are many fundamental practical questions that need to be addressed in connection with the issues surrounding Aboriginal heritage management and the repatriation of Aboriginal cultural items and associated materials, including documentary records. The fact that I have been directly involved in the study and repatriation of ancestral skeletal remains, cultural heritage site management, and research and curatorship for a period of almost two decades provides grist to my insights into these subject matters.

My personal belief is that one must understand the underlying philosophies and practices of the various government departments and other institutions that are in the business of preserving cultural items and housing information, in order to understand how they operate and how best Indigenous communities can interact with them. Examples of complex heritage management issues can be found all over Australia. The question must be asked, if an Aboriginal group was successful in gaining their cultural items from an institution either nationally or internationally, where would the material be housed? Where are the trained Indigenous people to conserve and catalog the material and related information? What assurances are there that the material and information is appropriately stored and curated? Many of these questions remain unanswered.

At present, there is in Australia a certain ungrounded approach to the issues that relate to the repatriating of Aboriginal ancestral remains and cultural material and the study and protection of Aboriginal sites and cultural objects and mythology. The discussions, debates, and commitments to best practice in relation to managing all aspects of Indigenous Australian culture need to be conducted at a higher level than they are at present. More discourse and commitment are needed by those involved in land management, heritage protection, Native Title, government programs and policy, and academia. Advancing Indigenous Australians' ability to deal with all aspects of cultural heritage management should be a priority for all stakeholders, including the Aboriginal community. Aboriginal people are aware of the sensitivities and the problematic "no-rules" approach surrounding basic issues that affect their daily lives. The practices that are allowed to distract us from the delivery of the basic requirements and needs of Indigenous Australians in managing and participating in their own heritage are daunting. Indigenous Australians' present position is like that of the many Indigenous peoples of the world: they are simply excluded from appropriately participating because they are not being properly equipped or qualified.

Some Aboriginal communities have taken custody of the material that they are related to and there is a growing desire for many more communities to take possession of material that they rightfully and ethically own. This means that right now, more than ever, people need to address a number of basic questions relating to how best to care for the cultural material, including associated records as well as the sites and artifacts themselves. Issues that need to be addressed and are imperative in the first instance are:

(1) deciding the place of lodgment,
(2) ensuring best practices are employed to curate and conserve the material items and databases,
(3) ensuring funds for training and employment of Aboriginal people are available long term,
(4) protection of both Aboriginal traditional sites and historical sites in the physical and legal senses, and
(5) learning from the material and/or place both culturally and academically.

I personally yearn for Aboriginal Australia to have a system similar to that of the Navajo Nation. The establishment of the Navajo Nation Tribal Museum in 1956 was the beginning of close tribal involvement in archaeology and historical research. With the establishment of the Cultural Resources Management Program in 1977, the Navajo became one of the most administratively advanced American Indian groups in relation to the discovery, description, and documentation of cultural resources on Indian-controlled lands in the United States (Watkins 2000:100).

One institution that is operated by Aboriginal people and is successful in aspects of curatorship, research, and training is the Koorie Heritage Trust in Melbourne. Upon entering the Trust building one gains a sense of best practice being implemented: This is a place where the living culture can breathe and the past come alive. The Koorie Heritage Trust is a place that semi-demystifies my argument. However, the existence of one place like that in Australia is not going to soften my complaints in relation to my gut-wrenching concern that Indigenous Australians have quality input, training, and jobs relating to their own heritage.

The debate about "who owns the past" goes on and on and on. On one side there are generally the institutions' and/or government's representatives and on the other there are generally the representatives of a more often than not impecunious Indigenous community. The institutions' or government's representatives will be persons with commonly accepted qualifications and experiences in cultural heritage matters, including major issues such as Native Title. Amongst the various Aboriginal community groups there is more variation. In some cases there are communities with knowledge of the issues, but in most instances there is very little if any understanding. Not a very fair situation, in other words, with one side being well versed in the subject matter and the other not so.

What is of concern are institutional practices aimed at ducking the issues and costs that relate to the conservation of Aboriginal cultural material, site protection, and/or determining who speaks for the country and material associated with it. Places such as museums and government departments are hiding behind policies such as "productive repatriation" and the policies and legal frameworks that govern them. Although many academics and government employees, a range of government policies, and billions of dollars have been involved over the past three decades, how far have we really come toward social justice for Indigenous Australians? First published in 1973, the late Kevin Gilbert's (1994) book *Because a White Man'll Never Do It* points out that the original Aboriginal Lands Rights Bill was drawn up so as to cover the whole of Australia excluding the external territories (e.g., Papua and New Guinea). Its main points were as follows:

(1) The return of all "Crown lands" recognized as Aboriginal reserves, deeded in perpetuity to the Aboriginal people and administered by them.
(2) That any other "Crown lands" which are of traditional or sacred significance to Aborigines be deeded to them in perpetuity.

(3)   That all sites of anthropological or traditional significance discovered apart from the reserves and "Crown lands" be preserved and made accessible to Aborigines.

(4)   That all hunting and fishing rights and areas be open to the use of Aborigines without fee or constraint.

(5)   That where Aborigines have been removed from lands in accordance with government land alienation polices and otherwise, fair land compensation grants be made, preferably from established "Crown lands" or areas bought by governments in reparation, to restore a land base to Aborigines and to purchase additional suitable land for Aborigines.

(6)   That Aborigines in each State be given corporate ownership and control of all reserves.

(7)   That all such lands be exempt from the provisions of the relevant mining legislation.

(8)   That in these areas, ownership rights be granted over minerals to corporate Aboriginal groups so as to give the effective priority in prospecting and mining rights.

(9)   That no mineral exploration or exploration occur in Aboriginal areas without consultation and approval by local Aborigines.

(10) That as an act of compensation for the loss of all other parts of the continent, a national Aborigines Trust Fund for Aboriginal development and enterprise be established. This is to be reparation and under Aboriginal administrative control and to be in addition to normal government assistance to Aborigines as Australian citizens (Gilbert 1994:56).

What has really changed over the past 30 years, given that there is still not a lot of land in the hands of the Indigenous people, there are still very few adequately trained Indigenous people, poverty and poor health are still at unacceptable levels, and there are far too many theories, policies, and strategies just sitting on shelves collecting dust? Where are the capable Indigenous communities in this country?

National and state institutions are in the business of collecting and researching material of importance and are also in the main in control of all aspects of Aboriginal welfare and well-being. The government's and institutions' reign over Indigenous groups' material culture and information has been one that generally excluded Indigenous Australians' input into the many matters related to Indigenous collections. Many Indigenous communities have places that are culturally important to their well-being. One could be easily led astray, thinking that many Indigenous groups and individuals are now participating and in some instances leading the way in the many areas of cultural heritage management. This perception has come about mainly because we have been led to believe that the ethical and moral battles that have taken place over the past have been put to rest. However, there is a great shortage of properly trained Indigenous people in the various heritage management fields in Australia and until this is rectified the country will continue to lose Indigenous input into Indigenous heritage at the same alarming rate we presently experience. As Aboriginal Elder Alfred Pettit (pers. comm. 1987) put it to me, "no one looks after or cares for the heritage more than Aboriginal people, but they must be supplied with the training and materials and resources to do that."

National and state institutions such as museums are recognized by most of the world's people as being pillars of society that should remain part of our world. Such institutions are not in danger of closing down, unlike present Indigenous community Keeping Places, which can and do close down overnight. The majority of Australian Indigenous communities do not have the infrastructure or the expertise to relieve national and state institutions of the responsibility to care for their cultural material. There are no guarantees set in place for Indigenous communities to adequately care for or take legal jurisdiction and responsibility over their own cultural material and information. The reality at present is that the majority of the Australian Indigenous communities do not have the money, either in government- or community-generated funds, to train Indigenous people to adequately care for the cultural material and associated items.

The present trend in Australia is that community-controlled Keeping Places receive government assistance for a period of three to five years. Everybody involved in heritage management should ask what would happen if Indigenous communities took legal responsibility of their cultural material and associated information from institutions such as museums and within a given time the government funds or the community-generated moneys either decreased or ceased? Would national or state institutions reaccession the cultural material and associated material? There are local and regional Indigenous Keeping Places within Australia, but how many have the capacity to ensure the collections' and employed staffs' well-being? If the option of giving the legal responsibility for Indigenous cultural material to relevant communities is to happen, that would mean national and state institutions such as museums would have to decentralize the present system to one that has an uncertain future. I would argue that major mainstream institutions and government departments should remain the legal owners of the material culture, ethnographic material, and associated information until Indigenous communities are ready to take full responsibility for their cultural material. Otherwise where would Indigenous groups house their cultural material – under community members' beds?

To give cultural property and related material back to relevant Indigenous communities should not be based just on morally superior talk. Ensuring present and future generations are able to appreciate and/or study cultural material and associated items from the past should be at the forefront of any dispute or decision. Solutions to cultural heritage management problems must be based on the practicalities of returning legal ownership to Indigenous communities. Until Indigenous communities either independently or in association with other groups can ensure funding and guaranteed training and employment of Indigenous people forever, it is imperative that permanent government institutions remain the legal owners of the cultural material and associated items. At present, such institutions are legally responsible for ensuring that expertise and moneys are made available to care for all cultural material and associated items that are contained within their walls (although one could easily argue that not enough is being done and that resourcing remains an issue).

Although most Indigenous material will remain in non-Indigenous institutions for the foreseeable future, Aboriginal communities need not necessarily lose control of their cultural property. In recent times it has been deemed ethically correct for Indigenous groups to have moral ownership of the cultural material to which they are related. Representatives from government institutions and departments must seek community views and invite community participation in decisions concerning the use of cultural items in exhibitions or research and seek the relevant Aboriginal communities' input into conservation and storage strategies. Yet understanding and employing best practice to care for cultural material and associated items is not achieved just by gathering together a group of Indigenous people to make up an advisory board to satisfy a higher-level board. Conserving cultural items and associated items is a discipline. It is about having people with expertise in their chosen field who can contribute to the cultural and scientific understanding of the many issues that relate to the matters at hand.

For this reason, social and political issues must become "ghosts" when you are doing your job. Whether data collecting, conserving, or exhibiting, it is not a game. When I am at work I hear the stories told to me as a child by Meemie (my grandmother) in my head whilst running a set of vernier calipers over either one of my people's or some other group's ancestral skeletal material or collecting data from their stone artifacts. At this point, I am at work and although my grandmother's stories are important to me I must concentrate on the job at hand. That is not to say that my history is not important, as I am constantly thinking of stories told to me by Indigenous Elders within and outside my group. What is important to me is that I do the job I have been trained to do, as professionally and culturally appropriately as I possibly can.

I remember being at primary school in the 1970s and my teacher interrupted our class show-and-tell and announced to the whole class that we come from the apes. She was referring to the australopithecine *Australopithecus afarensis*, the apelike ancestor of *Homo sapiens*. I clearly remember the effect that this news had on my young mind: I was devastated. At such an early age to be confronted with such news! Yes, I was deeply affected by this new scientific discovery, given that I was of an age when Meemie would put me to sleep most nights, at that time, with traditional stories and stories of post-contact events from our family, passed on to her by our now deceased Elders.

From this experience I now appreciate how Charles Darwin's theory affected the general public with the publication of *The Origin of Species* in 1859. Nonetheless, I believe that we all originated from early primates in Africa. Yes, I am a believer of evolutionary theory and yes, I am an Aboriginal man. Equally I believe that I come from a group of people that have always had a deep spiritual connection to this country we now call Australia. I am comfortable where I sit in the scheme of things. I think that it is far too easy for non-Aboriginal people to believe that all Aboriginal people think that they have always had their origins in Australia. I accept that hominids evolved out of Africa.

I clearly remember my first official day employed as a Cultural Heritage Officer in my community. I went out the doors of my workplace and into the cultural world of my region. I sat and thought, "Well, Mark, Mr Cultural Heritage Officer, what do you know and what is it you are going to do today?" I found myself near a place where I grew up as a child, the Many Waters Dairy Farm in northwestern Victoria. There I was sitting in the car with memories of my childhood for company. I had no idea of what it was I was meant to do or how I was to begin my work. I ended up driving around asking my ancestors for help, as to where to go and what to do. I can still recall the feeling of isolation in my new employment as a cultural heritage person. I was haunted regularly by a feeling of alienation, the idea that I did not fit into the general scheme of fieldwork like those who work in areas such as fisheries, town planning, flora and fauna, and so on: nothing seemed to connect with my job. This feeling was made worse by my lack of skills. How does one begin to protect the important areas that your Elders told you about as a child? I traveled into the bush and found myself at a place known as Karaodoc Swamp. There I located a large Aboriginal place, now known as a very significant Aboriginal occupation and burial site (see Luebbers 1995). I then traveled to an area near Monak in New South Wales and located a rather large midden site adjacent to the Murray River. I remember thinking, "That was a rather productive day on my first day out." Had the spirits shown me the way to these important sites? Or did I just have a good nose for finding cultural places?

How do I apply this gift of being able to locate cultural places either by the spirits giving directions or the fact that I had a good nose for it? What would happen when I needed to draw upon my ancestors or my nose to identify Aboriginal places, only to find out that either the spirits were looking after some other business or I had a cold? A rather intimidating thought crossed my mind, "What if I am standing in the landscape surrounded by people I do not know who want to understand my cultural landscape or do cultural business with me?" They ask me a question about cultural heritage/archaeology. I could just picture it. There I am either blowing my nose trying to get a good sniff or calling out to my ancestors in front of these people trying to tap into my rather limited toolbox for identifying Aboriginal cultural sites! Neither option appealed to me. If I talk to my ancestors I like to do it in private or with my people. Talking and listening to our ancestors is sacred to me and my people and is not for others unless invited, and if I have the flu I like to stay home in bed. I simply did not understand what sort of toolbox was required for this type of work or how to obtain one. Neither did anyone else in my State or the Aboriginal community at the time. It is not like you can go to the local hardware store and ask "I would like to purchase a toolbox to fix the cultural heritage in my region, how much do they cost? Oh, and do you have a specific one for the northwest of Victoria?"

During the next six years, prior to going to university, I worked with many field archaeologists, botanists, geomorphologists, and people from various state and regional government departments. We worked together on various projects, such as the archaeological study of Lindsay Island (Pardoe and Grist 1989), where I learnt to map Aboriginal cemeteries and isolated burials, hold a stadia rod, operate surveying equipment, record biological data and lithic artifacts, and map land-forms. Many of the people I worked with would go back to their respective workplaces and I would spend time with members of my community putting into practice and sharing some of my newly obtained skills and knowledge with some confidence.

Within my job description was the repatriation of ancestral remains from various institutions. It just so happened that the infamous Murray Black Aboriginal skeletal collection was from my area, some of the people in it being my direct ancestors. This material consists of more than 800 skeletal remains of Aboriginal individuals dated from 14,000 B.P. to several hundred years old. These remains were originally dug up (as opposed to being archaeologically excavated) by George Murray Black in the 1940s, acting on a commission from the University of Melbourne, and deposited in the university's Anatomy department. This was done without any consultation with the Aboriginal community. We may today ask how anyone could show such disrespect to a group of people. After holding discussions with my Elders, Colin Pardoe (then Visiting Fellow at the Australian Institute of Aboriginal and Torres Strait Islander Studies) and I agreed to collect data from the ancestral remains prior to me reburying them.

Over the years Colin and I would create makeshift labs within museums, learning institutions, sheds, old offices, hospitals, and on one occasion a coolroom. The place was not important, it was the activity over the years that was the reward. We measured thousands of individuals. I started off as a scribe, filling in the scores in the appropriate columns. I will never forget the first night I started on this venture, "nasio spinale to glabella 54 mm" (a major physical anthropological cranial measurement) and so on. I would then inscribe the data appropriately. I enjoyed this type of work. After a period of time the shiny stainless steel calipers were simply placed in my hand, with the instruction "you do it, take the measurement." "Hey," I said, "I fly my cousin Ronny Murray's beautifully crafted boomerangs and I ride European motorcycles, I like anything to do with precision." This was a great day, measuring and analyzing the skeletal material of my ancestors and collecting very important information. As you are reading these words, the information we collected almost two decades ago is still being used to locate and bring together my community's ancestors for reburial in our homelands.

I distinctly remember not accepting some of our ancestors' remains from a specific institution because of the simple fact that it was given back in no better state than a pile of bones in a dog's bowl. I said that I wanted to take the ancestors back to the institution and find the rest of their remains. I was not satisfied that everything that could be done had been done to ensure that my ancestors were put back as complete as possible and with some integrity. I took my ancestors back to the relevant institution and searched for the rest of their remains. Not only did my colleagues and I individualize my ancestors, we also found more remains that should have been with the original material being sent back to my community for reburial.

When writing this chapter, I went into my library one evening looking for an article. I noticed a tag with "Murray Black" written on one of my old university texts. I decided to have a look. I read the following quote in relation to the Murray Black Collection being returned to Indigenous communities for reburial: "Aborigines – like indigenous peoples elsewhere – tend to forget that not all of their recent forebears took pious care of the dead. But in view of Aboriginal sufferings at European hands, one must certainly look on their claims with sympathy" (Renfrew and Bahn 1991:465). I read this and was quite offended. I thought to myself, "I don't want sympathy, I want results." I was taught by my Elders, "What will sympathy give you or your people? Jack [nothing]." Give us training, employment, and the autonomy to work toward our own futures.

Over the years I can happily say that I have achieved results with my colleagues and my community. I participated in collecting physical anthropological data from almost the entire Murray Black Collection and data from other major skeletal collections both nationally and internationally. I created understanding of stone-tool procurement in my region (Grist 1995). I recorded numerous sites and put in place site management plans. This was not achieved through sympathy, it was achieved through hard work and being dedicated to achieving better outcomes for my culture and my people.

The information and data collecting that I have been associated with over the years has enhanced my understanding and my community's understanding of the heritage issues in our area. It is awe-inspiring to be directly involved and to witness the awareness and application to Aboriginal concerns in our region. Such activities include quantifying Elders' knowledge and comparing our oral history with data collected in the field, identifying our ancestors from collections from national and/or international institutions using the data collected from my people's traditional lands, learning about the lifeways of our people and how unique we were and are as a group of people, learning about the types of diseases and ritual practices of our people, and understanding how to predict Aboriginal site locations.

More needs to be done with government institutions and departments in developing a higher degree of genuine cultural protocols, polices, and input from Indigenous communities. Institutions and government must provide more traineeships and employment in all areas of relevance to Aboriginal people within national and state institutions and departments. Many more qualified and trained Indigenous people are needed in areas such as anthropology, archaeology, history, and conservation to ensure genuine Indigenous involvement in heritage-related matters, thus allowing Aboriginal people to fully partake in the interpretation of Indigenous objects, sites, and mythology. Further to this, many more departments and institutions must employ more Aboriginal people and provide them with sufficient training to rectify the growing shortage of properly trained Aboriginal people in all areas of Aboriginal affairs.

Elders with knowledge and those who hold traditional values and law need to take a lead in the direction of national and state bodies to ensure the past is properly brought forward and the integrity of past Aboriginal lifeways is properly documented. All of this costs money and lots of it. Where is the money to come from? Government funds? Philanthropic societies? This is a national issue and needs to be treated as such with the utmost haste and importance. There should be no question about returning Indigenous ancestral remains to relevant Indigenous communities that wish to return their ancestors back into the ground. What is important is that the community is satisfactorily aware of what science can offer, prior to reburying their ancestors.

During my on-the-job field training in bioanthropology with Colin Pardoe we collected data from my country and other Indigenous people's country throughout Australia and have also collected data from various institutions throughout Australia. It is this experience that gives me an understanding of being employed as a cultural heritage person and of the great mental anguish of not having the appropriate skills to successfully carry out the job required. More needs to be done to upskill more of our people. As long as the power and control of Indigenous heritage remain in the hands of Federal and state ministers there is no chance of survival for Aboriginal sites in this country. I don't see many Aboriginal people participating at the highest level, with real decision-making power. There is no real understanding of our landscape by others. More real power needs to be invested in the Aboriginal community (Sam Wickman, Indigenous archaeologist, pers. comm. 2004). Aboriginal people themselves need to run programs to bring on new blood within the Aboriginal community in heritage.

Elders such as Uncle Albert Mullett and Uncle Colin Walker in Victoria, who have been around for a long time arguing for a fair playing field in heritage management and the need to educate our own, should be offered positions in teaching heritage to the new people coming through. We have in this country some very talented Aboriginal people who are capable of teaching and coaching our own people in readiness for becoming Indigenous heritage monitors and Indigenous heritage officers. More must be done within universities to adequately equip the Indigenous people of this country in heritage management (David Johnston, Indigenous archaeologist, pers. comm. 2004).

Aboriginal involvement and control over archaeological fieldwork began in the early 1970s with demands that excavation be approved by traditional landowners. This was a time of drastic reappraisal of government policy toward Aborigines, with the dawn of an assertive Aboriginal nationalism, and with the struggle for legislative recognition of Aboriginal land rights that continues to the present day (Mulvaney and Kamminga 1999:6). Our people know who we are and where we have been. This knowledge has been passed down to us by our own system that is our way of doing and being. What is important is that people who are involved in managing our heritage be aware of the other players and how they input into managing and interpreting our heritage (Ricky Mullett, Indigenous archaeologist, pers. comm. 2004).

As Hodder (1994:166) recognizes,

> it can be argued that some movement in this direction has resulted from recent increased confrontation of "established" and "alternative" archaeological perspectives. By "established" I mean the archaeology written by Western, upper middle-class, and largely Anglo-Saxon males. The three "alternative" perspectives I wish to identify as having an emergent impact on the largely non-critical establishment position, are indigenous archaeologists, feminist archaeology, and working-class perspectives within the contemporary West. In all these instances, two points can be made: first the past

is subjectively constructed in the present, and secondly, the subjective past is involved in power strategies today.

Competency in the following areas would be a great start for any heritage person working in Indigenous site identification and/or protection:

(1)   Recording oral history
(2)   Map reading
(3)   Aerial photography understanding
(4)   GPS usage
(5)   Stone artifact identification
(6)   Basic understanding of the human skeleton
(7)   Landscape understanding/geomorphology (regional specific)
(8)   Scarred tree identification
(9)   Cataloging
(10) Public speaking
(11) Administration
(12) Knowledge of relevant computer programs.

Indigenous Australians are involved in heritage management and are making decisions on a daily basis with stakeholders from the wider community (Figure 18.1), including local governments, large and small-scale housing developers and industrial developers, mineral and energy consortiums, museums and various state and Federal government departments. People working in cultural heritage management need to be well versed in the above skills to make a contribution to Aboriginal heritage protection and interpretation.

To conclude, experts such as archaeologists, physical anthropologists, social anthropologists, archivists, and linguists, to name but a few, are not always available to the Aboriginal community and the Aboriginal people involved in Aboriginal heritage management are being called upon to give advice and/or direction to stakeholders on a daily basis. It is therefore imperative that Indigenous Australians who are involved in the management of heritage sites and artifacts and their interpretation are equipped with relevant skills both physically and mentally to conduct their work.

I am of the opinion that unless we invest in training many more Indigenous people in the areas addressed in this chapter we will not only be endangering Indigenous people's involvement in their heritage but we will be also hampering the further development of archaeology, heritage management, and museum best practice in this country. The need to identify training and employment pathways for Indigenous people in all aspects of Aboriginal land and cultural management is immediate. There also is an urgent need for educational courses to overcome the wider educational deficit in Aboriginal Australia, which is presently alive and well in many Aboriginal communities. Once there are more Indigenous people educated and a pool of expertise is gained we can then look forward to Aboriginal people

Figure 18.1 The author and Gunia/Kurni community members surveying Lake Glenmaggie. L–R Mick Harding, Mark Dugay-Grist, Tim Farnham, and Chris Johnson. (Photograph courtesy of the Aboriginal Affairs Victoria Library)

participating more actively and effectively in the areas I believe to be essential to the management of Aboriginal lands, objects, and information.

There are three key areas I believe should be incorporated across all levels: (1) Aboriginal community control of cultural heritage, (2) an integrated approach by government and other stakeholders around Aboriginal cultural heritage, and (3) broader knowledge and awareness of Aboriginal cultural heritage. We should also stop the Native Title circus and get on with respecting Aboriginal people as the rightful owners of their country.

A lot of this section deals with basic tools obviously not related to traditional Aboriginal lifeways. What I have tried to express is the need for our people to have the basic toolbox (both mentally and physically) to ensure our involvement in heritage management for the future. How and where Aboriginal oral history and cultural practices enhance the archaeology and cultural heritage management within Australia is a matter for each individual Aboriginal community. Science should be seen and used as a tool to enhance Aboriginal people's lives and not seen as something that is still strongly related to colonialism.

REFERENCES

Gilbert, K., 1994 Because a White Man'll Never Do It. Melbourne: Angus and Robertson.

Grist, M., 1995 An Archaeological Investigation into the "No Stone Saga" of Far North-West Victoria: A Study of the Berribee Quarries in the Landscape. B.A. Honours dissertation, Australian National University.

Hodder, I., 1994 Reading the Past: Current Approaches to Interpretation in Archaeology. Cambridge: Cambridge University Press.

Luebbers, R., 1995 An Archaeological Survey of Karodoc Swamp Northwest Victoria. Report of Survey Results to the Mildura Aboriginal Corporation, Mildura, Victoria.

Mulvaney, D. J., and J. Kamminga, 1999 Prehistory of Australia. Sydney: Allen and Unwin.

Pardoe, C., and M. Grist, 1989 Traces of the Aboriginal Past at Lindsay Island, Northwest Victoria. Report on a Survey of Burials, Artifacts and Sites in North-West Victoria.

Renfrew., C., and P. Bahn, 1991 Archaeology: Theories, Methods and Practice. London: Thames & Hudson.

Watkins, J., 2000 Indigenous Archaeology. American Indian Values and Scientific Practices. Walnut Creek, CA: AltaMira Press.

What is the Future of our Past?
Papua New Guineans and Cultural Heritage

Herman Mandui

Papua New Guineans have the right to be the end-products of some 50,000 years of cultural development. The country does not constitute one ethnic grouping, nor a linguistic unity or homogenous polity. Instead it is a country of five million people with well over 750 different languages and thousands of autonomous tribes that occupies the eastern half of the island of New Guinea, the Bismarck Archipelago and Bougainville, and the other islands of the North Solomons. This situation raises a fundamental problem. Any government that attempts to manage the nation will always be composed of representatives serving the interests of one or other of the many ethnic groups that make up the country's diverse population. Under these circumstances, the maintenance of diversity as a positive unifying force can only be achieved by understanding and preserving as much as possible of the nation's 50,000-year past.

In this general context, there are four specific reasons why it is important to protect Papua New Guinea's archaeological heritage. First, knowledge and understanding of our past can assist us to develop and sustain our common identity. Leaving aside an irony apparent to anyone who knows the nation, the call for Papua New Guineans to forget their characteristic tribal and regional loyalties and act like *Papua New Guineans* is a serious plea, yet there are no historical events (such as a war of independence) or documents (such as a treaty or bill of rights) to underpin the unity to which we aspire. We must therefore search for other symbols of the common identity which encourages nationhood. As my teacher and colleague John Muke once told me in a university lecture long ago, other countries have prehistoric and historical monuments that are above the ground. Our monuments lie beneath the ground and that is where we must seek them.

The second reason it is important to preserve Papua New Guinea's archaeological resources is that the nation's cultural heritage rests upon the materiality of those resources rather than the specifics of their abstract properties. In Papua New

Guinea there are many different perspectives on "knowing the past," but social actions are culturally and historically specific and the abstract meanings associated with particular practices can only be truly known to those who speak the languages entwined with those fields of action (Riches 1986:1; Harris 1990:72). A whole range of social actions, ideologies, rules, institutions, and subcultures within a sociocultural milieu contribute knowledge and understanding of a past which normally provides explanations for the present. Hodder's (1986) *Reading the Past* stresses that material culture is "often not a direct reflection of human behaviour . . . [but] an indirect reflection of human society . . . [and] its ideas, beliefs and meanings that impose themselves between people and things." The use of material wealth by contemporary big-men in the New Guinea highlands is a practical example of the use of material rather than abstract properties to justify one's standing in society. Although the abstract properties of the wealth items (such as pigs or ceremonial axes) may have changed dramatically over time, the concept of associating specific material forms with big-man status is symbolically adapted from a tradition that has been in place for millennia.

The third issue is that along with urban expansion and the construction of infrastructure (roads, dams), the rapid and exploitative expansion of commercially oriented development projects such as mining, agri-forestry, and commercial agri-industry is wreaking irreversible havoc on 50,000 years' worth of archaeological heritage. A representative sample of the nation's sites must be preserved. During the country's recent mineral boom, only one company seriously considered the significance of cultural heritage and actively engaged in the development of heritage management strategies. The need to preserve a sample of Papua New Guinea's archaeological history has often been raised but has been completely ignored by developers. Pamela Swadling, a past Curator of Prehistory at the Papua New Guinea National Museum, saw this as a major issue. As she rightly stated, "Steps must be taken to remedy this situation. It should not be forgotten that as each day goes by, the 'unwritten' record of the past is being eroded away by such events as the construction of roads, airstrips, housing and industrial estates, and so on" (Swadling 1983:ix). She noted that at the time of her writing, only two other archaeological salvage projects had been conducted in Papua New Guinea: her own Ramu Dam study in the Eastern Highlands Province (Swadling 1973) and Egloff and Kaiku's (1978) work on the Purari Dam in the Gulf Province. Things have not improved greatly in the two decades since.

The final reason it is important to preserve Papua New Guinea's archaeological heritage is that each site has its own intrinsic value. Indeed, an archaeological site with few remains can sometimes have more scientific or social value than a site with a rich record. It is thus critical to preserve a sample of *all* types of sites if we are to gain maximum benefit from our cultural property.

The 1965 National Cultural Property Preservation Act emphasizes "the need to conserve our natural resources" and so in many respects cultural heritage has been interpreted in terms of nature conservation, aims to protect cultural heritage, and prohibits the disturbance of traditional and archaeological sites. However, this Act is difficult to implement and enforce owing to a shortage of personnel trained in cultural heritage and to the failure of government to review and amend heritage legislation to incorporate not only the participation of other cultural institutions in addition to the Museum but also of other government departments and agencies as well. The lack of such a whole-of-government network has seen the rape of the country's patrimony to support a continual increase in cultural heritage smuggling. Moreover, although powerful global agencies such as the World Bank which are active in Papua New Guinea have adopted positive cultural heritage management policies, they are totally ignored on the ground.

The Bank provided the following guidelines against the destruction of archaeological and cultural resources (Goodland and Webb 1987):

(1)   Never destroy a site before a professional survey has been completed
(2)   Always survey a site even if it is thought that nothing of significance is present
(3)   Treat cultural sites and artifacts as finite resources that can never be replaced
(4)   Report all cultural sites and artifacts to the responsible authorities
(5)   Never dig an archaeological site or attempt to rehabilitate or preserve an important historical building or religious shrine without professional assistance.

Although Papua New Guinea's development is underwritten with borrowed money, none of these guidelines has been included in the policies of the country's borrowing institutions. This failure can only be viewed as a negative approach to development. Muke (1998:66–67) supports this view, noting that "many Papua New Guineans also have the mentality that traditional and archaeological sites are obstacles to development issues and therefore planners and policy makers often have the misconception that they should not waste money on an uneconomic enterprise." This mentality is strengthened by the negative attitudes of policy-makers who cripple non-profit-making institutions such as museums. In the end, the question thus remains: Who will take responsibility for management of Papua New Guinea's cultural heritage?

REFERENCES

Egloff, B., and R. Kaiku, 1978 An Archaeological and Ethnographic Survey of the Purari River (Wabo) Dam Site Reservoir. Purari River (Wabo) Hydroelectric Scheme Environmental Studies, vol. 5. Port Moresby: Office of Environment and Conservation.

Goodland, R., and M. Webb, 1987 The Management of Cultural Property in World Bank Assisted Projects – Archaeological, Historical, Religious and Natural Unique Sites. Technical Paper No. 62. Washington, DC: The World Bank.

Harris, C., 1990 Kinship. Buckingham: Open University Press.

Hodder, I., 1986 Reading the Past: Current Approaches to Interpretation in Archaeology. Cambridge: Cambridge University Press.

Muke, J., 1998 The Death (and Re-birth) of Kuk: A Progress Report on the Recent Development at the Kuk Prehistoric Site, Western Highlands Province. In Kuk Heritage: Issues and Debates in Papua New Guinea. A. Strathern and P. Stewart, eds. pp. 64–86. Port

Moresby, Townsville and Pittsburgh: The National Museum of Papua New Guinea, the James Cook University Centre for Pacific Studies and the Department of Anthropology, University of Pittsburgh.

Riches, D., 1986 The Phenomenon of Violence. *In* The Anthropology of Violence. D. Riches, ed. pp. 1–27. Oxford: Blackwell.

Swadling, P., 1973 The Human Settlement of the Arona Valley, Eastern Highlands District, PNG. Port Moresby: Papua New Guinea Electricity Commission.

——1983 How Long Have People Been in the Ok Tedi Impact Region? Record 8. Port Moresby: Papua New Guinea National Museum and Art Gallery.

Index

Page numbers in *italics* denote figure/map/illustration

Aboriginal Lands Rights Bill, 369
Aboriginal peoples, 5, 48
  affinities with Melanesians, 11
  association with Neanderthals, 63, 64
  dreaming beliefs *see* dreaming beliefs
  heritage management and repatriation of
    cultural items, 367–78
  invalidation of imposing ethnography of
    onto Australia's distant past, 65
  Keeping Places, 371
  lack of training for in caring for cultural
    material, 370–1, 377
  languages, 11
  and Murray Black Collection, 374–5
Admiralty Islands, 13
adzes, 97, 206
  basalt stone, 20–1, 306
'aggregation locale' concept, 110
agriculture, 7
  Australia, 6, 7, 15
  Bismarcks, 15, 196–7, 200
  conceptions of, 164–7
  Fiji, 17–18
  New Caledonia, 142
  New Guinea Highlands *see* New Guinea
ahupua'a (Hawaiian communities), 259–60,
    261–2, 268–80
  of leeward North Kohala, 269–80

  and resource productivity, 268
  topographic features defining, 268
Allen, J., 13, 191, 198, 199, 200, 206
Alocasia taro, 197
analogy
  as basis of ethnoarchaeology, 241, 242–3,
    244
  direct, 244, 245
'Ancestral Polynesian Society', 17, 19
Anderson, A., 19, 20
'Andesite Line', 20–1
Aneityum, 280
Angwurrkburna (Australia), 124
animals, 9–10
  'megafauna', 14
  translocation of in Bismarcks, 194–6
Anopheles mosquitoes, 10
Anson, D., 233
anthropomorphic sculptures *see tiki*
Aore Island, 234
Apia (Samoa), 346
Arapus pottery, 232, 236
Arawe Islands, 210, 220
arboriculture
  Bismarcks, 197
  New Guinea, 168, 169
Archambault, M., 324
architecture, ritual *see* ritual architecture

aridity
    impact of in Pleistocene Australia, 34,
        36–7, 38, 39, 43–4
Arnhem Land (Australia), 77, 90, 117
Arrernte country (Australia), 55, 62
Atanoassao site (Malo), 235
Athens, J., 309, 311
atoll societies, 21
Australia, 5–6, 321, 322
    agriculture, 6, 7, 15
    changing technological strategies in
        Holocene, 15, 69–91
    climate change and sea-level variation, 9
    cross-cultural engagements through
        indigenous rock art, 116–31
    dreaming beliefs of Aboriginal peoples,
        50–61
    heritage management and repatriation of
        cultural items to Aboriginal peoples,
        367–78
    initial colonization, 13–14, 31, 86
    interaction networks, 7
    language, 11
    maps, 33, 34
    Pleistocene use and occupation, 31–44
    rock art and social identity, 96–111
    significance of sea to inhabitants, 116–17
    topology and climate, 8
    see also Aboriginal peoples
Austronesian languages, 11–12
Austronesian settlers, 140
Austronesian/Lapita baseline, 139
Auwa quarry (New Britain), 211, 212, 213,
    215, 218
Auzépy, P., 252
Avias, J., 325
axes, 72, 83, 207
Ayres, W., 305, 306, 308

Babeldaob, 22
backed artifacts, 78–80, 79, 83, 84, 85,
    88–9, 91, 99, 100
Balme, J., 36
Balof rockshelter (New Ireland), 208, 234
bananas, 163, 166, 168, 170, 176, 179
Barham, A., 16
Barrau, J., 331
basalt shrines, 148, 153
basalt stone adzes, 20–1, 306
beachcombers (Levuka), 351

Bedford, S., 18
Beerroo, 52
being, 50
    Heidegger and meaning of, 49
Bellwood, P., 290, 303, 304, 315
Belt Collins and Associates, 354
Bernart, L., 309
bifacial tools, 76–7, 78, 85, 90, 212, 216,
    217, 217
biology, 10–11, 12
Bishop Museum (Honolulu), 363, 364
Bismarck Archipelago, 4, 139, 189–201
    agriculture, 15, 196–7, 200
    economic strategies, 194–5
    environmental manipulation, 195–7
    geographical background, 190
    initial colonization, 191, 192, 198
    Lapita culture/pottery, 138, 140, 229,
        231, 234
    map, 190
    pulses of deposition, 191–3
    social interaction, 199
    and strandlooper model, 194
    technological complexity evidence, 197–9
    translocation of animals, 194–6
    see also Manus; New Britain; New
        Ireland
Black, George Murray, 374
'blackbirding', 352
Bleed, P., 219
boats
    and cross-cultural interaction, 120–1, 130
    and rock art on Groote Eylandt see
        Groote Eylandt
Bole, J., 321–41
bonito fishing, 252, 253
Bowdler, S., 13, 39
breadfruit, 170, 291
breadfruit pits (ua ma), 296, 297
Britain
    annexation of Levuka, 352
    land clearance, 174
Buang Merabak (New Ireland), 191, 192,
    193, 194, 196
Buka, 190, 191–2, 195 see also Kilu
Buka-style pottery, 232
Burley, D., 353

C99 rockshelter (Australia), 38
Caldwell, J., 199

Calvert Ranges (Australia), 106, 109, 110
Canarium spp., 168, 206
canoe technology, 21
Cape Range (Australia), 38, 39, 40
Capertee 3 (Australia), 75
Caroline Islands, 21, 304
Carpenter's Gap 1 & 3 (Australia), 35, 36, 37
Cauchois, M-H., 363–9
Centre National Recherche Scientifique (CNRS), 364
ceramics *see* pottery
Chakobau, 352, 360
Chaloupka, G., 122, 128
Chang, K.C., 240
Chappell, J., 13, 14
charcoal samples, 53–4
Chathams, 20
Chauvet Cave (France), 64
chert
    at Yombon, 198, 211, 214, 218, 219
chiefdoms
    Hawaiian, 20, 260
    Micronesian, 21
    New Caledonian, 331
    Polynesian, 7, 19, 143
    Roviana Lagoon, 145–6, 148, 152–4
Chuuk, 21
Clark, G., 18
Clarke, A., 116–31
Clarkson, C., 76, 90
climate, 8, 9, 10
    effect of variability in on foraging risk and procurement costs in Holocene Australia, 88–9
    impact of aridity in Pleistocene Australia, 34, 36–7, 38, 39, 43–4
Clottes, J., 65
coastal colonization model, 13–14, 39
collective memories, 246
Colocasia taro, 163, 166, 168, 170, 174, 176, 179, 197
colonization, European, 5, 7, 321
colonization, initial, 1, 10–11, 12–13
    Australia, 13–14, 31, 86
    Bismarcks, 191, 192, 198
    Marquesas, 19–20
    Melanesia, 17, 140
    Micronesia, 21
    New Caledonia, 326–7

Near Oceania, 10–11, 12–13
    New Guinea, 13, 14
    Remote Oceania, 12, 235
    phases of, 5
    Polynesia, 19–20, 139, 140, 191
    Solomon Islands 13, 147, 191–2
composite tool forms, 218, 219, 220
Comtesse, S., 39
conical clan, 302–15
    and Leluh (Kosrae), 309–12, 313, 314, 315
    and matrilineal system, 303–4
    and Nan Madol (Pohnpei), 305–9, 313, 314, 315
    ranking, 303
Conkey, M., 110
Conte, E., 240–56
Cook, Captain, 332
Cook Islands, 20, 141
Cordy, R., 269, 309, 310–11, 312, 314
'Core Tool and Scraper Tradition', 15
cores, 74, 78
correspondence analysis (CA), 103–4
creation myths, 335, 336
crocodiles, 328
Crook, W., 289, 293
Crosby, A., 349
cross-cultural exchange
    through Australian indigenous rock art, 116–31
cultivation, 166
cultural continuity and change, 6–7
Cundy, B., 76, 90
Cyrtosperma spp., 168

Dant, T., 56
Darwin, C.
    The Origin of Species, 372
David, B., 16, 48–65
DeBoer, W., 289
Denham, T., 160–80
dentate-stamped pottery, 229, 232
Devil's Lair (Australia), 32
direct analogy, 244, 245
'direct historical approach', 244
districts, 280 *see also* moku territories
ditch-digging
    New Guinea wetlands, 176, *178*, 179
domesticated crops, 165, 166, 168–9
dorsal flaking, 216–17

Dortch, C., 44
double-notch tools, 212
dreaming beliefs, 50–63
    and Ngarrabullgan, 51–4, *52*, 62
    and place, 51–5
    and rituals, 55–6, 62
    and symbolism, 56–61, 62
    and Wardaman rock art, 57–61, 62
Dugay-Grist, M., 367–78
Durba Ranges (Australia), 106
Dye, T., 247

earth ovens (New Ireland), 206
Easter Island *see* Rapa Nui
Echymipera kalubu, 195
economic strategies
    Bismarcks, 194–5
    changes in early/mid-Holocene New
        Britain, 209–20, 222
Eekoo, 52
Efate Island, 17, 234
Effective Precipitation (EP), 87, 89
Egloff, B., 380
El Niño-Southern Oscillation (ENSO), 9,
    10, 88, 89, 90
Emory, K., 363–4
engraved art, 102, 103, 104, 105, 107, 108,
    109
environmental change, 6, 8–9
epistemology, 48
erosion, 6
ethnoarchaeology
    analogy as basis of, 241, 242–3, 244
    in Polynesia, 245–56
        direct use of ethnohistorical sources
            and continuing cultural traditions,
            245–7
        study of ancient fishing strategies,
            248–54
        using contemporary information to
            interpret archaeology of ancient
            past, 247–8
    use of ethnographic information in
        archaeology, 241–4
ethnographic mapping, 243
ethnographic writings, 334
European Palaeolithic, 98, 109
Europeans
    and colonization, 5, 7, 321, 332–3, 337–8

descriptions by as ethnohistorical source,
    246
encounters with people of Groote
    Eylandt (Australia), 119–20, 127,
    129
influence on indigenous societies, 321
exchange systems, 5, 145, 146
extinctions, 10

fauna *see* animals
Feru rockshelter (Santa Ana), 234
Fiji, 138, 336
    agriculture, 17–18
    cultural heritage legislation, 349, 360
    heritage management in Levuka *see*
        Levuka
    Lapita, 234
    pottery, 17, 18
Fiji Museum, 349, 357
Fiji Museum Act (1929), 349
Fiji Town Planning Act (1946), 349, 354
First Fleet, 100
fishhooks, 249, 250, 253, 254
fishing strategies
    ethnoarchaeological analysis of in French
        Polynesia, 248–54
flaked stone artifacts/technology 74, 80,
    100, 206–7, 208, 209–10, 216–17,
    220, 222 *see also* retouched flakes
Flannery, T., 14, 196
Flinders, M., 119–20
Flood, J., 58
foraging risk
    and changing technological strategies,
        69, 70, 71, 86–91
forest clearance, 171, 173, 197, 208, 327
'founder rank enhancement' model, 303,
    315
Frederick, U., 106, 116–31
French Polynesia *see* Polynesia
Frimigacci, D., 246
fruit bats, 10
Futuna, 246

Gadamar, H-G., 160
Galipaud, J-C., 228–37
Galt-Smith, B., 107
Gamble, C., 44, 107
gandawag (Moon), 57

Garanger, J., 246, 364
Gardin, J-C., 241
Garnawala rockshelter (Australia), 58, *60*, 62
Ghasarian, C., 255
Gibson, G., 359
Gilbert, K.
  Because a White Man'll Never Do It, 369
Gillen, F., 55
Gillin, T., 322
ginger, 168
Golson, J., 162, 163–4
Gordol-ya rockshelter (Australia), 61, 62
Gordon, Sir A.H., 352
Gorecki, P., 229
Gosden, C., 195, 197, 198, 199, 200, 206
Gould, R., 33, 106, 244
gourds, 169
Grande Terre (New Caledonia), 327, 328, 329, *330*, 331, 333, 338, 339
Graves, M., 259–80
Greater Australia *see* Sahul
Green, R., 17, 19, 20, 137, 140, 143, 228, 231, 235, 364
Groote Eylandt (Australia), 117–31, *118*
  boats and rock art, 121–4
  contact with Macassans, 119, 121–2, 124, 125–6, 129, 130
  encounters with European explorers, 119–20, 127, 129
  map, *118*
  people on boats in rock art, 122, 126–9
  prau images in rock art, 121–6, 128–30
  representing of cross-cultural relations through boat images, 129, 130
  rock art images of European sailboats, 121, 124, 125, 127, 129
  shaping of worldview by marine environment, 118
Groube, L., 230
Guadalcanal, 147, 154
Guiart, J., 248
Gulf of Caprentaria, 11
gulirrida (peewee birds), 57

Haberle, S., 162, 168
hafted tools, 76, 80, 85, 97, 218
Hage, P., 303, 304

Haka'iki, 291, 292
Hammersley Plateau (Australia), 39
Handy, E.S.C., 249, 293
Handy, W.C., 293–4
Hanlon, D., 306, 308, 308–9
Harris, D., 164–5, 166
Hather, J., 165–6
Hatiheu Valley (Nuku Hiva), 286, 290, 291, 292, 295–6, *295*
Hawai'i Island, 260, 321
  moku boundaries, *266*, 267–8
Hawaiian territories, 138, 259–80
  ahupua'a, 259–60, 261–2, 268–80
  chiefdoms, 20, 260
  emergence of territorial system from land-tenure system, 261
  formation and boundaries of moku 259, 260–1, 262–8 *see also* moku territories
  political and social organization, 260–2
  see also Hawai'i Island; Kaua'i; Maui; O'ahu
Hawkesbury Sandstone Formation (Australia), 102
Hawkesbury-Nepean River, 99
Hayden, B., 80, 81, 83
headhunting (Roviana Lagoon), 145, 146, 149, 152, 153, 154
Heidegger, M., 49
heritage management
  and Aboriginal peoples, 367–78
  conservation of colonial built-heritage, 350
  issues in Pacific Island, 347–51
  and legislation, 348–9
  Levuka (Fiji), 346–61
  limited human and economic resources, 347–8
Hiroa, Te Rangi (Sir Peter Buck), 335
Hiscock, P., 34, 35, 39, 69–91, 109
history
  colonial construction of, 335
  differences in perspectives between modern archaeology and indigenous traditions, 334
Hiva Oa (Marquesas), 287–8, 292
Hodder, I., 167, 173, 376–7
  Reading the Past, 380

Holocene
Australian rock art, 96–111
changes in Melanesia during early/mid-,
205–22
changes in technological strategies in
Australia, 69–91
and Near Oceania, 15–17
Hommon, R., 263, 268
Honiavasa, 149, 150, 153
Horton, D., 14
Hubbard, Timothy, 356

Ididubangara, Chief, 149
Illouz, C., 338
'indigenous archaeologies', 322
indigenous archaeologists, 339, 340–1
indigenous peoples, 64–5, 335, 336
archaeology and histories of, 321–2
attachment to land, 116
differences in historical perspectives
between modern archaeology and
traditions of, 334
influence of European colonization, 321
relationship with Europeans at Groote
Eylandt, 119–20, 127, 129
see also Aboriginal peoples
Indonesian Papua, 2, 14
information exchange theory, 97, 98, 105,
109, 111
Ingaladdi rockshelter (Australia), 74, 90
interaction systems, 16, 22
Inuit, 64
Island Melanesia, 2, 12, 18, 139, 142, 154,
322
'islands as laboratories' concept, 302
Isohkelekel, 306, 308

Jalibang (Australia), 58, 60
Jansz rockshelter (Australia), 38
Jochim, M., 72, 107
Jones, M., 165
Jones, R., 15
Jo's Creek site (New Guinea), 14
'Juan knives', 84

Kaalpi (Australia), 107–8
Kabris, 294
Kaiku, R., 380
Kakadu Sequence, 90
Kamehameha I., 260

Kamminga, J., 11
'Kanak', term of, 340
Kanaks, 248, 324, 325, 329–33, 336–7, 338–9
Karaodoc Swamp (Australia), 373
Katampul (Australia), 42–3, 106
Kaua'i, 260
moku boundaries, *265*, 267
Kauffman, P., 120
Kauffmann, C., 229
Kekehe complex, 149–50
Kellum-Ottino, M., 290
Keringke (Australia), 55, 56
Kermadecs, 20
Kilu (Buka), 191, 193, 194, 197
Kindeng (New Guinea), 161
Kirch, P., 17, 19, 20, 21, 141, 142, 143,
247, 255, 260, 262, 303
knapping strategies, 72, 76
Kohala *see* North Kohala
Kohala Field System, 277
Koné period, 232
Koolan 2 (Australia), 35, 37
Koorie Heritage Trust (Melbourne), 369
Kosipe (New Guinea), 171
Kosrae, 21, 280, 303
conical clanship, 314
Leluh site, 309–12, *310*, 313, 314, 315
multi-compound enclosures, 312
settlement hierarchy model, 311–12
Koster site (USA), 218
Krusenstern, A., 292
Kubo, 166
Kuhn, S., 71, 85
Kuk (New Guinea), 161, 162, 164, 168,
169, 173, 176
drainage systems at, 163, 174–9, *175*,
177–8
kula ring, 7
Kulpi Mara (Australia), 41, *41*, 42, 43, 105
Kweyunpe (Australia), 55, 56

Lachitu Cave (New Guinea), 14
Ladefoged, T., 259–80
land divisions
use of to reconstruct past patterns of
occupation, 246–7
landscape change
effect of on foraging risk and
procurement costs in Holocene
Australia, 86

languages, 11–12

Lapita, 5, 16, 18, 220–1, 222, 228–37, 335–6
  bias towards in Melanesian research,
    140–1, 142, 143
  chronology and continuity, 234–6
  development and expansion of, 17, 229,
    230
  ending of, 235
  origins, 16, 228–30
  and Solomon Islands, 147, 154
Lapita Cultural Complex (LCC), 140,
  162–3, 228–30, 326
Lapita Homeland Project, 138, 229
Lapita potters, 231
Lapita pottery, 17, 207, 228, 229,
    230–6
  ceasing of manufacture of, 235
  complex design system used by potters,
    231
  and dentate-stamping, 229, 232
  paddle-impressed styles, 234, 236
  and Plainware, 17, 19, 232–4, 236
  and Podtanéan pottery, 232–3, 236
  as potter's art, 231
  speed of spread of, 234
Last Glacial Maximum see LGM
Lawn Hill (Australia), 35, 40
Leavesley, M., 189–201
Lebot, V., 170
Lees, B., 87
Leeward Islands, 255
Lefebvre, H., 51
legislation
  and heritage management, 348–9
Leluh (Kosrae), 309–12, 310, 313, 314,
    315
Leroi-Gourhan, A., 63, 242–3
Levuka: Living Heritage, 359
Levuka (Fiji), 346–61, 348
  annexation of by Britain, 352
  brief history, 351–3
  declared Fiji's first 'historic town', 354–5
  as a heritage place, 353–7
  local community attitudes to heritage,
    359, 360
  location map, 347
  national and regional cultural
    significance of, 355
  and tourism, 350–1, 353–4, 360
  as world heritage site, 357–9, 360

Levuka Conservation Committee, 355
Levuka Heritage Committee, 358
Levuka Historical and Cultural Society,
  354
Levuka Town Planning Scheme, 349,
  354–5, 356
LGM (Last Glacial Maximum), 8–9, 32,
  35, 36, 38, 39, 40, 41, 42, 43, 105,
  109
Lifou, 331
Lightfoot, K., 244
Lightning Brothers, 58, 59
Lilley, I., 1–23, 31, 138, 139, 140, 191
Lime Infilled ware, 22
Lindsay Island, 373
Linton, R., 288, 290, 292
Little Ice Age, 9
Little Sandy Desert (Australia), 106
long chronology, 31
Loyalty Islands, 327, 328, 329, 331
Lurie, R., 218
Lütke, 311–12

Macassans
  contact with people of Groote Eylandt,
    119, 121–2, 124, 125–6, 129,
    130
  praus, 123–8, 130
McCarthy, F., 128
McConvell, P., 11, 109
McCoy, M., 277
McDonald, J., 96–111
Macknight, C., 119, 123, 125–6
Makue site (Aore Island), 234
Malea (Australia), 39
Malo (Vanuatu), 235
mana, 145, 152, 153
Mandu Mandu rockshelter (Australia),
  38
Mandui, H., 379–81
Mangaasi (Vanuatu), 17, 18
Mangaia, 280
Manus, 190, 192, 195, 197, 206
Maoris, 322
marae, 363
Marck, J., 304
Maré Island, 331, 338
Mariana Islands, 22, 229, 303
Marngkala Cave (Groote Eylandt,
    Australia), 124, 125, 130

Marquesas, 141, 284–98, 364
  anthropomorphic sculptures (*tiki*),
    286–9, *287*, *288*, 296, 297, 298
  archaeological art, 286–9
  domestic and ritual architecture, 289–95
  fishing techniques, 252–3
  houses, 289
  initial colonization, 19–20
  map, *285*
  petroglyphs/pictographs, 286, 296, 298
  sacred structures (me'ae/ahu), 284, 286,
    290–1, 294, 296, 298
  settlement patterns in Hatiheu Valley
    (Nuku Hiva), 295–6, *295*
  sleeping platforms, 289–90
  tribal ceremonial complexes (tohua),
    291–2, 293, 294, 296
  warriors' platform (tapu house), 293
  women and tribal ceremonial complexes,
    293–5
Marquesas Rock Art Project, 284
Marshall, B., 206
Marshall Islands, 304, 347
Marwick, B., 39–40
Mata, Roy, 245, 246
mateana, 151
Matenbek (New Ireland), 199–200, 207
Matenkupkum (New Ireland), 191, 192,
    193, 194, 195, 196, 199–200
matrilineal systems, 303–4
Maui, 260
  moku boundaries, *265*, 267
Maupiti (Leeward Islands), 255
me'ae (sacred structures), 284, 286, 290–1,
    294, 296, 298
Medieval Warm Period, 9
megafauna, 14
Melanesia, 17–19, 137–44
  changes in early/mid-Holocene, 205–22
  colonization, 17, 140
  definition, 2, 4
  differences between archaeology of
    Polynesia and, 138–44
  diversity of people, 137, 154
  emphasis placed on Lapita in research
    of, 140–1, 142, 143
  exchange systems, 5
  extent of archaeological coverage, 138–40
  language, 12

political history, 143
pottery, 141–2
social archaeology, 142–3
sociopolitical systems, 7
Melville, H., 293
Mennge-ya rockshelter (Australia), 60–1,
    62
Micronesia, 21–2, 350
  colonization, 21
  conical clan, 302–15
  definition, 4
  language, 12
  pottery, 236
  preservation of German colonial heritage,
    350
Millerstrom, S., 284–98
Milly's Cave (Australia), 39
Milly's Creek (Australia), 40
Minjigina (New Guinea), 161
Misisil Cave (New Britain), 193
moa, 21
Moberg, C., 241
moku territories (Hawaiian), 259, 260–1,
    262–8
  formation of, 262–3
  Hawai'i Island, *266*, 267–8
  Kaua'i, *265*, 267
  Maui, *265*, 267
  Moloka'i, 263–4, *264*
  O'ahu, 264, *264*, 266
  partitioning and subdivision of, 263
  use of topographic features to define
    boundaries, 262, 263
Moloka'i moku boundaries, 263–4, *264*
Montebello Islands, 38–9
Mooramully, 52
Morovo (Western Province), 154
Morphy, H., 117, 122–3
Morse, K., 38
mortuary architecture *see* tombs
Mountford, C., 123
Mugumamp, 176
Muke, J., 379, 381
Mullett, A., 376
multiple-origins model, 10
multivariate analysis, 104
Mulvaney, D.J., 11
Munda (New Georgia), 146
Munda Tradition (Roviana Lagoon), 148

Murray Black Aboriginal skeleton collection, 374–5
Musa phytoliths, 164
Mystery Islands, 4

Nan Madol (Pohnpei), 305–9, *305*, *307*, 313, 314, 315
Napuka, 251–2, 254
National Cultural Property Preservation Act (1965), 380–1
National Trust of Fiji, 349
National Trust of Fiji Act (1970), 349
National Trust of Fiji (Amendment) Act (1998), 349
native archaeologists, 364–6
Native Title, 36, 378
Navajo Nation Tribal Museum, 369
Near Oceania, *3*, 5–6, 137
  archaeological background, 12–17
  environmental variation, 8–9
  Holocene change in, 15–17
  initial colonization, 10–11, 12–13
  languages, 10–11
  Pleistocene, 12–15
  term of, 4
'Never-Never syndrome', 48
'New Archaeology', 243
New Britain, 190, 191, 206
  changes in settlement and economic strategies in early/mid-Holocene rain forest sites, 209–20, 222
  initial colonization, 198
  obsidian sources, 193, 206, 207, 208, 213, 327
  source selection, 198
  stone-working in mid-Holocene, 208
  volcanism, 210, 219–20, 221
  see also Yombon
New Caledonia, 18, 138, 139, 248, 321–41
  agricultural systems, 142
  archaeological research in colonial context, 323–6
  conflict of land control, 328–9
  creation of convict colony by French, 324, 333
  European arrival and consequences of, 332–3, 337–8
  forest clearance, 327

French colonization and treatment of Kanaks, 324, 332–3, 338–9
  initial colonization and 'first settlers', 326–7
  intensification of horticultural techniques, 329, *330*, 331
  Kanak societies and archaeology, 336–7
  Lapita pottery, 232–3, 234, *324*, 327
  and local archaeologists, 339–40
  map, *323*
  nineteenth century transformations and present day consequences, 337–9
  Podtanéan pottery, 232–3, 234–5, 327, 328
  prehistoric chronology of, 326–33
  revival of Kanak culture and calls for self-determination, 325, 333, 337
  rise of Kanak societies, 329–32
  taking root by Austronesian settlers and transformation of landscape, 327–8
  taro terraces, 329, *330*, 331
  trade, 331
New Georgia Island, 144, *144*, 145 *see also* Roviana Lagoon
New Guinea, 9, 14, 138, 206
  agriculture of Highlands, 6, 15, 160–80
  antiquity and origins, 162–3
  arboriculture, 168, 169
  archaeobotanical visibility, 167–8
  clarifying of terminology, 164–5
  drainage networks at Kuk, 163, 174–9, *175*, *177–8*
  and forest clearance, 171, 173, 180
  indigenist versus introduced debate over origins, 162–4
  signatures in material culture, 171
  starch staples, 168–9, 170, 179
  subsistence activities on wetland margins, 174–9, 180
  initial colonization, 13, 14
  language, 11
  map, *172*
  pottery, 229
  separation from Greater Australia, 9
  stone tools, 207
  topology, 8
  see also Papua New Guinea

New Ireland, 190, 206
    agriculture, 197
    earth ovens, 206
    fauna, 194, 195
    forest clearance, 208
    initial colonization, 191, 198
    and obsidian, 193, 197, 199, 207
    Plainware, 234
    shellfish selection, 195, 196
    source selection, 198
    translocation of animals, 192, 196
New Zealand, 4, 7, 10, 20, 21, 138, 321, 322
Newman rockshelter (Australia), 39
Ngarrabullgan (Australia), 51–4, 52, 62
Nissan, 200
Niuatoputapu (Tonga), 247, 248, 254
Noala Cave (Australia), 38–9
Nombe (New Guinea), 171
non-Pama-Nyungan, 11
Nordhoff, C., 249
North Kohala
    ahupua'a of leeward, 269–80
Northern Territory Tourist Commission, 48
Nuku Hiva, 284
    anthropomorphic sculptures, 287, 288
    Archaeological Field Survey (2002),
        297–8
    Hatiheu Valley, 286, 290, 291, 292,
        295–6, 295
    me'ae, 290
    petroglyphs, 286
    tohua, 291, 292
    warriors' platforms, 293
Nusa Roviana (New Georgia), 146, 149,
    150–2, 153

O'ahu, 260
    moku boundaries, 264, 264, 266–7
obsidian, 18, 229
    New Britain, 193, 206, 207, 208, 213,
        327
    New Ireland, 193, 197, 199, 207
    preference over chert in Bismarcks,
        198–9
    Yombon, 214
Oceanic Austronesian language, 12
ochre deposition, 61
O'Connell, J., 13, 292
O'Connor, S., 13, 14, 31–44
off-site sampling, 44

O'Neill, J., 347, 350
open sites, 44
oral traditions, 246, 247, 308–9, 321–2,
    334, 335
O'Regan, T., 366
ORSTOM, 364
Ottino, P., 249
Ouetcho, A., 321–41
Ovalau, 346, 356, 358
Ovalau Tourism and Promotion
    Committee, 354
Owl Dreaming story, 61

Pacific Area Travel Association (PATA),
    354
paepae hiamoe see sleeping platforms
Pahnwi tomb (Nan Madol), 305–6
Palau, 22, 303
Pama-Nyungan language, 11
Panakiwuk (New Ireland), 193, 206, 207
Pandanus spp., 168, 169, 171
Papua New Guinea, 4, 14, 138
    reasons for protecting archaeological
        heritage, 379–81
Pardoe, C., 374, 376
PATA study, 356, 358
patriclans, 55
Pavlides, C., 205–22
Pearson, J., 64
Peinkitel tomb, 306
Petersen, G., 22, 303, 308, 309, 313, 314
Peterson, N., 55
petroglyphs, 286, 296, 298, 329
Pettit, A., 370–1
Phalanger orientalis, 192, 195–6
pigment art, 102, 103, 104, 105, 107,
    108
Pilbara (Australia), 33, 34, 37, 39–40, 40,
    43, 106
Pilgonaman rockshelter (Australia), 38
place
    and dreaming beliefs, 51–5
Plainware, 17, 19, 232–5, 236–7
Pleistocene
    Bismarck Archipelago and Late, 189–201
    Near Oceania, 12–15
    settlement, subsistence and demography
        in Australia, 31–44
poata, 145
Podtanéan pottery, 232–3, 234–5, 236, 327

Pohnpei, 21, 280, 303
  conical clanship, 313, 314
  'culture-historical phases', 308
  and Isohkelekel, 306, 308
  Nan Madol site, 305–9, *305*, *307*, 313,
    314, 315
  and Saudeleur dynasty, 306, 309, 315
  value of oral history, 308–9
points, 76–8, 83, 84, 85, 88, 90, 91
Polynesia, 19–21, 137–44, 154
  archaeology in French, 363–9
  chiefdoms, 7, 19, 143
  definition, 4
  differences between archaeology of
    Melanesia and, 138–44
  ethnoarchaeology in, 245–56
  extent of archaeological coverage, 138–4
  initial colonization, 19–20, 139, 140,
    191
  languages, 12
  map of French, *252*
  monumental architecture, 19
  politics, 143
  pottery, 19, 141, 142
  social archaeology, 142–3
Polynesian Outliers, 4
Polynesians, 335
portable stone tools, 71
Porter, C., 291, 293, 294
post-processual archaeology, 302
potters, Lapita, 231
pottery, 22
  Lapita *see* Lapita pottery
  Melanesian, 141–2
  non-Austronesian/Austronesian, 229
  Plainware, 17, 19, 232–5, 236–7
  Podtanéan, 232–3, 234–5, 327, 328
  Polynesian, 141, 142
praus, 121–2
  depiction of people on praus in rock art,
    127–8, *127*
  rock art images of in Groote Eylandt,
    121–6, 128–30
Preservation of Objects of Archaeological
    and Palaeontological Interest Act
    (1940), 349
Pritchard, W.T., 352
procurement costs
  and changing technological strategies,
    70, 71–2, 86–9

Proto-Oceanic (POc), 303
Pryzywolnik, K., 38
Puntutjarpa, 106
Purari Dam (Gulf Province), 380
Puritjarra (Australia), 41–2, *41*, *42*, 43, 105

Rainbird, P., 302–15
Rainbow Serpent/Two Sisters, 57, 58, *60*
Rangiroa, 364
Rapa Nui (Easter Island), 20, 21, 138, 259,
  280
rats, 192, 195, 230, 328
Remote Oceania, *3*, 7, 8, 137
  archaeological background, 17–22
  environmental variation, 9–10
  initial colonization, 12, 235
  languages, 11–12
  Lapita Culture, 228–37
  term of, 4
Rennell Island, 357
resource reductions
  effect of on foraging risk and procurement
    costs in Holocene Australia, 86
retouched flakes, 74, 212, 213, 216–17 *see*
    also backed artifacts; points; scrapers
Richards, F., 51–2
ritual(s)
  architecture on Marquesas, 290–2,
    293–4, 298
  and dreaming beliefs, 55–6, 62
Riwi (Australia), 35–6, 37
Robertson, N., 195
rock art, 18
  Australia, 96–111, 116–31
    in arid zone (Western Desert), 98,
      105–10, 111
    correlation between stylistic variability
      with nature of social networks, 98,
      107
    cross-cultural engagements through
      indigenous 116–31 *see also* Groote
      Eylandt
    in fertile regions (Sydney Basin), 98,
      102–5, 110
    Wardaman, 57–61, 62
  Hatiheau Valley (Nuku Hiva), 296
  Marquesas, 284, 286–9
rockshelters (Australia), 35, 38, 52–3,
    58–61, 104
Roe, D., 154, 348

Rolett, B., 253, 290
Roquefeuil, C. de, 291, 294
Rotuma, 280
Roviana Lagoon (New Georgia Island),
    144–55, *144*
  archaeological sequence, 146–52
  Bao Period (700–400 B.P.), 148–50, 153
  development of chiefdom, 145–6, 148,
      152–4
  exchange system, 145, 146
  headhunting and skull shrines, 145, 146,
      149, 152, 153, 154
  hill fort on Nusa Roviana, 151–2
  initial colonization, 147
  and *mana*, 145, 152, 153
  Munda Tradition (700–100 B.P.),
      148–52
  politico-economic system, 145–6, *146*
  pottery, 147, 148
  Roviana Period (400–100 B.P.), 150–2,
      153
  settlement patterns, 153
  shell circulation, 152
  shrines, 148–9, 150, 151, 152–3, 154
  and Tiola, 151–2

Sackett, J., 103
sacred structures (Marquesas) *see* me'ae
sago, 163, 166
Sahlins, M.,
  Social Stratification in Polynesia, 302–3
Sahul (Greater Australia), 5, 8, 9, 13, 191,
    194
Samoa/Samoans, 7, 19, 228, 235, 335
Sand, C., 142, 233, 248, 321–41
sand painting, 96
Santa Ana, 234
Santa Cruz Islands, 220, 228
Sarazin, F., 324
Saudeleur dynasty, 306, 309, 315
sawei (Yapese Empire), 22
Schiffer, M., 244
Schneider, D., 309
scrapers, 74–6, *75*, 83, 84, 85, 88, 89, 91,
    212, 216
sea
  significance to indigenous Australians,
      116–17
sea levels, 8–9

sea temperatures, 8, 9
sedentism, 220–1, 222, 331
Serpent's Glen rockshelter (Australia), 35,
    37, 41, *41*, 42, 43, 106, 109
Setaria palmifolia, 168
shells, 21, 145, 152, 199, 206, 229, 306
Shepardson, B., 280
Sheppard, P., 137–55
short chronology, 31
shrines (Roviana Lagoon), 148–9, 150,
    151, 152–3, 154
Shulmeister, J., 87
Singapore, 350
single-origin model, 10–11
Sinoto, Yoshi, 364
skull shrines (Roviana Lagoon), 150, 151,
    152, 153
sleeping platforms (paepae hiamoe)
    (Marquesas), 289–90, 292, 296
Small Tool Tradition, 15
Smith, A., 19, 199, 346–61
Smith, C., 107
Smith, M., 34, 39, 41, 105
Smith, M.V., 44
Society Islands, 20, 249, 364
Solomon Islands, 4, 8, 21, 144, 154, 206
  economic strategies, 194
  geographical background, 190
  initial colonization, 13, 147, 191–2
  map, *190*
  and Roviana Lagoon (New Georgia
      Island) *see* Roviana Lagoon
Sorovi-Vunidilo, T., 336
Southeast Solomons Project, 140
spears, 72, 253
Specht, J., 196
Spencer, B., 55
Spennemann, D., 347, 350
Spilocuscus kraemeri, 195
Spriggs, M., 18, 19, 20, 141, 166, 174,
    179, 229
star-compass system, 21
stemmed tools, 213, 214, 215, 216, 217,
    217, 218, 219
Stevenson, C., 280
Stevenson, R.L., 350
stone tools/artifacts, 69–90, 99–100
  change in technology of as agricultural
      signature in New Guinea, 171

early Holocene Melanesia, 206–7
and early/mid-Holocene in Yombon, 210–19
extension-abundance continuum, 81, *82*, 83, 84–5
factors increasing foraging risk and procurement costs, 86–90
foraging risk and procurement costs, 69–73
hafted, 76, 80, 85, 97, 218
maintainable and reliable systems, 72, 73
mid-Holocene Melanesia, 208
portable, 71
production rates, 83, 84
and resharpening, 80, 81
retouched flakes *see* retouched flakes
scrapers, 74–6, *75*, 76, 83, 84, 85, 88, 89, 91, 212, 216
standardization of, 72–3
Sydney region (Australia), 89, 99–100
waisted, 14, 206, 215, 216, 217, *217*, 218, 219
stone-adze kit, 229
strandloopers, 194, 229–30
Stringer, C., 23
style
as a social strategy, 97–8
sugarcane, 168, 170, 176
Summerhayes, G., 230, 231
Suva, 353
Swadling, P., 229, 380
sweet potatoes, 166
Sydney Basin, 98, 99–105, 110
languages, 100, *101*
rock art, 102–5
social networks, 100
stylistic variability in engraved and pigment art, 103–4
Sydney Sequence, 89
symbolism
and dreaming beliefs, 56–61, 62

Tahiti, 280, 364
Tahuata (Marquesas), 287, 290
Takano, G., 360–1
Talasea (New Britain), 206, 207, 208, 210, 214, 313, 327
Talepakemalai (Mussau Islands), 234, 236

Tamariki Te Puka Maruia Association, 251
tapu house (warriors' platform), 293
taro
Alocasia, 197
Colocasia, 163, 166, 168, 170, 174, 176, 179, 297
Tasmania, 8, 9, 11, 15
Tautain, M., 294
technological strategies
Bismarcks, 197–9
changing of in Holocene Australia, 69–91
Tepoto Island, 246, 251–2, 254
Therreyererte (Australia), 55, 56
Thomas, J., 173–4
Thomson, D., 242
Thorley, P., 42, 105
tiki (anthropomorphic sculptures) 286–9, *287*, *288*, 296, 297, 298
Tikopia, 231
Tindale, N., 123
Tiola, 151–2
tohua (tribal ceremonial complexes) (Marquesas), 291–2, 293, 294, 296
tombs
Leluh (Kosrae), 311, 313
Nan Madol (Pohnpei), 305–6, 313
tomite system, 247
tomoko war canoes, 146
Tonga, 5, 17, 19, 228, 247, 321
tools, stone *see* stone tools/artifacts
Torrence, R., 72, 191, 206, 213
Torres Strait, 11, 15–16
Torres Strait Cultural Complex, 16
Torres Strait Islanders, 49
totems, 55
Town Planning Act (1946), 356
trading systems, 16
Traditional Kanak Cultural Complex, 331, 337, 340
trees *see* arboriculture
Triangle Polynesia, 4, 20
tribal ceremonial complexes *see* tohua
Trochus niloticus, 199
Tuamotu Archipelago, 246, 251, 252, 253, 255
tubers, 167–8
Tuggle, D., 262–3, 267, 268
tulas, 76, 97
Turbo argyrostroma, 199

Turner, D., 123
turtles, 328

Ua Pou, 290, 292
Underhill, P., 12
UNESCO, 356, 359
    World Heritage Convention (1972), 357,
        360
    World Heritage List, 346, 357
unifacial tools, 77, 78, 213, 216, 217, *217*
United States, 243
Urville, D. d', 310, 312

Vanuata Cultural and Historical Sites
        Survey, 348
Vanuatu, 17, 18, 21, 138, 139, 142, 234,
        235, 322
vegeculture, 165–6
Veitch, B., 39
Veth, P., 11, 31–44, 34–5, *34*, 39, 96–111
Vienne, B., 246

Waghi Valley (New Guinea), 161, 173,
        179
waisted tools, 14, 206, 215, 216, 217, *217*,
        218, 219
Waitangi, Treaty of, 321
Walker, C., 376
Walker Circulation, 88
Wallis, L., 90
Walter, R., 137–55
Wañlek (New Guinea) 171
Wardaman country (Australia), 57–61, 62
Warrawau Plantation (New Guinea), 161,
        169, 176
warriors' platform (tapu house), 293
Watom excavation, 229, 233
Western Desert (Australia), 33, 34, 36, 37,
        105
    language, 109
    occupation and social networks, 41, 42,
        43, 105–6, 108–9
    rock art, 107–10

Western Province 147 *see also* Roviana
        Lagoon
Whippy, David, 351
White Cockatoos, 60–1
White, J.P., 196, 206
White, N., 11
Widgingarri 1 & 2 (Australia), 35, 37
Wiessner, P., 105
Wik-Munkan Aborigines, 242
Wilkes, Lieutenant, 351
Wilson, J., 290
Wilson, M., 18–19
Windshuttle, K., 322
Witori, Mt. (New Britain), 210, 215,
        220
Wobst, M., 97, 105
women
    and tribal ceremonial complexes in
        Marquesas, 293–5
World Bank, 381
World Heritage Convention (UNESCO)
        (1972), 357, 360

yams, 163, 166, 168, 170
Yap, 5, 12, 22, 303
Yen, D., 168
Yeoh, B., 350
Yinumalyuwalumanja (Australia), 124
Yirra rockshelter (Australia), 39
Yiwarlarlay rockshelters (Australia), 58, *59*,
        62
Yolngu art, 117
Yombon (New Britain), 194, 198, 206
    chert, 198, 211, 214, 218, 219
    occupation, 193
    settlement and economic strategies in
        early Holocene, 212–14
    settlement and economic strategies in
        mid-Holocene, 218–19
    stone artifact production in early
        Holocene, 209–14
    stone artifact production in mid-
        Holocene, 214–19